sucess decided
by public opinion]
and CSB/CBS

The IRB

wrii..us
importators

Theme:
major influence
of church on politics

imp. of newsp: 244

gives the
data, makes
speculations
{
① speculation + uncertainty
② use of statistics
③ date of publishing
further out

BIG ISSUE: self-defence
IRB thrives on this issue

sources:
newspapers
previous scholarship
POLICE/intelligence records
memoires, etc

imp EDU

lim:
why do the
British care?

The IRB

The Irish Republican Brotherhood,
from the Land League to Sinn Féin

OWEN McGEE

FOUR COURTS PRESS

Set in 10.5 on 12.5 point Ehrhardt
by Mark Heslington, Scarborough, North Yorkshire for
FOUR COURTS PRESS
7 Malpas Street, Dublin 8, Ireland
e-mail: info@four-courts-press.ie
and in North America
FOUR COURTS PRESS
c/o ISBS, 920 N.E. 58th Avenue, Suite 300, Portland, OR 97213

A catalogue record for this title
is available from the British Library.

ISBN 978-1-84682-064-9

Printed in England by
MPG Books, Bodmin, Cornwall.

Contents

Illustrations

Acknowledgments

While working on my thesis on the IRB a few years ago, various individuals offered me some assistance. Special thanks are due to Thomas Bartlett for supervising my research and allowing me the intellectual freedom to pursue my own ideas, which I have continued to develop and revise since completing my degree. I also received help in locating useful sources and benefitted from discussions with various scholars. These include Gary Owens, Patrick Maume, Marta Ramón García, Carlo Maria Pellizzi, Donal McCracken, Michael Funchion, Máirtín Ó Catháin, Christopher Woods, David Doyle, Marie Coleman, Stephen Ball, Andrew Newby, Michael Ruddy, Jim Maher, Shin-ichi Takagami, Brian Maye, Christy Campbell, Helen Meehan, Catherine B. Shannon, Guy Beiner, Donald Jordan and James Quinn. Encouragement to persevere with my research was provided at times by Lawrence McBride, Jim Donnelly, Timothy Meagher, Vincent Comerford, Eunan O'Halpin and Joe Lee. Some descendants of men who were leading figures in the IRB during the later nineteenth century provided oral pieces of information or help in locating obscure written sources. These are Hilda Allan, Marie Fitzgerald, Louisa Nally, Harry Boland, Joseph McCullough, Ken Carroll, William Halpin, John C. Elliott, Denise Mell and Gerard McGowan. I wish to thank David Craig for allowing me to quote from documents and reproduce illustrations held in the National Archives, Gerry Lynne for permission to reproduce material held in the National Library, and The Board of Trinity College Dublin for allowing me to publish quotes from letters in the Davitt and Dillon papers held in the college's manuscripts department. Thanks are also due to John C. Elliott, Pam Rietsch and Hilda Allan for letting me reproduce illustrations in their possession. Finally, extra special thanks are due to my parents, Donard and Ailis, for their moral support.

Abbreviations

AOH	Ancient Order of Hibernians
CBS	Crime Branch Special (1887–1914)
CLS	Celtic Literary Society
CO	Colonial Office
CSB	Crime Special Branch (1882–1886)
DICS	District Inspector, Crime Special
DMP	Dublin Metropolitan Police
DPB	*Devoy's Post Bag*, ed. W. O'Brien and D. Ryan (2 vols, Dublin, 1979)
DUR	*Dublin University Review*
GAA	Gaelic Athletics Association
HGA	Home Government Association
HO	Home Office
HRCGB	Home Rule Confederation of Great Britain
HRL	Home Rule League
IAAA	Irish Amateur Athletics Association
INA	Irish National Alliance
INB	Irish National Brotherhood
INFA	Irish National Federation of America
INLA	Irish National League of America
IPHRA	Irish Protestant Home Rule Association
ISRP	Irish Socialist Republican Party
IRA	Irish Republican Army
IRB	Irish Republican Brotherhood
NAI	National Archives of Ireland
NBSP	National Brotherhood of Saint Patrick
NLI	National Library of Ireland, Manuscripts Department
NLS	National Literary Society
NMC	National Monuments Committee
OGBU	Old Guard Benevolent Union
PLC	Parnell Leadership Committee
PRO (London)	Public Record Office, London
Special Commission Report	*Special Commission Act, 1888: reprint of the shorthand notes of the speeches, proceedings and evidence taken before the commissioners appointed under the above-named act* (12 vols, London, 1890)

TCD	Trinity College Dublin, Manuscripts Department
UB	United Brotherhood (alternative title for Clan na Gael)
UCD	University College Dublin, Manuscripts Department
UIB	United Irish Brotherhood
UICA	United Irish Centennial Association
UIL	United Irish League
UILA	United Irish League of America
RIC	Royal Irish Constabulary
WTMC	Wolfe Tone Memorial Committee
YIS	Young Ireland Society
YIL	Young Ireland League

Introduction

There are inherent difficulties in writing a history of a secret organization like the IRB, which left few records behind and no one can claim to understand fully. Nevertheless, what I have attempted to do is to explain the IRB's politics from the 'inside-out'. In other words, instead of focusing on the reactions of political elites to its existence, which is the IRB's only claim to fame in most history books, I have tried to understand and explain what it sought to do itself. It is an attempt to write the first 'internal' history of the IRB. Very many of the 'grey areas' of the political history of Ireland under the Union, from the Great Famine to 'the Treaty', revolve around the history of the IRB and what it was *reputedly* doing, thinking, or stood for. I hope this book goes some way towards throwing much greater light upon these grey areas and that its arguments and conclusions are not read as being dogmatic. To examine the IRB's perspective on Irish politics and the relationship between Britain and Ireland does not mean retrospectively justifying its ideas or actions, but it is necessary to examine the IRB in depth if historical awareness of how and why a republican politics developed in modern Ireland is ever to improve. If the history of Irish republicanism is often seen as a contentious subject, this may well be because the actual evolution of republicanism in Ireland under the Union has never really been examined. As a result, historical understanding of the IRB has remained relatively slight or been shaped inordinately by anachronisms.

After spending eight years researching and writing about the history of the IRB, as well as doing biographical research on dozens of nineteenth-century republican activists, both well-known and obscure, for the Royal Irish Academy's Dictionary of Irish Biography project, I believe I have generally succeeded in establishing a suitable interpretative framework for understanding the IRB's politics. The first explanatory point that can be made is a deceptively simply one. To understand what it meant to be a 'republican' in nineteenth or early twentieth-century Ireland, one must examine the IRB in the context of the intellectual fashions of the proverbial 'long nineteenth century' of 1789–1914, which was a very different world, morally, politically and socially, to the age in which we now live. This is easier said than done. Republicanism, like liberalism, is to a large extent a form of political morality. Therefore, many are inclined to read the same meaning, or moral connotations, that such terms generally have today into their assessment of 'liberal' or 'republican' political activities in the past. However, just as the idea of a 'liberal' means something completely different today to what it meant in the Victorian era, the same is largely true of the meaning of the term 'republican'. This is something that modern liberal historiography in particular has often been inclined to ignore owing to its tendency to read a 'liberal' teleology of progress into the whole course of history and to overlook all other means of understanding the dynamics of political history.[1] A second explanatory point that can be made revolves around the question of why the IRB perceived itself, and was considered by its contemporaries, to be a 'revolutionary' movement. In our day and ever since the post-1918 period, most people's conception of the idea of a 'revolutionary' has been shaped by the revolutionary Marxist tradition, which was sparked off by the Russian revolution of 1917. Many historians are inclined to project this same perspective back into the past, reading a Marxist teleology of class conflicts into the whole course of history and identifying historical 'revolutionaries' solely on this basis. This, however, ignores the fact that in nineteenth-century Europe, which was a completely pre-democratic age dominated by monarchical and imperial governments, a 'revolutionary' was very often considered to be nothing more than an egalitarian democrat of any kind. Recognizing this is of critical importance in understanding the meaning of republicanism to contemporaries in nineteenth-century Europe and why the very idea of republicanism was something feared by political establishments across the continent.[2] Taking note of this reality is also important in contextualizing the political meaning given by contemporaries to the idea of 'nationalism' during this age of empires.

Various members of the IRB, whether in Ireland or in exile in America, left behind them personal memoirs or correspondence. Leaders as well as ordinary members of the IRB also wrote letters to the press quite frequently, or else made public speeches. By themselves, these sources do not necessarily reveal much, or indeed anything, of what the IRB was doing or thinking, because, for the most part, such letters and speeches only reflected personal standpoints and perspectives. Individual IRB men did not spell out ideological blueprints for a new society and the organization did not issue revolutionary manifestos of a similar kind. This is precisely because 'the organization' was not a revolutionary Marxist movement. It was a 'republican brotherhood' or an underground party that could accommodate diversity of political opinion. How then can we interpret what the organization as a whole was attempting to do from such sources? I believe that when the timing of these letters, or speeches, is examined closely, their meaning can become very clear. In particular, their tenor very often reflected either some progress, or setback, which the underground organization had just experienced, although for obvious reasons nothing was 'spelt out' in the public pronouncements. For this

1 Joyce Appleby, *Liberalism and republicanism in the historical imagination* (1992); P.N. Stearns (ed.), *A century for debate, 1789–1914: problems in the interpretation of European history* (New York, 1970), chapter 7, especially 188–90.   2 Phillip Nord, *The republican moment: struggles for democracy in nineteenth-century France* (Cambridge, 1994); Pamela Pilbeam, *Republicanism in nineteenth-century France* (London, 1995), 1–39.

reason, I believe one has to be familiar with both the mentalities and literary styles of the individuals who wrote them, as well as what was happening 'underground' at the same time these letters were written, before the whole scenario can start to make sense and a coherent (and hopefully accurate) chronological narrative can be put together.

For most of the IRB's history, the principal source of information available on its activities are the observations, speculations and information provided in the police reports of Dublin Castle, the IRB's great political enemy. These sources are invaluable for an illustration of the mentality of policemen and the workings of intelligence-gathering bodies, but they are inherently very unreliable sources for the history of the IRB itself. Owing to its subject matter, this book focuses specifically upon explaining the IRB and its moral world, rather than that of the 'other side', and, in this respect, I believe that the following factors must be taken into account to understand the nature of police documents. In the Victorian era, which was very much a pre-democratic age, the standard theory governing policemen's behaviour and sense of civic responsibility in the United Kingdom was that there existed a certain 'criminal class' in society which needed to be closely observed and contained; this class was invariably seen as synonymous with the working classes, as it was believed they were inherently the least inclined to welcome the restricting effect of police activities upon social and political behaviour.[3] As far as Dublin Castle and its police forces were generally concerned, the existence of nationalist sentiments among the working classes was the most likely factor to disrupt the political and social order in Ireland. As early as 1843, a 'political crime' detective department was established in Dublin to deal with this threat. By the 1860s, the threat of trade unionism to the existing social order in England, and what was generally known as 'Fenianism' in Ireland, preoccupied many politicians and journalists. They depicted this threat by warning people about various mongrel creatures who were threatening to emerge from the bowels of society and turn the decent, civilized world on its head. The language used in all police reports depicts the same picture. Police commissioners encouraged their subordinates to think in terms of combating a particular 'Fenian class' in society or, more specifically, a 'criminal subculture of Fenianism' that needed to be kept in check, equating this 'Fenianism' with any nationalist sentiment or agitation that appeared to be fermenting among the Irish lower classes. As a result, virtually any form of mobilization among the Irish lower classes in the Victorian era was frequently classified in police reports as an example of 'Fenianism'. For example, almost any congregation of urban workers found in public houses, temperance societies, reading rooms or trade union halls was

3 Jennifer Davis, 'The London garrotting panic of 1862 and the creation of a criminal class in mid-Victorian England' in Gattrell, Lenman, Parker (eds.), *Crime and the law: the social history of crime in western Europe since 1500* (London, 1980), 190–214; David Phillips, *Crime and authority in Victorian England* (London, 1977); Clive Emsley, *Crime and society in England 1750–1900* (London, 1987).

considered to belong to the 'Fenian class', just as the presence of boisterous or rowdy congregations of rural labourers in country towns on market days or at fairs were often described as a manifestation of 'Fenianism'. Any politician who exhibited nationalist leanings was likewise often suspected of being a 'Fenian'. As a general rule, I believe that the most suitable means of using police reports as a source for the history of the IRB is to pay attention to what they can tell us about the activities of those same men mentioned in republicans' correspondence and memoirs, and then consider how much can be corroborated by other sources of information, such as what is known regarding the opinions and mentality of the individuals in question from their own correspondence, reported speeches in newspaper columns and the manner in which they acted.

As noted, my main focus in writing this book has been to attempt to trace what the IRB was actually thinking and attempting to do at any one time, thereby establishing as accurate and as comprehensive a chronological narrative of its history as possible. While its activities are constantly set against the backdrop of what other political interest groups were doing, broader reflections on the degree to which the IRB succeeded, or failed, to affect the 'course of Irish history', and what its role was therein, have been confined mostly to the book's concluding chapter. This assesses the role of republicanism in Irish life under the Union, provides a complete overview of the IRB's history and offers a new interpretation of the origins and dynamics of the 'Irish revolution' of the early twentieth century by interpreting it in the context of the evolution of republican political activity in Ireland over the preceding fifty-odd years. As a concluding remark I might note that, while writing this work, a very different picture has emerged in my mind from the prevailing popular view of the nature of the IRB's politics, when it was at the height of its potency and as to what role it actually played in Irish history. In particular, I believe there is strong reason for arguing that the IRB made its most abiding impact upon Irish life not during the 'Fenian fever' of the 1860s or the 'Irish revolution' of 1913–1922, but rather during that period of history between the launch of the Land League and the formation of Sinn Féin. This is essentially why the book has been given its particular title. These were not only the most important years in the IRB's history, but they may well have been the most important years of modern Irish history in determining the social dynamics of all the political divisions that have affected the island of Ireland from 1916 down to our own day.

'An experiment should be made': the genesis of a republican brotherhood, 1848–67

On 17 March 1858 a half-dozen men launched an unnamed secret society in Lombard Street, Dublin, aimed at establishing an independent democratic republic in Ireland. These men constituted the remnants of an Irish revolutionary conspiracy started in 1849, which had been maintained in a very informal way primarily by young Protestant republicans in Dublin such as Philip Gray, a former mechanic, clerk and part-time medical student and Thomas Clarke Luby, a former law student turned journalist.[1] Their supporters included several Irishmen in the United States who had been forced to flee Ireland during 1848–9 following Dublin Castle's outlawing of their republican agitation. These emigrants had thought that the denuding of Ireland of British troops during the Crimean War might make it possible to launch a national insurrection and, although that war ended in 1856, they generally remained steadfast in this resolve. James Stephens, a 34-year-old private tutor in Dublin and former political exile of 1848, responded to their call but had different ideas regarding what form the conspiracy should take.

Stephens was convinced that 'to establish a democratic republic in Ireland; that is, a republic for the weal of the toiler' would require more than an insurrectionary conspiracy. He believed 'a thorough social revolution' would need to take place in Ireland before the masses could possibly become republicans. For this reason, Stephens desired to 'undertake the direction of a fraternal organization, to be composed of volunteers sharing my faith ... it seems to me such an experiment should be made'.[2] The movement he founded in 1858, rather than being a simple insurrectionary conspiracy, was a revolutionary fraternal organization determined to instill into the Irish masses the ability to think and act 'as befits citizens of a nation that is determined to be free'.[3] To reflect this objective, the movement soon chose to call itself the 'Irish Republican Brotherhood' (IRB). From its inception, its republicanism was defined far more so by its desire to act as an instrument of popular politicization than it was by its revolutionary ambition to form an Irish republic.

Stephens and the other IRB founders were typical nineteenth-century republicans; those 'bearded democrats', so familiar to French society, 'who do not believe in standing on ceremony', 'exercise an almost brutal freedom of speech', refuse to recognize anyone as their social betters and 'think they have

---

1 N.A. Leonard, 'Philip Gray', *Ríocht na Midhe*, 12 (2001), 165–75; T.C. Luby, 'Philip Gray – an Irish revolutionist', *Irish News* (New York), 17 Mar. 1857.   2 Desmond Ryan, *The Fenian chief* (1967), 133; James Stephens, 'Reminiscences of the commencement of the IRB' (chapter 20), *Weekly Freeman*, Feb. 1884.   3 *Irish Freedom*, Nov. 1910 (editorial on the purpose and history of IRB).

the monopoly of patriotism, just as the men in cassocks do of religion'.[4] In this extremely class-conscious and undemocratic age (when only 4 per cent of adult males could vote in the United Kingdom), politics was the concern only of the gentry and other elites privileged enough to own land and have access to higher education. In this political world of 'gentlemen', the likes of Stephens, a lower middle-class bohemian, or the working-class Chartists of Britain (with whom Stephens sympathized), simply did not count and were expected to act accordingly, deferring all judgment in political matters to the 'recognized leaders' of society. Conversely, being a democrat and egalitarian in mid nine-teenth-century Europe was tantamount to being a revolutionary.

During that century, in Ireland, as in France, to be a 'republican' was often considered nothing more than to be a champion of democratic liberty.[5] Concurrently, 'republicanism' was something that was feared by political establishments across Europe. Owing to their belief in 'the republican idea' that 'the common people are the [rightful] rulers of their own destiny', the IRB founders saw themselves as 'furious democrats in theory' and proclaimed the principles of their movement to be 'wholly and unequivocally democratic'.[6] If they favoured the idea of republican governments, this was generally simply because they were democrats. As two 'rank and file' IRB members of the 1860s recalled, the IRB's belief that 'a republic is the best and most sensible form of government' was based upon a firm conviction that monarchical systems of government of any kind 'breed flunkeyism and perpetuates silly class distinc-tions', both in society and in politics. The vast majority of IRB men detested this way of life, which they desired to see eradicated in Ireland, and were attracted to the idea of democratic republics because 'all were on a level of equality' in terms of their civic rights, irrespective of their social class.[7] A sense of excitement animated the IRB during the mid to late nineteenth century because it was seemingly 'the first really widespread, organized effort to bring about republican liberty in Ireland'; unlike 'previous organized efforts', it had actually 'arisen from the masses of the people themselves.' This perception gave rise to its so-called 'Fenian faith', which was that the very existence of their movement was proof that 'the spirit of liberty has been raised too high in the minds of the people to be crushed out by any power'.[8]

Stephens established a 'republican brotherhood' because he believed that any attempt to shape the political beliefs of the Irish people without directly

4 These quotations are translations of descriptions of contemporary French republicans in *Coup d'État* and *Boule de Suif*, stories by the French writer Guy de Maupassant (1850–93). 5 Philip Nord, *The republican moment: struggles for democracy in nineteenth-century France* (1994); Maurice Agulhon, *Marianne into battle* (1981).   6 Ryan, *Fenian chief*, 326; John O'Leary, *Recollections*, vol. 1 (1896), 245; Augustine Costello (IRB rebel of the 1860s) to *Freeman's Journal*, 27 Oct. 1891.   7 Mark Ryan, *Fenian memories* (1945), 211; Frank Roney, *Irish rebel and California labor leader* (1931), 53, passim; interview with Mark Ryan by *Irish Press*, reprinted in *Gaelic American*, 28 Nov. 1936.   8 Speech of Fred Allan (IRB), *Irish Daily Independent*, 26 Nov. 1894. 'An Ulsterman' [George Sigerson], *Modern Ireland* (2nd ed., 1869), chapter 2.

engaging with them through personal contact and actual political organization was futile. This belief in 'the principle of association' made him quite sceptical of the value of literary propaganda, or newspapers, as a revolutionary tool.[9] Like all European revolutionaries of 1789–1914, Stephens and the IRB believed that cultivating a 'spirit of fraternity' in a populace could spur it on to accomplish revolutionary changes in politics.[10] Whether they be republicans, socialists or communists, this concept of fraternity was associated in revolutionaries' minds with a philosophical belief in the equality of all men and a conviction that political liberty could be 'made known' to men of the lower classes often through a mere process of socialization, despite the perpetual claim of the 'gentlemanly classes' to the contrary.[11]

Like all revolutionary movements of its era, the IRB attempted to recruit people from all social classes and cultivate an egalitarian spirit within its organization, both to sustain its political resolve and to make a political impact, allowing artisans and labourers, for example, to hold higher positions in the organization than members of various middle-class professions.[12] By 1866, being thrilled that an egalitarian, fraternal spirit within his organization appeared to be making all its recruits 'consistent (else taught to be consistent) republicans',[13] Stephens professed that the Irish people had the potential to develop 'more republican lights and better republican principles than are to be found in any country in Europe'.[14] This over-confidence of Stephens was typical of revolutionaries of the time, and the magnitude of the task they faced, as revolutionary democrats, often led them to adopt very romantic attitudes indeed. For example, Stephens proclaimed that 'what we want is a nucleus' around which a new democratic political order could be built in Ireland, and the advice he gave to his followers was often nothing more than a simple, but dogmatic, order: 'Be you that nucleus.'[15]

This kind of rhetoric was not so naïve and simplistic as it might seem today, for in the nineteenth century such ideals had revolutionary connotations, culturally and politically. As James Billington has noted regarding this era of history, 'most revolutionaries sought the simple, almost banal aims of modern secular man generally. What was unique was their intensity and commitment to realizing them ... Their progress represented, for some, humanity emerging on wings from its cocoon; for others, a malignancy attacking civilization itself.'[16] Prior to the democratization of European governments in 1918 and especially in the completely pre-democratic age that was the mid nineteenth century, democratic politics did not signify electoral politics. It meant revolu-

9 Ryan, *Fenian chief*, 64. 10 A good description of the fraternal ethos of the IRB can be found in O'Leary, *Recollections*, vol. 2 (1896), 241–2. 11 James Billington, *Fire in the minds of men: the revolutionary faith* (1981), chapter 3. 12 Shinichi Takagami, 'The Dublin Fenians 1858–79' (unpublished PhD thesis, TCD, 1990), 81. 13 TCD, Stephens papers (included within Davitt papers), MS 9569d/30. 14 NAI, Fenian A files, carton 2, A180 (attached newspaper clipping from unidentified Irish-American paper, dated 24 Aug. 1866). 15 James Stephens, 'Personal recollections of '48', chapter 12 (originally published in *Irishman*, Feb–June 1882, bound in book volume in NLI, Ir. 92, s202).

tionary politics. This reality was reflected in the IRB founders' most famous (and most frequently misunderstood) verbal concoction. By calling upon all his 'brothers' to swear an oath to an 'Irish republic, now virtually established', Stephens asked each of his followers to see himself as 'virtually the citizen of our young republic', whereby all members of the organization automatically became equal to each other in their political rights, irrespective of their social class. In turn, Stephens equated this 'young republic' with 'the will of revolutionized Ireland',[17] or all those elements in Irish political society that might share the aspiration of this revolutionary, fraternal organization to destroy the old patriarchal order of political society and thereby keep a 'young republic', or democracy, alive. Anyone who identified with this broad revolutionary ideal could become a member of the IRB, provided he also swore to follow the orders of the organization's leaders.

As in provincial France, a republican politics developed and was sustained in nineteenth-century Ireland not least because of the power wielded by a Catholic political establishment that existed only to serve Catholic rather than 'national', or civic, ends.[18] There was more to the IRB's republicanism, however, than a desire to imitate French democratic radicalism. This was because it drew most of its political inspiration from the 'Young Ireland' movement, which was far more republican in its philosophy than were most contemporary champions of democratic liberty in France or England. A common perception of 'Young Ireland' in modern liberal Irish historiography is that it was simply a cultural and romantic nationalist movement, and its thinking has been analyzed with reference to liberal political ideas of both the nineteenth and twentieth centuries.[19] Certainly, like all nineteenth-century figures (even Marxist revolutionaries), the Young Irelanders were influenced heavily by romanticism, and their appeal through prose and ballad to the young to 'foster a public opinion' in Ireland that was 'racy of the soil' was partly an illustration of this.[20] Their belief that the 'risen and rising generation' would automatically take their side in any political dispute was shared by the IRB, which made sweeping declarations such as 'youth of Ireland ... you are our vanguard!', or 'it is the young men of Ireland who must and *will* obtain Irish liberty'.[21] Irish republican ballads of the nineteenth century, most of which dated from the 1840s, invariably exhibited the same enthusiasm.[22] The political

---

16 Billington, *Fire in the minds of men*, 13.   17 Jeremiah O'Donovan Rossa, *Rossa's recollections* (1898), quoted 274.   18 R.V. Comerford, *The Fenians in context: Irish politics and society, 1848–82* (1985), 212.   19 This is the model used in Richard Davis, *The Young Ireland movement* (1987), the only book written on the movement as a whole in the last sixty years.   20 Adam Zamoyski, *Holy madness: romantics, patriots and revolutionaries 1776–1871* (London, 1999). 21 'Owen Roe' [Eugene Davis] (ed.), *The reliques of John Keegan Casey* (1878), 229; T.C. Luby, 'Liberty or Destruction', *Irish People*, 23 Jan. 1864; 'National self-reliance', *Irish People*, 2 Jan. 1864. The names of the authors of articles in the *Irish People* were not published in the paper, but a bound volume of articles annotated with the names of the authors exists in NLI, John O'Leary papers, MS 18846.   22 *The Spirit of the Nation* (1843), the principal collection of such ballads, remained in print throughout the mid nineteenth century, going through fifty editions by 1870 but less than ten editions over the next sixty years and has never been reprinted since.

context of such sentiments was their expression of a hope in the eventual emergence of a democratic political order in Ireland. When declaring that 'the people' needed to be freed from 'the shackles of slavery', however, both the Young Irelanders and the IRB never placed their hope merely in the radical idea of democracy. Rather they hoped for the emergence of the basis of an independent civil society in Ireland, and this is why they could rightly be described as having been 'republicans'.

As Philip Petitt has emphasized recently, the ideological root of all true forms of republican political thought, ancient or modern, is the positing of a dichotomy between the political conditions of 'citizenship' and 'slavery'; these are synonymous with conditions of self-reliant patriotism (civic virtue) and political passivity (civic indifference) respectively.[23] Thomas Davis, John Mitchel and numerous other Young Ireland writers consciously made this republican dichotomy the basis of virtually all their propaganda, which was purposely written in a patriotic idiom. They claimed obsessively that it was an unavoidable truth of politics that every man was either a 'citizen' or a 'slave', 'for there is no middle term', and thus if a man was not to be a slave, he must assert his political rights in the manner of a citizen.[24] Because 'to act in politics is a matter of duty', according to Davis any man who was politically apathetic or concerned only about his own welfare was actually guilty of a sin, namely the 'sin against patriotism'.[25] There were two reasons why the Young Irelanders adopted this rigid republican philosophy; first, to highlight the lack of a strong civil society in Ireland, and, second, as a means of awakening the Irish intelligentsia to their responsibility to perform civic duties in Ireland itself.

Unlike most continental democrats, or republicans, and unlike almost all members of the IRB (with the noticeable exception of John O'Leary), the Young Irelanders had no inherent bias against the gentry and aristocracy. They desired to cultivate a patriotism among the gentry who could attend university, just as much as among the poor and self-educated. However, as in O'Leary's case,[26] either class of men was deemed worthy of respect by the Young Irelanders only in so far as they recognized the equality of *all* men through embracing the same patriotic political commitment. As republicans, the Young Irelanders believed primarily in the rule of the virtuous and the educated, regardless of what 'class' the virtuous and educated may have belonged to, and not so much in those democratic ideals of the French revolution which led most contemporaries (as it does down to the current day) to associate republicanism simply with the absence of a monarch and political self-determination for the masses. Like all republicans, instead of

23 Philip Petitt, *Republicanism: a theory of freedom and government* (1996), 31.   24 John Mitchel, *Jail journal* (Glasgow, c.1870), 25.   25 Arthur Griffith (ed.), *Thomas Davis: the thinker and teacher* (1914), 89.   26 This is clear from O'Leary's *Recollections* and the personal correspondence between Luby and O'Leary in NLI, O'Leary papers, MS 5926–7.

professing to hold a superior political ideology, the Young Irelanders and the IRB invariably claimed to possess a superior political *morality*. Their politics was always distinguishable by the claim that unless *their* critique of the political situation was accepted, Irishmen would remain slaves and could never become citizens.

The Young Irelanders quarrelled with the Catholic-liberal Daniel O'Connell over a number of issues, such as his refusal to accept anything but a Catholic university for Ireland and, most of all, his call for Irishmen to make no protest against Westminster's introduction of special legislation, not in force elsewhere in the United Kingdom, to deny Irishmen the liberty to bear arms. During the nineteenth century, the right to bear arms, rather than the right to vote, was seen as a basic token of citizenship, not least as it was a completely pre-democratic age. Consequently, this stance by O'Connell outraged the Young Irelanders, who denounced it as a contemptible, slavish act. As Thomas Davis noted, as 'to be without the power of resisting oppression is to be a slave', it does not matter whether a 'ruler says he will not rifle your altars, not pollute your hearths' or consistently proclaimed his desire 'to protect you'. If people do not possess the power to defend or advance their liberties, then they are inherently slaves. Davis also pointed out that, by definition, a nation is a political community that possesses both the ability and the resolve to 'vindicate its rights by the sword' if necessary: 'Ireland in this, as in other things, has been treated by England not as a nation, nor yet as a portion of herself, but as a right less dependant, an injured slave, disarmed and disabled ... lest she ever [attempt to] resume her rights.'[27]

Many Irishmen naturally felt a desire to bear arms and therefore members of the 'Confederate Clubs', founded by the Young Irelanders in a successful attempt to alter the basis of Irish popular politics, began arming themselves, not to express a desire for rebellion, but rather to demonstrate their willingness to stand up for their rights in the manner of free citizens, like all the other proverbial 'citizen-soldiers', or democrats, of the time.[28] Westminster responded, however, by outlawing the clubs, smashing their press and imprisoning all their leaders; this prompted many to reorganize themselves as a secret society, which was eventually transformed into the IRB.

Not surprisingly, later generations of republicans – particularly up until the Third Reform Bill of 1884 – felt the same way about this question because it was not until after the democratization of European politics in the wake of the First World War that this idea of the right to bear arms as a 'mark of citizenship' truly began to lose its relevance.[29] Volunteer movements were established frequently in nineteenth-century England to enhance men's sense of civic

27 Griffith (ed.), *Thomas Davis*, 67–9.   28 Gary Owens, 'Popular mobilization and the rising of 1848: the clubs of the Irish Confederation', in L.M. Geary (ed.), *Rebellion and remembrance in modern Ireland* (2001), 51–63.   29 Patrick Maume, 'Young Ireland, Arthur Griffith and republican ideology: the question of continuity' (1999), 157.

responsibility, but in Ireland this was neither encouraged nor allowed. As J.K. Casey, an IRB man and popular poet, noted that one reason for this was that 'if the House of Commons heard that a modern Napper Tandy had assembled 100,000 volunteers armed in the Phoenix Park', it was very likely that 'a bill for the repeal of the union would literally scamper through that body' if the government did not want to face an uprising. To prevent the Irish political community from ever being in a position to assert its right to act in this manner the special legislation was kept perpetually in place.[30]

In Ireland under the Union, the government (the Dublin Castle administration) was appointed by the British cabinet in London and was accountable only to the cabinet, not to the House of Commons at Westminster and certainly not to the Irish people or their political representatives. Irish MPs could speak at Westminster in protest about the actions of this administration, if they so desired, but its prerogatives were fundamentally unchallengeable since Irish representation in commons (one sixth of the total) was far too small to form a government in the British 'first past the post' system of majority governments. Hence, as T.W. Moody and Oliver MacDonagh noted, the government of Ireland under the Union was inherently a very irresponsible and essentially colonial form of government, no matter how much its leaders may have desired to govern Ireland fairly.[31] Republicans argued that whatever power which had been entrusted in Irish MPs by the electorate in Ireland was being denied proper expression. For this reason, they declared that Westminster could never be anything more than a 'talking shop' for Irish politicians. Those who were willing to enter it, rather than seek to win independence by mobilizing the masses at home, were forever described by IRB men as 'will-o-the-wisp-politicians' who were merely 'fritting away much of the best talent of our country' by slavishly acquiescing in the British government's attempts to deny Irishmen the right of meaningful political representation.[32] During 1847–8, Fintan Lalor and John Mitchel argued that only one logical conclusion could be drawn from this nature of British rule in Ireland under the Union: no valid form of social contract could be said to exist between the British government and the Irish people. From this premise, Lalor believed that Dublin Castle 'may be lawfully, and ought to be, resisted by any and every means of force whatsoever' and that Irishmen had both a perfect legal right and effectively a political duty to claim and exercise all the rights of government for themselves.[33] Likewise Mitchel proclaimed that neither Dublin Castle nor Westminster had any just legal claim to act as a government in Ireland because,

30 Davis (ed.), *J.K. Casey*, 233–6.   31 T.W. Moody (ed.), *The Fenian movement* (1967), 101; Ciaran Brady (ed.), *Interpreting Irish history* (Dublin, 1994), 106.   32 Patrick Cullen, 'James Stephens and the *Irish People* in the evolution of Irish nationalist politics in the nineteenth century' (1997), 93–4, 107; T.W. Moody, *Davitt and Irish revolution* (1981), 40; C.J. Kickham, 'Two sets of principles', *Irish People*, 19 Dec. 1863; T.C. Luby, 'Aspirationists', *Irish People*, 2 Apr. 1864; Fred Allan (IRB) to *Irish Daily Independent*, 6 Oct. 1894.   33 L. Fogarty (ed.), *James Fintan Lalor* (1918), quoted 75.

in a jurisprudential sense, it acted entirely 'above law', owing to its unaccountable nature.[34] Mitchel accused all politicians and writers who refused to
recognize this reality of engaging in sophistry and deliberately attempting to
mislead Irish public opinion for their own purposes.[35] Subsequent generations
of Irish republican activists invariably followed this particular example of
Mitchel to the letter. The IRB invariably demonstrated this resolve by
adopting a vanguardist mentality, proclaiming that the only Irishmen who
could justly claim to be called a 'patriot' or a 'nationalist' were those who
accepted these precepts of 'republican nationality' and attempted to assert the
Irish political community's rights accordingly. By contrast, all who continued
to operate within the Westminster arena were deemed by republicans as not
worthy to be considered as defenders of the rights of the Irish political
community.[36] Republicans who adopted this attitude claimed that they were
exercising 'the right to think, act and feel in accordance with the national will',
or the general will, of the Irish people. The IRB 'claimed on behalf of those
who advocate republican ideas and principles' the right to think and act in this
manner, just as had 'any section of our fellow countrymen' the right 'to pursue,
according to their own judgment, any course that seems best to them'. The
party-political line of the IRB was always to emphasize to the Irish public their
need to create a political movement that was 'most thorough and most national
in its republican discipline', by whatever means possible, to 'build up' the basis
of an Irish nation.[37]

When the IRB was established, Irish parliamentary representation was
divided exclusively along the traditional, English political affiliations of Whigs
and Tories, as had been the case for many years before and would be for many
years to come.[38] The individualism of all MPs in this pre-party-political age
only compounded this fact. Ever since the days of the Daniel O'Connell's
Catholic Association, Irish MPs at Westminster were also divided along
politico-religious grounds. Irishmen had no say whatsoever in how their
country was taxed or how the economy was managed: so the only questions
that Irish parliamentary representatives could concern themselves with related
to property rights and denominational education. As O'Connell had discovered so clearly during the 1820s, extra-parliamentary political agitations were
the only possible, effective means of championing other political reforms.
When the IRB was formed, however, such agitations were neither widespread
nor encouraged by most political representatives. This played a large part in
providing republicans with an opportunity to make their presence felt in the
popular political sphere.

In March 1861 the National Brotherhood of Saint Patrick (NBSP), a public
fraternal organization that quickly spread to several parts of the United

34 Mitchel, *Jail journal*, 24, 33.   35 Ibid., 24–6.   36 Davis (ed.), *J.K. Casey*, 238; John
O'Leary, 'Self-sacrifice', *Irish People*, 19 Dec. 1863; T.C. Luby, 'Aspirationists', *Irish People*,
2 Apr. 1864.   37 Speech of Patrick Hoctor (IRB), *Irish Daily Independent*, 25 Nov. 1895.
38 B.M. Walker, *Parliamentary election results in Ireland, 1801–1922* (1978).

Kingdom, was established and soon won a very large following. The NBSP was a similar type organization to the Repeal and Confederate Clubs of the 1840s, setting up political clubs and reading rooms specifically for the disenfranchised lower classes. As both movements were intended primarily to be instruments of popular politicization, not surprisingly they were heavily patronized and co-founded by republicans. In turn, the fact that the executive of the NBSP was not controlled by the MPs at Westminster, the Catholic hierarchy or other 'recognized leaders' of Irish public opinion meant that its existence was not welcomed by the political establishment in Ireland.[39] Many IRB men became active in the NBSP and, realizing that they identified with the republicans' democratic brand of politics, the NBSP's founder, Thomas Neilson Underwood, a Presbyterian barrister from Tyrone, and its secretary, Charles Guilfoyle Doran, a civil engineer from Wicklow (both of whom were descendants of prominent republicans of the 1790s) soon opted to become IRB leaders.[40] This helped the IRB to extend its secret organization through the medium of the open NBSP. The most notable single illustration of this took place in November 1861 when, through the medium of the NBSP (and with Irish-American financial assistance), the IRB was able to monopolize control of a monster funeral demonstration held in Dublin for a former popular leader of the Confederate Clubs, T.B. McManus.[41] This was considered as a landmark event by very many Irishmen during the later nineteenth century. As one journalist of the day noted, this was because previous agitations (particularly O'Connell's) had always been organized and based solely upon 'the ostensible leaders of public opinion of the day and the Catholic clergy'. The McManus demonstration, by contrast, was clearly 'organized by the people themselves', without the support or approval of either the 'ostensible leaders' of public opinion or the church.[42] In other words, it was a remarkable democratic political occurrence in the Ireland of that time. Owing to the fact that it collected subscriptions from the poor at church gates, O'Connell's Catholic Association (the branches of which were invariably led by parish priests) has traditionally been described by historians as a 'democratic' political movement, but it cannot be ignored that its purpose was only to serve the interests of Catholic elites, not at all to empower the poor, be they Catholic or otherwise.

Thanks to the huge social and political gulf separating the world of the gentlemen politicians at Westminster from the disenfranchised and apparently powerless workers and clerks of the NBSP, the niche established by republi-

---

39 Comerford, *Fenians in context*, 71–3. 40 Roney, *Irish rebel*, 156–7; John Daly, 'Recollections of Fenians and Fenianism', *Irish Freedom*, Sept. 1912, Mar. 1913. Underwood was descended, through his mother, from Samuel Neilson, while Doran was descended, through his mother, from Billy Byrne. 41 L.R. Bisceglia, 'The Fenian funeral of Terence Bellew McManus', *Éire-Ireland* (fall 1979), 45–64. 42 Richard Pigott, *Recollections of an Irish nationalist journalist* (Dublin, 1883), 115. On this theme, see also Davis (ed.), *J.K. Casey*, 229–38.

cans in Irish public life during the early to mid 1860s was certainly not a source
of great anxiety to the Whigs and Tories of Catholic and Protestant Ireland.
Rather it was generally of concern only to other political groupings that were
involved in the popular political sphere. The IRB soon found itself facing
numerous barriers in its attempt to revive the republican political enthusiasms
of the mid to late 1840s, and none was greater than the growing influence of
the Catholic Church after the restoration of the hierarchy throughout the UK
in 1850 by Whitehall and Rome. By the late 1850s, the *Nation* had fallen into
the hands of the Sullivans, a clericalist, Catholic political family from west
Cork. The Sullivans owned the *Nation* from 1855 until 1891, when they characteristically sold the newspaper to the *Irish Catholic*. Like all
formally-educated Catholics (most of whom were educated solely through
diocesan colleges), A.M. Sullivan felt a deep antipathy to republican notions of
political or constitutional liberty, which seemed only to produce rabidly anti-
clerical governments. Therefore, like O'Connell, his ideal of political liberty
was to achieve equality of status and power for Irish Catholics within the
empire, for he 'saw nothing to shake my conviction that Englishmen enjoy, on
the whole, more of solid, secure and substantial liberty without license than,
perhaps, any other nation in the civilized world'.[43] Sullivan knew that if the
Catholic Association's politics was to be revived, this could only be done by
centralizing control of Irish popular politics in the hands of moderates and that
this was precisely what the republicans were trying to prevent. Therefore he
was fiercely critical of the leadership of the NBSP, which was not cooperating
with his and the Catholic hierarchy's attempt to reestablish the Catholic
Association as the 'National Association'. To counter the influence of
Sullivan's new *Nation* and to defend the NBSP's right to its political independence, the IRB set up a rival newspaper, the *Irish People*, in late 1863. Stephens
immediately denounced Sullivan (not by name) in the *Irish People* as a 'felon-
setter', or a man who spoke of all democrats and republicans as if they were
criminals, and a hypocritical man who felt he had the right 'to denounce and
"warn" the People, when they presume to think and act for themselves and, at
the same time, to profess the utmost love for and devotion to the national
cause'.[44] Subsequent generations of IRB men often used this term of
Stephens, 'felon-setting', to denote the conservatism, or what they saw as the
hypocrisy of Irish Catholic political leaders who professed to hold nationalist
sympathies, yet evidently believed that any political movement in Ireland
which was not controlled by the gentry class, or the bishops, was of criminal
tendencies.

Owing to his control of the *Nation*, his very good relationship with the
Catholic Church and his popular histories which depicted 'Irish nationality' as
inherently Catholic, A.M. Sullivan was perhaps the single most influential

43 T.D. Sullivan, *A.M. Sullivan: a memoir* (Dublin, 1885), 7; idem, *Troubled times in Irish politics* (Dublin, 1905), passim.   44 James Stephens, 'Felon-setting', *Irish People*, 12 Dec. 1863.

writer in mid-to-late Victorian Ireland. Like many Irish Catholic politicians under the Union, he felt that the existing terms of the Union were unjust, yet decided to place his faith in that constitution 'which we may never feel or see',[45] namely the unwritten constitution of the United Kingdom. Republicans were always angry that the Irish middle classes usually adopted this attitude, but were very often powerless to reverse this development. They could argue, with good reason, that Westminster's continued authority over Ireland was designed only to exploit Irish resources for the empire. As the 'unwritten constitution' was totally flexible *in theory*, however, anyone could easily dismiss this argument by claiming that there was potentially no limit to the amount of progressive political reforms that Westminster could introduce in Ireland. This was the great quagmire in all Irish republican propagandistic efforts.

Up until his death in 1875, John Mitchel argued repeatedly that the political credibility of the 'unwritten constitution' among Irishmen was only being kept 'seemingly alive by the commercial world' and, in particular, by the 'canting spell' of the utilitarian political philosophy which the British empire had spawned.[46] Indeed, it is often forgotten today that the impulse which led to the creation of the utilitarian political philosophy during the later eighteenth century was not merely a desire to 'introduce economics into political philosophy' for the first time. It was also a direct response to the threat then being posed, militarily and morally, to the British empire by the new democratic republics of America and France. The British utilitarians purposely rejected the French and Americans' equation of political liberty with the existence of written constitutions and accountable governments. They argued that the test of good government was not whether it was accountable to a populace, or whether a people's liberties were defined by a written, that is, a republican, constitution. Rather a good government was one that saw it as its 'moral responsibility' to create economic and social circumstances whereby men could have greater opportunities for attaining self-fulfillment as individuals. This new 'liberal' philosophy, with its clarion calls of economic progress and 'morally responsible' government, became very influential throughout the United Kingdom, because of the unrivalled commercial success of the British empire. The resulting rapid industrialization of England, as well as many parts of Scotland and Ulster, created a higher standard of living for very many of its subjects and, in the process, seemed to validate simultaneously both the liberal philosophy and the institutions of the empire. Not surprisingly, as prosperity is most people's idea of liberty, the effect this had upon Irish political attitudes was considerable. Whereas democratic-republicans all over nineteenth-century Europe promised a future not only of greater liberty and equality but of greater prosperity as well, in Ireland, republicanism was invariably seen by the middle classes only as an argument against prosperity, since it entailed threatening the British connection. Sullivan's professed admiration for the fact that

45 T.D. Sullivan, *A.M. Sullivan* (Dublin, 1885), 7.   46 Mitchel, *Jail journal*, 25, 89.

the British constitution allowed men to enjoy substantial liberty 'without license' reflected this growing influence of English liberalism on Irish political attitudes. Most of all, it reflected the fact that Catholic social teaching invariably identifies with any political ideal which allows a people to thrive without being disturbed by the existence of a state. As Thomas Francis Meagher (one of the few Catholic 'Young Ireland' leaders and a man who considered Stephens to be 'the Wolfe Tone of our generation') lamented, this was why Catholicism and the civic philosophy of republicanism were destined to remain incompatible in most people's minds.[47]

By their very nature, both the state and Catholic educational system in Ireland under the Union taught Irishmen not to concern themselves with the arbitrary powers of interference held by the state, or the lack of definition to their liberties, thereby ensuring that they would not be influenced by the republican intellectual tradition.[48] They also subscribed to an aristocratic social ideal and this helped to negate the influence of democratic–republican radicalism in Ireland. John Mitchel knew that he could not alter the nature of the educational system in Ireland but he purposely wrote fierce polemics in an attempt to break up the hold of English liberalism upon Irish political leaders' attitudes. To do so, he rejected Victorian society's blind faith in the notion of 'progress' by arguing, in the manner of classical republican philosophers, that history will always follow a cyclical course, rotating between periods of barbarism and civilization.[49] He believed that the gross materialism of Victorian society was proof that an era of barbarism, not of so-called 'progress', was dawning, and he claimed that this trend had become most evident precisely in the way politicians were now asking men to be content with seeking greater material comforts, instead of the rights and duties of citizenship. Stressing that civic virtue cannot thrive in a culture that emphasized individualism and self-fulfilment, Mitchel believed that all Ireland's political woes and divisions stemmed from Irishmen's 'intellectual timidity' in the face of English liberal intellectual fashions, and, in their cowardly willingness to take part in the general race for prosperity, instead of demanding the rights and duties of citizenship.[50] Mitchel argued that any struggle for political freedom in Ireland inevitably 'will become a republican one in the long run', owing to the complete absence of a civil society in Ireland, and he based his prediction that 'the passionate aspiration for Irish nationhood will outlive the British Empire' upon this same reasoning.[51] However, the fact that Mitchel felt it necessary to

47 W.F. Lyons (ed.), *Thomas Francis Meagher* (London, 1869), 142–7. Ryan, *Fenian chief*, 155.
48 Senia Paseta, *Before the revolution: nationalism, social change and Ireland's Catholic elite, 1879–1922* (1999). Philip Petitt, *Republicanism* (Oxford, 1996), chapters 1–4, provides a brilliant scholarly analysis of the conflict between the republican and liberal intellectual traditions in modern political thought. 49 Mitchel, *Jail journal*, 88–9. For a liberal critique of Mitchel's writings, see James Quinn, 'John Mitchel and the rejection of the nineteenth century', *Éire-Ireland* (fall/winter 2003), 90–109. 50 Arthur Griffith (ed.), *John Mitchel's Jail journal* (1914), preface. 51 Mitchel, *Jail journal*, 26; *The last conquest of Ireland, perhaps* (Glasgow, n.d.), 220.

adopt such a polemical pose and reject completely the intellectual fashions of the day in order to make his point clearly shows that interest in republicanism was very slight in Ireland. This was perhaps best illustrated by the fact that Irish political society was divided on religious grounds and neither community exhibited any real conception of its civil liberties other than a desire to protect the influence of their respective communities and derive more benefits from the imperial economic system.

The IRB and the *Irish People* faced the same problems as the Young Irelanders did in pointing out the shortcomings of the liberal philosophy. The *Irish People* declared that the Irish middle classes' 'whine about the shortsighted policy of England, in making a foe of Ireland instead of a friend' by not championing the interests of the Irish population was 'all moonshine', for British state interests, never the economic or political wishes of Irishmen, would alone determine how Ireland was governed under the Union. Like Mitchel, the *Irish People* claimed that all Irish politicians and writers knew this to be the case, but were afraid to acknowledge it publicly either out of a slavish moral cowardice or a covert desire to prosper under existing political circumstances.[52] As Sullivan had turned the *Nation* into a self-consciously Catholic newspaper, the *Irish People* was also determined to revive the 'wise policy of Thomas Davis and the old *Nation* of intermeddling with no religious questions', as 'such irritating topics' only 'tend to produce bitterness among Irishmen of different persuasions'.[53] As did the *Nation* newspaper of the 1840s, the *Irish People* acted self-consciously as an organ to 'educate the people' in essentially moral, self-improving lessons.[54] Its calls for the lower classes to develop a spirit of 'political self-reliance' were also mingled frequently with declarations (in professing to be the true voice of 'the people') that 'superstition is fast yielding to common sense in this country. The ungenerous attacks of some of our priests can no longer warp the people from their efforts to be free ... Men think for themselves now-a-days.'[55] These calls by the *Irish People* for Irish Catholics to 'think for themselves' were clearly never intended (or presented) as an attack on religion, but were rather a call for Irishmen to assert their complete political independence from the influence of churchmen. Until this occurred, the IRB believed that Irishmen could 'not advance one step on the road to independence'.[56]

The IRB's propaganda campaign of the 1860s might never have attracted

---

52 C.J. Kickham, 'Two sets of principles', *Irish People*, 19 Dec. 1863; Luby, 'Aspirationists', *Irish People*, 2 Apr. 1864.   53 C.J. Kickham, 'Sectarianism', *Irish People*, 16 Apr. 1864. 54 T.C. Luby, 'Earnestness', *Irish People*, 16 Jan. 1864; 'Faith and Perseverance', *Irish People*, 30 Apr. 1864; 'National self-reliance', *Irish People*, 2 Jan. 1864; John O'Leary, 'Self-sacrifice', *Irish People*, 19 Dec. 1863. Most editorials of the *Irish People* had titles like these.   55 Denis Mulcahy, 'The Irish priests and the People', *Irish People*, 14 May 1864.   56 O'Leary, *Recollections* 2, 198–9 (quoting Kickham in *Irish People*). This argument would also dominate IRB propaganda in the later nineteenth century, particularly in the 1890s. A very good example is Fred Allan to *Irish Weekly Independent*, 6 Oct. 1894.

great publicity were it not that Tory newspapers which represented the
Protestant British political establishment decided to publicize and distort the
arguments of the *Irish People* with a view to widening the politico–religious gulf
in Ireland. To alienate the wealthy (mostly Protestant) sections of Irish society,
the Tory press irrationally accused the editors of the *Irish People* of being
enemies of religion and property rights, thereby reacting in the conventional
Victorian manner to the rise of any democratic challenges to authority.
Meanwhile, to alienate Irish Catholics, the Tories claimed that all Catholics
must realize that if the men behind the *Irish People*, with their 'despicable
ideas' inspired by the 'American democracy', were really intent on challenging
the British crown, then 'before they reach that throne, they must trample upon
the altar and walk over the prostrate body of the priesthood'.[57] As the Tories
expected, this created panic among the Irish Catholic hierarchy, who now
feared that Jacobins were in their midst. With the moral support of the clericalist Sullivan brothers (who denounced the *Irish People* for launching a
supposed 'anti-clerical crusade'),[58] priests began requesting that parishioners
inform the police of any secret societies in their parish and threatened to
excommunicate anyone who read the *Irish People* or was a member of a secret
society. Many Catholic IRB men listened in stunned disbelief when priests told
them that their political goals were 'illegal'; they were prompted to reply that
their goals were illegal only according to British law and had nothing to do with
their faith or the pastoral mission of the church, but these complaints were
invariably made to deaf ears.[59] As a result, IRB men in the cities became
quite anti-clerical, while in the small towns and villages, they generally played
a role similar to that of many republicans in provincial France; namely acting
as a rival community leader to the parish priest.[60]

The original IRB leadership of Stephens, Luby, O'Leary and Kickham all
professed never to have hoped to receive the support of the 'bourgeois' Irish
middle classes, and to be perfectly happy to rely on the 'men of no property' to
achieve their objectives.[61] The IRB leadership, as well as its 'rank and file'
(many of whom would later form the Land League), also possessed a strong
bias against the entire gentry and aristocracy of the country.[62] Be that as it may,
the vast majority of IRB leaders refused to tolerate the idea of instigating class
conflicts in the country. This was because their social radicalism never really
developed beyond a strongly egalitarian political commitment, desiring to
equalize the power of each class in the country. Hence although the IRB often

57 O'Leary, 'The *Times* on Fenianism', *Irish People*, 9 Sept. 1865; C.J. Kickham, 'The enemy's
press', *Irish People*, 7 Jan 1865.   58 T.D. Sullivan, *Troubled times in Irish politics* (1905), chapters 7–8.   59 Devoy, *Recollections*, 120–3; Roney, *Irish rebel*, 74–5, 148–9; O'Leary,
Recollections, vol. 2, 33–4. Cardinal Cullen, in particular, regularly described the IRB as an
'illegal' organization. Moody (ed.), *Fenian movement*, 109.   60 Comerford, *Fenians in context*,
212.   61 O'Leary, *Recollections*, vol. 1, 30–1; vol. 2, 147–9; C.J. Kickham, 'Ireland United',
Irish People, 26 Mar. 1864; James Stephens, 'Fenianism past and present' (NLI MS 10492),
Frank Roney, *Irish rebel*, chapter 2.   62 T.C. Luby, 'The elites of property', *Irish People*, 23
Jan. 1864.

spoke of the need 'to eliminate class distinctions' from Irish society and politics, it argued that this classless society could only be established by cultivating
an egalitarian political ethic among all classes and creeds, through their developing a common patriotism, or mutual concern for each other's welfare: 'what
we really require is this land of ours is a commingling of classes for the
common benefit of all'.[63] Adopting a Marxist perspective, some historians have
argued that this refusal of the IRB to promote class conflicts should be seen as
evidence that all the IRB really desired, subsconsciously, was simply greater
political mobility and power for the lower-middle classes in society, from which
its leadership was invariably drawn.[64] This argument is too simplistic, however,
for two reasons. On one hand, *all* people involved in politics, including Marxist
revolutionaries, inherently do so out of a desire to achieve, or maintain, power.
On the other hand, the goal of eliminating class distinctions was very much a
revolutionary one in the Victorian era and stood in direct conflict with all
aspects of the existing, aristocratic social and political order. It was a revolutionary idea for its time. What can be said about the IRB, however, is that its
revolutionary strategy was never clearly defined. It certainly possessed a hope
that it could force all classes to alter their politics through its strength in
numbers,[65] but as an organization, it was essentially just what the Confederate
Clubs had been: a conglomerate of democratic political activists (associated
with reading rooms, literary societies and trade unions), who possessed a desire
to act like a citizens' defence force. The only difference was that, after the
suppression of the Confederate Clubs, the IRB was necessarily a secret organization, and it could also draw upon the financial support of the Irish exiles of
1848. By 1859, these exiles had established themselves as a pressure group in
American politics known as the 'Fenian Brotherhood'.

The IRB's obsession with the importance of 'action' was central to its politics,
to such an extent that even the nomenclature it adopted to describe its organization or objectives was deemed unimportant.[66] In this respect, John Mitchel's
truthful philosophical observation that 'republicanism, or monarchism, *in the
abstract*, is nothing'[67] was an idea that shaped the attitudes of virtually all nineteenth-century Irish republicans. They understood, as did Mitchel, that
political ideas can have no bearing on reality whatsoever unless there is a willingness to implement them by *acting* upon them. The IRB often described
themselves as men 'who have set themselves in Ireland to teach republican principles and revolutionary action',[68] but did not distinguish between these two
facets of their activities. This was because they understood that unless Irishmen
were persuaded to take the revolutionary step of thinking and *acting* in the

---

63 C.J. Kickham, 'Ireland united', *Irish People*, 26 Mar. 1864; quotation: speech of P.N.
Fitzgerald (IRB), *Irish Daily Independent*, 25 Nov. 1895. **64** This is the interpretation of the
IRB offered in R.V. Comerford, *The Fenians in context*. See also T.W. Moody, *Davitt and Irish
revolution* (1981), 41. **65** C.J. Kickham, 'Ireland united', *Irish People*, 26 Mar. 1864. **66** John
O'Leary, *Recollections*, vol. 1, 119–27. **67** Mitchel, *Jail journal*, 88 (my italics). **68** Quotation
from Fred Allan (IRB) to *Irish Weekly Independent*, 6 Oct. 1894.

manner of republicans, then republican principles were an irrelevance and the
IRB's politics could not take effect. The Irish republicans of the 1860s – the
self-professed 'men of action' – invariably professed contempt for all those vain,
self-absorbed 'drawing-room patriots' and 'dilettantes' who were perhaps fond
of debating radical political ideas, but were actually incapable of, or unwilling to,
act upon them, because they could not transcend their personal class or religious
loyalties.[69] The members of the IRB, by contrast, saw themselves as 'men of
action' primarily because they were egalitarian democrats, committed to making
a real difference in the popular political sphere, and because they were ready to
launch an independence movement in the country.

As James Stephens was dependent on the Irish exiles of 1848 in America for
financial support (he did not attempt to collect subscriptions from IRB
members), he had to give much thought to their demand for rebellion in
Ireland. Consequently, on paper, he devised a system that would supposedly
allow his republican brotherhood to be transformed into a revolutionary army
if, or when, this became opportune. In such an eventuality, each 'centre' (the
term given to the leader of each revolutionary 'circle' or club of the IRB) was
to become a 'captain' and the centre's subordinates were to be assigned corresponding military ranks, in a descending scale. However, as this method of
organization was to be adopted by the IRB *only* when definite plans for a rising
were launched, Stephens always reminded his subordinates that, in all their
recruitment efforts, 'the question for you is not: "Will this man make a good
sergeant, captain etc." but, "Can this man organize, enroll, or enlist nine men,
ninety men etc. and keep them together till the time of action comes?"'[70]
Stephens was prepared to use Irish-American funding to buy arms in large
quantities only when Irish public opinion was clearly in favour of a rebellion.
In this respect, Stephens felt, as did the deputy IRB leadership of T.C. Luby,
Charles Kickham and John O'Leary (the three *Irish People* editors), that 'if the
Irish People be a failure', then the idea of rebellion, although perfectly justifiable in principle, was clearly out of the question, for the paper was published
'as a test' to see whether or not support for nationalist objectives actually
existed in the country.[71] In the meantime, Stephens discouraged all efforts to
import arms in regular small quantities, as he believed this would only make it
easier for Dublin Castle to track down their movements, seize the arms, arrest
the men involved and, consequently, suppress his organization.[72]

In its propaganda, the IRB always argued that Irishmen ought to possess a
willingness to bear arms to defend and to assert their liberties like freemen and

69 Luby, 'Aspirationists'; O'Leary, 'Self-sacrifice'; Kickham, 'Ireland united'.   70 TCD,
Stephens papers (included within the Davitt papers), MS 9659d/30.   71 Joseph Denieffe, *A
personal narrative of the Irish Revolutionary Brotherhood* (1906), 179–81.   72 O'Leary,
Recollections 2, 46; TCD, Stephens papers (included within the Davitt papers), MS 9659d/30.
73 Good examples are T.C. Luby, 'The use of arms', *Irish People*, 20 Feb. 1864; Davis (ed.),
J.K. Casey, 233–8; Bulmer Hobson, *Defensive warfare* (Belfast, 1909); John MacBride, 'Home
rule and an appeal to arms', *Irish Freedom*, Nov. 1912; P.S. O'Hegarty, *The victory of Sinn Féin*
(Dublin, 1924), 120.

to be ready to make a stand for Irish independence, but it never actually called for rebellion.[73] Owing to the special 'arms acts' which remained in almost perpetual operation in Ireland after 1845, the IRB was particularly at pains to emphasize that 'if Irishmen wish to be citizen-soldiers, if they wish for an impartial administration of justice', then 'they must look to themselves and not to English rulers for these great privileges'.[74] Under existing circumstances, however, owing to the arms acts and most Irishmen's fear of resisting them (thereby negating the possibility of forming *public* citizens' defence forces), the IRB had no option but to attempt to forward this goal solely through its own perseverance and stealth.[75] In so doing, it felt it was ensuring that Irish 'aspirations for freedom' could at least be 'brought within the range of practicality', for 'our nationality is frail unless it has stronger support than speech or song.'[76]

The IRB's desire to act as an instrument of popular politicization and its willingness to encourage the public to bear arms were closely related issues. The fact that all political leaders feared the idea of a democratic volunteer force being established in the country, as well as popular political movements (such as the NBSP) which they did not control, prompted the IRB to accuse them of deliberately assisting the British government attain its goal of leaving the Irish population forever powerless and unarmed, 'shouting and petitioning' for their rights like witless men who were 'striving to gain land in a boat without oars'.[77] In turn, republicans called upon 'the people' to take full control of their own political destinies, or, in other words, to 'cultivate civic virtue, through self-reliance'.[78] James Stephens proclaimed that 'the people' could become the rulers of their own destiny only if they developed 'the great, the essential, virtue of self-reliance': 'you, the strong of heart and arm' also needed to become sufficiently 'strong in intellect' to become 'fully equal to the conduct of your own affairs' and to develop 'the practical faculties needed to complete your task'.[79] Although 'the people' had always been led to believe by the Irish political establishment that they 'are powerless without leaders – without leaning on somebody', the IRB proclaimed that 'they should always remember it [politics] as a special business of their own – that by relying on themselves, nothing is impossible ... *Who would be free, himself must strike the blow.*'[80] These attempts to encourage the lower classes to be entirely self-reliant in their political conduct (whether by forming and leading their own political organizations or through being ready to bear arms like 'freemen'), were intended to fulfill the 'republican principle' of 'the extension of personal liberty' to members of

---

74 O'Leary, *Recollections*, vol. 2, 202 (quoting an article he wrote for the *Irish People*). 75 A good description of the purpose and difficulties involved in IRB arms importation efforts is William O'Brien's recollections of the Cork IRB in *Irish fireside hours* (Dublin, 1928), 114–22. 76 Davis (ed.), *J.K. Casey*, 236; quotation from 1883 IRB circular, which can be found in NAI, British in Ireland microfilm collection, Reel 4, Box 10, 200–3; Moody and O'Broin (eds.), 'The IRB Supreme Council 1868–78', Select Documents XXXII, *Irish Historical Studies* 19 (1974), 301. 77 Davis (ed.), *J.K. Casey*, 234; T.C. Luby, 'The use of arms', *Irish People*, 20 Feb. 1864. 78 Patrick Maume, 'Young Ireland', 157. 79 O'Leary, *Recollections*, vol. 1, quoted 169. 80 Davis (ed.), *J.K. Casey*, 238.

all sections of society,[81] and to muster a challenge to the political establishment by mobilizing a nascent, Irish democracy.

The IRB faced great difficulty in implementing its revolutionary strategy. Acquiring arms when this was forbidden by the British state required great conspiratorial expertise; moreover, the IRB, with its predominantly lower-class membership, had very limited funding, while firearms were expensive. Apart from the fact that its 'rank and file' could very rarely afford firearms, its members, most of whom were working five or six days of the week, were invariably nothing more than young men dreaming of being 'citizen-soldiers'. None of the IRB's founders had the slightest military knowledge or experience and, therefore, they could not train their men. During the early 1860s, this prompted those IRB men who *did* know something of military matters (such as John Devoy, a former member of the French Foreign Legion) to realize the necessity of recruiting from within the ranks of the British army. James Stephens's solution to this difficulty, however, was not to target the army; rather, he simply desired to ensure that his secret society was at all times 'governed by the spirit and letter of the discipline that governs an army', so it could develop 'a discipline never before equaled by men not trained in open war'.[82] His creation of a nominally autocratic structure for the IRB was intended to fulfill this same purpose, for, obviously, an army cannot elect its own leaders.[83] Stephens' belief that a secret society could possibly perform such a metamorphosis was undoubtedly very naïve. If many other IRB leaders possessed the same hope (which is by no means certain), this was no doubt because in its entire sixty-five year history only one IRB leader (J.J. O'Kelly) was ever a trained soldier.

Because Stephens made no systematic efforts to arm his followers, between 1858 and 1865 the IRB amassed a grand armoury of just pikes and little over one thousand antiquated rifles (essentially muskets),[84] which was all its members could afford. These weapons were either made or bought by 'rank and file' members of the organization, if only to express their personal desire to feel like 'freemen'. Not surprisingly, however, the IRB leadership of Stephens, Luby, O'Leary and Kickham (all of them permanently busy in the *Irish People* offices) had not the slightest intention of encouraging their followers to attempt to use, or even to display, these 'badges of freemen', because the IRB volunteers would have had no means of defending themselves. Not alone could they not possibly stand face-to-face with the British army, but the weapons at their disposal would not even have intimidated

81 'Faith of a Fenian: by an old member of the Brotherhood', *Irish Freedom*, Dec. 1910. 82 Denieffe, *Personal narrative*, 195; James Stephens, 'Personal Recollections of '48', chapter 19 (originally published in *Irishman*, Feb-June 1882, bound in book volume in NLI, Ir. 92, s202). 83 O'Leary, *Recollections* 1, 139, footnote 1; NLI, O'Leary papers, MS 5926, T.C. Luby to O'Leary (n.d., circa 1885); Ryan, *Fenian chief*, 320. 84 *Special Commission Report* (4), 573–6 (statement of F.F. Millen, IRB military commander, 1865, produced as evidence by Henri Le Caron); Takagami, 'Dublin Fenians', 141.

the British militia and semi-military police forces in Ireland, all of which were much better equipped and had a full military training. This was the reality of the IRB organization of the 1860s. In the public mind, however, there were false rumours that a potent insurrectionary conspiracy existed in Ireland that could easily erupt, for two reasons. On one hand, during the 1860s and subsequent decades, the upper or middle classes who controlled the Irish press were very anxious about the growth of democratic political activity in Ireland, which symbolized a threat of anarchy and revolution in their minds. On the other hand, after Anglo-American tensions erupted and war between the two powers was threatened in 1862, the Fenian Brotherhood in New York committed itself entirely to disseminating anti-British propaganda to fuel tensions and to muster American sympathies for the idea of Irish independence. This 'Fenian' propaganda was discussed regularly in the *Nation* and other Irish newspapers, though it was never taken very seriously. The Tories, however, were disturbed by this development, as they did not welcome the possibility of pro-American sensibilities developing in Ireland. They launched a propaganda campaign in the Irish press to discredit the American 'Fenians', not least by presenting them as enemies of Catholicism by quoting the negative comments of various American Catholic bishops. In Irish-America, as in Ireland and England, the Catholic hierarchy felt the development of a nationalist politics among Irishmen was inherently dangerous. It was feared that if Britain was given any reason to renew coercion in Ireland, then the church's increasingly successful efforts to persuade the government to tolerate and support Catholic interests in both Ireland and England would be undermined greatly.[85] The small class of Irish Catholic merchants, lawyers and gentry who had managed to prosper under the Union felt insecure for the same reasons. By 1864, the Tories had coined the phrase 'Fenianism' to describe all that was considered potentially troublesome among Irishmen on both sides of the Atlantic, including the *Irish People*. The same term was taken up by several members of the Irish Catholic hierarchy, which began denouncing 'Fenianism' in the name of the Catholic religion. The only *real* link between the IRB in Ireland and the Fenian Brotherhood in New York was financial. Not without reason the IRB journal, the *Irish People*, regularly professed to know nothing whatsoever of 'Fenians' or 'Fenianism'.[86] By 1865, however, the Irish public was fully conditioned, from a Tory as well as a Catholic perspective, to view any disturbances that might take place in Ireland as the work of the 'Fenians', and this is exactly what happened.

During the spring of 1865, as the American civil war came to an end, events suddenly began to overtake the IRB much faster than it could respond to them. The British-infiltrated American Fenian Brotherhood split and then decided of its own accord to send Irish-American army officers (all of whom were civil

---

85 For a much more comprehensive analysis of the full diversity of the church's thinking on 'Fenianism', see O.P. Rafferty, *The church, the state and the Fenian threat, 1861–75* (1999).
86 O'Leary, 'The *Times* on Fenianism', *Irish People*, 9 Sept. 1865.

war veterans) to Ireland, carrying orders to get in contact with the IRB and immediately place it upon a 'military footing'. To ensure continued American financial support, Stephens had made exaggerated claims regarding the strength of his organization and these were evidently taken at face value by the Fenians. As Anglo-American tensions were still very high, the Fenian Brotherhood claimed (rather foolishly) that if the IRB made a sudden, pre-emptive strike and attempted a rising in Ireland, then the United States might intervene as a revenge upon Britain for supporting the Confederate States during the civil war. Their revolutionary calculations were wholly American in both origin and inspiration, as was further demonstrated by the nature of their alternative plan, namely, to cause a pre-emptive strike in Canada, again as a means of straining Anglo-American relations to the limit and enacting revenge upon Britain for its support of the Confederacy.[87] Being the principal paymaster of the IRB, the American Fenians believed they had an inherent right to force Stephens and his organization to carry out their plans. Although it had a circulation of 10,000 copies a week,[88] the *Irish People* was not a financial success, due its failure to get businesses to advertise in its columns. For this reason, the IRB had not yet managed to become financially self-sufficient without Irish-American funding. Stephens was now put under great pressure and forced to concede to the Fenian Brotherhood's plans, despite the fact that they did not at all concur with his own.

During the summer of 1865, the IRB, now acting mostly under the American Fenians' direction, began to prepare for an insurrection. As the organization had no clerical records and little or no firearms, however, all that the IRB's centres could do was make some guesstimates of its following and present these figures to the Americans. Judging by the Americans' subsequent actions, they do not appear to have understood that these figures (such as 10,000 men in Dublin alone, 18,000 in England and as many as 80–200,000 in total)[89] were merely estimates of the amount of popular support the IRB centres felt they could receive from the general public in the event of a rising.[90] The actual sworn membership of the IRB at that time was very much smaller. Only 2,000 men, for example, generally responded to orders in Dublin,[91] which was the organizational nucleus of the IRB. Any surviving IRB membership figures from this era are all based on the idea that the organization could claim potentially the support of both 'sworn' and 'unsworn' members of the conspiracy, in the event of an 'emergency'.[92] Not until the IRB inaugurated a subscriptions scheme in 1869 to assist more regular arms importation was its

87 William D'Arcy, *The Fenian movement in the United States* (Washington D.C., 1947). 88 NAI, Fenian papers F Series, 8919R.   89 NLI, Devoy papers, MS 18025; Stephens papers, MS 10492, 'Fenianism: past and present'.   90 Gerald McGowan, a descendant of John O'Clohissey (1836–1902), compiler of the Dublin estimate from 1865, to author.   91 Shinichi Takagami, 'The Fenian rising in Dublin, March 1867', *Irish Historical Studies*, 29 (1994–5), 358.   92 O'Brien, *Irish fireside hours*, 107; Gerald McGowan to author.

following to become quantifiable for the first time on the basis of who was, or was not, subscribing to the organization at any one time.

In September 1865, before any plan could be put into operation, Dublin Castle decided to act, not least because the Irish-American civil war veterans were constantly loitering about the *Irish People* offices. Dublin Castle suppressed the *Irish People* and, in the process, was able to arrest most IRB leaders within its offices. They were also able to seize the vast majority of IRB funds as well as some (potentially incriminating) correspondence, both of which T.C. Luby had merely kept in an unlocked drawer in the newspaper's offices. In the trials that followed, which achieved great publicity throughout the United Kingdom, the *Irish People* staff were accused of being 'Fenians' (a label which stuck), charged of possessing all the motives which the Tory press had previously attributed to them, convicted of treason and sentenced from seven to twenty years' imprisonment.[93] The prisoners' refusal to disown their opposition to British rule in any way, or even protest against the false charges made against them when facing sentences of life-imprisonment, earned them the nickname of 'the bold Fenian men'. Subsequently, as a safeguard, Dublin Castle decided to suppress all forms of nationalist political activity in the country. In early 1866, the lower ranks of the British army was purged of suspected Irish nationalist sympathizers, Habeas Corpus was suspended in Ireland and, over the next eighteen months, more than a thousand people (mostly members of the NBSP, an organization which subsequently collapsed), were imprisoned without trial, on suspicion of being sympathetic to what was dubbed by the Tory government as 'Fenianism'; a fact that created much popular resentment in Ireland.

Shortly after he was rescued from prison in November 1865, James Stephens fled to the United States. At the request of the Fenian Brotherhood, the IRB leader spoke at several American public meetings during the summer of 1866 in an attempt to win American sympathies for Irish nationalism. By that time, however, the Fenian Brotherhood was in complete disarray. One faction wasted the organization's resources by performing futile raids into Canada. The other, believing that Stephens was unduly procrastinating in ordering a rising in Ireland, put a gun to his head in December 1866 and ordered him to give them complete control over the IRB organization or be immediately shot. What Stephens did on this occasion is unclear, but as he fled to Paris and deliberately isolated himself thereafter, it is quite likely that he bowed to their demands to save his own life and felt ashamed of what he had done, either for fear of the charge of cowardice or regret for the consequences he knew his actions would have. Subsequently the Fenian leaders sailed to Ireland and, claiming the right to depose Stephens (a right that was not generally recognized), split the IRB by trying to take command of the organization,

93 R.W. Kostal, 'Rebels in the dock: the prosecution of the Dublin Fenians, 1865–6', *Éire-Ireland* (summer 1999), 70–96. 94 Leon O'Broin, *Fenian fever* (1971); Takagami, 'Dublin Fenians'.

eventually leading about three thousand almost entirely unarmed men of the proverbial 'rank and file' into a completely hopeless attempt at a rising in Cork and Dublin during the first week of March 1867.[94] Had these Americans not taken this initiative, the abortive 1867 rising would never have taken place and the IRB would not have suffered from several years of intense factional strife thereafter.

T.J. Kelly, a Galway-born former lieutenant in the US army, directed the attempted rising of 1867 but he was soon arrested in Manchester, where he had set up his headquarters. In September 1867, the local IRB organization rescued him from a prison van but in the process an English policeman was shot dead by a poor Irish immigrant, allegedly by accident. The English public's reaction to this event was shaped by the fact that anti-Irish feeling was at an all-time high in northern England at that time because a great number of unskilled Irish rural labourers had recently begun entering their cities and depriving English labourers of jobs.[95] Amid great public outcry, three Irishmen were thereafter convicted in a Manchester police court, on doubtful evidence, of the charge of murder and were executed, being denied even a Christian burial.[96] While many Irishmen were outraged by the seeming injustice of the executions, the denial of burial rites was seen particularly by Catholics as a direct affront to their religion. As a result, A.M. Sullivan and other complete opponents of republicanism were prompted to describe the three men very sympathetically in the press as the 'Manchester martyrs', a fact that caused Sullivan to be imprisoned for a few weeks for seditious journalism. Thereafter the three men, best known for their cry from the dock, 'God save Ireland', were soon turned into Irish political icons by the popular Catholic press.[97] In subsequent years, the IRB (initially surprised by the great outpour of sympathy for their three deceased comrades) sought to make political capital of this, seeing it as a potentially useful propaganda coup, but it is doubtful whether or not this ever worked to a significant degree.[98] For many Irish Catholic observers, the Manchester 'martyrs' had an iconic status only because of their perceived religious affiliation and the general Irish Catholic community's sense of itself as being sufferers of victimization. In turn, the 'Manchester martyrs' and, more significantly, the 'Fenianism' they seemingly symbolized, became an object of scorn for many Irish Protestants.

The 'Manchester martyrs' cult launched by Sullivan (who after his release from prison wrote a highly influential book, *Speeches from the Dock*, which

95 W.J. Lowe, *The Irish in mid-Victorian Lancashire* (New York, 1989).   96 For the legal issues surrounding the trial, see Anthony Glynn, *High upon the gallows tree* (Tralee, 1967); Patrick Rose, *The Manchester martyrs* (London, 1970); Owen McGee, 'Manchester-martyr demonstrations in Dublin, 1867–1916', *Éire-Ireland* (autumn 2001), 39–41.   97 Gary Owens, 'Constructing the martyrs: the Manchester executions and the nationalist imagination', Lawrence McBride (ed.), *Images, icons and the Irish nationalist imagination* (1999), 18–36. 98 Owen McGee, 'Manchester-martyr demonstrations in Dublin, 1867–1916', *Éire-Ireland* (autumn 2001), 39–66.

portrayed all past rebels since 1798, including the IRB leaders tried in 1865, in the same light) played a major role in ensuring that 'Fenianism' began to be identified with Irish Catholicism; and this perception was heightened in the public mind by the reaction of the British government to the situation. During 1868, the new Liberal Prime Minister, W.E. Gladstone, responded to the recent embitterment of the Irish Catholic community by proclaiming that due to the 'intensity of Fenianism' in recent times, he felt it necessity to deliver 'justice to Ireland' and, in particular, to disestablish the Church of Ireland. Inevitably, the British and Irish general public saw this symbolic political reform of Gladstone's (which deeply upset many Irish Protestants and was celebrated by Irish Catholics) as a direct result of 'Fenian' activities. The Tories generally denounced it as being a surrender to 'the Fenians'. In turn, many confused Irish Presbyterians, amidst rumours in the Tory press of incipient Irish rebellion by huge (non-existent) 'Fenian armies', were quite naturally led to believe that all 'Fenians' (including the IRB leaders then in jail) were nothing less than 'an army of papists'.[99]

The 'Fenian fever' in the press between 1865 and 1868 left an indelible mark on the Irish and British public imaginations. Henceforth, the terms 'Fenian' and 'Fenianism' would be used perpetually by Tory, Whig-Liberal and Irish Catholic politicians or journalists (collectively, the political enemies of the IRB) in a way that caused the terms to symbolize in the public mind the entire political and religious divide within Ireland.[100] This, inadvertently, gave a greater opening for republicans to make an impact in Irish politics. After several years propagating republicanism in Irish popular politics without attracting much public attention, the IRB leaders now in prison suddenly acquired a life-long political notoriety and fame. The fact that this fame was received for 'all the wrong reasons' did not overly concern the IRB, as some publicity is always better than none for aspiring politicians. After 1867, slowly but surely republicans were able to assume a position of more central importance in Irish popular politics. As a result, by the time of the formation of the democratic organization of the Land League in 1879, the IRB found itself in a position whereby, for the first time, it could potentially become what it thus far had only dreamed of becoming: a dynamic organizational nucleus at the heart of an Irish revolution.

99 This is how Alice Milligan, a northern Presbyterian writer and poetess, would describe Ulster Protestants' perspective of 'the Fenians' during the 1860s in her popular poem, 'When I was a Little Girl'. 100 Peter Alter, 'Symbols of Irish nationalism', in Alan O'Day (ed.), *Reactions to Irish nationalism* (1987), 1–20.

2

A 'Fenian' opportunity: the IRB's role in the centralization of Irish popular politics, 1868–79

By 1869, the IRB had cut off all relations with the discredited Irish-Americans. An eleven-man elective executive, known as the Supreme Council, was put in place and an hierarchical structure of command devised. Almost every position in the movement was now determined by elections held every two years, rather than being simply appointed by its 'chief organizer'. To make itself financially self-sufficient, a new rule was introduced whereby every member of the IRB was expected to make regular small subscriptions; the mere taking of the oath being no longer a sufficient qualification.[1] Simultaneously, James Joseph O'Kelly, a cultured, Francophile republican (who was also a London-based journalist and former French soldier), inaugurated the first-ever, systematic attempt by the IRB at an arms importation scheme, but it was soon undermined and aborted because of the arrest of several agents. As had been the case in 1865, the organization could not afford anything but antiquated rifles; so the cessation of the scheme was not deemed a major setback.[2] Its one positive outcome was to alert the IRB to the potential financial support it could receive from the rural Irish community.

Once the IRB began importing arms, residents of rural Ireland would always be particularly willing to buy them, if only for self-defence or hunting reasons, and might even take the republican oath just to get their hands on them. By the time O'Kelly's scheme ended in the winter of 1870 when he fled for America, the IRB appears to have had as many as 40,000 subscribers or nominal members,[3] a peak figure it subsequently strove to maintain. This reality exercised a controlling influence over the IRB's organizational work throughout the remainder of the century. Although the leadership and core support was always urban in character, because Ireland was a predominantly rural country the financial well-being of the organization and, therefore, its capacity for taking constructive actions, was ultimately dependent on the degree to which the rural community remained willing to subscribe. The IRB did not grasp this fact fully until the mid 1870s when, starved of funds, it realized the uncomfortable fact that its rural, but not its urban, membership was generally willing to pay subscriptions *only* when they were receiving arms in return.[4] This is not surprising, as spare cash was certainly not something Irish

---

1 Moody, O'Broin (eds.), 'IRB Supreme Council'; John Daly, 'Recollections of Fenianism', *Irish Freedom*, Nov. 1912. 2 *DPB*, vol. 1, 489; T.W. Moody, *Davitt and Irish revolution* (2nd ed., 1984), 53; Ryan, *Fenian memories*, 38–40. 3 NAI, Fenian papers, F Series, 7931R. 4 NLI, Devoy papers, MS 18036; *DPB*, vol. 2, 142 (letter of O'Kelly); *Special Commission Report*, vol. 4, 505–11 (report by Devoy on IRB, produced as evidence by the British spy Henri Le Caron).

countrymen had in abundance but it became a major logistical problem for the IRB, whose capacity to import arms was also very restricted due to the arms acts and constant police vigilance.

A number of significant political developments took place during the late 1860s. In 1868, the United Kingdom increased its electorate greatly, thereby enfranchising as many as 10 per cent of adult Irish males, a figure that would increase to approximately 14 per cent by 1882 due to continued emigration.[5] Meanwhile an amnesty movement launched for the release of the Irish political prisoners soon won great support from the working classes. Greater debate began to take place upon Irish nationalism, including one revolutionary idea that had been raised during the 1840s. This was that Irish independence might be achievable if the MPs at Westminster were persuaded to withdraw and unilaterally set up an Irish government, which an Irish citizens' defence force could then defend. This so-called 'abstentionist policy' was always favoured by two IRB leaders, John O'Leary and C.J. Kickham, and it would become the official IRB policy by the mid 1870s.[6] The IRB considered calling for the establishment of a public citizens' defence force in 1869 through the medium of the amnesty movement. If this idea had been workable, it would have helped solve one very large practical problem: the near impossibility of a mere secret society being able to arm an entire community and thereby allow them to stand up forcibly in defence of their rights. During 1870, however, the arms acts were made more stringent than ever; meanwhile the lay and ecclesiastical leaders of the Catholic community denounced the idea of men bearing arms, not least because they feared this would provoke the government to renew coercion.

In 1846, when he refused to join in the Young Irelanders' protest about the arms acts, O'Connell invented a new form of political rhetoric. Although the Irish community had no right to determine its own political future, O'Connell argued that it could have faith that benign and enlightened liberal reformers at Westminster would respond to the 'moral force' of Irish MPs' speeches. To rationalize this claim, O'Connell tried to replace the ageless republican dichotomy of citizenship and slavery with a new one of his own. He dubbed his argument as one in favour of 'constitutional methods' and labelled everyone who disagreed with him as advocates of 'physical force', the supposed opposite of 'moral force'. Outside of Catholic political circles in Ireland under the Union, this distinction drawn by O'Connell was never (and has never been) adopted by any other political community because, literally speaking, it makes no sense. No politician or party can claim to represent a constitution, while force is an integral component of any state's constitution. O'Connell was also speaking nonsensically by making this argument as a *political* statement, because only the government, or lawyers and judges in their purely legal

5 B.M. Walker, 'The Irish electorate, 1868–1915', *Irish Historical Studies*, 18 (1972–3), 359–406. 6 *DPB*, vol. I, 162–5 (letter of Kickham, as IRB president); O'Leary to *Irishman*, 11 Jan. 1879, 20 Mar., 3 Apr. 1880; A.M. Sullivan, *New Ireland* (London, 1877), 394.

capacity, could have any right to speak of what was 'constitutional' due to the non-republican (unwritten) nature of the British constitution. Irish Catholic politicians who liked to call themselves 'strictly constitutional politicians' could be, and occasionally were, arrested just like their republican critics whom they had labelled as 'unconstitutional' politicians, whenever they were perceived by Westminster to be stepping outside the moral authority of the law. The only purpose of this rhetoric adopted by the Irish Catholic establishment was to claim on its own behalf a superior morality to that of the nationalist revolutionaries, and to rationalize the political and moral legitimacy that the British state had in its own eyes. Some historians have overlooked this reality by re-interpreting the political debates of this era in the light of late twentieth-century liberalism. One has even criticized the Young Irelanders for not following the intuition of the Hindu saint Mahatma Gandhi (1868–1948), whose 'moral force' teachings O'Connell supposedly prefigured.[8] What should be noted is that, during the 1840s, O'Connell's argument failed to convince anybody. By the late 1860s, however, the 'moral force' idea *did* begin to seem plausible to some contemporaries, if only because Gladstone had pledged himself never to neglect Irish Catholic interests and had disestablished the Church of Ireland. Thereafter the Catholic press in Ireland, as well as the Catholic clergy, tried to popularize O'Connell's rhetoric by pointing to Gladstone's actions as an example of its supposed truth.

Between 1869 and 1871, the Amnesty Association was the largest political organization in Ireland since the demise of the Repeal and Confederate Clubs of the 1840s, and it would remain in existence until 1878, when the last of the prisoners was released.[9] Its branches were led by various popular political activists, including many republicans, and consisted mostly of workers and clerks, many of whom were former members of the NBSP. The Catholic and Protestant political establishments were completely indifferent to the amnesty question, since only the poor had been (or were likely to be) arrested. Isaac Butt MP, a brilliant lawyer and former Tory, was appointed the nominal president of the Amnesty Association, in gratitude for his having defended the IRB prisoners in the dock in 1865, but the real leader of the organization was its secretary, John Nolan, a former journalist, clerk and Dublin trade unionist who was now a member of the IRB Supreme Council.[10]

In politics, the Amnesty Association was very opposed to the Catholic 'National' Association, which simply encouraged the Irish public to have total faith in Gladstone. The amnesty activists, by contrast, wanted to issue a strong protest against the government and opposed any Irish politicians who were prepared to work with it. Nolan was primarily responsible for organizing forty

8 Davis, *The Young Ireland movement*, introduction and conclusion. 9 Moody, *Davitt*, 121.
10 The best source on Nolan's remarkable career, and the general history of the amnesty movement, is Maurice Johnson, 'The Fenian amnesty movement' (unpublished MLitt thesis, Maynooth, 1980).

large amnesty rallies during 1869, including a monster rally in Cabra, Dublin that attracted 200,000 people and was addressed by various figures, including Butt. The Catholic press argued that these demonstrations were welcome proof that the unenfranchised Irish working class had faith in Gladstone's promise to deliver justice to Ireland. Republicans claimed, however, and quite convincingly, that 'those who argue in this manner forget that the people ... listened coolly enough' to the speakers, 'except when a prisoner's name was mentioned and then the ringing cheers showed how the feeling lay. Cheers for O'Donovan Rossa [who was being tortured in prison] rung, while the mention of Gladstone's name produced, in many cases, contemptuous laughter'.[11] Rossa's case achieved great publicity and the pioneering example of the Irish amnesty movement (which was supported by some radical English democrats)[12] helped to inspire the formation of similar movements abroad.

The amnesty movement quickly became a forum for various rising figures in Irish popular politics to make their mark. This was a development that was both welcomed by and caused concern to the IRB, for 'since the political prisoners were tried', many were speaking on public platforms 'on the glories of republicanism ... and receiving rapturous applause' from the workers, yet in other political meetings, many of these same men were making speeches 'of the most loyal character' before middle-class audiences.[13] To stem what was seen as a growing trend, John Daly, an intelligent Limerick labourer who soon became a Supreme Councillor, introduced resolutions at amnesty meetings that all Irish politicians should 'ask for, or accept, nothing from the British government but the unconditional release of the Irish political prisoners.'[14] However, few Irish politicians, other than republicans and the leaders of several workers' societies, were willing to second such resolutions. This prompted IRB members to realize that they needed to achieve much more influence in Irish public life if this trend was ever to change.

By 1871, after three years involvement in the branches of the amnesty association, the urban membership of the IRB (most of whom were former members of the NBSP) had become just as accustomed to being involved in public life as they were to being members of a secret revolutionary organization. A handful of republicans, most notably J.P. McDonnell, a Dublin printer and the first representative of Ireland on the communist Internationale, attempted to create a vibrant trade union politics in Ireland during the early 1870s.[15] Most of the clerks and artisans of the IRB, however, were not very concerned with labour politics. Instead they used the amnesty cause for holding protest demonstrations (principally in Dublin, Cork and Limerick), and tried to find new methods of spreading republican propaganda. In Dublin,

11 Davis (ed.), *J.K. Casey*, 238, 232. 12 Quinlivan and Rose, *The Fenians in England, 1865–72* (1982), chapter 11. 13 Davis (ed.), *J.K. Casey*, 239. 14 John Daly, 'Recollections of Fenians and Fenianism', *Irish Freedom*, Sept. 1912. 15 Sean Daly, *Ireland and the First International* (Cork, 1984).

the principal amnesty club was stationed at the Mechanics Institute, a centre for what contemporaries called 'scientific education' (meaning all practical forms of education) for artisans.[16] Republicans organized various committees that were based in the institute's building. The holding of Manchester-martyr demonstrations was outlawed in Ireland between 1868 and 1874, while the DMP suppressed a monster amnesty demonstration in the Phoenix Park by force in July 1871. Capitalizing upon the popular indignation this created, Dublin republicans started organizing 'monument committees', designed to erect monuments over the graves of deceased patriots, and collected funds for this purpose at amnesty demonstrations or at Glasnevin cemetery. This found a very receptive audience among Irish workers' societies and thus soon became an established feature of the republican movement's activities, as well as Irish popular politics generally.[17] The Catholic Church strongly resented republicans' frequent abuse of cemeteries (sacred ground) for political purposes, and threatened to take legal action against the republicans' little back-alley committees if they did not cease this activity.[18] Nevertheless this vibrant hive of activity continued and became a permanent feature of IRB propaganda work, just as similar activities frequently formed a basis for much popular, republican political activity in Paris.[19] If this helped to sustain republican enthusiasms in Ireland, however, it was not a basis on which any revolution was ever likely to be built – as the IRB leadership was fully aware. Consequently, the new young IRB leaders on the Supreme Council tried to persuade various well-known politicians to work with them.

John Martin, a northern Presbyterian and lawyer, was the most well-known and influential republican politician in Ireland. He paid for and erected the Manchester-martyr cenotaph in Glasnevin in April 1868. Later he assisted Nolan, Daly and other IRB leaders in promoting the amnesty agitation and in fighting against efforts by the Catholic hierarchy, the National Association and Butt to prioritize the questions of denominational education and tenant-right.[20] Martin entered into cordial correspondence with the IRB leadership, probably from the spring of 1869 onwards, when Charles Kickham and J.F.X. O'Brien were released from prison, and it is very probable that Kickham was made the Supreme Council's president, or chairman, at this time: being the only one of the four original IRB leaders then resident in Ireland and not in jail, he would have been the perfect choice for the position.[21] 'Honest John' Martin

16 Jim Cooke, 'The Dublin Mechanics Institute 1824–1919', *Dublin Historical Record* (summer 1999), 15–31. The Mechanics Institute building was on the site of the present Abbey Theatre. 17 Owen McGee, 'God save Ireland', 39–66; Gary Owens, 'Nationalist monuments in Ireland, 1870–1914: symbolism and ritual', in Raymond Gillespie & Brian P. Kennedy (eds.), *Ireland: art into history* (1994), 103–17. 18 NAI, CSORP 1877/18201; *Irishman*, 29 Nov. 1879. 19 Maurice Agulhon, *Marianne into battle* (1981); R.D.E. Burton, *Blood in the city* (London, 2001), 146. 20 David Thornley, *Isaac Butt and home rule* (1964), 74–6; NLI, John O'Leary papers, MS 5926, Martin to O'Leary, 1 April 1872. 21 NLI, John O'Leary papers, MS 5926 (correspondence of Martin with O'Leary, 1871–4); Martin refers in these letters to the fact that he was also corresponding for some time with J.F.X. O'Brien and Charles

MARTIN

(as he was popularly known) was always very determined to 'do no act to encourage the hateful fiction that Ireland enjoys constitutional rights and is a freely governed country',[22] and this was a resolution he generally maintained even after he was elected to Westminster for Meath in 1871 as the only Irish parliamentary representative who was not a Whig, Tory or Liberal. He described himself instead as an 'independent nationalist' and he would essentially remain one up until his death in 1875, refusing to vote on any pieces of Westminster legislation and speaking in the house only to issue nationalist protests. Martin always believed that a rebellion and the establishment of an Irish republic were perfectly just objectives *in theory*, but he felt that such a rebellion could only be justifiable *in practice* if it was supported by the majority of the Irish people. For this reason, during the early 1860s, he had been very uncomfortable about the rumours that a revolutionary movement existed that was determined to launch an insurrection regardless of the degree of popular support it might have. After 1869, once he realized that this was not the intention of the IRB, he was glad to act as a confidant to its leaders, but he could not suggest any initiatives and merely advised prudence and tolerance. On the other hand, G.H. Moore, a former Catholic Whig who, after 1867, described himself as an 'independent repealer', had a number of ideas.

MOORE

The IRB had taken note that Moore was the only champion at Westminster of the controversial amnesty issue, an issue that even Butt (despite his nominal presidency of the Amnesty Association) was afraid to raise, lest it cause offence to the English benches.[23] During 1869, Moore encouraged Kickham and O'Brien to adopt the novel initiative of nominating for parliament imprisoned republicans (knowing in advance that they would be immediately disqualified, if elected) to give maximum publicity to the amnesty cause; in one case, that of O'Donovan Rossa, this tactic succeeded. Apart from being an MP, Moore was also a local government official in Mayo. It was possibly through his influence that, by the time of his death in April 1870, IRB members of the Amnesty Association had decided upon another initiative, namely presenting amnesty petitions to local government officials looking for their support. These petitions, however, were ignored completely by the (non–elective) local government bodies, whose members, like the MPs, had no sympathy for the prisoners.[24] This fact may well partly account for the decision of the IRB Supreme Council to adopt a new policy in January 1870 of actually encouraging its members to run for election to local governmental office 'as a

speculation

Kickham, both of whom were released from prison in March 1869. John Devoy would later claim (from hearsay) that O'Brien (a contributor to the *Irish People* who attempted to take part in rebellion in 1849 and again in 1867) occupied the position of IRB president up until 1874, but O'Brien's own unpublished recollections indicate that he only ever held the position of the representative of Munster on the Supreme Council from 1869 up to 1871 and shortly thereafter left the organization. Pat McCarthy (ed.), 'James Francis Xavier O'Brien (1828–1905)', *Decies*, 54 (1998), 107–38. **22** Thornley, *Butt*, 57–8. **23** Johnson, 'Fenian amnesty movement', passim. **24** W.L. Feingold, *The revolt of the tenantry: the transformation of local government in Ireland, 1872–86* (1984), 82.

means of increasing the power and influence of the Irish Republic', or the IRB.[25]

The IRB decision to focus upon local government bodies was certainly a new departure in its politics, and it is quite likely that J.J. O'Kelly, the secretary of the Supreme Council, as well as Charles Doran (a former NBSP leader and a future Supreme Council secretary) were responsible for the initiative. O'Kelly and Doran were Francophile republicans who were aware of political developments in France.[26] During the reign of Louis Napoleon (1851–70), French republicans had concentrated upon getting elected to municipal office with a view to achieving a position from which they could slowly but surely reshape the tenor of political life in the country before attempting to overthrow the government and proclaim a republic.[27] Quite possibly, the IRB hoped to achieve a similar outcome in Ireland by concentrating upon local government bodies. In the short term, however, the practical benefits of this policy could not be substantial. In urban Ireland, although Charles Doran was elected as chairman of Queenstown (Cobh) Town Commission during the 1870s, very few IRB men owned sufficient property to be eligible to vote or stand for election to the city councils or town commissions. Meanwhile, in rural Ireland, the only elective, local government bodies were the poor law boards, and half their members were simply appointed by justices of the peace, who were invariably great landowners or British army officers.[28] Although not immediately effective, this focus on local government was never abandoned, primarily because republicans realized that, to accomplish their goals, they would need to have some sort of political foothold in the country.

Throughout the 1870s, James O'Connor, the Supreme Council's treasurer from 1869–72 and the former assistant manager of the *Irish People*, was assistant editor of the *Irishman*. This paper succeeded in winning much of the former readership of the *Irish People*, not least because it was a militant supporter of the amnesty movement. Unlike Sullivan's *Nation*, the *Irishman* (which had a circulation of about 10,000 copies a week)[29] had always sympathized with radical democratic movements. Being a purely commercial enterprise, however, its editorial policy was never defined clearly. The IRB's relationship with the *Irishman* was problematic. Although O'Connor republished American Fenian propaganda on a regular basis and encouraged republicans to give vent to their opinions by writing letters to the paper, the paper's proprietor and principal editor was Richard Pigott, a notorious swindler and unprincipled opportunist, whom the IRB distrusted, and for

25 Moody and O'Broin (eds.), 'IRB Supreme Council 1868–78', 310. 26 Doran was reputedly a correspondent of the first president of the Third Republic, Marshal McMahon, a relatively conservative figure. Although a Catholic, Doran always remained a strong sympathizer with the French Republic. *Rossa's recollections*, 134–40, especially p.140. The relationship of O'Kelly (who attempted to form an Irish brigade in France in 1870) with the French Republic will be noted later. 27 Nord, *The republican moment*, 190–218. 28 Feingold, *Revolt of the tenantry*, introduction, xxiv-xxv. 29 NAI, Fenian Papers F Series, 8919R.

good reason. In 1872, O'Connor decided to keep the IRB's funds in the safe in the *Irishman* offices, but Pigott stole this money once he discovered it, knowing that the IRB could not take legal action against him without exposing itself to the state. For the same reason, Pigott figured that he could get away with offering his services to Dublin Castle as an informant, but he was prevented from doing so because the IRB warned him that they knew exactly what he was doing.[30] The fallout from this event was O'Connor's replacement as IRB treasurer by Patrick Egan, a Dublin businessman, who, to solve this problem, decided in 1873 to buy out the *Irishman*, dismiss Pigott and turn it into a more reliable newspaper. Perhaps under different circumstances, the IRB could have accomplished this goal. By 1873, however, the funds the IRB expected to receive from its rural following were no longer forthcoming, since the Supreme Council had ceased to import arms.

During 1869–70, both John Daly and John Nolan had tried to put pressure upon Butt, in his capacity as president of the Amnesty Association, to organize public demonstrations in support of Irish independence. Meanwhile, since the abortive insurrection of 1867 and disestablishment, many leading Tories were discussing the potential advantage of the restoration of an Irish parliament, with very limited powers, as a means of preventing their influence in the country from declining further – a measure they described as 'home rule'. In an attempt to bridge both concerns, Butt decided to take up Nolan and Daly's idea of calling a national convention in Dublin but invited Irish Tories, Liberals, nationalists and amnesty activists equally to the meeting. On such an occasion, in May 1870, a body known as the Home Government Association (HGA) was launched under Butt's leadership. The HGA established a central committee of sixty-one members (half of whom were Tories), initially won the support of the Tory press and, within a year, had acquired a national membership of 800 men. Its influence was never felt far outside Dublin and it was never intended by Butt to be a popular political organization. Instead, its purpose was merely to provide a new forum for debate and to encourage Irish MPs of various hues to begin meeting on a common political platform.[31] Butt wrote a very novel pamphlet for the HGA, proposing the establishment of a new federal form of government for the United Kingdom, which he argued would accommodate Irish national aspirations, lead to the better government of Ireland and strengthen the empire. This failed, however, to arouse either the government or the Irish people's interest. John Martin, although an admirer of Butt's personal integrity, accused him of 'misrepresenting the nationalist feeling in the country', which Martin believed was in favour of complete separation from Britain. The IRB, by contrast, informed Butt that, while it would not support his proposed new organization, equally it would not attempt to thwart his federalist 'experiment'.[32]

30 PRO (London), Robert Anderson papers, HO 144/1538/8 (several letters of Richard Pigott to the Crown Solicitor, Under-Secretary and Lord Lieutenant, offering to be an informant on the IRB, Mar.-Oct. 1872); NAI, Fenian papers, 8021R; *DPB*, vol. 1, 55–6. 31 Thornley, *Butt*, 78, 84–5, 94–6.

Butt's idea was unworkable because the creation of a federal government for the United Kingdom would have necessitated drafting a written (republican) constitution, while the entire British system of government, the monarchy's role therein and its professed status as an empire, was totally dependent, legally speaking, on the unwritten nature of the British constitution. His idea might have appealed to English or Irish republicans, but few others. Reputedly, James Stephens favoured the idea of the United Kingdom becoming a federal republic (minus the crown and House of Lords), with both Britain and Ireland possessing an equal constitutional status, and that it was only because he realized its constitutional impossibility that he was a separatist.[33] His openness to various alternatives was perhaps best reflected by the fact that he tried to form an IRB alliance with the English republican movement during 1865. His intermediary on this occasion, Frank Roney, a Belfast labourer, found English republicans such as Charles Bradlaugh and even a young Joseph Chamberlain to be fairly sympathetic towards the IRB's political ideals. The English radicals' professed republicanism however did not extend beyond a resentment of the financial burden being placed on the general British public by a useless aristocracy – a conservatism on their part that Roney judged was rooted in their deep British nationalism.[34] Some contacts between English and Irish republicans continued to take place. In January 1867, Bradlaugh helped William Halpin, a Meath-born Irish-American soldier, draft a 'Proclamation of the Irish Republic' for the IRB (it was never used) and soon afterwards became a supporter of the amnesty movement.[35] Meanwhile, during 1870, several Irish-born trade unionists in London (where the IRB was particularly active) helped found and were leading figures in a short-lived English republican movement that was in favour of abolishing all feudal institutions (such as the House of Lords) and feudal privileges in the United Kingdom, such as the existing right of the English and Irish landed gentry, or aristocracy, to be the sole legal owners of virtually all land outside the cities.[36] These trends, although slight, help to explain why in Irish political circles during the early 1870s it was the English IRB organization that made the only determined effort to champion the federalist idea.

The Catholic Whig-Liberals, bishops and their 'National Association' initially opposed the HGA because of the Protestant Tories in its ranks, as well

32 Ibid., 91, 104. 33 An interview with Stephens by the Parisian correspondent of *The Times*, republished in the *Irish Nation* (New York), 10 May 1884, indicates this is what he always believed. At that time, however, numerous bogus interviews with Stephens were appearing in the British press. 34 Roney, *Irish rebel*, 117–22. For the history of English republicanism during this era, see Dorothy Thompson, 'The English republic', *The Republic*, 2 (spring/summer 2001), 72–80; F.A. D'Arcy, 'Charles Bradlaugh and the English republican movement, 1868–78', *Historical Journal*, 23 (1982), 267–82; Quinlivan & Rose, *Fenians in England*. 35 John Newsinger, *Fenianism in mid-Victorian Britain* (1994), 49–55; Bill Halpin (grandson of William Halpin) to author. This proclamation called upon the English workers to embrace republicanism and support the Irish republicans. 36 Royden Harrison, *Before the socialists* (London, 1965), chapter 5; Daly, *Ireland and the First International*.

as Butt's refusal to support their demand for state recognition of the Catholic University and his opposition to denominational education generally. When Butt tried to meet their demands during 1872, he lost all his Irish Tory support and the HGA virtually collapsed. In the summer of the 1873, however, a radical body known as the Home Rule Confederation of Great Britain (HRCGB) was founded by John Barry, a Wexford-born businessman and the Manchester IRB leader, and John Ferguson, a Belfast-born Presbyterian, leader of the Glasgow Republican Club, publisher and proud descendant of William Orr. The HRCGB was a much more popular, egalitarian and demo-cratic movement than the HGA (the membership of which was open only to a few hundred 'gentlemen') and it soon won the support of the English IRB and the Irish working class in Britain. Although Barry was its real leader, Ferguson (a future founder of the Scottish Labour Party) was perhaps the more gifted of the two men. Even though he generally preferred a British solution, Ferguson had a totally open mind regarding the question of Irish separation. He saw his republicanism and his support for Butt's federalist programme as intrinsically linked and was a friend of the young Scottish IRB leader, John Torley, who worked as a bank clerk and subsequently the assistant manager for a chemicals factory in Glasgow.[37] Emphasizing the popular support that the HRCGB was winning, Ferguson and Barry put much pressure on Butt to call another 'home rule' convention in Dublin and not to abandon his federalist scheme. Mostly as a result, an impressive convention was held in Dublin in November 1873 during which the HGA was reconstituted as the Home Rule League (HRL). Butt invited all kinds of people to the convention, which was attended by several members of the IRB Supreme Council,[38] who had taken an interest in Barry and Ferguson's initiative and may have been responsible for inspiring it.

During its first few months in existence, the HRL managed to acquire as many as 3,000 subscribers (or nominal members),[39] but it established few (if any) branches outside Dublin. Butt was opposed to its membership having any power to dictate policy to MPs, believing, in the best Westminster tradition, that every MP should follow only his own conscience in deciding what policy he would support. At the November 1873 convention, Joseph Biggar, a Belfast Presbyterian, son of the chairman of the Ulster Bank and leader of the small Belfast branch of the HGA, challenged this view. With Ferguson's support, Biggar proposed that all MPs who were either members or sympathizers with the league should be forced to take a pledge that they would follow its policy at all times and effectively act as a distinct party. Meanwhile, Charles Doran TC,

---

37 Elaine McFarland, *John Ferguson* (East Lothian, 2003), 56–7; Maírtín O'Catháin, 'John Torley' (unpublished article, courtesy of author); NAI, Land and National League reports, carton 2, speeches of John Ferguson in Monaghan and Armagh, 1887. **38** The Supreme Councillors in question were Charles Doran, John O'Connor Power, Matthew Harris, Patrick Egan and John Walsh. Power and Walsh were very closely associated with Barry and the Manchester IRB. **39** Thornley, *Butt*, 171–2, 242.

the secretary of the IRB Supreme Council, proposed that all MPs supportive of the federal programme should declare themselves willing to be held accountable before 'a great national conference, to be called in such a manner as to represent the opinions and feelings of the Irish nation ... in any emergency that may arise'.[40] The plan of the IRB president, Charles Kickham, was that if a 'great national conference' representing the views of general Irish public was held, owing to the numerical strength of the IRB (it had nominally some 35,000 members, or subscribers), it could dominate the proceedings and pressurize 'the MPs to take the first fitting opportunity to withdraw from the London parliament' as the first step in initiating a political revolution.[41]

Biggar's motion was defeated and Doran's adopted at this convention, but not for the reasons that the IRB wanted. Since 1870, it had been customary for the HGA to hold monthly meetings of its central council to discuss policy matters and, now that the HRL had been established, Butt and others were in favour of the idea of also holding annual general meetings. The 'great national conferences' envisioned by the IRB Supreme Council were not to be democratic gatherings, but merely another opportunity for the HRL's members to discuss policy matters in a strictly private setting. Butt, for one, made it clear that he had no intention of allowing himself to be held answerable to anyone but the 10 per cent of adult males who were wealthy enough to have the right to vote in his constituency.[42] Doran's resolution was accepted over Biggar's simply because, in practice, it did not place any definite restrictions upon Irish politicians' freedom to act as individual public representatives. The IRB, however, continued to test how far it could succeed in determining the direction that the 'home rule' movement would take.

In January 1874, as many as 59 MPs were returned nominally on a 'home rule ticket', but over half of these were Catholic Whig-Liberals who were not even members of the HRL. They had merely given a vague declaration of their admiration for the league's programme to boost their chances of winning a seat. In March, Butt raised the federalist idea in parliament for the first time, not as a demand, but as an issue that he felt ought to be discussed. The government refused to allow a debate to be held on the matter, however, the Attorney General stating that Irishmen's capacity for governing themselves was no greater than to sit on the poor law boards and therefore Butt's 'mischievous agitation' should cease immediately. Powerless before such a rebuff, as David Thornley noted, by the following month Butt had 'already abandoned any hope of achieving home rule.'[43] Over the next six years, most of the supposed 'home rule' MPs (who remained Whigs and Tories) took the government's side in opposing every bill Butt introduced; these included ones to increase the municipal franchise and funding for local government bodies in Ireland to the same levels as existed in Britain. By May 1874, the HRL had lost virtually all

---

40 Ibid., 164–5. 41 *DPB*, vol. 1, 162–5 (Kickham to Devoy). 42 Thornley, *Butt*, 168.
43 Ibid., *Butt*, 240.

its members, and its treasurer, Alfred Webb (a friend of Kickham and a Dublin Quaker bookseller whose attitude towards Irish nationalism was as open as Ferguson's), could not collect any funds for the home rule movement, which he felt was merely 'building castles in the air'.[44] Meanwhile republicans naturally started to express impatience. In August, John Daly (by now the IRB's chief travelling organizer) declared to the public that, 'on behalf of the democracy', his party 'must be told' by the HRL leaders what they intended to do, for the democrats had no intention of allowing 'a certain class of people' maintain the status quo 'while hunger exists in the land and the emigrant ships take our best men away to be slaves of other nations.' In a vain attempt to put pressure on the MPs to change their tune, Daly threatened that if the home rule 'representatives degenerated to Whiggery and Toryism' once more, the republicans would immediately 'unfurl the banner they struck under before.'[45]

By 1875, only a couple of factors were keeping the home rule movement alive. In England and Scotland, the HRCGB succeeded in attracting much publicity by holding large public meetings at Hyde Park, and, in June, it launched its own newspaper, the *United Irishman*, which (acting in line with the Supreme Council's policy) called upon the HRL to adopt and promote the abstentionist policy.[46] This propaganda, however, had no effect on the attitudes of the MPs or the Catholic-Whig press in Ireland, which were entirely conservative. Only two radicals had been elected as 'home rule' MPs during 1874. The first, W.H. O'Sullivan, a successful Limerick hotelier, land and amnesty activist (his son was an imprisoned IRB man), had launched his parliamentary career through first participating in local government. He cooperated and generally identified with the republicans' politics throughout the 1870s and despite facing intense clerical opposition throughout his career was re-elected several times for Limerick County.[47] Among the Irish political establishment, however, he was an object of ridicule. He was nicknamed 'Whisky O'Sullivan' owing to his common social origins and his desire to protect the Irish drink trade from Scottish competition. His more novel policies, such as forming a great union to protect the interests of both rural and urban labourers, his federalism (he was in favour of the UK adopting an American-style constitution and abandoning its sectarian ethos by completely separating church and state) and his revolutionary demand that women be given the right to vote and sit in parliament, were ignored completely.[48] The second radical elected was John O'Connor Power, an entirely self-educated former Lancashire labourer

44 M.L. Legg (ed.), *Alfred Webb: the autobiography of a Quaker nationalist* (1999), 36; Thornley, *Butt*, 175–7, 227–31, 241. 45 Thornley, *Butt*, 243–4. 46 Alan O'Day, 'The political organization of the Irish in Britain, 1867–90', in Swift & Gilley (eds.), *The Irish in Britain, 1815–1939* (1989), 193–8; John Denvir, *Life story of an old rebel* (London, 1910), 177–81; *DPB*, vol.1, 298. The *United Irishman*, which was both a literary and political journal, was edited by Henry Heinrick (1831–87), a Wexford-born schoolmaster in Birmingham, with some assistance from John Denvir, a Newry-born publisher and Liverpool IRB leader. 47 T.W. Moody, *Davitt and Irish revolution* (1981), passim. 48 W.H. O'Sullivan, *Speeches in and out of parliament* (Limerick, 1880).

who had worked as a history teacher in St Jarlath's College, Tuam, and was now elected for Mayo County. Power was an orator of great skill. He had been a travelling lecturer for the Amnesty Association in both Ireland and England since 1871 and was the only MP who dared to raise the amnesty issue after 1874. His politics, however, were a source of division to republicans. Apart from the fact that he was a member of the IRB Supreme Council and yet took a parliamentary seat and an oath to the queen, he had done something that was seemingly unforgivable. Unlike O'Sullivan, a successful businessman, Power had very little money. Therefore, it was widely believed (and was probably true) that the funds used for his election campaign and parliamentary expenses, including the great cost of accommodation in central London, were funds of the IRB. Consequently, a bitter controversy soon emerged.

The IRB had held its own 'national convention' of delegates in March 1873, four months before Barry and Ferguson formed the HRCGB and eight months before the HRL was established. On this occasion, the IRB resolved that, while it would continue to encourage Irishmen to prepare for the task of winning independence by force of arms, it would never actually launch an insurrection until 'a majority of the Irish people' was clearly in favour of the idea, and it enshrined this idea in its constitution. In the meantime, the IRB would prioritize the goals of 'the propagation of republican principles' and 'the spreading of a knowledge of the national rights of Ireland',[49] namely that 'the right of Ireland to self-government and independent nationhood' was 'inherent and inalienable'.[50] The republican movement resolved to 'lend its support' to any movement that it considered as 'calculated to advance the cause of Irish independence', so long as doing so was consistent with the 'preservation of its own integrity' as a distinct movement.[51] By the time the O'Connor Power controversy broke out, however, the efficiency of the Supreme Council system was being questioned by many republicans, because the IRB's capacity to act as an efficient, underground party was being lessened through its being pulled in so many different directions.

Since 1869, authority in the IRB had been decentralized greatly. Separate IRB leaders for each province in Ireland, as well as for three divisions in Britain (Scotland, Northern England, Southern England), effectively led their own organizations. About twice a year, each of these leaders met together, whenever and wherever practicable, to become the 'Supreme Council' (which did not exist at any other time) and to forward progress reports to the 'honorary Supreme Councillors', which included a chairman (or 'president'), secretary and treasurer. These three men were known as the 'Executive of the IRB' and the decision of any two of those three could be enforced as binding upon the whole organization if the Supreme Councillors ended up disagreeing with

49 Moody, O'Broin (eds.), 'IRB Supreme Council, 1868–78', Document C. 50 Ibid., Document A. 51 Ibid., Document C.

each other. This ensured that a strong central command was maintained within the organization, despite the decentralization of authority.

The position of president of the Supreme Council was usually given to a figurehead of the republican movement; he did not have to play a major role in shaping the IRB's policy or activities. Rather, he was generally called upon to make a decision only whenever there was disagreement between the secretary and treasurer of the Supreme Council, who had at all times a much more 'hands-on' responsibility in managing the movement. The treasurer, although a very important figure, performed an essentially clerical duty. The secretary, by contrast, was always the key position in the Supreme Council. The responsibility for the day-to-day management of the IRB, including the regulation of the other Supreme Councillors' activities, any arms importation efforts and negotiations with political prospective allies, fell almost entirely upon his shoulders. If the IRB did not have an efficient secretary, it would soon suffer the consequences. Effectively he was what Stephens had been prior to 1866, 'the chief organizer of the Irish republic', or in other words, the chief organizer of the IRB; but the onerous task of maintaining discipline over such a large movement was perhaps beyond the capacity of any one man.

After 1869, one of the IRB's chief concerns about discipline was that the elective system could easily cause personal rivalries between competing candidates for leadership, thereby creating factionalism, or allow popular men to be elected who lacked leadership abilities. Some republicans also felt that the chances of the IRB ever becoming a revolutionary citizens' army were lessened greatly under the new system. This idea was championed particularly by a small, rival IRB organization that, since 1867, was calling for Stephens to be reinstated as leader, but the distraught Stephens had no real intention of resuming his former career. This movement, often nicknamed as the 'Stephenites' or, borrowing from Bonapartist rhetoric, the 'Old Guard', denied the Supreme Council its right to call itself the IRB and tried consistently to win away the Supreme Council's following. For this very reason, the Supreme Council felt it necessary to change the IRB oath in 1869 from one to a 'virtually established' Irish republic to that of the authority of the Supreme Council, which was described as the 'sole government of the Irish Republic', or the sole government of the IRB – terminology that became enshrined in the IRB's constitution and would later give birth to some misunderstandings, although the actual meaning of the IRB oath had not changed. The 'Irish Republic' in question was still the same 'young republic' that Stephens had called upon his followers to embody and promote.

During the summer of 1873 the two key figures in the IRB (Charles Doran, its secretary, and John Daly, its chief travelling organizer) had calculated that it could only afford to concentrate upon attempting to democratize the 'home rule' movement for a maximum of three years.[52] This calculation was upset

---

52 John Daly, 'Recollections of Fenianism', *Irish Freedom*, Apr. 1913; Moody, *Davitt*, 123.

once Power became an MP in May 1874. The rank and file in Munster and Leinster now stopped paying subscriptions and threatened to break away from the Supreme Council, form a new movement or else join the Stephenite 'Old Guard', if they did not immediately get arms for their *past* subscriptions.[53] As a result, by 1875, the IRB lost almost half its subscribers. Despite assurances from the Supreme Council that it would start importing arms again, the rank and file, having lost confidence in their leadership, stubbornly withheld all financial support, pointing out that according to the IRB's constitution, three-quarters of all subscriptions were supposed to have been delegated to an arms fund.[54] As the Supreme Council could not revive arms importation efforts without continued financial support, it had no option but to follow the old treacherous path of looking to Irish-America. Consequently, Charles Doran began negotiating with the Clan na Gael, which had eclipsed the Fenian Brotherhood as the principal Irish-American revolutionary movement. Doran knew that as soon as an arms importation scheme was inaugurated with the Clan's assistance, the organization would become as numerically and financially potent as it had ever been. Accomplishing this goal now became his sole objective as the Supreme Council's secretary, but neither Kickham, the council's partly deaf and blind president, nor the IRB's treasurer, Patrick Egan (who had also become an assistant treasurer to the HRL), shared his concern.

The Clan na Gael was led by William Carroll, a Donegal-born Presbyterian, freemason, doctor and close friend and admirer of fellow northern republicans John Mitchel and John Martin. It had numerous talented former IRB organizers within its ranks, such as John Devoy (its secretary), John O'Connor (a brother of James and the Clan's leader in New York), J.J. O'Kelly, Jeremiah O'Donovan 'Rossa', T.C. Luby, Denis Mulcahy and others, several of whom had been released from prison in 1871 on condition that they never return to Ireland. During 1874–6, accepting an invitation from Doran, several Clan delegates visited Ireland and, together with Devoy and Rossa (who corresponded with Kickham) put pressure on the IRB president to ally the two organizations. Kickham, however, was indifferent to these proposals.[55] He also responded to Devoy's criticism of his hesitancy in coming to a final decision about Butt's movement by replying that 'we are not quite so benighted as ye seem to think' and expressed his opinion that the home rule movement might yet 'effect *some* good' in mobilizing greater popular support for the cause of Irish independence. He refused to condemn O'Connor Power's actions, stating that he believed he would serve a useful purpose by championing the abstentionist policy 'from within' the leadership of the home rule movement.[56] What Kickham (who was then spending most of his time writing fiction) did not

53 *DPB*, vol. 1, 131; NLI, Stephens papers, MS 10492 (correspondence of John Lucas and John Phelan); John Devoy, 'The story of Clan na Gael', *Gaelic American*, 15 Aug. 1923. 54 NLI, Devoy papers, MS 18036 (progress report on IRB). 55 NLI, John O'Leary papers, MS 5927, letter of Denis Mulcahy to O'Leary (n.d., *c.*1885) recalling his meeting with Kickham as a Clan envoy around 1875. 56 *DPB*, vol. 1, 162–5 (Kickham to Devoy).

seem to realize was that neither O'Connor Power nor any MP was promoting abstentionism at all. In fact, the only figure who was ready to do so during the mid 1870s was the man who had first suggested that the idea was a practical option: John Mitchel, the aging editor of the *Irish Citizen* (New York) who had worked with the IRB briefly during the late 1860s. With the support of the IRB and HRCGB, Mitchel was nominated for a Tipperary by-election in early 1875 on the understanding that he would not take his seat. He was elected twice by a very large margin, but (as an escaped convict) was declared non-eligible on both occasions; he died not long afterwards, shortly after attending the funeral of his brother-in-law, John Martin.[57]

During 1875–6 the IRB Executive was effectively being led by Patrick Egan and O'Connor Power, rather than Doran or Kickham; the latter did not even bother to attend Supreme Council meetings. As late as August 1876, Kickham wrote to Devoy expressing his hope that the 'great national conference' of the HRL (envisioned by Doran three years earlier) would soon be held,[58] but the league was almost totally moribund, having little or no popular support and it would soon fall into debt.[59] The Irish MPs at Westminster remained individualists who felt total contempt for the idea of promoting a democratic movement in Ireland since this would have been entirely contrary to their lifelong political sensibilities and social status as 'gentlemen'. Therefore, although public opinion was seemingly quite in favour of such an agitation, they were incapable of taking the necessary steps to launch it. For this reason, Egan and O'Connor Power hoped to win the leadership of the HRL away from Butt and other conservatives so that, with the assistance of the HRCGB, the republicans and democrats could refashion the movement to suit themselves. It was self-evident to Egan (less so to O'Connor Power) that if they were to succeed in such efforts, they would need to find a political ally of considerably greater social prestige than their own to lead their party, since most people in politics were prepared to follow only men of the gentry class. Egan found this ally in Charles Stewart Parnell, a high sheriff and member of the Wicklow gentry with a relatively distinguished family history, who had failed completely in his previous attempts to enter politics but was still eager of finding any means of doing so. Egan and fellow republicans provided him with his opportunity.

Parnell knew Egan as early as 1873, when the latter introduced him to the IRB leader John Daly to debate whether or not the 'home rule' movement could be democratized.[60] Subsequently, having been provided with a medium of communication with the IRB, Parnell tried to ingratiate himself with Charles Doran.[61] Following the death of the old republican John Martin in 1875, Egan persuaded Parnell to stand for Martin's seat in Meath and financially supported his campaign.[62] Parnell won the seat. Thereafter O'Connor

57 Thornley, *Butt*, 251–4. 58 *DPB*, vol. 1, 165. 59 Thornley, *Butt*, 245–6, 365, 370–1. 60 John Daly, 'Recollections of Fenianism', *Irish Freedom*, Apr. 1913. 61 F.S.L. Lyons, *Charles Stewart Parnell* (1977), 48–9.

Power advised him to build up a popular support base by championing the amnesty question and to begin working with the republican-led HRCGB.[63] Taking this advice, Parnell identified himself with the HRCGB, instead of the HRL. In August 1875, while the Catholic National Association and some nominal 'home rulers' (Catholic-liberals) held a large demonstration in Dublin to celebrate the centenary of O'Connell's birth, Parnell spoke instead alongside O'Connor Power and Joseph Biggar before a monster amnesty demonstration in Hyde Park, London, organized under the auspices of Ferguson and Barry's HRCGB, which had just formed the *United Irishman*. Subsequently, these three men (along with W.H. O'Sullivan) adopted an obstructionist policy at Westminster to attract as much Irish political attention to themselves as possible and, in the process, marginalize Butt and the conservatives.[64]

Together with James O'Connor of the *Irishman*, during 1875 Patrick Egan began promoting a fairly-active breakaway movement from the HRL, to put pressure upon the moderates of the HRL to follow the HRCGB's dictates. The '82 Clubs were founded in 1874 by P.J. Smyth, an old 1848 rebel (whose Confederate Club had also been known as the '82 Club) and a recently-elected 'independent nationalist' MP for Tipperary. Smyth opposed Butt's federalist ideas, supporting instead the complete repeal of the Union. Egan encouraged many IRB members to join the '82 clubs, particularly in Dublin, where republicans generally organized the society's political debates and subsequently swore many of the participants into the IRB.[65] Meanwhile, acting against Doran's wishes, O'Connor Power visited the United States and tried to persuade the Clan to collect funds in America for the HRL. This having failed, both he and Egan, in an effort to keep their political strategy alive, co-opted both Joseph Biggar, MP for Cavan, and John Barry of the HRCGB onto the IRB Supreme Council, possibly with Kickham's support.[66] Their co-opting of Biggar was a remarkable breach of IRB procedure. The Belfast man had never even been a member of the organization prior to his admission to its executive and he had absolutely no interest in its objectives, although he was a personal friend of the Belfast IRB leader, Robert Johnston, a wealthy timber merchant.[67]

Egan and O'Connor Power's strategy had a destructive effect on the IRB, causing the organization's leaders to start working at cross-purposes with each other. This fact was perhaps best demonstrated by a couple of incidental, yet revealing, events. In August 1875, to protest against the O'Connell centenary demonstration, Charles Doran, John Daly, John Nolan and the Dublin IRB carried black flags into the crowd, hurling abuse at all 'political place-hunters',

62 R.B. O'Brien, *The life of Parnell* (1910), 64–7. 63 Thornley, *Butt*, 252. 64 Donald Jordan, 'John O'Connor Power, Charles Stewart Parnell and the centralisation of popular politics in Ireland', *IHS*, 25 (1986), 46–66. 65 Thornley, *Butt*, 246; NAI, Fenian Papers F Series, 8992R, 9013R, 9103R; Crime Special Branch files, B198. The best source on the activities of the '82 Clubs are the columns of the *Irishman* from 1874–7. 66 Moody, O'Broin (eds.), 'IRB Supreme Council, 1868–78'. 67 Interview with Robert Johnston, *Irish Press*, 15 Apr. 1935.

only to find themselves attacked by moderate members of the '82 Clubs, who were armed with sticks.[68] The following spring, at an impromptu demonstration to celebrate the Clan's rescue of six IRB prisoners in Western Australia, IRB activists burnt an effigy of Prime Minister Disraeli on the streets of Dublin. At the same time, however, Matthew Harris, a Galway republican, building contractor, ex-arms agent and influential Connacht IRB leader, published a lengthy 'scientific' pamphlet he wrote, addressed to Disraeli and explaining how the government might make more effective use of the natural resources of the Shannon River and relieve impoverished communities in the west of Ireland.[69] In itself, Egan and Power's strategy was not necessarily inconsistent with the IRB's general policy, but they had made the preservation of the IRB's own integrity a very secondary consideration to their desire to democratize the home rule movement. In this respect, they were in direct breach of the IRB's 1873 constitution.

By the spring of 1876, Doran had completed his negotiations with William Carroll and established an alliance between the Supreme Council and the Clan. The only medium of communication between the two organizations was to be a 'Revolutionary Directory', consisting of three Supreme Councillors and three members of the Clan Executive. The sole ostensible purpose of this directory was to launch and sustain an arms importation scheme for the IRB.[70] At a Supreme Council meeting that August, Doran declared that the IRB must take a definite decision regarding the HRL. As the 'home rule' movement had failed to make any changes or headway in Irish politics, Doran moved that the Supreme Council should rule that any member of the IRB who was also a member of the HRL, or even the HRCGB, should be given but six months to leave these organizations or be expelled from the IRB. O'Connor Power, Barry and Egan (each of whom were HRL officials) protested against this. As only seven of the eleven members of the council were present at this meeting, they also demanded that no vote be taken on this issue until the full council was sitting. However, Doran's motion was passed by four votes to three, his own vote being the deciding factor.[71] As Kickham wrote to Devoy the same month defending Egan and O'Connor Power's policy against all criticism,[72] if he had attended this meeting, he would no doubt have taken their side. Indeed conceivably, if Kickham had attended this meeting, even if seven of the eleven Supreme Councillors took Doran's side, the motion could still have been defeated, as the combined vote of Kickham and Egan, as president and treasurer respectively, could technically have been made binding upon the whole organization. Evidently, Kickham was absent from this meeting either because Doran did not inform him that it was taking place, or else Kickham (who was

68 Thornley, *Butt*, 266–9. For taking part in this protest, John Nolan lost his job and was forced to emigrate to America, where he died in 1887, aged 40. His health had always been poor. 69 Terry Golway, *Irish rebel* (1998), 84; Matthew Harris, *The improvement of rivers and reclamation of wastelands* (Dublin, 1876). Harris' proposal was ignored. 70 *DPB*, vol. 1, 198–200, passim. 71 Moody, O'Broin (eds.), 'IRB Supreme Council'. 72 *DPB*, vol. 1, 162–5.

after all deaf and blind and could only converse by sign language) did not know what was going on. Whatever the case, by March 1877, O'Connor Power, Barry, Egan and Biggar had all been expelled from the IRB and the Supreme Council. However, O'Connor Power and Egan in particular were not ready to accept this decision; they believed that most ordinary IRB members would accept their judgment of the political situation if only it could be fully explained to them. Over the next year, this is what they attempted to do. Their expectations, however, were to be sorely mistaken.

The reality of the IRB's relationship with the HRL during the 1870s was that Power and Egan were the *only* IRB figures involved in that organization, which was completely moribund, notwithstanding the publicity won by the parliamentary obstructionists. The proverbial 'rank and file' had been very active in the Amnesty Association, but they had never been involved in the HRL, nor could they have been, even if they had wanted to, owing to its lack of branches and its elitist qualifications for membership. If only for this reason, the great bulk of the IRB's membership could not have had any intrinsic interest in the HRL, regardless of what they thought of its politics. Judging by the correspondence in the *Irishman*, they universally opposed it. As a result, in Ireland, the IRB's membership invariably welcomed Doran's policy. In England and Scotland, however, many IRB centres were uncomfortable about this decision as they were active in the HRCGB and felt loyalty towards the now discarded IRB leaders. In Edinburgh and Liverpool, many IRB men, resolving to stick with the HRCGB, were expelled from the organization, although, by 1878, the British IRB organization as a whole (excepting Edinburgh, where the IRB ceased to exist) had resolved, or were persuaded, to follow the Supreme Council's policy.[73] Thereafter they generally became only passive spectators of the activities of the HRCGB which, by August 1877, had made Charles Stewart Parnell its president.

It had not been possible to hold IRB elections since the O'Connor Power controversy broke out in 1874, possibly because the Supreme Council (acting mostly under Egan and O'Connor Power's direction), had prevented them. Around March 1878, following what appears to have been the first IRB elections held in five years, the republican movement underwent significant personnel changes at all levels.[74] Every position on the Supreme Council excepting that of the chairman (Kickham) and the representatives of the two smallest IRB divisions (Scotland and Southern England) was now occupied by a previously untested leader. Most of these men would play a key role in directing the policy of the republican movement over the next five to ten years. As he felt entirely responsible for all the problems that had faced the IRB since 1874 (its subscribing membership had halved) and was also extremely busy in his business career, Doran decided to step down as secretary of the Supreme

73 NLI, Devoy papers, MS 18036; *Special Commission Report*, vol. 4, 505–11; *DPB*, vol. 1, 349–51, 427. 74 NLI, Devoy papers, MS 18036.

Council. His regret was essentially misplaced as he had been more responsible for preserving rather than undermining the IRB over the past two to three years by prioritizing the rank and file's concerns. The services of four veteran figures were now availed of to help restore discipline and efficiency to the IRB: William Carroll, J.J. O'Kelly, John O'Connor and John O'Leary.[75] Although he would not be officially co-opted onto the Supreme Council until 1880, O'Leary almost immediately began playing a sort of guiding role of co-chairman (or deputy chairman) alongside the ailing Kickham. That Doran's policy was in the IRB's best interests was evidently something Kickham had come to understand by 1878, if not earlier, for henceforth he would become deeply suspicious of O'Connor Power and Egan's political clique and turned his attention away from the HRL.

The key change on the Supreme Council was Doran's replacement as secretary by John O'Connor, a 29-year-old medical student and freemason who, unlike his brother James of the *Irishman*, was 'neither a speaker nor a writer', although he was equally 'a man of intellect'.[76] O'Connor had been Stephens' mere messenger boy during the mid 1860s but sooned proved his ability by playing a significant role in establishing the IRB Supreme Council.[77] From 1869 to 1876 he had been a very effective leader of the Clan's 'Napper Tandy Club' in New York (the most important club within that organization) before the formation of the new 'Revolutionary Directory' prompted him to transfer his allegiance back to the IRB. He was to become, in John Devoy's estimation, the most efficient secretary the IRB ever had during its sixty-five-year history.[78] Doran's replacement as Munster IRB leader was Patrick Neville Fitzgerald, a 27-year-old former accountant from rural east Cork who had recently set up a public house on Prince's Street, Cork city with the help of his wife's dowry. A mostly self-educated man of strong democratic and egalitarian sensibilities, Fitzgerald had been a fanatical admirer of Thomas Davis's writings since a boy and followed his older brother into the IRB at the age of just fifteen after he witnessed the RIC opening fire upon a public demonstration while coming home from school in Midleton.[79] A very popular figure with the 'rank and file', he soon become the organization's chief travelling organizer, replacing John Daly. Like almost all IRB leaders, Fitzgerald was a man of very humble birth (the son of a gardener), but he was a close friend and trusted confidant of both O'Leary and Kickham, whose political sympathies he largely shared.[80]

Robert Johnston, a 38-year-old successful timber merchant and building contractor in Belfast, was elected as the Ulster IRB leader, replacing John Daly, who had been elected to this position by the Ulster rank and file in 1872 despite

75 *DPB*, vol. 1, 296–315. **76** *Gaelic American*, 5 Dec. 1908 (obituary). **77** Roney, *Irish rebel*, 154–6. **78** John Devoy, 'The story of Clan na Gael', *Gaelic American*, 6 Dec. 1924. **79** Tomas O'Riordan, 'Fenian and GAA pioneer: the story of P.N. Fitzgerald', *Cork Holly Bough* (Christmas, 1984), 20, 29; *Irish Nation* (New York), 13 Dec. 1884 (speech of Fitzgerald). **80** *Cork Examiner*, 9 Oct. 1907.

the fact he was a Limerick-man. Over the past ten years, Johnston had managed to assume an authoritarian discipline over the large Belfast IRB organization, despite the rank and file's dislike of his arrogant personality. A former friend of Biggar's and devoted admirer of Kickham, Johnston was a northern, self-made businessman (he was originally a labourer) of cultural nationalist leanings who was first won over to republican political beliefs by John Griffith, an obscure Presbyterian republican of the 1840s who had made independent efforts to sustain republican clubs in Belfast between 1848 and 1867 without being aware of the existence of the IRB.[81] Like Patrick Egan, Johnston's standing in society as a fairly influential businessman enhanced his tendency to view Irish politics from a purely practical standpoint and not to be too bothered by ideological scruples. The new Leinster IRB leader was James Mullet, a 28-year-old publican from Dublin who, despite his total opposition to the HRL, had been a close associate of Patrick Egan for several years. Mullet was drawn into the IRB only the previous year through attending Dublin debates of the '82 Clubs, during which he demonstrated strong republican proclivities. He replaced John Leavy, an uneducated Dublin shop-foreman who, though popular among various workers' societies in Ireland and England, had the reputation of being the most unintelligent man ever to be elected to the leadership of the IRB.[82] The new Connacht IRB leader was Matthew Harris, a 53-year-old building contractor from Ballinasloe, Co. Galway, who was originally a supporter of the Confederate Clubs and had been trying to sustain popular political activity in Galway ever since the early 1850s. During 1876, he created his own political organization, the Ballinasloe Tenants Defence Association, to defend the rural tenantry from eviction. A man intimately acquainted with the realities of Irish rural life, Harris viewed republicanism as synonymous with holding anti-aristocratic and democratic political sensibilities and so believed that destroying the political power of the landed aristocracy in Ireland should be the first priority of any sincere Irish republican.[83] The other new Supreme Council representative was Michael Davitt, a 32-year-old self-educated and very literate labourer who had been a 'rank and file' man in Lancashire during the late 1860s but was soon imprisoned, due to his involvement in J.J. O'Kelly's arms importation scheme. He was not released from prison until December 1877, when celebrations were organized by the Dublin IRB (which Parnell also attended) to mark his release and that of two other prisoners.[84] Davitt was elected as co-leader of the IRB in the north of England (alongside William McGuinness, a 23-year-old Preston publican) primarily to express sympathy with him for his having spent seven years in prison. Davitt, however, was only now beginning to formulate his political

81 Daly, 'Recollections of Fenianism'; interview with Robert Johnston, *Irish Press*, 15 Apr. 1935. Arthur Griffith's father, John Griffith, was a Presbyterian from Cavan, although this may well not have been the same man. 82 NAI, CSB files, B198; CSORP, 1877/91; Fenian papers, 9026R. 83 Matthew Harris, *The political situation* (Dublin, 1880), 1–4. 84 NAI, CSORP, 1878/875.

beliefs and would soon irritate his comrades on the Supreme Council by questioning the entire ethos of the IRB organization and championing a political stance akin to that of O'Connor Power, whom Davitt admired greatly and credited for having organized his release from prison.

Although the republican movement had tens of thousand of members and the HRL had only a few hundred, the IRB's policy during the 1870s failed because its members were not of sufficient standing to acquire influence in established political circles. In Ireland, most politicians who claimed to support the idea of 'home rule' did so only because they feared that a failure to do so might 'unite the democracy', which was their greatest worry.[85] In urban Britain, such concerns generally did not exist among the working and small middle-class Irish community that were behind the HRCGB; but republicans could not change the situation in Ireland. One member of the Irish gentry, Parnell, may have been willing to assume the presidency of the republican-biased HRCGB, but he was the only one seemingly prepared to act as a political ally. Meanwhile Egan and O'Connor Power's strategy had served merely to bankrupt the IRB. By 1878, it was self-evident to all Supreme Councillors that the organization would need to launch an extensive arms importation scheme to win back its following, particularly in rural Ireland. As the Amnesty Association had folded, the republican movement also needed to find a new 'public movement which will enable the young educated men to exert their proper influence'.[86] To this end, Kickham and O'Leary favoured taking up Patrick Egan's old plan of buying out the Irishman and establishing a new newspaper that would accurately reflect the state of opinion in the IRB and help popularize its political beliefs. Matthew Harris also supported this plan, but he and Michael Davitt were more interested in the idea of launching a radical land agitation under a democratic and republican leadership. Unlike all previous land agitations, this movement would champion only the tenants' rights and completely ignore those of the landed aristocracy and gentry. J.J. O'Kelly, by contrast, believed that the IRB could pursue its arms importation scheme while at the same time continue the old policy of trying to remould the HRL along democratic-republican lines. While in Paris working as a war correspondent during 1877, O'Kelly had met Parnell twice, befriended him and was impressed by his account of affairs in the HRCGB. O'Kelly became convinced that if a man of Parnell's social standing and political ability could be made to act as a spokesman for the republican movement, he could 'so remould Irish public opinion as to clear away many of the stumbling blocks in the way of progressive action'.[87] However, O'Kelly, who had grown up in London and had not been in Ireland for many years, did not realize how different the HRL was from the HRCGB.

During 1877–8, Carroll and O'Kelly contacted the Russian and Spanish governments (each of which held grievances against Britain at the time)

85 Thornley, *Butt*, 79, 101.   86 *DPB*, vol. 1, 384–5.   87 *DPB*, vol. 1, 267–70.

looking for promises of assistance in the event of a nationalist uprising taking place in Ireland sometime in the future. Neither government, however, could be convinced that there was any disloyalty to the British empire in Ireland since no nationalists were involved in public life. Even if a successful insurrection ever did take place, international approval for the establishment of an Irish state would almost certainly be needed; therefore this rebuff convinced O'Kelly that steps had to be taken by republicans to ensure that a nationalist public opinion developed in Ireland that would be recognized internationally. To achieve this, republicans would need more than just a strong influence in the popular political sphere. There would have to be Irish MPs who adopted an uncompromisingly nationalist stance at Westminster. Upon returning to New York, O'Kelly succeeded in convincing his best friend, John Devoy, as well as Carroll, of the truth of his assertions. As a result, in the autumn of 1878, while it simultaneously provided the IRB with a large amount of funds to help it inaugurate an arms subsidization scheme, the Clan, on the initiative of John Devoy, decided to publish a political programme in the Irish press without even consulting the IRB; this consisted of proposals which became known popularly as the 'new departure' programme.[88]

The republican exiles called for the establishment of the first-ever Irish nationalist parliamentary party in Westminster. They promised Irish-American aid if a party was established that supported Irish independence, rather than Butt's aim of a federal government for the United Kingdom. It was demanded that this new party would speak in defence of the right of all nations to political self-determination; would vote together as a party on all issues; would 'energetically resist coercive measures' introduced by the British government in Ireland and would support a 'vigorous agitation of the land question on the basis of a peasant proprietary'; the latter proposal having been inspired by Devoy's interviews with Davitt earlier that year. As Devoy openly called on all nationalists to 'come out of the rat-holes of conspiracy and take part in the public life of the country', the Catholic-Whig press presented the 'new departure' proposals to the public as meaning that the 'Fenians' had begun to favour 'constitutional' instead of 'physical force' methods. Some historians have presented the 'new departure' in precisely these terms,[89] but this is to misunderstand the entire reasoning of the programme. Devoy's appeal to the IRB to 'come out of the rat-holes of conspiracy' was not meant to denigrate its politics in any way (this was something that the IRB understood fully),[90] but was motivated by an understanding that, unless republicans and nationalists took a greater part in Irish public life, their politics would continue to be misrepresented, would never be properly understood by the Irish people and, as a result, would never have any great effect.

88 T.W. Moody, 'The new departure in Irish politics, 1878–9' (1949). 89 Although he understood the purpose of the 'new departure', T.W. Moody adopted this interpretative framework in his seminal work, *Davitt and Irish revolution* (1981) and this generally obscures what the 'Irish revolution' in question was all about. 90 *DPB*, vol. 1, 481.

In January 1879, a meeting of the full IRB Supreme Council was called in Paris to discuss the arms importation scheme and the idea of establishing a new republican newspaper. Devoy attended as a representative of the Clan's wing of the 'Revolutionary Directory' and raised the issue of the 'new departure' proposals. The IRB acknowledged the need for nationalists to become more active in Irish public life, but rejected the idea that they should help to create a new Irish party at Westminster.[91] It would be prepared to support such a party if it was ready to adopt the abstentionist policy, but it believed that current Irish political representatives had not sufficient 'public virtue' to act in this manner, nor was it likely that any MPs would be prepared to do so 'in any very near future', even though this might happen eventually.[92] The Supreme Council resolved to keep its focus 'well *in front* of the turmoil of everyday politics' in order to maximize its ability to determine an effective, long-term political strategy for the republican movement, and it believed the Clan was completely jumping the gun in believing that the sort of party it was envisioning could be created in the near future.[93] Knowing what had happened when O'Connor Power had stood for election, the IRB also knew the dangers involved in funding or campaigning for parliamentary candidates. The Supreme Council resolved to turn the organization's attention completely away from the 'home rule' MPs, although the Supreme Council had no intention of restricting IRB members' individual liberty to vote in parliamentary elections, if they so desired.[94] Speaking in defence of O'Connor Power's role as MP, Michael Davitt had recently accused most Irish revolutionaries of drawing 'a single line of distinction between a West Briton and the Irishman who accepted its programme',[95] but he believed with the rest of the council that the revival of arms importation efforts was a necessity. To make this clear to the Clan, the Supreme Council as a whole issued an official proclamation after this meeting making the simple statement that, ultimately, 'arms we must have or we have nothing'.[96]

The plan for the arms importation scheme was that the Clan would subsidize the costs of purchasing, packaging and transporting top-quality firearms with a view to reducing their cost to a level that the rank and file of the IRB could afford. The emphasis on acquiring quality firearms was central to the scheme. During the mid to late 1860s, the IRB had acquired a few thousand weapons that, by now, were in very poor repair and had been antiquated in the first place, although it did possess some revolvers.[97] Dublin Castle knew that it had nothing to fear from the IRB after it succeeded in several arms seizures in Dublin during the early 1870s; the idea of a band of Irish 'skilled musketeers'

91 Ryan, *Fenian memories*, 64–5. 92 O'Leary to *Irishman*, 11 Jan. 1879, 3 Apr. 1880. 93 *DPB*, vol. 1, 481 (quotation John O'Connor). 94 Devoy, *Recollections*, 314. 95 Speech of Michael Davitt, 5 Dec 1878 in Boston, reprinted in *Irish Nation* (New York), 17 Dec. 1881. 96 NLI, Devoy Papers, MS 18000 (2), statement of Supreme Council to Clan na Gael, Feb. 1879. 97 Takagami, 'Dublin Fenians', 141; NAI, Fenian papers, 7931R; *Special Commission Report*, vol. 4, 573–6 (evidence produced by the spy Le Caron).

being brought face to face with the British army seemed totally comical to Dublin Castle officials,[98] as no doubt it did to members of the IRB. As a result of Clan subsidization, however, the IRB could now afford large quantities of Schneider rifles, a top-quality, fully up-to-date firearm that was also the principal weapon used by both the RIC and the state militia in Ireland. The IRB still did not have sufficient financial resources to buy Martini-Henry rifles, the most accurate long range firearm then in existence which had been developed exclusively for the British army, but the qualitative difference between Schneider and Martini-Henry rifles was relatively slight. If the scheme was successful, therefore, the IRB could at least be sufficiently well equipped to make an attempt to fight some of the British armed forces in Ireland conceivable for the first time.[99]

In the spring 1879 the Clan sent F.F. Millen, a Tyrone Catholic, former Mexican general and the leader of the Clan's 'Military Board', to Ireland to carry out an inspection of the proverbial 'military organization' of the IRB, while John Devoy, the Clan secretary, was asked to examine its 'civil organization' (which was much the same thing). On his return, Millen stated to the Clan that the membership of the IRB, although eager to receive it, had no military knowledge whatsoever. To remedy this, Millen (an ex-British spy) had made proposals to the Supreme Council. He suggested that a 'military officer' of the Clan (such as himself) should be given 'entire control of the military department' of the IRB, be appointed an *ex-officio* member of the Supreme Council and allowed to superintend the election of all officers in the IRB so as to ensure that its 'circles', or revolutionary cells, were being led by men capable of turning their followers into nothing less than military companies.[100] Millen claimed that the Supreme Council was very enthusiastic about this proposal; hence, William Carroll's bewilderment when the Supreme Council ignored Millen's proposals. Writing to John O'Leary, Carroll warned that to 'simply report so many organizers, agents etc. are on the road' reorganizing the IRB was 'intolerable': the Clan needed to be convinced 'that at least the nucleus of an army is being formed or has been formed' if Irish-American funding was to continue and the Revolutionary Directory was to remain in existence.[101] It is perfectly clear, however, why the Supreme Council did not accept Millen's proposals: being aware of the unfortunate precedent of 1865, it was wholly opposed to the idea of the IRB ever being directed by an American military officer, whose first loyalty would no doubt be to his Irish-American friends, not the IRB. In addition, as John Devoy noted after performing his 'civil inspection' of the IRB, the organization was in no condition whatsoever to be turned into an army. Although the IRB leaders were 'very intelligent men' and 'good enough for their work', Devoy (a former soldier) judged that they were men of

98 NAI, Fenian papers, 7568R, 8053R, 8067R, 8551R; CSORP, 1880/5572. 99 *Special Commission Report*, vol. 4, 573–6 (statement by F.F. Millen to the Clan about the IRB's arms importation scheme in 1879, produced as evidence by Le Caron). 100 Ibid. 101 *DPB*, vol. 1, 430–1.

little or no ability as far as military matters was concerned.[102] Indeed, neither then, nor at any time in the IRB's history, was the republican movement's leadership elected on the basis of their knowledge of military stratagem or equipment.

The Supreme Council, not willing to work with Millen, sent him back to America, but as it trusted Devoy it let him stay in Ireland for a few more months and asked him to assist John O'Connor, P.N. Fitzgerald and others in reorganizing the movement. The first two arms agents employed by the Supreme Council during 1879 were Michael Hogan, a Tipperary IRB man, and Daniel Curley, a Roscommon-born carpenter and a Dublin IRB centre, men whom Devoy stated were only 'fairly competent' in their work, owing to their lack of a thorough military knowledge.[103] The IRB bought many arms in England with a view to sending them to Ireland, although it was expected that due to the vigilance of the police 'we must be prepared for that channel being closed some day'.[104] There was also a problem in finding an adequate system to store such arms. As a result, Devoy feared they could be easily seized by the police should it make a very vigilant search.

In August 1879 Devoy reported to the Clan that, in the past six months, newly appointed IRB organizers had travelled the country in an effort to convince men to rejoin the movement and prepare for an extensive arms importation scheme. The result was that after small quantities of top-quality firearms were produced, with the promise of much more to come, over 4,000 men rejoined the movement, or decided to pay their subscriptions once more.[105] Devoy broke down the current IRB membership in each of its seven districts (see Table 1):

Table 1

Ulster	10,266	North of England	3,685
Connacht	7,066	Scotland	1,000
Munster	4,798	South of England	734
Leinster	2,613		

This would indicate a nominal IRB membership of 30,162 men, but Devoy stressed that not all of these men (particularly in Munster) were in 'good standing', or regularly paying subscriptions and attending meetings.[106] In particular, the urban/rural divide in the IRB was still undermining its ability to organize itself in a systematic manner. While the discipline of the organization in the towns and cities was strong, the rural membership was far too 'easy going and careless', despite the fact that they were 'rather exacting with regard to their leaders'. Their 'great want of system' ensured that the Supreme

102 *DPB*, vol. 1, 404–7. 103 John Devoy, 'The story of Clan na Gael', *Gaelic American*, 13 Dec. 1924. 104 NLI, Devoy papers, MS 18036 (progress report of IRB). 105 This report by Devoy to the Clan can be found in the *Special Commission Report*, vol. 4, 505–11 (evidence produced by Le Caron). 106 NLI, Devoy papers, MS 18036 (progress report of the IRB).

Council was having much difficulty in maintaining constant communication with the centres in rural districts, who 'expect too much from the Supreme Council and do not stop to inquire where the resources are to come from to accomplish all they expect from it'. As they were still only ready to pay subscriptions when they were sure that arms were available, Devoy lamented that 'it will take long training to make the IRB, as a whole, a self-reliant, self-supporting organization, and to make the members in the rural districts understand that much more is necessary to sustain a great political movement than a mere willingness to risk life and liberty'.[107]

Once the IRB's arms importation scheme had got underway, it turned its attention to the idea of creating a new republican newspaper. William Carroll, the Clan chairman, believed from his past experience of talking with IRB leaders that they should be able to establish a paper that was 'equal to the ablest of our opponents in political debate' and be of sufficient literary quality to attract contributions from Irish intellectuals of all religious and political persuasions.[108] John O'Leary, however, did not think that it had enough men in its ranks of sufficient literary ability to do the job. He was no doubt quite right. Nevertheless Matthew Harris was delegated by the Supreme Council to negotiate with Richard Pigott to try and buy out the *Irishman* newspaper, but Pigott attempted to drive a hard bargain. This fact, combined with the IRB's general uncertainty as to who would be a suitable editorial team for the envisioned newspaper, prompted the IRB to suspend, at least in the short term, its newspaper project during the summer of 1879.[109]

In April 1879, Michael Davitt, John Devoy and Patrick Egan persuaded a reluctant Parnell to take up the land question. With the help of the Connacht IRB leader Matthew Harris and some of his subordinates, a monster land rally was held at Irishtown, Co. Mayo, on 20 April. This meeting was addressed by the parliamentary obstructionists (Parnell, O'Connor Power, W.H. O'Sullivan and Joseph Biggar), the HRCGB founders (John Barry and John Ferguson) as well as Matthew Harris and other local radicals, and marked the formation of the Land League of Mayo. Owing to continued distress in the west, arising from consecutive poor harvests, demands for a more extensive agitation continued. As a result, in October 1879, the Land League of Mayo was superceded by a body known as the 'Irish National Land League', which was established in Dublin with Parnell as its chairman, Michael Davitt (IRB), Thomas Brennan (IRB) and Andrew Kettle as its secretaries, and Patrick Egan, Joseph Biggar and W.H. O'Sullivan as its treasurers. As the IRB was still the most numerous political organization within Ireland, the Land League was naturally eager to win its support. Consequently, upon its establishment, the Land League's leading organizers claimed at public rallies that it was never

---

107 This report by Devoy can be found in the *Special Commission Report*, vol. 4, 505–11 (evidence produced by Le Caron).   108 *DPB*, vol. 1, 334–8.   109 *DPB*, vol. 1, 415–18, 437–41; *Gaelic American*, 8 Sept. 1906 (recollections of Devoy).

going to become the tool of Westminster politicians, but instead would commit itself entirely to bringing about an 'uprising of the democracy of Ireland',[110] a fact that immediately caused great consternation to the political leaders of both Catholic and Protestant Ireland. In so far as the Land League managed to live up to these credentials, there was certainly a strong possibility of its winning very considerable republican support.

During 1864, the *Irish People* had argued that an economy based on a system of peasant-proprietary was needed in Ireland to stem emigration, but it believed the issue could only be properly settled once an independent Irish state or, in other words, an Irish economy, had been established.[111] Similarly, during 1847, Fintan Lalor had been opposed to any attempts by MPs to raise 'the landlord-and-tenant question', since the landlords (who were also generally MPs) were 'a foreign garrison' and because 'the question of the tenure by which the actual cultivator of the soil should hold his land is one for an Irish parliament', not for Westminster. Lalor did, however, favour the idea of people making a direct attack upon the property rights of the landed aristocracy, 'the English garrison who stand here, scattered and isolated', by whatever means were possible.[112] The IRB's attitudes towards the Land League would be shaped by similar considerations. While it welcomed the challenge made to the aristocracy, first and foremost it wanted the Land League to be directed towards nationalist ends and was willing to give it full support so long as the agitation was not taken over by either Westminster MPs or by irresponsible peasant secret societies such as the 'Ribbonmen'. By 1880, the speedy success of the Land League agitation, as well as its own arms importation scheme, aroused much excitement among the IRB, leading many to judge that the potential of their revolutionary experiment was truly about to be tested for the first time. Indeed, if there was ever a time during the mid to late nineteenth century when the IRB could possibly have brought about a political and social revolution in Ireland, then the period 1879–82 was essentially that time.

[handwritten marginal notes: "L yrs of the land war"; "L transition!"]

110 NAI, Land League and National League reports, carton 2, speech of Thomas Brennan, Carrick-on-Shannon, 14 Dec. 1879. 111 Patrick Cullen, 'James Stephens and the *Irish People*', 117–19. 112 Fogarty (ed.), *Lalor*, 43–4.

3

'An uprising of the Irish democracy': the rise of the IRB and the Land League, 1879–82

The Land League could be described as having been a truly democratic political movement. It was both established and organized by lower-class politicians, and it *reputedly* won as many as 200,000 members (no actual statistics of membership have survived).[1] Unlike all previous land agitations, it was feared and almost universally opposed by the Catholic hierarchy, the press and all 'recognized leaders' of Irish public opinion, since it completely ignored the concerns of the landed gentry, whose property rights were challenged by withholding rents, and because its political leadership (excepting Parnell, its figurehead) was not at all composed of men of the 'gentlemanly classes'. This latter fact allowed Parnell to present himself to the Irish political establishment and to Westminster as the *only* Land League figure they could trust, and, in the process, acquire political influence. Parnell and other parliamentary obstructionists tried to act as the league's spokesmen in Westminster, but they spoke very rarely on league platforms in Ireland and they did not play a significant role in its organization. Republicans, by contrast, did almost all of the league's organizational work, particularly during the first year of its existence. They claimed that it was only due to the IRB that 'the manhood of Ireland now knows its rights and is determined to assert them' and that the Land League's real leaders 'are nationalists and so will not take a seat in the English House of Commons, even if sent there by every constituency in the land'.[2]

Although it did engage in relieving agrarian distress, the Land League was essentially a political movement with nationalist objectives. Many people who had no connection with the league engaged in relieving agrarian distress. For example, Edmund Dwyer Gray of the *Freeman's Journal*, a conservative Catholic-Whig, established a 'relief fund' at the Dublin Mansion House in January 1880, and this initiative soon won the support of the Catholic hierarchy and the propertied classes. However, neither Gray, the church nor the propertied classes were prepared to support the Land League, as they feared the possibility of democratic political activity taking place in the country. As a result, the funds that were used to set up branches of the political organization of the Land League came almost entirely from Irish-America.[3]

The Land League executive was controlled by Michael Davitt and Thomas Brennan, its two active secretaries, both of whom belonged to the IRB; and its

---

1 *DPB*, vol. 2, 21–5 (Davitt to Devoy, Dec. 1880). 2 NAI, Land and National League reports, carton 2, speech of Thomas Brennan, Carrick-on-Shannon, 14 Dec. 1879. 3 Comerford, *Fenians in context*, 234.

chief treasurer, Patrick Egan, was still closely associated with the IRB. Of these three, Brennan was the most responsible for organizing branches of the league, each of which had a right to elect its own leaders. The four principal travelling organizers of the league (Brennan, Matthew Harris, Michael Boyton and P.J. Sheridan), were all republicans of radical democratic and egalitarian leanings. Indeed, they could perhaps be described as socialist republicans. Contrary to the reputation he acquired in later years, however, Michael Davitt took a very different political line to these men. During his few speeches on league platforms in Ireland, he emphasized his belief that the Land League must adopt 'a platform of compromise' that could appeal to the middle ground of public opinion and even the MPs.[4] His commitment to this policy caused him to come into conflict with the IRB.

It was Davitt who devised the structure of the league, which was very unusual. While the executive organized the league's branches and directed the organization, the league also had a 'central branch' in Dublin that had a different purpose. Its members included several MPs, businessmen and parish priests, but the central branch itself had no power over the organization of the league.[5] Actually, the conservatives did not even want this power. During the 1880s, as in the past, men of the propertied classes had no desire to engage in popular politics and thereby have to deal directly with peasants or workers. As far as the conservatives were concerned, the only practical purpose of the league's central branch was to provide them with a new platform from which they could try to influence the policy of the leaders of the HRL regarding the management of parliamentary election campaigns. In effect, they wanted to turn the league into a pressure group. Unlike most other Land League leaders, Davitt was concerned with this type of political activity. This made him a trusted ally of Parnell and his supporters, who consequently lauded Davitt in the press (which ignored most Land Leaguers) and created a personality cult around him. The Parnellites would not have become involved with the league if it could not be used in some ways for MPs' purposes. Davitt, for his part, sought to convince the Clan that the Land League could be used for promoting the revolutionary ideals of the 'new departure' programme. Whether or not he believed this himself is unclear. In his own self-estimation, Davitt was essentially a reformer, not a revolutionary. He was always inclined to follow his own intuition, rather than act in line with party interests, and, to him, the publicity he received from the 'home rule' press was a sort of acknowledgment of his supposed reforming genius. In practice, he worked with Parnell in attempting to make the league's platform a consensual rather than a purely democratic or revolutionary one, without realizing that, in so doing, he was effectively undermining his own political influence in the long term.

Parnell spent the first two months of 1880 in America on a lecture tour,

4 NAI, Land and National League reports, carton 2, speeches of Michael Davitt (quotation from speech at Loughrea, 6 Jan. 1880). 5 Moody, *Davitt*, 341–3.

which was organized and promoted by the Clan at Devoy and Davitt's request. This worried British intelligence, which believed (not without reason) that no potent nationalist agitation could ever be launched in Ireland without Irish-American financial support. This was why British intelligence efforts regarding Ireland during the nineteenth century and well into the twentieth century were always concentrated upon Irish-America. This is also why the Tory press mounted sensational propaganda campaigns against the Parnellite movement whenever it looked to America for funding.

To appeal to the Clan, Parnell stated on some public platforms in America that he admired the politics of the 'Irish nationalist party', a term that, as Parnell himself noted, was understood by contemporaries to mean one thing only: 'the organization of the IRB'.[6] In press interviews, however, he generally stressed his commitment to revitalizing the HRL. He had, he said, become involved in the Land League only because the politics of the HRL 'was always upon a wrong basis and it was not composed of the kind of men to make it successful', but he believed he could alter this situation by finding a common ground between the Land League and the HRL.[7] When the Tory government fell in early March, Parnell announced his decision to return to Ireland and organize an electoral campaign. However, on 11 March, just before leaving, he proposed to a convention of Irish-American business leaders that a subsidiary organization to the Land League be established in New York. This led William Carroll, the Clan chairman, to realize that Parnell had no intention of relying upon his organization in any way, and to suspect (correctly) that he had no desire to commit himself to its 'new departure' programme either. As a result, he came to distrust Parnell greatly and tried to persuade the Clan to do likewise. He soon invited the IRB leaders John O'Leary and John O'Connor to America to help him.[8] In Ireland itself, however, republicans did not come to distrust Parnell until after the general election of March–April 1880.

The assistant secretary of the league, Thomas Brennan, a 26-year-old clerk and native of Meath, was perhaps its finest orator, often compared to Thomas Francis Meagher, both in appearance and for his eloquence.[9] While Davitt worked closely with the MPs, Brennan played the leading role in mustering support for the league in both urban and rural Ireland by using the party networks of the IRB and his influence as secretary of the Dublin Mechanics Institute. Popular among Dublin republicans, Brennan and his uncle, James Rourke (Egan's and later Davitt's business partner), persuaded many Dublin IRB men to view the land and labour questions as vital issues.[10] This trend was perhaps reflected by the fact that two young socialist-minded men, Thomas Fitzpatrick (a printer) and Fred Allan (a clerk), who joined the Dublin IRB during 1880 were soon able to rise rapidly in its ranks.[11] Brennan attended

6 *Special Commission Report*, vol.7, 88, 227 (evidence of Parnell). 7 *Irishman*, 14 Feb. 1880 (republished interview with Parnell). 8 *DPB*, vol. 1, 504–8, 516–8, 520–5, 529. 9 *Cork Examiner*, 24 Dec. 1912 (obituary). 10 NAI, CSORP, 1879/18042, 1879/23367; Fenian A Files, no. 634; CSB files, B260. 11 Owen McGee, 'Fred Allan: Republican, Methodist and

more meetings of the central branch of the Land League than any other man, yet he was completely indifferent to the question of parliamentary representation. Mostly due to his efforts in Dublin, it was possible to hold a monster meeting in the Phoenix Park on 14 March 1880. This was addressed by several members of the central branch of the league, but Brennan, Harris and Boyton adopted a very different stance from the other speakers, one that they would continue to champion at most league meetings for the rest of the year. According to Brennan, the true name of the league was not the 'Irish National Land League' but rather the 'Land and Labour League', which existed to defend the rights of both the urban and rural working classes, for 'whether the toiler had to contend against the heartless landlord or the exacting capitalist, the cause of labour was the same'.[12] Although socialism was neither popular nor generally understood in Dublin, the Land League undoubtedly boosted the level of political activism among the urban working classes. The first-ever Trades Union Congress in Ireland was held in Dublin that September, and many who attended it would later form the Dublin Trades Council (1886), which unanimously elected John O'Clohissey (an IRB man, best known in Dublin for having organized the McManus demonstration twenty-five years earlier) as its first president.[13]

Before Parnell arrived in Ireland in the last week of March, the Land League Executive issued an official pronouncement regarding the forthcoming general election. This attempted to marry the concerns of both the IRB and the Parnellite wing of the HRL. It stated that the league believed that Irishmen 'can expect nothing' from Westminster and therefore parliamentary representation was useless, but the general public should nevertheless 'see that no supporter of landlordism, Whig or Tory, or any other party, receives your assistance, or triumphs by your vote'.[14] This was consistent with the IRB's general stance on parliamentary elections. When Parnell arrived in Queenstown (Cobh), the Land League held a demonstration in his honour. When he reached Cork (where he was due to stand for parliament), P.N. Fitzgerald's local IRB following read an address to him, apparently on behalf of the whole IRB. Fitzgerald voiced IRB support for the Land League, but made the point that 'we must take this opportunity to express our clear conviction of the hopelessness of looking for justice to Ireland from the English parliament' and emphasized that the only 'practical national good' Irishmen could ever do was by engaging in political activity purely within Ireland itself:

Dubliner' (2003). Fitzpatrick joined the IRB in 1880, left during the late 1880s to commit himself entirely to socialist politics before returning to the IRB during the mid 1890s. NAI DMP files, carton 13, Report 3867, Assistant Commissioner Mallon, 7 July 1896. For his career as a socialist agitator, see Fintan Lane, *The origins of modern Irish socialism, 1881–96* (1997). **12** Moody, *Davitt*, 369 (quote Brennan). **13** Brendan McDonnell, 'Tradesmen, labourers and depression, 1886–9', *Dublin History Workshop* (1988), 26–7. John O'Clohissey (1836–1902) was the son of a Clare RIC officer and former British soldier in India before he became a jeweller and republican in the 1860s. **14** *Irishman*, 20 Mar. 1880.

Impelled by such conviction the Nationalists of the country [the IRB] have determined that, as a political party, they will take no part in the coming elections and, consequently, no part in the adoption, rejection or support of the parliamentary candidate [Parnell].[15]

Parnell thanked the IRB for their address, emphasizing that he 'would not criticise the policy of non-intervention',[16] which indeed could do him no serious harm; he went on to win the seat for Cork City.

John O'Leary did intervene in the general election, albeit in one way only. He criticized the Parnellites for trying to unseat Keyes O'Clery (MP for Wexford County), who announced his willingness to propose a bill in Westminster that a citizens' defence force be established in Ireland, which would be open to all creeds and classes.[17] This was a proposal that republicans naturally welcomed, although it was unlikely to win support from any Irish MPs. The Wexford clergy actually liked O'Clery, since he was a decorated ex-papal army officer, and they accused Parnell of attempting to dictate to the people who should stand for election when he tried to oust O'Clery. In Enniscorthy, Parnell was pelted with eggs, had his clothes torn and had to flee from the platform due to an angry mob, uttering cries of 'Down with dicta-torship' and 'Put Parnell down'.[18] As he had little funding, however, O'Clery polled very badly and lost his seat to two personal nominees of Parnell, John Barry, Parnell's deputy as leader of the HRCGB, and Garrett Byrne, its Liverpool leader, neither of whom was previously known to the Wexford people. The Wexford IRB, led by Charles Joseph O'Farrell, a 35-year-old clerk from Enniscorthy and self-educated Francophile republican, reputedly took part in the attack on Parnell, but this is not certain. In the aftermath of the contest, however, Wexford Parnellites resolved to 'go through every town and village in the county and make these men tremble, who dared to insult such a [aristocratic] man'. Meanwhile the clergy, effectively taking advantage of the situation, mounted their own independent campaign to have the anti-clerical O'Farrell dismissed from his job and socially ostracized.[19] As O'Farrell was also a leader of the Leinster IRB, this helped to alienate both Wexford and Dublin republicans from the Parnellite movement, for they felt Parnell's supporters were not only trying to turn their leader into 'a demigod', but were also seemingly as clericalist as the Sullivan brothers of the *Nation*, the old *bêtes noires* of the IRB.[20]

The Liberals won the election, which saw the return of as many as twenty-

15 *Irishman*, 27 Mar. 1880. The address was signed by Richard Cronin, P.F. Murphy, J.F. Canty (three IRB men who later became Cork city councillors), T. Christy and 'T.M. Fitzgerald', which was probably a mistaken reference to P.N. Fitzgerald, who (as an arms agent) did not want his real name to appear in public at this time.   16 Ibid.   17 *Irishman*, 20 Mar. 1880.   18 *Irishman*, 3 Apr. 1880.   19 *Irishman*, 10 Apr. 1880; *DPB*, vol. 2, 21–5; NAI, British in Ireland microfilm, C.O. 904/18/650, 904/18/815.   20 Letters of 'An Enniscorthy Nationalist' and Thomas Fitzpatrick to *Irishman*, 3 Apr. 1880.

four Parnellite candidates. Individual members of the league's central branch certainly supported the Parnellites, but none of the MPs were returned because of the league *per se*. As they were too poor, all the tenant farmers, labourers or urban workers who were members of the Land League branches did not have the right to vote.

One of the new Parnellite MPs elected in March 1880 was Tim Healy, the London correspondent of the *Nation* and a cousin of the Sullivan brothers, who won the seat for Wexford town. After the general election, Healy and a few other MPs started creating a personality cult surrounding Parnell as 'the true and only leader of the Irish people', 'the Chief' or 'the uncrowned King of Ireland'. Not surprisingly, this increased republicans' mistrust of Parnell, so much so that, by May, when Parnell was elected chairman of the HRL and announced his intention to launch a new party in Westminster, republicans within both the IRB *and* the Land League expressed fears that an attempt might be made to bring the league totally under the wing of Westminster MPs, rather than vice versa.

By late April 1880, both William Carroll and John O'Leary (effectively the chairman of the IRB, due to Kickham's illness) felt that the republican movement needed to decide soon 'what was to be done in view of the growing flunkeyism of Mr Parnell's worshippers and that gentleman's attempt to be the whole movement'. In their opinion, the cult of 'Parnellism' was a form of 'personal leadership idolatry that [will] drive away freemen from Irish efforts and bind those who remain hand and foot and soul to the chariot of political adventurers, masquerading and parading as *Liberators*'. It was believed that the only way to reverse this development was that men who are 'firmly grounded in real republicanism' made their voices heard and persuaded the Irish people not 'to be dazzled by the ephemeral glamour and claptrap of mere Parnellism', or what was described as 'Chieftain tinsel trickery'.[21]

This same point was made regularly on Land League platforms by its chief travelling organizers. Michael Boyton, a native of Kildare, sometime resident of New York and former soldier and labour activist in England, reminded his audiences that while 'you cheer for Parnell', 'Parnell is nobody without his followers'. Consequently, the political power of the league lay entirely in the public's hands, not Parnell's.[22] Emphasizing that the Land League was a 'republican, or democratic, agitation', Matthew Harris called upon all league supporters never to 'shrink before any man who has a good coat upon him' (meaning a wealthy or aristocratic man); otherwise, 'you will be ground down and trampled upon, for it is the slave that makes the tyrant all the world over'. Until 'the people' learnt this particular lesson, Harris believed that Ireland could 'never develop a wholesome state of public opinion'.[23] Thomas Brennan

21 John O'Leary to *Irishman*, 3 Apr., 8 May, 29 May 1880; *DPB*, vol. 1, 516, 520, 528, 531 (letters of Carroll to Devoy, Apr.–May 1880). The quotations are Carroll's. 22 NAI, Land and National League reports, speeches of Harris and Boyton, Newcastle, Co. Limerick, 7 Nov. 1880. 23 NAI, Land and National League reports, carton 2, speeches of Harris in Sligo and

was adamant that 'we have had enough of kings in Ireland, both native and foreign, both crowned and uncrowned', for all such men and their supporters really only 'despise the people on whose backs they climb to power'. The Land League, he noted, existed 'to teach that the people have their emancipation in their own hands' and to 'shut out that idea of leadership which was thought necessary to dazzle the Irish mind' by 'publicly sowing the seeds and principles of republicanism, which alone can raise an enslaved people':

> It is not necessary in Ireland today to raise up any idol for popular adulation … To attain your rights, it is but necessary that you *know* them …[then] neither the feudal power of the landlord nor the bayonet of a foreign government can keep you out of them.[24]

The IRB suffered from a serious defection during the 1880 general election when J.J. O'Kelly was persuaded by Davitt to run (successfully) for Roscommon, his candidacy being funded partly by the sale of his brother Aloysius's paintings. A friend of several leading French communards, O'Kelly was a sincere republican, yet upon his election he too started openly calling his friend Parnell the 'uncrowned King of Ireland' to the bewilderment of all his republican colleagues. No one was more hurt by this than John Devoy, his lifelong friend, who had no more time for 'Chieftain tinsel trickery' than any of his comrades. When Devoy pleaded with his friend to explain himself, O'Kelly stressed that he had spoken in an anti-republican manner, not from conviction, but simply because it was an unavoidable fact that there was 'a frightfully large element of the population who are not even up to the "King's" standard', 'who would smash your head and mine, as well as the "King's", at the bidding of the only two masters he recognises – the landlord and the priest.'[25] Meanwhile, O'Kelly justified his defection from the IRB by arguing that Kickham and O'Leary were leading it up a blind alley through their lack of initiative. He claimed that both he and Davitt wanted the Supreme Council to distribute arms for free among tenants in Connacht to give them a means of self-defence in the very likely event of their being evicted, and that many IRB leaders would have supported their plan of action if they were not unwilling to disobey Kickham or, more specifically, Kickham's mouthpiece, John O'Leary.[26] This, however, is very probably not true, as the IRB clearly did not want its arms to fall into the hands of non-members.

Following Parnell's election as chairman of the HRL, he asked Davitt to go to the United States to help establish an auxiliary wing of the Land League. The IRB Supreme Council, however, told Davitt not to go, since it had already ordered him to settle the affairs of the IRB in northern England. Davitt disobeyed the IRB's orders, and consequently he was expelled from the

Galway, 6 and 27 June 1880. **24** NAI, Land and National League reports, carton 4, speech of Brennan at Navan and Clonmacnoise meetings, 5 Sept. 1880, 5 Dec. 1880. **25** *DPB*, vol. 1, 538–39. **26** *DPB*, vol. 1, 483–4, 488–90, 496.

Supreme Council, a decision that Devoy and the Clan felt was unfair. The fact that Parnell and Davitt had been accosted by an 'Old Guard' IRB party at a recent political demonstration in Dublin also convinced Devoy that the republican movement in Ireland was becoming unduly reactionary. He responded to Davitt's dismissal by taking the bold move of forcing William Carroll to step down as Clan chairman on the mere technicality that he had invited O'Leary to attend Clan meetings without first seeking the approval of the Clan executive. Meanwhile, after Davitt's arrival in America, he wrote a pamphlet that was soon distributed *en masse* in the west of Ireland and was obviously meant for an IRB audience.[27]

To rally the IRB more fully behind the Land League, Devoy praised the efforts of men like Davitt, who he claimed had managed 'to attract the world's attention to Ireland' and 'to arouse the Irish people at home and abroad to the necessity of making an effort to lift the country out of bondage'. Meanwhile he criticized censorious members of the IRB like John O'Leary who 'have nothing to offer themselves' and 'are doing nothing to further their own principles', except for praising the examples of dead men like Thomas Davis and attempting 'to sit upon' those who did not agree with them. 'It is so much easier', Devoy noted, 'to dream of regenerating Ireland than to go out into the turmoil and strain of everyday politics', as the Land Leaguers were doing, 'and, with a fixed purpose ever in view ... help to give the people that political training without which a "free Ireland" would be almost useless.' All republicans, Devoy noted, gave 'infinitely more importance to the organization of the people and the work done in Ireland' than to any done in Westminster, and he believed that 'if our clever and ambitious young men would only look a little into the future', it should become clear that this 'extra-parliamentary' work would eventually 'accomplish more than all the Irish members put together, acting as one man inside parliament', could possibly ever achieve in preparing the way for 'an expression of the national will' and 'the solution of the national question'. Although 'the demands of the League will not be granted by a parliament of British landlords, of course they won't', so long as 'the people' developed a resolve 'to say how they would, if they had the power, settle all the great social and political problems', Devoy believed the republican cause would be well served. He concluded by expressing his belief that the republican movement in Ireland was wrong in suspecting that Parnell had ambitions to become 'a dictator' in Irish politics, or, that the Irish Party leader secretly desired to 'crush it out of existence'; Devoy had 'no fear' that this intention existed or, indeed, that this could ever occur.[28]

During the first year of its existence, John O'Leary did not actually oppose the Land League. Rather, he was critical of the Parnellite MPs' pretensions to be nationalists, noting that it was obvious that they had no intentions of

27 *John Devoy on the political situation* (Dublin, 1880); *DPB*, vol. 1, 531–5.   28 *John Devoy on the political situation* (Dublin, 1880).

adopting the IRB's 'Hungarian policy' (the abstentionist policy), and he wrote
letters to the press arguing that the political realities of rural Ireland were very
different to what the league's 'utopian' champions claimed.[29] Indeed, by June
1880, Thomas Brennan was claiming that the Land League had already
created a new, inviolable 'Magna Charta of Irish liberty' destined to unite the
Irish urban and rural working class for the first time, to 'bury the hatchet of
civil and religious strife once and for all' in Ulster and, after destroying the
'feudal power' of the English in Ireland and establishing an Irish republic, to
eventually 'take part in emancipating the world, in striking off the fetters of
men everywhere and writing on the tablets of the age: "Republican!"'[30] To
O'Leary and most outside observers, however, it was clear that the league was
a 'big thing' only because the rural poor were supporting it to protect their own
material interests, a fact which prompted John Boyle O'Reilly (a former IRB
arms agent, now editing the Boston *Pilot* in the United States) to complain
how 'petty-minded', 'jealous', and 'unrepublican' the vast majority of
Irishmen seemed to be.[31]

The Connacht IRB leader Matthew Harris responded to such criticisms of
the Land League by publishing a pamphlet in which he argued that the self-
interest of its supporters certainly did not mean that the league had no
revolutionary potential. It could only be inconsistent, Harris maintained, for
those 'republican and democratic' in their principles not to fully support the
league, for it was truly seeking to topple the 'tyranny' of the privileged classes
in society and advance the rights of 'all who live by their labour'; these sentiments, he noted, were also shared by the IRB founder, James Stephens.[32]
Harris argued that the league's call for a reduction in rents in Ireland could
easily be combined with a demand for national independence in a similar
manner to how 'America raised her voice against the tea-tax' and to how, 'in
the days preceding the French revolution ... the cry for bread mingled with
the cry for Liberty'. Although 'these views may be too utilitarian for some
patriots', Harris emphasized that 'the great army of toilers ... always come in
greatest numbers and strongest force when they bring the interest of their
calling with them'. This reality could not be ignored. As far as Harris was
concerned, Kickham and O'Leary's reservations regarding the moral justice of
the league's attacks upon the property rights of so many landlords (through
withholding rents) was 'not only immoral, but highly criminal' in the light of
how Ireland was actually governed by Dublin Castle and the role of the same
landlords in that government:

29 O'Leary to *Irishman*, 3 Apr., 8 May, 29 May 1880.   30 NAI, Land League and National
League reports, carton 2, speech of Thomas Brennan, Ballinlough, Co. Roscommon, 27 June
1880; carton 4, speech of Brennan, Ballyshannon, Co. Donegal, 26 Sept. 1880.   31 *DPB*, vol.
1, 546.   32 It is unclear what Stephens, who was effectively retired from politics, thought of
the Land League. At the time, he was in New York working with the moribund Fenian
Brotherhood organization and he allegedly refused an invitation to write a pamphlet criticizing
either Parnell or the Land League. *Irish Nation* (New York), 26 Nov. 1881.

I am not in favour of an agrarian war or any other war, he is a monster who would be; but I prefer war to slavery ... if we are not at war with them, they (the landlords) are at war with us ... If anyone concludes from these remarks that I think lightly of the higher efforts of public virtue, they are mistaken. The man who, in defence of liberty and truth, stands up ... as the men of '48 and '67 did, is to me the highest type of a good citizen.[33]

At many Land League meetings held in rural areas of Mayo, Galway and Roscommon during the summer of 1880, local IRB activists openly boasted about distributing arms, told the farmers how they might be used (to defend their homesteads or intimidate 'land-grabbers') and regularly called for and received enthusiastic cheers from the local tenantry for the establishment of an Irish republic.[34] As a surviving letter of an IRB centre in Clare demonstrates, the morale of the IRB 'rank and file' in rural Ireland was enhanced greatly at this time not only by the arrival of arms (which were 'much superior to the old ones') but because the existence of the Land League had boosted the political activism of the rank and file, who 'are at work now every day'.[35] The radical Land League organizers also concentrated upon giving the agrarian movement an overtly republican image and purpose, partly to win more Irish-American support. For example, in conjunction with Davitt's fund-raising lecture tour in America, both Brennan and Boyton organized 4 July celebrations under Land League auspices in honour of 'the Great Republic of the West' and spoke of a new Irish flag like that of the United States, with thirty-two shamrocks in place of the American stars. Boyton proclaimed that the time would eventually come for Irishmen to act like the Americans of 1776 and declare their independence not merely 'to the power that oppressed them and drove them to it, but to the whole world.' Although Irishmen were now beginning to have 'something in the shape of physical force' at their disposal (owing to the IRB's arms importation scheme), Boyton emphasized that, for the moment, what was most important was that all Irishmen learnt that they possessed 'the rights of a free citizen ... equal to your sovereign', noting that, for his own part, 'until Ireland can give me an equivalent of that', he intended to 'remain true and faithful to the allegiance I have sworn'.[36] During the autumn, when setting up branches for the first time in southern counties like Limerick and Tipperary, Harris and Boyton decorated all league platforms with blue, white and red banners bearing the French republican motto of 'Liberty, Equality, Fraternity'. Harris reminded his audiences that 'there can no approach to equality until the labourers of the country are taken care of', while Boyton emphasized that the Land League was ready to defend the

---

33 Matthew Harris, *The political situation* (1880). 34 NAI, Land League and National League reports, cartons 2 and 4, speeches of J.W. Nally, P.J. Gordon, Michael Fitzpatrick, Michael Burke, Joseph Huban (1880). 35 *DPB*, vol. 1, 493–4. 36 NAI, Land League and National League reports, carton 2, speeches of Boyton in Galway and Donegal, July 1880.

interests of all labourers, whether male or female, urban or rural. Boyton also stressed that, fundamentally, 'the right we ask is not tenant right, but manhood right – the right to guard what you have'. He predicted that as soon as Irishmen were 'able to achieve your social independence', they would make the decision to 'select an Irish national guard that, with the weapon of free men slung on their arm – the rifle – may take the place of that organisation [the Irish Volunteers] that 100 years ago gave Ireland a glimpse of liberty ... Do not depend on British legislation because the remedy is in your own hands.'[37]

By August 1880, the Catholic hierarchy, which thus far had merely expressed support for E.D. Gray's relief fund, felt they could ignore the Land League no longer. Its lower-class leaders were men whom they did not know and did not trust, prompting at least one bishop to denounce the league's leadership as 'godless nobodies'. In turn, the hierarchy re-asserted its demand, made ever since the days of the Catholic Association, that any political movement involving Irish Catholics must 'be guided, as of old, by their faithful allies, the priests ... [L]et no attempt at disserving so scared a union, fraught with blessings to the people, be tolerated'.[38] Subsequently, the bishops ordered priests to overcome their distaste for the league and begin forming their own Land League branches. Both MPs and parish priests now started accusing the Land League organizers of anticlericalism – accusations that were denied publicly by the likes of Sheridan and Harris, both of whom affected to believe that this was the basis of the charge of 'communism' that was made frequently against the movement.[39] They were indeed justified in denying that the league was anticlerical, for only one Land League speaker, P.J. Gordon, a Sligo shoemaker and former soldier in the Irish papal brigade, ever made anticlerical arguments on league platforms, accusing the clergy of living off the subscriptions of the poor while letting the people starve so the landlords and bishops' lifestyles would not be disturbed.[40] What really lay behind the clergy's accusations of anticlericalism was simply their anxiety regarding the league's non-sectarianism. For example, while establishing branches in the midlands and Connacht, P.J. Sheridan always emphasized that the Land League was completely non-sectarian, being as ready to defend the interests of 'atheists' as much as Catholics and Protestants.[41] Meanwhile, in an effort to illustrate the league's non-sectarianism and egalitarianism to north-erners, Thomas Brennan made sure that his Ulster tours in support of the league (which did not get beyond Donegal, Fermanagh and Tyrone, owing to the opposition of the Tory-Anglican upper class) were promoted by the

37 NAI, Land League and National League reports, carton 2, speeches of Harris and Boyton at Cahir, Limerick and Clonmel, Sept. 1880. 38 Moody, *Davitt*, quoted 308. 39 NAI, Land League and National League reports, carton 4, speeches of Sheridan and Harris at Clonmacnoise and Mount Irvine, Co. Sligo (1880). 40 NAI, Land League reports, carton 2, speeches of P.J. Gordon (1880). Gordon often described himself as being a 'Fenian' on league platforms, but he used this term as synonymous with simply being a nationalist (he believed 'all true Irishmen are Fenians') and he may well not have been an IRB man. 41 NAI, Land League reports, carton 4, speech of Sheridan, Clonmacnoise, King's Co., 5 Sept 1880.

Reverend Isaac Nelson, a Presbyterian clergyman from Belfast and enthusiastic Land Leaguer, who maintained that 'you will never find an honest Presbyterian who is not, at heart, a republican'.[42]

The IRB Supreme Council remained supportive of the Land League up until October 1880,[43] when the tenor of league rallies in the country began to change significantly. In late September 1880, the Land League was established in Co. Cork for the first time, and 'Long' John O'Connor, a very intelligent grocer-publican who was P.N. Fitzgerald's right-hand man in the Cork IRB, was elected its county secretary. He made his first speech at an event in Bantry, Co. Cork, on 17 October, when he denounced the fact that (according to his calculations) 742 people owned the entire land of Ireland and most of them never had to do a day's work in their lives. His speech was interrupted, however, by parish priests who were also on the platform. Supported by a local Catholic MP, they called for an agitation in defence of both the tenant and landlords' rights, denounced O'Connor for making seditious and socialistic arguments and forced him to stand down.[44] One week later a large Land League demonstration was held in Clonmel, the first to be managed purely by the bishops and clergy. The only speakers allowed were parish priests and MPs whom the hierarchy knew they could trust completely, such as T.D. Sullivan of the *Nation*. In complete contrast to the events organized by Brennan, Harris and company, all the speakers at this demonstration (who were heckled by a crowd of IRB protesters, led by P.N. Fitzgerald) condemned the attacks upon landlords' rights, as well as those 'bad men' within the league who were supposedly 'trying to throw enmity and strife between you and the clergy'. Sullivan and the clergy argued that the league must place their total faith in Prime Minister Gladstone.[45] On 7 November, at a large demonstration in Athlone chaired by a Catholic British army major and justice of the peace, Parnell and T.D. Sullivan (the principal speaker) proclaimed that the Land League would never encourage Irishmen to be disloyal to Queen Victoria.[46] Surprisingly, J.J. O'Kelly and James O'Connor stood on the Athlone platform, yet made no protests about Sullivan's speech,[47] and so P.N. Fitzgerald and his IRB followers disrupted this meeting through constant heckling.[48]

There were a number of reasons why the IRB began withdrawing its active

---

42 NAI, Land League and National League reports, carton 2, speech of Michael Boyton (quoting Rev. Nelson), 4 July 1880.   43 In his book, *Davitt and Irish revolution*, T.W. Moody presented the IRB as being wholly opposed to the Land League by citing some begrudging statements made by the 'Old Guard' in the *Irishman*, evidently without realizing that this was a different organization, with a very small following.   44 NAI, Land League and National League reports, carton 2, speech of O'Connor, Bantry, Co. Cork, 17 Oct. 1880.   45 NAI, Land League and National League reports, carton 4, report of Clonmel meeting, 24 Oct 1880.   46 Ibid., report of Athlone meeting., 7 Nov 1880.   47 The growing moderation of James O'Connor (with whom Kickham lived and who was John O'Connor's older brother) and his effective abandonment of the IRB was also a great surprise to Dublin Castle officials, who attributing it to the fact that he had 'become very domesticated' in the last few years, since he married and had children. NAI, Fenian A files, no. 701.   48 *DPB*, vol. 2, 21–5.

support from the Land League. P.N. Fitzgerald claimed (retrospectively) that the IRB 'felt acutely for the poor, who could not help themselves' and initially 'comprised the greater part of the agitation in the west of Ireland'. Once the MPs and priests began to monopolize control of the Land League rallies, however, 'a dry rot crept into the national opinion of Ireland' and the IRB felt that the league was becoming a lost opportunity.[49] By the autumn of 1880, Parnell had effectively launched his own party, the 'Irish Parliamentary Party', under his own chairmanship with two deputies who were intensely loyal to him, Justin McCarthy MP, a prominent London journalist and a Gladstonian liberal since the 1850s, and Joseph Biggar MP, the son of the chairman of the Ulster Bank. In conjunction with the bishops, all three men were eager to increase the MPs' influence over the Land League and to pressurize Gladstone into taking up the land question, thereby bringing the land agitation within the fold of British party politics. The IRB did not welcome this development for its principal *raison d'être* was to maintain the focal point of Irish politics within Ireland itself and thereby build up a 'young republic'.

P.N. Fitzgerald was ambivalent in his attitudes towards the land question. Like many a Land League orator, he often made enthusiastic statements like 'liberty is the right of all people' and 'no people should have the power or the right to subjugate others'. However, even though he felt that 'we ought to do our utmost to make living more pleasant and our people more happy', he believed that it was important

> to keep the hat of charity from going around begging of the civilised nations of the world. It is really a disgrace that artificial famines are brought about in this country by our English rulers and then the civilised world appealed to for alms to help our people to tide over the famine. If there is anything that ought to stimulate the nationalists of Ireland to increased activity it is the great desire to bring about results to stop this begging system.[50]

This was an elaborate way of saying he wanted Irish-American money to be used for nationalist purposes only and, in particular, for his own political organization. A greater concern for the IRB, however, was that it was importing a few thousand firearms into Ireland at the time and it wanted to make sure that these arms were not handed out to men who were not IRB members. For breaking this latter rule, P.J. Sheridan, the most active IRB and Land League organizer in north Connacht during early 1880, was actually expelled from the organization that summer, after an inspection tour of the Sligo organization and its armaments by John O'Connor and Fitzgerald. Subsequently, Fitzgerald, who chaired meetings of the Dublin IRB frequently

49 *Irish Daily Independent*, 10 Nov. 1894 (speech of Fitzgerald at Rotunda).   50 *Irish Nation* (New York), 13 Dec. 1884 (speech of Fitzgerald in Midleton, Co. Cork).

VIOLENCE STARTS!

during 1879–80, was delegated to perform Sheridan's IRB duties in addition to his own in Munster, meaning that he had to inspect every IRB circle in the west and south of Ireland at least twice a year.[51] He was now the chief travelling organizer of the IRB.

During the first year of its existence, most Land League demonstrations were simply events that marked the establishment of branches for the first time. By September 1880, however, few *new* branches of the league were being established and the 'land war' had effectively begun. Prolonged boycotts and withholding of rents were now taking place against members of the landed gentry in Mayo and Galway, a viscount was assassinated and agrarian outrages suddenly began to rise phenomenally. Between 1879 and 1881 in the five counties of Mayo, Galway, Clare, Kerry and Cork alone, 14,166 eviction decrees were issued by the landed gentry, forcing thousands of families to emigrate or enter the workhouse.[52] As a direct fall-out, between 1880 and 1882, as many as 10,457 agrarian outrages were committed in Ireland, including 57 homicides, and many of these were carried out by nominal members of, or subscribers to, the Land League.[53] It was not until the autumn and winter of 1880, however, that these outrages became frequent. Previously, leading IRB figures within the Land League, such as Harris, Brennan, and P.J. Sheridan (a Sligo hotelier and former workhouse supervisor), had not called for the use of violence against landlords or 'land-grabbers', but some low-ranking IRB centres in Galway, as well as the old English labour activist Michael Boyton, sometimes did not hesitate to tell crowds if they thought some tenant or landlord deserved to receive a 'pill', a synonym for a bullet.[54] To counteract this trend, most Land League leaders argued from September 1880 onwards that boycotting was the most effective (and non-violent) weapon at their disposal against land agents. The IRB's own feelings about agrarian violence was probably mixed. Most IRB Supreme Councillors, being men of humble birth, no doubt understood the frustrations from which agrarian violence emerged. Mark Ryan, whose Irish-speaking family had been evicted four times in rural Galway during the 1850s, felt incapable of condemning agrarian outrages born of social desperation, as did John O'Connor and James Stephens, while P.N. Fitzgerald and Robert Johnston, who originally came from very poor families in rural Cork and Antrim respectively, quite probably felt the same way.[55] However, Kickham and O'Leary (himself a landlord in Tipperary town) could not tolerate the idea that the IRB might become directly, or indirectly, responsible for this sort of activity. O'Leary stated during the winter of 1880–1 that should he ever find that an IRB member was engaged in agrarian outrages, he would immediately resign from the movement in protest;[56] an action, it might

51 *Special Commission Report*, vol. 3, 529, 540–1 (statement of informer Patrick Delaney).
52 Samuel Clark, *Social origins of the land war* (Dublin, 1979), 306.   53 Moody, *Davitt*, 565.
54 NAI, Land League and National League reports, cartons 2 and 4, speeches of J.W. Nally, P.J. Gordon and Michael Boyton, 1880–1.   55 *DPB*, vol. 1, 555; *DPB*, vol. 2, 39, 44, 74, 100; Ryan, *Fenian memories*, 68, 141.   56 *DPB*, vol. 2, 44–5.

be noted, that he never felt it necessary to take. John Mallon of the DMP (the most experienced and most knowledgeable Dublin Castle official in counter-acting the IRB) believed that it was the agrarian secret societies like the 'Ribbonmen', not the IRB, that were responsible for the agrarian outrages during 1880–1. As Mallon noted, however, dissident IRB men did occasionally pass arms on to members of agrarian secret societies and 'although it was never suggested to them to become members of the revolutionary society [IRB]' or to engage in outrages, 'the possession of a rifle or revolver suggested what use could be made of it' in the hands of socially desperate men.[57] Kickham and O'Leary's chief motivation in ordering the IRB to withdraw from the Land League agitation was to prevent this sort of thing from happening. O'Leary wrote to the press in early 1881 stating that the IRB felt 'little or no solidarity' with the Land League, 'strong though their fellow feeling with the oppressed tenants of Ireland may be', precisely because it was involved in agrarian outrages. He also denounced Parnell and other MPs for 'misrepresenting' the IRB by blaming it for the agrarian outrages which had taken place that winter, fearing the effect of this bad press.[58]

By October 1880, Matthew Harris had lost his position on the Supreme Council as Connacht IRB leader to P.W. Nally, a famous athlete, popular Mayo IRB leader and a wealthy land agent's son, and both Davitt and Brennan (who now began to distance himself from the IRB) were very unhappy at this election result, suspecting it was fixed.[59] Davitt, who was still in America, was bitter and angry when he learnt from Brennan that the IRB had begun withdrawing from the league, complaining to a credulous Devoy that he believed Fitzgerald and company were now out to destroy the league,[60] which was not true. The IRB had simply altered its focus and began to assert its independence from the Land League.

P.W. Nally, a close friend of Fitzgerald, was initially a strong supporter of the Land League and had been a key organizer of the Irishtown meeting. During 1879–80, like his far more gregarious brother John 'Scrab' Nally, a dandy and notorious womanizer who 'didn't give a damn about any bloody isms', he frequently expressed the desire to 'put these blasted landlords on the same way that we have been for years' (on the emigration boats) and declared that he had sworn to 'put down landlordism', even if this would only be possible 'at the point of a bayonet'. Unlike Harris, however, Nally had expressed no interest whatsoever in labour politics and spoke only in favour of the policy of calling for tenants to pay nothing more than those rents desig-nated in Griffith's property valuations of 1854. His only original idea was calling for the membership of the RIC, who invariably came from poor rural families, to support the Land League and turn against the Dublin Castle authorities.[61] Shortly after assuming Supreme Council duties, however, Nally

57 NAI, Fenian A files, no. 639. 58 O'Leary to *Irishman*, 19 Mar. 1881. 59 *DPB*, vol. 1, 555. 60 *DPB*, vol. 1, 555; vol. 2, 21–5. 61 NAI, Land League and National League

withdrew completely from the league, preoccupied himself entirely with assisting the arms importation scheme (he was soon able to import over three hundred rifles from Manchester) and wrote letters to the press condemning agrarian outrages and criticizing the Land League on this account.[62] This fact, combined with the weakening of Harris and Sheridan's influence over the IRB, quickly made the league very weak in its place of origin.[63]

In November 1880, shortly after Davitt returned to Ireland, the government threatened to instigate legal proceedings against the Land League owing to the boycotting and outrages. Meanwhile, 'Revolutionary Directory' meetings were held in New York between representatives of the IRB Supreme Council and the Clan. It was agreed that the IRB should concentrate purely upon advancing its arms importation scheme and cease to interfere with the Land League agitation, which would be let run its own course.[64] William Mackey Lomasney, a leading figure in the Clan in Detroit, Michigan (who had taken a prominent role in the attempted insurrection in 1867), was appointed as John O'Connor and P.N. Fitzgerald's principal assistant in the IRB's arms importation scheme, and they soon made an effective team: during the winter of 1880 and early spring of 1881, the IRB was able to import double the usual amount of arms into Ireland and, as a result, its recruiting efforts were going extremely well.[65] Through informers employed by the British consulates in the United States, the government was aware that the Clan and IRB were trying to import arms into Ireland, but it was unable to determine how it was being done or who was involved.[66]

In June 1880, Jeremiah O'Donovan Rossa formed a breakaway body from the Clan called the 'United Irishmen of America'. Like the original Fenian Brotherhood, it was an open movement governed by a secret caucus. Rossa's organization never assumed the menacing proportions that the British consulates in the United States feared (it had only a couple of hundred followers), but its policy was naturally a cause for concern. In the *Irish World* (New York) and his weekly 'American letter' in the *Irishman* (Dublin), Rossa had noted that, although 'I sincerely sympathize with the good-natured souls who imagine they can shame our enemy into doing justice', not until 'we show England that she is losing more than she is gaining by holding us ... will she sever the golden link that chains us to her'.[67] Since 1875 Rossa had argued intermittently in the Irish-American press that the only means to 'show England that she is losing more than she is gaining by holding us' was to make

reports, carton 4, report of meeting in Glenamaddy, Co. Galway, 20 May 1880; *Freeman's Journal*, 16 May 1880 (speeches of P.W. Nally); Louisa Nally to author. **62** Padraig O'Baoghill, *Nally as Maigh Eo* (1998), chpt. 11; Donald Jordan, *Land and popular politics in Ireland: county Mayo from the plantation to the land war* (1994), 280. **63** *Special Commission Report*, vol. 7, 93, 97 (evidence of Charles Stewart Parnell). **64** The outcome of this R.D. meeting in Nov. 1880 is explained by Devoy in his letter to the Clan chairman, James Reynolds, in *DPB*, vol. 2, 14–5. **65** UCD, Desmond Ryan papers, L.A. 10/k/23 (1), 25–9, 31–2 (statement of John O'Connor); *DPB*, vol. 2, 44, 56. **66** NAI, Fenian A files, nos. 622, 629, 637; CSORP, 1880/5572. **67** *Irishman*, 6 Mar. 1880.

direct attacks upon England itself, destroying government buildings and property with the new invention of dynamite. This idea was denounced by almost all figures within the Irish revolutionary movement as irrational, wasteful of revolutionary funds and highly immoral. Most believed Rossa's motivation was simply a feeling of vengeance for the way he was treated in prison. A 'Skirmishing Fund' set up by Rossa in New York for his 'devilish schemes' was taken over by the Clan, and there the idea would have ended, were it not for the passions evoked in Irish-America by the government's attempt to suppress the Land League during the winter of 1880–1.

In late December 1880, in a lengthy trial that achieved great publicity, fourteen Land League leaders, including Harris, Boyton, Sheridan, Brennan, Parnell and Egan,[68] were tried in Dublin for using seditious language or preventing the payment of rent. Simultaneously, the government prepared a 'Peace Preservation bill' to allow the police to suppress public meetings and perform arms raids upon any Irishman's home. The possibility that the Land League might be suppressed was intolerable to the Irish-American working class, for they had been primarily responsible for funding it and had made many personal sacrifices at a time when their community was hit very badly by a serious economic depression in America. As a result, while the trials were taking place in Dublin, several 'United Irish' agents were able to collect funds in New York for the purpose of causing explosions in Britain to punish the government for its 'tyranny'. On arrival in England and Scotland, they also tried (unsuccessfully) to win the British IRB's support for their plans.

After an attempt was made to blow up an army barracks in Manchester in early January 1881 (another attempted bombing took place in Glasgow), thousands of copies of a placard, evidently printed by the IRB, were posted in various urban centres across the United Kingdom. This warned that while the Irish people had 'a great cause for revolt', they were 'not yet prepared'. It claimed that by prosecuting the Land League the British government was seeking 'to provoke premature resistance', which could only deal 'a crushing disaster' to the revolutionary movement and 'would leave to the next generation the task of beginning anew the great work already so far advanced':

> Beware, then, of being misled by false and foolish friends, or goaded into the enemy by foolish outbreaks. The man who now incites you to attempts at insurrection is doing England's work and must be held guilty of treason to Ireland ... The most rigid discipline must be enforced and partial outbreaks prevented.[69]

68 The other figures on trial were John Dillon (MP), J.G. Biggar (MP), T.D. Sullivan, P.J. Gordon (reputed IRB), J.W. Nally (Mayo IRB), J.W. Walsh (Lancashire IRB), Michael O'Sullivan (ex-IRB leader in Galway town). *Weekly Freeman*, 18 Dec. 1880. 69 PRO (London), London Metropolitan Police reports on 'Fenianism', M.E.P.O. 3/3070 (3).

The action of the 'United Irishmen' had, indeed, very unfortunate repercussions for the IRB. Shortly after the attempted bombing in Manchester, William Lomasney noted that 'steps have been taken in such a manner to satisfy me' that British intelligence had received 'pretty accurate information' about the Manchester IRB organization.[70] Indeed, as soon as the police scare there ceased, the Manchester IRB leader 'entered into communications' with Robert Anderson of the Home Office: 'though he refuses, as yet, to give information ... he will prevent disturbances. I am still sounding him in hope of getting him into my confidence.'[71]

A pattern quickly established itself. On 16 March 1881, after hearing that the 'United Irishmen' were about to blow up the London Mansion House, a London IRB centre decided to become an informer to prevent an outrage which he completely opposed.[72] Thanks to the actions of the United Irishmen, the Home Office had discovered inadvertently a new and very potent means of counteracting the 'Fenian threat'.

A refusal to join, or a fear of being implicated in, a conspiracy against the property or lives of Englishmen naturally existed among the IRB's membership in Britain. Many were born in England, and all knew that any such incidents could only create intense communal hatred in what was already not always a hospitable climate for Irish workingmen. A risky, but potentially very profitable, course of action was now clearly open to British intelligence, which it soon would take. Instead of merely attempting to learn the intentions of the Irish-American revolutionary movement through spies, by using *agents provocateurs* to capitalize upon Irish-American extremism, it could potentially deal devastating blows to the IRB by prompting English IRB men to become informers. Since IRB organizers in Ireland frequently performed the same work in England, potentially British intelligence could acquire good knowledge about the whole organization this way.

By 1881, the semi-secret United Irish organization in New York had already been infiltrated by British intelligence and its correspondence was being intercepted. This fact soon allowed Dublin Castle to infiltrate the small 'Old Guard' IRB faction in Cork, Dublin and London, whose members corresponded with ex-members of the Fenian Brotherhood, some of whom were now in the United Irishmen.[73] Meanwhile the Home Office's chief spy in America, Thomas Beach (alias Henri Le Caron), was already a member of the Clan's 'Military Board', the purpose of which was to make 'military proposals' to the Clan Executive.[74] Consequently, British intelligence had some potentially very valuable weapons at its disposal in its espionage war against the proverbial 'Fenians'.

The Land League leaders escaped conviction at the Dublin trials in January

70 *DPB*, vol. 2, 37. 71 PRO (London), H.O. 144/1537/1, report of Robert Anderson, 29 Mar. 1881. 72 Ibid. 73 NAI, Fenian A files, nos. 629, 634, 647, 655, 663, 666, 668. 74 Henri Le Caron, *Twenty-five years in the secret service* (London, 1892), 119.

IRISH PARL. PARTY in effect

DAVITT
secretary
land
league

Brit. go
after
the
land
league

1881, but the government issued the 'Peace Preservation' act (known as a 'coercion act' to Irish nationalists) immediately afterwards, and it was clear that the league's future was far from safe. On 4 February 1881 Michael Davitt, the league's secretary, had his ticket of leave revoked and was re-arrested for no apparent reason. The following week Thomas Brennan, the assistant secretary, was imprisoned without trial for prompting crowds to boo a policeman. The day after Davitt's arrest, Parnell and numerous members of the Irish Parliamentary Party (bound together since December 1880 by a party pledge) protested at Westminster and, consequently, were suspended temporarily from the House of Commons. Expecting that an attempt to confiscate the league's funds would soon be made, Patrick Egan, its treasurer, fled to Paris, where he began discussing political matters for the first time in several years with the IRB leaders, John O'Leary and John O'Connor.[75]

The Land League's general reaction to the government's action was invariably bitter. At league rallies, several speakers began calling for a general rent-strike (a proposal favoured by Egan and Brennan), while John Dillon MP and Michael Boyton argued that the Land League members ought to hold onto their arms and continue to hold meetings, even if these were outlawed by Dublin Castle, since the British government was demonstrating once more that Irishmen had no constitutional rights.[76] In Dublin, the local IRB leader James Mullet tried to make a common cause with the Land League by holding a special meeting under his own chairmanship at a hotel near his Dorset Street public house. On this occasion, Mullet claimed (not convincingly) that 'commercial jealousies' between America and Great Britain would eventually lead to a declaration of war between the two great powers, thereby making Ireland a strategic 'Malta of the Atlantic'. In expectation of this future war, he encouraged all Irishmen to hold onto their arms and continue to attempt to acquire more. This argument, however, was not received as favourably as calls by a Galway land agitator to take reprisals against government officials for every Land League leader that was imprisoned, a suggestion that appears to have originated with the Irish-American press.[77] The government's obvious intention to follow up its coercive legislation by introducing a moderate land act to appease the better-off farmers was also discussed at the meeting, and all expected its passing would split the Land League, causing the moderates to withdraw.[78]

The most novel outcome of these Dublin debates upon the Land League was the creation of the Young Ireland Society (YIS), a nationalist literary and political debating club, on 25 March 1881.[79] This was the first of many branches of the YIS to be set up across Ireland over the next five years. It met

75 Henri Le Caron was also sent to Paris at this time to meet all three men. Ibid. 190–1.
76 NAI, Land League and National League reports, carton 2, speech of Dillon, Tipperary town, 27 Feb. 1881; speeches of Michael Boyton, Feb.–Mar. 1881. Even A.M. Sullivan was inclined to hold this view. T.D. Sullivan, *A.M. Sullivan*, 7–9. 77 NAI, Fenian A files, no. 639, 656. 78 Ibid., no. 639. 79 *Irishman*, 2 Apr. 1881.

at a room adjacent to the York Street Workingmen's Club that had previously been the home of a Dublin branch of the now defunct '82 Clubs', where James Mullet and others had been persuaded to join the IRB back in 1877. Dublin Castle believed that the IRB was directly responsible for the establishment of the YIS, a belief that prompted the DMP (taking advantage of the terms of the Peace Preservation act) to raid the Dublin YIS premises the day after its establishment, take down the names of all present and demand the right to know how and by whom the society was being funded; a fact that caused several short-lived protests.[80] Press reports indicate that its actual founders were a handful of Land League supporters who were some of George Sigerson's (a friend of Kickham and O'Leary) medical students at the Catholic University. These students chose John Dillon (formerly auditor of the Catholic University's Literary and Historical Society) as their honorary president, but only once did Dillon attend its meetings, owing to the demands of his parliamentary career. By contrast, the IRB did patronize this society, and several rising figures in the movement attended its meetings from a very early date, such as Fred Allan, a 20-year-old clerk from Ranelagh, Patrick Hoctor, a 20-year-old draper's assistant and son of a mill owner in north Tipperary, and John MacBride, a 16-year-old boy from a republican-minded family in Castlebar.[81]

The declared purpose of the YIS was to foster 'an interest in political debate' among the nationalist youth of the country with a view to educating them in 'the science of politics'.[82] Adopting the motto of the original *Nation*, 'educate that you may be free', as its own, the YIS also wanted to stimulate an interest in Irish history and Irish literature, as these subjects were intentionally not taught by the British education system in Ireland. As far as politics was concerned, the YIS was strongly sympathetic to the democratic-republican element within the Land League. Thomas Brennan was made one of its first vice-presidents and the society soon denounced Dublin Castle's attempts to suppress the league as a tyrannous act, worthy of the czar of Russia. Another vice-president was John Wyse Power, a talented journalist (and future IRB man) from a wealthy Waterford family who had been expelled from the civil service because he supported the recently established Ladies Land League. Power declared that the YIS existed to teach the Irish public that they 'must not rely on the assistance of the aristocracy or the leadership of any person ... in working out Ireland's freedom'. Instead, they must cultivate a spirit of 'complete self-reliance'.[83]

By August 1881, Parnell faced a serious problem. Gladstone had just introduced a moderate but practicable land act. Most MPs supported it, but the

---

80 *Irishman*, 7 May 1881. 81 NLI, Minute book of YIS 1881–4, MS 16095. Hoctor gave a lecture to the society on C.J. Kickham, the IRB president, while Allan gave a lecture on the theme of socialism. George Sigerson was related by marriage to the former Ulster IRB leader, T.N. Underwood. 82 *Irishman*, 2 Apr. 1881. 83 NLI, Minute book of YIS 1881–4, MS 16095, minute for 28 October 1881, quotation from J.W. Power.

Land League organization in Ireland itself generally did not. Indeed, they were seemingly unwilling to accept *any* terms of the government, a fact that only increased the government's resolve to suppress the league. Meanwhile, at a Clan convention in Chicago, John O'Connor and W.M. Lomasney revealed how far the IRB arms importation scheme had progressed, unaware that in so doing the British government would be able to find out its details, owing to the presence of a spy on the Clan executive, Henri Le Caron.[84]

The most promising sign for the IRB was that, although the Clan had subsidized arms transportation costs, the Supreme Council did not have to rely heavily on Irish-American financial aid. Of the £4,815 the Supreme Council had spent on firearms since 1879, £3,123 of this had come directly from the IRB rank and file itself and the Supreme Council still had £3,572 at its disposal. Since 1879, the IRB had purchased 4,018 firearms, including 2,844 Schneider rifles and 702 revolvers that had already been imported. As a result, the IRB had been restored to something 'close to its former dimensions' with a grand total of 38,181 members, although the loyalty of many of these men was no doubt conditional to their continuing to receive arms in return for their subscriptions. IRB membership in each of its seven divisions is given in Table 2.

Table 2

Ireland		Britain	
Ulster	12,748	North of England	4,477
Connacht	8,974	Scotland	1,326
Munster	6,403	South of England	570
Leinster	3,683		
Total in Ireland	31,808	Total in Britain	6,373

In most provinces, the membership increases since 1879 were evidently directly related to the importation of arms. The Munster IRB had acquired 1,173 rifles and 289 revolvers and saw its subscribing membership increase by 1,500; the Leinster IRB received 747 rifles and 176 revolvers since 1879 and its membership had an increase of 1,000; the same pattern holds for the IRB organization in Britain, which increased its membership and its total number of firearms by roughly a thousand over the space of two years. Although the Connacht IRB had received only 646 firearms, it had seen its subscribing membership increase since 1879 by nearly 2,000 men, no doubt because of the existence of the Land League. The high total of IRB members in Ulster is explained by the absence of any other nationalist organizations in Ulster and by the fact that it had long been the best-armed IRB division, possessing the

---

84 *Special Commission Report*, vol. 5, 143–4: statement of O'Connor and Lomasey produced as evidence by the Clan spy, Henri Le Caron. This is the source of the information listed.

vast majority of IRB firearms prior to 1879 (almost all of which were held in Cavan and Monaghan, where the IRB nominally had more members than in any other counties) and adding to this total at least 500 up-to-date rifles and revolvers over the next two years.[85]

The IRB was now better armed than it had ever been before, for as many as 7,371 members now possessed a quality firearm or, at least, had a right to one of the firearms held in the organization's secret depots. In addition to the 3,546 firearms recently imported, the IRB knew it possessed from former times 1,898 revolvers, 1,656 shotguns and 1,194 muskets,[86] but it now had no idea where at least 900 of these were held. Devoy noted in 1879 that very many of these were 'badly damaged through neglect, or entirely lost' since those who had control of them had left the organization several years previously.[87] Mark Ryan offered a reasonable explanation for this, noting that most of the firearms imported by the IRB during the late 1860s had to be dismantled and the various parts hidden or buried, to prevent their seizure in bulk. As many who were involved in this activity later left the organization, the arms became irretrievable.[88] Indeed, burying arms to ensure that the police were not able to find them was probably a standard tactic of the IRB in rural Ireland: on at least two occasions, informants in Connacht heard IRB organizers ordering their men to 'dig up' their arms and treat them with various substances to ensure they remained in a workable condition.[89] Meanwhile a standard tactic by the rank and file in urban Ireland was to move its firearms about from place to place whenever there were fears of a police raid, in order to minimize the chances of their seizure. With the continued operation of the arms acts, however, this sort of activity could not go on indefinitely without the men involved eventually being caught and the arms seized or falling into disrepair. Hence John O'Connor boasted to the Clan that 'only' 45 firearms (40 rifles and 5 revolvers) of those imported since 1879 had thus far been seized by the police; these were evidently those seized in Dublin by the DMP at Temple Bar, Aungier Street and the North Wall during the spring of 1880.[90]

The IRB may have had a fair share of armaments by the summer of 1881 but it did not yet have an applicable revolutionary strategy. John Mallon of the DMP was aware that 'revolt is not contemplated'. He believed the IRB 'have not amongst them persons having the knowledge' to drill recruits and it also had serious problems acquiring ammunition: 'they relied upon persons who are employed in the factory of Kynock and Co., Birmingham, to supply them with cartridges surreptitiously', but 'something has occurred in Birmingham recently that has made them less sanguine in this scheme.'[91]

85 NLI, Devoy papers, MS 18036. 86 Ibid. The shorthand notes have been interpreted as meaning revolvers, shotguns and muskets but this is uncertain. 87 *Special Commission Report*, vol. 4, 505–11, report of Devoy to Clan Executive, Aug. 1879, produced as evidence by Le Caron. 88 Ryan, *Fenian memories*, 40. 89 NAI, DICS files, carton 1 (Western Division), 4 June 1892; carton 4 (Midlands Division), 4 Oct. 1892. 90 NAI, CSORP, 1880/5572. 91 NAI, Fenian A files, a639.

An insurrection was obviously out of the question. According to Devoy's calculations, the British army had a total of 188,986 active members, 20,584 of which were stationed permanently in Ireland, and a total reserve force of 444,170 men.[92] Of course, the British navy was of equally formidable strength, while the RIC (numbering 12,000 men) had a full military training. There were 6,000 soldiers permanently stationed in the city of Dublin alone,[93] while the Dublin IRB had only 600, mostly unarmed and completely untrained, members.[94] The Clan suggested to the Supreme Council in December 1880 that the centenary of the establishment of the Irish parliament in 1782 might be a fit moment to inaugurate the 'new departure' programme, calling for the withdrawal of Parnell's party from Westminster and the unilateral establishment of an Irish government, which the IRB could defend. Pressure was put upon O'Leary to meet Parnell (whom he had not spoken to for two years) and discuss this alternative. O'Leary, for his part, had long felt that

> The best thing we could do would be to act like the Hungarians under somewhat similar circumstances: to refuse to send representatives to parliament at all. But this course would require an amount of public virtue we most certainly have not got at present and are not, I fear, likely to possess in any very near future. The next best course, *me judice*, would be to send men merely to protest and then leave the House, but that too is not at present, and probably will not be for a long time to come, within the region of what newspaper Solomons call practical politics.[95]

In April 1881, he dismissed the idea of trying to persuade Parnell and his followers to withdraw from Westminster as impracticable and soon afterwards pointed to Justin McCarthy's seniority in the Irish Party as an illustration of why this was the case.[96] O'Leary was convinced that the challenge of remoulding Irish public opinion along nationalist lines could be met only if some means was discovered of the IRB winning the intellects of the existing educated classes (a possibility he believed was very slight) or else a *new* strata of nationalist intellectuals was created in Irish society. For this reason, he took much interest in the YIS; a body that Chief Superintendent Mallon believed O'Leary was actually responsible for creating.[97]

In August 1881, Alec Sullivan, an astute lawyer as well as a Republican Party politician in Chicago, was elected Clan president. Like O'Kelly and Davitt, Sullivan believed that O'Leary and Kickham were far too socially conservative to be effective IRB leaders. His first action as Clan president was to issue a circular which claimed that, 'the leaders of the Land League are partly in

92 *Irish Nation* (New York), 14 Jan. 1882.   93 Tom Kennedy (ed.), *Life in Victorian Dublin* (Dublin, 1980), 74.   94 NLI, Devoy papers, MS 18036.   95 John O'Leary to *Irishman*, 3 Apr. 1880.   96 *DPB*, vol. 2, 72–3 (O'Leary to Devoy: Apr. 1881); O'Leary to *Irish Nation* (New York), 3 Dec. 1881.   97 NAI, DMP files, carton 12, report 2404 (giving history of the YIS since 1881), Chief Supt. Mallon, 25 Nov. 1892.

accord with us' and 'through them, we are likely to secure the assistance of a certain portion of the republican party of England and France'.[98] This, however, was a very unrealistic expectation. While a handful of Irish radicals within the HRCGB still maintained a republican outlook on English politics, the small English republican movement had essentially died as early as 1872. Some had become politically inactive socialist intellectuals. Others such as John Morley, the founder of the *Contemporary Review*, became leaders of Gladstone's Liberal Party.[99] Consequently, by 1881, most Irish republicans who kept a weather-eye upon British radicalism, such as Patrick Tynan, a militia-soldier and member of the London IRB, or Devoy in New York, were highly sceptical about *all* aspects of the politics of English radicals, who were considered to be merely 'ambitious businessmen' far less honest or consistent in their principles than the ultra-conservative Tories:

> The English radical humbugs ... are not democrats, or republicans; they have no real love for popular rights and only appeal to the workingman for help against the aristocracy by promises of small installments of rights which could be wrung with equal ease from the aristocracy if the Democracy of England was only organized and knew its power and its duties.[100]

A similar critique could have been made against many members of Parnell's young party. As for France, J.J. O'Kelly's friendship with Henri Rochefort, the editor of *L'Intransigent*, the leading and most notorious left-wing republican newspaper in Paris, ensured that articles sympathetic towards the Land League were occasionally printed in this paper during 1880–2, but the French left never had any sincere interest in Ireland. Indeed, the only practical support given to the Land League from Paris came from the opposite end of the political spectrum, namely from the Catholic archbishop of the city who, together with John P. Leonard, a Cork-born professor of English at the Sorbonne (and a friend of O'Leary), persuaded Parisian Catholics to raise funds for relief of the Irish peasantry.[101] In August 1881, Sullivan also argued that the Boers might assist the Clan because the Irish-Americans had supposedly provided assistance to them during their recent war against the British empire. This, however, was another idle boast. The Clan had done nothing except contact the Dutch government,[102] and the only Irish assistance of any kind given to the Boers came from a single man: Alfred Aylward, a very

98 NAI, Fenian A files, a705 (intercepted Clan circular, Sept. 1881). 99 For Morley's youthful republicanism and its role in inspiring the *Contemporary Review*, see Lord Morley, *Recollections* (1917), chapter one. 100 *Irish Nation* (New York), 31 Dec 1881. The *Irish Nation* was edited by Devoy, imported into Ireland and funded by the Clan and IRB through the 'Revolutionary Directory'. For Tynan's views on English radicalism, see P.J.P. Tynan, *The Irish National Invincibles and their times* (1894), passim. 101 Janick Julienne, 'John Patrick Leonard (1814–89)'. 102 NAI, Fenian A files, a705.

eccentric former Wexford IRB man who had been working in South Africa as a journalist before becoming a very popular and effective commando leader on the Boer side.[103]

The lack of revolutionary options available to Sullivan increased the influence within the Clan of its 'Military Board', which was led by Michael Kerwin, a native of Wexford, owner of the New York *Tablet* and a former American colonel, but also included the spy Le Caron among its ranks. In August 1881, this body proclaimed that there was very little chance that Britain would be involved in a major international war 'during the next few years' and, therefore, it believed that there was no longer any reason for the Irish revolutionary movement to continue to organize itself on that expectation. If a rising was not possible during the 'centenary year', 'we think that for many reasons a blow should be struck at the enemy's commerce and colonies and beg to suggest that the advisability of launching a cruiser against it ought to be carefully studied and pronounced upon'.[104] The 'cruiser' referred to was a prototype for a submarine, a new form of weapon invented by John Holland, a native of Clare, and not yet in use by any navy in the world. Since the mid 1870s, many within the Clan were enthusiastic about this idea, and Holland had already been commissioned by the organization to conduct his experiments.[105] The Supreme Council, however, was always opposed to this plan, considering it a waste of valuable funding.[106] Indeed, the Clan's very expensive prototype submarine (nicknamed the 'Fenian Ram') turned out to be a comparative failure; it sank after a trial run in New York harbour and, after being salvaged and made operable, was kept in a warehouse for many years before being donated to a museum. The principal significance of this plot was that it demonstrated the willingness of the Clan's 'Military Board' to support a policy similar to that of the discredited O'Donovan Rossa; namely destroying English property to weaken the empire commercially, rather than supporting the IRB policy of slow, but steady, arms importations until the day when a nationalist movement might emerge in Ireland. Le Caron may not have been responsible for creating this idea, but he could certainly use it to manipulate Clan opinion. This fact, combined with Le Caron's discovery in September 1881 that John O'Connor was the IRB's principal arms agent and that these arms were being acquired in England or Belgium rather than the United States (as the Home Office had suspected)[107] would be of great assistance to British intelligence over the next few years.

When questioned by the British government several years later, Parnell expressed his opinion that he managed to outmanoeuvre the IRB politically during 1881.[108] If this was the case, a key reason was Patrick Egan's estab-

103 K.W. Smith, *Alfred Aylward: the tireless agitator* (Johannesburg, 1983). 104 *Special Commission Report*, vol. 4, 582–3: evidence of Le Caron. 105 K.R.M. Short, *The dynamite war* (1979), 36, 170. 106 UCD, Desmond Ryan papers, L.A. 10/k/23 (1), 25–9, 31–2 (statement John O'Connor). 107 NAI, Fenian A files, no. 701, 702 and 705. 108 *Special Commission Report*, vol. 7, 88, 227 (evidence of Parnell).

lishment of the 'Irish National Publishing Company' in August 1881 under Parnell's directorship. This immediately bought out Richard Pigott's newspaper company, which had been the only Irish company that allowed republican propaganda to be published, and established a Parnellite newspaper in its place, *United Ireland*. Its editor was William O'Brien, a versatile journalist, former IRB man and native of Mallow, who had been a friend of P.N. Fitzgerald since 1871 but whose first loyalty was clearly to Parnell and the HRL. O'Brien was one of a number of Cork republicans who had sought to make their influence felt in Cork municipal politics during the early 1870s, but he chose to leave the IRB in 1875, owing to his suspicions that there was treachery in the organization, and many felt that his defection was a serious loss.[109] While all other Irish newspapers refused to champion Parnell or the Land League (though some Catholic papers had begun to tolerate them since the autumn of 1880), *United Ireland* was from its inception an uncritical champion of Parnell and constantly propagated a personality cult about him. The fact that O'Brien allowed the radical wing of the Land League to influence his journalism however meant that the establishment of his paper only increased the resolve of the government to suppress the league.

Because Parnell had managed to buy out Pigott's company before they could, the IRB and the Clan were reawakened to their need to establish a journal to represent their political views. Such a paper could well have been established in Dublin that autumn or winter were it not for the fact that Gladstone acted against the Land League in October 1881. The league was declared an illegal organization, Habeas Corpus was suspended and its leaders (including Parnell and several MPs) were imprisoned without trial. By the end of December, 334 league officials had been imprisoned without trial and *United Ireland* had also been suppressed.[110] Under such circumstances, it is not surprising that the proposed republican newspaper was published not in Ireland but in New York, under the editorship of John Devoy. The weekly *Irish Nation* first went to print on 13 November 1881, was financed by the 'Revolutionary Directory' and imported frequently into Ireland thereafter. Dublin Castle, however, seized most copies, as it did for all Irish-American newspapers.[111]

The Land League was determined to resist the government's coercion in

---

109 *DPB*, vol. 2, 101–2: Thomas Ronayne to John Devoy, 24 Sept. 1881, recalling events in the Cork IRB during 1875–6; Michael MacDonagh, *William O'Brien* (Dublin, 1928), 17–8; letter of P.N. Fitzgerald to GAA Executive about O'Brien, *Freeman's Journal*, 24 Nov. 1887. 110 NAI, CSORP 1881/35366, 1882/4305, 1882/4371; *Irish Nation* (New York), 31 Dec. 1881 (reprint from *Irish Times*). 111 *DPB*, vol. 2, 154, 191, *passim*. The importer was a Mrs. Keogh, a newsagent in Dorset Street who, for several years previously, had imported Irish-American newspapers. NAI, Fenian papers, 8980R; CSORP 1877/6742. Dublin Castle always restricted the importation of Irish-American newspapers not because they advocated the adoption of violent measures in Ireland (which they generally did not) but because, unlike Irish papers, they could publish very direct criticisms of the British government without being prosecuted or suppressed.

some way, but it had no real means at its disposal. Patrick Egan, who was funding the Ladies Land League, decided to set up an 'underground' edition of *United Ireland*, which was first published in Liverpool, then London and finally in Paris, where it was edited by Eugene Davis, a Cork-born popular poet and Francophile writer who also edited and published James Stephens's rambling recollections in the Irish press around this time.[112] Davis would later write several articles calling for the French to support the cause of Irish independence in the *Nouvelle Revue* (Paris),[113] as well as try to fulfill the dream of a moderate republican member of parliament of Irish descent of establishing a bilingual (French and English) Irish nationalist newspaper in Paris under Davis's own editorship.[114] Davis, however, was not a political journalist and did little for *United Ireland* except publish whatever he was asked. Most of its articles were actually written by William O'Brien and smuggled out of Kilmainham.[115] One of these was a 'no-rent manifesto', calling for tenants to withhold *all* rents until the prisoners were released. This manifesto was published as if it had the support of all the Land League leaders in jail (including Parnell), and it would become the principal topic for debate in Irish nationalist circles in the coming months.

The Irish press was hostile to the 'no-rent manifesto', which was really only promoted by a handful of members of the Ladies Land League as well as some members of the London HRCGB, including Frank Byrne (its secretary) and Patrick Tynan, who distributed copies of the manifesto in rural Leinster during the spring of 1882.[116] In Tipperary, a public campaign was launched to persuade C.J. Kickham to call upon all Irishmen to support the 'no-rent manifesto'. It was expected that the author of *Knocknagow*, who had a deep sympathy with the rural poor and whose own brother was in the Tipperary Land League, would support the campaign, but the ailing IRB president refused to do so. Although he desired that 'the toilers of the soil will win every atom of their rights', he believed that the no-rent manifesto was not really supported by Parnell or the Land League leaders and could not possibly lead to their release. Instead, it could only serve as 'a betrayal of the tenant-farmer cause' because it would reduce the tenantry to an even worse state of desperation and increase the likelihood of futile 'bloody collisions between the unarmed peasantry and armed soldiers and police'. 'If it must be fought', Kickham hoped comfortable farmers would respond to the no-rent manifesto

112 Owen McGee, 'Eugene Davis: a forgotten Clonakilty writer and poet', *Journal of the Cork Historical and Archaeological Society* (2004).   113 Janick Julienne, 'La question Irlandaise en France 1860–90: perceptions et reaction' (1997), 400–3. The *Nouvelle Revue* was a popular, nominally republican, literary and political journal owned and edited by Juliet Adam, a friend of the recently deceased Flaubert and publisher of Maupassant and Zola. Adam was one of the greatest patrons of the arts in nineteenth-century Paris. She was also fanatically anti-British. 114 Julienne, 'La question Irlandaise en France', 339–43.   115 John Denvir, *Life story of an old rebel* (1910), 209–18; Ryan, *Fenian memories*, 92.   116 NAI, British in Ireland microfilm, C.O.904/19/483.

by supporting the impoverished farmers in their distress; a very unlikely occurrence. Most of all, Kickham hoped that all the 'cowardly crimes' being committed in rural Ireland would cease.[117]

As editor of the *Irish Nation*, John Devoy's initial impulse was to support the no-rent manifesto, for 'the whole country is at the mercy of an absolute dictatorship'. He called upon all Irishmen to arm themselves and be ready to embrace revolutionary methods, now that the Irish Party leaders had been imprisoned and had 'accomplished, constitutionally, all that by mere agitation can be accomplished'.[118] After a short time, however, the *Irish Nation* championed Kickham's perspective on the no-rent manifesto, as it was supposed to represent the IRB's views. The paper emphasized that a political revolution was clearly not a possibility in Ireland at the time. While recognizing the value of withholding rents 'as a weapon against a class', the *Irish Nation* rejected 'the absolute no-rent policy' and denounced Patrick Ford's American labour journal, the *Irish World and American Industrial Liberator*, for continuing to champion it. Ford's paper had collected more money for the Land League than any other single source and had been imported into England since 1873, though Dublin Castle always tried (usually successfully) to prevent it reaching Irish readers. It was often very outspoken in its denunciations of the British government, and this alone was a cause of concern for the authorities. The Tory press in the United Kingdom detested the *Irish World*, which, for the most part, was simply a supporter of the American labour and 'populist party' cause; a short-lived attempt to break the monopoly held by the Democrat and Republican parties in American politics.[119] Both Devoy and Ford were members of the Land League of America, which was in favour of the no-rent manifesto. Specifically in the *Irish Nation*, however, Devoy emphasized that it was unlikely to win *any* popular support in Ireland itself. He believed it would 'uselessly involve thousands in misery' and 'provoke a premature conflict between the unarmed Irish people and their armed oppressors ... which could only end in slaughter', 'loss of material of war' and 'risk undoing all the work which has been steadily in progress for years', thereby 'casting our people for another quarter of a century into the slough of despondence':

> An appeal to physical force is not contemplated by any serious nationalist at the present day ... We have had enough of little spurts of insurrection and want no more Ballingarries [1848] or Tallaghts [1867]. We must work and watch and wait for years until we can strike with a force adequate to the task we have undertaken ... [and] we must have arms. Now is the time to get them.[120]

117 Letter of Kickham to Irish press, reprinted *Irish Nation* (New York), 3 Dec. 1881. 118 *Irish Nation* (New York), 3 Dec. 1881. 119 J.P. Rodechko, *Patrick Ford and his search for America* (1976). 120 *Irish Nation* (New York), 25 Feb., 11 Mar. 1882.

[handwritten margin note: no rights cb titles wry arms]

The suppression of the Land League, however, automatically forced the IRB to adopt a purely defensive posture. The British Army in Ireland (20,000 men) was mobilized to prevent any disturbances and both the DMP and RIC were ordered to devote *all* their energies to seizing illegally held firearms and guarding the country's ports.[121] Some success came quite quickly, to the joy of the Tory *Evening Mail* (Dublin), which quoted and mocked the propaganda of the *Irish Nation* and triumphantly celebrated the fact that Irishmen were completely powerless before the coercive power of the British state.[122]

Most of the raids performed by the police were unsuccessful and some were completely pointless: an entire family was imprisoned without trial in Waterford City for possessing a few rusty and unworkable revolvers dating from the mid 1860s.[123] Some successful arms seizures were made, however, against 'underground' branches of the Land League in Munster. These branches were generally sympathetic to the 'no-rent manifesto', but as they were now opposed by all the moderates who had withdrawn from the league, it is quite likely that these moderates acted as informants against them. A large quantity of rifles, bayonets and cartridges were seized in Kilkishen, Co. Clare (where they had been hidden in the vault of a Protestant church), several stand-of-arms and ammunition and pikes were seized at Listowel, Co. Kerry, some rifles were seized in Tralee, Co. Kerry and many revolvers were found in Millstreet, Co. Cork.[124] On 11 January 1882, the RIC raided an underground basement in an obscure laneway in Cork city and found a dozen Schneider rifles, well over a thousand bullets and forty pounds of dynamite, some of which had been stolen from an explosives firm two years earlier.[125] The most significant arms raid, however, took place in Dublin, not because of its scale, but because of its consequences.

On 16 December 1881, an arms depot held by a local 'Old Guard' IRB circle was raided and the police were able to arrest three men and seize two parcels of dynamite, 26 rifles, 6 revolvers, over 5,000 cartridges, 8 hand-grenades and 28 pounds of gunpowder.[126] Unlike the Dublin IRB organization under the Supreme Council, the Dublin 'Old Guard' movement had been under intense police scrutiny ever since it had assassinated the former head constable of the RIC ten years earlier as an act of revenge for his having joined the IRB and subsequently betraying his comrades during 1868.[127] The Dublin Old Guard leaders, James Carey, a building contractor and city councillor, and Jack Sullivan, a bookseller and auctioneer, were infuriated by the arms seizure, not least because it was made possible by an informer, Bernard Bailey, who was duly assassinated on their orders in February 1882.[128] Despite the offer of a

---

121 Ibid., 3 Dec. 1881.   122 Ibid., 18 Feb. 1882 (republished extracts from *Evening Mail*).
123 Ibid., 25 Mar. 1882.   124 *Irish Nation* (New York), 31 Dec. 1881, 4 Feb. 1882; *Irishman*, 7 Jan. 1882.   125 *Irish Nation* (New York), 28 Jan. 1882.   126 Ibid., 23 Dec. 1881.   127 NAI, Fenian A Files, no. 717.   128 NAI, British in Ireland microfilm collection, C.O. 904/18/1028; CSORP, 1882/33050, 1882/39290; NAI, DMP files, carton 1, Report of Supt. Smyth, 20 Aug. 1883; CSB files, B133, B149, B249.

huge reward of £500, no member of the public was prepared to give any information about the killing; a fact that was celebrated by Dublin street-balladeers.[129] The DMP, however, may well have been able to acquire the information it needed were it not that the 'Old Guard' had adopted some unusual tactics.

After Bailey betrayed their organization, Carey and Sullivan introduced a new controversial ruling (which was never introduced into the IRB) whereby anyone who disobeyed their orders would be shot.[130] Their motive in introducing this rule was simply fear for their own personal safety, since they suspected (correctly) there were other informers in their organization. The nightmare scenario that the Catholic clergy had always used to warn the public against joining secret societies had now come true. This ruling caused all the 'Old Guard' followers to want to join the IRB instead, thereby forcing Dublin IRB leader James Mullet and various other local centres to concern themselves with the dispute. The tensions arising from the Bailey murder were accentuated in March 1882 when the DMP responded to their failed attempt to catch Bailey's assassins by taking advantage of the suspension of Habeas Corpus, rounding up six Dublin suspects, who were sent to different jails across the country.[131] One of the men imprisoned was James Mullet and, as a result, the Dublin IRB was left without a central command at the worst possible moment. Meanwhile, Carey and Sullivan ordered another assassination (this time, the man killed was innocent) and the planting of a bomb outside the detective depot at Dublin Castle (it failed to detonate).[132]

John McCafferty, an Irish-American freelance revolutionary who had worked with Patrick Tynan and P.J. Sheridan in northern England during 1867, had been in London in October 1881. McCafferty had also been a leader of one of those Confederate guerrilla warfare units during 1864–5 that had resolved to kidnap President Abraham Lincoln and hold him to ransom until the Confederate leaders were released from prison; plots that ultimately led, inadvertently, to Lincoln's assassination. During 1874, McCafferty suggested to Kickham and the IRB that they should kidnap leading government officials until all the IRB prisoners were released, but the proposal was rejected.[133] It is highly probable that McCafferty suggested the same strategy to London HRCGB figures like Frank Byrne and Patrick Tynan after the Land League leaders and MPs were imprisoned without trial in October 1881, and, that this idea spread to Dublin after Tynan and P.J. Sheridan visited the country with funding to promote the 'no-rent manifesto'. Sheridan gave some money to James Mullet in December 1881. Mullet refused to support the no-rent campaign because Kickham and O'Leary were opposed to it, but Sheridan told him that they were 'old fogies' who were 'too fond of poetry'.[134] After Bailey's

129 G.D. Zimmermann, *Irish political street ballads* (1966), 279–80. 130 *Irishman*, 5 May 1883 (report of informer Thomas Devine's statements in court); NAI, CSORP, 1883/17078. 131 *Irish Nation* (New York), 25 Mar. 1882. 132 Ibid., 25 Mar., 1 Apr. 1882. 133 *DPB*, vol. 1, 67–9. 134 NAI, CSB files, B198.

murder and Mullet's arrest, James Carey managed to seize the funds Sheridan gave to Mullet and used this to build up a small band of followers (numbering at most 30 men) from *both* the IRB and the 'Old Guard' who would supposedly act as a sort of vigilance committee for the entire local underground movement. A new plot was also hatched.

By March 1882, the *Irish Nation* had adopted a 'declaration of principles' as its editorial policy, a statement shaped largely by the views of the IRB leaders Kickham and O'Leary, who considered Devoy's paper to be the first nationalist newspaper to exist since the days of the *Irish People*. 'While treating all Irishmen and all Irish parties who mean well to Ireland in a fair and friendly spirit', the paper would be 'absolutely un-sectarian', 'preach the doctrine that the Irish people alone are competent to make their own laws', 'advocate the establishment of an Irish nation in which all Irishmen shall be equal' and 'aim to sow the seeds of a more healthy and vigorous Irish public opinion' by 'reflecting the most advanced thought of Irish nationalists': 'in short, it will seek to have the direction of the national movement entrusted to the best intellects, most devoted patriotism and ripest political experience that the race can produce.'[135] Apart from Devoy, the editorial staff of the paper were John McInerney, a Limerick-born doctor, IRB arms agent and honorary member of the Supreme Council, and William O'Donovan, a Francophile journalist, formerly of the IRB and a close friend of John O'Leary.

During the spring of 1882, the *Irish Nation* published a diverse range of articles. O'Donovan translated French and German newspaper articles that were critical of the British government's suppression of the Land League and wrote a series on the history of European revolutionary movements. Extracts of journal articles relating to Ireland from American and Canadian periodicals were reproduced occasionally, with the assistance of Alec Sullivan and John Boyle O'Reilly of the *Boston Pilot*. Apart from writing most of the articles on contemporary politics, to help Irishmen come to their own decision about the no-rent manifesto, John Devoy reprinted numerous old articles by John Mitchel on the theme of the potential of an agrarian revolution to aid the cause of Irish independence. These articles, like a series of reprints of Thomas Davis's writings (selected for the paper at O'Leary's request by Sir Charles Gavan Duffy), came under the title 'Voice of the *Nation*: how the seed which today bears fruit was sown.' Thomas Clarke Luby, the old IRB founder who was currently an inactive member of the Clan, wrote articles on the political thought of Jonathan Swift and William Molyneux, as well as personal recollections of Fintan Lalor and the Irish revolutionary movement of 1849. The paper also regularly printed literary articles by Thomas O'Neill Russell, the leader of the Society for the Preservation of the Irish Language in Dublin, as well as John Murdoch, the editor of the *Highlander* (Inverness) and an old friend of William Carroll who believed Ireland could only become a nation if

135 *Irish Nation* (New York), 4 Mar. 1882.

the Ulster-Scots rediscovered their Gaelic heritage. Although it included articles on the Irish language, however, the *Irish Nation* did not actually feature an Irish language column, the only Irish newspaper that did so being James O'Connor's *Irishman*, which continued to exist after the establishment of *United Ireland* and featured regular Irish articles by Russell and George Sigerson.

As the ailing Kickham was dying and no other current Supreme Councillors had experience of the newspaper business, John O'Leary generally offered editorial advice to Devoy on behalf of the IRB.[136] This was not always accepted, however, because O'Leary's reaction to the suppression of the Land League had been very moderate. While O'Leary believed that the cause of tenant-right was 'a good one', just as was the cause of advancing education 'almost in any shape', he was convinced the Land League agitation could not possibly 'end in the abolition of landlordism and even if – *per impossible* – it did, it would not give Ireland either prosperity or happiness.' He expressed strong distaste at *United Ireland*'s descriptions of the imprisoned Land League leaders as 'martyrs' and Prime Minister Gladstone and Chief Secretary Forester as 'monsters' and 'priest hunters', as this was only inciting violence of emotion. He argued that the Parnellites could not claim to have a complete monopoly of political virtue in their recent quarrels with the British government and that Gladstone's land act was actually a good measure.[137] The Connacht IRB leader P.W. Nally also thought that the land act should have been accepted by the Land League and the league should now focus only on nationalist goals.[138] In response to criticism from Devoy, O'Leary promised that he would 'try to conform' a little more with the popular viewpoint. For the most part, however, he simply let Devoy decide what should appear in the paper and then, characteristically, criticized it.[139]

Kickham and O'Leary ordered the Supreme Council secretary John O'Connor to go to Ireland in February 1882 to work with P.N. Fitzgerald and others in trying to convince the 'rank and file' to conform to the organization's policy with regards to the no-rent manifesto and to do everything possible to ensure that the IRB's arms would not be seized. Upon his return to Paris the following month, however, O'Connor faced a rude awakening. In response to the demands of the Land League of America, Alec Sullivan had recently left for Paris to persuade Patrick Egan to return a lot of the funds of the suppressed Land League back to its American subscribers. Before leaving Paris, Sullivan also called upon O'Connor and made a startling announcement. Although John O'Leary had called for a meeting of the 'Revolutionary Directory' to take place in Paris at this time,[140] it seems clear that Sullivan called upon O'Connor totally unexpectedly and simply ignored O'Leary. Sullivan told O'Connor that the American wing of the Revolutionary

136 *DPB*, vol. 2, passim.   **137** O'Leary to *Irish Nation* (New York), 3 Dec. 1881 (reprint of letter to *Irishman*).   **138** Jordan, *Land and popular politics*, 280.   **139** *DPB*, vol. 2, 110–2 (O'Leary to Devoy, Mar. 1882).   **140** *DPB*, vol. 2, 127.

Directory (which since August 1881 consisted of himself, D.C. Feely and Michael Boland, two other lawyers) believed that the British government must be punished for suppressing the Land League by dynamiting government property in England. O'Connor later received letters from Sullivan stating that he did not support this idea at all, but in spring of 1882, when an incredulous O'Connor denounced and dismissed the idea out of hand, Sullivan appeared to be steadfast in this resolve. O'Connor complained to Sullivan that the Clan reported it had created a new 'arms fund' in December 1881 but the IRB was never told how much money it received. He also complained that the Supreme Council's calls to inspect the account books of the 'Revolutionary Directory' (which were managed on the American side) were being ignored,[141] despite the fact that the constitution of the 'R.D.' gave the IRB this perpetual right.[142] Sullivan, however, gave (or perhaps could give) no satisfactory explanation and the meeting ended quickly, as Sullivan had to return to the United States.

From information received from Michael Davitt (a long-term personal friend), J.J. O'Kelly and others, Alec Sullivan had been convinced since 1880 that so long as Kickham and O'Leary were on the IRB executive, 'no bold, effective work can be done' and 'I fear our work and money are wasted.'[143] It is very likely that he supported O'Kelly and Davitt's old plan to pressurize O'Connor into removing Kickham and O'Leary from the Supreme Council. Indeed, ever since the establishment of the 'Revolutionary Directory' in 1877, the Clan always saw it as a vehicle for bringing the IRB under an Irish-American directing influence, even though it had no right to do so, according to the directory's constitution.[144] Sullivan effectively acted upon this same premise, but the dynamiting proposal (as will be seen in the next chapter) was almost certainly not his idea. Rather it was the wish of Michael Boland, who was a strong sympathizer with the 'United Irishmen of America' and a member of the Clan's 'Military Board'.

By the late spring of 1882, the number of agrarian outrages in the country had decreased and the only recent political initiative taken in Ireland had come from the Catholic hierarchy. The hierarchy used its considerable political influence to ensure that Michael Davitt (who was in solitary confinement in Portland prison, London since February 1881) was nominated for a parliamentary by-election in Meath, thereby issuing a protest to the government. Davitt was duly elected in February 1882, but immediately disqualified, causing the hierarchy to push instead for the nomination of Patrick Egan for the seat, who would surely have won. The *Irish Nation* expressed strong opposition to this policy, arguing that Egan (then in Paris) could better serve

141 UCD, Desmond Ryan papers, L.A. 10/k/23 (1), 25–9, 31–2 (1889 statement of O'Connor regarding his role as secretary of the Supreme Council and IRB–Clan relations since 1881). 142 *Special Commission Report*, vol. 4, 493–502, constitution of R.D., produced as evidence by Henri Le Caron. 143 *DPB*, vol. 1, 549–50. 144 This is clear from the correspondence of William Carroll, Clan chairman, 1875–80, reproduced in *DPB*, vol. 1.

the nationalist cause by working outside of parliament. Alec Sullivan thought that Egan should go to Westminster and try to set an example for other Irish MPs to follow, by refusing to take the oath of allegiance and then withdrawing, but the *Irish Nation* dismissed this suggestion because 'the country is not ripe for such a movement' and, thus, the time had 'not yet' arrived to make this policy practical. After initially demonstrating some willingness to accept the nomination, Egan chose not to stand.[145]

In April 1882, after being granted parole to visit his sister in Paris, Parnell met with two friends of Gladstone. These were Justin McCarthy, a liberal MP and deputy chairman of the Irish Party, and William O'Shea, a Catholic army officer and Whig. They discussed upon what terms they could come to an agreement with the government. McCarthy later told their proposals to the Liberal government. This led to the so-called 'Kilmainham Treaty', whereby Parnell, Dillon and O'Kelly were let out of prison on 2 May 1882 on the understanding that they would suppress the no-rent campaign, not revive the Land League and cooperate fully with the government in the future. Four days later, just as Davitt was being released from Portland, James Carey's gang assassinated the newly appointed chief secretary of the British administration in Ireland and his under-secretary (or deputy) in the Phoenix Park, Dublin, in the process shocking the entire international community.

The Phoenix Park murders were condemned by all shades of Irish public opinion. How the conspiracy came into being was a mystery that was debated by the public for many years, and it has never been solved. The Tory press would always blame the Land League for the murders, and rumours were purposely circulated against all its former leaders, particularly Patrick Egan. He had been its treasurer, had funded the no-rent campaign and refused to bow to the Catholic hierarchy's demand that he use the defunct Land League's funds as a public reward to anyone who would give information to the police about the killings. When the killers Joe Brady and Tim Kelly were caught, tried and sentenced to death, John O'Clohissey was allowed to enter Kilmainham jail to bring a crucifix to them shortly before their execution. He claimed he was told that their only purpose was to kidnap, not assassinate, the chief secretary, to secure the release of the Land League prisoners.[146] There were still over three hundred league officials in jail at the time of the murders, and contemporary accounts do intimate that a struggle took place between the four men before knives were drawn and the two officials were killed. It is highly doubtful, however, that men would carry surgical knives with them if they merely intended to kidnap someone. The Phoenix Park murders were not, as Tory propaganda claimed, an inevitable outcome of the 'criminality' of the Land League, while the Tories' theory that the murders were planned by London HRCGB officials or political exiles like P.J. Sheridan is very probably

145 *Irish Nation* (New York), 25 Feb., 4 Mar. 1882. **146** Gerard McGowan, a descendant and owner of the property of John O'Clohissey (1836–1902), to author.

untrue.[147] It is more likely that the murders were the indirect outcome of James Carey's *ad hoc* efforts to build up an inner circle within the Dublin republican movement after the Bailey murder, effectively to save his own skin. As is well known, Carey eventually realized that there was only *one* way out of the mess into which he had got both himself and others, leading to still more tragic consequences.

After the murders, all newspapers in Ireland bore black borders to symbolize great popular mourning, while Parnell, Dillon and Davitt issued a manifesto condemning the event in the strongest terms. Meanwhile, the *Irish Nation* described the Phoenix Park murders as 'a tragedy' that could only be 'a pretext for new tyranny'.[148] Indeed, within five days of the murders, a new and more stringent 'crimes' act was introduced at Westminster.

For the IRB, the events at the Phoenix Park were undoubtedly a tragedy, for virtually all newspapers blamed and denounced the mysterious 'Fenian organization' for the murders. Parnell himself contributed to this development, arguing that the 'Fenians' were undoubtedly responsible for the murders and adding to the mystery by claiming to know that 'the responsibility must not be attributed to the whole association. It has numerous branches, possessing great independence. It may be indeed, and I am inclined to think it is, one of those branches composed of fanatics.'[149] Just as had happened during the mid to late 1860s, 'the Fenians' had suddenly resurfaced on the front pages of the press and both their character and motives were invariably interpreted in the light of the recent sensational events; thereby ensuring that the Phoenix Park murders, as well as the events of 1867, would ever-after be understood by the great majority of the British and Irish public as *the* defining illustration of what the politics of the so-called 'physical force party' in Ireland meant in practice. Not surprisingly, this troubled the IRB greatly. This public misconception of their politics was bound to have as negative an effect on the movement as the 'Manchester martyrs' incident had a positive one during 1867.

John O'Leary was determined to avert all blame for the murders from his party. Instead he blamed *United Ireland* for having written articles that had served only to incite men to irrational hatreds. O'Leary expressed great irritation about Parnell's recent remarks, which were full of 'the ambiguity which characterizes too many of his utterances', and stated that he 'wished that Mr. Parnell and the various public bodies of Ireland and America had not waited for the slaying of Lord Frederick Cavendish and Mr. Burke to issue indignant manifestos', for he could 'see no greater moral guilt in this particular crime' than in the 'cruel murders' conducted against the families of farmers in the west of Ireland. He also stated that he had 'not the slightest moral doubt that my views are shared by Mr. Stephens, Luby and every prominent nationalist in Ireland and America' and added that he could also 'speak

147 For a contrary view, see Tom Corfe, *The Phoenix Park murders* (London, 1968).   148 *Irish Nation* (New York), 6 and 13 May 1882.   149 Interview with Parnell published by *La France*, reprinted *Irish Nation* (New York), 20 May 1882.

authoritatively for Mr. Kickham' on this question.[150] As T.W. Moody noted, the Phoenix Park murders were undoubtedly a blessing in disguise for Parnell, for he was able to use the ensuing public outcry to justify both the compromise of the 'Kilmainham Treaty', and, his call for the public to rally themselves purely behind his own party in Westminster.[151] This marginalized all republican and democratic nationalists in Ireland who had been calling for the public to maintain a purely extra-parliamentary focus to their politics.

The IRB suffered a devastating propagandist blow as a result of the Phoenix Park murders, not least because of James Carey's betrayal of his comrades and their subsequent execution. A circular of the 'Executive of the Leinster IRB', led by Charles O'Farrell of Enniscorthy, and dating from the spring of 1883 lamented that 'a stigma has been cast upon the noblest cause that man has ever laboured to advance', and that it was no longer just 'the ultramontanes, lay or clerical' which were choosing to 'decry our ends as murderous and unholy'. It stated that, more so than ever, every member of the IRB needed to have the 'moral courage' to 'let the shafts of misrepresentation fly by him unheeded'. It was feared that the recruiting successes of the organization in recent years could now easily be undone ('heed not the falling away of a weak associate, for his loss but purifies our ranks') and that recruitment efforts would be very difficult in the future. This was because the Catholic clergy could now claim (after Carey's actions) that it was right all along about the great evils of secret societies and, in the process, easily persuade both young prospective recruits to the IRB and some existing members of the organization to have nothing to do with the movement. Hence the IRB circular lamented that 'the clergy, sons of Irish parents, men who are generously supported out of the scanty means of our people', were forever ready 'in obedience of orders from abroad ... to keep down even a thought of liberty' in Ireland, so that Britain 'might retain its grip on the throat of our mother country.' However, as 'it is not given to any man ... to anticipate the judgment of a God in whose sight right and justice rank far above expediency', the IRB called upon its followers to ignore those 'who assail your hopes of happiness hereinafter' and to 'rigidly adhere to principle; and, Brothers, you shall yet reap the reward of your devoted labours.' Specifically regarding the 'Invincible' conspiracy, the republican brothers did 'not wish to speak too harshly' about some of the men who became involved in it, but it 'cannot condemn too seriously' those 'who knew thoroughly that the line of conduct they pursued was in direct conflict with the principles of our organization' and who 'practically, if not openly, set at nought the authority of the Supreme Council' over the Dublin IRB:

> They knew, as every true Irishman knows, that crime and outrage are as
> foreign to our organization as the enemy is to our soil. Our constitution,

150 O'Leary interview, reprinted *Irish Nation* (New York), 20 May 1882. **151** Moody, *Davitt*, 538–9.

orders and addresses breathe alike the same spirit and point to the same ends; the use of all means commendable to every honorable and god fearing man ... Let not hatred of the foe impel us to such means; means that can bring about no good result and at whose adoption humanity itself revolts ... Remember you are called upon to make no great sacrifice and face no greater risk than good men have cheerfully done in the past.[152]

The IRB had rather more to worry about, however, than the moral credibility of its politics. The Phoenix Park murders prompted the British government to increase its 'anti-Fenian' espionage work to totally unprecedented levels. Between 1882 and 1887, Dublin Castle would spend roughly £70,000 on secret service work, an amount of expenditure equal to that spent in Ireland during the entire period (1919–21).[153] A small foretaste of what was to come for the IRB occurred in London on 17 June 1882. Possibly because of the effect the Phoenix Park murders had upon that same London IRB man who had offered his services to the government back in March 1881 to prevent the 'United Irishmen' from blowing up the London Mansion House, the recently established Criminal Investigation Department (CID) was able to carry out a raid on one of the IRB's largest arms depots. A total of 400 'small saloon pistols', 277 rifles, 276 bayonets, 30 revolvers, 7,925 cartridges for Schneider rifles and 600 cartridges for 'large pistols' were seized, having been found in a London stable. As London was the focal point of the IRB arms importation scheme (through which John O'Connor and fellow arms agents such as P.N. Fitzgerald, John Daly and John McInerney passed frequently), this event was a serious scare for the IRB, and Mark Ryan recalled that, thereafter, the republican movement 'decided not to attempt to send arms and ammunition to Ireland in large quantities, owing to the vigilance of the police'.[154] Police vigilance was increased exponentially in August 1882 when Dublin Castle established a new and extremely well funded intelligence body, the 'Crime Special Branch' under the direction of Colonel Henry Brackenbury, who later became the first director of British 'Military Intelligence' when that department was established in 1909. The Crime Special Branch was the first, permanent secret service department ever established in the British empire and it was set up with the sole purpose of infiltrating the IRB and breaking it up from within, by spreading fear and suspicions within its ranks until the day the organization would, it was hoped, totally collapse.[155] The writing was now clearly on the wall for the IRB.

152 A copy of this circular can be seen in NAI, British in Ireland microfilms, Reel 4 Box 10, Secret Societies 1882–4, 200–3. It was discovered in the summer of 1884 when the RIC performed an arms raid in Queen's County (Laois).   153 Eunan O'Halpin, 'The British secret service vote and Ireland, 1868–1922' (1983), 353.   154 Ryan, *Fenian memories*, 108, 171.   155 Richard Hawkins, 'Government versus secret societies in the Parnell era', in T.D. Williams (ed.), *Secret societies in Ireland* (Dublin, 1973), 113–25.

4

'The sword is sheathed by fighting men': the rise of Parnell and the defeat of the IRB by the Special Branch, 1882–5

During October 1882 two events of great long-term consequences happened in Irish nationalist politics, one taking place in a wave of publicity in Ireland and the other amidst the greatest secrecy in Irish-America.

On 17 October 1882, a large convention was held in Dublin to inaugurate a new political movement to replace the defunct Land League. Prior to this convention, a couple of Parnellite MPs and former Land League leaders such as Davitt, Brennan, Harris and Egan held negotiations to determine its programme. The latter group favoured the establishment of a wholly non-sectarian, nationalist and almost socialistic organization, whose leaders would be democratically elected and independent of the Irish Party's authority. This proposal might have won popular support were it not for the fact that Davitt (but not the others) stated publicly that he was also in favour of a policy of 'land nationalization', whereby the abolition of landlordism was to be accomplished by the state taking control of all property rights in the country – an idea that, not surprisingly, proved very unpopular. These proposals were submitted to Tim Healy MP and Tim Harrington, the owner of the *Kerry Sentinel* and a former (moderate) Land Leaguer, who were to draft the programme for the new organization. When the 'Irish National League' was founded on 17 October, however, the Irish Party (or in other words, Parnell) was given the right to have complete control over its executive. This idea outraged the former Land League leaders, as it was undemocratic. After quite a heated debate, a compromise was hastily accepted towards the end of the convention whereby the National League would be governed instead by a central council of 48 members, 16 of which were to be chosen by the Irish Party and the remaining 32 were to consist of one member to be elected from league branches in each Irish county. According to Parnell's wishes, however, this central council was never established. Parnell knew that if the movement was governed democratically, it would very soon come into conflict with the British government and the Kilmainham Treaty agreement, which had effectively saved his career, would be ruined.

The National League (like later bodies such as the 'Irish National Federation' and 'United Irish League') was governed only by a small, non-elective central organizing committee, nominated directly by the Irish Party's leadership. Tim Harrington (who became an MP in 1883) was made the National League's first secretary and would remain so for many years, with powers to disband any branches led by figures the Irish Party did not trust.

Catholic endorsement of the National League [handwritten marginalia]

Most branches came to be led by parish priests. Unlike the Land League, the National League had no real purpose except to act as an electioneering machine for MPs. Consequently, the HRL, which had been very opposed to the Land League, chose to amalgamate with the new National League. The conservative Catholic middle classes, which had never supported the Land League, also supported the National League and gave it financial support. As a result, unlike the Land League, the National League's support base was to be concentrated heavily in the prosperous midlands as well as urban areas. After 1882 Parnell and the Catholic hierarchy (which had previously distrusted the Irish Party leader) were both eager to reach a greater understanding. This goal would be accomplished during the autumn of 1884 when Parnell committed his party to championing the church's demand for greater public access to denominational education for Catholics at all levels of society. Although some radicals and democrats (including IRB men) would join the National League and try to reorganize it along Land League lines in the west of Ireland, the possibility of any Irish political grouping (excepting the Catholic Church) being able to influence the National League executive or pressure the Irish Party into adopting their policies had been completely prevented. Parnell now had a free rein to pursue whatever policy he wished and to bargain with the British government accordingly. As such, the formation of the National League marked Parnell's greatest triumph in Irish politics.[1] There was much truth in Davitt's later assertion that 'it was the counter-revolution … the complete eclipse, by a purely parliamentary substitute, of what had been a semi-revolutionary [democratic] organization … the overthrow of a movement and the enthronement of a man; the replacement of nationalism by Parnellism'.[2] In addition, across much of the country, it made parish priests the political leaders of the community once more instead of nationalists or republicans.[3]

Once the National League was formed, Alec Sullivan stepped down as Clan president to concentrate on the Land League of America, which was the leading Irish-American political organization of the day.[4] Anticipating that calls would be made for the foundation of an auxiliary wing of the National League in America, Sullivan decided to take the lead in helping to found such an organization. His greatest desire was to become as powerful a political spokesman for the Irish-American community in American politics as Parnell had become for the Irish political community in Westminster. As the new National League in Ireland was totally subordinate to the Irish Party, Davitt, Brennan and Egan did not want to be involved in it, but all three remained very sympathetic with the Land League of America, which continued to champion the same democratic-republican principles as had been championed by the Irish National Land League. This caused it to be demonized by the British

1 C.C. O'Brien, *Parnell and his party* (1957), chapter 4. 2 Davitt, *Fall of feudalism*, 377–8. 3 Ibid., 466–7. 4 UCD, Desmond Ryan papers, L.A. 10/k/23 (1), statement of Alec Sullivan in Clan 'trial' of 1888.

press, and it irritated Parnell, who feared the Irish-Americans' propaganda would undermine the trust established by the 'Kilmainham Treaty'. While Davitt (who rejected calls for him to stand as an MP) concentrated on working as a labour activist with the Irish community in Britain, both Egan and Brennan moved to the United States. They worked with Sullivan, as well as Patrick Ford (whose American labour journal, the *Irish World*, was sympathetic towards Davitt's stance and highly critical of the Kilmainham Treaty) in reorganizing the Land League of America. This formed the backdrop to the formation of the Irish National League of America (INLA) in April 1883, under the presidency of Sullivan. However Sullivan's stepping down as Clan president in October 1882 set off another completely different and very sinister chain of events.

Although Sullivan remained a nominal member of the Clan executive for another two years (he resigned completely from the Clan in April 1885 owing to quarrels surrounding the management of Devoy's *Irish Nation*),[5] in October 1882 control of the organization fell into the hands of Michael Boland, a former US soldier and financially-crooked lawyer in Kentucky who governed the movement in a virtually autocratic fashion.[6] In American politics, Sullivan's influence far outweighed that of Boland, who had a *public* reputation of being merely one of Sullivan's followers. Within the clandestine world of the Clan, however, Boland followed his *own* plan of action. Upon becoming the Clan leader, Boland formed a close working relationship with F.F. Millen, an ex-British spy who was soon to re-enter British pay and was secretly trying to form another revolutionary movement *within* the Clan connected with the extremist, spy-ridden 'United Irishmen of America',[7] which was still in favour of making terrorist attacks in London. These actions of Boland were evidently taken without the knowledge or consent of either Sullivan or Devoy, who had not been a member of the Clan executive since 1881. Both had forbidden Clansmen to join or associate with the United Irishmen (now led by Patrick Sarsfield Cassidy, a New York barman, whom O'Donovan Rossa believed was a British spy), and both also disliked and distrusted Millen. Devoy denounced Millen publicly as an unprincipled adventurer (which he was),[8] while Sullivan stated, just after stepping down as Clan chairman in October 1882, that he was opposed to Millen being 'entrusted with any responsible position' by his successor.[9] This understanding reached between Boland and Millen formed the backdrop to the launch of the infamous 'dynamite war' of 1883–85, which involved many British *agents provocateurs* and would deal devastating blows to the IRB.

John O'Leary no doubt replaced Kickham as IRB leader upon the latter's death in August 1882. He held great hopes for the *Irish Nation*, which

5 Ibid. 6 UCD, Desmond Ryan papers, L.A. 10/k/23 (1), statements of M.J. Ryan, Michael Biggane, Rev. Betts, H.J. Connolly and E.P. Lynch at a secret Clan meeting in October 1888. 7 Christy Campbell, *Fenian fire* (2002), 65–74; *DPB*, vol. 2, 53–4, 139. 8 *Irish Nation* (New York), 26 Aug. 1882. 9 *DPB*, vol. 2, 159.

continued to be imported into Ireland and was read by those IRB men who could get their hands on it. Up until 1885, O'Leary acted as an editorial advisor to the paper, and it continued to publish IRB-style propaganda. However, as Alec Sullivan was its principal shareholder after October 1882 and it was after all a New York newspaper, the greatest influence upon its propaganda was now the politics of the Irish-American community.

Devoy had been a prominent member of the Land League of America and he believed, mistakenly, that the political sensibilities of the leaders of the National League in Ireland and the Land League of America – soon to become the Irish National League of America (INLA) – were one and the same. Consequently, by the spring of 1883, he replaced the original 'declaration of principles' of the *Irish Nation* with a simple statement that, through the National Leagues of Ireland and America, it would be possible to bring about 'the complete unification of our people'. Furthermore, he stated that by giving 'unswerving support to the policy of the National League, as conducted by Charles Stewart Parnell', Irish nationalists would be 'preparing the way for the final settlement of the national question.'[10] John O'Leary was interested in all the developments that took place within the Land League of America during the autumn of 1882 and the spring of 1883, but this change of focus by the *Irish Nation* disturbed him. He wrote to Devoy that it was 'painful to me to find myself getting more and more out of harmony with the paper, which seems to me to be getting more and more into line with *United Ireland*', Parnell's totally uncritical champion. Indeed, *United Ireland* now began printing advertisements for Devoy's paper in its columns. O'Leary responded to Devoy's appeals for further Supreme Council funding for the *Irish Nation* by stating that 'I'd most certainly give nothing to keep it as it is, and most certainly should never have consented to give anything if I had known it was to be what it has been', for 'you have taken, or retaken, to constant laudation of a set of loose principled agitators as have ever disgraced Irish politics [Parnell and his party]'.[11] His subsequent attempts to persuade Devoy to alter his editorial policy were far from successful. O'Leary visited the United States in both the spring of 1882 and 1883 to confer with Sullivan and Boland, but he found it difficult to contact either. He complained to Devoy that he had been left with 'but the vaguest notion where authority resides' in the Irish-American revolutionary movement and so felt there was an urgent 'need of some consultation with a view to [establishing] some concert' between the IRB and the Clan,[12] but Devoy could not help him since he held no authority. This concern of O'Leary's became particularly strong after a mysterious event took place in March 1883, which disturbed the plans of *both* the IRB and Sullivan's party within the Land League of America.

10 Quotation from editorial policy of the *Irish Nation* (New York), written by John Devoy and printed on the back page of every issue from 1883 to 1885. 11 *DPB*, vol. 2, 165, 191, 222 (O'Leary to Devoy, 1883). 12 *DPB*, vol. 2, 115, 192, 194–5 (O'Leary to Devoy, 1882–3).

[handwritten: London — pub. opinion of IRB decreases, more opposition from the Brits   US Clan bombs   107]

In March 1883, shortly before a convention was held in Philadelphia to reconstitute the Land League of America as the Irish National League of America (INLA), a bomb exploded at the Local Government Board offices at Whitehall, London, and an unsuccessful attempt was made to blow up the offices of the London *Times*. With the aid of an informer within the dynamite team (William Lynch, a member of the United Irishmen of America, who may well have been an *agent provocateur*), an explosives factory was soon discovered by the police in Birmingham and the leading men involved (including Tom Clarke of New York, a future leader of the 1916 rising) were arrested and sentenced to life imprisonment.[13] The bombing outraged public opinion in England. More significantly, it aroused suspicions in the United Kingdom regarding the true intentions of the men who were about to set up the INLA. The Tories did their best to sustain these rumours by making the wildest charges against both it and Ford's *Irish World*, their purpose being to ensure that *any* public movement in Ireland that looked for Irish-American financial support (as the Land League had done and any nationalist movement generally needed to do), could be portrayed as being in league with terrorists. This was also intended to make Parnell's 'Kilmainham Treaty' compact with Gladstone more difficult to sustain, and indirectly to hurt the Liberals' electoral fortunes, which was the Tories' greatest concern. Parnell made a forceful speech in the Commons stating that he regretted and disapproved of what the Tories were doing,[14] but he nevertheless demanded that a resolution be passed at the inaugural convention of the INLA in April 1883 declaring that it would never consider supporting 'violent means' of furthering the cause of Irish independence. The INLA had nothing whatsoever to do with the explosions, but this resolution was introduced and passed by the Irish-Americans, not without some reluctance. This fact led the Tory press to issue propaganda for the rest of the decade in the English and Irish press about 'INLA dynamite conventions', all of which was pure nonsense. The INLA view was simply that, 'while an appeal to violence may never be needed', to 'dictate a policy to the people of Ireland' and argue that they did not have the *right* to fight for independence at any stage was fundamentally wrong, for, in the name of basic political liberty, no policy can be presented to any people 'as an ultimatum'.[15]

The London bombings not only helped the Tories give bad publicity to the INLA, but also outraged John O'Connor, who immediately demanded that a 'Revolutionary Directory' meeting be convened in Paris so that the Clan would explain its actions. Michael Boland did visit Paris, but did not give a satisfactory explanation as to why the attack was organized without the knowledge or approval of the Supreme Council, a fact that prompted an angry John O'Leary and John O'Connor to set sail to the United States shortly afterwards

---

13 Short, *Dynamite war*, chapter 5.   14 Davitt, *Fall of feudalism*, 460.   15 Sullivan to *Irish Nation* (New York), 25 Feb 1882.

to confer more extensively with the Clan leadership in Philadelphia. These meetings were inconclusive but, shortly after their return to Paris that autumn, O'Connor received two letters from Boland in which it was stated that the Clan had resolved 'to resume the original work and programme slowly', a statement understood by O'Connor to mean that the Clan would work only to aid the IRB's policy of conducting slow, methodical arms importations and that occurrences of the kind in London (or Birmingham) would never happen again.[16]

After organizing a large political funeral for C.J. Kickham in late August 1882, the IRB embarked on a number of endeavours that were in line with O'Leary's desires for the future of the organization and which also reflected the original editorial policy of the *Irish Nation*. The first of these was to concentrate upon the Young Ireland Societies (YIS) in an effort to recruit well educated young men – a policy that was first prioritized in Britain, probably because this was a trouble spot for the IRB ever since the first attempted Irish-American bombing in 1881. In the autumn of 1882, Mark Ryan (by now a London doctor) established the first IRB-governed branch of the YIS in London 'for the purpose of discussing Irish affairs and attracting educated young Irishmen who would make desirable recruits'.[17] The society soon acquired as members various clerks and junior civil servants of Irish birth. Simultaneously the Scottish IRB leader John Torley formed a number of YIS branches in western Scotland with the same object in view. His societies attracted a mostly working-class audience, some of whom were then becoming involved in Scottish labour politics and many were also former members of the '98 Debating Club' of Glasgow, which had argued that Parnell was 'misleading' Irish public opinion and his political strategy was 'detrimental to the national cause.'[18] The Glasgow-Irish community's interest in labour politics grew rapidly at this time, not least due to the influence of John Ferguson, the local leader of the Irish National League of Great Britain (INLGB), and Michael Davitt's great popularity in Scotland.[19] Both men were also friends of Torley, who argued frequently before the Glasgow YIS and in the *Glasgow Observer* that, 'if ever Irish liberty is to be gained', Irishmen must accept the simple fact that 'Ireland's independence must be won outside England' and thus 'the money employed in defraying the expenses of [Irish Party] members in the London talking-shop [Westminster] might be more profitably spent among the starving poor in Ireland'.[20]

There were also new branches of the YIS established in Ireland at this time.

---

16 UCD, Desmond Ryan papers, L.A. 10/k/23 (1), 25–9, 31–2 (statement of O'Connor); *DPB*, vol. 2, 191–2, 195 (letters of O'Leary); Report of E.G. Jenkinson, leader of the Crime Special Branch, in NAI, DMP files, carton 1, dated 29 Nov. 1883. 17 Ryan, *Fenian memories*, 171. 18 Maírtín O'Catháin, 'Association versus integration in the life of an obscure Fenian: John Torley (1852–97)', unpublished article, courtesy of author; *Irishman*, 26 Mar. 1881. 19 Maírtín O'Catháin, 'Michael Davitt and Scotland', *Saothar*, 25 (1999), 19–36. 20 E.W. McFarland, *John Ferguson* (2003), 89; O'Catháin, 'John Torley'.

In Cork City, a branch was founded by William Rowan, a clerk who could well have been an IRB man (he was a friend of P.N. Fitzgerald); in Kilkenny city, a small branch was formed by P.J. O'Keefe, a young local IRB leader and a clerk to the city council. Meanwhile in Dublin, following Thomas Brennan's leaving for New York in late 1882, the local YIS fell under the direction of Fred Allan who, by the summer of 1883, was both the Dublin IRB leader and the vice-president and secretary of the Dublin YIS.[21]

More information is available regarding the activities of the Dublin YIS than any other Irish branches, owing to the fact that reports of the debates at YIS meetings were almost never printed in the press, while only the minute book for the Dublin branch has survived. From this it is clear that its debates and lectures were as much upon literary as political matters. The general trend of thought in the society was best reflected by the outcome of debates it held upon the American and French revolutions, when it was argued that the only 'revolution' practicable in Ireland at the present time was 'such as would be brought about by the education and elevation of the masses.'[22] Another strong reflection of the political sensibilities of the YIS was its voting unanimously that Irish nationalists should never compromise their principles for the sake of appeasing English public opinion. Fred Allan gave lectures to the Dublin YIS during 1882–3 on the themes of 'Socialism', 'the Russian revolutionary movement' and 'the effect of the Manchester executions' and organized a debate upon the theme of 'whether a federal union with America would be more beneficial to Ireland than one with England' (the society ruled in favour of America).[23] Controversy emerged in the society, however, in May 1883, when James Shannon, a shop assistant and IRB man, proposed that a debate should be held on whether or not the recent resolution that Parnell forced upon the INLA was just. This led several Parnellite members (included J.J.Clancy MA and Daniel Crilly, two future Irish Party MPs) to resign immediately from the YIS, protesting against the mere introduction of such a topic of debate. Tim Harrington, the national secretary of the National League, was also angered by this event and, before the debate could be held, the Dublin YIS was formally expelled from ever again meeting in the premises of the National League headquarters, where some of its recent meetings had been held at Clancy's request. To defend his determination to hold the INLA debate, Shannon subsequently wrote a letter (co-signed by Allan) to the National League headquarters noting that the YIS was a strictly independent club and therefore it 'could not think of choosing a line of debate to suit the particular views of the National League or any other public body';[24] a policy that it had indeed followed since its inception. After relocating to its original meeting place (a rented room above the York Street Workingmen's Club), the

21 NLI, Minute book of the Dublin YIS, MS 16095. Reference is made in this minute book to these other branches being established. 22 NLI, Minute book of YIS, MS 16095, minutes for 26 Jan., 17 Mar. 1883, 22 Feb., 14 Mar. 1884. 23 Ibid., minutes for 17 Feb., 24 Feb. 1882, 27 Apr. 1883. 24 Ibid., minute for 7 May 1883.

Dublin YIS voted that the recent resolution of the INLA was 'not worthy of Irish support'; H.J. Coffey, a young college student, gave a lecture upon 'Ireland's latest struggle for freedom', which focused on the events of the mid 1860s; and a new society ruling (which offended some members) was introduced by Fred Allan, banning discussions and debates on any religious subject matters.[25]

Apart from becoming involved in promoting the YIS, another new IRB policy at this time was to consider forming a nationalist amateur athletics association as an alternative means of mobilizing and politicizing the masses to radical land agitation. The champion athlete P.W. Nally had supported this idea as early as 1877, not only for political reasons, and it also appealed greatly to P.N. Fitzgerald, who was a runner and footballer in his spare time and a close friend of Nally's.[26] This idea was supposed to be discussed at a London Supreme Council meeting in the summer of 1883, but a number of developments relating to the IRB arms importation scheme helped stall the progress of the plan.

A surviving report of John O'Connor from 1888 indicates that the IRB purchased roughly 1,500 rifles during 1882–4, although it was not generally able to import these into Ireland due to the vigilance of the recently established Special Branch,[27] which made sure that the police forces of Dublin Castle did not slow down in its efforts to track down the IRB's arms agents after the arrest of the 'Invincibles'. This vigilance of the Special Branch had a number of unfortunate consequences for the IRB. For example, during October 1883, with Special Branch assistance, the DMP was able to discover that Thomas Caffrey, a stoker who worked for a Liverpool shipping company in Dublin, had replaced the hanged 'Invincible' Daniel Curley as the Dublin IRB's principal arms agent, after Caffrey tried to receive information from detectives who were (supposedly) of divided loyalties.[28] Meanwhile, with the help of Special Branch funding, the RIC recruited a valuable informer, codenamed 'Quentin', who was apparently a native of Kildare and a former Land League organizer. 'Quentin', who received a huge salary, claimed to have known many IRB men in the midlands and was asked to trace its arms agents.[29] Acting on 'Quentin's' advice, Joseph Wall, a shop assistant and young Carlow IRB leader, was arrested by the RIC in the spring of 1883, nominally on the charge of larceny. During his subsequent imprisonment, Wall revealed under duress that the unaccounted-for money in his possession was not stolen but was in fact funds of the IRB. Thereafter he told the police all he knew about the IRB in rural Leinster. Wall also identified cryptic letters in his possession as being written

25 Ibid., minutes for 11, 18 May 1883. 26 W.F. Mandle, *The GAA and Irish nationalist politics* (1987), 2; Tomás Ó Riordáin, 'Fenian and GAA pioneer: the story of P.N. Fitzgerald', *Cork Holly Bough* (Dec. 1984), 20, 29; Louisa Nally to author. 27 UCD, Desmond Ryan papers, L.A. 10/k/23 (1), 25–9, 31–2 (statement of John O'Connor). 28 NAI, DMP files, carton 1, Sergeant Sheehan, 19 Oct. 1883, 1 Nov. 1883. 29 NAI, British in Ireland microfilm, C.O.904/183 (register of informants). 'Quentin' received £100 a year.

by the chief travelling organizer of the IRB and its principal arms agent in
Ireland, P.N. Fitzgerald, who had written to Wall stating that he was 'very
anxious to have you invest in the ironmongery trade' (an obvious reference, in
IRB parlance, to purchasing arms) and asking him to assist him 'see after those
country customers' and ensure that 'any letters addressed to me' were kept
safe.[30] Around the same time, Patrick Delaney, a former Dublin IRB centre
who turned informer to avoid being convicted of involvement in the Phoenix
Park murders, told the police that Fitzgerald was the chief travelling organizer
and arms agent of the IRB.[31] Consequently, E.G. Jenkinson, the Special
Branch leader and a former crown official in India, decided to appoint a plain-
clothes detective to follow Fitzgerald at all times and look for the first available
opportunity to arrest him.

Around the same time as the Special Branch was alerted to P.N. Fitzgerald's
central role in the IRB, Jenkinson was able to strike at the heart of the
Connacht IRB organization by acting upon information received (probably by
Robert Anderson) in Manchester. The RIC did not even suspect that P.W.
Nally, the Connacht IRB leader, was a republican activist. Indeed, in
December 1882, after he was elected a member of the Castlebar poor law board
(of which several republicans were apparently members), Nally had been
granted a gun licence for hunting reasons by the local district inspector, who
stated that he believed that Nally would 'lead a useful and loyal life' since he
came from a well-to-do family and thus was naturally considered to be beyond
suspicion.[32] Jenkinson, however, knew from his Manchester sources that Nally
had been an arms agent in northern England. Therefore a Special Branch
detective, Samuel Waters, was sent to Mayo and tried to convince the RIC of
the necessity of arresting Nally. Waters did this by acquiring the services of a
man named Andrew Coleman, who *claimed* to be a member of the IRB and to
know that P.W. Nally and Thomas McCauley (a medical student and Nally's
principal assistant in the Mayo IRB) were planning to assassinate a landlord's
agent in Crossmolina, Co. Mayo.[33] Using this evidence, the police arrested
Nally on 15 May 1883, and on 1 June he stood on trial in Castlebar with six
other men, including McCauley, on the charge of conspiracy to murder.

Public confidence in the British legal system was very weak at this time in
Mayo, particularly after a recent controversial trial when one man was hanged
and several others were sentenced to life imprisonment after being convicted
on doubtful evidence of involvement in the murder of an entire family in
Maamtrasna, Co. Mayo.[34] Nally's trial caused much unrest among the local

30 NAI, British in Ireland microfilm, Colonial Office, Reel 4, Box 10 Secret Societies 1882–4,
pp 183, 217–20, 233–8; *Irish Nation* (New York), 22 Nov. 1884.   31 *Special Commission
Report*, vol. 3, 529–31, 540–1 (evidence of Patrick Delaney).   32 O'Baoighill, *Nally as Maigh
Eo*, 176.   33 Stephen Ball (ed.), *A policeman's Ireland: recollections of Samuel Waters, RIC*
(Cork, 1999), 13.   34 Jarlath Waldron, *Maamtrasna: the murders and the mystery* (Dublin,
1992).

population in Castlebar because he had often totally denounced agrarian outrages in the local press and therefore was universally believed to be innocent of the charge. Fearing the influence this might have on the jury, Dublin Castle ordered that the trial in Castlebar be cancelled and that it should reconvene in Cork in December under the same judge who had recently convicted the 'Invincibles' in Dublin. In the meantime, the RIC was ordered by Waters to carry out regular arms searches of the Nally family home at Mayo Abbey, Balla, Co. Mayo, an action that the *Irishman* believed was intended only to 'have the effect of prejudicing the minds of the jury'.[35] Two men testified against Nally in Cork, namely Coleman, who emphasized his intimacy with McCauley, who had been arrested before for Land League activities, and an unnamed Manchester informant, who provided the court with a rulebook of the 'north of England division' of the IRB. They both identified Nally as an arms agent. Ultimately, after eleven months in police custody, on 28 March 1884 Nally was sentenced to ten years' imprisonment on the charge of conspiracy to murder. Nally was sent to Downpatrick prison while McCauley and three other men were given sentences of seven years imprisonment and sent to Mountjoy.[36]

The belief that Nally was completely innocent was widespread. Parnell, in having to respond to local feeling in Mayo, would say in 1885 that Nally was 'one of the victims of the infamous system which existed in this country during the three years of the [1882] coercive act' whereby, in their desire to suppress all forms of land agitation, Dublin Castle decided to imprison men 'whether they were innocent or not'.[37] While the desire to suppress land agitation may have formed a backdrop to Nally's arrest and imprisonment, the real reason for his conviction was the Special Branch's awareness of his prominence in the IRB, a role that, secretly, Parnell was also aware of, through speaking with Davitt.[38] According to the Nally family, the men imprisoned due to the 'Crossmolina conspiracy' were, as the Special Branch believed, all members of the IRB, but they were not in any way involved in planning the assassination of land agents, as Waters' agent, Andrew Coleman, claimed and for which charge they were convicted and imprisoned.[39]

P.W. Nally's arrest in May 1883 meant that he could not attend a meeting of the Supreme Council that was due to take place in London the following month, when a sub-committee was to be founded to consider the idea of launching an amateur athletics organisation. Consequently P.N. Fitzgerald, Nally's closest friend on the Supreme Council, was appointed in charge of the committee. The other members of the committee were Patrick Hoctor, an intelligent 22-year-old draper's assistant from a relatively wealthy background

35 *Irishman*, 22 Dec. 1883.   36 Tom Donohue, 'The Crossmolina Conspiracy 1880–84', *North Mayo Historical and Archaeological Society Journal*, 1 (1985), 18–21.   37 *United Ireland*, 7 Nov. 1885 (speech of Parnell at Castlebar).   38 *Special Commission Report*, vol. 7, 6, 97 (evidence of Parnell).   39 Louisa Nally to author.

who operated his own vibrant branch of the YIS in Newport, Co. Tipperary, James Menton, a solicitor's clerk from Wicklow town, and Jim Boland, a native of Manchester, Dublin corporation foreman and formidable hurler, who was a very popular figure in the Dublin IRB. Fitzgerald's committee does not appear to have accomplished much during the remainder of the year, other than winning support for the plan from James O'Connor's *Irishman* and Michael Cusack (who preferred to be known as 'Citizen Cusack'), an influential journalist, athlete and former IRB man, who had also been a close friend of Nally's and shared his desire to form a nationalist amateur athletics association.[40]

By the beginning of 1884, there were two principal channels of republican propaganda in operation and the most influential of these remained Devoy's *Irish Nation*, which was still read by members of the IRB. Extracts of INLA pamphlets were frequently reprinted in the *Irish Nation*. These argued that, in Ireland, 'nationalists are the only real constitutionalists' as they believed governments 'should be controlled by the governed'. Those opposed to this republican definition of constitutional politics were portrayed as 'interested supporters of an absolutely despotic system'.[41] In his lecture tours for the INLA, Alec Sullivan emphasized this point by arguing that 'in all modern countries', it was recognized that governments should 'endure or perish' depending upon the degree to which they satisfied the public that they were exercising 'judicious collection and application of public revenue'. In the United Kingdom, however, ever since 1862, no account of the expenditure of Irish revenue was published by the British government, not least (so Sullivan believed) because it was afraid of the possibility of a growth in Irish nationalism. That year, he noted, one half was spent in support of the imperial army, less than one-fourteenth was spent on education and the remainder was only used to pay off some interest on the imperial debt, and 'we may reasonably assume that the same proportions exist in the application of Irish taxes now'. Noting that 'for grievances far less than these our fathers resorted to revolution and drove out the British crown', Sullivan believed nobody could deny that 'the right of the British crown in Ireland depends wholly on the arms by which it maintains itself there' and thus 'were it in their power to do so, the people would be perfectly justified in its expulsion', for it 'prevents the Irish people from actualizing the theory of government which is settled in the intelligence of the Irish people' and 'if history teaches one truth clearly, it is that no people are well governed except by themselves'.[42]

The *Irish Nation* also advertised the INLA lecture tours of Thomas Brennan, who criticized the National League in Ireland for acting only as a support body for Westminster politicians. He believed it should be doing what

---

40 W.F. Mandle, 'The IRB and the beginnings of the GAA', *IHS*, 20 (1977), 418–38. 41 *Irish Nation* (New York), 16 Feb. 1884 (extracts from INLA pamphlet, *What is Castle government?*). 42 *Irish Nation* (New York), 2 Aug. 1884.

the Land League had done: to pay 'sole allegiance to the sovereign will of the people'. Brennan believed that so long as Irishmen were 'counselled to place chief reliance on themselves and not on the men in the House of Commons; to depend on their own activity and organization', it was inevitable that they would become 'content with nothing less than the national sovereignty of our country', whereby 'Irish intellect shall mould Irish law', and would desire to establish a republic, 'the most perfect of all forms of government'. If the republican example of the Land League continued to be followed in Ireland, Brennan believed that ultimately it would not matter if the Irish Party 'from Parnell down, were to pass away tomorrow', for 'the movement itself will remain and work its way in triumph … It is a movement of principles and ideas.' Brennan, however, also felt that the Parnellite movement was assisting the republican cause in one important respect, namely by seeking to improve people's material welfare and educational opportunities, for 'people who are steeped to the lips in social superstitions, who are constantly striving to keep famine from the door, cannot be expected to cultivate a high patriotism.'[43] This later view was not generally shared by the IRB, or, at least, it refused to admit that this was the case. The Irish Party was dependent on the British government to implement any reforms and therefore the IRB refused to encourage people to support it. Most of all, the IRB was obsessed with the duplicity of the propaganda of the 'home rule' press. John O'Leary's complaint during 1884 that the public's acceptance of the emotionally nationalist, but politically loyalist, editorial policies of the Parnellite press 'all but too clearly shows' that the vast majority of Irishmen lacked 'that sort of education that tends to make a nation free' was a typical IRB argument.[44] Republicans often spoke as if the press alone was the great perpetrator of all Irish political evils[45] – a rather naïve attitude that never quite left the organization.

The other principal channel of republican propaganda in operation during 1884, apart from the *Irish Nation*, emanated from the work of the Dublin YIS, which launched a movement commemorating deceased Irish rebels. This propaganda was generally prioritized at the *expense* of the IRB's clandestine activities because the Dublin IRB leadership was particularly concerned at this time about the endemic disorder in its ranks in the wake of the Phoenix Park murders and the trial and execution of the 'Invincibles'.[46]

A special curfew was in operation in Dublin during 1882–3 whereby the DMP had the right to arrest anyone on the streets of the city after 6 p.m. if they could not prove they were on legitimate business, a law which James

43 Ibid., 26 Jan., 16 Feb. 1884 (Brennan's lecture tour).   44 O'Leary to *Freeman's Journal*, 14 June 1884.   45 The greatest single example of this is Tynan, *Irish national invincibles*, passim. 46 These events prompted Jack Sullivan and the imprisoned James Mullet, and his brother Joseph, to make statements to the police to prevent life-threatening sentences being brought against them for their supposed connections with the 'Invincibles', but they generally gave no information about anyone in the IRB except themselves. NAI, CSB B files, nos. 1 & 198. James Mullet was imprisoned until 1891, Joseph until 1893, Sullivan was imprisoned only briefly.

[handwritten margin note: NO GOOD EDUCATION! So not enough nationalist support in Ireland]

O'Connor believed was turning Ireland's fair city into nothing less than 'the devil's place to live'.[47] The general community's fear of arrest was enhanced by the fact that, during the 'Invincible' trials, the DMP, with the assistance of the royal marines, carried out about a dozen raids upon public houses in the poorer quarters of the city, taking down the names of *all* present and adding these names to their 'suspects' lists, just as it had done following the suspension of Habeas Corpus in 1866.[48] For many ordinary people, this helped to make the imprisoned 'Invincibles' a symbol of government oppression, just as IRB leaders had been turned into such symbols following the mass arrests and suppression of the NBSP during 1866–8. What the prisoners stood for politically was not necessarily the public's concern.

Violence on the streets was quite frequent ever since a riot took place following the suppression of the Land League and the arrest of all its leaders in October 1881.[49] While the determination of Carey's gang to do anything to escape the noose accentuated this trend, it occurred mostly because of the Dublin working classes' great hatred for anyone suspected of being willing to work with the police. Rowdy mobs, in which the police believed the IRB was not involved, boycotted or physically attacked various innocent individuals. Some people (often wives of imprisoned men) became informants to save themselves from having to enter the workhouse, while cranks, who had nothing to do with any political organization, wrote threatening letters to intimidate the police or jury members.[50] On the morning Joe Brady was hanged, five thousand people, many singing the Manchester-martyrs anthem 'God save Ireland' (which was now being called the 'Irish national anthem' by *United Ireland*) gathered around Kilmainham jail, prompting the DMP to call for the army's protection in case of disturbances.[51] Public collections, supported by *United Ireland*, were made for the families of executed, or imprisoned, men.[52] The trial and execution of a Donegal labourer Patrick O'Donnell for assassinating James Carey on a boat off the coast of South Africa led to protest demonstrations in Dublin, as well as London.[53] The arrest, imprisonment, trial and execution of Joseph Poole (whose impoverished brother-in-law William Lamie informed and testified against him) in December 1883 on the charge of shooting an informer in July 1882, served to demonize secret societies in the Dublin public mind almost as much as Carey's

47 *Irishman*, 25 Nov. 1882; *DPB*, vol. 2, 231 (O'Connor to Devoy, 7 Dec. 1883). 48 NAI, DMP files, carton 1, report of Chief Supt. Corr (and attached reports), 13 Mar. 1883; Takagami, 'Dublin Fenians', 70, 193, 207. 49 NAI, CSORP, 1881/35366. 50 *Irishman*, 25 Nov. 1882; NAI, CSORP 1883/806, 1883/7163, 1884/9803; DMP files, carton 1, Supt. Mallon, 3 Aug., 17 July, 16 Oct., 16–7 Nov. 1883; DMP files, carton 5, Chief Supt. John Mallon, 12 June 1884, attached to Report 1434, dated 15 May 1889. 51 NAI, CSORP 1883/13980. 52 DMP files, carton 1, Supt. Mallon, 3 Aug., 17 July, 16 Oct., 16–7 Nov. 1883. 53 *Irishman*, 22 Dec. 1883. In Irish-America, an unsuccessful appeal was made to the American government to defend O'Donnell on the grounds of his (possibly genuine) American citizenship. J.P. O'Grady, *Irish-Americans and Anglo-American relations, 1880–88* (1976), 191–4; *DPB*, vol. 2, 229–30.

actions, for most people in Dublin believed (correctly, as Chief Superintendent Mallon later admitted in private)[54] that Poole was innocent of this crime; a fact that eventually forced both Parnell and William O'Brien to protest Poole's innocence in the House of Commons, a year after his death.[55]

Against this backdrop, Fred Allan, who was more than familiar with all the problems facing the Dublin IRB,[56] sought to focus the Dublin republicans' attention upon the YIS and, in particular, a subsidiary organization to the YIS he founded called the 'National Monuments Committee' (NMC), which was designed to raise money to erect monuments over the graves of deceased patriots; the poet James Clarence Mangan being a popular choice. The first priority of the NMC was to erect a large monument over the 'Fenian plot' in Glasnevin Cemetery (where T.B. McManus, John O'Mahony and others were buried); an objective the IRB had held for several years, particularly in Dublin itself.[57] Branches of the NMC were soon set up for this purpose through the medium of local branches of the YIS. Michael McGinn, a baker, Tyrone IRB leader since the early 1870s and passive supporter of the National League, formed a branch in Omagh; John Torley formed a branch, in Glasgow, and republicans in Clare and Tipperary did likewise. John O'Leary immediately wrote from Paris declaring his support for this new initiative while John Devoy advertised for the committee in the *Irish Nation* at Allan's request.[58] The NMC never became a large organization or one with a high public profile, since the middle classes always refused to give it any financial support, but it would long outlive the YIS, eventually becoming a parent body of the 'National Graves Association' in 1926.

54 NAI, CSB files, carton 1, 860/s, Chief Supt. Mallon, 8 July 1890. Mallon noted that the police had insisted on Poole's conviction, not because they believed he had murdered John Kenny (the crime for which he was executed), but because an 'Old Guard' circle reputedly under Poole's command was believed to have been responsible for the death of a policeman in November 1882, when armed DMP detectives (acting upon the orders of a nervous and inexperienced officer, set out to catch the 'Invincibles') opened fire on a crowd of people on Middle Abbey Street late on a Saturday night, when one was seen with a revolver in his jacket. The police opened fire first, resulted in a shooting spree that left one policeman and one reputed member of the 'Old Guard' dead. In his speech from the dock, Poole, a carpenter from Gardiner Street, protested his innocence, stated he had been in the IRB since the age of eighteen and was 'proud to go the scaffold for being a member of the Irish Republican Brotherhood'. He emphasized that 'our objects are not for murder' and cried 'three cheers for the Irish Republic and to hell with English tyranny.' *Irishman*, 22 Dec. 1883. 55 *United Ireland*, 29 Nov. 1884. 56 Fred Allan, 'Behind prison bars', *Irish Weekly Independent*, 28 Apr. to 4 Aug. 1894. 57 This work began when James Carey and others founded the 'Stephen O'Donoghue Memorial Committee' in 1869. *Irishman*, 27 Nov. 1869. Stephen O'Donoghue was an IRB man and the only figure who was killed during the attempted rising in Tallaght in March 1867. After John O'Mahony was buried alongside T.B. McManus in 1877, this committee amalgamated with another committee, set up by Patrick Egan and others, to erect a monument for O'Mahony. Advertisements for the 'Stephen O'Donoghue and John O'Mahony Memorial Committee' appeared occasionally in the *Irishman* from 1877–81. 58 NLI, Minute book of YIS, MS 16095, Nov. 1883-May 1884; NAI, DMP files, carton 4, Report of Supt. Reddy, 24 Nov. 1883; O'Leary to *Irishman*, 1 Dec. 1883; *DPB*, vol. 2, 221; *Irish Nation* (New York), 29 Nov. 1884.

At the same time as the NMC was launched as a focus for the passions of the Dublin 'rank and file', the IRB began to push for the creation of a federation of all branches of the YIS under the central leadership of the Dublin branch. During the spring of 1884, new branches of the YIS were established in Galway, Limerick and Dundalk, their founders being IRB centres,[59] while the Dublin branch began to focus its members' attention more upon Irish public life.

By the spring of 1884, it was well known that Gladstone intended introducing a new franchise bill, which would enfranchise roughly half the adult male population in the United Kingdom and, in the process, at least triple the franchise in Ireland. This led the Parnellite press to argue, or to profess to hope (unrealistically), that if the English working class was enfranchised it might persuade English MPs to create an Irish parliament. However, in conjunction with John Clancy, a Sligo-born publican and the sole IRB man on Dublin City Council, the Dublin YIS emphasized its belief that any attempt by Irishmen to form 'an alliance with the English democracy' could not be 'conducive to the welfare of Irish nationality', and, 'that anything short of universal suffrage is inconsistent with true liberty'.[60] Subsequently, to commemorate the fourth of July, the Dublin YIS drafted a resolution, 'to be presented to the presidents of the American and French Republics', emphasizing the society's wish 'in unison with the American and French Republics' (both of which had implemented universal male suffrage)

> To offer a humble tribute to the memories of the men who, in these countries, struck the first great blow at tyrannical institutions in the new and old worlds, thereby placing upon perpetual record examples in principle and action to peoples struggling against monarchical power.[61]

During 1884, Fred Allan championed women's rights before the Dublin YIS, most notably the right to receive higher education (which would not be allowed in the UK for many years to come), while Michael Seery, a 20-year-old commercial traveller and athlete from Dublin who soon became an IRB leader, spoke in favour of the traditional IRB demand for 'the elimination of all class distinctions' from politics, emphasizing that, as a republican, he believed all classes in any political society should have an equal right to determine their country's future.[62] In April 1884, the Dublin YIS passed a

---

59 NLI, Minute book of YIS, MS 16095, Nov. 1883-May 1884. The men in question were Dick Troy (Limerick), a farmer, and James Johnston (Dundalk), a solicitor's clerk and son of Robert Johnston. For their IRB connections, see John Daly, 'Recollections of Fenians and Fenianism', *Irish Freedom*, Sept. 1912-Mar. 1913. Who exactly founded the Galway branch is unclear, but it was later led by J.P. McCarthy (1844–94), a solicitor from Loughrea and IRB arms agent. 60 NLI, Minute book of YIS, MS 16095, minutes for 7 Mar., 18 April 1884. 61 Ibid., minute for 4 July 1884. This resolution was drafted by Charles McCarthy Teeling, a brother-in-law of P.W. Nally & grandson of Bartholomew Teeling, as well as Fred Allan. 62 Ibid., minute for 8 and 29 Feb. 1884. The right of women to higher education would be

resolution (subsequently distributed to all members of Dublin City Hall) denouncing the corporation's 'toadyism' in sending a vote of condolence to Queen Victoria upon the death of a member of the British royal family.[63] This was a reaction to a recent debate in City Hall, when John Clancy argued that all city councillors should be there only 'to do civic duty' and not to 'take part in toadyism to any foreign prince'. In making this argument, Clancy said that he did not mean any personal disrespect to Queen Victoria, 'who is an estimable lady and a good mother', but he argued that there were thousands of Irish mothers 'just as good as she' who had been sent on the emigration boats and whom the corporation would never honour. He described this as a base denial of the reality of human equality. Clancy's speech won great cheers from some members of the general public who were present in the gallery, but his motion was not seconded and he left the hall so as not to be present when the mostly Parnellite city council voted unanimously in favour of the royalist resolution.[64] A few months later, Cork city appears to have elected its first republican mayor.[65]

Whenever opportunities were not available for republicans to advertise their political beliefs during 1883–4, they sometimes cynically promoted Davitt's land nationalization policy, not because they agreed with Davitt's ideas, but simply to break the Parnellite press' monopoly over Irish nationalist propaganda.[66] The most notable example of this occurred in Belfast, where John Duddy, a publican and IRB man, managed to get himself appointed as leader of the National League in the city and the league's principal promoter and organizer right across Ulster during 1883. Subsequently he championed Davitt's policy to ferment serious dissent within the National League in Ulster, an activity which Michael McGinn (who was briefly a member of the National League at this time) also appears to have promoted, with Robert Johnston's support.[67] Parnell, however, would have none of this, and shortly before the Ulster Convention of the National League was held in the summer of 1884, he ordered that the convention be postponed until Duddy was removed from his position of authority, which he duly was. Davitt, who evidently thought Duddy was sincere in championing his politics (it is possible that he was), recalled this event as evidence of Parnell's dislike for all 'staunch nationalists' who 'followed principles and not persons' and 'dared to think for themselves on the land question'.[68]

championed in Ireland later that decade by Alice Oldham, a lecturer in Alexandra College Dublin and sister of C.H. Oldham, a prominent figure in the Dublin YIS during 1885–6. **63** Ibid., minute for 18 April 1884.   **64** *Irish Nation* (New York), 26 Apr. 1884.   **65** Ibid., 6 Dec. 1884: 'Mr. John O'Connor, a Parnellite, has been elected lord mayor of Dublin and Mr. Madden, a Nationalist, mayor of Cork.' Madden was denounced by Dublin Castle and the Catholic hierarchy for being a 'Fenian'. Mandle, *GAA*, 20, 68.   **66** *DPB*, vol. 2, 264 (O'Kelly to Devoy).   **67** NAI, Police reports, ref. 3/715 carton 1, packet (iii), reports of E.G. Jenkinson, 5 Mar. and 9 Aug. 1884; Chief Inspector Townsend to E.G. Jenkinson, 16 Oct. 1884; DICS reports, carton 5 (Belfast Division), reports of D.I. Seddall, 2 Oct. 1889, 1 Apr. 1890 (report of IRB holding funeral for Duddy upon his death); NAI, British in Ireland microfilm, C.O.904/18/719.   **68** Davitt, *Fall of feudalism*, 502.

In October 1884, the Gaelic Athletics Association (GAA) was founded at a meeting in Thurles, Co. Tipperary. Over the previous seven to eight months, Michael Cusack, a member of the Dublin YIS, had appealed to various figures to act as patrons of the proposed association, including William O'Brien MP, the recently elected president of the Cork YIS,[69] Michael Davitt and surprisingly Justin McCarthy MP. No MP or clergyman was present at its inaugural meeting, however, when Maurice Davin, a great athlete and friend of Cusack and Nally, was appointed as its president. Its three secretaries were Cusack, J.W. Power, editor of the *Leinster Leader* (Naas) and a former vice-president of the Dublin YIS, and John McKay, a Belfastman and journalist with the *Cork Examiner* associated with the YIS in Cork and Belfast. Several Tipperary IRB activists well known in local popular politics, most notably Joseph K. Bracken, a building contractor and mason from Templemore, were also present. All agreed that the GAA should be a nationalist, yet non-political, sporting organization that, unlike the National League, would elect its own leaders. Essentially, the GAA was founded as a result of the social networks being built up in journalistic circles through republicans' efforts to federate branches of the YIS. During the first ten months of 1884, however, while the YIS and the GAA experiments began to take shape, the IRB's arms importation scheme and the revolutionary dimension to its politics were compromised and effectively defeated by E.G. Jenkinson and the Crime Special Branch.

In the summer of 1883, Jenkinson was informed by the British consulates in the United States that John Daly (who was last in Ireland in August 1882 when, at the Supreme Council's request, he delivered the graveside oration at the funeral of C.J. Kickham) was on his way to Britain. Consequently, a plain-clothes Special Branch detective was delegated by Jenkinson to follow Daly at all times upon his arrival. Since 1881, Daly had been embroiled in the quarrel between the Clan and the United Irishmen of America, despite the fact that the IRB understood that he was working only with his fellow Limerick-man and cousin, John McInerney of the *Irish Nation*, in ensuring that the untrustworthy Clan remained supportive of the IRB's arms importation scheme.[70] It is very probable that he was sent to Britain by Michael Boland. In August 1883, Daly was seen by Jenkinson's detective calling upon three men, John Torley in Glasgow, Robert Johnston in Belfast and Mark Ryan in London, thereby alerting the Special Branch to their importance in the IRB. He then

---

69 In this capacity, William O'Brien, a one-time deputy Munster IRB leader who was still on friendly terms with P.N. Fitzgerald, had also attended a public Dublin YIS event in Nov. 1883, when he praised Fred Allan's lecture on the Manchester martyrs, and then noted, ambiguously, that, on his return of London, he would 'tell our friends, the enemy [the British government], that, bad as they considered the [Parnellite] members of parliament, they might go farther and fare worse ... The next generation [?] of young fellows they will have to deal with will be persons to whom even the present representatives are reactionary.' *Irishman*, 1 Dec. 1883.
70 NAI, British in Ireland microfilm, C.O.904/17/130 (police biography of Daly).

settled in Birmingham where he stayed with James Egan, an old friend and generally inactive IRB man who, like Daly, was originally from Limerick city.[71]

Jenkinson was wholly committed to the policy of using *agents provocateur* in an attempt to convict republicans. The first *agent provocateur* used was 'Red' Jim McDermott, a former member of the Fenian Brotherhood in New York. In the spring of 1883, McDermott was able to persuade a handful of IRB men (mostly from the 'Old Guard' faction) in Cork and Liverpool to join a (bogus) dynamite plot, and he subsequently secured their arrest by betraying them.[72] It was possibly these Liverpool arrests which persuaded Dan O'Neill, a republican and local IRB centre, to offer his services to the government to help counteract the 'dynamite war'. O'Neill was 'approached' by Major Nicholas Gosselin,[73] Jenkinson's unofficial deputy who was based in Manchester. This infiltration of the Liverpool IRB organization alerted Jenkinson to the fact that arms were being smuggled into south Ulster by the IRB via the Liverpool–Newry ferry. Recently, while attempting to track down arms agents, a Special Branch detective had requested that the RIC charge twelve Crossmaglen men with conspiracy to murder. These men were sentenced to, on average, nine years' imprisonment, but local nationalists (backed up by Tim Healy MP) claimed that no conspiracy ever existed and that it was merely invented by Dublin Castle to incriminate various young men in the vicinity, thereby intimidating the whole nationalist community.[74]

Despite the assurances given to the Supreme Council by Michael Boland that the 'dynamite war' would cease, terrorist attacks continued to take place in London during late 1883 and early 1884, including several attempts to plant bombs (or instigate bomb scares) in the London Underground – actions that could have served no other purpose but to terrorize ordinary English civilians (nobody was killed as a result of the 'dynamite war') and arouse intense anti-Irish feeling. These events helped Jenkinson and Gosselin in persuading Dan O'Neill to betray John Daly, who had arrived in northern England to work with the IRB. In late March 1884, O'Neill asked Daly to deliver sealed cases to some associate of his in London. On 11 April, Daly was arrested in the outskirts of Liverpool as he was about to board the train to London and explosives were found in the cases he was carrying. As Daly was being arrested, the police raided the Birmingham home of James Egan (where Daly was staying) where explosives were allegedly found buried in Egan's garden as well as documents providing a total breakdown of IRB armaments,[75] indicating

71 Ibid. 72 Short, *Dynamite war*, 155–8. McDermott was a former papal brigade officer, educated at Clonliffe College, Dublin. 73 Christy Campbell, *Fenian fire* (2002), 139. 74 NAI, Police reports, 3/715 carton 1, packet (ii), two reports entitled 'Secret Societies in Armagh', dated 9 and 16 April 1883; Report of Inspector Law, 9 June 1883; E.G. Jenkinson to Major Gosselin, July 1884; Report of Special Branch agent Samuel Waters, 14 Sept. 1884. For Tim Healy's view of the 'Crossmaglen Conspiracy' see his article, 'A prison murder' (one of the Crossmaglen prisoners died during 1884, allegedly due to the prison authorities withholding medical treatment), reprinted *Irish Nation* (New York), 17 Apr. 1884. 75 NAI, British in Ireland microfilm, C.O.904/17/130 (police biography of Daly).

[handwritten annotation: extreme measures of the special branch ... IRB]

Daly's heavy involvement in the arms importation scheme (Egan would not have held any such documents). Daly and Egan were sentenced to life imprisonment on 11 August 1884 on the charge of being the leaders of the 'dynamite war', and the British government always denied that they were framed. In 1889, after a retired Birmingham police commissioner made a death-bed confession that Daly and Egan had been framed,[76] Gosselin was asked by the government to account for himself, but his emphatic protestations that Daly really was 'the most bloody minded fanatic since the days of Guy Fawkes' were accepted by the Tory cabinet at face value and the case was not reopened.[77] Surviving correspondence of Jenkinson to Earl Spencer, the crown's representative in Ireland and Jenkinson's former boss in India, proves beyond doubt, however, that Daly was framed:

> Yesterday I heard of the arrest of Daly by telegraph 'with the things on him' ... Our difficulty was to get the things passed to Daly and then to arrest him with the things on him, without throwing suspicion on our own informant.[78] Two plans missed fire – Daly was too suspicious – but the third plan succeeded.[79]

[handwritten annotation: UNCERTAIN!]

Within twenty-four hours of Daly's arrest, a more devastating blow was dealt to the IRB as a result of a series of events that no doubt also involved a serious element of treachery. Patrick Sweeney, who went under the alias 'Skeritt', was appointed by Boland as the treasurer of the 'Revolutionary Directory' during 1882–3 and was sent to London, where he was delegated to work with the IRB.[80] It was quite possibly Sweeney that Daly was asked to call upon by O'Neill in London. Since the summer of 1883, a Special Branch detective had been shadowing P.N. Fitzgerald as he travelled from Cork to Dublin, from Dublin to Belfast, from Belfast to Glasgow and, after a series of detours across England, eventually arriving in London sometime during late March 1884, where he stayed at Sweeney's home not far from London Bridge.[81] It seems clear that Sweeney was a British spy. During 1883 Jenkinson alerted the DMP to Fred Allan's role in the Dublin IRB after he had entered

76 NAI, Crime Branch Special files, 9156/s. 77 PRO (London), H.O.144/196, Gosselin to Matthews, 20 Jan. 1891. 78 Gosselin had three informants working on this case and closely related ones. Ibid. 79 Campbell, *Fenian fire*, quoted p.144. Campbell's source: British Library, Althorp papers, KS247, E.G. Jenkinson to Earl Spencer (lord lieutenant of Ireland), 12 Apr. 1884. 80 *DPB*, vol.2, 189–90, passim. British intelligence later referred to a man named John Sweeney (who also went under the alias Skeritt) as a suspected 'secretary of the IRB' during the early to mid 1880s. NAI, Crime Branch Special reports, carton 1, 533/s; NAI, British in Ireland microfilm collection, Memorandum on the IRB, C.O.904/16. That Sweeney was *not* secretary of the Supreme Council, however, is proven by John O'Connor's statement regarding his role as secretary of the Supreme Council since 1881 before a secret meeting of the Clan in September 1888 and the recollections of John Devoy. UCD, Desmond Ryan papers, L.A. 10/k/23 (1), 25–9, 31–2; John Devoy, 'The story of Clan na Gael', *Gaelic American* (Aug. 1923–June 1925). 81 *Irish Nation* (New York), 22 Nov. 1884 (report of trial of Fitzgerald).

into correspondence with and had recently stayed at the London home of 'an American agent named Sweeney'.[82] On 10 April 1884, shortly after leaving Sweeney's home, several members of the London CID (acting on Jenkinson's orders) surrounded Fitzgerald, wrestled him to the ground and forced him into a police vehicle, and he was driven off to Scotland Yard. Upon being searched, cryptic letters and bundles of money were found in his possession.[83] The following day, Sweeney posted to 'J.C. Percy' in Paris a large packet that had been brought to London by Fitzgerald, but acting on orders previously received from Jenkinson, the Royal Mail, on receiving this envelope, immediately sent it to the British Home Office.[84] When it was opened it was discovered that it contained four separate packets of IRB documents, providing progress reports on the condition of the IRB throughout the UK, reports evidently destined to be read at the next meeting of the Supreme Council. There can be little doubt that the reason why Special Branch decided to arrest Fitzgerald in this sudden manner, without even having a warrant, was because they had been somehow informed that a collection of important IRB documents was in his possession in London and, sensing a great opportunity, decided to act quickly. Sweeney's decision to post a large quantity of IRB documents to Paris via the Royal Mail made no sense: members of the Supreme Council always transported reports of this level of importance purely by hand, rather than through the British postal system, for the IRB was well aware that Dublin Castle and the Home Office always ordered that any letters posted by Irish political suspects should be opened by post office officials and copied.[85] As Fitzgerald was the chief travelling organizer of the IRB at the time, it was his duty to travel across the whole United Kingdom, collect the progress reports of all IRB circles, and then deliver these documents by hand to the IRB executive at the next meeting of the Supreme Council. Had Fitzgerald not been arrested, this is exactly what would have happened. Instead, due to Sweeney's actions, all the internal progress reports of the IRB were now in the hands of the British Home Office, who dubbed these documents the 'Paris Letters'.[86]

82 NAI, DMP files, carton 1, Report of E.G. Jenkinson, 29 Nov. 1883; NAI, British in Ireland microfilm collection, C.O.904/17/1. 83 *Irish Nation* (New York), 19 Apr. and 26 Apr. 1884. 84 At press reports of the ensuing trial of Fitzgerald, the police claimed that Sweeney attempted to claim the return of the envelope, but the Dead Letter Office told him there was no one of the name of Percy at the specified address in Paris and apparently indicated that the envelope was lost. *Irish Nation* (New York), 22 Nov. 1884. It is clear, however, that the envelope was never posted it the first place and that it was simply handed, on the orders of the Special Branch, to the Home Office. In 1888, in response to accusations by Michael Boland that several of his letters to O'Connor during 1884 went missing, O'Connor replied that he 'had no reason to doubt the safety of my address', indicating that these letters posted were never actually sent and were not meant by the IRB to be posted. UCD, Desmond Ryan papers, L.A. 10/k/23 (1), 25–9, 31–2. 85 Ryan, *Fenian memories*, 60. 86 Virtually nothing is known about Sweeney's activities after 1884, except that, during 1892, the Special Branch knew that he had just died in Australia; a country where all British spies and informers during the 1880s (including Patrick Delaney and Dan O'Neill) were sent once their usefulness expired. NAI,

Now that they had P.N. Fitzgerald in their custody, the police had to offer some reason to the press why he had been arrested without a warrant. The London CID sent a report to all the press agencies stating that Fitzgerald was a leading member of 'an Irish murder society' and was going to be tried for alleged involvement in an outrage that took place on a remote Sligo farm during 1881. When asked by *Freeman's Journal* journalists why Fitzgerald was not allowed to speak to them, the London CID stated that he could not be granted these privileges because he was ready to inform against his Sligo associates and thus needed government protection.[87] A similar ploy seems to have been used in Nally's case the previous year.[88] In due course, heavily surrounded by policemen, Fitzgerald was transferred from Scotland Yard to Dublin and thence to Sligo jail, without at any stage being allowed to speak to the press, a solicitor or a doctor.[89] As the trial regarding the Sligo outrage was not due to take place until November, Fitzgerald was held in Sligo jail for six months and only once was he able to get a message through to the press (through the medium of Dr. George Sigerson, a friend of O'Leary's who visited Fitzgerald in jail, ostensibly to give him a medical examination) to deny the rumour circulated by the police that he was an informer. Meanwhile Fitzgerald's wife Ellen instigated a public protest at her husband's treatment, as well as the way she was being treated by the police, for Special Branch detectives had called upon her more than once, stating that the only way she could save her husband from being sentenced to life-imprisonment or worse was by giving evidence for the crown in court. Two leading members of the Irish Party also protested in Westminster at Fitzgerald's treatment, namely William O'Brien and Thomas Sexton.[90]

At the same time as Daly and Fitzgerald were arrested, all the Clan's correspondence with John O'Connor stopped. As a result, O'Connor had no means of knowing when or where the next Clan convention, which he was due to attend as envoy of the IRB, was to be held.[91] Michael Boland did not want O'Connor present at this convention because he knew he would denounce the 'dynamite war' policy – a policy which Boland had led the Clan to believe had the full support of the IRB by making false claims in its internal circulars over the past eighteen months.[92] When O'Connor did visit America, he only managed to contact Boland with the help of Alec Sullivan, who asked Boland to call at his Chicago legal office where, to Boland's surprise, O'Connor was waiting for him. Boland told O'Connor that the 'Revolutionary Directory' had recently been dissolved, unilaterally, by the American wing and would never be re-established unless O'Connor authorized a false statement in the

British in Ireland microfilm, Memorandum on the IRB, C.O.904/16. 87 *Freeman's Journal*, 12 Apr. 1884. 88 *Irishman*, 22 Dec. 1883. 89 *Irish Nation* (New York), 3 May 1884; 10 May 1884. 90 Ibid., 10 May, 26 May 1884. 91 John Devoy, 'The story of Clan na Gael', *Gaelic American*, 10 Nov. 1923. 92 All these circulars were produced as evidence by the British spy, Henri Le Caron, at the Special Commission. *Special Commission Report*, vol. 4, pp 489–631; vol. 5, pp1–187 (evidence of Le Caron).

Revolutionary Directory's account book stating that $75,000 had been sent recently to the Supreme Council to carry out the 'dynamite war' policy. This, of course, O'Connor refused to do, whereupon Boland (who was undoubtedly in British pay) produced a revolver and threatened to shoot him if he did not do so. This prompted Sullivan, who remained present and was always armed with a revolver, to come to O'Connor's defence and forcibly eject Boland from the building.[93] Not surprisingly, shortly after this meeting, Sullivan resigned completely from the Clan (which, by this stage, he regretted ever having joined), while the distraught O'Connor turned immediately to the only Clan figure whom he knew he could trust completely, namely, John Devoy.

Devoy responded to O'Connor's appeal by issuing circulars to all Clan camps accusing the organization's current executive of being entirely corrupt and calling for the immediate establishment of an entirely new Clan executive that would be accountable to the Clan's 'rank and file' and, more importantly, the IRB Supreme Council. Very many Clan camps (now realizing that the IRB was opposed to the 'dynamite war') expressed strong support for this initiative of Devoy,[94] but they were expelled from the organization for doing so by the British spy, F.F. Millen, acting on Boland's direct orders.[95] Not only was Jenkinson dealing crushing blows to the IRB at this time, but he could now manipulate the Irish-American revolutionary movement any way he pleased, noting gleefully to Lord Spencer that he had been able to take advantage of the conflict between the IRB and the Clan caused by the 'dynamite war' to the fullest possible extent.[96]

While Jenkinson, a prominent Gladstonian Liberal, wreaked havoc on the clandestine world of Irish revolutionary politics, the Tories responded by mounting a new propaganda campaign, which effectively began in May 1884, when an article appeared in the *Contemporary Review* (London) entitled 'Ireland and the Franchise bill' under James Stephens's name, but its real author was Richard Pigott, a man now secretly in the pay of the Irish Loyal and Patriotic Union (ILPU), a Tory propaganda body.[97] The common trend in all this propaganda, which flooded the international press from April 1884 onwards, was to ascribe views and intentions to various 'Fenian' revolutionaries in Paris to fuel the fears of an ignorant British and Irish public. During 1884–5, these fictitious revolutionaries claimed they were behind the 'dynamite war', thereby helping to alienate the Irish public from the republican movement. Later, when it appeared that a Liberal government might

---

93 John Devoy, 'The story of Clan na Gael', *Gaelic American*, 10 Nov. 1923.   94 Ibid.
95 Statements of John O'Connor, M.J. Ryan, Michael Biggane, Rev. Betts, H.J. Connolly and E.P. Lynch at a secret Clan meeting in October 1888 reproduced in a lengthy Clan circular from 1889 which can be found in UCD, Desmond Ryan papers, L.A. 10/k/23 (1).
96 Campbell, *Fenian fire*, 154.   97 'James Stephens' (Richard Pigott), 'Ireland and the Franchise Bill', *Contemporary Review* (May 1884). This purpose of this article was to abet Tory criticisms' of Gladstone for introducing the franchise bill. Michael Davitt later found conclusive proof (when taking control of the deceased Pigott's papers in 1889–90) that Pigott wrote the article. Davitt, *Fall of feudalism*, 571.

become sympathetic to some form of 'home rule', the fictitious revolutionaries claimed (most spectacularly in a bogus statement of the IRB Supreme Council, published on the front page of the London *Times*)[98] that it was only because of the IRB 'dynamitards' and 'the much maligned Ribbonmen' that Parnell had his political power, and 'that great English statesman' Gladstone was now ready to bow down to the terrorists' demands. This was obviously designed to prompt the British voting public to adopt a more hard-line Tory stance.

Both Pigott and F.F. Millen[99] were closely associated with Chester Ives, an Englishman who edited the *Morning News* (Paris), which was the principal source of bogus reports that later flooded the international press, the second port of call invariably being the *London Standard*. Ives had long been an expert in such work. In July 1880, while working with Millen as the editor of the *New York Herald*, Ives published a bogus interview with a supposed 'Fenian' leader in Ireland, which claimed that Davitt had recently been expelled from the movement (which Millen knew to be essentially true)[100] and that he was going to be shot as a traitor, which was entirely false. The article nevertheless helped to ensure that Davitt (who felt deeply betrayed for having his IRB membership exposed) was alienated completely from the IRB, at least in the short term,[101] and, consequently, fought actively against its policy for the Land League;[102] unaware that, in so doing, he was effectively undermining his own influence in the league and boosting that of the MPs.

During 1884, John O'Leary protested bitterly about the Tories' propaganda campaign, noting that 'no human being who knows anything about the working of newspapers believes one word of all this', but 'unfortunately, most newspaper readers know nothing of their working and a large percentage of them are more or less inclined to believe anything they see in print':

> No Irishman here [in Paris] is safe. The other day they gravely announced that I 'was not a *practical* dynamitard.' This is certainly literally true, but seems to suggest a very ugly and stupid falsehood. I, for instance, do not believe that Mr. Ives, the editor of the *Morning News*, is a practical assassin, or a practical forger or a practical swindler ... but I

98 *Times* (London), 21 June 1886. This was also written by Pigott. Davitt, *Fall of feudalism*, 493.   99 Copies of the Pigott's forged letters, and letters Millen was writing claiming that Parnell told him he approved of the Phoenix Park murders, can be found at PRO (London), Sir Robert Anderson Papers, HO 144/1538 (1).   100 Millen had been removed from the Clan Military Board in June 1880 (*DPB*, vol.1, 534), a month after Davitt's demotion from the Supreme Council, which was an issue discussed in high Clan circles at that time. Davitt, however, had not actually been expelled completely from the movement.   101 During 1880 Davitt began denouncing figures like P.N. Fitzgerald, Charles Doran and James Mullet in letters to Devoy. Once he came to learn what was going on during the mid 1880s, however, he befriended such figures (especially Fitzgerald) once more, even though he followed a different politics. Davitt and Fitzgerald socialised regularly while the former was writing his *Fall of feudalism* book in the early 1900s.   102 *DPB*, vol.1, 546–9.

most strongly believe that he is earning his living by a very discreditable and disgusting trade.[103]

Most of Ives' articles were based upon tit-bits of information received from Carroll Tevis, a former French general and papal count who, while a British spy (he had also been in British pay while leading the Fenian Brotherhood into Canada during 1870), was made the accredited Parisian 'agent' of the United Irishmen of America by Patrick Sarsfield Cassidy in the spring of 1883,[104] a responsibility that, in practice, meant nothing. Together with Pigott and Stuart Stephens, a former British army captain in Africa who had been cashiered for drunkenness, Tevis attempted to acquire information from Eugene Davis and particularly Patrick Casey, two journalists of republican sympathies who had been organizing Parisian St Patrick's Day demonstrations since 1881.[105] Both Casey and Davis knew nothing about Irish revolutionary affairs except rumours, but they freely told stories and these were subsequently redrafted, evidently without their knowing, into sensational articles in the British press; articles that later became the basis of top-selling pieces of Tory nonsense such as *The Repeal of the Union Conspiracy, or Mr. Parnell and the IRB* (1886, written by Stuart Stephens)[106] and *Incipient Irish Revolution: an exposé of Fenianism today* (1889, author unknown).

This new style of 'Fenian fever' Tory propaganda in the British and Irish press was so prevalent that many contemporaries, as have some historians, believed that an Irish revolutionary movement existed in Paris during the 1880s. This was not the case.[107] Furthermore, it can be noted that the IRB Supreme Council was never *based* in Paris, or indeed anywhere else for that matter, for it existed only at those moments when its members were free to temporarily leave their employment and travel to *any* location that suited all concerned.[108] That some Supreme Council meetings were held in Paris between 1879 and 1891 (several others were held in Dublin, London, northern England, Rouen or Antwerp)[109] was due only for the sake of convenience. John O'Leary could not return to Ireland until his ticket-of-leave expired in 1885 (he did so at the first available opportunity), and John O'Connor lived in Paris because he had married a German-born lady living in Paris and had raised a non-English speaking daughter. However, O'Connor performed all his IRB duties in the UK, rather than in Paris, using various false names, disguises and his membership of the freemasons as a means of avoiding Special Branch surveillance.[110] If O'Connor kept records for the administration of the IRB

---

103 John O'Leary, 'Parisian *canards* [lies]', *Irish Nation* (New York), 28 June 1884.   104 For Tevis's career as a British spy, see Christy Campbell, *The Maharajah's box* (2000).   105 *Irishman*, 26 Mar. 1881.   106 Campbell, *Marahajah's box*, 110, 114. This republished the bogus Supreme Council document of the London *Times*, and was later taken to be genuine by G.A. Lyons (1879–1950), a friend of Leon O'Broin. O'Broin used it as a historical source in *Revolutionary underground* (1976), 41.   107 Julienne, 'La question Irlandaise' (1997), 331–8.   108 *DPB*, vol. 1, 384.   109 Ryan, *Fenian memories*, 64; NAI, Crime Branch Special files, carton 1, 533/s.   110 *Gaelic American*, 5 Dec. 1908 (obituary for O'Connor); *DPB*, vol. 2,

(which, it appears, were generally nothing more than figures and symbols, written in a cryptic short-hand) they were no doubt kept permanently in Paris, but that is all.[111]

The Tory propaganda war was a major irritant to the IRB, proving once again that it could never exercise any control over its public image. Its purpose, like the Liberals' espionage war, was to cripple the Irish revolutionary movement as much as possible before Parnell's party got a chance to take advantage of the franchise bill. Both the Tories and the Liberals feared that the IRB and various ex-Land League radicals might be able to force Parnell's party to adopt the abstentionist policy and thereby make a stand for Irish independence should it triumph at the next general election.[112] Consequently, the republican threat needed to be negated as much as possible before this general election could be held.

When P.N. Fitzgerald (together with nine Sligo suspects) was finally brought into the dock at Green Street Court House, Dublin on 5 November 1884, the crown could produce only three witnesses against him. One of these was the detective who had been following Fitzgerald's movements since August 1883, but he could not produce any incriminating evidence, other than questioning Fitzgerald's *bona fides* as a commercial traveller (he was a genuine one) and by claiming that he had raided a hotel room in which Fitzgerald was staying and found his case contained no samples, only a revolver and a prayer book. The other two witnesses were John Moran, a Sligo farmer who claimed that Fitzgerald was the Sligo leader of the 'Invincibles' (a claim that could not be proved, for obvious reasons), and Patrick Delaney, a man who had testified against the Dublin 'Invincibles' and who was now let out of prison for the day, having been offered his release if he could help to convict Fitzgerald. The charge that Fitzgerald was involved in a Sligo murder or 'Invincible' conspiracy could not be taken seriously. Consequently, Delaney was the principal witness against the IRB leader and his evidence, combined with the 'Paris Letters' and a handful of cryptic letters found on Fitzgerald during his arrest, were used against him. One of the latter (which Fitzgerald had evidently intended to be distributed to a subordinate in the IRB) clearly indicates that the Supreme Council was having great difficulty in continuing its arms importation scheme and maintaining discipline over its ranks, no doubt as a result of a growing paranoia and mutual distrust in the organization brought about by the numerous arms seizures, arrests, betrayals and hangings that had taken place since the winter of 1881–2:

> Please forward me a receipt for £20 which I have paid to you … You are
> as fickle at times as a London Fog. In your last, you say to me at present

375. 111 When O'Connor died, the Clan was concerned about the whereabouts of certain documents (*DPB*, vol.2, 372–3), but this concern related to affairs during the 1900s (which are explained in chapter 10) and had nothing to do with affairs during the 1880s. 112 Gladstone's views are quoted in O'Brien, *Parnell and his party*, 162; Campbell, *Fenian fire*, 185.

you will, or would, not advise forwarding grain[113] to the city by the hill [Cork]. And now you tell me you have written for final ... Such business can't be done by post; try and remember what you are asked to do ... Rest easy on this score and I will attend to the matter. You will, therefore, relieve your mind and your pen entirely in this regard. If you fit in, I will give you timely summons ... I asked you not to call on, or see, or meet, or consort, or recontre etc. Stock, especially either of K[ynock] and Co's gents at London.[114]

Accidentally you meet me if there and, as if instigated by the devil and without the fear of God in your heart, you arrange to meet the one. God knows 'tis beautiful. You could not be alone – no, not for one week – no, not if it were to be the means of getting you to be alone for perhaps a year, or two, or ten, or twenty, and others as well. You will say somebody must run risks and do *you*, in order to prove your own argument, run these risks and make others too? I asked you for your address. I did not ask you whether the place was quiet or old fashioned, or hoppy or stoppy. Face the music. Tell me where you are stopping or don't. I should be most happy to learn that you were as careful about yourself as you advise in Kemston's case. Talk about running risks, why it strikes me that you have been looking our most carefully when and where you can do most in that line. Naturally you won't see this in the same light as I do ... As you won't keep away from people I spoke about, I have written them to keep away from you. If this won't be done, there will be bloody noses. Rest and be thankful. Your Uncle John.[115]

Some of the 'Paris Letters' were produced before the court and were used, in conjunction with Delaney's evidence, to indicate that Fitzgerald was a 'Fenian' and thus potentially guilty of treason-felony. During the five-day trial, however, Delaney's evidence was deemed too unreliable to convict Fitzgerald of any charge, due to Delaney's criminal record (he was a former highway robber) and the fact he perjured himself at one stage. Meanwhile the 'Paris Letters' were eventually deemed to be too unsuitable as evidence to be presented before the court, owing to their highly cryptic nature. Dublin Castle no doubt knew all along that neither Delaney nor the highly cryptic 'Paris Letters' would be sufficient to convict Fitzgerald. Rather, his lengthy imprisonment and trial was intended to justify the strange circumstances under which he was arrested in April and, more specifically, to spread a fear within the IRB that their chief organizer might have broken down under constant police interrogation during the past six months and, in the process, compromised the entire organization.

113 Probably either subscriptions or arms.   114 These are arms dealers. A different part of the letter refers to another arms firm, Pollards.   115 Letter read at Fitzgerald's trial, reproduced *Irish Nation* (New York), 22 Nov. 1884.

Fitzgerald was released on 10 November. Shortly afterwards, to express sympathy with his ordeal, a public testimonial was established for him by the Cork Chamber of Commerce, to which seven Cork city councillors, seven Parnellite members of parliament and the lord mayors of Cork, Dublin and Limerick subscribed.[116] The leaders of the Cork City IRB, a couple of whom were also city councillors, presented its own testimonial and address to Fitzgerald at a protest demonstration it organized in the city, which was very well supported by the local population. Fitzgerald was too ill to speak at this demonstration, though J.C. Flynn of the IRB denounced the Special Branch at length for trying to 'consign him [Fitzgerald] to a doom worse than death', and prophesized (incorrectly) that 'Jenkinson and his spy system are doomed'.[117] The reality, however, was that the IRB was losing badly the amoral battle of wits with the elusive and formidable enemy that was the British secret service as a direct result of the latter's ability to manipulate the Clan, the IRB's nominal allies.

As Fred Allan had taken a prominent role in organizing P.N. Fitzgerald's defence and was already a target of Jenkinson's, the Special Branch ordered the DMP to raid the Allan's home on the North Strand in Dublin on 2 November, three days before Fitzgerald's trial began, presumably looking for more evidence. Allan, not realizing that he too was a target, was taken completely by surprise and was arrested immediately for possession of suspicious documents. He was held in prison for two weeks before being brought before the Northern Police Court in Dublin (a week after Fitzgerald's release), where preliminary hearings took place to test whether or not he could also be charged of the capital offence of treason felony.[118] The police had only one witness to testify against Allan, namely, a man who used to work with him during 1880 in the clerical department of the Great Northern Railway (Ireland) who claimed on examining the documents that several of the 'Paris Letters' were in Allan's handwriting. As the 'Paris Letters' had, by this time, been deemed too cryptic to be used as evidence in the trial of Fitzgerald, however, this evidence was dismissed, prompting Jenkinson himself (as there was no other possible witness against Allan) to take the stand and claim that one of the documents found in Allan's home was evidently an IRB constitution. Allan did not employ a lawyer to defend himself, but the *Freeman's Journal* hired Tim Healy MP to act in his defence, since Allan (the chief clerk in its advertising department, soon promoted to business manager) was one of its most promising young employees. Healy, then making his debut as a defence lawyer, was able to convince the jury that the mere possession of such a document by a journalist and researcher like Allan was insufficient

---

116 *Irish Nation* (New York), 13 Dec. 1884.   117 Ibid., 13 Dec. 1884. This demonstration took place on 18 November 1884.   118 *United Ireland*, 9, 15 and 22 Nov. 1884 (reports of arrest and trial of Allan).

evidence to press charges against him, least of all for treason-felony. As a result, the charges against him were not prosecuted and he was granted bail.[119]

Although the actual 'Paris Letters' have not survived, many of them were produced as evidence at Allan's trial. The terms used in the letters (such as 'grain', 'cows' and 'firms', as well as letters of the alphabet and numbers) meant nothing in a literal sense, but the crown prosecutors interpreted the ones in Allan's hand (no doubt correctly) to refer to the Leinster IRB organization and its resources. These indicate that, across eight of the ten counties in Leinster, the IRB had a total of 3,372 members, 428 rifles and between three and four hundred revolvers, indicating that the Leinster IRB organization was slightly stronger during 1884 than it had been during the days of the 'land war'. In Dublin, the IRB had 650 subscribing members (an increase of 75 members over the past five years, probably as a result of the existence of the YIS);[120] it had roughly 500 members in both Co. Louth (based mostly in Drogheda) and Co. Wexford (based mostly in Enniscorthy); 332 in Co. Kilkenny (based entirely in Kilkenny City); a similar-size membership in Co. Wicklow (confined mostly to the Bray and Rathdrum areas) and a following in rural north Kildare, as well as in Meath and Westmeath, but its following here was not very large: in Westmeath, for example, the IRB had only 147 members.[121] From Joseph Wall's information, Dublin Castle already knew that the weakness of the IRB in much of rural Leinster stemmed from the lack of 'travelling organizers' who would keep its members in regular communication with the movement's leadership. John Mallon believed these communications had been more frequent in the past because some of the Dublin IRB centres, hanged or imprisoned for their involvement in the 'Invincible' conspiracy, were natives of rural Leinster and used to keep in frequent contact with the IRB following in these locations. The rural Leinster IRB organization itself had also been partly compromised earlier that year, after the Special Branch informer 'Quentin' had told the RIC to carry out an arms raid upon the home of Stephen Delaney, a shop assistant and the IRB leader in Queen's County (Laois). Although no arms were found, an IRB circular was discovered, as well as letters which provided the police with the names of men who may have been IRB leaders in Queen's County, King's County (Offaly) and Carlow, most of whom were publicans.[122]

The effect of the setbacks the IRB suffered during 1884 was diverse. As John O'Connor recalled, the Supreme Council brought a complete and sudden halt to its arms importation scheme that year, due to the arrests of John Daly

119 *Irish Nation* (New York), 22 Nov. 1884 (report of trial of Fred Allan). 120 Police intelligence indicates that the 'Old Guard' IRB organization in Dublin, which was independent of the Supreme Council's authority, was of similar dimensions. NAI, CSORP 1880/3723; Fenian A files, no. 590 and 612; Takagami, 'Dublin Fenians', 331. 121 *Irish Nation* (New York), 22 Nov. 1884 (evidence produced at Allan's trial). 122 NAI, CSORP 1879/18042; British in Ireland microfilm, Colonial Office, Reel 4, Box 10, Secret Societies 1882–4, pp 181–3, 200–3, 209–20, 233–8.

and P.N. Fitzgerald, the imprisonment of P.W. Nally, the seizure of the 'Paris Letters' and the cessation of the Clan alliance – very disturbing events all of which took place within the space of just two weeks. Owing to the cessation of its alliance with the Clan, there was also a strong chance that its arms importation scheme could not be revived. The IRB knew that its rural 'rank and file' would soon react very negatively to this development, in particular, by withholding their subscriptions, thereby potentially bankrupting the organization. All it could do was attempt to limit these effects, while trying to deal with the uncomfortable reality that the chances of ever again reviving an arms importation scheme on a similar scale to that of 1879–84 were very slim.

The IRB's self-confidence must have been undermined greatly as a result of these setbacks, especially if one considers the fact that, since 1865, no leading member of the IRB had ever been arrested, let alone imprisoned, nor had so many IRB documents fallen into Dublin Castle's hands. From prison, John Daly wrote to Devoy expressing his belief that the IRB was finished for good.[123] John O'Leary, by comparison, felt that the IRB could still thrive, so long as it altered its political focus and did not allow itself to become embroiled in problems it could not solve. O'Leary did not know what to think of the 'dynamite war' and had no idea who caused it. He just hoped it would be short-lived, noting that he would 'begin to despair of our future if I did not believe that this was a mere passing craze – the Irish form of that general nihilistic movement which, in some shape or another, seems spreading everywhere at present'.[124] He was evidently very concerned, however, about the forces imperilling the IRB, and it is not a coincidence that he decided to give a lecture during the mid 1880s (subsequently published by the YIS, but very probably addressed originally to a purely IRB audience) in the IRB's troublespot of northern England specifically on the themes of the necessity of organizational discipline, and, not allowing unnecessary militaristic sentiments to emerge, for they could easily obscure political judgments or, more importantly, cause the movement to fall prey to dangerous and completely unnecessary vices:

> I have been constantly hearing … of the necessity of what is called deceiving the enemy. Well, of course, that may be right in a sense of war … but, in point of fact, we have little to do with that. We are not at war and, as a matter of fact, we seldom or ever deceive the enemy, which knows little and cares less about our small machiavellisms [this was a false

123 *DPB*, vol. 2, 244: 'It's damn hard, Jack, to think of the amount of traitors our business has produced, everywhere you turn, betrayed, betrayed. Parnell and his party betraying the nation for the grand living 'tis giving them, while we seem to produce nothing but Jim Careys. To have to live the rest of my life perhaps in a prison is very hard, but knowing I was handed over to England by one who stood over Kickham's grave with me [Dan O'Neill] is harder still.' O'Neill was later tracked down in Australia by an agent sent by John O'Connor. John Devoy, 'Jack Daly', *Gaelic American*, 15 Mar. 1924.   124 O'Leary to *Freeman's Journal*, 14 June 1884.

presumption]; but to my certain knowledge, we are constantly deceiving each other – saying to each other the things that are not, counter-combining, counter-plotting and of course, as a consequence, counteracting each other in many ways. I should have said nothing of this, if it were merely a thing of the past, but unfortunately all the forms of ugly activity enumerated are in the fullest operation at this very moment ... There may be no need of working towards war, as there seldom or ever is of talking about it ... I would mildly suggest, again in the words of Davis, that 'Not peace itself is safe but when the sword is sheathed by fighting men'.[125]

As the IRB did not know what was going on in the Clan, it had absolutely no means of knowing how the British secret service had manipulated events, and it is also evident that it did not know how exactly, or to what extent, its organ-ization in England had been compromised. These two forms of leverage would allow British intelligence to continue to deal crippling blows to the Irish revolutionary movement whenever it attempted to flex its muscles. To avert this danger, in subsequent years, the IRB purposely focused purely upon propagandistic work. Following O'Leary's advice, as a general rule, it avoided doing anything that might potentially bring it into conflict with the state or cause any of its members to risk imprisonment.

The Special Branch was delighted at its success in counteracting the IRB. Jenkinson boasted to the lord lieutenant (his former boss in India and the only man to whom he was prepared to reveal what he was doing) that he had seriously compromised the entire IRB organization in England through manipulating the 'dynamite war', as there was such 'a strong feeling against the dynamite policy' in the IRB that its continuance had led many to 'retire from the field altogether', owing to their refusal to have anything to do with the Irish-American extremists. Meanwhile, owing to the willingness of some English IRB men to become informers to prevent English lives from being endangered, 'in some places, the organization is almost under our management and control'. With this foothold established in England, and America, Jenkinson felt confident that 'in the IRB, nothing of importance [endangering national security] can be done we should not know of', for through having infiltrated the Clan and the IRB in England, advance warning of any threat-ening initiative originating in Ireland, as well as a means of compromising such initiatives, could be available.[126] Jenkinson also knew that exposing leading members of the IRB, by arresting them on circumstantial evidence and putting them on trial, was potentially even more valuable than actually convicting such men. This was because fears that the individual in question may have broken down under interrogation could either occur naturally, or,

125 John O'Leary, *What Irishmen should know and how Irishmen should feel* (1886), 10–2.
126 Campbell, *Fenian fire*, 154, 165 (Campbell's source: British Library, Althorp papers, KS 250, E.G. Jenkinson to Earl Spencer, 1 Mar. 1885).

in the more likely scenario, be actually created and perpetuated thereafter by whatever spies and informers the government *did* have. Hence after F.F. Millen was added to the Special Branch payroll during 1885 (quite probably having been transferred from the payroll of the British consulate in New York), Jenkinson stated to his secretaries that Millen would 'not be entitled to the full remuneration' (£2,500)[127] until more of the IRB leaders 'have been arrested and returned to trial', but noted that 'it is not part of the stipulation that a conviction should be obtained'.[128] The Special Branch believed that only if members of the IRB 'felt that there is no safety' and began to fear that their own leaders were betraying them that there would ever be a chance that the organization would 'fall to pieces'.[129] As it turned out, this strategy was not very successful, but it undoubtedly helped achieve some of its objectives, not least because widespread fears *already* existed in the IRB, as a result of the actions of men like James Carey and William Lamie.

Jenkinson's strategy had proved to be very potent during 1883–4, but his policy of abetting the 'dynamite war' ultimately backfired on himself. Although most Irish-American dynamite teams of the mid 1880s were either created by *agents provocateurs* or involved spies, a couple of them did not. One of these made a partly successful effort in May 1884 to blow up the offices of the recently established London office of the Crime Special Branch (known as the Special Irish Branch), in the process destroying much of its records.[130] This did not concern the government very much, but on 23 January 1885, another dynamite team from Philadelphia (led by Luke Dillon, then wavering between support for Boland and Devoy's wing of the Clan) caused minor explosions at Westminster (not during a parliamentary session) and the Tower of London. This event prompted Gladstone's cabinet to call an emergency meeting and demand that Jenkinson make an immediate report as to how this could possibly have happened.[131] Not coincidentally, this was something that never occurred after all the other 'dynamite war' episodes that had terrorized the general public in London. Jenkinson did not find the Clansmen responsible for the January 1885 bombings and thus, perhaps inevitably, he was forced to retire but not before being knighted by the queen. Jenkinson's 'Crime Special Branch Department' was closed down by the government the

127 In the 1880s, this was roughly six or seven times the annual salary of a bank manager or a lawyer. 128 Campbell, *Fenian fire*, quoted p. 169. Campbell's source: PRO (London), F.O.5/1932, Jenkinson memo, 30 May 1885. 129 Richard Hawkins, 'Government versus secret societies: the Parnell era' in T.D. Williams (ed.), *Secret societies in Ireland* (Dublin, 1973), quoted 105. 130 Short, *Dynamite war*, 184–6. 131 Short, *Dynamite war*, 211–12. Several historians have quoted as authoritative one of the pieces of information Jenkinson produced before the cabinet in January 1885, but this was false. This was a report supposedly read before the August 1884 convention of the Clan claiming that the IRB had 47,500 members (Short, *Dynamite war*, 211–12), but no IRB man actually attended this convention, while the rounded figures given for IRB membership in each province in Ireland did not correlate in *any* way with the information revealed at Allan's trial or with previous reports of the Supreme Council had made during the period of the 'land war'. It is probable that by 1884–5, the IRB's following had dropped from the 38,000 men it had in 1881.

following year, although it was revived six months later on a different basis by the Tories under the title the 'Crime Branch Special Department' which was directed by Major Gosselin in Manchester.[132]

On 6 December 1884, the British government introduced its 'Third Reform Act', which enfranchised half the adult male population of the United Kingdom and tripled the parliamentary franchise in Ireland. The municipal franchise, which was proportionally smaller in Ireland than in Britain, remained in same. After the passing of this act, tens of thousands of Irishmen were excited by the strong possibility of the first-ever landslide victory for men of Catholic-nationalistic sympathies in the majority of British parliamentary constituencies in Ireland and therefore enrolled *en masse* in the National League and subscribed to the Irish Party's coffers. Previously, the National League had not acquired many members in Ireland. Only halting efforts by some of its members to revive the land agitation, combined with the militant rhetoric of *United Ireland*, had generally served to sustain any political enthusiasm for the Parnellite movement during 1882–3. From the summer of 1884 onwards, however, its subscribing membership reached extraordinary heights. The IRB altered its propaganda accordingly.

In December 1883, the IRB president John O'Leary had written to the press stating that he had 'too much confidence in the rising manhood of Ireland' to believe that the majority of them would ever believe the irrational delusion, propagated by loose-principled men posing as Irish nationalists at Westminster, that Ireland could achieve its independence through an act of legislative reform by a British government.[133] From the summer of 1884 onwards, however, O'Leary was arguing in his letters to the press that, although he had not altered this opinion and, of course, would not 'while God grants me full possession of my faculties', since the majority of Irish public opinion was now seemingly prepared to support the Parnellite political enterprise, so long as that remained the case, all Irishmen of his way of political thinking had an obligation to recognize this fact and be tolerant of the Parnellites.[134] This is essentially what the IRB did in coming years. It continued to concentrate upon the YIS and the GAA and considered the possibility of reviving arms importation efforts or publishing a new journal, but it did not at any time openly criticize, or praise, the Irish Party. During 1884–5, most contemporaries believed that the shape of Irish politics would alter completely after the next general election. Many republicans were no doubt also fascinated by this possibility. Parnell had on more than one occasion intimated that he might be willing to adopt the abstentionist policy and although the IRB believed (by 1880) that Parnell did not have this intention, the question of what the Irish Party leader would or would not do *if* he won a clear majority of the Irish seats had yet to be decided.

132 The nature of the Crime Branch Special will be described in the next chapter.
133 *Irishman*, 1 Dec. 1883.   134 O'Leary to *Freeman's Journal*, 14 June 1884.

If a general attitude can be attributed to the IRB on the eve of Parnell's year of opportunity, it was no doubt similar to that of P.N. Fitzgerald, its chief travelling organizer. Prior to his release from prison on 10 November 1884, Fitzgerald had never spoken on a public platform but, now that arms importations had ceased, he became a fairly regular public speaker, particularly at republican commemorative events. He made his first speech on 25 November in the town where he grew up, Midleton, Co. Cork. As might be expected, he emphasized his belief that Ireland's future would eventually be worked out by the IRB, praised Mitchel and Tone's example, said that Irishmen should never be satisfied until Emmet's epitaph was written and argued that every policy adopted by Britain was designed to subjugate the Irish population and deny it its right to political freedom. For the most part, however, he spoke only about his hopes for the emergence of an Irish democracy:

> I firmly believe that the present generation will witness great changes in the political relations of this country … In Ireland, at present, we are arriving at a time when the forces of the future will compromise two parties – one I should designate as the party of progress, or the educated democracy; the other, the coalition party, comprising a combination of Whigs [Liberals][135] and Tories of every grade and religion, whom I would call the party of retrogression. Twixt those two powers all the political struggles of the country will lie. I will not insult your intelligence by asking you which party will ultimately be the governing power; educated, intelligent democracy battling for the rights of man will sweep all obstacles from its path … The guiding motive power of that party in Ireland, I need not tell you, my friends, is nationalism. No power of England can crush it; no persecutions or imprisonments can kill it. I will say nationalism – call it what name you please – till it [the IRB, presumably] has accomplished its mission, men will be found ready to dare and to do all for Irish liberty … Liberty is the right of all peoples, be they black, copper-coloured or white. God created all men equal and I believe he invested no people with the power or the right to subjugate others. The onward march of the party of progress is slowly cementing a common feeling of *brotherhood* amongst all classes of our people at present. From that common feeling of brotherhood, I look forward to great results in the near future … It is the duty of every man in the community to take an intelligent view of the affairs of his country, to teach lessons of practical patriotism and sow broadcast the seeds of Irish nationality … In spite of famine, emigration and political ignorance amongst the masses, this spirit of nationality is growing stronger and it only remains for the young men, such as I see around me today [IRB], to

135 He meant Liberals. Nineteenth-century Irish republicans always spoke of the Liberal Party as the Whig party to portray it as a retrogressive influence, and to deny its right to any claim to being liberal.

keep sowing the seeds of Irish nationality so that, by and by, we might
reap an abundant harvest ... and so that when the time comes when we
may be called on to stand up in defence of a principle, no Irishman need
hang his head for shame ... Keep spreading and sowing the doctrines of
pure nationality; I would ask you to be prudent, and in the words of a
Young Ireland poet I say to you: Be patient, oh! Be patient! For the germs
of mighty thought, must have their silent undergrowth, must underground be wrought; but as sure as there's a power that makes the grass
appear, our land shall with liberty, the blade-time shall be here.[136]

Over the next two years, for the first time, the politics of 'home rule' would
begin to take a definite and final shape. The role, or lack thereof, that the
republican movement was to play in the future of Irish political life was largely
determined too. Now that Gladstone had suppressed the democratic Land
League and the Special Branch had rendered the IRB impotent as a revolutionary underground, it was up to Parnell to decide whether he would make a
stand for an independent Ireland or else compromise with Gladstone. Most
contemporaries had no idea what he was going to do. However, as Parnell's
political career had essentially been saved by the terms of the 'Kilmainham
Treaty' of 1882, and as 'the squire of Avondale' had entered Irish politics not
least due to his fear of the IRB,[137] it was perhaps inevitable what choice he
would make.

136 *Irish Nation* (New York), 13 Dec. 1884 (speech of P.N. Fitzgerald).   137 J.H. Parnell,
C.S. Parnell (London, 1916), 127.

Republican propagandism and Parnell's opportunism: the redefinition of 'home rule', 1885–7

Following Fred Allan's release from prison in November 1884, the Dublin YIS organized a testimonial to him and unanimously elected John O'Leary as its president for the forthcoming year, now that his ticket-of-leave had expired and he could legally return to Ireland for the first time in twenty years. The first thing O'Leary did upon arriving in Dublin was to announce at a public YIS meeting at the Rotunda what he believed needed to be done. He stressed his belief that 'of all the revolutionary forces, education is still the greatest'. More importantly, as Irishmen's 'supply of the right sort of things to read is of the most limited kind', there was a clear need for the creation of a new literary-political movement of comparable merit to the Young Ireland movement of the 1840s. He believed that 'the Fenian movement did comparatively little for Irish literature and the Land League[1] one has done far less' and that this was the principal weakness of both: 'at nearly every step of both these movements, men gave constant evidence of the need they had to know more, in order to do more, and above all, to avoid doing much which they ought not to have done'.[2] O'Leary noted that he had not returned to Ireland to preach rebellion or to concentrate primarily on 'those thorny political paths where my footsteps have hitherto chiefly lain'. Instead he wanted to turn the YIS into a movement that would help improve the quality of Irish public life by reawakening Irishmen to their need for much greater debate upon political principles. He believed that 'in the Ireland of today', and 'among all classes, creeds and conditions of Irishmen', 'there is no right so steadily denied and the assertion of which is so severely punished' than 'the right to differ' and that this was creating great problems. O'Leary believed that there could never be political freedom in Ireland unless there was intellectual freedom, and, that complete freedom of expression must be allowed to all Irishmen, even the gentry. He did not criticize Parnell and the National League directly, but his argument was nevertheless a veiled criticism of the predominant trend in

---

1 In referring to the Land League in the present tense (over three years after its suppression), O'Leary may have been doing what many contemporary political commentators did, which was to refer mistakenly to the National League as the same organization as the Land League. It is unclear, however, whether or not this is what he meant. 2 O'Leary was criticized by many republicans for making this argument, none more so than by his old friend Denis Mulcahy. NLI, John O'Leary papers, MS 5926 (letters of Mulcahy to O'Leary, n.d., circa 1885–6). O'Leary's reasoning, however, was his awareness that much of the 'rank and file' of the IRB and the Land League were men who lacked sufficient education to have good judgment. This is also why IRB leaders sometimes spoke in a relatively, patronizing manner to

Parnellite propaganda since 1882 of denouncing all who did not completely support the policy of Parnell and his party as 'factionists'.[3]

Like most IRB men, O'Leary was completely ignorant of economics, a fact that his friend Sir Charles Gavan Duffy believed was his greatest failing, for while O'Leary could 'deliver ingenuous criticisms of whatever is being done', the lack of an economic dimension to his arguments meant that he could 'influence the current of affairs in no appreciable degree.'[4] O'Leary, however, was convinced that it would be possible to create the sort of public opinion he desired to see in Ireland 'if not at present, then at least in the future',[5] so long as there was greater freedom of debate in the country, the branches of the YIS federated and that those who promoted his political viewpoints (the IRB) did not engage in too much 'over-wise talk' or promote 'actively injurious controversy': 'failing to do so, we are little likely to get out of any of our old troubles and very likely to fall into new ones.'[6]

The IRB had some success during 1885 in spreading its political beliefs within the YIS and the GAA, but Parnell's party dominated Irish politics that year. One illustration of this was its success in winning over prominent IRB men to its ranks, a goal that was made much more possible because of the recent setbacks the republican movement had suffered.[7] Following P.N. Fitzgerald's release from prison in November 1884, Parnell (MP for Cork City) made it his business to 'talk to him … whenever I see him'. The two men soon became on 'personally friendly terms' but, as Parnell noted, they could not agree about political matters: 'he always tries to reason me out of the error of my ways, and I try to reason with him, and neither of us has any success.'[8] Although Parnell did not succeed in winning over Fitzgerald, he did win over two other Cork City IRB leaders, James Christopher Flynn (who had organized the IRB demonstration in honour of Fitzgerald in November 1884) and 'Long' John O'Connor, both of whom stood successfully as Irish Party candidates during 1885 and were evidently eager to leave the potentially dangerous underworld intrigues of the IRB far behind them. At his own admission, from January 1885 onwards, O'Connor became the Irish Party's chief instrument in Munster in persuading other republicans to follow his example, and he claimed to have succeeded in some 'illustrious cases'.[9] To encourage this trend of defections from the IRB, the Irish Party ran a radical general election campaign in 1885, during which the Parnellite movement deliberately presented itself not only as nationalistic, but as motivated by democratic, or republican, principles as well.

their followers. 3 Davitt, *Fall of feudalism*, chapter 38: 'the danger of uncrowned kings'. 4 NLI, John O'Leary papers, MS 5927, Duffy to O'Leary, 25 Apr. 1886. 5 O'Leary, *What Irishmen should know*, 11. 6 John O'Leary, *Young Ireland: the old and new* (1885). This is a copy of O'Leary's speech to the YIS on 19 January 1885 at a public meeting at the Rotunda, Dublin. 7 NAI, DMP files, carton 1, report Chief Commissioner Harrel, 15 Oct. 1885 (attached report of E.G. Jenkinson). 8 *Special Commission Report*, vol. 7, 276 (evidence of Parnell). 9 Ibid., vol. 10, 22–3 (evidence of 'Long' John O'Connor).

Parnell & nationalism

In Cork city on 21 January 1885, Parnell made what ultimately became his most famous political speech, although it was certainly not his most characteristic one. He argued that although 'we cannot, under the British constitution, ask for more than the restoration of Grattan's Parliament', 'no man has a right to fix the boundary to the march of a nation' and he stated that this was a cardinal belief of his party, which he claimed 'have never attempted to fix the *ne plus ultra* to the progress of Ireland's nationhood, and we never shall'. Mark Ryan recalled (and lamented) that many IRB men were influenced strongly by such pronouncements, made frequently on Parnellite platforms during 1885, and some became willing, to the dismay of the Supreme Council, to abandon the IRB and support the Irish Party, thinking it was now best placed to forward nationalists' interests.[10]

The first general Parnellite appeal for republicans' support occurred in April 1885, when Gladstone sent the Prince of Wales to Ireland in an attempt to win over the population. This plan could go ahead because Earl Spencer, the lord lieutenant, assured the cabinet on 23 March (ten days after he was informed by Jenkinson that the IRB threat had been effectively contained) that the 1882 crimes act could now be repealed. One year before, John Clancy of the IRB had been denounced by the Parnellite Dublin City Council for opposing a royalist resolution, but now the Prince of Wales' visit to Ireland was being described by at least a dozen Irish Party figures on platforms up and down the country as a piece of 'royal buffoonery' and a futile effort to restore the loyalty of Irishmen to the crown. This stance was supported by members of the corporations of Dublin, Cork, Limerick, Waterford, Clonmel, Kilkenny, Wexford and Drogheda, as well as 84 town commissions and 160 poor law boards, all of which boycotted the prince's visit,[11] possibly more as a simple act of obedience to the Irish Party's orders rather than to express any real identification with egalitarian, republican principles. Meanwhile in Dublin, William O'Brien MP, the editor of *United Ireland*, arranged private meetings with various local republicans, in an effort to persuade them to support the Irish Party. His most notable recruit was the 44-year-old John Clancy, who joined the National League and was soon elected sub-sheriff of Dublin, thereby making a republican the chief registrar of the parliamentary and municipal electorate of Ireland's principal city.[12] Similar appeals for republicans' support occurred in the provinces.[13] For example, in Gorey, Co. Wexford, William Redmond MP (while campaigning for his brother John for the local parliamentary seat) proclaimed that 'no Irish patriot' could justly refrain from supporting the Irish Party anymore because it really wanted Ireland to be no less politically free than the American Republic:

attempt the IRB into DKN party (Parnell)

10 Ryan, *Fenian memories*, 134. 11 Boyce & O'Day (eds.), *Ireland in transition, 1867–1921* (2004), 51; NAI, Land and National League Reports, cartons 2–3 (reports of MPs' speeches during spring 1885). 12 NAI, DMP files, carton 1, report Chief Commissioner Harrel, 15 Oct. 1885. 13 NAI, Land and National League reports, carton 3, speeches of J. Maher and T. McDermott, Kildare and Sligo town, May 1885.

> We want no kings or queens in this country any more, God knows! ...
> Irishmen can look forward to full freedom and prosperity in the future,
> to a form of government that will be democratic and that will be repub-
> lican, giving out fully and fair play to every citizen, rich and poor alike.
> We will not have kings. We will let the world know our movement is as
> democratic as it is republican.[14]

All IRB men who were won over to the Irish Party during 1885 professed,
while running for election, that they were joining a party that could advance
the cause of republicanism. In east Galway, Matthew Harris overcame his
lifelong strong prejudice against entering 'that English house' by accepting a
Parnellite nomination for parliament. In December 1880, as a Ballinasloe town
councillor, Harris had dismissed Irish Party calls for him to stand for
parliament, stating that 'I would be degrading myself as an Irishman if I
entered that House,' to the cheers of local nationalists.[15] By the autumn of
1885, however, Harris was arguing that every Irishman should be a member of
the National League and he emphasized that if he was about to enter 'the
citadel of the enemy', 'I do not go there for the purpose of assisting that
House' and he promised to withdraw and promote the abstentionist policy if
it were not possible to advance republicans' goals there in the near future:

> I shall not deviate a hair's breadth from principle ... I shall endeavour to
> bring about such a state of things in this country that, instead of men
> going beyond the Atlantic and using their intelligence to build up the
> American Republic, we will have a republic of our own. We will be able
> to build it up, so that no power on earth can ever pull it down again.[16]

The Parnellite endeavours to win republicans' support received a significant
boost as a result of a demonstration held in Mullinahone, Co. Tipperary, on
23 August 1885. This event was held to commemorate the third anniversary of
the death of Charles Kickham and to collect funds to erect a monument in his
memory in Tipperary town, the latter project being the initiative of P.N.
Fitzgerald, who was a friend of some Tipperary town councillors.[17] At a well-
attended meeting chaired by Fitzgerald, John O'Leary addressed the crowds
and during his speech he noted that, at least at present, it was clear that

> Mr Parnell is the choice of the Irish people and, as long as that is so, I
> think it is the duty of all Irishmen, even Irishmen of my way of thinking
> [IRB], to take heed that they throw no obstacle in the way of his carrying
> out the mandate with which he has been entrusted.

14 Ibid., carton 3, speech of William Redmond, 23 Aug 1885. 15 Ibid., carton 2, speech of
Harris, Ahaseragh, Co. Galway, 19 Dec. 1880. 16 Ibid., carton 2, speeches of Harris at
Athenry and Gurteen, 26 Oct 1885 and 29 Nov 1885. 17 *Cork Examiner*, 7 and 9 Oct. 1907
(obituary and report of funeral of P.N. Fitzgerald).

O'Leary's speech was intended as a profession of political neutrality, but within days of this event 'Long' John O'Connor cited these particular comments of O'Leary on National League platforms throughout Munster as evidence that republicans wanted everyone to support the Irish Party.[18] Like Harris and Parnell, O'Connor claimed that the Irish Party would be perfectly willing to 'stand aside' and 'leave the assertion of the independence of Ireland to other men' if their demand for 'national self-government' was refused at Westminster in the near future. In calling for all republicans to support the Irish Party, he also claimed that if a 'home rule bill' was ever passed, 'it will be beyond the power of any nation on earth' to rob Irishmen of their independence, and that if the British government ever attempted to do so, 'they will have to march over our dead bodies'.[19] However this claim, like that of Harris's, was very disingenuous, for the legal reality was that the British government could at any time unilaterally dissolve an Irish parliament established through an act of Westminster legislation, since no parliament has a right to bind succeeding parliaments; a fact that John O'Leary was reminded of during 1886 by James Bryce MP, the distinguished Belfast-born professor of civil law at Oxford and the Liberal under-secretary for foreign affairs, after O'Leary asked him whether or not the government intended to make any 'home rule' measure a permanent one.[20]

J.J. O'Kelly MP, who was a member of the central committee of the National League, was Parnell's closest personal friend in the Irish Party, excepting perhaps William O'Brien, and throughout 1885 he tried to influence the Irish Party's selection of candidates for the next general election, only to be very disappointed at the sort of candidates the party was choosing. O'Kelly still had many contacts with the IRB,[21] and a letter he wrote to John Devoy in September 1885 indicates that, at least within some sections of the Irish Party, the desire to win over republicans was motivated by more than mere political opportunism.[22] O'Kelly noted that, 'happy as outside appearances are', the Irish Party had 'to face serious difficulties under the surface' not least because the National League was coming under the control of the Catholic hierarchy ever since Parnell accepted its educational policy the previous autumn. Although the church's support was 'a source of great immediate strength for

church

18 Ibid., carton 3, O'Connor's speech at Newport, Co. Tipperary, 30 Aug 1885 (quoting O'Leary). Newport was the home of Patrick Hoctor's branch of the YIS, the centre of the Tipperary IRB organization. 19 Ibid. 20 NLI, John O'Leary papers, Ms 8001 (7), Bryce to O'Leary, 20 May 1886. Apart from the huge difference in the terms of the legislation, this, of course, was the major difference between the 'home rule' bills of 1886, 1893 and 1912 (which were the prerogative only of the British government) and the Anglo-Irish Treaty of 1921, for a treaty is by definition an agreement between two sovereign states that requires ratification by two national governments. The treaty, as such, could neither have been drafted nor come into existence were it not that the British government effectively recognized Dáil Eireann, albeit very reluctantly, when it entered into the treaty negotiations with the Irish government. 21 *DPB*, vol. 2, 142. 22 Another letter he wrote, dating from December 1885, indicates the same thing. *DPB*, vol. 2, 267.

the present' for the Irish Party at the polls, O'Kelly expressed serious doubts as to 'whether it will continue to be so in the future', for the bishops were forcing the National League to choose candidates for parliament who were not at all nationalists or men 'that can be depended on to lay the foundation of Irish self-government on a secure and lasting basis'. If more IRB men had been willing to enter the Irish Party, O'Kelly believed that this problem could have been averted and, therefore, he lamented that:

> The mistaken attitude [of refusing to run for parliament] taken up by the leading men representing your friends [IRB] in this country has thrown back an enormous political power into the hands of the Church Party … Should any evil result, your friends will be held largely responsible before history for the failure of a movement which, if allowed to develop rationally, promised to make a real and, what is better, a permanent revolution in Irish politics.

Like Devoy himself, O'Kelly believed that 'even should we [the Irish Party] fail ultimately the country will be in a better position than it ever was before to adopt any policy in replacement of parliamentary action that may seem good to the people. This fact must be clear to all men of intelligence, though it does not by any means seem clear to some men who ought to be intelligent [IRB]'.[23]

John O'Leary's rigid attitude to Westminster politics no doubt limited the possibility of many IRB men joining the Irish Party for, as Devoy noted, O'Leary was 'unalterably opposed … to nationalists entering the British parliament', even though 'he was very tolerant of men who held a different opinion, provided they were not Fenians [members of the IRB].'[24] The greatest barrier to O'Kelly, O'Brien and Parnell's strategy of trying to get republicans to join the Irish Party, however, was no doubt P.N. Fitzgerald, who exercised the single greatest influence in maintaining discipline within the organization in Ireland. Responding to widespread rumours that Parnell had asked him to stand for parliament, Fitzgerald told the Dublin YIS in November 1885 that he would have no problem with running as an Irish Party candidate only so long as it was understood that he would not take his seat if elected.[25] It is likely, therefore, that the chief reason why Parnell and Fitzgerald could not agree on political matters during 1885 was that Fitzgerald was only prepared to join the Irish Party and ready to encourage (or order) other IRB men to do so, if it committed itself officially to the abstentionist policy *prior* to the election, so it could impose terms upon the government when the election was over, but Parnell refused to do this.

---

23 *DPB*, 2, 264–6 (O'Kelly to Devoy, Sept. 1885). Devoy made this same argument, albeit not very convincingly, while attacking James Stephens, in *Irish Nation* (New York), 7 June 1884. 24 Devoy, *Recollections*, 283. 25 NLI, Minute book of Dublin YIS 1885–7, MS 19158, minute for 7 Nov. 1885 (meeting chaired by Fitzgerald).

One possible indication that P.N. Fitzgerald was actively trying to promote the abstentionist policy during 1885 was that the Mayo IRB persuaded the local National League not to support the Irish Party candidate for the local parliamentary seat and instead put forward the imprisoned P.W. Nally as an abstentionist candidate. This prompted Tim Harrington MP, the very authoritarian secretary of the National League, to call a special meeting in Castlebar, where Parnell, Dillon and O'Kelly pleaded directly with local nationalists to withdraw Nally's nomination. While all spoke very highly of Nally, they argued that every Irish county must be represented by a man who could sit and vote in parliament. John Dillon claimed to know that this was the wish of all Irish-American revolutionaries and Parnell said that if 'ninety honest Irishmen are returned to the English House of Commons' in the forthcoming election, he guaranteed that 'it will be the last time they will ever [need to] be returned there'.[26] The issue was not resolved, however, until a couple of weeks later, when Parnell persuaded J.F.X. O'Brien (an ex-IRB man formerly of Cork city, now a London tea merchant and business partner of W.H. O'Sullivan)[27] to stand as the Mayo Irish Party candidate. O'Brien, an 1849 rebel and former college lecturer in Louisiana, had not been a member of the IRB for thirteen years (though he remained a friend of Kickham) and it was well known that he had taken a leading role in the attempted rebellion in Cork in 1867. He told the Mayo people he would demand that Nally's case be reopened in parliament.[28] This satisfied the Mayo National League. Nally's nomination was withdrawn and O'Brien was duly elected, to the chagrin of Mayo IRB which, within two months, complained bitterly that the Irish Party was refusing to take up the Nally case (it never did), and made the begrudging argument that 'if the people of this country had worked as earnestly for true principles of liberty as they have worked to get relief measures', then they would not now be attempting simply to justify themselves in the eyes of English MPs but instead 'would, like men, be prepared to risk all to achieve their independence, or die for it.' Acting in line with O'Leary's policy, however, the Mayo IRB stated that it 'will not call for disunion' among Irishmen at the present time, but instead would 'prepare for any crisis.'[29]

---

26 NAI, Land and National League reports, carton 2, speech of Dillon (Castlebar, 3 Nov. 1885), carton 3, speech of Parnell (Castlebar, 3 Nov. 1885); *United Ireland*, 7 Nov. 1885. 27 Bowing to pressure from the Catholic hierarchy, the National League forced W.H. O'Sullivan not to stand for re-election in 1885. O'Sullivan was quite willing to do so, for he felt the Irish Party had become too focused upon British politics and he had always refused to move to London, spending all his life in his hometown of Kilmallock, Co. Limerick. He died in 1887, aged fifty-eight. *Freeman's Journal*, 28 Apr. 1887. Two other leading Irish MPs of the 1870s that had been forced to retire by Parnell were John O'Connor Power and P.J. Smyth. 28 NAI, Special Branch biographical report of J.F.X. O'Brien (this report can be found in a folder, misfiled in DICS reports, carton 3, containing Special Branch biographical reports of about half the members of the Irish Party compiled at the time of the Special Commission). 29 NAI, Land and National League reports, carton 2, speech of Richard Hastings, Louisburg, Co. Mayo, 10 Jan. 1886.

The last man to defect from the IRB during 1885 was Thomas Condon of Cashel, a Tipperary IRB leader who had stood alongside Fitzgerald and O'Leary at Mullinahone in August, but three months later (on the eve of the general election) was persuaded (probably by 'Long John')[30] to stand as a Parnellite. Condon, the founder of the *Tipperary Nationalist* and a future leader of the 'Plan of Campaign', promised his would-be constituents that he would be 'no shilly-shally, milk and water politician', as 'I believe in the principles of O'Donovan Rossa and John Mitchel' and would always be 'ready to adopt different tactics' (presumably the abstentionist policy) if the Irish Party failed to achieve independence in the near future.[31] Once Condon achieved parliamentary honours, however, he found himself not so eager to relinquish them and, like so many of the rising stars of the Irish Party of 1885, he ended up moving to London and becoming an insignificant backbencher, remaining on the Irish benches at Westminster for another thirty-three years.

Parnell made determined moves to enhance his control over the press during 1885, which was already substantial. Ever since 1882, *United Ireland* (now edited by Tim Healy as much as William O'Brien) had used semi-military nationalist rhetoric while championing Parnell to ensure that the radical image he acquired prior to the 'Kilmainham Treaty' never evaporated, despite the fact that he had long since abandoned the Land League policy, if he had ever supported it at all. Furthermore, as *United Ireland* was the fastest growing newspaper in the country, both the rapidly expanding provincial Irish press and the Catholic-Liberal national press (the *Freeman's Journal* and, to a lesser extent, the *Nation*) generally had to emulate its rhetorical example to prevent it from winning over their readership.[32]

The Parnellite press of the 1880s was characterized by fairly conventional reports and editorial columns on British parliamentary politics, but it also denounced Gladstone or celebrated him as Ireland's saviour depending upon the course of the week's events in British politics. Many articles were printed describing all Catholic priests as 'patriots' and many made bitter, satirical attacks upon the personnel of the Dublin Castle administration; the latter being a tactic which caused *United Ireland* and many recently established, provincial newspapers (which were often even more aggressive in their rhetoric) to be prosecuted and sued for libel several times during the 1880s.[33]

---

30 Around this time, O'Connor married a wealthy daughter of J.P. Leonard and began studying to be (and soon started practising as) a barrister in London, where he lived till his death in 1928. Devoy never liked him since he first met him in 1879 and considered him to be a true *Bel Ami* type character, though this was rather unfair. Devoy, 'Story of the Clan', *Gaelic American*, 15 Aug. 1923.   31 NAI, Special Branch biographical report on Thomas Condon (this report can be found in a folder, misfiled in DICS reports, carton 3, containing Special Branch biographical reports). Condon won P.J. Smyth's former seat.   32 James Loughlin, 'Constructing the political spectacle: Parnell, the press and national leadership 1879–86', in Boyce & O'Day (eds.), *Parnell in perspective* (1991), 220–34; S. Warwick Haller, *William O'Brien and the Irish land war* (1990), 50.   33 Warwick Haller, *William O'Brien*, 70–4; Legg, *Newspapers and nationalism*, 136–8, 168–9.

Thanks to T.P. O'Connor, the president of the INLGB who soon founded the *Star* and the *Sun*,[34] Parnell also had at his disposal the 'Irish News Agency',[35] which disseminated Irish Party pamphlets (usually written by the old liberal Justin McCarthy) in Britain, designed to win the Liberal party vote, just as similar pamphlets were issued in Ireland to appeal to the Irish Liberal constituency.

In April 1885, in his capacity as director of the Irish National Newspaper Company, Parnell shut down the *Irishman* and James O'Connor was made to join the *United Ireland* staff instead. During the same month, Devoy's *Irish Nation* collapsed due to bankruptcy, not least due to the costs of legal proceedings Devoy had foolishly brought against August Belmont, a New York banker who had seized Fenian Brotherhood funds in 1865. Over the previous six months, Alec Sullivan (who was eager to leave the Clan and formally left on 9 April 1885) had refused calls from Devoy to fund his dying paper. Instead he asked Devoy to repay him loans that he had made to the *Irish Nation* in the past.[36] As a result, the cantankerous Devoy blamed Sullivan *entirely* for the collapse of his paper and thereafter became one of his fiercest critics in Irish-American politics. Sullivan had actually withdrawn significantly from *Irish-American* politics after resigning as president of the INLA in August 1884 in favour of Patrick Egan, but he was a powerful 'boss-politician' in *American* politics in the mid-west by 1885; he had even secured some Republican nominations for the vice-presidency of the United States. However the fact that Sullivan had been the Clan president when Devoy last held any footing in the revolutionary organization (August 1881) led Devoy to believe that Sullivan was the mastermind behind *both* the public and secret Irish-American nationalist movements and was at the root of all the Clan's troubles since 1883–4. Some Clansmen (Democrat) who resented Sullivan's (Republican) status as the leading Irish-American politician in the United States gave lip service to this idea, but it was entirely false, and Devoy's subsequent controversial attempt to make Sullivan's personal integrity (or lack thereof) the main issue in the struggle between the two wings of the Clan only helped to cripple the movement further by inadvertently splitting it along class and party-political lines. The IRB was indifferent to and did not understand the Devoy-Sullivan quarrel, but the collapse of the *Irish Nation* was considered a serious loss, as its demise (as well as the *Irishman*) had left republicans without any journal to give voice to their opinions. Therefore, efforts

importance of printing

34 Unlike the modern-day tabloids, these were originally radical papers of a literary quality, but with a strong bias in favour of popular politics; a fact that ensured they were ridiculed by the *Times* and most English national papers. The agnostic O'Connor, who was opposed by the clergy but supported by republicans when running for Galway in 1880 (he won the seat), had an eye for various young literary talents, such as George Bernard Shaw, who was the first music critic of *The Star*. 35 This existed in Ireland as well and was operated by J.J. Clancy, MP for Dublin North. 36 *DPB*, vol. 2, 257–64; UCD, Desmond Ryan papers, L.A. 10/k/23 (1), statement of Sullivan.

were made by the IRB during the summer and autumn of 1885 to launch a new paper in conjunction with the YIS.

In June 1885 Patrick Hoctor, who now worked as a commercial traveller and was emerging as P.N. Fitzgerald's chief assistant in the Munster IRB, was appointed in charge of a YIS subcommittee, the purpose of which was to federate all branches of the YIS under the direction of the Dublin branch. This initiative was set back because the two other leading YIS branches in the country, those of Cork and Belfast, were effectively governed by Parnellites (William O'Brien MP and Michael McCartan, a Newry-born Catholic businessman soon to be an MP) who did not care to have their societies affiliated with John O'Leary's branch in Dublin. For this reason, it seems the proposed federation never came about, even though the Cork YIS would later boycott a public lecture given by Justin McCarthy, the vice-president of the Irish Party, on the grounds that he was not a nationalist.[37] P.N. Fitzgerald did not attend the Cork YIS frequently, as he was essentially not a literary man and was more preoccupied with the GAA. It was on his initiative, however, that a Dublin YIS meeting was held in November 1885, under his own chairmanship, to discuss the newspaper idea. J.K. Bracken (a building-contractor, IRB man and GAA founder from Tipperary) and Patrick Hoctor (who had recently established the first-ever GAA clubs in Clare, as well as some clubs in Tipperary)[38] called for a new national newspaper to be established, which would advocate 'the principles which have been inherited from the Young Ireland leaders' and be independent of the Parnellite movement. Not surprisingly, all the IRB men in the Dublin YIS supported the idea, but most non-IRB members of the society felt there was no need for such a paper and that the existing Parnellite press was truly representative of Irish nationalist public opinion.[39] The poor timing for the introduction of this proposal (made on the eve of the 1885 general election) may well explain why it won little support, but it did receive enthusiastic support from one influential member of the society. This was T.W. Rolleston, a recent prize-winning graduate of Trinity College Dublin and a literary critic who had founded the monthly *Dublin University Review* (*DUR*) nine months earlier.

Rolleston, who came from a Wicklow Tory background, was one of a small number of Trinity scholars who had attended Dublin YIS meetings that spring, when Henry Dixon (IRB, a solicitor's clerk) and James Shannon of the IRB gave lectures on the need to protect Irish industries and the 'relationship between industry and nationality', Fred Allan organized a YIS Bodenstown

37 PRO (London), 30/60/1, Arthur Balfour papers, intelligence notes 15 to 30 Nov. 1889. O'Leary had argued before that the fact that McCarthy was vice-president of the Irish Party proved it had no nationalist credentials. O'Leary to *Irish Nation* (New York), 3 Dec. 1881. 38 Nancy Murray, 'Joseph K. Bracken: GAA founder, Fenian and politician' (1985); Floyd Collins, 'The beginning – Pat Hoctor' in *By the Mulcaire banks: the story of the Tipperary GAA* (Tipperary, 1986), 25–30.   39 NLI, Minute book of the Dublin YIS 1885–7, Ms 19158, minutes for Nov. 1885.

demonstration, and Patrick Hoctor gave a lecture entitled 'Writers and Writing', in which he argued that Ireland needed to develop a new 'national literature'.[40] After listening to Hoctor's lecture on 8 May, Rolleston asked to join the society and later that same evening was introduced to John O'Leary for the first time along with two other outstanding, young Trinity graduates. The first of these was Charles Hubert Oldham, another prize-winning graduate of Trinity and the co-founder of the *DUR*, who came from a well-established Dublin family of merchants that supported the Liberal Party. The other was Douglas Hyde, the son of a Protestant clergyman who had been strongly influenced politically as a teenager by John Lavin, a Castlerea grocer, Irish-language enthusiast and the leader of the Roscommon IRB.[41] A lasting friendship soon developed between these young men and O'Leary, who admired their Trinity publication because Rolleston and Oldham (its editor) desired that it would become a forum for sophisticated and non-partisan political, literary and 'scientific' debate among Irishmen generally, rather than for Trinity students only.[42] Other figures from the same circle that O'Leary managed to win over were William Stockley, who became a distinguished academic, and the very different figure of Charles Johnston, son of Billy Johnston (the Grand Master of the Orange Order) of Ballykinlar, Co. Down. Later, in New York, Johnston also befriended John Devoy.[43]

Although the proposal to establish a new newspaper in November 1885 failed, the IRB would, in the not so distant future, launch a journal for the GAA under Hoctor and O'Leary's editorship, which would reflect the political opinions of the YIS and the GAA, and, at the same time, feature numerous literary contributions from *DUR* contributors, including Rolleston, Hyde and a young poet named W.B. Yeats. The final act the Dublin YIS undertook during 1885 was the holding of a monster Manchester-martyr demonstration two days before the general election. This was addressed jointly by P.N. Fitzgerald and Michael Davitt, two men whose paths crossed quite frequently and seem to have had a love-hate political relationship. The National League did not want the demonstration to be held, fearing it might have a negative influence on voters.[44] On the day, Fitzgerald unveiled NMC Celtic crosses over the graves of two deceased IRB men (J.K. Casey and Stephen O'Donoghue) and stated that Irishmen should all swear never to be satisfied with less than 'the sovereign independence of our country.'[45]

The British general election of November-December 1885 was a great triumph for the Irish Party, which saw it winning 85 of the 103 Irish seats at Westminster, or one-seventh of the total number of seats in the House of Commons. As a result of the unusually narrow margin between the amount of

40 Ibid., minutes for Feb-June 1885. 41 Ibid., minute for 8 May; Dominic Daly, *The young Douglas Hyde* (1974), xviii, 22, 25, 44, 46, 53, 56, 201. 42 C.H. Oldham, 'Introductory Article', *Dublin University Review*, 1: 1 (Feb. 1885), 1–2. 43 *DPB*, vol. 2, 268; *Gaelic American*, 26 Mar. 1907 (O'Leary obituary). 44 NAI, CSORP 1885/21082. 45 *Nation*, 28 Nov. 1885.

Gladstone turning events for power [handwritten marginalia]

seats won by the Liberals and Conservatives, the Irish Party temporarily held the balance of power in the House of Commons (by one seat) and, by siding with the Tories, was able to oust Gladstone's government. As his party had just been removed from power only because of the Irish Party's vote and (reputedly) the sizeable Irish vote in Britain (directed by the radical liberal T.P. O'Connor), shortly afterwards Gladstone announced to the public his sudden 'conversion' to the home rule cause in an attempt to get back into power. The very weak Tory government under Lord Salisbury lasted only a matter of weeks and, by February 1886, Gladstone had again been returned to power, to the jubilation of the Parnellite press, which, notwithstanding the fact that he had suppressed the Land League and introduced the coercion act of 1882–5, now showered praise upon him as Ireland's saviour. In turn, the Parnellites, having presented themselves virtually as republicans for electoral gain during the election campaigns of 1885, now emphasized that they were wholly opposed to 'separation'. *United Ireland* maintained that the idea of separating Ireland from the United Kingdom was completely contradictory to all Irish political aspirations, past and present. It reminded its readers of the fact that, 'with the exception of the great organization of the Irish Republican Brotherhood', there had never been a single movement in Irish history 'deliberately formed with the object of separation', for both the United Irish and Young Ireland movements 'were not beyond the range of reconciliation' with Britain, and had been turned from 'reformers into revolutionists' solely because the government tried to suppress their right to hold meetings and act as members of 'a free-spoken debating society.' It was also argued that both the United Irish and Young Ireland movements had been initially founded with the aspiration to achieve for Ireland just what 'Mr. Gladstone is said to be now meditating – the gift of an honest Irish parliament, purged of English corruption and intrigue.'[46]

Long prior to the 1885 general election, the Liberal and Tory parties had been managing the 'home rule' issue through engaging in secret negotiations, of which the general Irish public was totally unaware. The Liberals' chief instrument was Cardinal Manning, the Catholic archbishop of Westminster and one of Gladstone's key advisors on the 'Irish question' since 1868. On Gladstone's behalf, Manning contacted the Irish Catholic hierarchy (his ecclesiastical juniors) and Parnell regarding what sort of settlement could win over the Catholic population wholly to the Union. Meanwhile, during the summer, Earl Carnavon, a leading Tory, debated the same issue in private with both Parnell and Sir Charles Gavan Duffy.[47] Joseph Chamberlain's idea, first presented to Parnell through Manning, to grant Irishmen greater autonomy over local government bodies instead of a powerless parliament, was dropped. It was considered too dangerous. Mostly through Cardinal Manning, an

46 'A chat about separation', *United Ireland*, 21 Jan. 1886.   47 O'Brien, *Parnell and his party*, 92–103.

understanding was reached between Parnell, Gladstone and the Irish Catholic hierarchy that some sort of powerless parliament might be established in Ireland that would be allowed to promote the Catholic educational system, though it would not be allowed to interfere with the existing schools. This promise of security naturally appealed greatly to the church, which had no political interests other than denominational education and its own property rights. In turn, on 16 February 1886, the Irish Catholic hierarchy announced for the first time their total support for the undefined concept of 'home rule'. Previously, in order to guarantee the church's future support for the Irish Party, Parnell and Tim Harrington had granted the hierarchy the right to be *ex-officio* members of the National League executive. This potentially gave the hierarchy a power of veto over the choice of all Irish Party candidates. This is probably why, very shortly after 1886, J.J. O'Kelly was demoted from the National League Executive and ceased to play an important role in the Irish Party. In return for Gladstone's promise to play the 'home rule' card, Parnell formed an electoral-pact, or party political alliance, between the Irish Party and the Liberal Party. This effectively turned the Irish Party into the Irish wing of the Liberal Party, even though its politics was essentially that of the Catholic party in British politics; a brand of politics that the non-conformist Liberals detested even more so than the Tories. This conflict of interests would soon harm the Irish Party, through its being pulled in two different directions. The Tory leadership responded to Parnell and Gladstone's dealings with the church in an equally opportunistic fashion by 'playing the Orange card'. The Tories told Ulster Protestants that 'Home Rule means Rome Rule', thereby polarizing Ireland on politico-religious grounds to a far greater degree than before and, of course, potentially boosting the Tories' electoral fortunes against the Liberals not only in Ulster but in Britain as well.

By the time Gladstone's 'home rule bill' was introduced in the Commons on 8 April, Joseph Chamberlain and George Trevelyan, a former chief secretary at Dublin Castle, had resigned from the government as a protest, taking many followers with them to form what they called the 'Liberal Unionist Party'. As a result, the Liberal Party had technically split, although they still generally voted together on most other issues. The defeat of the bill in the commons was expected and it could not possibly be acceptable to the House of Lords. The bill itself provided for the establishment of an Irish parliament, with an upper Irish house, consisting of non-elective nominees of Dublin Castle, that would have powers of veto over all legislation proposed by the elective house, which could raise special taxes to help pay off the imperial debt. Meanwhile the Imperial parliament in London was to maintain its existing complete control over general taxation in Ireland (customs and excise) and the management of the economy, as well as all defence matters, such as the ports, the army, the militia and (for an unspecified time period) the armed police forces as well. The elective house could nominate judges to the upper house (again subject to the veto of upper house), but otherwise control of the legal system remained unchanged. Parnell, though critical of some of its clauses, welcomed the bill as a 'final settlement' of Irish nationalists' demands, but on 8 June the bill was defeated in commons, since it was considered a very impractical and unworkable form of devolution, and there the matter ended for the time being. Two weeks later, speaking at Portsmouth, Parnell spoke again in favour of such a bill as Gladstone had proposed, for he believed its passing was essential to win over the bulk of the Irish population perpetually to the Crown and make them refuse to listen to arguments in favour of an independent Ireland, which he described as the 'most absurd talk that ever was given utterance to'. If an attempt was ever made in the future to create an independent Ireland following the granting of a devolved 'home rule' parliament, Parnell claimed that the crown's 'moral power' over the Irish population would have become so strong that the Irish people themselves would desire to crush the effort as soon as possible.[48] Over the next four years, the Irish Party leader resided permanently in England with Captain William O'Shea's family in Brighton. He only once returned to Ireland (for two days), and attended numerous Liberal Party conferences in England and Scotland in an attempt to persuade a not entirely convinced body of English liberal opinion that Gladstone's measure was the surest means of safeguarding the future of the Union. Parnell adopted a 'hands-off' approach to managing the Irish Party after 1886 because he knew it was now almost inevitable that his party's nominees would be returned (invariably unopposed) in all general elections for the foreseeable future. This was because the only people who could possibly afford to run for parliament without the Catholic hierarchy's support in the vast majority of Irish constituencies were the landed gentry and aristocracy, who had absolutely no chance of being elected to the popular house in the wake of the democratic-republican agitation of the Land League and the Third Reform Act, and so were not about to waste their money by standing. Nevertheless, as many had the right to sit in the House of Lords, they had no real need to have voting powers in the House of Commons.

Following the 'home rule' negotiations of 1885–6 which led to the intro-duction of Gladstone's bill (which was almost identical to bills introduced in 1893 and 1912),[49] in practical terms, the politics of 'home rule' had been set on definite terms: Gladstone's. Gladstone (and subsequent Liberal govern-ments who acted likewise) would never have introduced a 'home rule' bill in the first place were it not that he was dependent on the Irish Party to maintain his chances of keeping his own political party (the weaker of the two British parties) in power. As such the Liberal government(s)' actual motivation in introducing any such bill was party-political, to defeat the Tories in the race to form a cabinet at Whitehall. Although they differed in their party-political manifestos on the question of 'home rule' and championed a different moral

---

48 Lyons, *Parnell*, 353.   49 The main difference was that, under the later measures, a large percentage of Irish MPs would have had to continue to sit in Westminster as well.

[handwritten: HR would not ↓ GB power / just colonial tax]

posture on questions of political reform, the Liberals and Tories' basic policy regarding Ireland was exactly the same: to strengthen the Union, negate the IRB or Irish nationalist threat and maintain the existing colonial system of taxation in Ireland. 'Home rule' would not have lessened the authority of Westminster. Nevertheless from 1885–6 onwards, the Parnellite press consistently propagated the idea that the philanthropist Liberal prime minister wanted to 'make Ireland a nation' out of the goodness of his own heart, and that a 'union of hearts' now existed between the Liberal Party and the entire Irish nationalist community, because of the Liberal-Parnellite party political alliance against the Tories. Meanwhile, both lay and clerical Catholic elites denounced all who opposed the Irish Party as 'factionists', while the ownership of many provincial newspapers passed into the hands of MPs who were lay graduates of Catholic diocesan colleges.

Numerous Irish MPs in Westminster may have claimed that the existing terms of the Union were unjust, but, as in O'Connell's days, they generally only ever protested against the Union as a means of trying to persuade Westminster to pass reforms. Gladstone seemingly validated their grievances by making the buzzword 'home rule' a live issue in British party politics for the first time during 1886. In reality, however, this 'home rule' issue was never anything more than Gladstone and Parnell's implementation of a strategy designed to manage hitherto the Catholic vote in Ireland in line with the Liberals' interests in Westminster in return for a promise to promote Catholic interests. This was the bedrock of Gladstone's policy regarding the 'Irish question' since 1868 and it would continue to be the *only* practical basis of 'home rule' politics over the next thirty years until both the Liberal Party and the Irish Party disintegrated. Having apparently finally succeeded in acquiring a hold over the majority Catholic vote in Ireland, the Liberals were willing to allow the Tories to acquire the minority Protestant vote. As the Liberals and particularly the Irish Party gave constant lip service to the National League's slogan 'Ireland a Nation' after the cementing of the Liberal-Catholic voting alliance, the Tories responded with their own propaganda, telling Irish Protestants that, if Gladstone's and Parnell's opportunist politics really represented the views of 'Ireland a Nation' (as the Parnellite, Catholic and, to a lesser extent, Liberal, press universally claimed), then clearly there were 'two nations' in Ireland; a Catholic and a Protestant one. In effect, because Parnell was willing to allow the weaker of the two British parties define the so-called politics of 'Ireland a Nation', the dominant Tory party, which had already created the popular idea of 'Fenianism' in the British and Irish public mind, was now able to claim as its own reserve the rhetoric of nations and nationality in Ireland as well, and confuse it with British party politics. The Liberals played the same game, with the Irish Party's support.

The most significant result of the 'home rule' episode was the complete alienation of Ulster Protestants. After Gladstone's bill was introduced, there were massive sectarian riots in Belfast that continued to take place for the rest

[handwritten margin note: religious split]

of the summer, and occasional sectarian brawls between Protestants and Catholics also took place in working-class Dublin.[50] Many Ulster Protestants began to bear arms, sometimes at the behest of Tory army officers, sometimes of their own accord.[51] Ulster Presbyterians in particular now felt that they were 'under siege' and many began to distrust the RIC, owing to its rural and predominantly Catholic social composition.[52] Mass political activism among Ulster Presbyterians was not frequent prior to 1886, but henceforth they felt compelled to adopt a militant Tory stance. The Tory leadership revived the Orange Order, which was traditionally the preserve of the Church of Ireland only but now began to be run by Ulster Presbyterians, who probably would never have joined the order if they did not feel that their religious liberties were somehow now under threat. The Tory mantra 'Home Rule means Rome Rule' was thereafter made a platform for a new brand of Ulster-centred politics. Unsure what to call their politico–religious concerns, many Ulster Presbyterians defected from Gladstone's party to the Tories and chose to adopt the same title for their movement (minus the tag 'liberal') as had Joseph Chamberlain's group when they defected from Gladstone's party in England: 'The Unionist Party'. Over the next five to seven years, another new idea emerged in Ulster politics. Being indifferent to the fate and opinions of the mostly Church of Ireland Protestants elsewhere in the country, Ulster Presbyterians argued that if a ridiculous 'home rule' settlement was ever forced upon Ireland by a Liberal government, then the only way it could be tolerable, and a politico–religious civil war avoided, was if Ireland was effectively partitioned and a separate Ulster parliament established; this option being considered the lesser of two great evils.[53] Such a parliament, like the Gladstone's envisioned parliament in Dublin, would have little or no legislative power and obviously would not be a proper form of government, but it could at least protect or prioritize a social and educational policy that would be in line with the sensibilities of the predominant religious grouping within its jurisdiction.

Many of Parnell's supporters felt they were breaking the mould of Irish

---

50 Mark Radford, 'The RIC and the Belfast riots of 1886', paper delivered at American Conference for Irish Studies, University of Limerick, 28 June 2000; Martin Maguire, 'The organization and activism of the Dublin's Protestant working class', *IHS*, 29 (1994), 76–7. 51 NAI, British in Ireland microfilm, C.O.904, reel 110/box 182 and reel 12/box 28. 52 Radford, 'The RIC and the Belfast riots of 1886'. Hundreds were injured in Belfast and of the 32 people killed, 24 were shot dead by the RIC. The men shot by the RIC were all Protestants that were burning down Catholic property (including 28 pubs) in what were colloquially referred to as 'Protestant districts' of the city.   53 NAI, DICS files, carton 6 (Northern Division), District Inspector Gambell, 6 Mar., 5 June and 4 Sept. 1893. The Special Branch believed that it was 'undoubtedly a fact' that the Orange Order could get all the arms they wanted 'at a moment's notice', if they desired, presumably from the British army. They did not begin secret and slow methodical arms importation solely because 'the Orangemen say that they do not see any good in getting a lot of arms, keeping them secretly and thus allowing them to get into disrepair', as happened quite often in the IRB. NAI, DICS reports, carton 5 (Belfast Division), DI Seddall, 9 Oct. 1892.

politics by supporting the Irish Party and, in one sense, they were. The idea of having 'strength in numbers' had shaped the Catholic community's imagination since O'Connell's days, but this ideal was never reflected in parliamentary election results before the 1885 general election. The fact that the National League was not allowed either to develop a policy or to influence the one that Parnell took at Westminster was considered unimportant. The illusion of power was sufficient to make them feel that they had been empowered, just as this was sufficient to make the Irish Protestant community feel as if the Ireland they knew was somehow under siege. The politics of 'home rule' during 1885–6 and its outcome effectively illustrated the continued absence of the basis of a civil society in Ireland. The creation of a pan-Protestant Irish political alliance under a Tory banner as a reaction to the seeming arrival of an Irish Catholic party at the heart of British politics was the direct consequence of Parnell's purely opportunistic political strategy. Had he supported the old non-sectarian and federalist policy of Isaac Butt, his party could not possibly have risen to such dominance after just five years in existence and would not have been able to triumph so completely after the 1884 franchise act either, as he would never have won the support of the Catholic Church. The Irish Party possibly might have done so after a very much longer period, but Parnell was not willing to risk the possibility of democrats or nationalists finding a way to acquire any greater political influence than what they already had. Neither, of course, were Gladstone, the church, the upper classes and, indeed, much of the middle classes. This is why the politics of 'home rule' generally remained acceptable to the 'recognized leaders' of society after 1886.

Parnell knew that the IRB might well be able to impose a policy upon him if the National League was governed democratically. The desire of conservative National League leaders to have parish priests as its branch leaders emanated from this same concern. This was, in a sense, only natural. The predominant social ideal within the United Kingdom and within the Irish Catholic community, as upheld by its upper classes and bishops, was aristocratic. They saw themselves as the natural leaders of the Catholic community as a whole by virtue of their social status, and they desired any form of government that represented this social ideal, even if this was nothing more than a caretaker British administration monopolized by Catholics, such as was proposed by Gladstone's measure. The introduction of the 'home rule' measure was celebrated because it was felt to be tantamount to real recognition by Whitehall of their social prestige; this had never happened before. In the minds of Catholic elites, the Liberals were promising Catholics a status of equality within the empire and the fact that the Liberals were supposedly the more 'progressive' party in British politics enhanced their sense of self-importance all the more. After 1886, T.D. Sullivan and his *Nation* newspaper (read by the Catholic lower middle class) sold cheap icons of Gladstone to the general Irish public, while Archbishop Croke of Cashel erected stately marble busts of Gladstone and Parnell in his palace in Thurles, as if these two

Westminster MPs had already made 'Ireland a Nation', but neither Sullivan nor Croke could probably explain their reasoning for doing so. They were certainly expressing confidence in the future well-being of Catholic Ireland, but they were essentially celebrating a political consensus that did not exist beyond their own imaginations.

Most Parnellite contemporaries understood that because Westminster was very much an aristocratic institution (as it would remain up until the late Edwardian and Georgian eras), and, as the Irish benches were completely powerless in their own right, only Irishmen of a very high social standing could be taken seriously by the British political establishment or potentially be able to achieve any political influence or bargaining powers with the London government. This was the only means whereby Irishmen could have any real influence upon how the country was governed. In this respect, things had not essentially changed since O'Connell's days, notwithstanding the Third Reform Act or the introduction of Gladstone's bill. It was politically necessary throughout its history for the Irish Party to choose a leadership from the only three proverbial 'home rulers' who (in the wake of the Land League agitation) ever belonged to landed gentry, namely Charles Stewart Parnell (already an established political figure by 1882) and two men who were only beginning to make their mark, John Dillon and John Redmond. The National League *had* to rely on Parnell, and the Catholic political establishment's raising of as much as £38,000 (which was far more than they collected for the Land League organization) during 1883 just so that the 'uncrowned King' of Avondale could continue to live in his mansion and pose as an aristocrat was the supreme demonstration of this.[54] This structural reality to British politics was the main reason why many English contemporaries, as much as the Irish, considered Parnell as head-and-shoulders above virtually all other Irish politicians of his day and would remember him as such.

As the Irish Party needed men capable of brokering political deals with the government if it was to have any voice at all, apart from its gentrified leaders and the Catholic hierarchy, it always needed to rely very heavily upon established English political figures that had already acquired the confidence of the British political establishment. During the 1880s, these were primarily Justin McCarthy (a London Liberal since the 1850s and an effective Irish Party leader up until the mid 1890s), William O'Shea (a Galway-born Whig, British army captain, friend of Gladstone and member of the landed gentry, who Parnell made an Irish Party MP in 1885 and a chief intermediary in the 'home rule' negotiations) and R.B. O'Brien (a very influential London Liberal journalist). In later years, during the Edwardian era, the Irish Party would rely very heavily, or almost entirely, upon the Liverpool MP T.P. O'Connor once

---

54 To put this figure in context, it is worth noting that a bank-manager's, lawyer's or newspaper owner's annual salary and earnings during the 1880s was generally between £400 and £500.

his democratic brand of politics in northern England began to be considered as 'respectable' by the British political establishment for the first time. As the rest of the Irish Party and National League movement consisted wholly of men of a lower middle class background, as well as various obscure Catholic businessmen who were encouraged to enter politics by the hierarchy only to represent their interests, they could never do more than vote with the Irish Party leaders: 'foot-soldiers' was the rhetoric the Irish Party's press always used to describe them from the mid-1880s onwards. Men like Tim Healy and William O'Brien generally had influence among the party leadership only because they were relied upon to act as the party's chief propagandists in the press, whose purpose was to capture the new lower middle class vote, and because of their closeness to the rank and file of the National League. This is why, throughout its history, the Irish Party was always graphically portrayed by British political satirists as a single aristocratic figure (first Parnell, and later Redmond) surrounded by various popular Irish Party MPs who lacked a high social status (more often than not Healy and O'Brien) who were caricatured as country bumpkins or bawling children to denote their closeness to the rabble.

It would be mistaken to believe that the Irish Party brought about any form of class unity in Ireland along nationalist lines during the 1880s. The Irish Party was intensely divided among itself, as was the National League, and the semblance of unity they presented was very often nothing more than the unity of the Catholic Church which, between 1884 and 1886, had assumed a controlling influence over both. There would never have been any 'home rule' bill introduced unless there was agreement between the British government, Parnell and the Catholic hierarchy to allow for the advancement of Catholic interests in return for Catholic electoral support for the Liberal Party.

Like all Irish contemporaries, the IRB was not in a position to make an impact in the 'home rule' negotiations, which were confined purely to Parnell, the Catholic hierarchy and select governmental circles, although John O'Leary did manage to learn a little of what was taking place, owing to his friendship with Sir Charles Gavan Duffy. As the IRB was an underground organization with no newspaper, it was completely silent regarding the 1886 bill, although something of its attitudes can be ascertained. P.N. Fitzgerald's general attitude to the 'home rule' issue during 1886 was no doubt virtually the same as it was a couple of years later, when he noted that 'there is no such thing as half-way houses to liberty' and that it was 'a crime' that some Irishmen were now helping the British government to 'tune their fiddles to catch Paddy's ear with a new tune of a cheap form – a home rule bill'.[55] Patrick Tynan, a former 'rank and file' IRB man who was now a resident of New York, wrote during 1886–7 for his own amusement a lengthy critique on the duplicity of Parnellite

<hr />

55 *Freeman's Journal*, 24 Nov. 1887 (speech in Limerick City), 4 Sept. 1890 (speech in Glasnevin); *Daily Independent*, 10 Nov. 1894 (speech in Rotunda, Dublin).

politics, which he described as 'provincialist' rather than 'nationalist'. By examining its terms, he explained why the Irish parliament proposed by Gladstone's bill could not be considered as a proper form of government, emphasizing in particular the taxation and defence clauses.[56] Such may well have been the general attitude within the IRB during 1886. It was certainly the prevalent view in Irish-America, where the INLA ceased to hold any conventions after 1886, having lost all faith in Parnell and his party, since it did not make any sense to people living under American political institutions why anyone could possibly support such a measure. Mark Ryan recalled many years later that the attitude of the IRB towards the 1886 home rule bill was that it was a 'miserable measure', since it provided the proposed Irish parliament with no executive power and was obviously so 'designed, not to remove foreign domination, but to make Ireland safe for the British Empire'. The IRB was particularly grieved by the fact that the Irish Party's press ignored the great weaknesses of the bill, attempting instead to persuade the 'unthinking thousands' in Ireland to regard the leader of the English Liberal Party 'as the saviour of our country and the measure he had introduced as a great charter of Irish freedom.'[57]

The response of the Dublin YIS to the home rule issue during 1886 was shaped by the fact that, by January 1886, both the editors of the *DUR* managed to get themselves elected as vice-presidents of the society. C.H. Oldham even succeeded in defeating Charles McCarthy Teeling (IRB), P.W. Nally's brother-in-law and a grandson of Bartholomew Teeling, in an election for the position. Oldham, who also operated an elitist 'Contemporary Club' on College Green in conjunction with the *DUR*, was a budding economist and Gladstonian liberal who once gave a talk to the YIS in praise of J.S. Mill, but his attitude to 'home rule' was shaped mostly by his reading of Thomas Davis's writings, which O'Leary had given him. Oldham argued that it was the fundamental duty of all Irishmen to attempt 'the building-up of the shattered fabric of an independent, self-reliant citizenship among their countrymen' by 'gathering together and the glorification before us of an ideal … a soul of citizenship', but the British political system was so designed as to prevent 'the growth of public spirit' in Ireland.[58] He invited John F. Taylor (a Catholic barrister and the Dublin correspondent of *Manchester Guardian*) to give a public YIS lecture at the Rotunda in January 1886, during which Taylor denied the claim of the Tories that the Act of Union was a 'fundamental law'

56 Tynan, *The Irish National Invincibles* (1894), especially 372–94. Tynan's critique of Irish politics was originally never supposed to see the light of day and was ultimately published (in 1894) only because he was persuaded to do so by a publisher friend whom, presumably unknown to Tynan, was actually being funded to do so by the ultra-Tory, London *Times*, for the reason that Tynan had played up the association between the Land League and the Phoenix Park murders. PRO (London), Sir Robert Anderson Papers, H.O.144/1537/3–4. 57 Ryan, *Fenian memories*, 133. 58 C.H. Oldham, 'The prospects of Irish nationality', *Dublin University Review*, 2: 6 (June 1886), 457–68.

of the (unwritten) British constitution.[59] Oldham also invited Roman Ivanovitch Lipmann, a Russian Jew and member of the small Dublin Socialist League (which was then seeking to win over the local IRB), to deliver a lecture to the YIS upon the theme 'Nationalism and Internationalism'. Fred Allan, the Dublin IRB leader (who also gave a lecture on Emmet and organized a Bodenstown demonstration for the YIS that year), was given the responsibility of responding to Lipmann's paper, which he praised highly. However, Allan's motion that the adoption of internationalist views by Irishmen could in no way help to improve the political situation in Ireland so long as they were governed by a regime of the character of Dublin Castle was unanimously passed by those present, excepting Lipmann.[60] Meanwhile the other YIS vice-president, T.W. Rolleston, wrote an article for the *DUR*, blaming Parnell's decision to allow Catholic clergymen the right to be *ex-officio* officers of the National League for the growing politico-religious polarization in Ireland. Rolleston, who reputedly became an IRB man at this time, believed most Irish Catholics felt that clergymen were 'the last class in the nation' that ought to possess such powers over the principal political organization in the country. Since January 1886, Archbishop Walsh of Dublin and Archbishop Croke of Cashel were being given a free rein by Parnell to denounce critics of the National League as enemies of the Catholic Church, despite the fact that 'it should not be open to an archbishop, or to anyone else, to require that the opponents of his politics ... should keep silence about them, simply because those politics are the politics of an archbishop or of twenty archbishops.' Rolleston pointed out that a nation was inherently something 'which includes all classes, all creeds, all political divisions' and that 'such, however poorly and inadequately expressed, is the gospel of nationalism as it was handed down to us by Tone and Emmet, by Davis and O'Brien and even by fierce John Mitchel himself.' From this standpoint, he maintained it was self-evident that 'no man who preaches any other doctrine than this, however influential he may be as the champion of a class or a creed, is likely to wear in history the title of Irish patriot' and that if the Irish Party did not begin to live up to these credentials, then the IRB party was 'destined to become the bulwark of the civil rights of the Irish laity' since it was the only political movement in Ireland since the days of Young Ireland that was 'wholly independent' of the churches in political matters.[61]

John O'Leary did not remain completely silent during the 'home rule' debates. In April 1886, he wrote to a Liverpool newspaper condemning an Edinburgh speech of Parnell (not reprinted in Irish newspapers) in which the Irish Party leader argued that, as a security precaution, Westminster should keep total control of the RIC if an Irish parliament of any kind was ever estab-

59 NLI, Minute book of the Dublin YIS, MS 19158; J.F. Taylor, 'Is the act of union a fundamental law', *Dublin University Review*, 2: 2 (Feb. 1886), especially 89–91. **60** NLI, Minute book of the Dublin YIS, MS 19158, minutes for Feb. 1886. **61** T.W. Rolleston, 'The archbishop in politics: a protest', *DUR*, 2: 2 (Feb. 1886), 98–103.

lished.[62] Although this stance by Parnell was contrary to the official demand of the National League as set down in its constitution (namely an Irish parliament with complete control over the police and taxation), the Parnellite press remained completely silent about Parnell's statement, to the great anger of O'Leary ('this is the conspiracy of silence with a vengeance'),[63] who thereafter contented himself with holding his opinions in private. Indeed, it is probable that IRB protests about the bill *were* issued during 1886) but the Parnellite press would not allow such criticisms to be published.

Partly from debating the question with Duffy, by the winter of 1885 O'Leary was convinced that any Irish parliament ought to have two houses, with the upper house there to represent the gentry's interests (an idea to which Davitt was totally opposed),[64] and Duffy subsequently took the liberty of sending a copy of an interview with O'Leary 'to Mr. Gladstone, as evidence that representative Fenians would accept a parliament of two houses.'[65] O'Leary also began a correspondence with James Bryce, a leading Oxford jurist and the Liberal undersecretary for foreign affairs (they probably first met at Oldham's 'Contemporary Club'), debating the American constitution and the question of bicameral parliaments.[66] He also visited Bryce and a few other Liberal MPs at Westminster to discuss the issue further.[67] O'Leary's general view was that an Irish parliament established through an act of British legislation could be acceptable only if the parliament had 'a separate executive',[68] for the least which Irishmen could be satisfied with was 'repeal of the union, pure and simple', but Gladstone's measure 'stops far short of it'.[69] He dismissed the argument that Irishmen should 'take any measure of self government the English may grant us' because they would be able to 'make use of it, to squeeze more out of them', noting that 'I cannot believe in the possibility of snatching liberty by lies', for without a separate executive, this could never be possible. He believed it was many Irishmen's inability to 'face facts' that was causing them to be 'living in a sort of fool's paradise in Ireland just now' and to suffer from 'the most serious of all delusions', 'to think we are within a measurable distance of our goal'. Even if Westminster, in theory, became ready to set up an Irish parliament with a separate executive (which O'Leary doubted would ever happen), the passing of such a bill would still be

62 O'Leary referred to his actions in this manner in his letter to the *Freeman's Journal* on 1 Dec. 1890. 63 NLI, John O'Leary papers, MS 8002, 'Unionist and Home Rule Delusions' (unpublished paper). 64 Daly, *Young Douglas Hyde*, 72–3 (Hyde's report of debate between O'Leary and Davitt at the Contemporary Club). 65 NLI, John O'Leary papers, MS 5927, Duffy to O'Leary, 5 Apr. 1886. 66 Ibid., MS 8001 (7), Bryce to O'Leary, 20 May, 2 Aug., 30 Dec. 1886; Daly, *Young Douglas Hyde*, 71. 67 NLI, O'Leary papers, MS 5927, Duffy to O'Leary (n.d., 1886): 'I am glad you saw those representative Englishmen. We cannot do without them and they ought to know that there are other Irishmen than those who go to bawl at Westminster.' 68 O'Leary to *Freeman's Journal*, 8 Dec. 1889; Devoy, *Recollections*, 282; *Gaelic American*, 12 Dec. 1908 (article on O'Leary); O'Leary, *Recollections*, vol. 1, 122. 69 NLI, O'Leary papers, MS 8002, 'Unionist and Home Rule Delusions' (unpublished paper, written *c*.1886–8).

entirely 'in the power of the House of Lords', which was wholly opposed even to Gladstone's limited measure.[70] In short, O'Leary was opposed to any measure that did not grant Ireland real autonomy and believed that Irishmen would be 'better wait another century for the right-sort of home rule than take an altogether wrong sort.'[71] The mere fact, however, that O'Leary was willing to conceive the *possibility* of a British settlement of Irishmen's demand for independence being acceptable caused him to be subject to criticism from two of his oldest friends, C.G. Doran and Denis Mulcahy, the latter declaring that to recognize Britain's right to settle Irish affairs in any way 'is to renounce Irish national independence.'[72] The attitude no doubt existed in the IRB as well, which had long maintained this stance in its pronouncements. As far as O'Leary was concerned, however, this was essentially a pointless debate upon a hypothetical question, as it was not of contemporary relevance. It is possible, however, that others felt differently.

One possible indication that O'Leary was subject to criticism from other IRB leaders because of his general attitude towards the 'home rule' debates is that he felt it necessary to write to the IRB founder T.C. Luby in New York during the winter of 1886, specifically asking him for an explanation of the IRB's republican oath, which he himself had never actually taken, since he could never understand how anyone could talk of an Irish republic being 'virtually established', since no republican government of any kind existed.[73] Quite possibly, the meaning of the oath may have confused some other IRB men as well. Luby replied to O'Leary that the meaning of the IRB's oath (Stephens's 'young republic' theory) 'is a very complicated one', which had nothing to do with the idea of republican governments and 'is by no means the simple question you seem to think it is.' He simply advised O'Leary that, as the leader of the IRB, 'you *should* be "politic", within just bounds' in interpreting its application.[74] The IRB's general response to the 'home rule' debates of 1886 was certainly 'politic' for, although it opposed the home rule bill and the Irish Party's stance on the bill, as Mark Ryan recalled, its only real concern was forwarding its own Irish nationalist aims:

> We could make little progress while so many of our people laboured under the delusion that the home rule bill meant the end of English tyranny and freedom for Ireland ... We therefore did not feel unduly depressed when the Gladstone home rule bill was rejected but went on with our work, preaching the republican gospel and trying to secure recruits for our organisation by means of public propaganda and private canvassing.[75]

70 Ibid. 71 Ibid. 72 Ibid., MS 5926, letter of Mulcahy to O'Leary (n.d., 1885). 73 O'Leary, *Recollections*, vol. 1, 122. 74 NLI, O'Leary papers, MS 5927, Luby to O'Leary, 7 Jan. 1887. On the same point, see Rossa, *Recollections*, 274 (1859 letter of Stephens explaining the meaning of IRB oath and noting O'Leary's failure to understand it). 75 Ryan, *Fenian*

The Parnellite-Liberal rhetoric of the existence of a so-called 'union of hearts' between the Irish nationalist community and Gladstone was something the IRB detested, for, as O'Leary noted, its only purpose, apart from helping Gladstone's party at the polls, was to attempt to undermine Irishmen's political self-reliance, by calling upon the general Irish public 'to want just what English Liberals, in their changing fancies, choose to think we want.' Noting that 'it is not a union of hearts, but some sort of harmony of heads the time and situation need', O'Leary feared greatly for the future of Irish public life if a more rational form of public debate upon the Irish Party's politics did not take place in Ireland.[76]

The IRB was always officially committed to combating sectarianism, but it was ill equipped to do so in one notable respect, namely the lack of influential members of the Protestant communities within its ranks. Indeed, very few Protestants seem to have been in the IRB at all, except a few dozen poor members of the Church of Ireland in Dublin, and some isolated dissenters who were actually free-thinkers with no time for parish life, like the Derry IRB leader Louis Smyth, a nominal Presbyterian from Magherafelt, and the Dublin IRB leader Fred Allan, a Methodist turned theosophist. Meanwhile, although O'Leary was an agnostic, most other IRB leaders of the 1880s, including P.N. Fitzgerald (who sent his only daughter, Mary, to a Belgian convent school),[77] Mark Ryan and Robert Johnston of Belfast, while completely non-sectarian and relatively anti-clerical in their political attitudes, were in their private lives devout Catholics, with relatively little experience of interacting with Protestants on a social level. As such, while the IRB could combat sectarian attitudes within the Catholic community, it could not, in itself, bring about greater interaction between the two polarized communities because of its lack of influence with the Protestant community. John O'Leary did, however, attempt to 'reach out' to the Protestant community during 1886 by taking advantage of the existence of the sectarian 'Irish Protestant Home Rule Association' (IPHRA), a small body established by James Bryce MP in Belfast in March 1886 after a recent Liberal Party convention in Belfast when virtually all remaining Irish Protestant Liberals voted to leave the party.[78] Irish Catholic Liberals had already joined Parnell's Party without feeling they had changed their political allegiance in any way.

C.H. Oldham, the vice-president of the Dublin YIS, established a more nationalist-based branch of the IPHRA in Dublin, which attracted O'Leary, who believed that, if 'the Pope ... still sits heavily on the souls of many Protestants in Ulster and other parts of Ireland', this was primarily because of 'the prominence of the priests in the present agitation [National League]'. Although O'Leary thought that economics, far more so than religion, was the

---

memories, 133–5.   **76** NLI, John O'Leary papers, MS 8002, 'Unionist and Home Rule Delusions'.   **77** Marie Phelan (née Fitzgerald) to author. Fitzgerald's daughter later became a teacher and then a nun.   **78** Loughlin, 'The Irish Protestant Home Rule Association'.

1

2

3

1 James Stephens (1824–1901), photographed shortly before his death. It was this bohemian, Francophile figure who formed the IRB in 1858 and led the organization during the 1860s. 2 C.G. Doran (1835–1909), photographed here in 1873, was the pivotal figure in the IRB during the 1870s and later became the first leader of the National Council/Sinn Féin in Cork. 3 Thomas Brennan (1853–1912), photographed here in 1904 as a successful American businessman, was assistant-secretary to the Land League and the most enthusiastic republican propagandist during the 'land war' of 1879–81.

4

5

6

4 Matthew Harris (1825–90) was a leading figure in the IRB and popular politics in Galway for many years. He championed the Land League's aims in, and out of, parliament throughout the 1880s.
5 J.J. O'Kelly (1845–1916), a Francophile republican, IRB activist and the effective author of the 'new departure', he was the most republican-biased member of the Irish Party during the Parnell era.
6 Fred Allan (1861–1937), a socially-radical Methodist and Dublin IRB leader for almost thirty years, he served as IRB secretary in 1895–1902 and 1910–12 and later took a small part in the 'war of independence'.

7

8

9

7 P.N. Fitzgerald (1851–1907), the chief travelling organizer of the IRB during the Parnell era; his arrest in 1884 was a major turning point in the IRB's history. 8 John O'Leary (1830–1907), photographed here in 1894, was an editor of the *Irish People* during the 1860s and oversaw the IRB's progress from the days of the Land League to the beginnings of Sinn Féin. 9 P.W. Nally (1855–91), a champion athlete and Connacht IRB leader; he was wrongfully convicted in 1884 and died under unusual circumstances in Mountjoy jail.

VOL. IV. No. XLIV.   NEW YORK, SUNDAY, NOVEMBER 10, 1895.   PRICE 5 CENTS.

IRISH NATIONAL

land's difficulty her opportunity and to use all possible means to create that difficulty. "In view of these facts the members of | "All authority to organize must come from the national executive. "The initiation fee shall be $1, payable in advance and 50 cents quarterly dues. | Municipal Councils shall be met by special assessment on Local Councils in such State or Municipal district. | tail; but no more will come of it all than of the imposing declarations with which we were familiar while the Corinto incident lasted," and so continues for two columns.

10 Title page of the controversial *Irish Republic* (New York), published between 1893 and 1898 and the sister publication of the *Shan Van Vocht* (Belfast).

11 William Lyman (1854–*c.*1910) was the proprietor of the *Irish Republic* and a leader of the Irish National Alliance and Clan na Gael during the 1890s.

11

12

13

12 John Daly (1845–1916), on the left, and John Devoy (1842–1928), photographed in New York in 1898. Daly, an IRB leader of the 1870s, spent twelve years in prison after being framed by an *agent provocateur* in 1884 and was an inspirational figure to many young IRB men up until his death. Devoy, editor of the *Irish Nation* (New York) and *Gaelic American* (New York), is often considered the greatest Irish revolutionary propagandist of his generation, and acted as a constant supporter of the IRB leadership in Ireland. 13 John O'Connor (1849–1908), doctor, freemason and the IRB secretary during the Parnell era, he was the most successful arms agent in the IRB's sixty-five-year history.

14 Arthur Griffith (1871–1922), the chief Sinn Féin propagandist and later the chairman of the provisional government of the Irish Free State, photographed here during the late 1890s. He was active in the republican movement from boyhood.
15 P.T. Daly (right) with James Larkin outside the Dublin police court. Daly (1870–1943) was IRB secretary during the 1900s, a life-long labour activist and among the first to call for the establishment of an Irish Labour Party.

14

15

16

16 John MacBride (1865–1916), IRB activist and rebel commando leader in the Boer war, speaking at a republican rally *c*.1907. He was considered a potential IRB president during the early 1900s and was later executed for his part in the 1916 rising. **17** Mark Ryan (1844–1940), the London IRB leader for over twenty years and financier of the pro-Boer movement, receiving a presentation of a portrait, jointly commissioned by all parties in the Dáil, 3 March 1936. Present from left to right, W.T. Cosgrave, Leo Whelan (artist), Anthony MacBride, Alfie Byrne (mayor of Dublin), Justice O'Byrne, Sean T. O'Kelly, James Ryan (government minister), Conor Maguire (attorney general), Mark Ryan, James Hamilton Delargy, Eamon de Valera and Chief Justice Kennedy.

17

18   19

20

18 Tom Clarke (1857–1916) and Sean MacDermott (1883–1916), the organizers of the 1916 rising. 19 Michael Collins (1890–1922), the co-ordinator of Ireland's struggle for independence and the last active president of the IRB. 20 'Chess Final': Fred Allan (IRB) vs. Jimmy Mallin (IRA) in Ballykinlar Jail, Co. Down, March 1921, illustration by Sean Milroy (SF).

main reason why most Ulstermen were opposed to Irish independence, he believed that Ulster Protestants 'when properly appealed to (as they have not yet been during the present [Parnellite] movement), are quite capable of seeing again as they saw before, that our country is also theirs and things can never be altogether well with Ulster while they are [or continue to be] ill with the rest of Ireland.'[79]

During 1886–7, the IRB leader wrote articles for both the *DUR* and the IPHRA's official organ, *North and South* (also edited by Oldham),[80] on the question of the place of Protestants in Irish political life and the immorality of boycotting. In the review article, O'Leary argued that as 'more than a proportionate share' of the privileged classes or intelligentsia in Irish society were Protestants, and, as Protestants composed more than 20% of the population, they should not have any great reason to fear that they would be unable to protect their own interests in an Irish parliament of any kind. O'Leary believed that the question of denominational education was the central factor in creating political divisions in Ireland along religious lines, and he blamed MPs willingness to concede to the churches' demands for denominational education for bringing about this development. He noted that most Protestants and lay Catholics in contemporary Ireland were not really in favour of denominational education, having 'no definite ideas on the subject and no strong feeling one way or another.' Were it not for the harmful influence of clericalist politicians in Irish politics, O'Leary was convinced that this divisive question of denominational education would never have raised its head, as it was a

> Self-evident fact that many of the so-called Catholics, here as elsewhere … are in point of fact either broad, or, if you like it better, loose Protestants or freethinkers of very varying hue and dye. Orthodox people in Ireland, whether Catholic or Protestant, do not like to face this fact, but surely all facts will force their way into notice in the long run.

O'Leary argued that Irishmen 'will have to fight the matter' of the need for a secular education system 'out here, as it has been (and is still being) fought out in Belgium and elsewhere', if political-religious controversy and tensions were ever to subside in Ireland in the future. He believed that 'in our modern societies, you can draw no definite lines between Protestants and Catholics' or pretend, as if 'one could omnisciently enter into the shifting minds that make up the numbers', that the numbers of 'Protestants and Catholics on the census papers' provided sustainable evidence of how a country would be governed. He cited the example of Belgium as being significant here, noting that since

79 NLI, John O'Leary papers, MS 8002, 'Unionist and Home Rule Delusions'. 80 Loughlin, 'The Irish Protestant Home Rule Association', 354. On the whole, O'Leary's letters to *North and South* during March 1887 were more in criticism of the Plan of Campaign and the approach of the National League towards the land question than the activities of the clergy.

Catholic Belgium's separation from Protestant Holland in 1830, although 'the proportion of Protestants to Catholics is roughly somewhat the same in Belgium as in Ireland' and 'religion, directly or indirectly, plays a great part in Belgian politics, as it may here', 'the Liberal party, which is there opposed to the Catholic party, has ruled the country for more than half the time since the Revolution of 1830'. He argued that strong anti-Protestant prejudice existed in much of the Irish Catholic lay community, not because they held feelings of religious intolerance (as all forms of clergymen claimed), but simply because 'most of the landlords are Protestants' and 'because most of the Protestants are West-British' in politics. As a corollary of this, he believed that sectarianism in Irish society could be completely eradicated through purely political means. He was convinced that the prevailing mentality of many Protestants, of feeling 'under siege' and desiring 'guarantees' that their religious or material interests would never be undermined, could easily disappear if greater interaction between the Protestant and Catholic lay communities could be brought about. Noting that 'trust begets trust', he suggested that 'when Protestants cease to fear' interacting with the Catholic community they would surely feel that had 'advanced far on the road to safety.' From this standpoint, he suggested that the interests of the Protestant community in Ireland, as well as that of the Catholic community, could be best advanced if they worked together in Ireland itself, and ceased to 'hug their chains' to Britain or to continue depending upon Westminster to solve their problems (as the Irish Party was doing). O'Leary hoped that most Protestants would eventually realize the necessity of doing this, for 'surely it is only to the soul of the slave that there can ever be any question as to whether it is better to be safe and in bondage or be free and in danger.'[81]

In an attempt to encourage Irishmen to believe in the necessity of non-denominational schools, O'Leary organized a public YIS lecture in November 1886 by James Poole, a postgraduate student of modern history at Trinity College and a moderate Dublin socialist. This event, however, had a disastrous effect on the YIS. When Poole praised the National Schools for being non-denominational and was very critical of the Christian Brothers' schools for encouraging anti-Protestant feeling, Joseph Kenny, a Dublin Parnellite MP who was present, objected strongly to Poole's attack on the Christian Brothers and prompted others to do likewise. Some IRB men present, while admitting the value of non-denominational schools, also refused to praise the National Schools, owing to the fact that they did not teach Irish history. Poole responded by arguing that, as a student of modern history, he could state with certainty that there was no such thing as Irish history because they were living under laws 'which were moulded upon English history' and that by studying the history of the United Kingdom, Irishmen's 'moral fibre' (which he

---

81 John O'Leary, 'Some guarantees for the protestant and unionist minority', *DUR*, 2: 12 (Dec. 1886), 959–65.

inferred was inherently inferior to that of Englishmen) would be improved. According to the report of a DMP detective present, this caused a lengthy and very bitter row to break out at this meeting, which O'Leary failed to control. A good indication that this detective was not exaggerating the bedlam that broke out after this little speech was that all the pages of the YIS minute book regarding this meeting (and all subsequent ones) were later ripped out.[82] The public boycotted the Dublin YIS after this meeting and, to all intents and purposes, it had only a nominal existence thereafter. O'Leary's solution to its imminent demise was to take up Fred Allan's idea of setting up a 'National Club' in the city as a new meeting room for the YIS. Allan had tried, but failed, to collect funds for this purpose among YIS members earlier that year. As a result it appears that when the 'National Club' was finally opened at 41 Rutland (now Parnell) Square in June 1887, the money required came largely from the IRB's coffers. One source indicates that as much as £2,000 was spent on the National Club, although it is unclear whether the building was actually purchased or merely rented and renovated.[83] Another setback to the YIS venture was that, in the same month as the National Club's establishment, Oldham and Rolleston's *DUR* was forced to close down, as it had been boycotted by Trinity College students because it encouraged freedom of debate on the 'home rule' question and had not sold well otherwise. Although the National Club formed its own 'National Club Literary Society', run by IRB men like Henry Dixon and Patrick Lavelle BA, and had its own library and reading room, most of the students and Dublin intellectuals who had formerly frequented the YIS generally kept their distance, not least owing to the growing attraction of other *purely* literary societies not just in Dublin but in London as well, where most Irish writers, publishers and journalists could only ever find work. As a result, the principal function the National Club would serve, apart from being a social outlet (it also had its own gymnasium and bar), was to provide a convenient venue for IRB meetings.

While O'Leary and Fred Allan had concentrated on the IPHRA or YIS during the autumn of 1886, P.N. Fitzgerald and Patrick Hoctor turned their

---

82 NAI DMP files, carton 2, Supt. William Reddy, 15 November 1886; NLI, Minute book of the Dublin YIS 1885–7, MS 19158. Fifteen years earlier, James Bryce Killen, a prize-winning graduate of Queen's University Belfast, poet and close associate of Poole's in Dublin labour politics, was expelled from the prestiguous Belfast Literary Society and denounced publicly as a 'Fenian' for arguing that there *was* such a thing as Irish history. Killen, a Presbyterian and former barrister, was imprisoned for supporting the Land League and was a journalist for *United Ireland, Irishman* and the *Irish World* during the 1880s. He supported all republican commemorative work, wrote a very popular pamphlet on Anglo-Irish relations called *The Incompatibles* (1882) and wrote in 1878 that he wanted to see the creation of a United States of Europe, called 'the European Union'. He died in great poverty in Dublin in Dec. 1916. 83 In a letter to John O'Leary around this time, Sir Charles Gavan Duffy advised him strongly against spending £2,000 on a club premises in Dublin (an apparent reference to the National Club) as such places only tended to attract 'bad characters and ill-educated persons ... who will slander you'. NLI, John O'Leary papers, MS 5927, C.G. Duffy to O'Leary (n.d.).

attention to the GAA. Both men had been very active in promoting it in Munster (and attempting to use it as a recruiting ground for the IRB) since 1885. This had been done without coming into any conflict with the National League, although one slight exception to this general rule took place in Tralee. The Kerry IRB leaders were William Moore Stack, a 43-year-old solicitor's clerk and former Land Leaguer who was reputedly very anticlerical, and Maurice Moynihan, a 23-year-old former lay student at a diocesan college in Listowel, where he had been sworn into the IRB by his lecturer, Michael Power. Stack and Moynihan formed the first branches of the Kerry GAA during May 1885 and mounted a propaganda campaign against the Irish Amateur Athletics Association (IAAA). This was an Irish wing of an English organization, which confined its membership exclusively to the middle classes and had been established in Ireland three months earlier to combat the social and cultural influence of the GAA among the lower classes. Edward Harrington MP, the editor of the *Kerry Sentinel* and the county leader of the National League, promoted the IAAA in Kerry. As the GAA was more popular, the National League in Tralee attempted to and did depose Harrington as the leader of their organization in favour of the republican Stack. This prompted Harrington to appeal the case to his brother Tim (who controlled the Central Executive of the National League) who dissolved the Tralee National League until such time as it accepted his brother back as leader.[84]

During the summer of 1886, Patrick Hoctor and John Boyle O'Reilly (IRB, a shop-assistant and prominent member of the Dublin YIS), managed to get themselves elected as the vice-presidents of the GAA and, by October, they had persuaded the GAA Central Executive to appoint John O'Leary as the association's fourth official patron, alongside Parnell, Davitt and Archbishop Croke (none of whom took any part in its activities). Although the GAA already had tens of thousands of members, it required patrons who could fund the association since its membership was confined to the lower classes. In April 1887, Patrick Hoctor launched the *Gael* (Dublin) under his own editorship as the official journal of the GAA,[85] while John O'Leary was made its 'literary editor'. It is probable that its publication was financed by the IRB. The principal editorial policy of the *Gael*, apart from providing reports of the association's progress, was to emphasize that all members of the GAA must be, in Davis's words, 'kindly Irish or the Irish, neither Saxon nor Italian' or, in other words, entirely non-sectarian. While promoting or establishing many GAA clubs in Munster during 1886–7, P.N. Fitzgerald was adamant that members of the GAA must promote social and political attitudes that were

---

84 J.A. Gaughan, *Austin Stack* (Dublin, 1977), 11–17; idem, *A political odyssey: Thomas O'Donnell, M.P. for west Kerry* (Dublin, 1983), 22–3 (biography of Moynihan). William Moore Stack was Austin Stack's father. Maurice Moynihan was the father of Maurice Moynihan (1902–99), secretary to the department of the Taoiseach, 1932–57.   85 At this time, the ex-GAA president, Michael Cusack, also operated his own short-lived newspaper, the *Celtic Times*, to promote the GAA and all 'Gaelic pastimes'.

acceptable to men of all religious denominations.[86] The *Gael* reprinted lectures that O'Leary gave to the Dublin and Cork YIS and published original verse and articles by W.B. Yeats, Douglas Hyde, Katherine Tynan and T.W. Rolleston. Much of this work, including Hyde's 'Death Lament of John O'Mahony' (the founder of the Fenian Brotherhood) and 'The Marching Song of the Gaelic Athletes', was later republished as the *Poems and Ballads of Young Ireland* (1888), edited by Rolleston and dedicated to O'Leary and the GAA. It was effectively the swansong of the Dublin YIS. O'Leary suggested in the *Gael* that the GAA's motto should be 'mind will rule and muscle yield, in senate, shop and field, while we've still our strength to wield, let us take our own again.' Meanwhile Hyde's 'marching song' for the GAA (which was later set to music) emphasized the patriotic spirit that IRB men were then trying to promote within the GAA: that 'the numerous men of Eire', 'glorying in our Gaelic manhood', should always be ready to 'arise', if need be: 'see the weapons on our shoulders, neither gun nor pike we bear, but should Ireland call upon us, Ireland soon should find them there.'[87]

The IRB's principal motive in promoting and organizing the GAA was to discourage the general lower class rural community (including its own 'rank and file') from becoming involved in peasant politics and instead remould their attitudes along more republican lines. For example, the Kerry IRB leader, Maurice Moynihan, and the Cavan IRB leader, Terence Fitzpatrick (a publican in Cavan town), after becoming the leaders of the GAA in their county, encouraged GAA members to boycott agrarian secret societies and instead to support the local, strictly non-sectarian branches of the YIS, of which they were also the leaders and which were used to encourage debate upon republican principles among National League members.[88] T.B. Kelly, a Ballina publican who had replaced the imprisoned P.W. Nally as the Mayo IRB leader, did the same thing while promoting the GAA in northern Connacht.[89] This IRB work did not affect the activities of the rural National League, which, in October 1886, following the lead of four MPs, Matthew Harris, William O'Brien, John Dillon and David Sheehy, launched a 'Plan of Campaign', calling for tenants to demand rent reductions on particular estates of the landed aristocracy.

Apart from relieving agrarian distress, the motive in launching the Plan of Campaign was to ensure that the tens of thousands of Irishmen who suddenly

86 Statement of Fitzgerald before the Central Executive of GAA regarding his role in the GAA since 1885, *Freeman's Journal*, 24 Nov. 1887. **87** *The Gael*, 9 Apr. 1887; John Kelly, 'Aesthete among the athletes', *Yeats: an annual of critical and textual studies*, 2 (1984), 75–143; T.W. Rolleston (ed.), *Poems and ballads of Young Ireland* (Dublin, 1888); H.B. Leech, *The continuity of the Irish revolutionary movement* (2nd ed., London, 1912), 32–3. **88** NAI, British in Ireland microfilm, C.O.904/18/707, C.O.904/17/264; CBS reports, carton 1, 1181/s; DICS files, carton 2 (Southwest Division), reports 4 April, 4 Sept., 1 Nov. 1888, 2 May 1889; PRO (London) 30/60/2, Arthur Balfour papers, intelligence notes, 1 to 15 Jan. 1890. **89** NAI, DICS reports (Midlands Division), DI Alan Bell, 3 Mar. 1890 (intercepted IRB–Clan correspondence).

began enrolling in the National League during 1884–5 would not resign
following the collapse of the 'home rule' demand and the return of the Tories
to power in the summer of 1886. Just as the IRB could never depend upon the
rural community's support if it was not importing arms, the National League
and Irish Party could never depend upon the rural community's support if it
was not prepared to launch a land agitation along Land League lines. Irish
countrymen expected to get value for their money. Parnell was very opposed
to the launching of the 'Plan of Campaign', fearing it would hinder the Irish
Party's alliance with the Liberals and lead to renewed coercion, but nevertheless it went ahead. The Tories proclaimed this agitation as illegal in
December 1886, but the 'Plan of Campaign' continued, thereby making the
passing of a new (and rather draconian) coercion act three months later
virtually inevitable. Under its terms, Dublin Castle would suppress or
prosecute thirteen provincial newspapers and sentence their editors, including
a half-dozen members of the Irish Party, to imprisonment for several weeks
(with or without hard labour) for having expressed support for the Plan of
Campaign.[90] Many of the leaders of the Plan claimed that Irishmen were
perfectly within their constitutional rights (as per the unwritten English
common law) in resisting unjust rents (they frequently cited the example of
the Magna Charta), but the Tories were free to interpret these actions as
evidence that the National League was seditious, claiming that it was championing an alternative 'unwritten law' to that of the state.[91] Such was the nature
of the 'unwritten constitution' of the United Kingdom as it operated in
Ireland. By August 1887, the National League had been officially proclaimed
as 'a dangerous organization' and the RIC thereafter began suppressing many
of its branches in rural Ireland. This led to the RIC being stoned by crowds
numerous times during the late 1880s in counties like Donegal, Limerick,
Tipperary and Kerry; the latter county being a particularly disturbed area
owing to the fact that over five hundred tenant farmers were forced to
emigrate during 1887–9 after the RIC had prevented local National League
supporters from introducing a 'no rent manifesto'.[92] These tensions would
reach their greatest height during 1889 when National League supporters in
Tipperary (without any IRB involvement) caused three riots and four explosions, including the throwing of a bomb at the RIC barracks in Tipperary
town, during confrontations with the police, while the RIC shot three people
dead and wounded several others in Mitchelstown, Co. Cork after angry
crowds threatened to stone the police for attempting to prevent a National
League demonstration from taking place.[93]

90 Legg, *Newspapers and nationalism*, 136–8, 168–9; Haller, *William O'Brien*, 70–4; L.M.
Geary, *The Plan of Campaign* (1986), passim.   91 Donald Jordan, 'The Irish National League
and the "unwritten law"' (1998).   92 PRO (London) 30/60/2, Arthur Balfour papers, intelligence notes, 1 to 15 Jan. 1890; NAI, DICS files, carton 2 (Southwest Division), DI Jones, 22
Feb. 1889; DI Gambell, 2 Nov. 1889.   93 PRO (London) C.O. 903/2, Intelligence notes,
series 15, 10; PRO (London) 30/60/2, Arthur Balfour papers, intelligence notes, 1 to 15 Jan.

This pressure being put upon the National League came not merely from the RIC, but also from the Crime Branch Special (CBS), the prerogatives of which were very different to that of its predecessor, the Crime Special Branch. The CBS did not work as a distinct department to counteract the IRB. Instead its forces were delegated by the Tory administration to work under newly established Divisional Magistrates (or 'Special Residential Magistrates') in assisting the RIC and the Residential Magistrates to reassert their general moral authority over the community. An entirely new group of Special Branch detectives were recruited, who were virtually all Englishmen with no prior experience of life in Ireland and so were inclined to believe anything they heard. They became known as 'District Inspectors, Crime Special', were integrated into the regular police forces, and recruited informers within the National League, the Tenants Defence Association, the GAA, the Irish National Foresters, the Trade and Labour Association, the Temperance Societies, the Ancient Order of Hibernians and virtually any body of lower-class Catholics in Ireland, *all* of which were suspected of holding seditious views, or being susceptible to what Dublin Castle described as the 'criminal subculture of fenianism'.[94] The CBS was more effective as an auxiliary police force than an intelligence body. As very many people did not support the Plan of Campaign, the CBS was able to recruit hundreds of informants, or informers, against those 'underground' branches of the National League which attempted to keep the agitation going. These men generally spoke only of rumours, personal vendettas and little more than what could be read in newspapers, but their services were kept to give the RIC every available source of help in counteracting the Plan.

Even before the introduction of the new coercion act in March 1887, the new Tory policing policy in Ireland had aroused the indignation of several influential commentators, such as Archbishop Croke of Cashel and Michael Davitt, two of the four patrons of the GAA. In February 1887, while John Dillon and William O'Brien were on trial in Dublin for promoting the Plan of Campaign, Croke wrote to the press denouncing the RIC as a completely irresponsible and needlessly violent police force, while Davitt, who had long maintained that the RIC was nothing less than a 'standing army of semi-

1890. **94** The CBS 'secret societies register of home associations' and 'register of secret society suspects in Ireland' (NAI, British in Ireland microfilm collection, C.O.904/16–8) shows how it did not distinguish between any social or political movement of professedly nationalist sympathies, all of whom were portrayed as criminals and somehow associated with 'fenianism'. As a result, every lower-class political agitator was suspected of being a member of the IRB. This is equally evident in the thousands of CBS reports, referring to the activities of these various organizations, in NAI, DICS reports, Special Branch (all RIC divisions), carton 1–6, 1887–95, as well as in some DMP reports (especially NAI, DMP files, carton 2, report of Supt. William Reddy, 19 Nov. 1886). Carton 3 of the DICS reports also includes CSB biographies of about half the members of the Irish Party compiled in 1887. The CBS Special Branch 'register of informants' (NAI, 'British in Ireland' microfilm, CO904/183) shows how it recruited informants in virtually every single social and political organization in Ireland involving lower-class Catholics during the late 1880s.

military police', argued that the Dublin Castle administration was a mere 'prostitution of the names of government and of law' and a 'negation of almost every right of political liberty': 'no stronger indictment ever toppled monarchies from the throne of state amidst the plaudits of the world than that which we can substantiate against England rule in Ireland.'[95]

On 27 February 1887, just days after the outbursts in the press against the RIC by Croke and Davitt, Patrick Hoctor and the republican members of the GAA Executive introduced a new rule banning all members of RIC from becoming members of the GAA.[96] As any sporting association was allowed to make its own club membership rules, neither Dublin Castle nor anyone else could protest at this ruling, which Hoctor claimed had made the GAA 'the first association to introduce home rule into Ireland' because it made disapproval of the institutions of the British state a communal way of life.[97] Simultaneously, the GAA Executive introduced a rule giving its members the right to be *ex-officio* members of all county committees of the GAA; a ruling that mirrored the action that the National League had taken on behalf of the Catholic hierarchy. This GAA ruling was justified on the grounds that it could bring the various GAA branches around the country under some form of central control for the first time (an obvious necessity), but it was no doubt intended to give republicans greater ability to shape the ethos of the young association. Maurice Davin, the GAA president and a distinguished athlete, was not present when these rules were passed and, as he approved of neither of them, he stepped down as president as a form of protest. Being unhappy at this development, the GAA Executive left the president's position unoccupied, pleading with Davin to reconsider, while Hoctor was delegated as the acting president of the GAA in the meantime.

Two parties in Ireland were particularly hostile to the GAA at this time. The Tory press (then promoting the gentlemanly IAAA) accused the GAA of being a 'Fenian' conspiracy because it was a movement of the lower classes and it pointed to O'Leary's patronage of the association and editorship of the *Gael* as proof of this.[98] The Catholic clergy was bitterly hostile to the GAA Executive because the *Gael* and many county leaders of the GAA were seeking to eradicate all sectarian attitudes within the lower-class rural community. The clergy viewed the GAA as a threat to their authority in the community and looked with horror upon the possibility of GAA clubs being exposed to viewpoints similar to those recently championed by O'Leary in the YIS and the *DUR*. Owing to the National League's dependence upon clerical support, it was unlikely to back up the republicans if the clergy mounted a campaign to have the *Gael* shut down or to alter the GAA Executive, but the clergy still

95 Archbishop Croke to *Freeman's Journal*, 17 Feb. 1887; Moody, *Davitt*, 318; Leech, *Continuity of Irish revolutionary movement*, 7.   96 W.F. Mandle, 'The IRB and the beginnings of the GAA', *IHS*, 20 (1977), 418–38; idem, *The GAA and Irish nationalist politics, 1884–1924* (1987), 38.   97 *Freeman's Journal*, 27 July 1887.   98 Kelly, 'Aesthete among the athletes', 79.

needed to have some excuse with which to criticize them. Irish provincialism gave them their opportunity.

In July 1887, a Dublin GAA club refused to allow Francis Dineen to collect gate money at their matches simply because he was a Limerick man rather than a Dubliner. Patrick Hoctor (a Tipperary man resident in Dublin) responded in a high-handed manner by suspending this Dublin GAA club and placing a placard in Dublin ordering GAA members to boycott it. The *Freeman's Journal*, which had organized its own Dublin GAA club for its staff, criticised the Central Executive for taking this action, as did a number of other Dublin GAA clubs. Unlike most GAA clubs during the 1880s, the *Freeman's Journal* club consisted mostly of middle-class individuals and was very opposed to the GAA rule (introduced by Cusack) preventing its members playing of 'foreign games' like cricket and rugby. For this reason, Hoctor responded to the *Freeman's Journal*'s criticism of the GAA Executive by accusing it in the *Gael* of exhibiting 'metropolitan snobbery' and of being 'a weak minded, dissentient clique' that was 'acting under the control of the worst form of the West British element.'[99] Owing to its respectable public image, the *Freeman's Journal* was the paper to which the Catholic hierarchy always contributed. Hoctor's creation of bitter hostility between the *Gael* and the *Freeman* meant that the clergy could thereafter use the latter paper freely to mount a propaganda war against the *Gael* and the GAA Central Executive, which is precisely what they did.

On 9 November 1887, the Central Executive voted at the annual convention of the GAA in Thurles to abandon the rule regarding the collecting of gate-money, which had sparked off so much controversy in Dublin. It also voted to abandon the rule granting its members the right to be *ex-officio* members of the county committees of the GAA, for fear of appearing dictatorial. These resolutions were introduced by P.N. Fitzgerald who, though not a member of the GAA Executive, had been asked to chair the convention by Patrick Hoctor as well as Alderman John Horgan, a former mayor of Cork City who was disliked by the clergy and a close confidant of Cork republicans. Fitzgerald genuinely believed that both these GAA rulings had been unnecessary and potentially harmful to the association. However the parish priest of Thurles, Fr John Scanlan, objected strongly to his chairing the meeting and proposed instead that this honour be given to a Catholic, former British army major who was a member of a GAA club previously expelled by the Central Executive for its opposition to the ban on the RIC.[100] Not surprisingly, this caused a bitter row to break out, during which (priests later claimed) Patrick Hoctor started 'hooting' the clergymen present in 'a most bitter and aggravating tone',

---

99 Mandle, *GAA*, quoted 41. 100 Mandle, *GAA*, 50–1. Mandle generally presents a very false picture of the political context of republican-clerical controversies in the GAA during the late 1880s by relying on CBS informers' reports, which purposely portrayed the conflict in even more polemical terms than the clergy did, and by failing to understand the politics of the CBS, the Catholic hierarchy or the IRB.

causing Scanlan and his party to walk immediately out of the courthouse (as they no doubt had intended doing all along) with delegates from several Dublin and Tipperary GAA clubs. Thereafter Edmond Bennett (IRB), the chairman of the Ennis Board of Guardians, was elected president of GAA. Supported by Fitzgerald, Bennett then introduced a rule that no GAA club should 'officially take part in any public political meeting or demonstration'. This rule was supposedly to advertise the non-political character of the GAA but it did not include Manchester-martyr demonstrations within this ruling, for, as did the non-partisan Dublin Trades Council, the GAA considered these as 'national' rather than 'political' events.[101] Bennett had no problem with calling for GAA clubs to attend a Manchester-martyrs demonstration in Ennis two weeks later, which was addressed by John O'Leary, P.N. Fitzgerald and himself. This 'non-political' ruling inadvertently created a controversy, however, for when it was proposed at the convention that the GAA Executive should officially pass a resolution of sympathy with the immensely popular William O'Brien MP (then in prison for his involvement in the Plan of Campaign), Bennett ruled the idea out of order as 'we are after putting a resolution not to take part in politics'.

Upon leaving Thurles town hall, while the GAA convention was still going on, Fr Scanlan and several other priests told waiting *Freeman's Journal* journalists outside that the men in charge of the GAA must be 'put down', as they were 'Fenians', 'spies' and 'informers' who desired only to use the GAA to assist Dublin Castle undermine the National League or 'turn the people away from their priests'. The *Catholic Press* immediately supported this view, but no other Irish newspaper did, although the *Freeman's Journal* allowed the clergy to give a voice to their opinions in its columns without making any editorial comment. In subsequent weeks, the *Freeman* printed numerous letters from Catholic priests from Munster who denounced Fitzgerald, Hoctor and O'Leary as men who were 'playing the game of the English papers' by 'vilifying the Irish priesthood' and who were obviously 'doing the work, the sad, disgusting work of [Chief Secretary] Balfour and Company' for if they were not all CBS spies, then they surely would be 'instantly arrested'.[102] Fr Scanlan accused John O'Leary of preaching 'physical force' and of having attempted to destroy the National League ever since his arrival in Ireland in 1885 and he denounced him as a man whom no Irish Catholic could listen to, for he 'is not a religious man'. Archbishop Croke also issued a statement calling for a change in the way the GAA was governed. He accused the organisers of the Thurles Convention of being anticlerical men who were trying to secure 'a party triumph' by 'placing fully *fifty thousand* young and enthusiastic Irishmen under the irresponsible control' of men who were 'either wholly unknown, or *not* favourably known to the country', which was tantamount to saying that they were not favourably known to the Catholic hierarchy.[103]

101 Boyle, *The Irish labor movement*, 248. 102 *Freeman's Journal*, 29 Nov. 1887. 103 Fr Scanlan and Archbishop Croke to *Freeman's Journal*, 29 Nov. 1887.

This dispute was of a very similar nature to that which arose in the days of *Irish People* and the Land League, for once republicans began speaking out against sectarian attitudes on public platforms, the Catholic clergymen invariably denounced them as 'godless nobodies' or even British agents. Fr Scanlan, for instance, argued at his public rallies during November 1887 that because the GAA executive did not call upon Archbishop Croke to settle the dispute with the Dublin clubs, it was inherently a dangerous, anticlerical faction whose attitude was

> *We don't want him* – we don't want priestly patronage ... but you will speak out in trumpet tongues today and proclaim your resolution to follow the new path ... the path that will lead to assured and speedy triumph ... Here's how the cause stands. On one side, the Archbishop of Cashel and the priesthood of Ireland ... on the other, a physical force policy, secret societies, government emissaries and informers! Which will you follow! (Mass response: 'We'll follow our priests!')[104]

John O'Leary was determined that the republican party would exercise caution in responding to the clergy's campaign. While noting that he had 'said many words, and meant to say many more, against the particular acts [boycotting and outrages] of many of the agitators' in the Plan of Campaign, O'Leary denied the claim that he had sought to undermine the National League in any way. He also denied that the GAA executive had the slightest intention of fermenting rebellion in the country and regarding 'Father Scanlan's general utterances on Fenianism, separatism and the like', O'Leary argued that 'neither I, nor any man, need say anything whatever',[105] his attitude to this dispute being 'the least said, the sooner mended'. Many IRB men, however, found it impossible to restrain themselves in the controversy and openly accused the clergy of 'raising this disturbance for their own purposes' and 'casting aspersions on the intelligence of the Irish people' by making 'the most wild and vicious charge' that anyone who did not follow the priests in politics were British spies.[106] A statement issued by the GAA Central Executive on 23 November 1887 claimed that the clergy behaved in an 'excited and violent manner' at the Thurles convention while the chairman, P.N. Fitzgerald, exhibited 'the moderation of conscious strength'. It also claimed that the *Freeman's Journal* had purposely exaggerated greatly the number of delegates who left the convention with Fr Scanlan, which were 'not 200 ... but only some thirty or forty'.[107]

As much of the clergy's propaganda had circulated around P.N. Fitzgerald's role as chairman at the Thurles convention, after discussing the matter with Michael Davitt, he felt obliged to make a public statement. Fitzgerald stated that

104 *Freeman's Journal*, 21 Nov. 1887.   105 O'Leary to *Freeman's Journal*, 21 Nov. 1887.
106 Letters of Pat McInerney (Ennis IRB leader) and Keith O'Brien to *Freeman's Journal*, 29 Nov. 1887.   107 *Freeman's Journal*, 21 Nov. 1887.

he believed that the GAA must be allowed to have 'complete freedom of action' and that 'the Gaelic Association should be open to all – an Irish nation must include *all* sections of Irishmen – to make independence easy, Ireland requires the aid of all her sons.' Noting that he was 'partly responsible for the non-political resolution' at the convention, Fitzgerald denied that any insult was meant to William O'Brien MP, for 'we have been friends for sixteen years, and are so still'. He suggested that a motion of sympathy with O'Brien be passed and emphasized that both he and the GAA executive wanted to see O'Brien released from prison as soon as possible. He denied completely the clergy's accusations that either he or the GAA executive sought to undermine the National League (then being suppressed in Munster by the RIC) and expressed strong resentment at the 'unfair manner' in which the *Freeman's Journal* had assisted the clergy 'raise such false issues from the altar and elsewhere'. He stated that priests were not attacked or subject to verbal abuse at the convention and he would not have allowed any such actions to be made. He believed that 'all intelligent readers' and 'any ordinary politician' could see the total unreality of the whole issue. Indeed, apart from those league officials who were clergymen, the National League was evidently indifferent to this whole controversy. Commenting on the aftermath of the Thurles convention, John Dillon MP also stated publicly that he believed the GAA executive should be allowed to adopt any policy it desired.[108] Few Irish Party MPs other than Dillon, however, could afford to risk losing the necessary financial support to sustain their parliamentary careers by potentially attracting the wrath of the Catholic bishops. Finally, Fitzgerald noted that 'I really thought that with the spread of political knowledge the days of felon-setting [Irishmen talking of republicans as criminals] were over', but he felt confident that, 'when the smoke has cleared aside', most Irishmen would have the intelligence to realize the petty purpose of all such talk, for 'that game is now too stale'.[109] Fitzgerald, however, was to be sorely disappointed in his expectation.

Although few, if any, GAA followers appear to have accepted the priests' claims that the GAA executive was attempting to undermine the National League or that it was riddled with CBS spies, many *did* feel that 'the *soggarth aroon*, who through weal and woe in the chequered history of our country has been guiding light of our people', had been 'derided and condemned' by the existing GAA executive and therefore its personnel must be changed completely.[110] At a conference chaired by John O'Leary in early December 1887, the GAA central executive and appointees of Croke agreed that elections for a new, enlarged GAA executive should take place the following month. At this tense convention on 4 January 1888 the priests' nominations succeeded in winning a majority of the seats, a result that Fitzgerald begrudg-

---

108 NAI, Land and National League reports, carton 2, speech of Dillon in Drogheda, 10 Nov 1887.   109 Letter of Fitzgerald read at meeting of the GAA Central Executive, *Freeman's Journal*, 24 Nov. 1887.   110 This is the predominant tone of the letters of many GAA clubs to the *Freeman's Journal*, 23–29 Nov 1887.

ingly accepted, but added that 'if we had been in the majority we would not trample on the right of a minority.'[111] Not surprisingly, the first action of the new clericalist executive was to close down the *Gael,* prompting a dejected Hoctor to leave for the United States where he would remain until the spring of 1890. As John Kelly has noted, the closure of the *Gael* was a 'most serious loss' to Irish literature, for its literary columns were of a much higher quality than any other popular journal in Ireland at the time.[112] It was perhaps an even greater loss, however, to the IRB, which could only have been demoralized greatly by the fact that its harmless efforts to champion non-sectarian attitudes had backfired so completely in the YIS and in the GAA, in town and in country.

R.V. Comerford has argued that the structural basis of Irish life during the nineteenth century dictated that no political movement (even if it was urban based) could possibly succeed if it did not uphold and accept 'the Catholic, rural-orientated and property-conscious values of the dominant social ideal' of the farming community in what was a rural and parochially-minded country.[113] The events of the late 1880s certainly validate this view. During 1886–7, the IRB's efforts to prioritize O'Leary's policy and effectively ignore the Plan of Campaign had proved entirely counter-productive. Retrospective comments of P.N. Fitzgerald on the setbacks the IRB suffered during the mid 1880s indicated that many republicans felt that their failure to advance their brand of politics was due to their having been victimized. Speaking regarding the arrests of P.W. Nally and himself during 1884, Fitzgerald noted that they were neither 'political fanatics' nor 'scheming agitators', yet they were tried on the charge of 'conspiracy to murder' by justices of the peace who had since become enthusiastic supporters of the 'home rule' movement; something Fitzgerald felt was a complete 'satire on Irish nationalism'. Meanwhile as the Irish Party was 'having the pudding and the profit' and helping to ensure that 'the clergy are now the stronger power in rural Ireland', 'the poor Fenian, condemned by Church and State' was left having to face 'his countrymen's ingratitude' while he attempted 'to carry out his ideal of Ireland a nation, free and independent.'[114] The 'unwritten law' that Dublin Castle felt was ruling the National League by 1886–7 was effectively nothing more than the collectivist mindset of a political community that not only upheld 'the Catholic, rural-orientated and property-conscious values of the dominant social ideal' but also refused to tolerate any other form of political behaviour or standards. These same factors in Irish political society that had helped to remove the IRB's foothold in Irish popular politics during 1885–7 would soon serve to topple Parnell himself. Not until this occurred did the Irish political community begin to re-examine its standards and would John O'Leary's belief that Irish society was in a dire need of a proverbial republic of letters begin to find more than a handful of adherents.

111 *Freeman's Journal,* 5 Jan. 1888. 112 Kelly, 'Aesthete among the athletes', 133. 113 Comerford, *Fenians in context,* 248–9. 114 *Irish Daily Independent,* 10 Nov. 1894 (speech at event in honour of P.W. Nally at Rotunda).

6

'Condemned by Church and State?': the eclipse of the IRB and Parnell, 1887–91

P.N. Fitzgerald's professed belief in an 'onward march of a party of progress' among 'the intelligent, educated democracy' of Ireland; his complaint about people's 'ingratitude' to republicans for failing to recognize that they were trying to lift them 'out of political slavery'; and his prediction that 'governments might persecute, but the more persecution, the better for the cause and the stronger it will grow',[1] was a rhetoric very typical of democratic-republican radicals or revolutionaries in nineteenth-century Europe. The same was true of the arguments of Tom Brennan and the republican propagandists of the Land League during the earlier part of the decade, who were just as inclined to denounce 'the people' for their lack of self-reliance in the same breath as they were calling upon them to take control of their own political destinies. The reality of Irish life during the 1880s, however, was that this rural-orientated country was very deeply divided in virtually every way possible, social, political and religious, and this virtually ruled out political mobilization along any ideologically-motivated lines. The Tory policy for governing Ireland during the late 1880s was designed to capitalize upon this reality. In particular, the Tories knew as well as did John O'Leary and the members of the Contemporary Club and YIS in Dublin that if the material interests of the farmers and the church were served, both would cease to pretend to have any interest in Irish nationalist politics and the heart would be taken out of the National League.[2]

The Tories' suppression of branches of the National League, imprisonment of newspaper editors and baton charging public meetings may have been draconian, but notwithstanding the popular press' talk of 'Bloody Balfour', very many people actually supported the government's efforts to combat the 'Plan of Campaign'. The Tories soon realized that, with the possible exception of William O'Brien, 'those who have suffered imprisonment' for having supported the Plan of Campaign 'show no inclination to again earn the plank bed',[3] and that endless numbers of assistants to the police, or informers, could be recruited for all sorts of reasons. For example, Matthew Harris' Trade and Labour Association, a novel attempt to defend the rights of skilled and unskilled labourers in country towns, was opposed by most farmers in the prosperous midlands who supported the National League. They told the police bluntly that they wished to see both the Plan of Campaign and Harris's agitation 'put down', for the labourers in town and country now

1 *Freeman's Journal*, 4 Sept. 1890 (speech at Glasnevin). 2 Daly, *Young Douglas Hyde*, 71.
3 NAI, DICS reports, carton 2 (Southwest Division), DI Jones, 4 Apr. 1888.

'thought themselves as good, or better, than the class above them' and 'they should be kept in their proper place'.[4] Many farmers had a great distaste for the GAA for the same reason and were very opposed to the fund-collection efforts of the Tenants Defence League, one Tipperary farmer telling a CBS agent, for example, that most 'respectable' people's view was 'to hell with the National League, Tenant League and every other damn league; what have we been doing, as gentlemen, but supporting a pack of bloody cut-throats and ruining ourselves and our families'.[5] The prevalence of such feeling in the country placed republicans and various other radical democrats in a very precarious position.

As the National League had been outlawed in various parts of the country, many (including some Parnellite journalists with provincial newspapers) were willing to inform against those who tried to keep the branches going on an underground basis. This made any attempt to redistribute IRB arms in rural Ireland during the late 1880s a very risky strategy and a couple of arms seizures took place, the most successful one occurring in Roscommon. During 1887, Jim Boland brought arms from the trouble spot of Liverpool to Dublin, before sending them on to Athenry, Co. Galway, where they were collected by Thomas Ryan, a local hotelier, a brother-in-law of P.W. Nally and a leading Connacht IRB man. Some of these arms were then sent to John Lavin, the Castlerea IRB leader, who drilled recruits regularly and also operated the Roscommon YIS. Lavin, however, was not able to fulfil his desire to keep the local IRB out of the Plan of Campaign agitation. J.J. O'Kelly, the local MP, supported the Plan of Campaign and also ran a radical 'Boyle Democratic Club', where republicans had taken to meeting, but an informer against the Plan of Campaign in Roscommon soon enabled the RIC to seize much of Roscommon IRB's arms in Ballaghadereen and Boyle.[6]

CBS informers recruited against the Plan of Campaign could help the police combat the IRB in several rural areas. In Cavan, for example, the local IRB leader Terence Fitzpatrick was unable to keep his local following away from the Plan of Campaign agitation and the suppressed branches of the National League. As a result, the CBS was able to recruit a very valuable informer against the IRB in the county.[7] Clare and Galway were the only counties where the IRB was perpetually involved in land agitation, because the Supreme Council could never persuade them to do otherwise. Clare IRB leaders like Patrick McInerney, an Ennis town commissioner, were arrested a couple of times during the 1880s for encouraging boycotting and the intimi-

4 NAI, DICS reports, carton 3 (South East Division, including Tipperary), DI Bouchiers, 4 Dec. 1890. 5 NAI, DICS files, carton 2 (South West Division), DI Jones, 12 Aug. 1889. 6 NAI, DMP files, carton 2, Report of Supt. William Reddy, 20 April 1887; Jim Maher, *Harry Boland* (Cork, 1998), 9–10 (Jim Boland was the father of Harry Boland); NAI, DICS reports (Western Division) reports of DI Gibbons, 6 Mar., 6 Apr, 10 Sept., 10 Nov. 1888, 6 Apr., 7 Aug. 1889. 7 NAI, DICS reports, carton 4, Midlands Division, reports 1887–95 (detailed and apparently authoritative reports were received every month regarding the Cavan IRB).

dation of landlords' agents. In Clare, numerous poor tenant farmers were recruited as informers against the National League and, in turn, those branches of the league in which local IRB circles had become involved. In 1888, the Galway IRB leader, J.P. McCarthy, a leading Loughrea town councillor and National League activist, ordered an arms raid upon the Galway Naval Reserve Battery and subsequently distributed these arms to men involved in the Plan of Campaign. He also spoke alongside James Redpath of the Clan on National League platforms in Galway in favour of tenants arming themselves to defend their homesteads; an idea that Matthew Harris MP (who was now seriously ill; he died from stomach cancer in 1890, aged sixty-five) also supported.[8] Informers, however, generally kept the CBS well informed of what McCarthy was doing. The Plan of Campaign divided, rather than united, the general populace in rural Ireland.

The National Club in Dublin was effectively the IRB headquarters during the later 1880s and it became a nucleus for various other republican activities. The DMP believed that the Dublin IRB leadership held meetings in this club on a fortnightly basis and that, on more than one occasion, IRB conventions (chaired by P.N. Fitzgerald) of centres from all around the country took place in the club's private rooms, but they were unable to learn what was discussed at any of these meetings.[9] The National Monuments Committee (NMC) also held its meetings here. The club's patrons, apart from John O'Leary, were Michael Davitt and John Clancy, who had recently resigned from the National League and still associated principally with republicans. The club's secretary was Michael Seery (IRB) of the Dublin GAA, a young commercial traveller whom O'Leary claimed was his most inspirational advisor and more than 'any single person', gave 'the most faithful and effective support' to his plans ever since he had returned to Ireland in January 1885.[10] During 1888, P.N. Fitzgerald spent much of his time in Dublin, working with Clancy in setting up various other political clubs in the city. These included the 'Commercial Club' in Ringsend and the 'City Club' on St. Andrews Lane, the members of which boycotted the 'Catholic Club', which met in the National League headquarters on Sackville (O'Connell) Street. The Catholic Club, unlike the others mentioned, was reported to be very hostile towards the politics of the members of the National Club, indicating that its republican antecedents and proclivities were well known in the city.[11]

Other republican clubs or societies in Dublin included Fred Allan's 'Robert

8 NAI, British in Ireland microfilm, C.O. 904/18/958; NAI, DICS reports, carton 1 (Western Division), reports 6 April 1889, 4 April 1892; *Special Commission Report*, vol. 3, 540–1.   9 NAI, DMP files, carton 3, report 825, Sergeant Montgomery, 21 Nov. 1887; reports 1191, 1212, 1250 and 1264, Supt. William Reddy, 30 Aug., 24 Sept., 16 Oct., 24 Oct. 1888; carton 6, report 1714 and 1766, Supt. William Reddy, 11 and 19 May 1890.   10 *Irish Daily Independent*, 23 Nov. 1897 (speech of O'Leary at a Rotunda demonstration in honour of Seery).   11 NAI, DMP files, carton 3, report 1125, 21 July 1888, various authors; report 1212, Chief Inspector Peter Hughes, 30 Aug. 1888.

Emmet and John Mitchel Debating Societies', and the Leinster Debating Society (LDS), which was run by James Doyle (a socialist printer and lifelong member of the NMC) and Denis Seery (IRB), Michael's younger brother. The LDS's membership included a well-known labour activist John Masterson as well as former members of the 'Junior Young Ireland Society' (designed for school children) such as William Rooney and Arthur Griffith, the latter having been first introduced to the writings of John Mitchel when presented with a prize of his books by John O'Leary in 1885.[12] The LDS met at the same venue on Marlborough Street as a number of other clubs that were promoted by individual republicans or socialists, most notably the 'Progressivist Club'. William Swords, a former 'Old Guard' activist and prison warden, established a wing of the principal American labour organisation, the Knights of Labor, in Dublin, while Thomas Fitzpatrick, a printer who served intermittently as the deputy leader of the Dublin IRB, was the most notable champion of small socialist clubs in Dublin. At the time, the *Commonweal*, the principal British socialist publication, was describing Fitzpatrick as 'the greatest hope for indigenous Irish socialism' (along with Davitt) and he was invited to address socialist conventions in Copenhagen, Chicago and other cities.[13] Fitzpatrick's activities might have reflected a slight trend in IRB circles. At the end of the decade, for example, Michael Davitt's short-lived socialist Irish Democratic Labour Federation (which championed the rights of both the skilled and unskilled working classes and demanded universal male suffrage) reputedly found its greatest support in Cork from IRB men.[14] Meanwhile the RIC believed that the IRB was responsible for circulating 'atheistic books which go to encourage disbelief in God and in a future state' (an apparent reference to radical socialist literature) in Enniscorthy, Bray and north Kerry during the late 1880s, and for establishing an independent labourers' league in Thurles.[15] On the whole, however, it is very probable that the IRB was not actively promoting socialism, even if its members viewed greater political activism among the working classes as 'a hopeful sign'.[16]

During the later 1880s, the IRB continued to concentrate upon the GAA rather than the 'Plan of Campaign' and promoted the NMC as well. The problem facing the organization, however, was that its failure to import arms meant that its 'rank and file' ceased to subscribe in many parts of the country and began to drop out.[17] Manchester-martyr demonstrations were prohibited by the Tories in all counties where the 'Plan of Campaign' was in operation

12 NLI, Minute book of the Leinster Debating Society (renamed Leinster Literary Society in 1890), MS 19935; Brian Maye, *Arthur Griffith* (1997), 13.   13 For Fitzpatrick's career see Lane, *The origins of modern Irish socialism, 1881–96.*   14 NAI, DICS files, carton 2 (Southwest Division), DI Jones, 3 Feb. and 2 May 1890.   15 PRO (London) 30/60/2, Arthur Balfour papers, intelligence notes, 1 to 15 Apr. 1890; NAI, DICS reports, carton 3 (South East Division), Sergeant Collins, 2 Sept. 1890.   16 NAI, DICS files, carton 3 (South East Division), DI Bouchiers, 7 Oct. 1890 (report of speech of Patrick Hoctor in Tipperary town, 21 Sept. 1890).   17 NAI, DICS files, carton 2 (Southwest Division), DI Jones, 1 Oct. 1889; DI Gambell, 2 Nov. 1889.

between 1886 and 1891; those that were held were invariably suppressed by force, often resulting in riots.[18] As it was no longer possible for the IRB to collect funds for the NMC by this means, the GAA in Londonderry, Enniscorthy and Dublin regularly donated a percentage of their gate-earnings to the NMC to keep the organization alive.[19] Republicans also contributed to keeping the GAA alive. In Dublin, for example, Michael Seery and Jim Boland arranged and completed a financial deal with the owners of Clonturk Park (renamed as Croke Park in 1912) so that the grounds could be used for GAA tournaments and finals in the future (no such grounds existed previously).[20] Elsewhere in the country, however, the Catholic clergy continued to denounce the GAA from the altar whenever it was suspected of falling under the republicans' influence. The bishop of Cork warned his parishioners, for example, that he had been informed that some men in the GAA were secretly acting under the direction of 'something called a Supreme Council' and that anyone who supported such men would not only be excommunicated but deserved to be ostracized by the whole community.[21] Not surprisingly, the CBS welcomed the willingness of the clergy to denounce the GAA from the altar whenever it fell under republicans' influence (especially in Munster and south Ulster), considering this as 'a good safety valve'.[22] The IRB, however, was a serious threat neither to the church nor the state during the late 1880s. Instead it was simply trying to maintain its political influence in the country through setting up various clubs and societies. The most important centre of Irish 'revolutionary' affairs was essentially Irish-America, where British intelligence continued to concentrate its efforts.

Major Gosselin received all the reports of the CBS in Ireland, but was essentially indifferent to what they said. He knew the most important aspect of Irish revolutionary politics was what was happening in America, for without Irish-American financial assistance, the IRB could not be a serious threat. Furthermore, if the Irish-American movement could be compromised further, the IRB could potentially be as well. The fact that the Clan was split also gave British intelligence numerous opportunities, and it seems clear that most of

---

18 *Nation,* 1 Dec. 1888, 25 Nov. 1890; *Freeman's Journal,* 24 Nov. 1891; *The People* (later known as the *Wexford People*), 21 Nov. 1891; *Western People,* 28 Nov. 1891. One of the worst cases occurred in November 1887 when P.N. Fitzgerald, Patrick Hoctor and the lord mayor of Limerick, W.P. McCormick, attempted to organize a Manchester-martyr demonstration despite Dublin Castle's ban upon the event. They brought with them John McInerney of New York to unveil a ceremonial cross in honour of the 'martyrs' in the city. When McInerney started to make a republican speech, the RIC dispersed the crowds forcibly, resulting in the police being stoned and a lengthy riot. *Freeman's Journal,* 28 Nov. 1887. 19 NAI DMP files, carton 3, Report 1288 and 1290, Supt. William Reddy, 26 Nov 1888; DICS reports, carton 3, South East Division, report 4 Sept. 1888; DICS reports, carton 6 (Northern Division), reports of 19 Sept. 1888, 4 Jan. 1889, 5 July 1890. 20 NAI, DMP files, carton 6, Report 1727, Supt. William Reddy, 21 May 1890. 21 NAI, DICS files, carton 2, South West Division, DI Jones, 3 Feb. 1890. 22 PRO (London) 30/60/1, Arthur Balfour papers, intelligence notes 16 Oct–1 Nov. 1889; NAI, DICS reports, carton 4 (Midlands Division), DI Bell, 5 Sept. 1889; carton 6 (Northern Division), DI Reeves, 4 Jan., 4 Mar. 1889.

the Special Branch's funding continued to be used to recruit agents in America.

Since 1884, John Devoy was trying to gather together the various Clan camps expelled by the British spy F.F. Millen and establish a rival Clan executive to that led by Michael Boland, but this work went very slowly and it was not until 1887 that he was able to create an alternative wing, or executive, of any kind. Even then, the dividing line between the two wings of the Clan was far from clear. By 1886 the Michael Boland wing of the Clan had renamed itself as the Irish National Brotherhood (INB) to distinguish itself from the seceding faction of the Clan, which retained the official title of Clan, the United Brotherhood (UB), and was led by Luke Dillon (who ran a credit union in Philadelphia) and Devoy.[23] Although Devoy favoured restoring the Clan's alliance with the IRB on the Supreme Council's terms, the UB preoccupied itself mostly with trying to win away the INB's following. It claimed that the INB neglected the family of W.M. Lomansey (the IRB's military adviser during 1880–1), who, notwithstanding his previous denunciations of the 'dynamite war', was killed during December 1884, reputedly while trying (inexplicably) to detonate a bomb under London Bridge. The UB claimed that he had been sent on a 'mission' by Boland's group, but it is equally likely that Luke Dillon was responsible for inadvertently sending Lomansey to his death, since Dillon was in London at the same time on a so-called 'mission'. Spies were in *both* wings of the Clan. The INB wing took over complete control of the funding of what was formerly the 'Revolutionary Directory'; a body that had originally been central to the IRB's success during the period 1879–81 and was now nothing more than a medium for British intelligence to create mayhem. For this reason, any efforts the IRB might make to restore its alliance with the Clan were a recipe for disaster. John O'Leary's decision in 1884 to cease communicating with the Clan was motivated by this reality, but the IRB could not ignore the fact that it would not be able to improve its political capacity without Irish–American financial backing. It was in a no-win situation.

In Paris, John O'Connor received some letters from Michael Boland and his secretary, John D. Carroll, during 1885–6 stating that there would be no question of the 'Revolutionary Directory' ever being re-established or the IRB receiving its funding if the Supreme Council did not cooperate fully with the 'dynamite war' policy. They offered to re-enter negotiations with the IRB 'provided you are not corresponding with others on this side.'[24] O'Connor ignored these letters, but supposed followers of Devoy, most notably W.M. Browne of New Jersey, were also demanding that the IRB ought to be supporting the dynamite war or was 'not worth bothering about'. During June 1886, with the support of Luke Dillon, Browne became a UB leader and

[margin handwritten note: probs. w/ Amer. funding & GB intell.]

23 *Special Commission Report*, vol. 5, 45–6 (statement of the spy Le Caron regarding his role in the INB). 24 UCD, Desmond Ryan papers, L.A. 10/k/23 (1), 25–9, 31–2 (statement of John O'Connor); John Devoy, 'The story of Clan na Gael', *Gaelic American*, 17 Jan. 1925.

pressurized John McInerney in New York into giving his delegate, a 'J. Gallagher' of New Jersey, all the names and addresses of the Supreme Council. McInerney refused, but gave him some old contact addresses for Mark Ryan and John Torley.[25] It is known that a 'Gallagher of Jersey City' was a leading British spy in the Clan for very many years, as was John Groves, a fervent supporter of the 'dynamite war' who wavered between both wings during the mid 1880s.[26]

In July 1886, O'Connor travelled to New York, soon to be followed by Mark Ryan, to work with McInerney and Devoy in trying to overthrow the leadership of the INB.[27] The INB responded by sending the British spy F.F. Millen to London in the winter of 1886 to get in contact with the Supreme Council. Millen was able to learn from John Ryan, a Chelsea shoemaker, IRB veteran of the 1860s and the South of England representative on the Supreme Council, that a Supreme Council meeting was due to take place in a hotel in Rouen, France on 2 January 1887. Probably because Millen had been an accredited delegate of the Clan to the IRB in January 1879, Ryan evidently thought he was doing a good thing by letting Millen come with him to Rouen. Upon their arrival, John O'Connor objected strongly to Millen's uninvited presence, but it appears that some other Supreme Council members thought that there was no harm in at least hearing what the INB's delegate had to say, so they could learn *something* of what was happening in the Clan. O'Connor suspected that Ryan had been followed to Rouen by London detectives (which is probable, considering Millen's presence) and so he ordered the other Supreme Council members to disperse and to reconvene in Paris, on 4 January. From a Home Office report of the time, it is known that Millen and a UB delegate (quite possibly Gallagher) were permitted to attend this meeting and, consequently, Major Nicholas Gosselin was able to learn the exact names of the IRB leadership for the first time.[28]

Seven of the eleven members of the Supreme Council attended this meeting, namely O'Connor himself and six of the seven divisional leaders of the IRB. These were P.N. Fitzgerald (Munster), C.J. O'Farrell (Leinster), Michael O'Hanlon (Ulster), John Torley (Scotland), William McGuinness (a Preston publican, north of England) and John Ryan (south of England). The British agent, or agents, gathered from speaking with the ordinary members of the Supreme Council that the other, honorary members on the council, apart from O'Connor, were John O'Leary, John McInerney of New York and a man named as 'John Sweeney'. Although there was a John Sweeney in the Galway IRB (who could well have been the Connacht representative), the fact that this Home Office file was annotated with the remark that Sweeney also went under the alias 'Skeritt', *could* mean this man was Patrick Sweeney of 'Paris Letters'

25 *DPB*, vol. 2, 272, 274–5, 284–5. 26 NLI, Devoy papers, MS 18008 (5), Thomas Markham (keeper of records at Dublin Castle) to John Devoy, 9 Aug. 1924. 27 *DPB*, vol. 2, 288–90. 28 NAI, CBS files, carton 1, 533/s (attached reports of Major Gosselin from Jan. 1887 regarding the Supreme Council's meeting in Paris).

fame, who was apparently working with the Clan in New York. If this was the case (which is by no means certain), the Supreme Council was rather naïve to keep such a man among their counsel. As O'Connor chaired the meeting, British intelligence became convinced that he was the IRB president, but IRB and Clan sources indicate that O'Connor (who deferred to the judgment of O'Leary in political matters) remained the secretary.

It was also learnt that the current paid travelling organisers of the IRB were Patrick Hoctor, who was then doing organizational work in Glasgow, and P.J. Boland, who was due to visit Ulster. The identity of 'P.J. Boland' is unknown, but this was probably a mistaken reference to J.P. Boland, otherwise known as 'Jack Boland', who together with his brother Jim was a leading figure in the Dublin IRB. A good reason for believing this is that in subsequent years one of Gosselin's principal tactics in trying to undermine the IRB was to subject Jack Boland (while in New York as an IRB envoy) to the intrigues of an *agent provocateur*, William Jones, a native of Armagh, who may well have first won Boland's confidence in the past, while he was in Ulster.[29] Millen's proposal of a Supreme Council alliance with the INB was rejected firmly, owing to his call for it to support the 'dynamite war' policy, which the Supreme Council 'unanimously condemned'. O'Connor was the only member who remained apprehensive that further outrages might take place, probably because he was the only member who knew anything of Clan affairs.

Apart from discussing affairs in the IRB in England (the IRB leadership suspected that its Liverpool organization was infiltrated),[30] the Supreme Council discussed the possibility of delegating IRB funds to import more firearms into Ireland via England, probably meaning some of those firearms it had purchased prior to 1884. Commenting on this, Major Gosselin of the Home Office reported to Dublin Castle that 'you will hear from me' as soon as any attempt was made,[31] presumably because of his many informers in the IRB in northern England, where he was based. This may well have been an idle boast, but it might help to explain why the DMP knew when Jim Boland imported arms from Liverpool during the spring of 1887 to distribute to the Connacht IRB, quite possibly at J.P. McCarthy's behest.[32]

In February 1887, Luke Dillon, the chairman of the UB, learnt that Millen had been able to find the 'grand connecting link in the chain that binds us to the people at home' and resolved to do all in his power 'to get at the bottom of Millen's overtures'.[33] Through his own informers in the United Irishmen of

29 Ibid. The activities of William Jones will be explained in the next chapter. 30 Although Dan O'Neill was tracked down in Australia, he may well have convinced the IRB agent that he was not an informer, and that someone else in Liverpool was. This is hinted in the ambiguous comments made in Devoy's article 'Jack Daly', *Gaelic American*, 15 Mar. 1924. 31 NAI, CBS files, carton 1, 533/s. 32 In 1882, McCarthy persuaded the Dublin IRB to distribute arms to Galway, indicating that it was standard procedure in the Galway IRB to make such appeals. *Special Commission Report*, vol. 3, 540–1 (report of informer Patrick Delaney on McCarthy). 33 *DPB*, vol. 2, 300.

America organization, Dillon knew that its leader Patrick Sarsfield Cassidy, whom O'Donovan Rossa was convinced was a spy, and Millen were planning to revive the 'dynamite war' by planting a bomb in London to disrupt Queen Victoria's golden jubilee celebrations. The British secret service's principal target in this plot was the Irish Party rather than the IRB. Prior to forming his 'dynamite team', Millen was ordered to introduce himself to a few Parnellite members of parliament in London, so that, when the plot was exposed and Millen was arrested, the Tory government would be able to prove that the Irish Party was in league with terrorists, as Tory propaganda liked to claim.[34] The British prime minister, Lord Salisbury, and the proprietor of the London *Times* both appear to have been aware of the Millen plot and approved of it.[35] If this plot had succeeded, it would have served the dual purpose of helping the Tory government deflect criticism from its introduction of a draconian coercion act in Ireland on 7 March 1887 and, at the same time, constitute a great propaganda success for the London *Times*, which had published the first of its infamous 'Parnellism and Crime' series of articles (many of which were written by Sir Robert Anderson of the London CID)[36] on the same day as the coercion act was introduced. Ultimately, however, the 'Jubilee Plot' came to nothing except the arrest and imprisonment of a handful of Millen's dupes in London.[37]

The fiasco of the Jubilee plot created great suspicions about Millen in the Irish-American revolutionary movement, where Gosselin wanted him to do most of his work. Consequently, his services were soon dropped,[38] and, lacking any protection, he met a perhaps inevitable fate. Millen was found dead in his *New York Herald* office on the morning of 10 April 1889, having locked himself into his offices the previous night. He may have committed suicide from fear of exposure and, indeed, by the time the 'Parnellism and Crime' propaganda campaign led to the creation of the Special Commission (1888–90), Michael Davitt had somehow discovered (probably from Jenkinson, who was being blackmailed by ex-agents he employed)[39] that Millen had been a spy. In March 1890, Tim Harrington MP stated in the House of Commons that he had proof Millen had been employed as an *agent provocateur* by the British government in order to help the *Times* press its charges against Parnell, but no parliamentary debate was allowed to be held upon the question and consequently Millen's treachery was soon forgotten.[40]

Millen was not alone and British intelligence was relentless in its anti-Irish

---

34 PRO (London), Sir Robert Anderson papers, H.O.144/1537/2, report of James Monroe, London CID, 4 Nov. 1887 (report on Jubilee Plot).   35 This is the theme of Christy Campbell, *Fenian fire: the British government plot to assassinate Queen Victoria* (London, 2002). 36 Leon O'Broin, *The prime informer: a suppressed scandal* (1971), 120–1. Anderson made a public confession in 1910, much to the embarrassment of the then Home Secretary, Winston Churchill.   37 PRO (London), Sir Robert Anderson papers, H.O.144/1537/2, report of James Monroe, London CID, 4 Nov. 1887 (report on Jubilee Plot).   38 PRO (London), F.O. 5/2044, Fenian Brotherhood files, vol. 47, 317.   39 Campbell, *Fenian fire*, 309–11.   40 Ibid., 353–6.

espionage work during the late 1880s. As no actual alliance existed between the UB and the IRB, the INB was still able to cause trouble by sending various spies or *agents provocateurs* to Ireland. Following the fiasco of the Jubilee Plot in London, two INB *agents provocateurs* were sent to Ireland, namely John Groves of Omaha, Nebraska, and Joseph McKenna of New York. They met IRB men in Dublin, Mayo and London. Although they failed to get these men involved in bogus plots, they did persuade some men (such as John Merna, a publican and Dublin IRB centre) to open correspondence with their wing of the Clan, thereby ensuring all their letters fell into the hands of British intelligence.[41] As will be seen later, there is strong reason to believe that Merna was eventually persuaded to become a spy and *agent provocateur* himself.

Another notable success for British intelligence occurred in Belfast, where the IRB had more members (950) than in any other single city in the United Kingdom. The Belfast IRB was prone to factionalism ever since Robert Johnston attempted to ferment dissent in the National League by promoting Davitt's policy during 1883–4. Several local centres opposed this policy on the grounds that they believed the IRB should not become involved with the Parnellite movement. It was possibly for this reason that Johnston evidently lost his position as the Ulster representative on the Supreme Council to Michael O'Hanlon at the next IRB elections. As Johnston's job involved international trading in timber, by 1885, though he continued to spend a lot of time in Belfast, he spent *most* of his time in Canada and New York, where he interacted frequently with members of the Clan. To re-assert his authority over the Belfast and Ulster IRB, Johnston sought to win the support of the various Clan leaders he met, and to get them to send agents to Belfast to help fund or organize the IRB on his behalf. As the Clan was split, however, probably unknown to Johnston, many he met were associated with Boland's wing of the Clan. Probably for this reason, in December 1885 (shortly before his retirement), E.G. Jenkinson succeeded in getting an agent (probably an American one) into the Belfast IRB, codenamed 'Fox', who was ordered to 'utilize to the uttermost any line of cleavage between Robert Johnston and his confederates of the IRB'. American envoys continued to come to Belfast occasionally, where they were met by Johnston and a young rising Belfast IRB leader, Daniel McCullough, a publican in west Belfast who was currently promoting the GAA. Michael O'Hanlon and other local IRB leaders were annoyed that Johnston was still trying, with considerable success, to direct the organization, despite the fact that he officially held no authority. As a result of this factionalism, 'Fox' was able to ferment divisions and get himself elected as one of the Belfast IRB leaders, thereby allowing Dublin Castle to learn the

41 NAI, DMP files, carton 2, Report 724, Chief Commissioner Harrel, 10 Oct. 1887; report 719, attached report of James Monro (London CID), 3 Oct. 1887 and report of Home Office, 12 Dec. 1887; carton 3, Report 1001, Supt. William Reddy, 21 Mar. 1888, reports from Robert Anderson (London CID), 9 and 30 Aug. 1888; carton 5, report of James Monro (London CID), 20 June 1888.

names, addresses and occupations of the local leadership and keep the RIC very well-informed of matters in Belfast for several years.[42]

The IRB was evidently blissfully unaware that the Irish-American revolutionary movement was almost completely compromised by British intelligence during the 1880s. It had no *real* reason to doubt that the seeming extremism of the Clan's leaders ever since the suppression of the Land League was, if misguided and counter-productive, nevertheless genuine. For example, although it promised that it would someday ally itself with the IRB and support *its* plans, the Dillon-Devoy wing of the Clan (which was very much in the minority) also had genuine sympathizers with the 'dynamite war', not least of whom was Dillon himself. The IRB, however, refused to give up on the Clan and simply hoped Devoy would be able to accomplish his mission of removing the corrupt members of the Clan and reunite it on terms favourable to the IRB. During 1888–9, this hope came close to being realized only to be dashed completely.

During the summer of 1888, Patrick Hoctor, John Torley, Mark Ryan and John O'Connor were in New York to assist Devoy in reuniting the Clan. British intelligence learnt this quite probably because Patrick Sweeney was heavily involved in the Clan's intrigues in New York.[43] A 'trial' of the Clan leadership took place in New York that September, at which delegates from both wings of the Clan were present to speak, but only John O'Connor was allowed to speak on behalf of the IRB. At Devoy's insistence, *all* Clan leaders since his own demotion from the Clan executive in August 1881 were put on 'trial' and, therefore, Alec Sullivan was forced by his old friends to take part. At this meeting, Michael Boland accused the IRB Supreme Council of having betrayed to the British government all the men involved in 'active work' (the dynamite war) in recent years; a claim which many INB men present professed to believe. O'Connor could not *prove* otherwise, but he stated that the Supreme Council would never betray any Irish revolutionary and that, while it was firmly 'opposed to the kind done in '83 or '84' (the dynamite war), it was no means opposed to other kinds of 'active work'.[44] Michael Kerwin, the ex-leader of the Clan Military Board (a former US colonel who was also editor of the *New York Tablet* and a future leader of the New York Police Department), stated at this meeting that he was solely responsible for *financing* the dynamite war, but he had no involvement in organizing or selecting the dynamite teams. The man directly responsible for this could not be identified (Kerwin and the other INB leaders refused to speak on the matter), but as Boland was shown to have governed the organization in an autocratic fashion since 1883, he was no doubt the key figure. Alec Sullivan was censured, retro-

42 NAI, British in Ireland microfilm, C.O.904/18/609, C.O.904/183 (register of informants); DICS reports, carton 5, (Belfast Division), reports of DI Seddall, 2 Oct. 1889, 1 Apr. 1890, 3 June 1890, Annual Report (1891), 14 May 1892.   43 NAI, CBS files, carton 4, 4755/s (1892 report of Gosselin on events of 1888).   44 UCD, Desmond Ryan papers, L.A. 10/k/23 (1), 25–9, 31–2.

spectively, for his refusal to cooperate with the IRB during 1882, but he was found 'not guilty' of any offence, while Boland was found guilty of misappropriating Clan funds, breaking the Clan's constitution (by indiscriminately expelling camps) and for breaking the alliance with the IRB.[45] Boland was expelled from the Clan and this naturally put an end to his chairmanship of the INB. Consequently, the Clan began to reunite and a renewal of its alliance with the IRB in the near future became likely. This was prevented, however, by 'the prince of spies', Henri Le Caron, who, as a member of the INB executive, was present at this trial. He evidently reported to British intelligence in London that Boland was now gone and that he no longer felt entirely safe. The Home Office responded by asking Le Caron to come to London, where he appeared before the Special Commission, produced copious amounts of Clan documents before the court (all of which, Devoy later admitted, were genuine),[46] spoke about his role in the Clan in Chicago and claimed that there were four other British secret service agents holding senior positions in the Clan's ranks.[47] This had great repercussions.

Philip Cronin, a Cork-born doctor in Chicago and a leader of the UB, was present at the 'trial' in New York during September 1888. All records regarding this 'trial' were supposed to be destroyed, but Cronin stated that he would turn its findings into a UB circular, which he did,[48] and this was then distributed among many Clan camps to win over the INB 'rank and file', by showing them how corrupt their leaders had been. Cronin, however, was also a very bitter rival of Alec Sullivan in Chicago municipal politics and he threatened to reveal to the *public* at the next convention of the INLA that Sullivan had been a leader of the Clan. To do so could serve no purpose whatsoever other than to destroy Sullivan's influence in American politics. Cronin may well not have intended acting upon this threat, but several Chicago Clansmen took it into their heads that Cronin must be one of the four British secret agents Le Caron had talked about in London and, therefore, he was murdered on 4 May 1889.[49] This had two major consequences.

Sullivan's intense political rivalry with Cronin in Chicago was well known and so he was called before the trial that followed but was soon acquitted of any involvement in the murder. It was proven, however, that prominent Irish-American members of the Chicago police force were responsible for the murder *and* were members of the Clan. As a result of this corruption in the Chicago police department, the trial achieved national publicity in the United States and the American public held a series of large public demonstrations,

---

45 Ibid., L.A. 10/k/23 (1). **46** John Devoy, 'The story of Clan na Gael', *Gaelic American*, 15 Aug. 1923. **47** *Special Commission Report*, vol. 4, 489–631, vol. 5, 1–187 (evidence of Le Caron). **48** The minutes of the trial, reprinted in an 1889 Clan na Gael (UB) circular held in UCD, Desmond Ryan papers, L.A. 10/k/23 (1), are in fact Cronin's notes of the proceedings, which may well explained why it has an appendix attributing various comments to Sullivan that he probably never made. **49** Michael Funchion, *Chicago's Irish nationalists* (1976), 103; John McEnnis, *The Clan na Gael and the murder of Dr Cronin* (Chicago, 1889).

denouncing the Clan for its 'un-American' behaviour and questioning the loyalty of all so-called Irish-American 'nationalists' to the American way of life.[50] The social tensions arising from this development were very great, resulting in thousands of ordinary Irish-Americans (many of whom had now acquired 'respectable' middle class social status) to withdraw from both the INLA and the Clan (they never returned) for fear of becoming social pariahs.[51] Irish-American 'nationalist' politics would never be the same again.

The second major consequence of the Cronin murder was that because John Devoy (who lived in Chicago from 1886–92) was Cronin's right-hand man and best friend in the local UB he was convinced every day for at least three years that he too might be assassinated at any moment.[52] As secretary of the UB, Devoy began issuing circulars stating that a prominent UB official (Cronin) had been assassinated at the behest of the INB and though this claim was generally denied by the INB (many members of the UB also did not believe it), owing to Devoy's influence in the Clan and the paranoia which spread in its ranks as a result of these rumours, the movement could not be reunited.

One other consequence of the Cronin murder was that Devoy, being unable to identify his invisible would-be assassins, started accusing Alec Sullivan *publicly* of desiring to kill him. Sullivan's good name in American politics had already been destroyed by his having come before the court in the now nationally famous Cronin case, and he had since become a recluse. He wrote to Davitt that he feared being killed by one of Devoy's many admirers. Two other figures who stood by Sullivan, other than Davitt, were Patrick Egan, now US minister to Chile, and Thomas Brennan, whom Sullivan had helped to become an attorney and who was now working full-time in running Minister Egan's mortgage and real-estate company in Omaha, Nebraska.[53] Sullivan's name would also be tarnished when Le Caron, at the request of the Tory London *Times*, published his best-selling book, *Twenty-five years in the secret service* (London, 1892) that, for obvious reasons, made no mention of Michael Boland (who was no doubt a British agent) or *agents provocateurs*, but instead portrayed Alec Sullivan, Patrick Egan (the presidents of the INLA, 1883–6) and the *Irish World* editor Patrick Ford as the leaders of the 'dynamite war' in an attempt to substantiate all the Tory nonsense about INLA 'dynamite conventions' funding Parnell that had flooded the British press during the mid 1880s.

---

50 Henry Hunt, *The crime of the century or the assassination of Dr Patrick Henry Cronin: a complete and authentic history of the greatest of modern conspiracies* (New York, 1889). 51 Funchion, *Chicago's Irish nationalists*, 112. 52 The intensity of Devoy's fears at this time (which some of friends feared had made him temporarily 'a little insane') is well illustrated by the fact that as late as 1925 he could remember the events and passions he felt in Chicago during 1889–92 as vividly as if they had occurred only yesterday. Devoy, *Story of the Clan*, passim. 53 TCD, Davitt papers, MS 9432/2584–2606 (correspondence of Sullivan 1889–93).

The Special Commission, which was founded in August 1888 and sat from October 1888 until November 1889 before issuing its verdict in January 1890, was a very strange event. The Tory government provided a single party-political and commercial English newspaper, the *Times*, with Dublin Castle records (including Special Branch records) to use as evidence in support of *press* allegations made against over sixty Irish elected public representatives at a government-founded commission. As several historians have noted, this was essentially illegal,[54] but no member of the public realized the source of the information used. The main claim to fame of the event was the sensational side of the commission, namely Parnell's desire to clear his good name after the publication in the *Times* of a forged letter claiming he supported the Phoenix Park murders, and the exposure of Richard Pigott as the forger, leading to his suicide. The Irish Party may have known all along that Pigott was the forger, thanks to Davitt's success in manipulating Jenkinson, who was being blackmailed by his ex-agents, and Patrick Egan's role in identifying Pigott's handwriting.[55] Parnell knew what was going on between Davitt and Jenkinson as well as early as 1885.[56] Whether or not Parnell or Davitt told IRB leaders like P.N. Fitzgerald what was taking place is unknown. They probably preferred to keep them in the dark. The Pigott case, however, was not the real purpose of the Special Commission.

At the end of the commission, many figures (including Davitt, who 'defended' himself), were found 'guilty' of the charge of holding nationalist ambitions and of having encouraged the non-payment of rents, but the Special Commission was not a trial. No prosecutions did, or could, occur. Rather, the Special Commission was an attempt by the Tories and the *Times* to restore what they considered to be standards of decency in British public life by calling upon various ex-Land League supporters who were now MPs to admit to, or repent for, their past 'criminality' through their association with the IRB. The remarkable thing is that so many MPs chose to do so. Davitt was not an MP, but he volunteered to take part anyway and subsequently published his lengthy *Speech in defence of the Land League* (London, 1890) as a top-selling book and, in the process, saw his political fame rise to a great height for the first time since 1882.

Henri Le Caron appeared at the Special Commission a week before Pigott. His evidence undermined the credibility of the Irish revolutionary movement on *both* sides of the Atlantic, for he was able to produce IRB progress reports

<hr />

54 T.W. Moody, 'The *Times* versus Parnell and Co., 1887–90', *Historical Studies*, 6 (1968), 147–82; O'Broin, *The prime informer*; Margaret O'Callaghan, *British high politics and a nationalist Ireland* (Cork, 1994), 104–23. 55 Campbell, *Fenian fire*, 309–11; Davitt, *Fall of feudalism*, 546. 56 When questioned what he knew about J.P. Hayes, an *agent provocateur* who had worked for Jenkinson and was still in British pay, Parnell stated that 'I sent for that Hayes to come over from America to see Mr. Davitt in Paris' in 1885, once he knew that Jenkinson and Davitt were in communication with each other. *Special Commission Report*, vol. 7, 279, evidence of Parnell.

to the Clan dating from the period 1879–81. Pigott was questioned before the commission only for a short time during February 1889 and was very quickly exposed, yet the commission sat for another seven months. Mark Ryan believed that 'the Irish Party should not have bothered about the Commission after the Pigott forgeries had been exposed'[57] and it is clear why. Virtually all Irish Party MPs, including Parnell, 'took the stand' *after* the exposure of Pigott and the defeat of the *Times* charges, and stated all that they knew about the IRB. The only logical explanation as to why the Irish Party did this was that it was so wholly committed to the Union that it was fully prepared to join with the government in attempting to undermine the republican movement as much as possible.

Although sections of the National League had been prosecuted, neither the National League nor the Plan of Campaign were mentioned at all at the commission. Instead, the entire focus was upon the days of the Land League and whether or not it was designed to bring about Irish independence; the idea that the National League or the Irish Party might have had this ambition since 1882 was not taken seriously by either the *Times* or the government. Meanwhile the litmus test of supposed 'criminality' was how far the Irish Party had been prepared to work with 'the nationalist party' [meaning the IRB] All Irish Party figures downplayed the extent to which the original Land League agitation had been based upon the nationalist movement. Ex-IRB figures like Matthew Harris, J.J. O'Kelly and 'Long' John O'Connor, while agreeing to talk (selectively) about their past role in the IRB, generally refused to describe their past politics as criminal.[58] In May 1889, however, Parnell was asked directly whether or not he disapproved of 'the aims – whatever the aims are – of the nationalist party?' and replied that he did 'most undoubtedly', noting that 'I have always disapproved of it from the first time that I entered political life until now' and viewed Irish nationalists' goals and methods 'as useless and criminal':

> My position with regard to the opposition of the nationalists is this: that the organization in Ireland – the organization of the IRB – according to the best information, constantly and consistently opposed the Land League from first to last ... They were the sons of farmers, the sons of labourers and shopkeepers throughout the country and I think it was a mistaken policy of the nationalist organization to oppose us.[59]

Early interviews with Parnell, when he made statements like 'as to the nationalists? They are a body whose earnestness and readiness for sacrifice I have always respected', were quoted against him, but he said these were views he no longer held.[60] Parnell expressed his belief that 'up to the date of the formation

---

57 Ryan, *Fenian memories*, 144. 58 *Special Commission Report*, vol. 10, 22 (evidence of O'Connor). 59 *Special Commission Report*, vol. 7, 219, 227 (evidence of Parnell). 60 Ibid.,

of the National League', the term 'nationalist' was always understood in
Ireland to be a reference only to the IRB, but this was no longer the case, and
he claimed rather perversely that the Land League was responsible for this: 'it
accomplished a revolution.'[61] When the *Times* prosecutors asked Irish Party
MPs during the summer of 1889 if they were opposed to the aims of the
nationalist movement, they generally replied that they were opposed to
'physical force', and referred to the IRB as 'the physical force party'; the
favoured rhetoric of the Irish Catholic establishment. The *Times* prosecutors
went along with this, even though it made no literal sense and was not a direct
answer to their questions.

If the Tories' 'Parnellism and Crime' articles were intended to throw bad
light on the Irish Party to hurt their Liberal electoral allies, after the exposure
of the Pigott case, the purpose of the Special Commission was essentially only
to destroy whatever political credibility the IRB might have had left in Ireland.
Although it had nothing to do with the nominal purpose of the commission
(testing the charges brought against Parnell by the *Times*), the informers used
against P.N. Fitzgerald and P.W. Nally in 1884 (Patrick Delaney and Andrew
Coleman) were asked to state before the commission, in evidence which often
lasted over several days, all that they knew about the IRB; men such as John
Leavy (an impoverished ex-foreman and former Leinster IRB leader who was
ejected from the organization in 1880 for reputedly swindling his employers)
were also paid to give evidence about the IRB; while (unsuccessful) attempts
were made to persuade several IRB leaders in prison, most notably P.W. Nally,
to give evidence before the commission in return for their release.[62] Although
the Supreme Council could take some comfort from the fact that the information revealed at the commission by informers like LeCaron, as well as past
IRB members who were now MPs, was now long out-of-date, any ordinary
IRB man who possessed a blind confidence in John O'Leary's bluff that the
government 'knows little and cares less about our small machiavellianisms' was
no doubt shaken by these events. The political purpose of the questions that
were asked and answered by the Irish Party MPs at the commission was never
stated directly, but it is not coincidental that Parnell was asked if he suspected
that men he had spoken to in the past like John O'Leary, John O'Connor, John
McInerney, P.W. Nally, P.N. Fitzgerald, Mark Ryan and John Torley were
leaders of the IRB specifically 'during the year 1884';[63] a question that would
have had no special relevance to contemporaries except to the members of the
republican movement. The *Times* may have hired the lawyers for the event and
felt it was on a moral crusade against Parnell, but for the government, the
Special Commission was essentially a means of enhancing the fears that
already existed in the IRB regarding what the government did, or did not,

228. **61** Ibid., 13, 88. **62** Ibid., vol. 3, 522–79 (evidence of Delaney); vol. 6, 207–56
(evidence of Coleman), 370–81 (evidence of Leavy); PRO (London), C.O.903/2, Intelligence
notes, series 15, 24–30; O'Broin, *Prime informer*, 129–31. **63** *Special Commission Report*, vol.
7, 276–7 (evidence of Parnell).

know. It was doing publicly what the Special Branch and CBS were up until now doing (and continued to do) covertly.

The IRB Supreme Council no doubt knew as well as the government that Dublin Castle could not suppress the republican movement, but the 'rank and file' could not have known this. After the Special Commission, little or no member of the Irish general public was likely to join, or perhaps want to remain, a member of a secret and oath-bound revolutionary organization, the recent internal history of which had seemingly become front-page tabloid news on a constant basis for a whole year. This was something the organizers of the commission, as well as all its participants, understood fully. The Irish Party could have exposed Pigott without going through the charade of the Special Commission. Unlike the nonsensical Tory propaganda war of 1884–6, much of the information presented before the commission was correct, as it came from the mouths of ex-IRB men. What exactly the IRB leadership of the time thought of the whole affair is unknown. Quite probably it felt very betrayed. At the time, the IRB was merely keeping its revolutionary under-ground organization alive and concentrating upon attempting to maintain a foothold of some kind for republicans in Irish public life or political debate, through the GAA or the various political and literary clubs. For this reason, it had every reason to be sensitive about its public image. The Parnellite press presented the Special Commission as being solely about the personalities of Parnell and Pigott, resulting in a moral vindication of 'Ireland a Nation' against all Tory criticisms. In effect, however, for the Irish Party the Special Commission was a means of deflecting all potential criticism of its politics from nationalist and republican quarters, and, to continue to present itself to the Irish public as the only political alternative. It was a party triumph over the IRB as much as it was over the *Times*, and the Parnellite press, as much as the bishops, generally encouraged the public to look on *each* in an entirely negative light. How far the general Irish public went along with this is unknown and impossible to ascertain: who in Irish politics was really 'playing the game of the English newspapers' and informing against their comrades at this time? It is very likely that the general Irish public had no definite opinions on this question but, be that as it may, the IRB had clearly suffered yet another devastating propagandist defeat and had little or no political credibility left.

In the midst of the Special Commission, a retired Birmingham police officer who had formerly cooperated with Jenkinson made a deathbed confession that John Daly had been framed.[64] This prompted the Limerick IRB leaders, John Crowe, Dick Troy and Patrick O'Brien (who were leading figures in the GAA and YIS in Limerick City) to establish 'The Irish Political Prisoners Committee' with the support of sections of the Limerick working class. Meanwhile in Dublin, Jim Boland (who operated a 'P.W. Nally Club' of

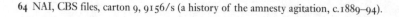

64 NAI, CBS files, carton 9, 9156/s (a history of the amnesty agitation, c.1889–94).

the GAA) revived public interest in Nally's case by working with T.J. O'Reilly, the secretary of the Dublin Trades Council, in establishing a small number of amnesty clubs in Dublin. As members of both organizations had been imprisoned, the question of political prisoners was the one issue upon which the Clan and IRB could agree. Probably for this reason, Patrick Hoctor was able to return to Ireland from New York with some Irish-American funding during February 1890. Only then were the amnesty clubs able to hold any public rallies. Between March and September 1890, public amnesty demonstrations for Daly and Nally took place in Ennis, Limerick, Kilkenny, Dundalk, Tralee and Tipperary, but some of these attracted only several hundred people (mostly IRB and GAA men). All of the demonstrations were boycotted by the National League and the clergy, while the Parnellite press refused to report on most of the events. During 1890, O'Leary's friend George Sigerson published a book entitled *Political prisoners: at home and abroad*, a very sophisticated treatment of a complex question. The Liberal MP James Bryce was asked to write a forward for Sigerson's book, since he had been critical of the Tories for imprisoning (briefly) Irish Party MPs during the late 1880s for supporting the Plan of Campaign. The Irish Party, however, still refused to take up either Daly or Nally's case.[65]

The Limerick and Kilkenny amnesty demonstrations were large events, since the local branches of the Trade and Labour Association supported them,[66] and Matthew Harris may well have taken part in the campaign had he not died in April. Many local republicans and some Irish Party figures attended Harris's funeral in Ballinasloe, which was a large event at which William O'Brien (who had recently been released from prison only to be rearrested again shortly) gave a rebellious graveside speech, taunting the RIC officers who threatened to suppress the funeral demonstration. O'Brien was the only Irish Party member to give the amnesty agitation any moral support during 1890.[67]

At the Kilkenny demonstration, organized by Patrick Hoctor, John Crowe and W.J. O'Donnell (the lord mayor of Limerick), both Hoctor and his best friend John Torley (the Scottish IRB leader, who had recently become a popular city councillor in Glasgow), prompted the crowds to boo the Catholic bishop of Limerick because he had expressed opposition to any attempt to reopen John Daly's case. In an effort to undo the bad publicity given to the IRB at the Special Commission, they also tried to convince their listeners that neither Daly nor anyone else who believed in his IRB principles should ever be considered as being guilty of a crime, because 'in the national catechism that John Daly has given to the students of Irish politics, there is nothing that could

65 NAI, CBS files, carton 1, 824/s, 838/s, 876/s; NAI, DICS files, carton 2 (Southwest Division), DI Gambell, 31 July 1890; DI Jones, 3 Apr., 1 Oct. 1890; PRO (London) 30/60/2, Arthur Balfour papers, intelligence notes, 16 to 31 Mar. 1890. 66 NAI, DICS reports, carton 3 (South East Division), Report of DI Bouchiers, 7 Oct. 1890 (attached press report). 67 *Freeman's Journal*, 15 and 18 Apr. 1890.

induce them to take part in a criminal conspiracy to degrade the national honour.'[68] 'Long' John O'Connor MP was also booed in Kilkenny for having admitted at the Special Commission that he had been an agent in winning people away from the Munster IRB and he was thereafter driven away from an IRB political funeral (organized by Charles Doran) in Cork for having taken 'the oath of our country's slavery' when he had become an MP.[69]

Two days after the Kilkenny amnesty demonstration, Michael Seery died aged just twenty-six, apparently of natural causes, whilst promoting the GAA in Connacht.[70] After his death, however, the top-paid informer in Ireland, 'Nero', was declared to be 'invaluable' by one of his employers, for he claimed to have known that Seery had been in possession of important IRB documents, the whereabouts of which were now unknown.[71] There may well be no truth in this story. 'Nero' (who got £200 a year) was first employed during June 1887 to combat the Plan of Campaign and the GAA and most of the stories he told to the CBS were evidently false. His speciality was in capitalizing upon the insistence of his employers (a Welsh and English army officer) in viewing the Plan of Campaign, the National League and insurrectionary republicanism as part of the same conspiracy. Therefore, he was able to convince his superiors that the president of the South of Ireland Cattle Trade Association was an IRB leader, simply because he had expressed passive support for the Plan of Campaign, and that fifteen of the seventeen seats on the executive of the National League in Cork City had just been won by IRB men, just because Parnell (the MP for Cork City) was being questioned at the Special Commission in the same week about his relationship with the IRB, which according to 'Nero' was still led by James Stephens.[72] 'Nero' was very probably Patrick Cogan, a Cork journalist, who belonged to the Cork 'Old Guard' faction which was ready to disband and trying to amalgamate with the 'Supreme Council party'.[73] After attending a meeting at the National Club in

---

68 *Freeman's Journal*, 1 Sept. 1890. **69** Ibid. NAI, CBS files, carton 1, 631/s. **70** *Freeman's Journal*, 2 and 4 Sept. 1890. **71** NAI, DICS files, carton 2 (Southwest Division), DI Jones and DM Turner, 1 Oct. 1890. **72** NAI, DICS files, carton 2 (Southwest Division), reports of DI Jones, 1 June 1889, 2 Sept. 1889; 3 Apr. 1890, 31 May 1890, 1 Oct. 1891. PRO (London) 30/60/2, Arthur Balfour papers, intelligence notes, 1 to 15 June 1890. **73** 'Nero' was hired by the Special Branch in Cork in June 1887. NAI, British in Ireland microfilm, CO 904/183 (register of informers). He claimed to know the local leaders of the Plan of Campaign, as well as P.N. Fitzgerald (who was originally a member of the Old Guard during the early 1870s) and members of the Old Guard faction in Cork well, and made reports up until February 1893, when the Cork IRB reportedly stopped holding meetings owing to their belief they had been betrayed by one of their members. NAI, DICS reports, carton 2 (Southwestern Division), reports for July 1887 to 6 March 1893. In March 1893, a Cork-man named Patrick Cogan arrived in Dublin, offered his services to the DMP, claimed to know P.N. Fitzgerald and members of the Cork Old Guard well and was given a great deal more money than was usual for informers. Although the names of informers are never mentioned in police reports, John Mallon made an uncharacteristic slip on this occasion by referring to his name, background and occupation. NAI, DMP files, carton 12, Report 2451, Chief Supt. Mallon, 30 Mar. 1893. The Dublin IRB had long made attempts to receive information from policemen of divided

NO DOUBT

Dublin, he once claimed that he could report the names of many of the recently elected county officers of the IRB, and this was no doubt the source of information used in the next 'Annual Report' of the CBS, which lists the names of believed IRB leaders in fifteen different Irish counties. This information was undoubtedly false however, for the names in question were just the editors and proprietors of those provincial Parnellite papers (including MPs) that had recently been prosecuted for having championed the Plan of Campaign.[74] Due to 'Nero', rumours seem to have been spread in the Cork IRB that P.N. Fitzgerald (who was spending much of his time in Dublin) had misappropriated their funds;[75] a claim that was no doubt false. During the late 1880s, however, any such rumours could easily spread and sap the morale of an already demoralized organization.

The Special Commission was a great embarrassment to the London *Times* because it evidently did not realize that Pigott's letters were forged and resented the fact that the government made it pay most of the costs for the proceedings. Naturally, it was determined that Parnell was not to have the last laugh. The CBS leader Major Gosselin was a close friend of the proprietors of the *Times* and, after Pigott's exposure, Gosselin ordered a London CID detective to keep the entrances to William and Katherine O'Shea's home in Brighton under constant surveillance. By November 1889, the Special Branch leader had also introduced himself to O'Shea's solicitor.[76] It was a well-known secret in Irish Party circles that Parnell was having an affair with Katherine O'Shea and was a 'house guest' in William O'Shea's home. A serious controversy had almost broken out during 1885 when Parnell insisted on making William O'Shea an Irish Party candidate, despite grave reservations expressed by several leading Irish Party colleagues, who knew that O'Shea was totally opposed to the party's politics. As both Katherine and William O'Shea had been go-betweens for Parnell and Gladstone during the secret 'home rule' negotiations of 1885–6, it is likely that the Liberal party leader knew the secret story of their relationship as well.

In December 1889, William O'Shea, who had been completely indifferent to his wife's affair with Parnell for years, filed a petition for divorce. The public was made aware that Parnell was cited as a co-respondent in the case in January 1890 but the matter did not raise much attention: the National League simply expressed its confidence in Parnell's claim that his name had been brought into

loyalties and Jim Boland received a letter from a policeman stating than the Dublin police had just acquired the services of a man with the '*nom de plume* Nero'. Jim Boland papers (private collection, courtesy of Annraoi O'Beolain) This letter to Boland is undated, but glued onto the front cover of a notebook containing some records of Dublin GAA finances. Boland was chairman of the Dublin GAA during 1893. **74** PRO (London), 30/60/2, Arthur Balfour papers, intelligence notes, 1 to 15 Jan. 1890; NAI, CBS Annual Report (all RIC Divisions, Jan. 1891), misfiled in DICS files, carton 5 (Belfast Division). **75** NAI, CBS files, carton 1, 1128/s, British in Ireland microfilm, C.O. 904/17/251; NAI, DICS files, carton 2 (Southwest Division), DI Jones, 1 Oct. 1889, 1–4 Mar. 1890; PRO (London), 30/60/2, Arthur Balfour papers, intelligence notes, 1–15 Jan., 1–15 May 1890. **76** Campbell, *Fenian fire*, 352.

the case only because the *Times* was seeking revenge for its failure to use the Pigott forgeries against him the previous summer (which it was). The matter was then ignored. When the O'Shea divorce proceedings finally took place in mid-November 1890, the Irish Party, to express their loyalty towards their 'Chief', unanimously re-elected Parnell as its chairman on 25 November 1890. The following day, however, Gladstone (whose popular persona in England was that of a philanthropist of the highest moral standards) wrote to the *Pall Mall Gazette* stating that the retention of Parnell as chairman of the Irish Party 'would be productive of consequences disastrous in the highest degree to the cause of Ireland' because it would render the chances of 'my retention of the leadership of the Liberal party ... almost a nullity'. Immediately, many Irish Party members turned against Parnell, who had every reason to feel deeply betrayed by Gladstone, whose political career was certainly not dependent on Parnell's personal life and whose real motive in taking this action was to put more pressure upon the Irish Party to continue to act as the Irish wing of the Liberal Party, thereby increasing the likelihood of his seizing power once more in Britain.

Sensing an imminent disaster in his political career, Parnell responded by publishing a manifesto in the *Freeman's Journal* criticizing those Irish Party members who were ready to abandon him and stating that Gladstone's attempt to influence 'the decision of the Irish Party in the choice of their leader and claiming for the Liberal party and their leaders the right of veto upon that choice' was an attack upon the independence of the Irish Party and its basic right to be 'independent of all English parties'. Parnell maintained that the Irish Party's relative success during the previous ten years would not have been possible but for its independence (although it had not been independent since 1886), and, that the loss of the Liberal alliance would be preferable to what he described ambiguously (and meaninglessly) as 'a compromise of our national rights'.[77]

On 1 December 1890, the Irish Party began a week-long conference in a private committee room in the House of Commons to decide the future of the party and Parnell's position. Parnell set out a new programme for his party whereby it would reassert its complete independence from the Liberals for the first time since 1885, but many Irish Party members (who were simultaneously negotiating with Gladstone) refused to support this idea, for the party's political credibility among the propertied classes since 1886 rested largely on the value of the Liberal alliance. The Catholic hierarchy was equally as determined as Gladstone to capitalize upon the controversy regarding Parnell for its own ends. For example, Archbishop Croke of Cashel wrote to Archbishop Walsh of Dublin that

> I go with you entirely in thinking that they [the Irish Party] make small or no account of Bishops and priests now as independent agents, and only

77 *Freeman's Journal*, 29 Nov. 1890.

value them as money gatherers and useful auxiliaries in the agitation. This I have noticed for a considerable time past; and I believe we shall have to let them see and feel unmistakably that, without us, they would simply be nowhere and nobodies.[78]

The Catholic hierarchy had indeed made the Irish Party the power that it was since 1884. On 4 December, the entire Irish Catholic hierarchy published a statement in Ireland which declared that 'as pastors of this Catholic nation', 'we give it as our unanimous judgement' that Parnell was not fit to be 'the leader of the Irish people'. Furthermore, it declared that 'we see nothing but inevitable defeat at the approaching general election' if Parnell was retained as its leader, for 'surely Catholic Ireland, so eminently conspicuous for its virtue and purity of social life' would not vote for a party that was led by an adulterer.[79] Irrespective of the question of the Liberal alliance, this action by the Catholic hierarchy effectively ensured that every Irish Party MP who had been nominated or elected to parliament with the clergy's support and who was not willing to risk losing his seat at Westminster had no choice but to abandon Parnell, who was clearly going to be opposed by the entire Irish Catholic Church in the next elections. Consequently on 6 December, before any decision was reached at the Irish Party's convention in London, forty-five members of the Irish Party simply walked out of the committee room, and issued a manifesto stating that they no longer recognized Parnell as the leader of their party. More were to follow. The *Times* had indeed got the last laugh.

Over the past seven years, the IRB had suffered greatly at the hands of the Liberals, Tories, Irish Party and the Catholic Church, each of which had used their powers to combat its influence. In the short term, however, it was specifically the combined influence of the Catholic Church and the Irish Party-Liberal alliance that had crowded republicans completely from Irish public life since 1886 and had undermined their attempts to create an Irish nationalist public opinion through encouraging freedom of debate and non-sectarian attitudes in Ireland. As both these powers had now been turned against Parnell, the IRB had every reason to believe that if Parnell was utterly defeated, so too would the chances of ever re-asserting the influence of republicans in Irish public life.

On 1 December 1890 John O'Leary wrote to the *Freeman's Journal* that, although 'I am not and never was a follower of Mr. Parnell and therefore am, in a sense, out of court' in expressing an opinion regarding the Irish Party's problems, he felt he had 'quite as good a right as another to have a say in the

78 Noel Kissane (ed.), *Parnell: a documentary history* (Dublin, 1991), 85. 79 *Freeman's Journal*, 4 Dec. 1890.

matter' since the outcome of the dispute would undoubtedly affect the future well being of the Irish political community as a whole. Although he considered Parnell to be 'no more immaculate as a politician than as a man', O'Leary believed the principal of Parnell's recent manifesto, of re-asserting the independence of the Irish Party from the Liberal Party, was 'of great importance' and it would be 'stupid and cowardly' for the general Irish public to reject its wisdom, or to abandon Parnell, just 'because Mr. Gladstone and the whole howling voice of prurient British hypocrisy' had called for his resignation.[80]

Two days after the Catholic hierarchy's denunciation of Parnell, a body known as the Parnell Leadership Committee (PLC) was established at the IRB's National Club to support Parnell's stance in the controversy. This was the initiative of John Clancy, the sub-sheriff of Dublin. The purpose of the PLC, which consisted entirely of Dublin city councillors (excepting Henry Dixon, the leader of the 'National Club Literary Society'), was to create an alliance between local governmental officials across the country with a view to consolidating Parnell's political support base. It immediately sent appeals to town councillors and poor law guardians all over the country to join their new body.[81] Fred Allan turned up at one of its first meetings, but not to express support for Parnell. Instead he introduced a resolution (which was passed unanimously) denouncing leading anti-Parnellites such as Tim Healy and Justin McCarthy for having 'slandered the men of '67' in the past, and calling upon 'every man who has the smallest respect for the memory of the men of '67 and for the honesty of those who follow them to protect them from the insults of those who pretend to be leaders of Irish nationalists'.[82] On 10 December 1890, a mob led by John Clancy of the PLC, Jim Boland of the Dublin IRB and Parnell himself attempted to take control of the offices of *United Ireland* by force. Its acting editor, Matthias Bodkin JP (William O'Brien had fled to France to escape re-arrest for promoting the Plan), had already taken the anti-Parnellite side. As this paper had created the Parnell personality cult, without it Parnell would obviously lose much of his power. A futile brawl took place during which Parnell was cut and bruised badly and Boland was concussed by having a chair smashed over his head.[83] The fact that the old republican James O'Connor, a sub-editor with *United Ireland*, was badly hurt by the mob persuaded him to support the anti-Parnellites, despite the fact that he had long been a critic of the Liberals and a man of anticlerical views. He certainly would have been indifferent to the controversy surrounding Parnell's affair and his illegitimate children, as he believed that condemnations of extra-marital love affairs made purely 'according to some civil or religious formula'

80 John O'Leary to *Freeman's Journal*, 1 Dec. 1890. 81 *Freeman's Journal*, 8 Dec., 15 Dec. 1890. 82 *Freeman's Journal*, 13 Dec. 1890. 83 Frank Callanan, *The Parnell split* (1992), 64; Leon O'Broin, *Revolutionary underground* (1976), 46–7. 84 *DPB*, vol. 2, 275.

were 'barbarous and brutal and ought to be relegated to the dark ages in which the savage idea originated.'[84]

On 13 December, John O'Leary wrote to the press denouncing the anti-Parnellite manifesto as the most 'nerveless, boneless, sapless production' he had ever read, written by forty-five young men who had no more courage than 'an old woman'. He called on the public to support the Parnellite candidate (Vincent Scully) in the forthcoming Kilkenny by-election.[85] Parnell himself was determined to take a very prominent role in promoting Scully's candidacy, but as the National League in Kilkenny had already turned against him, he clearly needed some extra help. The man he looked to was P.N. Fitzgerald, who was made assistant director of Scully's campaign alongside Parnell himself.[86] According to 'Fox', the CBS's most reliable informer, the IRB in Belfast and several other parts of the country were encouraged to send some of their members to Kilkenny to support the Parnellite candidate.[87] This order may well have originated with Fitzgerald, although it could have originated with Robert Johnston who had already taken the lead in organizing support for Parnell in Belfast, after virtually the entire membership of the National League in the city (over 3,000 men) had turned against him at the behest of the local priesthood. By January 1891, Johnston had formed a branch of the PLC in the city under his own chairmanship, with Samuel Jordan, the leader of the IPHRA in Belfast, as vice-chairman, and Daniel McCullough, the local IRB leader, as treasurer.[88]

The anti-Parnellite candidate in the election, Sir John Pope Hennessy, was a Catholic, former Tory MP and governor in India who, although 'a Conservative in principle', had declared himself a believer in the Irish Party in the past six months.[89] Michael Davitt became Hennessy's principal election-eering agent, having taken the anti-Parnellite side because of his desire to re-establish his influence in Irish politics. Davitt accused P.N. Fitzgerald of 'hiring a mob' during the election, a claim Fitzgerald denied and retorted by questioning why any sincere nationalist like Davitt should be prepared to support someone like Hennessy who 'has got a pension from the Tory government'.[90] Fitzgerald's stance in this little quarrel with Davitt was backed up fellow IRB man P.J. O'Keefe, a corporation official in Kilkenny city and local labour activist, but Tim Healy (a more effective electioneering agent than either Fitzgerald or Davitt) realized that the decisive factor in the election would not be the relative merits of the two candidates, or the opinions of Fitzgerald and other nationalists of the lower classes, many of whom did not have voting rights and who Healy characteristically dismissed as 'the rabble'.[91] Just as the two leading British principal parties were fond of ridiculing Irish Party MPs as country bumpkins, the Irish Party MPs were fond of ridiculing

85 John O'Leary to *Freeman's Journal*, 13 Dec. 1890. 86 Callanan, *Parnell split*, 66, 77 (footnote 38). 87 NAI, DICS files, carton 5 (Belfast Division), DI Seddall, 1 Jan. and 3 Feb. 1891. 88 *Freeman's Journal*, 9 Jan. 1891. 89 Legg, *Newspapers and nationalism*, 144–5. 90 *Freeman's Journal*, 17 Dec. 1890. 91 Callanan, *Parnell split* (Cork, 1992), 69.

republicans as 'hillside men'. Healy effectively sealed the fate of the Parnellite candidate by getting the local Catholic or 'home rule' press to champion Hennessy as 'the selected one of the bishops and priests of Ireland' and by capitalizing upon bourgeois opinion regarding the scandal surrounding Katherine O'Shea.[92] Hennessy won the election with almost a two-thirds majority, which was a bad result for Parnell not least because, as Frank Callanan has noted, it 'shattered his mystique of electoral invincibility.'[93] Parnell did not hesitate after his defeat, but immediately sailed to Boulogne in an attempt to win over to his side the political exiles William O'Brien and John Dillon, who had escaped to France with John Clancy's help. This caused grave concern to the anti-Parnellites, for few men possessed more influence within the Irish Party and among Irish public opinion generally than O'Brien and Dillon, the popular heroes of the Plan of Campaign. O'Brien was deeply opposed to Healy's slanderous political tactics during the split and remained very sympathetic to Parnell, while Dillon was more concerned with ensuring that neither Tim Healy nor Justin McCarthy was allowed to become the Irish Party leader; a position for which he felt more suited. The Boulogne negotiations proved inconclusive and both O'Brien and Dillon were arrested shortly after their return to Ireland, owing to the warrants still standing for their arrest, and were held in prison for five months, unable to take any part in the struggle for power. In the meantime, Parnell had little choice but to continue to look for Irish nationalists' support if he and his ever-decreasing circle of followers were to weather the coming political storm. Strangely enough, the man Parnell relied upon most to help him in this task was R.B. ('Barry') O'Brien, a distinguished London-Irish Liberal Catholic journalist and barrister who had effectively invented the 'union of hearts' rhetoric during 1886, but had now taken the Parnellite side mostly due to his strong personal admiration for 'the Chief.'

Barry O'Brien took a prominent role in the Kilkenny by-election and, several years later, he recalled meeting a leading 'Fenian' in Kilkenny (probably Fitzgerald) who reminded him that although 'we are here to help Mr. Parnell', 'we are not his people' and were offering their services only voluntarily and certainly not indefinitely. This same man claimed that the Irish Party would be powerless to shape the outcome of the split, for the Catholic bishops were the real leaders of the National League 'and the only power that can stand up to the Church is Fenianism [the IRB].'[94] This was probably a generally held conviction in the IRB. According to W.B. Yeats, one of the first things John O'Leary told him was that 'in this country, a man must have upon his side the Church or the Fenians'.[95] It was not possible to have both.

Upon returning to London, Barry O'Brien started working with Mark Ryan, who befriended him, closed down his local branch of the YIS and estab-

92 Legg, *Newspapers and nationalism*, 145.   93 Callanan, *Parnell split*, 69.   94 O'Brien, *Life of Parnell*, 515, 517.   95 C.C. O'Brien, *Passion and cunning* (London, 1990), 25.

lished a branch of the PLC. After being elected vice-president of the London PLC, Ryan was introduced to Parnell (for the first time) and was encouraged by the latter to become a member of the Parnellite wing of the INLGB.[96] Meanwhile O'Brien appealed directly to O'Leary to encourage P.N. Fitzgerald to come to London to help himself and Ryan get the local National League branches into 'good hands'. O'Brien told O'Leary he believed that the involvement of republicans in the split was essential if Parnell was to triumph and if public opinion in Ireland was not to return to the 'contemptible state' it had been during the mid-Victorian period, for 'without P.N. Fitzgerald and his men', Parnell 'could not have carried on the war at all' during the Kilkenny by-election.[97] Fitzgerald does not appear to have left for London, but it is known that Ryan agreed to become one of the two treasurers of the INLGB in April 1891, 'not', so Ryan recalled, 'because I believed in parliamentarianism [the Irish Party], but because I felt that it would help the cause with which I had been so long identified, if we could smash English dictation' over Irish political attitudes.[98] Excepting the Tyrone IRB leader Michael McGinn, who worked as the chief organizer of the National League in Ulster from March until October 1891 before withdrawing from the Parnellite movement,[99] Ryan (who had not been a Supreme Councillor for some time) was the only prominent IRB figure to join the Parnellite National League in either Ireland or England during the 'Parnell Split' controversy. Indeed, even though his first loyalty was probably still with the republican movement, Ryan remained a committed leader of the INLGB (serving for a time as its president) up until 1895. In most instances, however, IRB-Parnellite cooperation during the 'split' was a typical scenario whereby very different parties who are equally adept at the political game were willing to become temporary bedfellows, as is perhaps best illustrated by Barry O'Brien's colourful description of his short-term political friendship with a certain well-known Cork rebel:

> I like P.N. Fitzgerald. He said he would hang me when he got the chance and I agreed to deal equally liberally with him when I become Chief Secretary. On this basis, we worked smoothly together.[100]

Republicans were naturally on their guard in offering support to Parnell during 1891, for they had to be sure that they had something to gain from doing so. The clearest illustration of this was the politics of the PLC. Although it met in the National Club, very few IRB men attended in the month after the Kilkenny by-election. Fitzgerald turned up at only one

96 Ryan, *Fenian memories*, 151–3, 171. 97 NLI, John O'Leary papers, MS 5927, R.B. O'Brien to O'Leary, 15 Mar. 1891. 98 Ryan, *Fenian memories*, 154. 99 NAI, DICS files, carton 6 (Northern Division), District Inspector Gambell, 3 Feb. 1892. 100 NLI, John O'Leary papers, MS 5927, R.B. O'Brien to O'Leary, 15 Mar. 1891.

meeting, when he expressed his belief that, while 'the common sense of the people will decide the question', 'wherever the intelligence of Ireland exists, it is upon his side' in the dispute. Fitzgerald declared that he 'supported Mr. Parnell on principle', that the PLC must do everything in its power to fight English influences of any kind in Irish public life (he made no mention of electioneering) and seconded a resolution that for the Irish Party to bow down to Gladstone's wishes 'would be an act of national baseness and degradation' which would 'merit the contempt of the nations of the world'.[101] Not until February 1891, when Parnell himself visited the National Club and expressed strong support for the IRB's amnesty agitation (asking to become an ordinary member of one of the local amnesty clubs), did Jim Boland and several prominent IRB figures begin to attend meetings of the Dublin PLC. The DMP believed that the Dublin IRB thereafter held private 'inner circle' meetings at the National Club to discuss what had taken place at each PLC meeting, who might make useful recruits and how the amnesty agitation could be boosted.[102]

By March 1891, the new anti-Parnellite 'Irish National Federation' had succeeded in winning over most branches of what was formerly known as the 'National League', and Tim Healy had established a new, intensely partisan and clericalist organ, the *National Press*, which was remarkably successful in focusing the public's attention purely on Parnell's adultery rather than his politics. Several IRB leaders, however, still refrained from entering the controversy. The Scottish IRB leader John Torley simply proclaimed that he was glad the true character of the Irish Party had been shown up to all who foolishly believed it had any nationalist credentials in the past,[103] while his best friend, Patrick Hoctor, as well as Maurice Moynihan and Charles Doran also refused to enter into the dispute in any way. Meanwhile other republican figures, such as the Clare IRB leader, Patrick McInerney, did nothing except offer a small financial contribution to the PLC and was at pains to emphasize that he was doing so only to 'protest against the miserable clique' behind the anti-Parnellite party that were attempting to 'sap the blood of the nation', not because he believed in Parnell's politics.[104]

Although there were a few IRB men in local government (including McInerney), the IRB itself had nothing much to gain from the creation of a federation of Parnellite city and town councillors across the country. Consequently, it had no great reason to work with Clancy's PLC. Hence when the PLC made a direct appeal to the IRB president John O'Leary to support Parnell in March 1891, he responded bluntly that 'I can barely conceive the possibility of my party being with him at any time. I condemned many things

101 *Freeman Journal*, 24 Jan 1891.   102 *Freeman's Journal*, 9 Feb. and 16 Feb. 1891; NAI, DMP files, carton 8, Chief Supt Mallon, 7 Feb., 4 Mar., 14 Mar. 1891.   103 E.W. McFarland, *John Ferguson* (East Lothian, 2003), 203–4.   104 McInerney to *Freeman's Journal*, 10 Mar. 1891.

he said and did in the past and I condemn them still.' He did, however, express a hope that Parnell would in the future start taking a stand 'for an Irish parliament with independent powers'. He also pointed to Archbishop Croke's boast that three-quarters of the wealthy classes in Irish society were against Parnell as another illustration of the 'old story' of the comfortable classes' complete indifference or hostility to Irish nationalist politics. Nevertheless, he professed (rather uncharacteristically) to take comfort from the fact that, ultimately, 'the classes always go down before the masses.'[105]

The key factor that drew the IRB further into the Parnell Split controversy was essentially the question of money. John O'Leary, P.N. Fitzgerald and Fred Allan did not become active in the PLC, but by late March 1891 all three men had become members of the executive of a new, associated body, the 'Parnell Leadership Fund', the other members of the executive being George Coffey B.L., formerly of the YIS, John Wyse Power, also formerly of the YIS and a sub-editor with the *Freeman's Journal*, Henry Dixon (IRB), John Clancy and William Field, a butcher and the Parnellite MP for the liberties area of Dublin.[106] While the main purpose of the National League was to pay MPs expenses, the purpose of the Parnell Leadership Fund was to raise funds to maintain a Parnellite presence in the press. Edmund Dwyer Gray, the proprietor of the *Freeman's Journal*, was one of its treasurers, but the sales of his paper had already dropped considerably (and would continue to do so) owing to his support for Parnell, and so it was already expected by March 1891 that he too would soon turn anti-Parnellite. By becoming involved in the Parnell Leadership Fund, therefore, the IRB hoped to be able to assume a strong influence over whatever new Parnellite paper might be established. One strong reason why it could expect to be able to do this was that Parnell had already decided to send a delegation of MPs to Irish-America to raise funds for this purpose, and this fund-raising tour was to be organized (as a response to Parnell's personal request) by the UB secretary, John Devoy.[107]

The Parnellite delegation to America consisted of J.J. O'Kelly, 'Long' John O'Connor, William Redmond and Henry Harrison. The latter, a very wealthy Oxford-educated Liberal and a descendant of Henry Joy McCracken, became Parnell's and Katherine O'Shea's closest confidant during the controversy of 1890–1. During February 1891, acting under Parnell's orders, Harrison had worked with Robert Johnston and his son James Johnston (IRB, a solicitor and town councillor in Dundalk) in an effort to get possession of the books of the National League in Belfast.[108] Upon Harrison's arrival in America, Devoy's group managed to raise several fund raising ventures,[109] but the Parnellite mission to America was not very successful, partly because Michael Davitt, who was very influential in Irish-America, was actively trying to persuade people to support the anti-Parnellites. Alec Sullivan supported Davitt's efforts, albeit only in a small way, in Chicago.[110] By May 1891, Thomas Addis Emmet, a wealthy New York banker and the grandson of the United Irish leader of the same name, succeeded in winning over much of the former members of the INLA to the 'Irish National Federation of America' (INFA), an anti-Parnellite body. However with the assistance of William Carroll (now an active member of the Republican Party, who had not taken part in Irish-American politics for ten years), Devoy and others were successful in keeping the INLA organization specifically in New York in support of Parnell during the spring and summer of 1891. They also held a particularly large convention in the city later that year.[111]

Devoy was particularly grieved that William O'Brien and John Dillon, two men whom he respected, took the anti-Parnellite side upon their release from prison in July 1891. That summer Devoy made a number of futile attempts to change their minds by corresponding with them, adopting a conciliatory tone.[112] The main reason why he supported the Parnellites during 1891 was that he believed if Parnell was removed from the political stage, the Irish Party would be forever at the 'mercy of English whims and Irish cranks' and the Catholic hierarchy would be able to convince the British government once and for all 'that *they* and they alone were the people to deal with in the settlement of the Irish question'. Devoy believed that if the 'supreme parliament of bishops' succeeded in overthrowing Parnell, it would ensure that the international community could never be convinced that a desire existed in Ireland for independence, and, would also ensure that 'home rule', if it ever came about, 'would be in the strictest sense of the word, Rome Rule and, for my part, I most decidedly prefer English rule to that.'[113]

As was long expected, ultimately Gray and the *Freeman's Journal* turned against Parnell in September 1891 and the 'Parnell Leadership Fund' was closed down, but not before it had collected over £5,000 for the Parnellite cause.[114] These funds were kept in the possession of the PLC, rather than the National League; a fact that would have significant consequences later that year.

In rural Ireland and the provinces, the Parnell Split controversy had two principal political consequences. First, it put an end to the 'Plan of Campaign' agitation, which had all but been suppressed already by the Tory administration, and gave all well-to-do farmers who had never supported the agitation

Sullivan 1889–93). 111 Irish National League of America, *Union for Ireland: Principles before men: proceedings of the conference of the Irish National League, New York, November 26th 1891* (New York, 1891). 112 *DPB*, vol. 2, 319–29; TCD, Dillon papers, MS 6837/20–22 (Devoy–Dillon correspondence). 113 *DPB*, vol. 2, 316; TCD, John Dillon papers, 6837/17a, John Devoy to Joseph Patrick Ryan (secretary of INFA), 14 July 1891. 114 *Freeman's Journal*, 6 Aug. 1891 (at this stage, the fund had £4,673). 115 NAI, DICS files, carton 2 (South West Division), report of DI Jones, 1 Jan. 1891.

a welcome opportunity to 'place their faith in the government' once more.[115] The agrarian wing of the Irish Party was solidly anti-Parnellite not least because they believed, in the light of Tory's recent actions, that only the Liberals might be prepared to listen to their demands. The fact that priests who had been active in the Plan of Campaign were entirely anti-Parnellite no doubt also influenced their decision. The second consequence of the Parnell Split in the provinces was that it revived the struggle between the republicans and clergy for control of the GAA.

Owing to republicans' continued influence in the association, the GAA was the principal source of Parnellite support in many of the towns and villages of rural Ireland. Immediately the Parnell Split controversy broke out, a Sligo parish priest told a Special Branch detective that priests were 'under orders' from their bishops to do everything in their power to combat the IRB's powers of influence within the GAA, particularly during the current political controversy.[116] The GAA president, P.J. Kelly (a farmer, friend of P.N. Fitzgerald and reputed IRB man), took the Parnellite side in January 1891 and together with J.P. McCarthy of the IRB (the only significant political figure in Galway to take the Parnellite side) formed branches of the PLC in Athenry and Loughrea, as well as a branch of the strictly non-sectarian YIS in Galway town.[117] In the midlands and west of Ireland, Dublin Castle believed that the IRB was the only party that was 'soundly Parnellite' both in the villages and country towns, as well as the only movement that was indifferent to both the land question and the opinions of the Catholic clergy.[118] The clergy's influence, however, remained paramount. For example, when Kelly presented a Parnellite motion to the GAA county boards of Connacht, half the men present left without voting, apparently because they were afraid to vote for Parnell in the presence of their priests. Indeed, these same priests afterwards set about blacklisting all those GAA men who had been prepared to vote for Parnell, resulting in many of them losing their jobs.[119]

In May 1891, pastoral letters from three bishops were read out in all Catholic churches in the midlands denouncing both Parnell and 'secret societies'; an action that Dublin Castle welcomed, for any alleged connection between Parnell and secret societies of any kind (even semi-public ones like the IRB) would inevitably erode Parnell's support among the Catholic middle classes and especially the comfortable farming community.[120] Priests were the most active promoters of the Irish National Federation throughout rural Ireland and although very many Catholics were apparently still sympathetic towards Parnell as a politician, few were prepared to defy their priests. The announcement from the altar of Bishop McNulty of Meath that Catholics were forbidden to vote for 'either a Protestant or a Parnellite' did not create the

116 Ibid., carton 4 (Midlands Division), DI Bell, 4 Jan. 1891. 117 Ibid., carton 1 (Western Division), DI Gibbons, 11 Jan., 5 June 1891. 118 Ibid., carton 4 (Midlands Division), DI Bell, 4 Jan., 4 Feb., 4 Mar. 1891. 119 Ibid., 4 Mar. 1891. 120 Ibid., 11 June 1891. 121 Ibid., 3 Feb. 1892.

(handwritten margin note: Church against Parnell)

same sort of outraged reaction in this part of the country that similar type pronouncements did in Irish cities.[121] As a result, the bitterness of the Parnell Split died out more quickly in rural areas than anywhere else. Meanwhile, in several midland counties, under the weight of clerical denunciations, the GAA simply ceased to exist and the only midland county where the clergy was unable to have its own way with the GAA was Cavan. This was because the local GAA and PLC leader was also the local IRB leader, Terence Fitzpatrick, a publican who also ran the Cavan branch of the YIS that, as elsewhere, was a strictly non-sectarian organization that encouraged men of all religious denominations to join.[122] In August 1891 Bishop McGinnis of Kilmore denounced the local GAA organization from the altar, to little effect, although the clergy nevertheless succeeded in blacklisting Fitzpatrick by degrees, by regularly entering his public house and accusing him before all present of being a government spy because he was not a member of the anti-Parnellite Irish National Federation.[123] Eventually, as his business was collapsing, by the mid 1890s Fitzpatrick was forced to immigrate to Glasgow. One rare exception to this general rule of priestly supremacy in rural Ireland was in south Tipperary, where the IRB's old enemy, Fr Scanlan of Thurles, was for the first time unable to have his way with the local GAA, which responded to his condemnations of all Parnellites by threatening to throw him into the Suir River, as some Parnellites had reputedly done to their local parish priest in Waterford City.[124] As a result, whenever Patrick Hoctor or P.N. Fitzgerald called upon Tipperary GAA clubs, they were received with open arms for the first time since prior to the republican-clerical controversies in the GAA during 1887–8.[125]

One of the many reasons why the Parnellites became dependent on republicans' support during 1891 was the fact that the MPs generally lacked the capacity to be popular political organizers: they could speak at political rallies and get their names in the newspapers, but could not actually organize rallies themselves. They relied upon their support organizations to do that. Hence while priests organized most National Federation demonstrations during 1891, as the National League was moribund, it was the republicans who organized several of the largest Parnellite demonstrations held that year. In April, P.N. Fitzgerald, together with T.B. Kelly (IRB) of the Mayo GAA and the Nally and MacBride families, took the lead in organising two large Parnellite rallies in Mayo, which were addressed by Parnell and a number of local, republican ex-Land Leaguers. One of these took place on the twelfth

---

122 Ibid., 5 Dec. 1890, 4 Feb. 1891. 123 Ibid., 4 Mar., 4 July, 4 Sept. 1891, 4 Oct. 1892; British in Ireland microfilm, CO904/17/264. 124 In actual fact, what occurred in Waterford was that the local parish priest stood on a street near the quays telling people that all who attended a Parnellite meeting in the city would be damned. When he was heckled, he started hitting people in the crowds with his umbrella and, in a tussle, he was simply knocked over. 125 NAI, DICS files, carton 3 (South East Division), DI Bouchiers, 5 May, 5 Sept., 3 Oct 1891.

anniversary of the famous Irishtown meeting of 1879 and attracted around 11,000 people, despite the Catholic clergy's denunciations of all who attended the event.[126] Meanwhile in Dublin, Fred Allan (who also helped organize and spoke at the second-ever May Day demonstration in Ireland that year),[127] together with John Clancy, took the lead in organising a couple of large supposedly Parnellite 'labour' rallies in the western suburbs of Dublin in June 1891, both of which were attended by over 10,000 people and addressed by Parnell.[128] In Belfast, Robert Johnston was responsible for hiring the prestigious Ulster Hall on 24 May for what was Parnell's only well-attended public lecture in Ulster during 1891.[129] Various IRB men from across the province (including Henry Diver, a Letterkenny shopkeeper and the old Donegal IRB leader, who had seen his followers desert him for his non-participation in the Plan of Campaign) travelled to Belfast especially for the occasion, while Parnell stayed at Johnston's Belfast home for the duration of his visit to Ulster.[130] In the same month, Mark Ryan played a prominent role in organizing Parnell's only public lectures in London, during which Parnell's speeches (like most he delivered that year) included some obvious attempts to appeal to the IRB's sensibilities.[131] The Parnellites were willing to return this favour offered by the IRB to some degree. On 14 April, the Commercial Branch of the Parnellite National League, led by Patrick O'Brien MP (a former Liverpool IRB leader), together with the Dublin Trades Council and a number of IRB men from across the country, organised a monster amnesty meeting in the Phoenix Park to attract attention to the cases of Nally and Daly.[132] The unresolved problem remained, however, that Parnell did not want to be committed to Irish nationalists' politics in any way, just as the IRB did not want to be manipulated by Westminster MPs.

As the Parnellites prepared to meet for their first-ever 'National Convention' in Dublin on 24 July to create a new executive for the National League, DMP detectives observed leading Parnellite MPs holding lengthy interviews with Robert Johnston and P.N. Fitzgerald at the Gresham and Imperial Hotels, evidently in an attempt to win them over to the National League. Several Parnellite MPs also met Johnston, Jim Boland and other Dublin IRB leaders in hotel bars late at night to discuss the amnesty question, what sort of agitation Irish-Americans might be prepared to support financially and how the political influence of the clergy might be combated.[133] When the Parnellite National Convention eventually took place, however, no

---

126 Ibid., carton 1 (Western Division), D.I. Gibbons, 10 May 1891.   127 Lane, *Origins of modern Irish socialism*, 177.   128 *Freeman's Journal*, 8 June 1891; NAI, DMP files, carton 11, Reports 3132 and 3185, Chief Supt. Mallon and Supt. Thomas Byrne, 8 June 1891.   129 *Belfast Morning News*, 4 May 1891.   130 NAI, DICS files, carton 5 (Belfast Division), reports for May 1891, 6 June 1891; interview with Robert Johnston, *Irish Press*, 15 May 1935.   131 Ryan, *Fenian memories*, 155.   132 *Freeman's Journal*, 15 Apr. 1891; NAI, DMP files, carton 8, Report 2044, Chief Supt. John Mallon, 15 Apr. 1891.   133 NAI, DMP files, carton 11, reports of Chief Supt. Mallon, 6 and 25 July 1891; carton 8, Report 2131, Chief Supt. Mallon, 25 and 28 July 1891; Ryan, *Fenian memories*, 65.

IRB leaders were present; a clear indication of their refusal to be drawn into the National League.

Tensions were very evident at this convention between the MPs present and various popular political activists in the country who had taken the Parnellite side. C.H. Oldham of the IPHRA, T.J. O'Reilly, president of the Dublin Trades Council, Francis Dineen, the GAA vice-president, and leaders of the PLC in Dublin and Cork all argued that the new National League executive must include representatives from the PLC, the amnesty clubs, the GAA, the IPHRA and the Trade and Labour Association so that the policy of the Parnellite MPs would be decided at grassroots level for the first time, rather than at Westminster, and so MPs could be held accountable to their constituents.[134] This may well demonstrate that many who took the Parnellite side during 1891 did so out of a desire to undo the undemocratic system of governing the National League that had been in place ever since its establishment. Tim Harrington MP, the old secretary of the National League, was irritated greatly by these suggestions, partly because they seemed to him as impractical but mostly because he could not tolerate the idea of being made accountable in any way to working-class men like the Trades Council leader O'Reilly, whom Harrington denounced violently at the convention as 'a troublemaker'. This caused a lengthy and bitter quarrel to break out, which was solved only when Parnell, after leaving the hall for a few minutes to gather his thoughts, intervened and managed to silence opposition, arguing that those who had not even been members of the National League in the past were hardly entitled to hold positions of authority in the movement now. Afraid to challenge Parnell to his face, one-by-one, O'Reilly, Dineen and others slowly withdrew their motions and later a central committee of the National League was appointed directly by Parnell himself, with Tim Harrington once more serving as its leader.[135] This ensured that, as had been the case in the past, the National League executive would never be made accountable to anyone other than the MPs in Westminster and that its branches could not decide policies for themselves. Instead they were supposed to act purely as an electioneering and fund raising machine and 'trust in their leaders'. John Dillon ensured that the same system was maintained in the National Federation and thus the structural basis of Irish politics remained unchanged, although, in time, Tim Healy and later William O'Brien tried to change this in their own idiosyncratic ways. In turn, these two ex-*United Ireland* editors, who had done so much to build up the political reputation of the Irish Party during the mid 1880s, would have their own former rhetoric turned against them and be denounced as 'factionists' by the 'home rule' press.

If the Parnellites and IRB were not prepared to cooperate with each other on any issue outside that of promoting the amnesty agitation, they had a

---

134 *Freeman's Journal*, 25 July 1891 (speeches of Oldham, Shanks, Dixon and O'Reilly at Parnellite National Convention).   135 *Freeman's Journal*, 25 July 1891 (report of Parnellite National Convention).

shared interest in altering the tenor of the national press, which was decidedly unfavourable to both of them. Archbishop Logue of Armagh, the Catholic primate of all Ireland, was determined that no newspaper read by Catholics would take the Parnellite side during 1891 and feared that an Irish 'anti-clerical crusade' might be launched,[136] but he had no real reason to be anxious. Most editors of the 'home rule' newspapers were lay graduates of Catholic diocesan seminaries who were always very proud of the Irish Party's status as *the* champions of Catholic interests in British politics. As if to affirm this commitment, in July 1891 T.D. Sullivan MP decided to sell to the *Irish Catholic* the franchise for the old *Nation* newspaper, which had once been the wellspring of both nineteenth-century Irish republicanism and non-sectarian nationalism, but which had been slowly but surely turned ever since the mid 1850s into a clericalist organ by the Sullivan brothers. By August 1891, the *Freeman's Journal* was ready to turn against Parnell and only a handful of its staff were opposed to this change, including Fred Allan (advertising manager), and two sub-editors of the paper who were friends with many republicans but may not (though the DMP believed otherwise) have been members of the IRB: John William O'Beirne and John Wyse Power. On 17 August, Parnell wrote a letter (whether it was addressed to O'Beirne or Allan is unclear – it was repro-duced by O'Beirne many years later in the *Irish Press* to commemorate Allan and Robert Johnston's death) asking for a conference to be organized among those *Freeman* staff who were favourable to the idea of launching a new 'independent national daily paper'.[137] O'Beirne recalled that, together with Allan and Power, he thereafter mobilized support for this plan through the PLC, which, by July 1891, had won the support of about two hundred town councillors and poor law guardians across the country and essentially became the backbone of Parnellite support in the country.[138]

The IRB exercised no actual control over the PLC, even though Fred Allan became a member of its executive in June. As its headquarters were based in the National Club, however, its membership interacted continually with republicans, as well as the membership of all the Dublin clubs and societies founded during the late 1880s, for which the 'National Club Literary Society' (which organized Bodenstown demonstrations) was intended to be a magnet.[139] During the summer of 1891, members of these literary societies turned up frequently at Dublin PLC meetings and were responsible for drafting most of its resolutions. Henry Dixon and James Shannon (IRB) intro-duced resolutions (which were passed unanimously) on themes such as that no English politician 'should be permitted to dictate or interfere . . . in any way in our politics'; that Irishmen 'will not tolerate autocracy, whether it be from

136 Callanan, *Parnell split*, 69.   137 J.W. O'Beirne, 'The story of Parnell's newspaper: recol-lections of an old Dublin nationalist', *Irish Press*, 5 May 1937.   138 *Freeman's Journal*, 25 July 1891.   139 The leaders of the society were David Fagan (president), Henry Dixon, John Murphy, R.J. O'Duffy, P. Lavelle (BA), T.C. Woods, George Lynch, M.S. Connell (committee). Fagan, Dixon, Murphy and Lavelle were almost certainly IRB men.

England or Rome'; and that 'the lessons of history teach a policy of independence, upholding the national dignity and devoid of sectarian colour, is the only effective method of winning a nation's liberty'.[140] The National Club Literary Society's initial response to the Parnell Split was to emphasize its republican commitment to popular politicization, noting that, in the light of recent events, there was a greater need than ever to combat in Ireland

> The utter absence of an independent judgement and the tendency of the multitude to adopt their opinions at second hand on vital questions of principle. To make every man a circumspect politician may be an impractical object … but we must avail of every means of disseminating political information … All that is wanted is earnest endeavour.[141]

The LDS, which was renamed as the Leinster Literary Society (LLS) by its new leader Arthur Griffith (who was probably in the IRB by this time) during November 1890, was equally active. It issued its own political statement during the run up to the Kilkenny by-election, declaring its support for Parnell. This was published in two national newspapers, although Griffith insisted in taking this action that the minute book would record that 'Mr. Griffith spoke as one who was never a supporter of Mr. Parnell, but was an independent nationalist.'[142] Since the age of eighteen, Griffith had given literary lectures to the society and introduced and defended topics of debate such as 'the Catholic Church is opposed to civilization' and 'that ancient [classical] civilization is superior to modern civilization'.[143] During the Parnell Split controversy, in a debate upon the French revolution Griffith disagreed with the argument of Edward Whelan (a socialist and fellow impoverished Dublin printer) that the revolution was inspired by the writings of Voltaire and Rousseau, but instead described it as a simple 'outburst of popular feeling against the corrupt and debauched nobility and clergy who governed the land'. He also 'palliated the excesses of the revolutionists' against the clergy and nobility.[144] He argued that the presence of priests in politics was 'fatal to the progress of nations'.[145] The society as a whole then issued an address to Parnell, arguing that it did not matter if the Irish Party 'seeks fusion with any English party' or if 'ecclesiastical domination on the one side, or Dublin Castle influence on the other prevail', for Irishmen's duty would remain the same:

> The path of independence is before us. Independent of English politicians, and without Irish traitors and cowards we will seek for freedom; or failing to obtain it, we will, like the Carthaginians of old, retire behind the

---

140 *Freeman's Journal*, 3 and 20 Aug. 1891.   141 *Freeman's Journal*, 23 Jan. 1891.   142 NLI, Minute book of the Leinster Debating/Literary Society (1888–92), MS 19935, minute for 28 Nov. 1890.   143 Ibid., minutes for 12 Apr. 1889, 28 Mar. 1890.   144 Ibid., minute 6 Mar. 1891.   145 Ibid., minute for 6 Feb. 1891.

embattlements of our rights and refuse to obey the dictation of any leader of any alien people. And we hereby emphasize that resolve by declaring, in the words of John Mitchel: 'all Whig [Liberal][146] professions about conciliatory and impartial government in Ireland are as false as the father of Whiggery himself.'[147]

This activism of the National Club Literary Society and the LLS throughout the Parnell Split controversy, combined with republicans' growing influence among Dublin journalistic circles, helped to revive the IRB policy, which had been defeated during 1886–7, of attempting to create a federation of literary and political debating clubs. In May 1891, while planning a Bodenstown demonstration, the National Club Literary Society called for 'a convention of the Young Ireland Societies and other literary associations which uphold the principle of independence in Irish politics and opposition to all English and other dictation' with a view to furthering 'a scheme of national education through the medium of literary societies and otherwise'.[148] Many different societies were asked to support the initiative, including the YIS in Cavan and Limerick and five different branches in Co. Cork.[149] As a result, on 17 September 1891, at a convention chaired by John O'Leary at the Rotunda, a body known as the 'Young Ireland League' (YIL) was founded. The YIL declared that its principal objective was 'to carry into effect the principles of the Young Ireland movement and, for these purposes, to promote independent, national opinion', a resolution that could be interpreted as having a republican purpose, or Parnellite connotations, or both. The IRB president explained that the rules of the YIL 'do not necessarily commit members of this society to any theory about Irish government or an Irish constitution. We don't mean to force men to take the field against England.' Rather, their purpose was to encourage all Irishmen to 'read and think' for themselves, 'to be opposed to dictation from any person, or creed or class in this country, or in any others' and then to encourage them 'to spread such light as they have then gathered over wider and wider areas'. O'Leary believed that if the YIL was able to forward this goal, 'we will have succeeded in a great many things however we may fail in some others.'[150]

While the YIL was being formed in the Rotunda, the PLC decided that it would hold a convention on 12 October to launch a new independent, national newspaper and Parnell himself would be asked to chair the meeting.[151] To the

146 Republicans always cited the Liberal Party as the Whig party, to portray it as being a retrogressive influence on Irish politics, and the LLS's use of Mitchel's quotation was supposed to be read this way. 147 *Ibid.*, minute for 2 Aug. 1891. The society's committee was Arthur Griffith (president), Edward Whelan (vice-president), James Doyle (treasurer), J.R. Whelan (secretary), Peter White and William Rooney. 148 *Freeman's Journal*, 14 May 1891. 149 NLI, Minute book of the Leinster Debating/Literary Society (1888–92), MS 19935, minutes for 11 June 1891. 150 *Freeman's Journal*, 18 Sept. 1891 (report of inaugural meeting of YIL). 151 O'Beirne, 'The story of Parnell's newspaper'.

surprise and shock of all, however, Parnell died in Brighton on 6 October from pleurisy and over-exhaustion. Parnell's funeral in Dublin on 11 October was a massive affair, which was long remembered in the city. It was organized mostly by the PLC and was attended by several IRB leaders, as well as the long-retired James Stephens, who had recently been allowed by the government to return to Ireland (provided he did not take part in politics) after John Clancy persuaded Parnell to negotiate his safe passage.[152] The PLC convention went ahead on 12 October, but it was to be the last meeting of the PLC, as it no longer had a reason to exist now that Parnell was dead. On the occasion, in honour of Parnell's memory, the chair was left vacant and the Rotunda was kept in complete darkness and silence for half-an-hour before the six-foot-four figure of Robert Johnston, attired in a top-hat and a long goatee beard, stood up and opened the convention theatrically by shouting out in the darkness and silence a quotation from one of Parnell's last speeches: 'if I were dead and gone tomorrow, the men who are fighting against English influence in Irish public life would fight on still.' This meeting, at which William Redmond MP played the most conspicuous part, declared that a new independent nationalist newspaper must be launched, but Tim Harrington, the secretary of the National League, later attempted to thwart the project, as he feared that the formation of a stridently 'Parnellite' paper would only perpetuate the political hatreds aroused by the split and prevent the reunification of the Irish Party, which was a possibility now that Parnell was dead. Nevertheless the Parnellite *Irish Daily Independent*, a noticeably anti-clerical paper by contemporary Irish standards, went to press for the first time on 18 December 1891, thanks not least to the determination of Pierce Mahony MP.[153] Fred Allan was appointed manager of the 'Independent Newspaper Company', J.W. O'Beirne was made a sub-editor of the *Daily Independent*, while J.W. Power (whose wife subsequently published a book of Parnell's speeches) became the editor of the *Evening Herald*, which came into being the following summer. By 1893, the *Weekly Independent*, edited by John Murphy of the National Club Literary Society/YIL, had also been established. British intelligence suspected that William Redmond MP was sworn into the Clan during his 1891 American tour, but this seems unlikely. He did write to Devoy, however, in December 1891 asking him to sell shares for the *Independent*, and claiming that the new independent Irish party intended to make sure that 'no sham settlement of the Irish question will be regarded as satisfactory'.[154]

The formation of the Independent Newspaper Company was a significant event for the IRB, for during the 1890s republicans were allowed to give an airing to their viewpoints in its newspapers, thereby exposing their opinions to a national readership for the first time since the demise of the *Irishman* and the

---

152 Parnell to John Clancy (n.d.), on display in the Parnell Museum, Avondale House, Rathdrum, Co. Wicklow; Ryan, *Fenian chief*, 326. 153 O'Beirne, 'The story of Parnell's newspaper'. 154 *DPB*, vol. 2, 328–9.

Irish Nation (New York) in April 1885. Tim Harrington, who eventually succeeded in getting himself appointed as a director of the Independent Newspaper Company, was but one of several influential Parnellites who were totally opposed to republicans being allowed to express their opinions in the press. Consequently, he used all his influence to have Fred Allan and the IRB clique removed from the *Independent* offices, yet failed to do so. Very probably, republicans' ability to maintain a foothold in the *Independent* originated with the fact that Fitzgerald, O'Leary and Allan, combined with Devoy in America, had played a prominent role during the first half of 1891 in raising money for the 'Parnell Leadership Fund', the funds of which (following Parnell's death) were expended almost entirely in setting up the Independent Newspaper Company. In effect, with Fred Allan as the paper's manager and a handful of his friends in editorial positions with the company, the IRB was able to ensure that it received something in return for its financial stake in the newspaper company, even though its directors were conservative MPs. As most businesses outside Dublin refused to place advertisements in its papers' columns, the Independent Newspaper Company was always in a precarious position financially and, this also helped republicans' to keep their stake in the paper, for the Redmond brothers (its principal directors) would have to call upon Devoy in New York twice during the mid 1890s looking for his financial support.[155]

On 15 October 1891 the UB wing of the Clan (which had only 5,000 members, less than a quarter of the Clan's membership during the early to mid 1880s) issued a circular announcing that, after a recent Supreme Council meeting in Paris, 'a complete and satisfactory union' between the IRB and the UB had been established for the first time since 1882. The UB promised that it would regularly send 10% of its funds to the IRB in the near future. Meanwhile it noted that both the Clan and the IRB believed that many of those Irishmen who had stood up against the Liberals and the church during 1890–1 had become 'sufficiently advanced to make good members of our order' of republican brothers.[156] If all this was hopeful for the IRB, however, subsequent events would show that the diverse problems created for the republican movement during the mid-to-late 1880s were irremediable.

IRB ⟨+⟩ US clan

155 NAI, Home Office précis, carton 2, 12946/s, 13738/s. 156 NLI, Devoy papers, MS 18015 (5), Circular of UB Executive, 15 Oct. 1891.

The Parnellite quagmire and the
semi-retirement of the IRB, 1892–4

Despite the renewal of the IRB's alliance with the UB, the formation of the YIL and the existence of the Independent Newspaper Company, things began to turn very sour for the republican movement from the winter of 1891 onwards. The mutual animosity between the two wings of the Irish Party and their supporters was enhanced greatly by Parnell's unexpected death, and some republicans attempted to capitalize upon this, not least by mustering bitter anticlerical feelings. For example, Robert Johnston's branch of the Belfast PLC sent wreaths to Parnell's funeral bearing the words 'Murdered' and 'Avenge' in red flowers (an event that attracted much publicity) and posted many outrageous placards in Belfast with the caption: 'Parnell Murdered. Is it true? Say you priests, is it true?'[1] In Kilkenny city, the local workingmen's club, led by P.J. O'Keefe (IRB), provoked violent anticlerical behaviour after Parnell's death, a fact that prompted a local Franciscan priest to call upon his parishioners to pray for God to 'wreak His vengeance upon the club', which he described as nothing less than 'the council room of the devil' and 'a synagogue of Hell'.[2] Some rural IRB leaders held very extreme anticlerical sentiments during the early 1890s. Patrick McManus, a Donegal schoolteacher who lost his job due to the clergy and soon moved to Paris, told John O'Leary that he considered all priests as 'castrated animals' who did not deserve to be called men.[3] The fact that priests denounced virtually all YIS and GAA clubs in Irish country-towns that were led by republicans no doubt only sustained, or created, such hostility. In Cork city, Charles Doran actually tried to defend the clergy from unfair criticisms in the wake of Parnell's death, only to be booed by his own IRB following.[4] The most derided figure in Irish politics at the time, however, was certainly not any of the clergy, but rather Tim Healy, who had asked for police protection earlier that year after being accosted by angry Parnellites on the streets of Dublin for his scurrilous verbal abuse of Katherine O'Shea, soon to be Katherine Parnell.[5]

If amusing, none of this was of the slightest concern to Dublin Castle or British intelligence. Meanwhile, it did not take long for the authorities to learn that the alliance between the IRB and the Clan (UB) had been restored. Once William O'Shea petitioned for his divorce, Major Gosselin turned his attention to the British intelligence network in Irish-America, which had been

---

1 NAI, DICS files, carton 5 (Belfast Division), DI Seddall, 4 Nov. 1891 (monthly report). 2 *Kilkenny Moderator and Leinster Advertiser*, 28 Oct. 1891. 3 NLI, John O'Leary papers, MS 8001(37), letters of McManus to O'Leary (undated letter, c.1893). 4 NAI, British in Ireland microfilm, CO 904/17/151. 5 NAI, DMP files, carton 8, Report 2044, Chief Supt. Mallon, 15 Apr. 1891.

crumbling since Millen and Le Caron's departure. In 1890, he sent a couple of his informers to America as well as a new spymaster, who was able to recruit seven prominent figures in the Clan (mostly in the INB) as spies in a relatively short time, and one of these was on the seven-man executive of the UB.[6] In so far as the IRB operated as a 'revolutionary underground', British intelligence had been able to manipulate it ever since 1883–4 through the medium of American envoys. During the 1890s, Gosselin remained well informed of the Clan's dealings with the IRB, and whenever it attempted to finance the 'home organization'. Although British intelligence could not persuade any member of the UB to act as an *agent provocateur* to undermine the IRB, it did have several such agents in the 'United Irishmen of America' and, in particular, in certain clubs of the INB in New York, which had been trying to manipulate Dublin IRB opinion ever since 1887. As a result of this latter network, on 26 October 1891, a bomb exploded in the offices of Tim Healy's *National Press*, the first of several explosions in Dublin. The 'dynamite war' had spread to Ireland for the first time and, not surprisingly, it had very negative consequences for the IRB.

BOMBS but for IRB

Many years later, in his recollections, Tim Healy made an outlandish claim that Parnell had ordered P.N. Fitzgerald and Jim Boland into the *National Press* offices during 1891 to make death threats against him (a claim not at all substantiated by contemporary records of the DMP, who were protecting Healy at the time), and that Boland had planted the *National Press* bomb.[7] Healy did have *some* reason to suspect that Boland planted the bomb, for within a couple of days of the explosion, Michael Davitt (who had managed to expose Pigott) told him that he strongly suspected that one of the Boland brothers 'planned, if he did not carry out' the explosion at the *National Press* and was secretly acting as a British *agent provocateur*.[8] This rumour about the Boland brothers soon spread in Dublin, no doubt thanks to Healy rather than Davitt, and it made life very difficult for Jim Boland (Jack Boland was in New York), who was then a leader of the GAA, an amnesty activist and a member of the Commercial Branch of the Parnellite National League. The police

6 O'Broin, *Revolutionary underground* (1976), 75–6. The UB Executive spy may well have been 'J. Gallagher', who was sent by W.H. Browne of Jersey City as the UB envoy to the IRB in 1886–7 (when British intelligence learnt the names of the men on the Supreme Council), and was one of the seven-man executive of the UB in the 1890s. *DPB*, vol. 2, 284–5, 299, 336; NLI, Devoy papers, MS 18008 (5), Markham to Devoy, 9 Aug. 1924. Thomas Markham was appointed in charge of Dublin Castle by Michael Collins in 1922 and was asked by Collins to find as many secret service papers as possible before they could be taken away to London (as the Home Office was attempting to do).   7 Tim Healy, *Leaders and letters of my day* (1928), vol. 2, 368–70; NAI, DMP files, cartons 10–11.   8 UCD archives, Tim Healy papers, p.6/b/33, Davitt to Healy, 28 Oct. 1891. Davitt was able to learn the names of some spies from E.G. Jenkinson after two of Jenkinson's former agents, Matthew O'Brien (a Parnellite journalist) and Red Jim McDermott, blackmailed him at the time of the Special Commission. Campbell, *Fenian fire*, 309–11.

suspected that Boland was opposed to the idea of bombings (though he certainly detested Healy), and the Parnellites evidently trusted him as well.[9] The apparent truth of the bombing (and all subsequent ones that took place in Dublin) was clarified five years later, following the 'Ivory' court case in Glasgow arising from a bogus INB plot to cause explosions in London during the Queen's forthcoming jubilee celebrations. In this trial, one of the *agents provocateurs* in the plot,[10] William Jones, revealed in court that for several years he had been a spy in the 'United Irishmen of America' and New York INB. He claimed that both organizations had managed to make contacts with two Dublin IRB men (John Merna and John Nolan, a gas-fitter and amateur boxer) and that he had won the confidence of Jack Boland, an active member of the Clan in New York, formerly of Dublin.[11] Jones's evidence during 1896 explains why, not long after the bombing of the *National Press*, the DMP was absolutely certain that John Merna was being funded by the New York INB to cause various bombings in Dublin.[12] Merna's correspondence with the INB had been 'intercepted' by Dublin Castle as early as 1887 and he was eventually assassinated in Washington DC as a spy for betraying John Nolan and Luke Dillon in another plot.[13] It is very probable that he was the man who launched the Dublin 'dynamite war' in conjunction with the *agents provocateurs* of the New York INB.[14]

Merna and his sidekick John Nolan were members of Jim Boland's P.W. Nally Club in Dublin and, as Boland was suffering from a brain haemorrhage, for most of the early 1890s they effectively ran the club in his absence. Upon their visits to New York, they formed a 'P.W. Nally Club', of which Jones was a leader and upon which Jack Boland and others (including Robert Johnston)

---

9 NAI, DMP files, carton 12, Report 2458, Chief Supt. Mallon, 22 Feb. 1893; *Evening Herald*, 14 Mar. 1895 (obituary). 10 The other agents were John F. Kearney, a Glasgow-born labourer and United Irish/INB activist from 1880 until 1898, who launched the first 'dynamite war' attack in 1881 (for his career, see Short, *Dynamite war*) and John P. Hayes, who attempted to incriminate Mark Ryan (Ryan, *Fenian memories*, 127–9). During the 'Ivory case', extradition warrants were reported to have been issued for both men, as they were for Patrick Tynan (who was also involved in the plot) but were denied by the Dutch and French governments. PRO (London), Sir Robert Anderson papers (H.O.144/1537/3–4). 11 *Times*, 9 and 14 Nov 1896 (press cuttings of these articles are held in the Davitt papers at TCD, demonstrating that he was following this trail of events closely). 12 NAI, DMP files, carton 12, Report 2395, attached report of Chief Supt. Mallon, 17 Oct. 1892. 13 PRO 30/60/28, Gerald Balfour papers, Report of Chief Comm. J.J. Jones to Under-Secretary, 9 Jan. 1900; NAI, DMP files, carton 7 (packet for 1900), report 5527, J.J. Jones, 28 March 1900. Jones was unsure whether Merna had been killed or committed suicide, but it is more likely he was killed. Nolan and Dillon were sentenced to life-imprisonment. C.J. Brannigan, 'The Luke Dillon case and the Welland Canal explosion of 1900' (1977). 14 Shortly before his retirement in 1901, John Mallon revealed that he had known that Merna had custody of all the dynamite imported into Dublin during the early 1890s by the spy-infiltrated Nally Club of New York and where exactly it was held, thus making it quite possible that Merna ordered the assassination of Patrick Reid in November 1893 to deflect suspicion from himself. NAI, CBS files, Home Office précis, carton 3, 25520/s. For Gosselin's attitude to the Reid murder, see O'Broin, *Revolutionary underground*, 75–6.

called regularly.[15] During the early 1890s, the *agents provocateurs* had two principal causes they could use to incite men to commit bombings, and subsequently secure their arrest. On the one hand, the New York agents visiting Dublin tried to convince local republicans that causing explosions could force the government to free all political prisoners; a suggestion that nobody apparently believed. They also attempted to incite republicans by speculating upon the unusual circumstances surrounding the death of P.W. Nally in Mountjoy Prison.[16]

P.W. Nally was due to be released from prison in mid November 1891 and large demonstrations in his honour were planned by senior IRB, GAA and Parnellite figures. Just days before he was to be released, however, he died in Mountjoy prison, aged thirty-six, apparently from typhoid fever. As Nally was a champion athlete reported to have been in good health not long before his death, Joseph Kenny, a Parnellite MP and the City Coroner of Dublin, held an inquest. On 16 November, the jury found that Nally's 'naturally strong constitution' has been 'shattered' and made 'susceptible to the disease to which he succumbed' because of 'the harsh and cruel treatment to which he was subjected in Millbank prison, for refusing to give evidence on behalf of the *Times* at the Special Commission' and the further harsh treatment he received more recently (for the same reason) while held in Downpatrick prison.[17] At the large funeral that followed, which was attended by many GAA, IRB and Parnellite leaders, the symbolic gesture was made of covering his coffin with the same green flag that was placed over Parnell's coffin two months earlier. Many IRB men were naturally very suspicious of the circumstances surrounding Nally's death.[18] The P.W. Nally Club of New York, together with Merna in Dublin, demanded that explosions take place to punish the government and the prison authorities. A series of strange and purposeless bombings followed, including the detonation of a bomb in the cellar of an unoccupied building in Dublin Castle in December 1891; an explosion outside the detective depot of Dublin Castle one year later, which was placed too far from the wall to cause any damage to the detective depot, but killed an unfortunate novice DMP constable who unintentionally set off the bomb by picking

15 *Times*, 9 and 14 Nov 1896 (statements of Jones in court). 16 NAI, DMP files, carton 12, Report 2432, 2459 and 2498, Chief Supt. Mallon, 4 Jan., 30 Mar. and 24 June 1893. 17 *Freeman's Journal*, 12 and 17 Nov. 1891; *National Press*, 17 Nov. 1891. Tom Clarke was also pressurized to give evidence (O'Broin, *Prime informer*, 129–31), as reputedly were James Egan and James Mullet. Tom Clarke, *Glimpses from an Irish felon's prison life* (1922), passim. 18 Nally's brother, Jeremiah (IRB), the coroner for south Mayo, attended all the inquests in Dublin and presumably examined his brother's body. He believed that his brother was treated badly in prison due to his membership of the IRB, rather than his refusal to give evidence at the Special Commission, and, in particular, was made to clean out cesspits in addition to his 'hard-labour' prison duties as a punishment for his political sympathies. However, unlike a number of IRB figures, he also believed that his brother's death was not planned, and the collapse of his health stemmed partly from the fact that he suffered from a rare stomach condition, inherent in the family, whereby he could not eat certain foods, but the prison authorities refused to accommodate his expressed dietary needs. Louisa Nally to author.

it up; and a failed attempt to blow down a single wall of an army barracks at
Aldborough House, Dublin.[19] The last of these attacks took place on 25
November 1893 and was carried out by a New York labourer named Walter
Sheridan, who was arrested while shopping on Henry Street, Dublin the
following day for inexplicably having several detonators and explosives in his
pockets, which needless to say the police knew were there in advance. Merna
responded by ordering the assassination of Patrick Reid, a low-ranking Dublin
IRB member and a brother of a popular UB leader, for supposedly betraying
Sheridan.[20] The DMP, being well aware of what was taking place,[21] immediately arrested Merna and Nolan (the man who was apparently ordered to kill
Reid, his best friend; Nolan later suffered from severe mental problems) and
put them on trial for Reid's murder.

Fred Allan responded to this development by establishing a 'Fair Trial
Fund' to organize a defence for Nolan and Merna, and the police suspected
that Allan's motive in doing this was that Nolan knew a good deal about
Dublin IRB activities, despite holding no senior rank in the organization.[22]
However it appears that Allan was responding solely to a demand made by
Devoy and the UB, at the request of Reid's brother, that the case be sorted out,
as from what they knew of Dublin IRB affairs, it made no sense to them how
Reid could have been shot.[23] Thereafter English anarchists visited Allan at the
Independent offices, asking that the funding of Allan's committee be used to
promote the case of their own prisoners as well, an appeal that was refused.
These anarchists were the same men that were behind the attempted bombing
of an observatory in Walsall during 1892.[24] It was this event, as well as a
number of interviews held with Sir Robert Anderson (the man behind the
Special Commission and many 'dynamite war' intrigues of the 1880s), that
inspired Joseph Conrad to write his famous novel, *The Secret Agent*.[25] Nolan

19 NAI, CBS files, carton 4, 4418/s; carton 5 (this carton includes reports only on the explosions); DMP files, carton 12, Report 2435, Chief Supt. Mallon, 3 Jan. 1893. 'Detonators of
American origin' were found near the Four Courts within days of Nally's death in November
1891 and a small explosion also took place outside the Four Courts in May 1893, shortly after
an 'American suspect' was seen in the region. NAI, DMP files, carton 12, Report 2481, Chief
Supt. Mallon, 15 May 1893; carton 13, report 3035, Assistant Commissioner Mallon, 28 Feb
1895. 20 NAI, DMP files, carton 12, Report 2701, Assistant Commissioner John Mallon, 10
Apr. 1894. 21 John Mallon used the Dublin 'dynamite war' to convince his superiors that an
Invincible-style terrorist conspiracy existed in Dublin, causing Dublin Castle to increase its
security precautions for the second time in five years and to reward Mallon for his vigilance by
promoting him to Assistant Commissioner of the DMP, the 'first Catholic' ever to hold that
position; an achievement of which Mallon was very proud. NAI, DMP files, carton 12, Report
2451, Chief Supt. Mallon, 2 Mar. 1893; report 2468, Assistant Commissioner Mallon, 11 April
1894. 22 Interviews with Fred Allan, *Irish Weekly Independent*, 27 Jan. and 3 Feb. 1894; NAI,
DMP files, carton 13, Report 2872, Ass. Comm. Mallon, 8 Oct. 1894. 23 John Devoy, 'The
story of Clan na Gael', *Gaelic American*, 15 Aug. 1923. 24 NAI, DMP files, carton 13, report
2720, Ass. Comm. Mallon, 26 Apr. 1894 (attached report of Gosselin). 25 See Conrad's
introductory 'author's note' to the 1920 edition of his novel, which was first published in 1907.
26 Fred Allan, 'Behind prison bars', *Irish Weekly Independent*, 28 Apr. to 4 Aug 1894; Davitt,
Fall of feudalism, chapters 35–37 and 43–49. Davitt was better informed than Allan, although

and Merna were released, as it (presumably) could not be proved that they had ordered or committed the assassination of Reid. Thereafter Allan wrote a lengthy series of articles for the *Weekly Independent*, 'Behind Prison Bars', to promote the amnesty agitation and to show up government intrigues (this was also a favourite hobby of Michael Davitt),[26] and slowly but surely wrested control of the P.W. Nally Club out of Merna and Nolan's hands and then shut it down.[27] This put an end to the Dublin 'dynamite war', which was sanctioned neither by the IRB nor Clan leadership (including, at least reputedly, that of the INB) and which served only to enhance the conviction of many in the IRB that its Irish-American contacts, as well as its own underground ethos, had become far more of a liability than an asset to the organization. The price Allan had to pay for getting involved in this mess was the rise of a determined clique in the *Independent* offices that wanted to have him dismissed from his job, and to be subject to every intrigue John Mallon could conceive of against him. This no doubt partly helps to explain why, for mental relief, Allan became drawn to the contemporary vogue for theosophy, séances and spiritualism.[28]

The intrigues surrounding the Boland brothers stemmed from the fact that British intelligence believed that both men (as well as Merna) had been closely associated with the 'Invincibles' during 1882 and, as was the case with all men associated in any way with the members of that conspiracy, or indeed the 'dynamite war', the police could always approach them and attempt to persuade them to become spies, or else be brought before the courts and meet the same fate as Joseph Brady. After a lengthy period in hospital in a state of complete delirium, Jim Boland died from his brain haemorrhage on 11 March 1895, aged thirty-eight, and his funeral was quite a public event, primarily because his head injury was received (or so it was generally believed) while shielding Parnell from what probably would have been a fatal blow during the *United Ireland* brawl of December 1890. In honour of Boland, during the funeral the Parnellite Dublin City Hall lowered their flag to half-mast and all three Parnellite members of parliament for Dublin attended, as did two former Parnellite MPs, as well as leaders of the GAA and Dublin and Cork corporations. Patrick O'Brien, a Parnellite ex-MP and former IRB man (who was re-elected to parliament for Kilkenny in the summer of 1895), later paid for the education of Boland's three sons, Gerry, Harry and Ned, all of whom joined the IRB as soon as they reached the age of eighteen.[29] Meanwhile Jack Boland, who had become relatively wealthy from entering into business deals

he later admitted to have got several things totally wrong in his investigations, particularly regarding his suspicions of the moral character of Eugene Davis. UCD, Desmond Ryan papers, Michael MacDonagh to Desmond Ryan, 8 Nov. 1937. MacDonagh, a leading journalist/historian, was a friend of both Davitt and Davis. For Davis's life, see McGee, 'Eugene Davis: a forgotten Clonakilty writer and poet' (2004). **27** NAI, CBS files, carton 9, 9814/s; DMP files, carton 13, report 3904, Ass. Comm. Mallon, 8 Aug. 1896. **28** Hilda Allan to author. **29** *Irish Daily Independent*, 12 and 15 Mar. 1895; *Evening Herald*, 15 Mar. 1895;

with William Lyman (a very prosperous New York builder and the new INB leader), died later that same year, apparently from typhoid fever, while sailing from New York to England. He was thirty-three. He was buried in Liverpool, his funeral being attended by many local IRB men and John O'Leary, who made the trip from Dublin especially for the event.[30] William Jones revealed at the 'Ivory Case' in November 1896 that he had acquired all Jack Boland's correspondence after his death, including letters to Mark Ryan and Robert Johnston.[31]

Two historians have accepted as true informers' rumours that Boland was an *agent provocateur or double agent*,[32] and while this is possible, it is a great mistake to interpret such police reports at face value. The history of British *agents provocateurs* in New York was a very long one, dating back to 1881. They constantly attempted to corrupt Irishmen in America, Ireland and Britain and there was probably not a single man who did not have an 'informer' accusation thrown against him at one stage. It was to bring about *exactly* this type of scenario that the Special Branch had been set up and provided with copious funding. Jack Boland was but one of many who were brought into close association with the heartland of Irish revolutionary paranoia and *agents provocateurs* in New York, which O'Donovan Rossa had escaped from as early as 1883. The 1890s were a decade when endless anarchist plots on the continent became front-page news (they almost invariably ended with everyone involved being hanged) and caught the public imagination, and while there were many adherents of anarchism and terrorism in the Fabian society of Trinity College,[34] it is doubtful if there were any in the club rooms of the IRB. The amnesty clubs, the supposed centres of 'the extreme party' in Dublin (according to informers' colourful reports), denounced terrorism and anarchism during the 1894 May Day events, as did O'Donovan Rossa, who came to Dublin to give a short lecture tour on his prison trials in June that year; events that Jim Boland was mostly responsible for organizing.[35] G.K. Chesterton's surreal and allegorical fantasy, *The Man Who Was Thursday* (1908), could be said to have been a more accurate reflection of the idealistic moral world of nineteenth-century secret societies than Joseph Conrad's sinister and macabre *Secret Agent* (1907), which reflected the moral world of

Jim Maher, *Harry Boland* (1998), 11–2. **30** *Irish Daily Independent*, 30 Nov and 2 Dec. 1895. **31** *Times*, 9 and 14 Nov. 1896 (Jones's statements in court). Many newspaper cuttings surrounding this trial and related events can be found in TCD, Davitt papers, MS 9469/4137–71. **32** David Fitzpatrick, *Harry Boland's Irish revolution* (2004), 18–29; O'Broin, *Revolutionary underground*, 59, 102. **34** NAI, DMP files, carton 13, report 2720, Ass. Comm. Mallon, 26 Apr. 1894. Over two hundred students listened sympathetically to Faustus MacDonald (PhD) of London justify terrorism in a lecture entitled 'Anarchism and Darwinism'. **35** *Weekly Independent*, 13 Jan. 1894 (Rossa interview), 12–26 June 1894 (public celebrations in Dublin in honour of Rossa and accounts of his lecture tour); *Irish Daily Independent*, 20 Apr. 1894 (amnesty association and trades council statement regarding May Day).

spies and informers. By the time both these novels were written, however, this nineteenth-century political culture of idealistic secret societies generally no longer existed in Europe. That reality, as much as the successes of British intelligence during the 1880s, partly helps to account for the fact that the IRB began to slowly but surely fade away from the early 1890s onwards.

William Lyman, who became the INB leader in 1891, was a 37-year-old native of Roscommon who had worked originally as a plumber in Brooklyn but later became wealthy through speculating in real estate and so joined the US Republican Party. He was elected treasurer of the nominally Parnellite INLA in October 1891 and afterwards played a prominent role in Irish–American politics. John Devoy effectively controlled the INLA branches specifically in New York in the Parnellites' interests, but the *official* policy of the INLA, as laid down by Lyman, was that it could never consider encouraging the Irish-American community to support either wing of the Irish Party unless it reunited; a rather unlikely occurrence.[36] A month before the July 1892 general election (which saw the return of Gladstone to power and the election of but nine Parnellite MPs, as opposed to seventy-one anti-Parnellites), Lyman and O'Neill Ryan, a St Louis judge, former INLA secretary and nominal INB man, travelled to Ireland in their capacity as leaders of the INLA. They held brief interviews with John Redmond in Dublin regarding the possibility of reunifying the Irish Party, but the anti-Parnellites refused to meet them. Upon returning to New York in July, Lyman issued an INB circular, subsequently distributed in Ireland, which stated that the INB would be prepared to reopen communications with the IRB leadership, if it ceased to associate itself with the Parnellite cause and adopted an insurrectionary policy.[37] This did not evoke any immediate response from the IRB, but it did arouse the curiosity of many of its members, since the INB was by far the larger of the two Clan factions and had reputedly put the 'dynamite war' idea behind it.

Shortly after Lyman's return to New York, two UB members, including a Boston judge, held a meeting with Fred Allan, Robert Johnston, Jim Boland and John Wyse Power in the *Daily Independent* offices and offered a large amount of funding to boost the amnesty agitation in the country.[38] With the help of this funding, a monster amnesty meeting was held in the Phoenix Park on 24 August 1892, after which the 'Irish National Amnesty Association' was officially established. Thereafter the IRB attempted (albeit with little success) to make the amnesty issue the principal public issue of the day, rather than the rivalries of the Irish Party factions or the apparent readiness of Gladstone to reintroduce his home rule bill. As a propagandist exercise, it was also hoped that the raising of the black-and-white question of political prisoners would put an end to 'that absurd prating of the "union of hearts"' between Irish

36 NAI, CBS files, carton 4, 4642/s. 37 NAI, DMP files, carton 12, Report 2355, Chief Supt. Mallon, 22 July 1892. 38 Ibid., Report 2374, Chief Supt. Mallon, 3 August 1892.

nationalists and the British government which the Irish Party had been propagating since 1886.[39] Several IRB men were made members of the executive of the Amnesty Association: Fred Allan was the vice-president, while P.N. Fitzgerald, Mark Ryan of London and Thomas O'Gorman of the Limerick Amnesty Association were made 'honorary' vice-presidents, but its actual president was Pierce Mahony MP, a director of the Independent Newspaper Company. Meanwhile, its principal treasurer was Ffrench Mullen MP (whose brother was in the INB) and, indeed, its executive was essentially controlled by a handful of Parnellite MPs, even though republicans ran most of the association's branches in Ireland.[40] This placed the IRB in a problematic position, for it needed to cooperate with the Parnellites to make a success of the amnesty agitation yet, at the same time, it did not want the amnesty question to become a purely party-political issue, or a mere electioneering aid to the Redmondites. This conflict of interests would dictate the nature of the IRB's relations with the 'Parnellite Party' over the next two years when it struggled, but failed, to wrest control of the association out of John Redmond's hands.

Instead of boosting the morale of the Irish nationalist movement, the IRB's alliance with the UB actually lowered it greatly, for almost all of the UB's financial resources were used after 1891 solely to win the battle for survival between the two wings of the Clan – a tactic that was justified in the UB's internal circulars by arguing that 'progress here in America' for the UB faction 'cannot fail to bring progress at home' for the IRB.[41] O'Leary and the IRB Supreme Council (who were constantly expectant of UB aid, only to be perpetually disappointed) remained totally committed to the alliance, for although the INB had far greater financial resources,[42] it was felt it could not be trusted, owing to its past record. Not least because of the Dublin 'dynamite war', Fred Allan refused to accept *any* financial support from the INB but, in London, Mark Ryan (a leader of the INLGB, who no longer held rank in the IRB) was willing to accept INB aid to boost the London Amnesty Association (of which he was a leader) and believed that the republican movement as a whole should do the same. As a result, a Dublin–London divide began to emerge in the republican movement through the medium of the amnesty movement. The Supreme Council was already impoverished because of the huge fall-off in rank and file subscriptions during the late 1880s and as it necessarily delayed the implementation of various plans until the UB funding arrived, many IRB circles began to lose faith in the organization, which had seemingly come to a complete standstill policy-wise. As there was already division of opinion within the IRB regarding whether or not Parnell deserved

39 This is evident from Fred Allan's articles on the amnesty movement, entitled 'Behind prison bars', *Irish Weekly Independent*, 28 Apr. to 4 Aug. 1894 (the quotation is from 28 Apr. 1894). 40 NAI, CBS files, carton 9, 9156/s. 41 NLI, Devoy papers, MS 18015 (5), eight UB circulars dating from 1890–1897, quotation from circular dated 1 Oct. 1896. 42 NLI, Devoy papers, MS 18015 (7), (8), (9), (11), (13), (14), (15), statistics of Clan membership

to be supported during 1890–1, the absence of any new initiative by the Supreme Council in the wake of Parnell's death inevitably led some members to suspect (incorrectly) that the organization's leadership had 'sold out' to the Parnellites. As will be seen, the reaction of a few prominent IRB men to the 1892 general election helped to sustain these rumours.

Although the *Independent* newspapers championed a rhetoric implying that the Parnellite Party wanted to create a new body of 'independent, nationalist opinion' in the country as a means of 'separating the wheat from the chaff once and for all' in Irish political society,[43] the predominantly-urban Parnellite movement of the 1890s was characterized neither by political independence nor uniformity of opinion. In Cork City, for example, the Parnellite movement during the early 1890s was nothing more than a conglomerate of conservative business leaders and city councillors who formed electorate alliances with the Tories to defeat the anti-Parnellites at the polls; a fact which ensured that William O'Brien, rather than John Redmond, remained the most popular political figure in Co. Cork, and that P.N. Fitzgerald and the Cork IRB had no time at all for the local Parnellites. In Cork, more so than anywhere else, republicans' plans had been based on the eventuality that UB funding would arrive very quickly, as Fitzgerald promised, and the fact that this funding did not arrive at all turned several local IRB centres against Fitzgerald (who 'Nero' had already attempted to portray as dishonest in money matters) and they refused to forward subscriptions to him. Ultimately, in March 1893, once the Cork IRB heard (through Jim Boland) that an informer ('Nero') had been in their ranks, many of the already demoralized local centres fell into mutual recriminations against each other and their loyalty to the organization disappeared. Many resolved to leave the IRB altogether and act merely as individuals within the amnesty and NMC clubs.[44] This not only left Fitzgerald out on a limb but also effectively led to the demise of the Munster IRB organization, the enthusiasm of which was now confined mostly to Limerick City, where the IRB's amnesty clubs had strong popular support. In Kilkenny City, the Parnellite movement was very different in character, having more in common with the Dublin, as opposed to the Cork, Parnellite movement, owing to its having a more working-class social profile. The local Parnellite MP, Patrick O'Brien, was an old Liverpool republican who was a strong supporter of both amnesty and the GAA, and this fact convinced the militant local IRB leader, P.J. O'Keefe, that the Parnellite movement was worth supporting. In 1892, O'Keefe supported Edward Keane TC in forming the Parnellite *Kilkenny People*, which championed O'Keefe's local branches of the Trade and Labour Association, the YIS and his 'workingmen's club'.[45] If republicans in Kilkenny and Dublin could feel some identification with the

1874–1897. **43** *Freeman's Journal*, 25 July 1891 (speech of William Redmond at inaugural convention of Parnellite INL). This subsequently became the tone of the Parnellite press. **44** NAI, DICS files, carton 2 (South-western Division), DI Jones, 1 May 1892; DI Patterson, 5 Mar. 1893. **45** NAI, CSB files, carton 10, 10231/s, 10418/s.

Parnellites, however, this was not the case in Wexford, where Parnellite support was confined largely to wealthy and conservative farmers. As a result, C.J. O'Farrell and his followers no doubt felt out of touch with Kilkenny and Dublin republican circles. These trends in Munster and Leinster helped to demoralize the IRB greatly, by causing it to feel as if it had lost its sense of direction. Meanwhile in Connacht and Ulster, this process of demoralization was much stronger, owing to the fact that some local republican leaders were actually prepared to defect to the Parnellite movement.

The Parnellites were naturally eager to win IRB men over to their party. Both Jeremiah Nally (brother of P.W. Nally) and Mark Ryan were asked to stand for parliament during 1892–3 for Connacht constituencies, although they declined.[46] However, J.P. McCarthy, the IRB leader in Loughrea (the key centre of Connacht IRB activities in recent years), did accept an invitation to run for parliament and was also seemingly prepared to abandon his old policy of prioritizing radical land agitation – a fact that possibly explains why one of McCarthy's associates of the late 1880s, possibly out of pure spite, informed the RIC of the whereabouts of his arms depot.[47] McCarthy, who failed to win the seat, died from tuberculosis in April 1894, aged fifty, and the divided and demoralized Galway IRB organisation virtually died with him, due to the absence of any acceptable local leadership. Meanwhile in Ulster, Robert Johnston (who, like Mark Ryan, had not been a Supreme Councillor since 1882) managed to persuade many republicans to defy the orders of Michael O'Hanlon (the Ulster IRB leader) and assist the Parnellites in the 1892 general election, both in Ulster and north Leinster. This prompted O'Hanlon and many others to retire from the IRB, justifying their decision by expressing disgust at what was happening to the republican movement.[48] According to well-placed informers in Belfast and Cavan, Robert Johnston and Terence Fitzpatrick had told the Ulster IRB during the summer and autumn of 1891 that they should try to ensure that those who stood by Parnell during the split in fighting 'English and clerical dictation' would now join their ranks,[49] and this was evidently the general IRB policy. However, the fact that Johnston actually stood (unsuccessfully) as a Parnellite candidate for the small parliamentary constituency of Newry in July 1892 naturally led many republicans in Belfast, as well as Ulster generally, to suspect that the IRB leadership had promoted this policy only to help launch parliamentary careers for themselves. Johnston denied this. He claimed that Parnell had asked him in May 1891 to

---

46 Arthur Lynch mentions this in an interview in *Irish Weekly Independent*, 3 Feb. 1894. Lynch, an Irish-Australian republican whose father (along with a brother of Fintan Lalor) had led the Eureka Stockade of 1854, was co-leader with Mark Ryan of the London Amnesty Association. Lynch stood unsuccessfully for Galway as a Parnellite in 1892.   47 NAI, DICS files, carton 1 (Western Division), report of DI Gibbons, 10 May 1891; report of DI Otter, 4 Apr. 1892.   48 NAI, DICS reports, carton 6 (Northern Division), DI Gambell, 1 Mar. 1892.   49 NAI, DICS files, carton 4 (Midlands Division), District Inspector Bell, 3 Dec. 1891; carton 5 (Belfast Division), DI Seddall, 5 Aug. 1891.

stand for Newry in the next election and he refused, but Parnell had stated that there was absolutely no chance of a Parnellite candidate being returned for Ulster and that by running for election Johnston could at least help to maintain *some* sort of Parnellite agitation in the province, which could serve both the Parnellites and the republicans' interests. Johnston claimed to have stood only to fulfil this last wish of Parnell,[50] and this may well have been true, for he and all other Ulster IRB figures did cease their association with the Parnellite cause after the 1892 general election.[51] This, however, did not heal the debilitating division that had been created in the Ulster IRB during 1891–2 as a result of his actions.

The IRB seems to have expected that the revival of an amnesty agitation could increase the republican party's influence in popular politics in a similar manner to what had occurred during the 1870s. For this reason, the failure of the Irish National Amnesty Association to become a truly popular movement during 1892–4 demoralized the IRB and served to convince many republicans that 'the future will be very black indeed'.[52] Both republicans and Parnellites adopted a similar rhetoric on amnesty platforms, citing the Liberal government's refusal to release the prisoners as evidence of the falsity of the 'union of hearts' idea. Fred Allan and Maurice Moynihan cited this as proof that the Irish Party's past endeavours to make 'respect for English opinion' and trust in Westminster the 'all-pervading factor' in Irish life had created a 'most artificial public life' in the country that 'misrepresents the true feelings of our people'. Parnellites who criticized the 'union of hearts' idea at amnesty demonstrations, however, did so only to back up their claims that Parnell's decision to sideline temporarily the Liberal alliance during 1890–1 was wiser than what the anti-Parnellites had anticipated.[53]

As had been the case during the 1870s, the IRB was determined that the amnesty clubs would not be allowed to be used by MPs for electioneering purposes, and many Irish-Americans desired this as well. Consequently, after attending the inaugural meeting of the Amnesty Association of America in New York in June 1893, Fred Allan introduced a resolution before the executive of the Irish National Amnesty Association stating that no political party should have any control over the policy of the association, which must be completely independent. The Parnellite MPs on its executive, however, refused to accept such a resolution, and as a result Allan, P.N. Fitzgerald and five other IRB members of the association officially resigned from its executive.[54] This was hardly a practical stance to take. John Redmond's very ambiguous remarks on the question of whether or not men like John Daly

50 Interview with Robert Johnston, *Irish Press*, 15 May 1935. **51** NAI, DICS files, carton 6 (Northern Division), District Inspector Gambell, 3 Aug. 1892, 4 Feb. 1893. **52** Allan, 'Behind prison bars', 4 Aug. 1894. **53** *Kerry Sentinel*, 29 Nov. 1893 (speech of Maurice Moynihan); Allan, 'Behind prison bars', 28 Apr. to 4 Aug. 1894; *Daily Independent*, 26 Nov. 1894 (speech by Allan); J.E. Redmond, *Political and historical addresses, 1883–97* (1898), chapter entitled 'Amnesty'. **54** NAI, British in Ireland microfilm, CO 904 / 17/ 1.

should be considered as guilty of a 'crime' certainly annoyed many IRB men, prompting John O'Leary, for example, to write a particularly caustic letter to the *Daily Independent* in October 1893,[55] criticisms which 'greatly pained' Redmond,[56] who, unlike Tim Harrington, was eager to maintain the IRB's support and to win away its following to his own party. Unlike the IRB in Ireland, Mark Ryan (who was chairman of the INLGB by 1894) and the London Amnesty Association had absolutely no problem with the Parnellites' control over the amnesty movement because they felt that Redmond was giving the movement valuable assistance in numerous ways. It was through Redmond's appeals to the Liberal government, for example, that members of Ryan's association were allowed to interview Tom Clarke and John Daly in prison, to give greater publicity to their cases. Meanwhile, during 1894, by speaking alongside Fred Allan at a handful of amnesty demonstrations at Cork, Limerick, Waterford and Dublin, Redmond was responsible for encouraging many indifferent Parnellites to promote, or found, amnesty branches in each of these cities;[57] something that Allan on his own could surely not have achieved. Likewise, Mark Ryan would not have been able to launch the Amnesty Association of Great Britain in August 1894, under his own presidency, were it not for Parnellite assistance, as the association was based not upon English IRB circles, of which very few still survived, but rather branches of the INLGB throughout England.[58]

The clearest indication that the IRB was in danger of collapsing during the early 1890s is that by 1893 it could no longer afford the costs of maintaining the National Club in Dublin, which had been its effective headquarters during the late 1880s. As a result, the Parnellites took over the management of the premises, the directors of which (by 1894) no longer included John O'Leary or any other IRB leaders, but consisted exclusively of Parnellite MPs.[59] It was now more of a Parnellite, rather than a republican, recruiting ground. Simultaneously, the Parnellites attempted to capitalize upon the political bankruptcy of the republican party by using its powers of patronage to attempt to win over various republicans who no longer held political influence, or who simply lacked a good job. This trend was particularly evident in Dublin. Henry Campbell (MP for Fermanagh South, 1885–92) had been Parnell's personal secretary during the 1880s and was now the town clerk of Dublin City Hall, thereby effectively placing him in charge of all municipal appointments. He wrote to the Dublin IRB leader Jim Boland (a corporation foreman) in April 1894 that:

---

55 *Daily Independent*, 24 Oct. 1893. 56 NLI, John O'Leary papers, MS 8001 (49), Redmond to O'Leary, 24 Oct. 1893. The best of example of Redmond's very ambiguous attitude towards the prisoners was his speech at the 1894 Parnell National Convention in Dublin. *Irish Weekly Independent*, 7 Apr. 1894. 57 NAI, DICS files, carton 2 (South Western Division), DI Morrison, 4 Oct. and 4 Nov. 1893; CBS files, carton 9, 9156/s. 58 Ryan, *Fenian memories*, 174. 59 *Irish Daily Independent*, 26 Apr. 1894 (report of Annual General Meeting of the National Club).

I need not, I trust, assure you that anything I can do, at anytime, on behalf of any of your [IRB] friends will not be neglected. I am quite certain that you would not recommend Hogan or anyone else if they did not possess the proper brand. If there is anything I can do for him later on, or for you, at all times command me.[60]

John Clancy, who continued to keep a foot in both the republican and Parnellite camps (he rejoined the National League in 1891) owed his prominence in City Hall to these patronage networks run by the Irish Party ever since 1885. From the 1890s onwards, he began actively using them both to build up his own political support base and to secure lucrative employment for his son; a fact that led many republicans to criticise him, although (as Campbell's letter to Boland indicates) it is probable that many republicans would have done the same to forward their own personal careers, if they had had an opportunity of doing so.

During September 1892, Clancy persuaded the mostly Parnellite city council (by a very slight majority) to refuse to make an address of welcome to the new (Liberal) lord lieutenant, despite the fact that Gladstone had promised to reintroduce his 'home rule' bill in the near future. Not surprisingly, those councillors who opposed the address represented lower-class constituents, while those that represented the business classes (both Protestant and Catholic) were entirely in favour of a loyal resolution, as they had prospered under the existing, colonial system of taxation in the country. John O'Leary was very happy with this result, noting that although he saw 'no marked improvement of any sort in Ireland of late', 'I must confess that in this one small matter of the Dublin Corporation we have improved ... Flunkeyism no longer reigns predominant and that is much.'[61] O'Leary was also pleased that Clancy managed to give publicity to the amnesty movement, by taking up a propaganda campaign against the Liberal chief secretary, John Morley, for his refusal to tolerate the amnesty agitation, despite his frequent criticisms of the Tories for imprisoning Irish Party supporters in the past. This campaign essentially began in 1893 when Morley visited the trouble spot of Co. Clare to try and understand the history of the 'Plan of Campaign' and the nature of Irish politics; an action he deemed necessary because, like virtually all other Englishmen who governed Ireland during the nineteenth century, he had never been in Ireland before his appointment and knew nothing of life in the

---

60 Henry Campbell to Jim Boland, 27 Apr. 1894 (private collection, courtesy of Annraoi O'Beolain). Boland was inquiring as to who was to receive the job of Joseph Bolger (IRB) as assistant secretary to the corporation's Public Health Committee now he was leaving for America. The job was eventually given to James Collins, a young IRB man who collected funds for a monument to be erected at the 'Croppies Hole' (a site along the Dublin quays where many United Irishmen were executed in 1798) and later, between 1912 and 1919, acted as Archbishop Walsh of Dublin's chief informant on the IRB. NLI, Sean T. O'Kelly papers, MS 27, 728 (1–3). 61 *Freeman's Journal*, 26 Sept. 1892; O'Leary, *Recollections*, vol. 2, 77; NAI, DMP files, carton 12, Report 2396, Chief Commissioner Harrel, 26 Sept. 1892.

country. After asking the local Catholic bishop and newspaper editors who was the most representative nationalist political figure in the county, Morley was advised to call upon Patrick McInerney of Ennis Town Commission, the Clare IRB leader, whom Morley liked and spoke freely to (not knowing McInerney's actual political affiliation), only to be bitterly disappointed when McInerney subsequently revealed in the newspapers that Morley was opposed to the amnesty cause and denounced him in the strongest terms.[62] Thereafter, like all other chief secretaries, Morley no longer engaged with the Irish public, but stayed in aristocratic social circles at Dublin Castle and the Viceregal Lodge and looked forward to returning to England once more.

During 1894, Clancy persuaded Dublin City Hall to present an amnesty petition to Morley, but he refused to meet the lord mayor's deputation or even accept its petition, prompting Dublin Corporation to pass a resolution (again on Clancy's initiative) denouncing the chief secretary's action and demanding that he would resign. John Redmond supported this campaign, while P.N. Fitzgerald obliged his friend Clancy by bringing a draft of the corporation's resolution to various municipal bodies across the country and persuaded many of them to sign it.[63] Fred Allan, who 'had no faith in Morley as a politician', but 'had considerable admiration for his writings and teachings in other directions', also gave vocal support for this campaign, but it did not have any effect on the Liberal government, partly because, as Allan himself noted, there was 'really very little deep interest in the amnesty question' among the general Irish public.[64]

The reason why IRB leaders had been reduced by 1894 to distributing petitions – a form of political agitation that it had always detested for being too servile in nature – was that the organization's leadership had effectively resigned themselves to the fact that the republican movement was on its last legs. From British intelligence received at UB conventions in the United States (which IRB men attended yearly to forward progress reports), it is clear that by 1894 less than one in four of the roughly 30,000 men in the United Kingdom who had taken the IRB oath ever attended IRB meetings or paid subscriptions any more, and this figure was *still* falling.[65] Since the cessation of its arms importation scheme in 1884, the IRB's rural following had slowly but surely fallen completely away. The few thousand urban followers left were now both demoralized and divided and the men on the Supreme Council no longer

---

62 Lord Morley, *Recollections* (London, 1917), vol. 1, 333, vol. 2, 31–2. 63 Redmond, *Historical and political addresses*, 363–4; NAI, CBS files, carton 9, 9238/s. 64 Allan, 'Behind Prison Bars', *Irish Weekly Independent*, 4 Aug. 1894. Allan's admiration for the writings of John Morley (who like Allan was initially a Methodist, before embracing the more fashionable 'positivist' philosophy) probably stemmed from the fact that Morley's *Contemporary Review* was perhaps England's finest journal for political debate and that, at least during his early university days, Morley was sympathetic towards continental republicanism; a fact that prompted Lord Morley to title the first part of his *Recollections* (1917) as 'The republic of letters'. 65 PRO (London), CO 903/7, Chief Secretary Office miscellaneous intelligence notes (W Series), 1–10, p. 44.

held any real party control over their nominal following. As the IRB had no apparent means possible of remedying this problem, the organization was almost set to retire during 1894.

In the summer of 1894 the 58-year-old John O'Clohissey, who had been reasserting his influence in Dublin republican circles since 1885,[66] created a public IRB veterans association (under his own presidency) known as the 'Old Guard Benevolent Union' (OGBU), soon to be renamed simply as the Old Guard Union; a body that survived until at least 1917 and was always strongly supported by the Dublin Trades Council. The initial membership of the OGBU consisted mostly of former members of the 'Old Guard' IRB organization, which had already ceased to exist a few years previously, but very many of the 'Supreme Council party' of the IRB also joined. The rules of the Old Guard Union stated that any member of the public could subscribe to the association 'to pay the honours due to them as patriot soldiers', in their retirement. The nominal purpose of the association was to vindicate the principles of the IRB in the eyes of the younger generation, thereby undoing the very harmful negative publicity drawn to Irish republicanism by the dynamite wars and Phoenix Park murders. The OGBU desired to be seen by the nationalist youth of the country 'as the Main Guard of Our Nation' and as a purely idealistic body of men whose sole purpose was to form with 'their sons and sympathisers … a bond of United Brotherhood, in promoting the indestructible rights of our race to self-government'; to 'guard against any attempt … to lower the Irish flag on its onward march to freedom'; and to 'discourage rash, unwise and reckless action, no matter from whom they may spring, having in our ranks men who have stood by the sacred cause in every struggle of our times, men of wisdom and experience'.[67] A body known as the 'IRB Veterans Association', which lasted until the late 1930s, was also established in New York around this time, while it is surely not coincidental that both John O'Leary and O'Donovan Rossa began writing and publishing their recollections in the press in serial form during 1894, telling the story of a movement and a brand of politics which they believed no longer existed. Younger IRB leaders took a somewhat similar line.

In his articles on the amnesty agitation and his public platform speeches on the amnesty question during 1894, Fred Allan occasionally referred to 'the IRB' and its political legacy in the past tense. He cited its republican example and principles as 'still the best hope' in Ireland for the elimination of British-style class distinctions from Irish politics and for realizing the Young Ireland ideal of building 'a firm imperishable bridge' between Protestant and Catholic. However, while attempting to explain why he believed that the republican cause 'would never die' so long as democracy could be sustained in Ireland, Allan in the same breath also referred to the IRB as 'that movement just now

---

66 NLI, John O'Leary papers, MS 5927, Luby to O'Leary (n.d., 1885). 67 Manifesto of the Old Guard Benevolent Union, Sept. 1894 (courtesy of Annraoi O'Beolain).

passing away'.[68] At a demonstration chaired by O'Leary to mark the third anniversary of P.W. Nally's death at the Rotunda in November 1894, P.N. Fitzgerald stated that 'unfortunately in this country, we have not been successful at revolution' and the Irish nationalist movement had failed. Fitzgerald argued that the only hope that could sustain the IRB's ideals was that once a generation of more politically-aware Irishmen existed, the correctness of their political judgement would be recognized, for 'revolutions are to nations and humanity what instruction is to individuals', an unavoidable learning process that cannot be shirked.[69] Like Fitzgerald, Fred Allan believed that the 'noble fight for liberty of political opinion' in Ireland against English and clerical influences was one that self-evidently would 'have to be fought out and won before Ireland can even honestly aspire to nationhood'. He noted that this 'fight' had been fought by republicans constantly, long before the Parnell Split controversy had broken out, and argued that the battle could have been won by republicans 'fourteen or fifteen years ago', during the Land League era, were it not that Parnell deliberately tried to 'draw much of the power out of the revolutionary organization of that time' by bringing the Land League under the wing of the clergy and the politicians at Westminster, 'the home of the will-o-the-wisp of Irish politics'.[70] All the woes of Irish politics during the 1890s were believed to have stemmed from this fact, for the Irish Party's politics, by its very nature, could not possibly achieve anything except 'be the means of putting one government out, and getting in another', pushing for 'a few reformed Land Bills' and 'creating some ignorant JPs in the country ... Ireland, now as then, cannot expect nationality through its means'.[71] It was also during 1894 that the NMC, having been funded almost exclusively by the GAA, spent £500 on a seventeen-foot high, three-figure white marble monument that was dedicated in memory of 'the members of the Irish Republican Brotherhood ... outlaws and felons according to English law, but true soldiers of Irish Liberty'. This monument was completed during November 1895 and was supposed to be erected and unveiled by John O'Leary in Glasnevin cemetery,[72] but its erection was prevented by Archbishop Walsh and the Catholic Cemeteries Committee, which did not allow it to be placed over what was popularly-known as the 'Fenian plot' in Glasnevin until 1933, long after the IRB had ceased to exist.[73]

Perhaps more so than anything else, it was the IRB's failure to capitalize upon the Parnell Split and turn the controversy into a proverbial 'republican

68 *Daily Independent*, 26 Nov. 1894; 23 Nov. 1895 (speech of Allan in Belfast National Club). 69 *Daily Independent*, 10 Nov. 1894 (speech of Fitzgerald at Nally commemoration at Rotunda). 70 Ibid.; Fred Allan to *Irish Weekly Independent*, 6 Oct. 1894. 71 Ibid. (quotation from Fitzgerald) 72 *Irish Daily Independent*, 22 Nov. 1895. 73 In the thirty-eight intervening years, the monument was held in a stonemasons yard in Glasnevin and was looked after mostly by John O'Clohissey and his descendants. It was taken over by the National Graves Association in 1926 and ultimately unveiled by Maurice Twomey, the leader of the IRA. Gerard McGowan to author.

moment' in Irish politics that led it to feel that its political prospects had passed. Fred Allan wrote to the press in October 1894 complaining that most of those who had taken the Parnellite side in 1891 had failed completely to live up to their original professed desire to fight against English and clerical influences in Irish public life and thus a 'parting of the ways' between republicans and Parnellites would take place 'in the near future'.[74] Allan, who soon afterwards became the treasurer of the Irish Journalists Association (the national trade-union for journalists), credited three Parnellite newspapers as having maintained non-sectarian and republican political principles in the public eye since 1891, namely the *Weekly Independent*, *Leinster Leader* and the *Westmeath Examiner*.[75] Only a couple of weeks after his article was published, however, the last of these papers was condemned publicly by Dr Nulty, the Bishop of Meath (with the written support of Rome) as a paper that 'exposed Catholics faith and feelings to grave and serious danger'. The *Leinster Leader*, 'in the name of individual civil liberty', denounced this attack, which it claimed had been made at the bidding of 'eminent theologians such as Messrs [Tim] Healy and [T.D.] Sullivan'. Meanwhile the *Daily Independent*, for which J.J. O'Kelly (who narrowly lost his parliamentary seat in 1892 after the clergy made his bigamy and reputed atheism a key issue in the campaign) was now a leading columnist, proclaimed that it was supposedly 'a mortal sin' to read the *Westmeath Examiner* only because it had criticised a new Mullingar water works scheme in which Bishop Nulty was the principal shareholder.[76] However, the editor of the *Westmeath Examiner* soon lost his job at the request of the local Catholic community and this served as a clear warning to the directors of the Independent Newspaper Company. John Redmond, Tim Harrington and Pierce Mahony had never desired that anticlerical sentiments would be promoted or spread by their party in the first place and, after this controversy broke out about the *Westmeath Examiner*, they were no longer prepared to allow republicans, or others, to use the Parnellite press to speak out against 'clerical dictation', for they knew this would be electoral suicide for their party. As a result, the trend of anticlericalism in Irish popular politics during the early 1890s, which had only been half-hearted at best, did effectively disappear by 1895. The rhetoric of fighting 'English and clerical dictation' in Irish politics had ceased to strike a chord with the general public.

The only constructive initiative the IRB actually *did* take during 1894 was to instigate a plan designed to create a new republican movement that could replace the old secret organization. On 9 March 1894, a group of Wexford émigrés in New York formed a UB committee which declared that the republican movement in Ireland should cease to organize itself as a network of secret societies, but instead work along the basis of a network of open clubs designed to promote awareness and revive popular interest in the ideals of the United

74 Fred Allan, 'Parnell's legacy: is the fight flagging?', *Weekly Independent*, 6 Oct. 1894.
75 Ibid. 76 *Leinster Leader*, 17 Nov. 1894; *Daily Independent*, 12 Nov. 1894.

Irishmen in the run up to the centenary of the 1798 rising. This policy was immediately taken up by (or perhaps originated with) Fred Allan, Henry Dixon and the YIL Executive. In early 1894, this body decided to prepare for the centenary year by organising numerous commemorative events up until 1897, and, thereafter they would establish 'centenary clubs' accepting as members *only* those men who believed in the United Irishmen's principles and intended to carry them into practice.[78] It was felt that this alone could sustain a republican movement in Ireland and, in the meantime, it was decided to keep a skeleton IRB organization alive merely to help see the policy through.

As John O'Connor had given up hope in the republican movement and retired, Fred Allan was made the secretary of the new skeleton IRB organization during 1894–5, despite the fact that his responsibilities with the *Independent* and the Irish Journalists Association dictated that he could no longer act as a traditional-style IRB 'travelling organizer'. Instead, from his private office at the *Independent*, Allan merely issued circulars to what was left of the secret organization calling for any apathetic member to leave, but not before they handed over whatever firearms owned by the organization they had to younger or more determined members. Simultaneously, in conjunction with the YIL executive, former IRB organizers (who now had effectively nothing left to organize) attempted to lay the grounds for the launch of a 1798 centenary movement. P.N. Fitzgerald helped revive and maintain the tradition of annual Bodenstown demonstrations; the old Leinster IRB leader C.J. O'Farrell began organizing annual commemorations of the United Irishmen at Vinegar Hill,[79] while the new Ulster IRB leader, Neal John O'Boyle, a farmer from Staffordstown, Co. Antrim, held annual commemorations of the United Irishmen at the 'Temple of Liberty' in Toome, Co. Antrim.[80] As 'Manchester-martyr demonstrations' had been banned by the Tory government of 1886–92, these events were renamed as 'Decoration Day' and their purpose was no longer only to commemorative the 'noble-hearted-three' but also the memory of all 'deceased patriots'.[81] Patrick Hoctor announced in November 1894 that 'Decoration Day' was so-called to emulate events of the same name held by the Republican Party in the United States, during which the graves of all men who died for their country were decorated, and as every nation on earth promoted such activities, he believed Irishmen should do the same.[82] Thereafter, at all 'Decoration Day' events organized by republicans, the public were called upon to study the history of the United Irishmen and

77 See reports of the origins of the 1798 Centennial Association of America in *Daily Independent*, 12 and 17 Apr. 1897.   78 *Daily Independent*, 6 Jan. 1897. See speech of Henry Dixon (IRB), chairman of YIL, on the origins of the centenary movement in Ireland. Fred Allan co-chaired this meeting.   79 'Remember '98', *Weekly Independent*, 19 May 1894.   80 NAI., DICS files, carton 6 (Northern Division), District Inspector Gambell, 4 Dec. 1893.   81 McGee, 'Manchester-martyr demonstrations', 47, 55.   82 Hoctor to *Daily Independent*, 26 Nov. 1894.

the IRB in their locality, search for their graves and decorate them each year; an example that was followed particularly in Cork and, to a lesser extent, in Dublin, where the policy was encouraged by the IRB veterans associations.[83] The 64-year-old John O'Leary was still nominally the president of the IRB, but his health had deteriorated greatly over the past five years, following the death of his last remaining sibling, and he had no policy or suggestions left to guide the organization. At the November 1894 Nally commemoration, all O'Leary said (apart from the fact that he had probably not much longer to live) was that he believed political matters in Ireland would undoubtedly 'take a turn very much for the worse before taking any turn for the better.'[84] Indeed, as the IRB had now been reduced to a policy of merely commemorating its own history, it could no longer act as a nucleus for radical popular political activity in the country, nor essentially be the source of any fresh new departures in republican propaganda. This reality ensured that whatever new nationalist movement might emerge in the coming months, or years, would be one from which the old secret organization of the IRB could derive little real benefit.

83 This activity only occasionally was reported in the press. *Irish Daily Independent*, 25 Nov. 1895.   84 *Daily Independent*, 10 Nov. 1894.

8

Republican propaganda and activism: from the *Irish Republic* to the 1798 centenary

The defeat of the 1893 home rule bill (which was actually passed by commons, but rejected totally by the House of Lords) led to Gladstone's retirement from politics and his replacement as the Liberal leader by the earl of Rosebery. Rosebery never raised the 'home rule' issue, because he knew his party had no electoral need to do so, and so it was clear that the question would not be raised again or, at least, not for many years. Following the defeat of the bill, many anti-Parnellite MPs opted to leave the party. The cost of permanent accommodation in London, just so they could attend Westminster sessions, had proved expensive enough to bankrupt many a newspaper editor or lawyer within the party. Some former MPs opted to become justices of the peace in Ireland and thereafter acted as faithful servants of the Dublin Castle administration. Meanwhile both wings of the Irish Party and the new Tory government turned their attention towards rationalising Westminster's system of taxation in Ireland. It was found that the Irish population had long been overtaxed compared to the rest of the United Kingdom and the Tories promised that this imbalance was going to be rectified, but naturally the question of how Irish taxation was actually *spent* by the government was not even brought into the discussions. As a result of all these demoralizing developments, the INLA folded and the nominally anti-Parnellite INFA became a totally moribund organization. Meanwhile in Ireland the membership of both the National Federation and National League plummeted, their combined active, subscribing membership soon dropping to little more than 10,000 men.[1] The Ulster Unionist Clubs, by contrast, were by far the most popular political movement in Ireland, having somewhere between 75,000 and 90,000 members (most of whom were now also members of the Orange Order) during 1893; a significant illustration of how the state of Irish representation at Westminster was very often a poor reflection of the realities of grass-roots politics in Ireland.[2] Despite their lack of popular support, the two Irish Party factions combined still held four-fifths of all Irish parliamentary seats and would continue to do so, because no one except the landed aristocracy could afford to stand against them in most Irish constituencies. Meanwhile Ulster unionists' greater sense of purpose and activism reflected a well-founded confidence that, in the future, they, rather than the Irish Party, would be able to win the spoils arising from the Tories' and Liberals' perpetual opportunism in dealing with Irish political movements.

1 NAI, CBS files, Home Office précis, carton 2, 18623/s. 2 NAI, DICS files, carton 6 (Northern Division), DI Gambell, 6 Mar., 5 June and 4 Sept. 1893.

The public's unwillingness to subscribe to the coffers of the National Federation led to a very embarrassing situation for the anti-Parnellite Party. During August 1894, it was revealed to the public that many of its members had been dependent since 1891 on financial support from the English Liberal Party.[3] Many of those who did not avail of this patronage would see their political careers end and William O'Brien, perhaps the most popular figure in Irish nationalist politics, retired (temporarily) during 1895 because he had been bankrupted by the costs of trying to sustain his parliamentary career. This growing serious problem facing the 'home rule party' was alleviated only by Justin McCarthy's success in October 1894 in acquiring legal rights to the disputed 'Paris Funds' of the semi-revolutionary Land League; Irish-American money that had been held in a Paris bank for the past thirteen years and which had been subscribed for a very different purpose to that for which it was now being used.[4] Against this backdrop, after disbanding the INLA in October 1893, William Lyman founded the *Irish Republic* (New York), a weekly paper which was subsequently imported into Ireland by republicans and members of the YIL, its principal agent being William Hartnett BA, a Dublin chemist. Like most Irish-American papers that republicans had imported into Ireland in the past, the *Irish Republic* did not refrain from highlighting certain realities of Irish politics which the 'home rule' press either feared to raise, or else simply did not wish to see raised, while Dublin Castle did everything in its power to confiscate whatever copies were imported. Charles O'Connor McLaughlin, a graduate of Queen's College Galway who was originally a literary columnist with the *Freeman's Journal*, was the first editor of the *Irish Republic*, which adopted George Washington's motto 'Resistance to Tyrants is Obedience to God' as its own.

Although the *Irish Republic* had a sufficiently large circulation to stay in print for five years, strangely no copies of this paper have survived in any Irish, American or British archives, except an occasional issue, or extracts from its columns, attached to various Dublin Castle intelligence reports. From these sources it appears to have been of very variable quality.[5] Its small editorial staff changed frequently, its focus was on American more than Irish affairs and it was not of the same literary quality as Devoy's old *Irish Nation*. O'Neill Ryan was the most talented columnist of the *Irish Republic*. He argued that the Irish Party had become 'a permanent conspiracy against every form of independence in Ireland', for the fundamental purpose of the party and its 'electioneering clergy' ever since the 'new departure' experiment failed in 1886 had been to act as 'a centralist caucus for the suppression of independent ability and free election'. Ryan declared that if Irish public did not want to 'allow yourselves and your posterity to be sold as slaves', they needed to realize that 'no compromise can there be on the question of nationhood and liberty.'

3 F.S.L. Lyons, *The Irish parliamentary party, 1890–1910* (1951), 49–50. 4 Ibid. 5 One complete copy of the paper, dating from 10 Nov. 1895, can be found in NAI, CBS files, carton 10, 10878/s.

By consenting to work with 'the terrible oligarchy of England', which 'no air of modern emancipation has touched', the Irish Party was ensuring that 'every nominal reform is made a bulwark of the old ascendancy' and 'law and religion are doled out through the caste'. He emphasized the fact that 'in the immense imposture called the English Constitution', 'the people do not exist as a constitutional power' and consequently it was impossible that Ireland could ever achieve independence without separating itself from the United Kingdom. The paper called on all Irishmen to cease supporting Westminster MPs, who only 'sprawl in the smoking rooms of the London Liberal Clubs' and 'lengthen the tails of Whig divisions in the alien parliament'. It declared that 'the people of Ireland are a sovereign people' by their very 'birth right' and 'the only hope for Ireland lies in a revolution'.[6] As far as Dublin Castle could tell, most readers of the *Irish Republic* belonged to the urban middle classes. It certainly received occasional praise from the Parnellite *Weekly Independent*.[7] The *Irish Republic* initially confined most of its criticisms of the Irish Party to the anti-Parnellites and this could easily have made some Parnellites sympathetic to its arguments. The fact that it printed literary-historical articles similar to those which appeared regularly in the *Weekly Independent* and reprinted some writings by members of the recently established Gaelic League (including Douglas Hyde),[8] would also have made it attractive to supporters of the YIL, although not all those who were associated with that body had a strong interest in politics.

Unfortunately the location of the minute books of the YIL (which ultimately fell into Arthur Griffith's hands) is currently unknown,[9] but something is known of the organization's activities. Many IRB figures such as P.N. Fitzgerald joined the YIL at its inception in September 1891. However apart from helping to organize, or speaking at, many of the commemorative events it held, these men otherwise played little or no part in the YIL. Many would have found themselves in the same situation as Mark Ryan, who noted with regards to himself and his medical doctor friends in London that 'we were not literary men' and so could contribute relatively little to Irish literary societies of the 1890s.[10] John O'Leary's almost apologetic tones when launching the YIL, noting that many had advised him 'that the Young Ireland Societies did not succeed and so neither will this'[11] may well indicate that few other IRB leaders were enthusiastic about the idea. Even some literary IRB

6 *Irish Republic* (New York), 6 Aug. 1896 (attached to NAI, DMP files, carton 13, report of Ass. Comm. Mallon, 9 Sept. 1896); M.F. Fanning (ed.), *The new movement convention* (1896), 88 (speech of O'Neill Ryan). 7 NAI, CBS Précis reports, carton 1, 11678/s; 'The *Irish Republic* asks some straight questions', *Irish Weekly Independent*, 3 Mar. 1894. 8 NAI, CBS files, carton 10, 10878/s. 9 The last known location of the minute book of the YIL was the library of Arthur Griffith's grandson, Neville Griffith, who died in 1999 and was the last surviving member of the Griffith family (Maye, *Arthur Griffith*, p.15; Brian Maye to author). Unfortunately, however, its current location is unknown (current owner of Neville Griffith's estate and library to author). 10 Ryan, *Fenian memories*, 162. 11 *Freeman's Journal*, 18 Sept. 1891.

figures such as Charles Doran, who owned one of the finest private libraries in Ireland, did not believe that the republican movement could be sustained by focusing on literary societies. T.C. Luby had expressed doubts about the idea as early as 1885, since literary movements, by their very nature, could not be turned into disciplined bodies of leaders and followers.[12] Another possible reason for this reluctance is that many of the old IRB organizers, such as P.N. Fitzgerald, Robert Johnston and others, were used to the political power they formerly wielded in popular politics through the IRB, and they had no desire to attempt to assume the same levels of power and influence, if that was possible, through participating in literary movements. Whatever the case, it is known that about a dozen YIS branches existed in Ireland during the 1890s, with a total membership of roughly 2,000 men. Those most closely federated with the YIL executive were evidently those in Dundalk, Midleton, Tralee, Listowel, Cavan and Ennis, as these were called upon at the end of the decade to create a new 'national republican association' in the country.[13]

During the mid 1890s, the YIL Executive was led by Henry Dixon, Patrick Lavelle B.A. and John MacBride of the 'National Club Literary Society', Patrick O'Loughlin (a Tullamore teacher and friend of John Nolan) and J.W. O'Beirne of the *Daily Independent*. These same men also managed the local NMC and organized most republican commemorative events.[14] Meetings of the YIL Executive were always held in the rooms of the National Club Literary Society, but this society seems to have made little progress. John MacBride wrote to the press in April 1894 complaining that its library was still of a poor quality and that it had become more of a social outlet than a centre for intellectual debate.[15] The potential of the YIL was lessened by the fact that former leading branches of the YIS, such as those in Belfast and Cork as well as Louis Smyth's branch in Magherafelt, had suffered badly and virtually collapsed as a result of the Parnell Split. In Belfast, owing to the anti-Parnellite bias of the local YIS, Belfast republicans such as Henry Dobbyn, a small-time building contractor formerly from Magherafelt, established the 'Independent Young Ireland Society', which met in the recently established 'National Club' of Belfast. This society, which was soon renamed as the 'Henry Joy McCracken Literary Society', federated itself with the YIL, but never acquired a large membership and thus its powers of influence were limited, although it would later succeed in publishing its own journal. In Cork, William O'Brien was expelled from the YIS for being an anti-Parnellite, but with the support of the local Catholic bishop he managed to win over most of its

YIS on parnell's side

12 Ibid. (O'Leary speech, mentioning Doran); NLI, O'Leary papers, MS 5927, Luby to O'Leary (n.d., circa 1885). 13 PRO (London), CO 903/7, Chief Secretary Office miscellaneous intelligence notes (W Series), 1–10, p. 44; *United Irishman*, 11 Mar. and 12 Aug. 1899. 14 NAI, DMP files, carton 12, report 2348, Chief Supt. Mallon, 20 June 1892; carton 13, reports 2928 and 3212, Assistant Commissioner Mallon, Nov. 1894; CBS précis, carton 1, 11613/s; *United Irishman*, 8 Apr 1899 (article on Bodenstown and history of YIL); *Shan Van Vocht*, Apr.–Dec. 1896. 15 *Irish Daily Independent*, 26 Apr. 1894.

members to the 'Cork National Society', leaving the Cork YIS in a completely moribund condition: it ultimately folded in March 1896.[16] If Cork failed to produce a new literary movement at this time, however, the two most notable literary societies affiliated with the YIL in Dublin are justly famous: Arthur Griffith and William Rooney's Leinster Literary Society (soon to be renamed as the Celtic Literary Society), and, W.B. Yeats' National Literary Society (NLS), which was established in Dublin in June 1892 as an offshoot of Yeats' London Irish Literary Society at Bloomsbury Mansions.

Yeats' relationship with the YIL explains why many republicans doubted the value of the project. At O'Leary's request, the young poet was made one of the three principal speakers at the inaugural meeting of the YIL, but thereafter he took no interest in the YIL Executive at the National Club because he found their company uninspiring. For similar reasons, during the 1880s Yeats had only turned up at one meeting of the YIS. By 1893, Yeats' NLS won the support of O'Leary, Sigerson and a few members of the same literary coterie that had become interested in the Dublin YIS during 1885–6, as well as a couple of literary editors with the *Weekly Independent*. The society held many lectures and debates, but these focused entirely upon cultural matters, as Yeats forbade all political subjects of discussion.[17] This ruling was nominally justified on the grounds of avoiding all the bitterness created by the Parnell Split, but its real purpose was to help fulfil Yeats' only real ambition, namely to form a movement that could instigate more creative, or artistic, literary endeavours, and establish a literary reputation for himself in Dublin as much as in London. During 1894–5, he quarrelled with the pedantic figures of Sir C.G. Duffy and John O'Leary for failing to prioritize the works of young, creative writers and this quarrel essentially broke his friendship with O'Leary. Ultimately, Yeats was able to realize his dream of creating a new mythology-based art by launching the Irish Literary Theatre in conjunction with Lady Gregory and the NLS in 1899. During the 1798 centenary, he would become associated with the republican movement briefly (he even contributed once or twice to the *Irish Republic*),[18] but it would be wrong to consider him as having ever being wedded to any political project. He was genuinely excited by the idea of promoting knowledge of literature among the masses, but as he was preoccupied mostly with his own personal, artistic development and possessed a good deal of social snobbery, he never actually engaged in any such mundane work among the general public. By contrast, Griffith and Rooney's considerably less prestigious Leinster Literary Society (LLS) did far more practical work in forwarding these goals.

Although the LLS temporarily collapsed in November 1892 owing to a political quarrel instigated by Griffith (who thereafter became much less active

16 NAI, British in Ireland microfilm, CO 904/16/301–2 (memo on YIL/YIS).   17 NLI, Minute book of the National Literary Society, MS 645.   18 NAI, CBS Précis reports, carton 1, 13738/s.

in the society), William Rooney revived it three months later under the title of the Celtic Literary Society (CLS). Thanks to the energy of Rooney (whose father was a leader of the OGBU), the CLS organized many political and historical debates, both public and private, as well as free classes for the poor in the Irish language, history and music every week, which attracted many young self-educated and working class people (including a few socialists like James Connolly and Fred Ryan) to its meetings by the mid 1890s. Eventually, the various events it organized soon became a regular feature of Dublin social life, involving scores of people.[19] In contrast to the artistic and idiosyncratic figure of Yeats, Rooney was a classic nineteenth-century example of a lower-class activist whose populism and character as an autodidactic radical allowed him to inspire many with his missionary-like, personal fervour. The fact that his enthusiasm was generally greater than his talent made him all the more effective. The DMP soon became convinced that Rooney's CLS was nothing more than an IRB recruiting ground,[20] although the society's minute-book tells a different story. Members of the CLS, unlike the members of Yeats' NLS, did take part in various republican commemorative events organized by the YIL Executive, but no obvious IRB clique existed within its ranks. Instead the IRB men on the YIL Executive (most notably Henry Dixon) simply kept in close touch with the society's activities, while Fred Allan did much the same, not least by acquiring employment at the *Daily Independent* for the numerous printers who attended the society occasionally, including Griffith and the future labour activist, P.T. Daly.

James Egan (who was imprisoned in August 1884 on the grounds of being John Daly's associate) was released in September 1893, and the following year he became the principal travelling lecturer for Mark Ryan's Amnesty Association of Great Britain, which later sent him to the United States to collect funds for the amnesty cause. While giving a lecture tour in America, Egan became aware of many Clansmen's great dissatisfaction with the republican movement in Ireland. He answered some allegations that it had become too closely linked to the Parnellites by writing to the *Irish Republic* to point out that it had remained a totally 'distinct body', and, that 'if in aiding Parnellism in the past they were wrong, it was with a view to hold onto principles which appeared to them to be sound … and not for the purpose of abandoning the old cause.' Fred Allan also wrote to the *Irish Republic* during 1894 to the same effect.[21] Shortly after Egan's arrival in America, calls were made in the *Irish Republic* and *Chicago Citizen* for the launch of a new organization in the United States to replace the moribund INFA. This new organization would call on the Irish and Irish-American public to ignore the Irish Party and attract

19 NLI, Minute book of the Celtic Literary Society, MS 19934. **20** NAI, DMP files, carton 13, report 2928, Assistant Commissioner Mallon, 8 Nov. 1894; CBS files, carton 10, 10885/s, Assistant Commissioner Mallon, 25 Nov. 1895. **21** NAI, CBS files, carton 10, 10712/s; Fred Allan to *Irish Republic*, undated extract attached to NAI, DMP files, carton 13, Report 2832, Ass. Comm. Mallon, 13 Sept. 1894.

the attention of the international community to Irishmen's desire for complete political independence. This idea was the initiative of William Lyman, the INB leader. Mark Ryan learnt of Lyman's plan upon Egan's return to London. Meanwhile Robert Johnston (who knew Lyman well and was in New York for much of the mid 1890s, securing contracts for his timber business) also became enthusiastic about the plan. He informed his Belfast associates, most notably Henry Dobbyn, of Lyman's intentions during his brief returns to his hometown. As a result, Ryan and Dobbyn began calling for the republican movement to reorganize itself by affiliating with the new public movement that was soon to be launched in America. To this end, Ryan stepped down as chairman of the INLGB (a position now given to Arthur Lynch) and, through his capacity as president of the Amnesty Association of Great Britain, tried to launch a new secret movement under his own leadership. This would operate under the cover of the amnesty clubs and work in cooperation with Lyman and the 'new movement' in America.[22]

Lyman's unnamed 'new movement' was formally launched on 26 September 1895 at a convention in Chicago and it chose to call itself the Irish National Alliance (INA), which was intended to be a confederation of all Irish organizations in the United States that desired to draw the world's attention to Ireland's 'full claim' and 'God-given right to complete and absolute independence'. Lyman was made its president, but he was neither a gifted orator nor writer, and thus its true spokesman was its vice-president, O'Neill Ryan, a St. Louis judge and future Clan president who wrote all INA manifestos. These were published in the *Irish Republic* and the *Chicago Citizen*, but were almost totally ignored by all Irish and most Irish-American newspapers. Although the INA won the support of many lawyers, doctors, judges, senators, businessmen, army officers, artists and politicians in the American mid-west, on the east coast (the heartland of Irish-America) it evoked no response or outright hostility, not least because by the mid 1890s a significant percentage of the Irish-American community had become fully integrated into the American middle classes and were more concerned about acting as political spokesmen for the American Catholic community than having anything to do with Ireland.[23] Indeed, the INA never became a powerful or influential organization. Rather than providing any financial assistance to Mark Ryan and his associates in London, it merely provided Lyman, a member of the US Republican Party, with some greater powers of leverage in American politics. Its establishment, however, helped inadvertently to create bitter divisions within Irish republican circles in the United Kingdom as a result of the response of John Devoy to Lyman's initiative.

Devoy's principal concern about the INA was that it might easily become a medium for the INB to win away his followers in the UB and, in the process,

22 NAI, CBS files, carton 9, 9130/s, 9317/s; carton 10, 9862/s, 10738/s.   23 Fanning (ed.), *The new movement convention*; D.N. Doyle, *Irish Americans, native rights and national empires* (New York, 1976).

undo all the progress recently made by his organization, which had begun to win the struggle for control of the Clan.[24] Anticipating the launch of the INA, as early as May 1895, he had launched a similar type organization in America known as the 'Irish Confederated Societies of America', which was inaugurated in Pittsburgh and found some support in eastern American cities. Owing to the bitter struggle for power that was taking place between the UB and INB (much of which revolved around Devoy's own cantankerous personality), the UB leader was deeply antagonistic towards both the INA and the *Irish Republic*. To discourage the American public from supporting the INA he published manifestos on behalf of his own organization that alleged that several of the INA's leaders were British spies and former supporters of the 'dynamite war'. This was a rather malicious criticism, but Devoy's allegations were not totally unfounded: John F. Kearney, a British *agent provocateur*, was in fact one of the INA's leaders in New York and the branch Kearney operated was very closely linked with William Jones's circles in the INB. At Devoy's request, many of these manifestos of the 'Irish Confederated Societies of America' were sent to P.N. Fitzgerald, who was the last IRB figure to attend a UB convention in the United States (in July 1894), when the Corkman made a last, futile plea with the Americans to cease quarrelling over who killed Dr. Cronin and to reunite and help save the IRB from collapsing.[25] It is unclear whether or not Fitzgerald distributed these manifestos, but he certainly took care not to repeat any of Devoy's controversial allegations when he spoke about the INA in public. Instead he expressed his belief that the foundation of the 'new movement' was an interesting but probably not very significant development, and he dismissed its political relevance with the ambiguous remark that 'too many new departures we have had already'.[26] Fred Allan, however, made a great *faux pas* by writing letters to the *Daily Independent* and *Evening Herald* in which he quoted directly and at length from the allegations made in Devoy's manifestos, that the men behind the INA (of which Allan naturally knew little or nothing) were all former members of 'the disgraced and discredited Triangle' who were directly responsible for the murder of Dr. Cronin.[27] This action by Allan was not forgotten about for many years and turned Mark Ryan, Patrick Hoctor and others against him, owing to the great hopes they had for the INA. One old Cork IRB man, now based in London, denounced Allan particularly violently, writing to the *Freeman's Journal* that 'I did not think any Irishman would stoop so low as to call 1,000 delegates of our countrymen in America murderers!'[28]

Allan did eventually realize his mistake in having acted as Devoy's mouthpiece in Ireland over the INA dispute. Many years later he complained to

24 NLI, Devoy papers, MS 9823–5.   25 NAI, CBS Précis reports, carton 1, 11225/s.
26 *Daily Independent*, 25 Nov. 1895 (Manchester martyrs speech at Tralee). Maurice
Moynihan made the same argument at this demonstration.   27 Allan to *Evening Herald*, 21
Sept. 1895; *Irish Daily Independent*, 26 Sept. 1895.   28 William Healy to *Freeman's Journal*,
3 Oct. 1895.

Devoy that he had acquired several long-term 'enemies' in the republican movement solely because of 'the bad feeling created against me some years ago' when 'I took perhaps an unwisely strong part in advocacy of your side of the house ... over the split in the American company [Clan].'[29] His actions certainly served to accentuate greatly the already noticeable Dublin-London divide in the republican movement. From Dublin, O'Leary, Fitzgerald and Allan were committed to a simple strategy of preparing the way for the 1798 centenary and keeping a skeleton, yet vibrant, IRB organization alive that might be able to launch new initiatives in the wake of the centenary. This policy was in line with the views of the Executive of the YIL. From London, however, Mark Ryan and his supporters (including Patrick Hoctor, Robert Johnston and several others) had far greater ambitions, believing that the establishment of the INA in the United States was just the lifeline that the republican movement needed not only to stay alive but also to become a very potent force once more. As the *Irish Republic* was a strong champion of the INA and exaggerated its strength, its propaganda helped to complicate the matter further. This was no real concern of the IRB, but O'Leary and Allan in particular would soon become very angry at the paper, as a result of the activities of the (anonymous) Dublin correspondent of the *Irish Republic*.

The DMP claimed to know that the Dublin correspondent of the *Irish Republic* was D.J. O'Riordan, a native of Cork and former Parisian journalist who had worked with Richard Pigott in attempting to blackmail the Land League treasurer Patrick Egan during 1882, and had now returned to Dublin to join the Old Guard Union.[30] His articles often called for the adoption of violent measures to secure the release of the political prisoners and were certainly unlike the other columns in the paper. Devoy later accused the Dublin correspondent of the *Irish Republic* (whose identity he did not know) of 'practically, if not openly, doing the work of the British secret service' and for having forced John O'Connor to leave the IRB by printing 'a series of dastardly exposures' that 'without giving his proper name, gave such descriptions of his movements and of his personality as made the work of Scotland Yard and the Irish Police comparatively easy.'[31] O'Riordan does seem to have been in government pay. In May 1894 O'Riordan wrote an article denouncing the IRB leadership for not having supported the Phoenix Park murders and the dynamite war, claiming that this had reduced the movement to impotence, and stated that, as the IRB was still led by the same men and these were 'gulling the young men as before', he would reveal their names and their movements to the public in the near future to force them to retire, if they did

---

29 *DPB*, vol. 2, 401–2: Allan to Devoy, 4 Mar. 1912.   30 NAI, CBS files, carton 10, 10878/s. 31 *Gaelic American*, 5 Dec. 1908 (obituary for John O'Connor). O'Connor spent the rest of his life working as a medical assistant in Paris and living in poverty and relative isolation with his German-born, Parisienne wife and one child, a well-educated daughter who spoke only French and German. She would eventually be taken care of by Devoy in America following her mother's death in 1924.

not do so voluntarily.[32] In subsequent months, he denounced Fred Allan for being too close to the Parnellites. In October 1895, after Allan had denounced the INA, O'Riordan (seeking to capitalize upon the recent outbursts made against Allan) accused him of working for Dublin Castle ever since his imprisonment in 1884.[33] This incensed the Dublin IRB, as well as some Parnellites and figures on the Dublin Trades Council, who jointly held a special meeting at the Rotunda solely to vindicate Allan's good name, and prompted an irate John O'Leary to denounce the *Irish Republic*, writing that 'I do not well see how I could touch that paper, and especially that article, without soiling my hands.'[34] Allan, however, continued to be subject to abuse, for his unusual position of being both a very public figure and an IRB leader made him a very easy target for political opponents of any kind. In December 1895, for example, Tim Harrington, the editor of *United Ireland*, accused Allan and 'his staff at the *Independent*' of being men who 'spend half their time drinking with detectives' (a remark he subsequently apologized for), after a Dublin republican, Patrick Gregan, was elected to Dublin City Hall as a labour-republican candidate, defeating Harrington's candidate, with Allan's support.[35]

It is clear that Major Gosselin had valuable informers within the higher echelons of the northern England IRB organization. It is probably for this reason that as soon as Mark Ryan formally launched his new secret organization in London, following the formation of the INA, a copy of its constitution fell into British hands.[36] The organization had the same name as Lyman's wing of the Clan, the 'Irish National Brotherhood' (INB), and was structured on the exact same basis as the IRB, except that its officers and executive had different titles. Meanwhile members, rather than taking an oath, took a pledge that they 'agree' to become a member of the INB and 'to do all in my power to establish the Independence of Ireland and to keep secret all transactions relating to the organization.' The plan was to establish branches of the INA in Ireland and England that would be allied with the American organization of the same name and that these would then be used as recruiting grounds for the secret organization. While the INB's constitution stated that 'all members should, when possible, learn military drill and study the art and science of war', its declared objects were far from revolutionary in tone: 'to encourage as far as possible the extension of national feeling among all classes of Irishmen', 'to take all proper opportunities of promoting common action for national objects' and to 'encourage as much as possible the study of Irish history, of the Irish language and of all subjects likely to promote the national spirit.'[37] This reflected Ryan's belief that the cultural nationalist organizations, more so than anything else, were playing an important role in

32 NLI, Devoy papers Ms 18062, extract from the *Irish Republic*, 5 May 1894. 33 NAI, DMP files, carton 13, Report 3454, Ass. Comm. Mallon, 8 Nov. 1895 (attached extract, *Irish Republic*, 13 Oct 1895). 34 *Irish Daily Independent*, 29 Nov. 1895 (report of meeting in honour of Allan and letter of O'Leary's). 35 *United Ireland*, 28 Dec. 1895. 36 Its constitution can be found in NAI, CBS files, 12474/s. 37 Ibid.

overcoming political apathy among the nationalist youth of the country. He intended to make the INA a similar type organization to the YIL. Small branches of the INA were established in Belfast and Dublin, mostly around the basis of the GAA, and a larger branch was established in London, which included W.B. Yeats, T.W. Rolleston and other figures of the Bloomsbury Irish Literary Society. How far the INB succeeded in establishing a secret organization is unclear: statements purportedly from the Supreme Council reproduced in UB circulars claimed it had no real organizational basis anywhere and that it had the support of only a handful of long-inactive IRB men.[38] Curiously, in his recollections (which made no reference to the INB), Mark Ryan referred to T.W. Rolleston and John MacBride as men he 'recruited' into the IRB at this time,[39] although MacBride was evidently in the IRB for many years previously, while Rolleston, even if he did take the INB 'pledge' (which is doubtful), certainly had not committed himself to secret revolutionary politics of any kind. Together with Arthur Griffith, however, MacBride did collect funds for Ryan's London branch of the amnesty association after they immigrated to South Africa during 1896.[40]

The first man delegated to perform an inspection tour of Ryan's nascent organization during early 1896 was none other than the British spy William Jones.[41] In Dublin, Jones called upon Patrick Tobin, a clerk who was seeking to establish the INA in the city. Tobin, a man who was well known in popular Parnellite circles in Dublin, had replaced the deceased Jim Boland as the Dublin leader of the GAA. He told Jones that he believed Mark Ryan's blueprint for the INB was flawed, for the secrecy of any movement could not possibly be maintained by a mere pledge and because the headquarters of the INB ought to be in Ireland and not in London, but Mark Ryan refused to listen to either complaint. Upon travelling to Belfast, Jones was told the exact same thing by Henry Dobbyn, who had attended the inaugural INA convention in Chicago.[42] Although the *Irish Republic* was being distributed in Munster and promoted the idea of forming a 'new movement' in Ireland, Dublin Castle believed that the rank and file of the Munster IRB felt antipathy to the idea for the same reasons as Tobin and Dobbyn.[43] Curiously, Dobbyn also told Jones that if Ryan or Lyman provided him with enough funding, he could import enough firearms from Scotland to arm 'the whole of Ulster'.[44] This was probably a reference to the same stock of firearms that had been stored by John O'Connor in western Scotland during the early 1880s. Dublin Castle believed that Patrick Hoctor, who had offered his services to Ryan's INB, was trying to import arms from western Scotland into Tralee and Limerick, the latter apparently being accomplished by using a ferry business on the Shannon owned by Anthony Mackey, formerly a Limerick IRB rebel

38 NLI, Devoy papers MS 18015 (5), UB circulars, 20 Oct. 1894, 20 June 1895. 39 Ryan, *Fenian memories*, 62, 174. 40 *Shan van Vocht*, Nov. 1896. 41 NAI, CBS Précis reports, carton 1, 12836/s, 12946/s (reports of spy William Jones) 42 Ibid. 43 Ibid., 11952/s. 44 Ibid., 12836/s, 12946/s (reports of spy William Jones)

and now a somewhat more politically reticent and very wealthy Parnellite businessman.[45] That Dobbyn and Hoctor were apparently considering seizing the IRB's arms for the 'new movement' was perhaps the greatest illustration of the growing divide within the republican movement, and this would soon start to undermine even the plans for the 1798 centenary.

On 23 November 1895, the day after Fred Allan addressed a meeting of the 'Henry Joy McCracken Literary Society' in the Belfast National Club,[46] Alice Milligan, daughter of Seaton Milligan (a former member of Yeats' Bloomsbury society), and Anna Johnston (the poetess 'Ethna Carbery'), daughter of Robert, established the *Northern Patriot,* a monthly paper of the McCracken Literary Society. This paper circulated chiefly in Belfast and was intended to revive popular awareness of the United Irishmen in the run up to the 1798 centenary. The McCracken Literary Society had long been supported by Neal John O'Boyle (the official Ulster IRB leader) and James Johnston, son of Robert and the leader of the Belfast 'National Club', which reputedly had several Presbyterian members of strong republican sympathies.[47] During 1895, the McCracken Literary Society began to thrive due to the support it received from Seaton Milligan and John Clarke, the librarian of the Linen Hall Library. However petty divisions soon emerged in the society after Maud Gonne, a member of the London INA who operated her own branch of the YIS in Paris (which was often attended by French ladies, together with Patrick McManus, W.B. Yeats and Arthur Lynch), gave a lecture to the society on the amnesty movement. For a long time Gonne had been a very close associate of the principal British spy in Paris, Carroll Tevis, who had first introduced her to Irish political circles.[48] In 1895 she sent a resolution of support to the inaugural convention of the American INA and was appointed by Mark Ryan as a travelling lecturer for the Amnesty Association of Great Britain.[49] Within republican circles in Ireland, however, Gonne was always distrusted, because she used to socialize at Dublin Castle, and she was also disliked as a histrionic figure.[50] Therefore Belfast IRB men protested when she was invited to speak before the Henry Joy McCracken Literary Society and the *Northern Patriot* reported favourably upon her lecture. Offended by the hard men's criticism of their fellow female patriot, Alice Milligan and Anna Johnston (with Robert Johnston's financial support from New York) left this

45 NAI, DICS files, carton 6 (Northern Division), DI Gambell, 6 Mar. and 5 June 1893, DI Seddall, 5 Oct. 1893; CBS Précis reports, carton 1, 10712/s, 10882/s, 11032/s, 11538/s. 46 *Daily Independent,* 23 Nov. 1895. 47 Helen Meehan, 'Shan van Vocht' (1997); NAI, CBS Précis reports, carton 1, 10165/s, 11032/s; carton 1, 12836/s, 12946/s (reports of spy William Jones). 48 Campbell, *Fenian fire,* 310 fn. 49 NLI, CBS Précis reports, carton 1, 9670/s, 11104/s, 13738/s. 50 Davitt distrusted her as well, after Tevis introduced her to him while he was tracking down spies in 1885 (Campbell, *Fenian fire,* 310 fn.). Davitt also knew of a case of a rich, female *agent provocateur* working in Dublin the previous year. Davitt, *Fall of feudalism,* 438–41. Later that same year, Gonne, while trying to befriend Davitt, was admitted to the Contemporary Club, where she met John O'Leary. Maud Gonne MacBride, *A servant of the queen* (London, 1938), 85–90.

society, formed their own 'Charles Kickham Literary Society' as well as another monthly journal, the *Shan Van Vocht*.

Both the *Northern Patriot* (whose new editor was John Clarke) and *Shan Van Vocht* were similar in style, and the same group of people generally contributed to both papers, even if there was some rivalry and differences of opinion between their respective editors. Each had a circulation of about 2,500 copies, although the RIC seized many copies of both at the Belfast ports. In Dublin, both papers were sold in a shop owned by Jim Boland's widow.[51] The *Northern Patriot* expressed support for 'Decoration Day' and the amnesty movement but, for the most part, it was a promoter of the 'educational programme' of the YIL only in its broadest sense. It purpose was to serve 'as the meeting ground of many who differ in opinion as to the methods by which Ireland may best be served.' Its propaganda mirrored that of the *Weekly Independent*. Several Parnellite papers advertised it, namely the *Kilkenny People*, *Munster Express* (whose former editor, W.G. Fisher, now worked for the *Irish Republic*), *Derry Journal*, *Carlow Vindicator*, *Dundalk Democrat* and *Waterford News*. In turn, the *Northern Patriot* advertised for several Parnellite papers, such as the *Westmeath Examiner* and *Limerick Leader*.[52] The *Northern Patriot* was essentially a literary-historical, rather than a political, journal. While it praised the Bodenstown demonstrations, only Henry Dixon (the leader of the YIL) generally wrote any political letters to the paper, emphasizing Ireland's need for non-denominational education.[53]

The *Shan Van Vocht* was distinguished by the fact that, from the autumn of 1896 onwards, it contained far more columns on political matters. It also welcomed contributions from various Irish radicals, including the socialist-republican James Connolly.[54] Since it was funded by Robert Johnston, the *Shan Van Vocht* was a little more inclined to identify with the INA rather than the YIL. It also publicized the *Irish Republic*, for which Anna Johnston's future brother-in-law, Patrick McManus of Donegal and Paris, was a leading contributor.[55] Indeed, the *Shan Van Vocht* was essentially the sister publication of the *Irish Republic*. Some columns of the *Irish Republic* were reprinted in the paper, declaring that 'we have come in earnest to the parting of the ways ... the home ruler must henceforth be looked upon as quite as inimical and dangerous to the cause of nationality, as were the loyalists during the American revolution.' The *Shan Van Vocht* also publicised the activities of both Irish-American and London-Irish nationalists' societies.[56] In particular, as Mark Ryan had recently helped establish a branch of the Gaelic League in London,

---

51 NAI, CBS Précis reports, carton 1, 11104/s, 11414/s. 52 *Northern Patriot*, Oct. 1895-Jan. 1896 (editorials). 53 *Northern Patriot*, July 1896. John Murphy, editor of the *Weekly Independent* and a reputed IRB man, addressed the Bodenstown demonstration that year. The following year Charles Doran gave the Bodenstown speech. *Shan Van Vocht*, July 1897. 54 Connolly to *Shan van Vocht*, Nov. 1896, Jan. 1897, Aug. 1897. 55 *Shan Van Vocht*, Apr. 1896; NAI, CBS Précis reports, carton 1, 13738/s. McManus soon left for Buenos Aires where he enlisted the support of William Bulfin for the *Irish Republic*. 56 *Shan Van Vocht*, Sept. 1896.

it praised that association, as well as the amnesty movement. In turn, the *Irish Republic* began supporting the Gaelic League, while the *Shan Van Vocht* started to be distributed in America through INA channels, as well as in London and Paris by Mark Ryan and Maud Gonne of the London INA.[57] The general ethos of the *Shan Van Vocht* was perhaps best reflected by a letter of T.W. Rolleston to the paper. He argued that

> If we have nothing better to give young minds in Ireland than the worn out old formulas of which Irish patriotic history is composed, be assured they will seek the intellectual nourishment they crave from English sources, and nationalism in Ireland will remain a subordinate feature of the land question instead of being an ideal movement enlisting the best the nation produces in character and intellect.[58]

In August 1896, an emaciated John Daly was finally released from prison. This was partly because he had gone on hunger strike and was partly because a public inquiry had found that he had been poisoned with arsenic by the prison authorities, reportedly by mistake. The previous year Daly was elected unopposed to parliament for Limerick City and his candidacy, of course, was disqualified. Very shortly after his release, Daly was met by Fred Allan and sent to New York, where he began working for Devoy and the UB, who were trying to undermine Lyman's influence in the Amnesty Association of America.[59] No doubt to vindicate his claim that Daly should never have been released and was the true mastermind of the 'dynamite war', once Daly arrived in New York, Major Gosselin (who had actually framed Daly) ordered British *agents provocateurs* within the New York INB to leave for Britain, ostensibly to plant explosives to disrupt the Queen's forthcoming jubilee. This led to the 'Ivory Case' in Glasgow that November, when William Jones, the trans-Atlantic organizer of the INB, testified in court and revealed that he knew Robert Johnston well and had acquired numerous letters of the recently-deceased Jack Boland, as well as letters from William Lyman and Mark Ryan.[60] This caused great embarassment to Ryan, who wrote to the *Evening Telegraph* claiming that his letters produced in court by Jones were forgeries,[61] though there can be little doubt that they were genuine. According to the recollections of Maud Gonne (who organized Ivory's defence), Mark Ryan felt deeply betrayed by Lyman after this event,[62] but he appears to have continued to work for Lyman for some time afterwards.

57 *Shan Van Vocht*, Mar. 1897. The *Shan Van Vocht* was publicized by the *Irish American* (New York), *Citizen* (Chicago), *Irish Republic* (New York), *United Irishman* (New York) and *Irish World* (New York). Most of these papers were identified in some way with the INA, although only the *Citizen* and *Irish Republic* actively championed it. 58 Rolleston to *Shan Van Vocht*, Nov. 1896. 59 *DPB*, vol. 2, 338. 60 *Times*, 9 and 14 Nov. 1896. 61 *Evening Telegraph*, 14 Nov. 1896. The *Shan Van Vocht* also dwelt a good deal upon the 'Ivory Case'. 62 MacBride, *A servant of the queen*, 179–81, 228.

In December 1896, Patrick Gregan T.C. made the long awaited call for the establishment of a 1798 centenary movement. A provisional 1798 centenary committee was thereafter formed in Dublin, consisting of Henry Dixon and Patrick Lavelle of the YIL Executive, Dublin IRB leaders Fred Allan, Thomas Fitzpatrick and John O'Shaughnessy, and the editor of the *Weekly Independent*, John Murphy. This body maintained that only those who upheld the United Irishmen's principles in practice should be involved in organizing the centenary celebrations.[63] In late January 1897, the IRB president John O'Leary accepted the presidency of this committee and subsequently intimated to the public its general political intentions. O'Leary noted that there was much debate, 'mostly, I think, rather foolishly', during the past year about the potential value in a reunification of the Irish Party. Although 'I too am all for unity' among Irishmen, O'Leary desired this would be brought about 'rather on the lines of the United Irishmen than on any other I know of'.[64]

In early February, P.N. Fitzgerald chaired meetings of the YIL executive on the planning for the centenary movement, Gregan persuaded Dublin Corporation to allow the committee to use City Hall for its meetings, and a few thousand circulars were distributed across the country appealing for support for the committee's plans.[65] These circulars were reportedly sent to representatives of all shades of Irish nationalist opinion but it seems clear that none were sent to Irish Party members. Among the men invited to take part at the inaugural convention of the 1798 Centenary Committee on 2 March 1897 (apart from many IRB men from across the country) were several prominent members of staff of the Independent Newspaper Company, leaders of Irish literary societies in Dublin, Belfast and London, the mayors of Cork, Dublin, Waterford, Wexford and Kilkenny and the chairmen of the town commissions in Dundalk, Monaghan, Longford and Carlow.[66] The exact political affiliations of these local government officials are unclear. Mark Codd, the mayor of Wexford, was an old republican and friend of P.N. Fitzgerald, while another, Patrick Meade, the recently-elected Parnellite mayor of Cork, was believed by Dublin Castle to have been an IRB man,[67] if only because of his prominent role in promoting the 'Decoration Day' tradition in Co. Cork. Meade was a leading shareholder in the Independent Newspaper Company, and both Fred Allan and, to a lesser extent, P.N. Fitzgerald had been involved in selling shares in the company to the general public in the recent past. James Casey, the national secretary of the Gaelic League, was also invited to attend, as republicans had started to become interested in that movement through the influence of William Rooney's CLS.[68] James Daly, the fiercely-independent

63 Gregan to *Daily Independent*, 1 Dec. 1896; 'Formation of '98 committee', *Daily Independent*, 6 Jan. 1897. 64 Letter reprinted *Daily Independent*, 6 Feb. 1897. 65 *Daily Independent*, 3 Feb. 1897; O'Riordan, 'Fenian and GAA pioneer', 29. 66 *Daily Independent*, 3 March 1897. 67 NAI, British in Ireland microfilm collection, C.O.904/18/718. 68 NLI, Minute book of the Celtic Literary Society, MS 19934; Ryan, *Fenian memories*, 165–6.

proprietor of the *Connacht Telegraph* (who always refused to support the Irish Party and was still best known in Ireland for his prominent role in founding the Land League), was also invited, as was John Hutchinson, a Dublin city councillor and the leader of the Irish National Foresters, the principal workers' benefit organization in the country. The Foresters had always patronized Manchester-martyr demonstrations and had a strict tradition since its foundation in 1877 of maintaining a policy of complete political independence. They had been the only public body of professedly nationalist sympathies not to take sides during the Parnell Split of 1890–1 and were generally opposed to MPs taking part in the centenary movement.[69]

All parties invited by the IRB to take part in the centenary movement soon did, but many were not present at the inaugural convention, when Fred Allan and the YIL Executive proposed to appoint an executive for the '1798 Centenary Committee' that was almost identical to the existing provisional committee. Complaints were made against this idea by a party led by William Field MP, a butcher who represented the liberties area of Dublin as a Parnellite and who was also a member of the GAA Executive, the only Westminster MP ever to hold that honour. Field had recently been instrumental in repealing the ban on RIC members joining the GAA[70] and, together with two London-Irish journalists and Dr. Joseph Kenny (a former Parnellite MP for Dublin), he suggested that no executive or 'national council' of the 1798 centenary movement should be appointed until a sufficient number of branches had been established in both Ireland and England so that a truly representative executive could be elected by branch members. Several figures identified with Ryan's London movement supported this policy, including J.K. Bracken, Alice Milligan of the *Shan Van Vocht*, Henry Dobbyn of Belfast and D.J. O'Riordan, the Dublin correspondent of the *Irish Republic*. Henry Dixon, John O'Leary, Fred Allan and Patrick Lavelle dismissed the suggestion, claiming that from the circulars already distributed across Ireland, as many as five hundred members of the public had asked to join the committee, thereby undoubtedly making it a representative body of Irish opinion. This, however, was conveniently ignoring the fact that the actual executive of the committee had not been elected. To defeat Field and Bracken's amendments, P.N. Fitzgerald and P.J. O'Keefe introduced resolutions stating they had confidence in the existing Dublin provisional committee to accommodate all interest groups and govern the movement satisfactorily, and this resolution won the support of the majority present. As a result, the existing provisional committee, consisting only of about a dozen IRB figures, assumed control of the Executive of the 1798 Centenary Committee when it

69 Although a strictly non-sectarian organization in theory, the Foresters' membership was predominantly Catholic and this fact shaped its public image and also influenced its leadership's willingness to accept the Catholic Church's teaching regarding the evils of secret societies. Dublin Castle generally viewed it as associated with the IRB, if only because of its working class profile, but this was hardly true. 70 Mandle, *GAA*, 96–7.

was officially established two days later.[71] The committee itself, which nominally had about three hundred members, was dominated by Dublin men, but it also included many local politicians or GAA figures from the rest of Ireland. At Charles Doran's request, it was soon expanded to include (at least nominally) several former leading republican activists of the 1860s and 1870s who now lived abroad, such as J.P. McDonnell, Hugh Brophy, Denis Mulcahy, O'Donovan Rossa, D.F. McCarthy, Eugene Davis and John Finerty.[72] Three MPs were also members of the ordinary committee, including two Parnellites, William Field and John Redmond (who was not invited to the convention, but had written to O'Leary asking to join the committee), and one anti-Parnellite, J.P. Farrell, the MP for Cavan West.[73] However these men, having no authority over the executive, could play no part in the subsequent evolution of the centenary movement.

Although its personnel was altered a number of times, the political profile of the 1798 Centenary Committee established in March 1897 essentially remained unchanged over the next year. This fact would eventually create controversy because the centenary clubs quickly became the fastest growing nationalist movement in the country (they had 10,000 members by July 1897)[74] and thus the question as to who should have control became an important and divisive political issue. The first party to express dissatisfaction with O'Leary's committee were the small Parisian and London branches of the YIS. These bodies had been among the first to express support for the provisional centenary committee in January 1897,[75] but were denied representation on the executive of the association in March. Subsequently, with Lyman's support, they formed their own body known as the '1798 Centenary Committee of Great Britain and France', whose leaders, W.B. Yeats (president), Mark Ryan (treasurer), Maud Gonne and Frank Hugh O'Donnell (ex-MP), were all members of the London INA. Yeats began contributing to the New York *Irish Republic* on the centenary movement and, in turn, this paper backed up Yeats' claims that many of those present at the Dublin convention in March were denied a hearing; a claim that O'Leary rejected. Although a member of the Dublin committee, Patrick Hoctor supported the stance of the London-based centenary movement and expressed his belief that

---

71 *Daily Independent*, 5 Mar. 1897.   72 *Daily Independent*, 26 May 1897. Most of these men were now newspaper editors. J.P. McDonnell now edited the *Patterson Labor Standard* (New Jersey). Mulcahy and McCarthy (a relative of P.N. Fitzgerald who took part in the Catalpa rescue of 1876) were associated with Rossa's *United Irishman* (New York), which now identified itself with the *Shan Van Vocht*. Davis, who died in late 1897, had worked as an assistant editor of the *Boston Pilot* and Finerty's *Chicago Citizen*, while Brophy (the most important Dublin IRB centre of the 1860s whose brother William was associated with the Old Guard IRB during the 1880s) was a newspaper editor in Melbourne, Australia. John Finerty was the chairman of the inaugural convention of the INA in September 1895. 73 *Daily Independent*, 3, 5, 6 Mar. 1897; NLI, O'Leary papers Ms 8001 (49), John Redmond to O'Leary, 27 Feb. 1897.   74 *Shan Van Vocht*, July 1897.   75 *Daily Independent*, 6 Jan. 1897.

a new, larger executive for the centenary movement should be appointed 'to obviate delays which are bound to arise hereinafter through confusion.'[76] No move to rectify the situation was made, however, for another few months.

In April 1897 the 1798 Centenary Committee issued appeals for clubs to be set up in 'every town and parish in Ireland and in every district out of Ireland where Irishmen are resident', emphasising that 'every Irishman, irrespective of creed, class or politics ... should be eligible for membership.' This policy was generally followed by the various centenary clubs. The sole stipulation was that the leaders of all centenary clubs should affiliate themselves with the Dublin committee and, in line with the policy of the executive of the association, 'should preserve a neutral attitude with regard to present-day party politics.'[77] By championing this non-party stance, the republican-controlled executive of the association hoped to ensure that the rival Irish Party factions were not provided with *any* grounds upon which they could criticise the management of the centenary movement. Owing to the ongoing bitterness of the Parnell Split, however, it often proved very difficult for republicans to implement this policy, and its first serious setback occurred in Cork city that May. With the assistance of Patrick Meade, P.N. Fitzgerald organised a large convention to set up a local centenary committee (subordinate to the Dublin committee) but most Parnellites used the occasion merely to shout abuse at all the Dillonites present, leading to the latter's withdrawal from the convention. Fitzgerald appealed to the Parnellites to 'let their bitter feelings subside', but in vain.[78] As a result, the Cork centenary movement got embroiled in the quarrel between the rival Irish Party factions and, as Fitzgerald feared, the Dillonites became determined to take control of the centenary movement themselves.

In June 1897, a move was made for all republican factions to unite. This was supported by the *Irish Republic* as much as Fred Allan and the IRB.[79] In the same month, all republican parties, including James Connolly's recently established very small Irish Socialist Republican Party (ISRP), came together in Dublin to formalize plans to erect a monument to Wolfe Tone in Dublin; establish a 'literary committee' to republish the memoirs of the United Irish leaders and create a new larger executive for the centenary movement. Many ballot papers had been distributed in recent weeks and the results of the elections saw John O'Leary being re-elected president, Henry Dixon as vice-president and Fred Allan as the principal treasurer and secretary. Five new 'assistants' to Allan were elected, however, including Maud Gonne of London, Patrick Gregan T.C., William O'Brien, Count George Plunkett and William

76 *Freeman's Journal*, 6 and 7 Apr. 1897 (letters of Yeats, O'Leary, Hoctor read at centenary club meetings); NAI, CBS Précis reports, carton 1, 13738/s. **77** *Daily Independent*, 14 Apr. 1897. **78** *Freeman's Journal*, 15 May 1897; *Daily Independent*, 26 May 1897. **79** *Shan Van Vocht*, July 1897. Some ISRP members began contributing to the *Irish Republic* at this time, although Patrick McManus dismissed Connolly's idea of forming a new republican party at Westminster as impractical. *Shan Van Vocht*, Aug. 1897. Milligan supported McManus against Connolly in the debate. *Shan Van Vocht*, Oct. 1897.

Martin Murphy. Given this profile to the movement's executive it is not surprising that John Dillon's party and the National Federation became convinced that the centenary movement was out to undermine its public influence.

William Martin Murphy, a prominent Dublin businessman, was a former anti-Parnellite MP who, since 1896, was supporting Tim Healy's breakaway group from the National Federation, the People's Rights Association. This was in favour of democratizing control of the 'home rule' movement by putting an end to the Irish Party's control over the National Federation and National Leagues. Murphy had recently launched a newspaper, the *Daily Nation*, which championed the non-party policy of the 1798 Centenary Committee (a fact that probably explains his election) and which also promoted greater understanding between the Healy and Redmond parties. Meanwhile Count George Plunkett, a Parnellite who had stood unsuccessfully for Tyrone in 1892, was a strong supporter of Redmond's recent initiative in launching the Irish Independent League (IIL), which virtually replaced the dormant National League; a body which, under Harrington's influence, had sought a rapprochement with the Dillonites. The IIL was officially opposed to any moves towards a reunification of the Irish Party. Shortly before it was launched in Dublin, Redmond had called upon Devoy in America looking for financial support for the *Daily Independent*. At least according to Dublin Castle, 'in well-informed circles' it was known that Redmond launched the IIL only because he had been promised extensive financial support by John Devoy if he launched such an organization.[80] Just like the IRB, Devoy's UB was opposed to any moves to reunite the Irish Party because it was known that a reunited Irish Party would attempt to achieve a complete monopoly over Irish nationalist propaganda and crowd the republican party out of Irish public debate. Acting upon this motivation, Fred Allan, P.N. Fitzgerald and P.J. O'Keefe attended the inaugural meeting of the IIL on 20 April 1897, while Robert Johnston (who continued to spend most of his time in America) was soon elected onto the IIL's provisional council, as was J.K. Bracken and John Clancy, the sub-sheriff of Dublin.[81] Excepting Clancy, however, none of these men subsequently attended any IIL meetings.

If only because republicans had taken the lead in forming most centenary clubs, they generally dominated the various sub-committees that were elected during July 1897 to govern the centenary movement in the provinces. Of the ten men elected to the Dublin committee, the men who received the most votes (J.W. O'Beirne topped the poll) were generally republicans of the lower-middle or skilled-working classes, while former Parnellite MPs (then working for the *Independent* newspapers) such as Alex Blane and Edward Leamy came only seventh and eighth place, just ahead of Patrick Hoctor. Mark Codd, the

80 NAI, DMP files, carton 14, Report 4268, Ass. Comm. Mallon, 28 Apr. 1897; CBS Précis reports, carton 1, 12946/s, 13686/s, 13738/s, 13748/s.   81 *Daily Independent*, 21 Apr. and 5 May 1897.

mayor of Wexford, topped the poll for the Leinster provincial committee, which also included a few town councillors. James Moore, a prominent amnesty activist and the leader of the Old Guard Union in Dundalk, came second, while Luke Hayden, the Parnellite proprietor of *Westmeath Examiner* (who had recently lost his seat in parliament) came fifth, just ahead of the chairman of Carlow Town Commission, P.J. O'Keefe and some old (soon to be deceased) IRB leaders from Kings County and south County Wicklow. Surprisingly C.J. O'Farrell, the aging Enniscorthy IRB leader who had taken a prominent role in preparing for the centenary year (and who Dublin Castle claimed to have known was the IRB's medium for receiving UB funds), failed to be elected; a fact that excluded him from the centenary movement thereafter.

In Connacht, Barry McTernan, a Sligo figure of only local repute, topped the poll just ahead of two Connacht IRB leaders: John Lavin, a very popular but ailing republican from Castlerea (he died not long afterwards and a monument was erected in his memory by the local community)[82] and T.B. Kelly, the leader of the Mayo GAA. The leader of an obscure Ballinasloe workingmen's club (which had originally been formed by Matthew Harris) won more votes than the famous James Daly of the *Connacht Telegraph*, or Joseph MacBride TC, the Castlebar IRB leader, and Maurice Shine, the chairman of Tuam Town Commission and a well-known Galway GAA leader of republican sympathies. In Munster, except for one Tipperary Parnellite journalist (who came third) and one obscure Waterford figure (who came sixth), the men elected were all old IRB men. John Daly, who had recently been elected president of the 'Limerick '98 Committee', topped the poll just ahead of P.N. Fitzgerald, while the Limerick amnesty leader John Crowe, Maurice Moynihan of the Kerry GAA, John (later Sean) O'Keefe of the Cork IRB, Charles Doran and J.K. Bracken were also elected. In Ulster, John Clarke, the proprietor of the *Northern Patriot*, topped the poll ahead of old republicans such as Michael McGinn of Omagh, Patrick Russell of Belfast and Edward Madden of Monaghan. Neal John O'Boyle, the Ulster IRB leader, came fifth, while Alice Milligan, Anna Johnston, Henry Dobbyn and an alderman of Londonderry municipal council of unknown political antecedents also made it into the 'top ten'.[83]

The Dillonite *Freeman's Journal* and Tim Harrington's *United Ireland*, both of which were only now beginning to take an interest in the centenary movement, claimed that these elections were rigged, alleging that William O'Brien, Count Plunkett and William Martin Murphy were evidently 'qualified' to be elected onto the executive of the association solely because they were no longer members of parliament, whereas John Dillon, John

---

82 Lavin died on 8 March 1899 and a monument was unveiled in his memory in Castlerea on 8 September 1901. Approximately 500 people attended the demonstration, including Maud Gonne and J.P. Hayden, MP for South Roscommon. PRO (London), C.O. 903/7, miscellaneous intelligence notes, W series 1–10, 30–1. **83** *Daily Independent*, 14 July 1897.

Redmond and Tim Healy were 'disqualified' simply because they were 'the leaders of the Irish nation' in London. Against this backdrop, William O'Brien felt it was politically necessary to decline the honour of having been elected as a member of the executive of the 1798 Centenary Committee, for the reason that 'the elected [parliamentary] representatives of the Irish people appear to be wholly – and it cannot be doubted designedly – excluded from the committee.'[84] Throughout the remainder of the year, the *Freeman's Journal* and *United Ireland* propagated such conspiracy theories regarding the 1798 Centenary Committee and demanded that control of its executive be simply handed over to Irish Party leaders. William O'Brien supported this campaign, albeit cautiously, not least owing to his fear that his ambition to launch a new, radical land agitation in Connacht could be frustrated if he alienated the still highly influential Land League founder James Daly, who was a strong supporter of O'Leary's committee. The Independent Newspaper Company refused to bother about the Dillonite campaign against the 1798 Centenary Committee and thereby gave the committee implicit support, while Murphy's *Daily Nation* came out strongly in defence of the representative nature of the centenary committee, despite the absence of Westminster MPs. It maintained that the arguments of John Dillon's party were based 'on the prosperous and absurd theory that the moment a man becomes a member of parliament he becomes, in some mysterious manner, a superior being' and a member of 'a superior caste' in society. According to the *Daily Nation*, the sole object of the promoters in Irish public life of this distorting perspective was an undemocratic desire to have the Irish public perpetually 'bound to themselves', whereas the reality was that 'the people know their members of parliament' and their politics and 'there is not even one amongst them who possesses a sacrosanct character in their eyes.'[85]

Just like the annual elections to the GAA executive, the results of the centenary movement's elections do appear to have been genuine results. The ability of republicans and purely local political activists to be elected onto either body, rather than Westminster MPs (most of whom resided in London), was a natural result of the fact that these men were involved in both movements, while the MPs were not. As had been the case with the GAA and Land League during the 1880s, the only party the MPs could generally rely upon to help reverse this situation was the Catholic Church. During August 1897, the Catholic clergy began to form their own 1798 centenary clubs and, unlike all the other clubs formed so far, they refused to affiliate themselves with the executive of the 1798 Centenary Committee. In Ulster, some parish priests warned parishioners that, from information received 'on good authority', it was known that 'there is an organization in our midst known as the I.R. Brotherhood' and that a certain dangerous individual from Omagh 'is going

84 *United Ireland*, 17 and 24 July 1897; *Freeman's Journal*, 19 July 1897. 85 *Daily Nation*, 27 Sept. 1897; 18 Jan. 1898.

from town to town spreading such an organization throughout the country'; a man whom everyone in the community knew to be Michael McGinn (IRB), who had been recently-elected deputy leader of the Ulster executive of the 1798 Centenary Committee and who was then promoting the establishment of '98 clubs across Ulster.[86] During the first eight months of 1897, McGinn along with fellow republicans James Johnston and James Moore had formed many centenary clubs in Ulster, which were supported by numerous town councillors and trade union figures.[87] Things began to change, however, in late August when Joseph Devlin, the leader of the National Federation in Belfast, managed to persuade John Clarke, the leader of the Ulster executive of the 1798 Centenary Committee, to cease to work for the Dublin committee and instead join forces with the clergy and the Belfast leadership of the National Federation and National League in forming the 'Belfast United '98 Centenary Association', which would direct all local centenary events and support William O'Brien's policy of reviving a land agitation in the west of Ireland.[88]

The first public meeting of the Belfast United '98 Centenary Association was held on 4 October 1897 when John Dillon MP, Tim Harrington MP and William O'Brien spoke about the need for the Irish Party to reunite. Anticipating this development, in late September, Patrick Dempsey of the IRB (a leader of the Belfast '98 movement) had written to the press denouncing John Clarke's change of heart and resolving that because of 'determined attempt now being made by a political organization in Belfast to use the '98 centenary movement as an election machine', a new executive for Belfast and the entire province of Ulster must be established, to be composed only 'of office bearers from all *bone fide* '98 clubs and associations.' This action received 'the highest recommendation' from Fred Allan in Dublin, and the Dublin central committee requested that a new Ulster council for the centenary movement would be elected in Belfast on 14 October, the anniversary of William Orr.[89] This meeting did not occur, however, for Joseph Devlin was able to win the support of most Belfast Catholics for an Orr commemorative demonstration that was purely an Irish Party political event, during which he spoke alongside Dillon, Harrington and O'Brien about the leadership quarrel within the Irish Party and the land question.[90] On 9 November, when the meeting suggested by the Dublin committee finally did take place in Belfast, it was chaired by members of the Dublin committee, such as Henry Dixon, rather than by Belfast individuals. This initiative did win the support, however, of several small Belfast '98 clubs, as well as Milligan and Dobbyn and numerous '98 clubs from across the province, many of which were led by republican figures such as McGinn, John Traynor (now a town councillor in Armagh), Edward Madden (an old Monaghan IRB leader and prominent town councillor), Henry Diver and James Gallagher of

86 *Daily Independent*, 30 Aug. 1897.   87 *Freeman's Journal*, 13 Apr. 1897; *Daily Independent*, 19 Apr., 4 May 1897.   88 *Daily Independent*, 3 Sept. 1897.   89 *Daily Independent*, 27 Sept. 1897.   90 *Freeman's Journal*, 15 Oct. 1897.

Letterkenny and the McManus family of Mountcharles, Co. Donegal. This new Ulster '98 body elected the retired political figure of James Stephens as their president; a position that the IRB founder accepted, but which involved no responsibilities and so he never had to travel to Ulster or Belfast.[91] The only public action Stephens performed during the 1798 centenary was to unveil a Manchester-martyrs memorial in Manchester; an event that was organized by Yeats' 1798 Centenary Association of Great Britain and France and which attracted about ten thousand people.[92] The real leaders of the new Ulster '98 body were Neil John O'Boyle (IRB) and Louis Smyth of Magherafelt, one of the few Presbyterian IRB men in the province. Neither was able, however, to stem the growing influence over the Ulster centenary clubs of Joseph Devlin, who revived the sectarian Ancient Order of Hibernians (AOH) in Ulster with the clergy's support to counteract the republicans.

Devlin's initiative won much support from the clergy and from local Dillonite and O'Brienite politicians in north Connacht, and this greatly enhanced the young Belfast man's public profile. In October 1897, the entire priesthood of County Mayo issued a statement to the *Freeman's Journal* expressing their support for O'Brien's proposed land agitation and argued that the 1798 Centenary Committee must be controlled by the Irish Party, not the infidel O'Leary.[93] Meanwhile, with the support of Devlin and O'Brien, P.A. McHugh, a Dillonite MP originally educated to be a priest (he was mayor of Sligo and owner of the *Sligo Champion*), began organizing 'centenary clubs' in north Connacht that affiliated themselves with Devlin's organization and expressed support for O'Brien's call to revive the land agitation in the west of Ireland. With the support of *United Ireland* and the *Freeman's Journal*, McHugh also condemned O'Leary as a 'factionist' who had supposedly 'insulted' the Irish MPs by not automatically making them the *ex-officio* leaders of the 1798 Centenary Committee.[94] O'Leary responded by dismissing McHugh and his arguments as 'scarcely worth referring to', while several other members of the Dublin Executive pointed out that the MPs were not elected simply because they had never been involved in organizing any centenary clubs.[95] Elsewhere, the Catholic clergy continued to form their own '98 clubs across the country, usually at the request of their bishops, and affiliated themselves with Devlin's rather than O'Leary's group. During August and September 1897, virtually every parish priest in Co. Wexford formed a centenary club under his own leadership and subsequently arranged a large '1798 demonstration' in the county, when the speakers talked only of Westminster politics. This demonstration was held just outside Enniscorthy on 4 October 1897 and was addressed by John Dillon, John Redmond and Tim Healy, the three rival leaders of Irish Party, who now realized their need to abandon their mutual bitterness towards each other in order to reassert the

91 *Daily Independent*, 10 Nov. 1897. 92 Ryan, *Fenian memories*, 188–9. 93 *Freeman's Journal*, 26 Oct. 1897. 94 *Freeman's Journal*, 12 Nov. 1897; *United Ireland*, 13 Nov. 1897. 95 *Daily Independent*, 10 Nov. 1897; *Daily Nation*, 13 Nov. 1897.

no clearly support for O'Leary

MPs' control over the Catholic community and guarantee the bishops political support.[96] The tide now quickly began to turn against O'Leary's party in Dublin.

To resist the clergy's demands to have the Irish Party in control of the centenary movement, in September 1897, all republican factions came together to ensure that the 1798 Centenary Committee would continue to operate as planned. John O'Leary, Fred Allan, P.N. Fitzgerald, P.T. Daly, Jack O'Hanlon, P.J. O'Keefe, Maurice Moynihan, Patrick Hoctor, Henry Dobbyn, Alice Milligan, John O'Clohissey and J.P. O'Brien (who collectively were the leaders of the IRB, Old Guard Union and what remained of the INA party in Ireland) resolved that the executive of the committee should be expanded in January 1898 to include various figures. These were the mayors and chairmen of town councils from all across the country, as well as the presidents and secretaries of several bodies, such as the Amnesty Association (which, since John Daly's release in 1896, had become a small body of only 3,000 members that was governed by members of the Old Guard Union, rather than Parnellite MPs), the Trades Council of Dublin (which was currently led by the republican Thomas Fitzpatrick), the Irish National Foresters, the GAA, the Old Guard Union, the CLS, the NMC and the Gaelic League.[97] P.T. Daly, a printer who was emerging as Allan's right-hand man in reorganizing the IRB, as well as John O'Clohissey, were delegated to work with the Foresters, Trades Councils and GAA to attract crowds to the forthcoming demonstrations and collect funds for the proposed Wolfe Tone memorial. P.N. Fitzgerald, N.J. O'Boyle, Charles Doran, T.B. Kelly, James Daly and Joseph Nannetti (Old Guard Union, a popular Irish-Italian Dublin city councillor and future mayor) were delegated to work with the corporations and town councils of Cork, Belfast, Carlow, Wexford and Dublin in securing hotel accommodation for members of the 1798 Centennial Association of America, who were due to arrive in Ireland the following year. Finally Alice Milligan of the *Shan Van Vocht*, Patrick Lavelle, William Rooney, W.P. Ryan (secretary of the London Gaelic League) and Edmund Leamy (ex-MP) of the *Weekly Independent* were delegated to organise historical lectures and exhibitions about 1798.[98] The IRB secretary, Fred Allan, who played the principal role in affiliating centenary clubs with the central branch, subsequently reached an understanding with William Lyman and the American INA regarding their plans to come to Dublin the following year, while the *Irish Republic* organized its own collection in New York for the Wolfe Tone memorial committee in Dublin, of which Allan was the leader.[99] All these activities contrasted singularly with those of the '1798 clubs' set up by Devlin and the clergy, none of which were making any preparations for 1798 centenary demonstrations but

96 *Freeman's Journal*, 11 Oct. 1897; *Daily Nation*, 28 Oct. 1897. **97** *Daily Independent*, 6 Sept. 1897. **98** *Freeman's Journal*, 13 Sept., 9 Nov. 1897. **99** *Daily Independent*, 22 Nov. 1897. The *Irish Republic* collection began in May. *Daily Independent*, 12 May 1897.

instead were simply organizing public meetings where calls were made for the Irish Party to reunite as soon as possible.

As leader of the 1798 Centenary Committee, John O'Leary portrayed the centenary movement as having a purely 'educational' purpose, attempting to revive the public's interest in the United Irishmen's writings through republications. This was a purpose he lauded in an (unpublished) article of the time entitled 'What Irishmen Should Think' and which the committee generally fulfilled, by publishing pamphlets and organizing history lectures.[100] Apart from resisting all efforts to turn the centenary movement into a platform for the MPs, this was generally all that the IRB party was trying to do at this time. James Connolly, who ran the 'Rank and File '98 Club' of Dublin, was very dissatisfied with this approach, however, arguing that if the 'democratic and republican principles of the United Irishmen' were to become relevant to the public once more, the committee should be making immediate attempts to turn all Irishmen into 'earnest democrats' or revolutionaries.[101] Recently Connolly's ISRP had instigated public protests in Dublin against the holding of diamond jubilee celebrations of Queen Victoria's reign and both Maud Gonne and Patrick Gregan (who raised a black flag over Dublin City Hall for the event) supported Connolly's endeavours.[102] W.B. Yeats, the president of the 1798 Centenary Committee for Great Britain and France, had also made several speeches in London at this time which proclaimed that the centenary movement was the ultimate riposte to claims that Irishmen were loyal to Queen Victoria, but the IRB leadership, or rather the leadership of the Dublin centenary committee, patronized no such protest movements. This was partly because O'Leary 'abhorred flash-in-the-pan exploits' but was also because the IRB was focused first and foremost upon making a success of the forthcoming centenary celebrations, before claiming some of the spoils of that success.[103]

In November 1897, bowing under the pressure of the *Cork Examiner*, William O'Brien's *Cork Free Press*, the Catholic bishops and the Cork Trades Council, Patrick Meade (a vice-president of the Dublin body) invited several leading Dillonite MPs to become vice-chairmen of the local centenary committee.[104] This action greatly disappointed the Dublin committee and John O'Keefe, the Cork IRB leader, who felt that Meade had made a big mistake by giving 'a handle to those who had been anxious to manipulate the movement'.[105] Within a month of their assuming authority, the anti-Parnellites defeated motions of P.N. Fitzgerald, O'Keefe and Meade that the Cork committee should remain affiliated with 1798 Centenary Committee and called for it to unite with Devlin's body.[106] As a result, in December 1897, with

---

100 *Daily Independent*, 10 Nov. 1897; NLI, John O'Leary papers, MS 8002 ('What Irishmen should think'). **101** *Daily Independent*, 1 Dec. 1897. Connolly made this same argument in the *Shan Van Vocht*, June 1897. **102** NAI, DMP files, carton 14, report 4346, Ass. Comm. Mallon, 14 July 1897. **103** G.A. Lyons, *Some recollections of Griffith and his times* (1923), 17. **104** *Daily Independent*, 22 Nov. 1897. **105** *Daily Independent*, 29 Nov. 1897, 14 Dec. 1897. **106** *Daily Independent*, 21 Dec. 1897.

the support of the Dillonite *Freeman's Journal* and the Catholic clergy, Joseph Devlin's 'Belfast and Ulster United Centenary Association' was able to ally itself with the centenary committees of Galway, Cork and a few other towns to launch a rival organization to the Dublin committee, known as the 'United Irish Centennial Association' (UICA). The UICA mounted a bitter propaganda campaign against the 1798 Centenary Committee, called for the Irish Party to be made the leaders of the committee and announced its intention to launch a land agitation in the west of Ireland.[107]

The centenary year began as the IRB had generally hoped, with torchlight '98 demonstrations in almost every major town in the country; the most provocative being that held in Kilkenny City where, 'just as the first stroke of twelve rang out, a salute of twenty-one shots was fired by the rifle corps attached to the [workingmen's] club' at the bidding of PJ O'Keefe TC, Alderman Joseph Purcell of the GAA Executive and the Dublin militant, John Nolan.[108] John O'Leary, however, felt that if the forthcoming centenary celebrations were not to turn out a fiasco, some sort of compromise needed to be reached with the UICA. With apparent reluctance, Fred Allan produced a letter of O'Leary's before the Executive of the 1798 Centenary Committee on 16 January 1898, which proposed 'that the different sections of the Parliamentary Party be requested to appoint representatives to act on the Executive Committee of the '98 Committee'. Together with Patrick Lavelle, however, Allan later introduced an amendment (which was passed unanimously) to O'Leary's proposal, arguing that a convention could be held at a later date to decide upon this question, but that no action should be taken as yet.[109] Dublin Castle believed that IRB-patronized 1798 clubs could not tolerate the idea of 'oath of allegiance men' being involved in managing the centenary movement, although in public, the 1798 Centenary Committee never made reference to this issue, but only proclaimed that the clubs should not attend 'any meetings ostensibly called to support the '98 Centenary, but which may be really called from party motives.'[110] Indeed, it was self-evident that the meetings of Devlin's new association were called only for Irish Party motives. During January 1898, the UICA held a number of demonstrations, including a large gathering of MPs and journalists to discuss the future of the Irish Party at the Westminster Palace Hotel in London (the most patriotic of all 1798 demonstrations, according to the *Freeman's Journal*), and a large land demonstration at Westport, which was addressed by O'Brien, Dillon, numerous priests and Tim Harrington.[111] At the Westport demonstration on 23 January, William O'Brien argued that 'if Mr John O'Leary will only broaden out the sensible and patriotic proposals he has made [of including MPs], there can be no difficulty about coming to a general understanding that will save us from the discredit of anything like [the need for] rival organizations.'[112]

107 *Freeman's Journal*, 17 and 31 Dec. 1897. **108** *Daily Independent*, 1–4 Jan. 1898. **109** *Daily Nation*, 17 Jan. 1898. **110** *Freeman's Journal*, 13 Sept. 1897. **111** *Freeman's Journal*, 5 Jan., 7 Jan., 20 Jan., 24 Jan. 1898. **112** *Freeman's Journal*, 24 Jan. 1898.

The week before the Westport demonstration, O'Leary had travelled to Mayo with John Simmons (a leader of the Old Guard Union and secretary of the Dublin Trades Council) to supervise the election of an executive for the 'Connacht '98 Council', which was to remain under the central committee's authority in Dublin.[113] This election took place in the Claremorris hotel of the local IRB leader, Thomas Ryan, and resulted in James Daly of the *Connacht Telegraph* being elected as president. Daly's first action in this capacity was to denounce O'Brien's attempt to induce O'Leary to accept 'such a soft-headed policy' for the centenary movement, arguing that it could 'not be expected that believers in the Union of Hearts, worshippers of the Union Jack, or such other hypocritical policies, would honestly and befittingly celebrate the centenary of the brave martyrs of liberty of the 1798 movement.' Daly noted that the Connacht '98 Council had boycotted the Westport meeting, for they did not consider it to have been a 1798 demonstration at all, despite the claims of the *Freeman's Journal* to the contrary.[114] Indeed, the focus of the speeches at this demonstration were not at all upon 1798, but rather upon the legacy of O'Connell, the present situation in the House of Commons and in making calls to 'divide those great ranches up' for farmers in the west of Ireland.[115] Within a couple of days of this Westport demonstration, its organizers announced their intention to form a new organization known as the United Irish League (UIL), which was to be built upon the basis of the UICA, to push for the reunification of the Irish Party and to launch a widespread land agitation in the west of Ireland.[116]

As most Irish Party figures were still hedging their bets whether to follow Dillon, O'Brien, Redmond or Healy and not all were in favour of O'Brien's proposed land agitation, the UIL did not win their immediate support. Its creation, however, effectively solved the difficulty that the Catholic political establishment had faced in recent times in reasserting their control of popular political activity in the country. This was done not merely by championing the land question but also by attempting to capitalize upon popular enthusiasm for the 1798 celebrations. Reflecting its intrinsic link with the UICA, every UIL membership card bore a picture of Wolfe Tone surrounded with pikes and the slogan 'who fears to speak of '98', thereby portraying the UIL as a militantly nationalist movement.[117] This belied the fact that the movement was not at all founded to revive public interest in the example of the United Irishmen, but rather to reassert the authority of the Irish Party over the community through attempting to persuade the government to provide material assistance to the farmers. Not coincidentally, most UIL branches were led by parish priests. Writing to the English liberal journal, the *Contemporary Review*, the UIL leader William O'Brien argued that 'it would be living in a fool's paradise to

113 *Daily Independent*, 17–18 Jan. 1898.   114 James Daly to *Daily Independent*, 26 Jan. 1898.
115 *Freeman's Journal*, 24 Jan. 1898.   116 *Freeman's Journal*, 28 Jan. 1898.   117 A copy of one of these membership cards can be seen in Fr Conal Thomas, *The land for the people: the United Irish League and land reform in north Galway, 1898–1912* (Galway, 1999), 37.

affect not to see that popular confidence in the effectiveness of constitutional agitation [the Irish Party] is being seriously shaken' because 'serious influences in Ireland ... seem to be lending themselves, consciously or unconsciously, to the work of paralysing the Irish party in Westminster.' O'Brien predicted that Ireland 'may be nearer to another such calamity' as occurred in 1798 than many people believed, for not only 'hot-blooded young Irishmen' but 'even a good many cool headed ones' had become contemptuous of Westminster politics and all it symbolized. Tim Harrington also expressed a fear that 'the great bulk of the people of Ireland' might be ready to consider 'if they should not once and for all, abandon any expectation of getting anything from the English parliament.' He expressed the same firm resolution as O'Brien, proclaiming 'God save Ireland from such troubles' and warned the British government of the folly of not cooperating fully with the Irish Party.[118]

Naturally the Tory government already had its own plans to deal effectively with this potential difficulty. In February 1898, the government introduced a bill that would create a system of local government similar to that which had existed on the island of Britain for ten years previously. This would allow for the creation of elective, county councils, as well as urban and rural district councils that were subordinate to the county councils. These could impose rates and appeal to the Treasury for funding to implement a certain amount of administrative reforms. While the British municipal authorities also controlled judicial responsibilities, in Ireland, control of judicial functions would remain with non-elective grand juries, controlled by the landed aristocracy. Chairmen of the county and district councils would have the option, however, of becoming justices of the peace to assist the magistrates, provided they took an oath of allegiance to the queen. This bill would become law in August 1898 and was praised by Irish MPs of all persuasions (William O'Brien even proclaimed that it would undo the Norman conquest), but its true purpose, as far as the Tories were concerned, was simply to dissuade the Catholic middle classes from supporting Irish nationalism by increasing their belief in the benefits to be derived from the Union. This strategy was perhaps best reflected by Arthur Balfour's decision to follow up the local government act by promising that the government would commit itself to granting state recognition for the Catholic University in Dublin;[119] an idea that English Liberal public opinion had long refused to tolerate, but which had been the long sought after dream of the Irish Catholic political establishment ever since 1845, when the Catholic hierarchy forced Daniel O'Connell to take up the issue, just as virtually every Irish Catholic MP in Westminster was prompted to do from that date onwards.

It is probable that O'Leary's 1798 Centenary Committee would not have evoked as much hostility from the Catholic political establishment since the

---

118 *United Ireland*, 19 Feb. 1898 (editorial and extract from O'Brien's article).   119 Alan O'Day, *Irish home rule, 1867–1921* (1998), 186–7.

counter factual

summer of 1897 were it not that the Dillonites suspected O'Leary's party of having a definite bias in favour of Redmond's IIL; allegations that Alice Milligan, the *Shan Van Vocht* editor, also believed, leading her to criticize the committee for this reason,[120] although her main grudge was that the Parnellite *Daily Independent* had published a couple of articles that were critical of the *Irish Republic*, supposedly for being 'too outspoken'.[121] The non-party stance of the 1798 Centenary Committee was intended to boost republicans' levels of influence in Irish political society as much as possible before the Irish Party could possibly be reunited. The committee, however, was not working to support the actual purpose of the IIL, which was to boost Redmond's personal powers of leverage in the struggle for control of the Irish Party, now that the Parnellite faction had virtually disintegrated. Likewise Redmond did not support the republicans' purposes, but it would suit him if the Dillonites were unable to achieve their objective of using the centenary movement as a means to give them an insurmountable power in dictating terms to the IIL. In other words, no real understanding existed between Redmond and the IRB during 1897, but both realised that they could benefit from the other's politics. On the republican side, this was illustrated by their attendance at the inaugural meeting of the IIL in April 1897. On Redmond's side, this was reflected by his becoming a 'rank and file' member of the 'Wexfordmen's Association' (a Dublin body led by P.T. Daly, which petitioned against the singing of 'God save the Queen' in Irish theatres) and his volunteering to help the IRB pay the costs of a memorial erected seven years earlier for Michael Seery; a decision that O'Leary and Allan felt was 'a gracious act' on Redmond's behalf.[122] By February 1898, however, O'Leary realized that the rumours that the 1798 Centenary Committee had a Redmondite bias were harming its progress. As a result, he modified his usual statement to the press that the '98 clubs were open to all 'but a '98 association, as an association, has no business whatever to mix and meddle with any present day party politics' with an added qualification that no member of the 1798 Centenary Committee should attend a Dublin meeting to welcome John Redmond home from the United States; a policy that was subsequently followed to the letter by the movement's executive.[123] This declaration by O'Leary was interpreted by the *Freeman's Journal* as a 'manly and outspoken' repudiation of the policy of the 'factionist' IIL and this development did much to moderate the criticisms of the 1798 Centenary Committee by the Dillonite press.[124] This did not alter the fact, however, that there were still two very different centenary movements in existence.

120 Milligan to *Daily Independent*, 26 June 1897.   121 *Shan Van Vocht*, May 1897 (editorial). Fred Allan was inclined to defend the Parnellite press from criticisms of the *Irish Republic*. *DPB*, vol. 2, 338.   122 *Daily Independent*, 9, 23 and 29 Nov. 1897; *DPB*, 2, 338: Allan to Devoy, 29 Dec. 1897. Redmond helped pay the costs of the memorial by giving a lecture at the Rotunda on 1798, an event that was attended by six Redmondite MPs (and two ex-Parnellite MPs) and John O'Leary.   123 *Evening Telegraph*, 1 Feb. 1898; *Daily Independent*, 4 Feb. 1898. 124 *Freeman's Journal*, 2 Feb. 1898.

The emphasis in the speeches made at various centenary events during the spring of 1898 differed significantly depending on whether or not they were organized by the 1798 Centenary Committee or the UICA. In Munster, for example, Maurice Moynihan argued that Irishmen were 'not worthy of '98, or worthy to celebrate '98, if we do not make an effort to imitate their principles and their patriotism'. To do this, he believed Irishmen must 'create and foster a spirit of brotherhood amongst themselves' based upon the United Irishmen's republican principles and be ready to arm themselves, if necessary, to defend their liberties, for 'the day might come during the present generation when we should be called upon to fight for our national existence'. Likewise, P.N. Fitzgerald proclaimed that until the day arrived when Irishmen followed the United Irishmen's principles exactly, they would be 'forever under the heel of the Saxon' and remain 'slaves'.[125] The largest event organized by the 1798 Centenary Committee that spring was a monster '98 demonstration in the Phoenix Park. At this event, which attracted 20,000 people, Henry Dobbyn and Charles Doran argued that Irishmen should be ready to bear arms in defence of their liberties, while Louis Smyth proclaimed that the 'only way' Ireland 'may take her place among the nations of their earth' was if the Irish people resolved 'to propagate a great, democratic republic' amongst themselves and turned their attention completely away from Westminster.[126] By contrast, on UICA platforms, most speakers who did speak at all about 1798, rather than the land question or the prospects of the Irish Party, did so only to portray the rebellion as having been an act of self-defence specifically by the Catholic population against coercion. Fr Patrick Kavanagh, the most popular historian of 1798, did occasionally praise the United Irishmen's non-sectarian ideals, but his proclamations that Irishmen should 'rejoice' in the centenary year now that 'the time of judgment for the Pharisee of Nations and the scourge of our country is drawing nigh, when the children of St Patrick, like those of Israel, shall chant a hymn of triumph over the fall of their ancient foe', undoubtedly had sectarian undertones.[127] Despite the popularity of the song 'who fears to speak of '98', UICA speakers portrayed the rebellion as having been a disastrous event and argued that Irishmen should do all in their power to ensure such a disaster would never occur again. No UICA speaker at the 1798 centenary events ever dealt with the question of the United Irishmen's republicanism, except for John Dillon. He suggested that the modern principles of political liberty which were given nascent expression by the United Irishmen's republicanism later found fuller and more mature expression in the liberal politics of Daniel O'Connell and W.E. Gladstone. The Irish Party leader thereafter produced a letter (a 'St Patrick's Day gift') from the retired and soon to be deceased 'grand old man' of English liberalism (whose biography was currently being written by Justin McCarthy)

125 *Daily Independent*, 11 Jan. 1898 (speech by Maurice Moynihan at Tralee); *Freeman's Journal*, 18 Apr. 1898 (speech of P.N. Fitzgerald at Mallow). **126** *Daily Nation*, 14 Mar. 1898. **127** *Irish Times*, 22 Sept. 1897; *Daily Nation*, 13 Jan. 1898.

announcing that 'the Irish nation' would soon achieve all its desires through its electoral pact with the minority party sitting in opposition at Westminster.[128]

By March 1898, the controversy regarding the 1798 Centenary Committee's apparent antipathy to the Irish Party had still not been resolved. W.B. Yeats took the lead in attempting to solve this problem by attending a Dublin meeting of the 1798 Centenary Committee as an 'accredited delegate' of the trans-Atlantic INA. He proposed that, to bring about the unification of the two bodies, 'six members of the different sections of the parliamentary party be co-opted onto the general executive – one from the Parnellite, two from the Healyite and three from the Dillonite section, their election to be based on their standing as Irishmen, and not as members of parliament.' This suggestion was immediately objected to by James Connolly who, supported by John O'Clohissey, moved that 'as this convention does not recognise the right of the British parliament or government to govern Ireland, we cannot see that membership of that parliament gives any right to membership in commemoration of the men of '98.' Connolly's motion was defeated, however, P.T. Daly reminding his friend that 'no rule ever existed' excluding MPs from the centenary movement. Daly, who had become the principal organizer of the centenary clubs since January, proposed that the 1798 Centenary Committee maintain its existing policy, namely that only men elected by the various branches of the association could be admitted to the central committee and no *ex-officio* members (the MPs) should be allowed. This proposal was carried with the support of Fred Allan and Henry Dixon. The latter then passed another rule that anyone who was also a member of the UICA would be immediately expelled from the 1798 Centenary Committee; a policy that was denounced by Patrick Hoctor for its intolerance and did help to perpetuate discord.[129] The *Freeman's Journal* responded to this challenge to the UICA by again demanding that John O'Leary be replaced by John Dillon as president of the 1798 Centenary Committee. It also denounced the 1798 Centenary Committee's official policy of excluding clergymen of all religious denominations from its membership, stating that 'priests and people must be together, as in '98'.[130] Meanwhile William O'Brien revived his absurd claims that the 1798 Centenary Committee was acting against the wishes of five-sixths of all Irishmen by not trying to prevent Westminster MPs from continuing to seem 'detestable' to the general Irish public.[131]

Thanks mostly to P.T. Daly, the 1798 Centenary Committee continued to establish 1798 clubs during March and April 1898, but O'Leary was finding the likely prospect of the forthcoming centenary demonstrations being a failure due to the opposition of the Irish Party and Catholic hierarchy more intolerable by the day. As a result, a series of negotiations took place at

128 *Freeman's Journal*, 18 Mar. 1898. 129 *Daily Independent, Daily Nation* and *Freeman's Journal*, 14 Mar. 1898. 130 *Freeman's Journal*, 4 Mar. 1898. 131 *Freeman's Journal*, 18 Mar. 1898.

O'Leary's request between Fred Allan and the UICA, and on 21 April 1898, the 1798 Centenary Committee capitulated to demands that the two centenary associations be united. The UICA initially proposed that the entire Irish Party (meaning Dillon's party) be made *ex-officio* members of the executive of the new centennial association, but this was immediately rejected by Allan, who instead proposed that the six members of the UICA executive could be added onto the executive of the centenary committee; a modification of the proposal initially championed by Yeats. Allan maintained that the executive of this new 'United 1798 Centenary Committee' should have just one president (which he insisted should be John O'Leary), secretary and treasurer. As the 1798 Centenary Committee was the larger of the two '98 movements, Allan's terms were accepted by the UICA and were generally welcomed by the Dillonite press. Only a few members of the Executive of the 1798 Centenary Committee, most notably Henry Dixon, the leader of the YIL, expressed serious reservations in public.[132] Republicans' plans suffered two unexpected setbacks, however, within days of this agreement.

Due to the outbreak of war between the United States and Spain over Cuba, the 1798 Centennial Association of America issued a manifesto (signed by Devoy, Lyman and others) announcing that it could not bring 100,000 men or indeed *any* Irish-Americans to Ireland that summer to support the '98 demonstrations, as previously planned, as 'it is the paramount duty of every American citizen to remain at the disposal of his government while there may be need of his services.'[133] Around the same time, the *Irish Republic* ceased publication, mostly due to William Lyman's growing serious financial difficulties arising from failed property investments; a development that also led to a serious decline in the American INA. Whatever about the demise of the *Irish Republic*, the abandonment of the American expedition was undoubtedly very unfortunate for the republican movement, for it negated almost all of the committee's plans for the demonstrations that had been arranged the previous September; a fact that demoralized many of the committee's members. It was also known that the leaders of the 1798 Centennial Association of America would have given a huge boost to the republicans' propaganda campaign if they had arrived as planned and were able to address many centenary demonstrations. The UICA, realizing this, held out against committing itself to the arrangement agreed with Allan in April, demanding that more negotiations take place. This continued right up until mid May, a week before the principal centenary events were to begin. Not until 18 May 1898 did the proposed amalgamation officially take place, but according to terms which indicated that Allan was forced to make a much more significant capitulation to the UICA's demands than was originally envisioned.[134] The UIL leader William O'Brien and as many as sixteen MPs were admitted to the executive of the new 'United

132 *Freeman's Journal*, 22 Apr. 1898; *United Ireland*, 23 Apr. 1898; *Daily Independent*, 25 Apr. 1898. 133 *Daily Independent*, 3 May 1898. 134 *Daily Nation*, 19 May 1898.

1798 Centenary Committee' without ever having been elected. These men did not even attend its meetings, which continued to be run mostly by Allan and Dixon. The MPs did avail of this new position, however, to ensure that they, as well as the priests, could address *all* principal centenary meetings in the country, thereby ensuring no more monster '98 demonstrations could take place like that held in the Phoenix Park during March, from which Westminster politicians had been excluded and during which republican speeches had been made before as many as 20,000 people.[135]

The UICA formally ceased to exist on 26 May 1898, but not before its members were ordered to boycott all the various torchlight demonstrations which were held by republicans across the country that week. As a result, these demonstrations often attracted as little as 1,000 men, almost exclusively of the working classes.[136] Large UIL demonstrations, which were called 1798 demonstrations by the *Freeman's Journal,* were held that week in the west of Ireland. At Westport, William O'Brien chaired a large '1798 demonstration' in which he spoke almost entirely about Gladstone and Parnell's legacy regarding the land question, while John Howard Parnell (brother of C.S. Parnell), when chairing the Arklow '98 demonstration during the centenary week, spoke merely about the contrasting attitudes of Chamberlain and Balfour regarding the local government bill currently being debated in Westminster. Republicans would appear to have been excluded (or excluded themselves) from the Vinegar Hill and New Ross demonstrations held on 29–30 May, addressed by Redmond, Healy, T.D. Sullivan, Fr Kavanagh and many priests.[137] Indeed, although republicans spoke at several demonstrations in the forthcoming months (and were often the only speakers at Dublin meetings), the Irish Party's much greater influence over the centenary movement was now evident; a trend perhaps best reflected on 'Wolfe Tone Day', an event which took place in Dublin on 15 August to unveil the foundation stone for a Wolfe Tone monument. This was the largest of all the centenary events that took place during 1898, attracting well over 100,000 people. Fred Allan, P.T. Daly, John O'Clohissey and others played the principal role in winning the support of trade bodies for the event and in organizing the huge procession, while John O'Leary performed the ceremonial role of unveiling the foundation stone, but the Irish Party was able to ensure that the main political speeches for the event were delivered by MPs, who consequently derived perhaps the biggest political benefit from the event.[138]

The 1798 centenary celebrations had a fairly positive effect on the republican movement. The propaganda of the *Northern Patriot* and especially the *Shan Van Vocht,* together with the Dublin committee's pamphlets of United Irish writings and books such as the *Songs and Ballads of '98,* did make a deep

---

135 *Daily Nation,* 14 Mar. 1898.   136 *Daily Independent,* 24–9 May 1898.   137 *Freeman's Journal,* 24 May 1898, 1 June 1898; *Daily Nation,* 30 May 1898; *Daily Independent,* 10 June 1898.   138 *Freeman's Journal,* 16 Aug. 1898; *Daily Independent,* 16 Aug. 1898; Ryan, *Fenian memories,* 188.

impact upon many intelligent, literate young nationalists, both Catholic and Protestant, who joined '98 clubs in Dublin, Belfast and Cork and some of them later joined the IRB. Be that as it may, G.A. Lyons, a young Protestant clerk and a particularly active figure in the CLS and Dublin '98 clubs, complained that 1798 Centenary Committee's capitulation to the UICA's demands in April 1898 was unforgivable, since it allowed the Irish Party to 'absorb the only available vehicle for the propagation of the Fenian faith', caused the centenary movement to prematurely 'fizzle out' and led many of the 'original founders of the '98 centenary movement' to become apathetic, demoralized and give up hope in the republican movement.[139] Many figures in the Dublin IRB (which Allan had managed to rejuvenate since 1895) and the CLS were adamant that, once the centenary celebrations ended, the '98 clubs affiliated with the 1798 Centenary Committee should be kept in existence permanently and that a great republican movement could be built on this basis. Their hopes were based upon the fact that by December 1898 (when the celebrations were over), there were still about 30,000 nominal members of the clubs, which was three times the membership of the UIL and more than any other single organization in the country, excepting the Ulster Unionist Clubs.[140] The problem, however, was that most ordinary members of these clubs were certainly not political enthusiasts of any kind. This was something of which O'Leary, Allan and Fitzgerald were fully aware, and thus the centenary events did little or nothing to revive their fading political enthusiasms. By contrast, many of the young men who had either joined or become associated with republican circles during the period 1894–8, whether through the YIL, the INA or the Dublin centenary clubs, believed that the future was literally theirs to mould as they pleased. As a result, in the wake of the centenary movement, many young activists began to either dictate IRB policy themselves or else follow their own initiatives in forwarding Irish nationalists' goals.

139 Lyons, *Recollections of Griffith*, 6–7. **140** NAI, CBS files, Home Office précis, carton 2, 18623/s (attached statistical report, dated 31 Dec. 1898). The Ulster Unionist Clubs now had 33,000 members.

9

Local government, Cumann na Gaedhael and the re-invention of Irish nationalist politics, 1899–1902

The establishment of the county, urban and rural district councils in 1899 played a significant role in redefining the nature of Irish politics because it created a new strata of independent activists who were not prepared to allow any party dictate how they should fulfil their responsibilities to the newly enfranchised municipal electorate. The Irish Party feared this prospect.[1] Following the reunification of the Irish Party in 1900, the editorial policy of those newspapers that the party controlled, most notably the *Freeman's Journal*, as well as some provincial papers (especially P.A. McHugh's *Sligo Champion*) revived the rhetoric that had been used by *United Ireland* during the mid 1880s, the Irish Party's moment of nationalist opportunity. They argued that the Irish Party in Westminster was a living embodiment of 'Ireland a Nation', its new chairman, John Redmond, was often referred to simply as 'The Leader', and any dissenters from the party's politics and that of its 'patriot priests' were still described as 'factionists'. Once people began to experience civic life for the first time through the means of local government, however, this brand of politics, as well as the entire Catholic establishment of the nineteenth century, which was both created by and dependent on (materially and politically) the whims of the two principal British parties in Westminster, began to lose much of its political and moral authority.

The democratization of local government had unsettling consequences for republicans as well. In the past, the 'travelling organizers' of the IRB and particularly its 'county centres' had effectively always been popular politicians, working on a local level. The authority of the republican party, just as in the case of their arch-rivals, the parish priests (who were now forbidden by law from holding any municipal office), rested upon the fact that Irish politics had always been divorced from public office, both on a local and a national level, owing to the great strictures imposed on political life in the country by the Union. Most Irish political activity prior to 1899 could be maintained only by the propaganda of local newspapers and relatively powerless community-based political, sporting and literary clubs that could not shape the policy of the MPs. Political reforms could not be implemented by either the MPs or the general community. Whitehall decided everything. Even if half the adult male population in Ireland had a right to vote since 1884, they still had no opportunity to act and thereby generally think like citizens. This is why, under the

---

1 Feingold, *The revolt of the tenantry* (1984), epilogue. For Dublin Castle's interpretation of this reality, see NAI, CBS files, Home Office précis, carton 3, 25191/s (Aug 1901), 26398/s (Feb. 1902).

Union, political discourse in Ireland generally was (and essentially could be) nothing more than a debate upon questions of political morality, irrespective of whether or not these debates took place within nominally 'nationalist' or 'unionist' communities. A republican politics developed and was sustained in nineteenth-century Ireland not least because of the centralized and very distant nature of national government and the power wielded by a Catholic establishment that served Catholic, rather than national or civic, ends. When the focal point of Irish politics came to rest upon the practicalities of local government across much of Ireland, however, there was an end to the old politics of parish priests and maverick republicans vying with each other perpetually to mobilize the community around their respective poles. The parish priest could no longer present himself in public as the authoritative, political spokesman for the community (although the Irish Party's press continued to present him as such) and neither could the freelance republican rebel. For many politically idealistic and ambitious young men in Irish country towns, the presence of elective, local governmental bodies also meant that there was no longer any need for the covert existence of an Irish republican brotherhood to serve as a medium to fill the huge, gaping void in the Irish political experience. Something like a civic society could now well and truly begin to develop in the community for the first time, on a local, if not on a national, level. This reality slowly but surely remoulded the nature of Irish politics between 1899 and 1910.

The first democratic local governmental elections took place in Ireland between January and April 1899 and saw 75 per cent of all seats being won by Catholics of professedly nationalist persuasions. Officially, members of the IRB were allowed to enter municipal office, just as they were allowed to vote in parliamentary elections, if they desired to use that particular outlet to 'exert their proper influence in public affairs', but it does not appear that the IRB had ever developed any real faith in the policy it had first experimented with in 1870, of encouraging its followers to run for local office 'as a means of strengthening the power and influence of the Irish Republic.'[2] Perhaps the main reason for this was that, after 1882, many of the town commissions and poor law boards, having little or no authority to collect rates for administrative reforms, had become mere platforms for struggles between the National League and the Tories for local powers of patronage and jobbery. They could do little else, and any republican who had entered this world prior to 1899 generally operated according to its terms. In some cases, like that of John Clancy, they actually built their careers upon it. Accustomed to this reality, in the short term, republicans did not consider the democratization of local government to have been a very significant development. Consequently, the IRB stated that while men could run for election and 'the individual member

---

2 In Cork City, some republicans appear to have occasionally been elected to high municipal office during the 1880s, but this seems to have been exceptionable rather than a pattern. Mandle, *GAA*, 20, 67–8.

might take what part he pleased in local affairs' and his freedom of action would 'not be circumscribed', the republican movement must be on guard against the 'risk of being made, in its whole or in its parts, subservient to the parochial ambitions of petty men.'[3] Equally, however, republicans desired that voters would 'reject with equal contempt the slavish home ruler and the knavish unionist and vote for representatives, regardless of their party politics, who are honest men.'[4]

At Dublin Castle, the Crime Branch Special statisticians, who compiled statistics regarding every aspect of Irish life, estimated that 114 county councillors and 486 district councillors elected to local government office immediately after the democratisation of local government in 1898 were IRB men.[5] Another statistical estimate indicated that the IRB party won 10 per cent of all county council seats, 5 per cent of all district council seats and twenty-three positions as chairmen of either district or county councils in the 1899 local government elections.[6] These estimates, however, are virtually impossible to quantify and are very possibly gross exaggerations, for since the 1860s Dublin Castle had labelled a wide variety of Irish political activists and individuals as 'Fenians' depending upon all sorts of unreliable criteria, such as their class position and their general attitude towards British rule. The fact that no IRB leaders ran for office indicates that 'the organization' was not directly concerned with the elections, although some republican figures were undoubtedly elected to local government office during 1899, invariably on the strength of the labour vote. These included John Daly, elected mayor of Limerick, Anthony Mackey as chairman of Limerick county council, Edward Madden, chairman of Monaghan town commission and P.J. O'Keefe who was elected deputy mayor of Kilkenny. Most republicans who had held office in previous years (such as James Johnston, C.G. Doran, Maurice Shine, Patrick McInerney and Michael O'Sullivan) in towns like Dundalk, Cobh, Tuam, Ennis and Galway were re-elected, while in Dublin, a couple of young IRB men, following in the footsteps of Patrick Gregan, were elected to City Hall to represent the labour interest. The new deputy-chairman of Wicklow town council was obviously a republican as well.[7] These men, however, clearly acted in a purely individual capacity and did not constitute a distinct republican party in any of the areas where they had been elected. Even those who were still loyal to the IRB necessarily became most responsive to those trade and labour associations that had elected them. In their new responsibilities, none could act according to the ideal of ignoring mere class or sectional interests in

---

3 *United Irishman*, 29 April 1899.   4 *United Irishman*, 26 Mar. 1899 (editorial).   5 NAI, Crime Special Branch précis reports to the Home Office, carton 2 (1897–1900), files 18240/s, 18257/s, 18259/s, 18263/s, 18272/s, 18287/s, 18340/s, 18345/s, 18488/s, 18586/s, 18696/s, 18595/s, 18711/s, 18733/s, 18846/s, 18851/s, 19071/s, 19074/s, 19100/s, 19257/s (all dating from the spring of 1899).   6 NAI, Crime Branch Special reports, 18168/s; C.B. Shannon, *Arthur Balfour and Ireland* (1988), 309.   7 *United Irishman*, 29 July 1899.

politics. This was well illustrated in case of John Daly, who remained mayor of Limerick (despite clerical opposition) up until the beginning of 1902. He acted nominally in republicans' interests by removing the royal coat of arms from City Hall and granting the freedom of the city to Tom Clarke and (following the outbreak of the Boer War) to the president of the Boer Republic. His first responsibility, however, was always to his constituents, who demanded that he act as a labour politician. As a result, in September 1900, Daly issued a manifesto on behalf of the new 'Limerick Labour Party' calling for one of their leaders to run as an independent labour candidate for Westminster; an initiative that needless to say was immediately denounced by the Irish Party as that of a 'factionist' and surprised republicans, who noted that Daly would be 'censured' should he run for Westminster and take his seat,[8] which ultimately he did not.

Owing to a strong history of labour activism in Limerick, John Daly could easily identify with an urban labour cause, rather than the rural-orientated UIL. Most republican figures elected to local government during 1899, however, naturally cooperated closely with the mostly UIL councillors in such bodies. This created no intrinsic problem for republicans except whenever the small non-elective national executive of the UIL in Dublin attempted to enforce a policy upon the county councillors through the medium of the local UIL branches. For example, in Castlebar, the town commission was very much republican, but upon being elected a leader of Mayo county council, James Daly was pressurized by the UIL into becoming a justice of the peace. In this latter capacity, Daly would have had to take an oath of allegiance, something he initially totally refused to do, but he eventually relented (in 1901) after it was 'explained to me' by the UIL leader William O'Brien (whom Daly had formerly denounced) 'that it was not an oath, but a kind of pledge.'[9] Once Daly became a JP, however, his popularity and that of his paper, the *Connacht Telegraph*, began to drop, as he had become divorced from Mayo popular politics for the first time in his lengthy career. The UIL leadership also put pressure upon P.N. Fitzgerald's former right-hand man, J.K. Bracken (a founder of the GAA), to become a justice of the peace, after his being elected a Tipperary county councillor and chairman of the district council of Templemore, Co. Tipperary, in March 1899. He could not ignore the demand, as local Tipperary papers, which were owned by MPs, had put pressure on him to do so. To avoid becoming a JP and taking the oath of allegiance, Bracken stepped down as chairman of the local town council and subsequently attempted to act as the council's unofficial chairman through operating a personal clique; an action which slowly but surely alienated the local UIL. This went on for two years until, ultimately, 'furious that his own people had let his down, he decided to shake the dust of the town off his feet', leave the

8 *United Irishman*, 8 and 15 Sept. 1900. 9 *United Irishman*, 26 Jan. 1901.

council and effectively retire from politics, still convinced that no Tipperary man possessed greater political virtue than himself.[10] The reality of the situation, however, was essentially that there was no longer any room in local politics for men like Bracken who, for a generation, had been able to maintain their political standing in the community simply because of their status and reputation as republican patriots, rather than their actual record of public service. That game could no longer be played. Be that as it may, Bracken and Daly were certainly not isolated figures in desiring to serve the community through local government while refusing to act as servants to the British state. Several UIL leaders of the county councils, who may have had no connection with the republican movement, refused requests from the Irish Party and the UIL central branch in Dublin to become justices of the peace because of the required oath of allegiance to the British crown.[11]

Between roughly 1898 and 1904, at very large public demonstrations, dozens of memorials of Irish rebellions were erected by county and town councillors in conjunction with local centenary clubs,[12] but once this work was performed, all such clubs not controlled by republicans invariably disbanded. This was partly a natural development, but it was also the result of a conscious decision by the Dillonite elements in the UIL not to allow republicans to take advantage of the situation. In Belfast, for example, Robert Johnston spent £500 during early 1899 is setting up a meeting hall for all local '98 clubs, but at the clergy and Joseph Devlin's request this was boycotted by the local population. As a result, the Belfast clubs disbanded.[13] The Wolfe Tone Memorial Committee (WTMC), which was founded in June 1898 under O'Leary's presidency and one year later led by Fred Allan, had the support of several Dublin '98 clubs that remained in existence for many years. These local centenary clubs soon became known as the 'Wolfe Tone Clubs'. They met at the former site of the Dublin National Club, which was closed down in June 1899 by John Clancy but the premises was then sold to the Irish National Foresters, who rented it to the WTMC.[14] These clubs formed the basis of Dublin republican politics over the next ten years and had a total membership of several hundred men. It did not prove easy, however, to use the centenary clubs for a similar purpose outside Dublin.

IRB activists such as John Daly, P.T. Daly, Maurice Moynihan, T.B. Kelly and John O'Keeffe formed small branches of the WTMC in Drogheda, Kilkenny, Tralee, Ballina, Limerick and Cork during 1899, but these did not prove to be popular organizations and they were also isolated from each other. As was the case with the WTMC in Dublin, their fund-collecting efforts for

10 Brendan Bracken, 'An Irishman's Diary: J.K. Bracken', *Irish Times*, 28 Aug. 2004; NAI, CBS précis reports to the Home Office, carton 2, 18696/s, 19203/s, 19208/s; Murray, 'Joseph K. Bracken'.   11 NAI, CBS files, Home Office précis, carton 3, 25191/s (Aug 1901), 26398/s (Feb. 1902).   12 Owens, 'Nationalist monuments in Ireland 1870–1914', 103–17.   13 NAI, CBS files, Home Office précis, carton 2, 18948/s.   14 NAI, DMP files, carton 14, reports 5286–8, Supt. Lanktree, 21 to 27 June 1899; Home Office Précis, carton 2, 14920/s.

the proposed Wolfe Tone monument were very unsuccessful outside of very select GAA circles. Seventy-six different Dublin labour bodies had made vague promises to support the WTMC on 'Wolfe Tone Day',[15] but the Catholic middle classes refused to give it any support and, without the support of the propertied classes, it could hardly raise the £8,000 necessary for the endeavour.[16] The UICA was not essentially a 1798 centenary movement, but rather a ruse designed to lay the groundwork for the establishment of the UIL. It had organized land rallies but no actual centenary commemorations (though the *Freeman's Journal* presented a different picture), and by the autumn of 1898 several of its former leaders and many Irish Party MPs were campaigning for a monument to be erected in Dublin in memory of Gladstone, instead of one in memory of Wolfe Tone.[17] This idea was turned down by a Redmondite Dublin city council, but it was no more in favour of the idea of a monument to Wolfe Tone being erected in Dublin than the UICA. On the first anniversary of 'Wolfe Tone Day', with the support of John Redmond, the City Council established a 'Parnell Monument Committee', which deliberately competed with the WTMC and planned putting a monument of Parnell at the top of O'Connell Street instead.[18] Fred Allan, as president of the WTMC, had been engaged in negotiations with Daniel Tallon, the Parnellite mayor, regarding the erection of the Tone monument, but after Tallon supported the Parnell monument, many republicans were opposed to the WTMC having anything to do with City Hall and called upon Allan to withdraw; a highly impractical stance that seriously undermined the project.[19] A foundation stone for the Parnell monument was laid by Dublin City Hall within two months during a demonstration that attracted very few people compared to 'Wolfe Tone Day' and to which the DMP believed the Dublin working class was hostile.[20] Owing to the support of the business classes, however, the Parnell monument was erected within twelve years. Meanwhile despite the best efforts of the IRB and WTMC (which remained in existence until 1921, but never collected much more than several hundred pounds), the proposed Wolfe Tone monument at the top of Grafton Street was never erected, due to opposition from Dublin City Hall and the UIL and the indifference of Irish society generally, except for the republicans and sections of the urban working class.

Republicans had two principal objectives during 1899: to launch a new public movement based on the centenary clubs, and to maintain a foothold in the press. This latter objective was deemed crucial because, due the growing rapprochement between the different wings of the Irish Party, the Redmondites decided to sell the franchise for the Independent Newspaper Company to an English firm associated with the Liberal Party in February

15 *Daily Independent*, 1 Aug. 1898. 16 NAI, Home Office Précis, carton 2, 20110/s and 20270/s. 17 *Shan Van Vocht*, Sept. 1898. 18 NAI, DMP files, carton 14, Report 5307, Sergeant Montgomery, 15 Aug. 1899. 19 NAI, Home Office précis, carton 2, 20022/s. 20 NAI, DMP files, carton 14, Report 5343, Chief Commissioner J.J. Jones, 9 Oct. 1899.

1899. The new board of directors immediately fired Fred Allan and the republican clique that had influenced the editorial policy of the *Daily Independent* and especially the *Weekly Independent* in the past.[21] Many republicans were angry with John Redmond for taking this action, for they and the Clan had invested in the paper and now this investment, like the 'Paris funds' the Irish-Americans had subscribed to the Land League, had been misappropriated as far as they were concerned. On 4 March 1899, within days of the republicans' losing their foothold in the Independent Newspaper Company, a 'national weekly review', the *United Irishman*, was launched, edited by William Rooney and Arthur Griffith of the CLS. This paper continued and significantly expanded upon the propaganda campaign formerly run by the *Weekly Independent*, patronizing the YIL and GAA and printing either biographical articles about, or selections from the writings of, past republican rebels in virtually every issue. Reflecting the trend of opinion in Rooney's CLS, it also championed the Gaelic League (as had the *Shan Van Vocht*) and encouraged the public to buy only Irish-made products: a 'new patriotism', commonly known as 'Irish-Ireland' nationalism, which informed all of Rooney's propaganda, if not that of Griffith. The paper was funded mostly (no doubt at the Supreme Council's behest) by the IRB's official allies, the UB,[22] but during its first year of circulation it published not more than 1,000 copies a week and effectively did little more than capture the former readership of the *Shan Van Vocht*, which ceased publication in April 1899 because the demise of the American INA deprived it of funding.[23] The propaganda of the *United Irishman* was also of a noteworthy quality and, over the next five years, its journalism slowly but surely achieved its principal objective, which was to reflect the shifting trends in Irish nationalists' politics.

The *United Irishman* truly was a 'national weekly review' that was concerned with literature as much as politics. It was written mostly by members of the YIL and CLS, not all of whom were members of the IRB. The principal figures in maintaining this little circle of propagandists were Henry Dixon and William Rooney, both of whom had been primarily responsible in recent years for keeping the focus of their respective literary circles upon the nationalist ideals of Davis, Lalor and Mitchel. All their writings had been republished in recent years, as were the writings of some United Irishmen, in a very cheap format by the republicans' small committees attached to the 1798 Centenary Committee. The declared purpose of the *United Irishman* was 'to make the people think and create a healthy and fearless public opinion, not as an end, but as a means to an end' and its establishment

21 NAI, CBS files, Home Office précis, carton 2, 18948/s. In 1903, the franchise for the *Daily Independent* was sold by this English firm to William Martin Murphy, who launched a new paper, the *Irish Independent*, which (although known colloquially as 'the Daily') had little or nothing in common with its predecessor of the 1890s.   22 John Devoy, 'The story of Clan na Gael', *Gaelic American*, 8 Sept. 1924.   23 NAI, Crime Special Branch, Home Office précis, carton 2, 19257/s.

could be said to have marked the fulfilment of John O'Leary's ambitions for the YIS project ever since 1885. On a propagandist level, the purpose of the *United Irishman* was to encourage the public to associate the ideal of creating greater freedom of political debate in Ireland with the ideals of republicanism and to call for the establishment of a new public 'national republican organization' in the country.[24] The IRB leadership was evidently supportive of and quite probably responsible for this proposal, because the exact same policy was championed at Bodenstown in June 1899 at a demonstration that was chaired by P.N. Fitzgerald and Fred Allan. This demonstration was patronized by the Wolfe Tone Clubs and attracted over 8,000 people, about half of whom were from Dublin. Maurice Moynihan, the speaker for the occasion, denounced the Irish Party's press as 'the most potent and most dangerous auxiliary of the English garrison in Ireland ... which masquerades in nationalistic garb', called upon all nationalists to support 'that sturdy and patriotic little sheet, the *United Irishman*' and advocated the establishment of an 'open organization', because 'political opinion in Ireland at this time is in too unsettled, too chaotic a state to start a real revolutionary movement'. Moynihan declared that the proposed new public organization should have nothing to do with 'the politically deranged gang of parliamentarians' and could easily ignore 'the rules prescribed by the British constitution' without coming into conflict with the state, but it need not 'decry any existing organization, whether connected with land or labour.' As a Kerry IRB activist, he particularly lamented that 'the abolition of landlordism is in the minds of the masses, outside the towns and cities, the be-all and end-all of nationality' and, for this reason, he felt certain that it was 'to the young men of the cities and towns we must look for the formation of a national organization'. Most of all he hoped that the formation of this public movement would encourage many lapsed, republican activists to overcome their growing political apathy, for 'it is little short of criminal on the part of men who have the ability and the influence to continue passive spectators of this process of demoralization going on before their eyes'.[25]

Not surprisingly, many columnists of the *United Irishman* argued that the new public 'republican association' in the country should be based around the centenary clubs, one contributor arguing that 'if we had a '98 club in every town in Ireland, working as I know at least one to be working in Dublin, we would not fear for the future of an Irish republic'.[26] As republicans had very little control over the centenary clubs outside of Dublin, however, this policy was very difficult to realize. Most columnists who dwelt on the idea focused instead upon what principles the new 'open' republican movement should be based. In this respect, the paper's contributors emphasised Irishmen's need to do away with the politics of the Parnell era. As 'believers in republican systems of government', they argued there was a necessity for every Irishman to be free

24 *United Irishman*, 4 Mar., 11 Mar., 29 April, 6 May 1899.   25 *United Irishman*, 1 July 1899.
26 G.A. Lyons to *United Irishman*, 23 Sept. 1899.

to think and act 'like every citizen of a free state': 'this is unity amongst freemen, not the hideous thing we have been accustomed to for so long in Ireland, which throttled and gagged every man who differed from the majority'. During Parnell's day, the paper emphasized, Irishmen had grown accustomed to sacrificing their 'liberty of thought, speech and action' by subscribing to a monolithic political platform in an attempt to maximize the power of the Irish Party on the Irish benches at Westminster. This Irish Party policy of the mid 1880s had brought 'degradation in the national character' but most of the Irish political community had supported it as a temporary, expedient measure, 'most of us thinking it patriotic, some of us doubtful, and a few us knowing it to be wrong, but unable to revolt, or fearing of being stoned as blasphemers if we did.'[27] The *United Irishman* believed that this malaise in Irish politics should 'have ended the day C.S. Parnell died', but the Irish Party was still keeping Irishmen bound by 'the habits of servitude' by attempting to make Westminster the centre of their attention and seeking to re-establish the unnatural monolithic, political platform of the mid 1880s.[28] Henry Dixon, in particular, attributed all Ireland's current political woes to the country's 'failure to cultivate a free, healthy national opinion between 1880 and 1890' and, in particular, to the Irish Party's efforts to 'stifle any attempt at its growth between 1885 and 1890'.[29]

The *United Irishman* proclaimed that the Irish Party's press was purposely trying to 'mislead the public mind' by keeping the public ignorant of the true meaning of 'home rule' ('a modification of foreign domination') as well as the true meaning of constitutional politics.[30] The latter point was one with which Arthur Griffith was particularly preoccupied. This concern had also been reflected in his sole contribution to the centenary movement of 1897–8, when together with John MacBride and John Geraghty of Glasgow (who soon became the Scottish IRB leader), he issued a manifesto from south Africa calling upon the Irish people to use the 1798 centenary as an opportunity to 'declare to the world that there is no constitution and law in our country' and to 'repudiate forever ... the sham miscalled "constitutional action"'.[31] Several of the paper's contributors emphasized the fact that 'there is no constitution in Ireland', for a constitution, by definition, is something 'founded by the people and for the people',[32] and it was argued that for any political community to refuse to accept and *act* upon this reality 'daily enfeebles the oppressed, whilst it more than in the same proportion strengthens the usurper'.[33] The *United Irishman* pointed out the fact that 'in Irish newspapers and in Irish

27 'A National Organisation', *United Irishman*, 29 April 1899.   28 *United Irishman*, 4 Mar., 11 Mar., 29 April, 6 May 1899.   29 *United Irishman*, 22 Apr. 1899 (speech of Henry Dixon at the CLS).   30 *United Irishman*, 8 Apr. 1899.   31 *Daily Nation*, 13 July 1897 (manifesto issued from South Africa, signed by Arthur Griffith, John McBride and John Geraghty). Upon his return to Glasgow, Geraghty became the Scottish IRB leader, replacing John Torley TC, the leader of the Glasgow YIL who died in November 1897, aged forty-five, from respiratory problems due to prolonged exposure to toxic chemicals in the chemical factory for which he worked.   32 John MacBride to *United Irishman*, 18 Jan. 1902.   33 *United Irishman*,

histories we often see mention made of moral force and physical force', as well
as proclamations that 'constitutional agitation' was only something 'very
vague' denoting 'continued peaceful action', and this had raised an entire
society that had 'no clear idea of what they are talking about' regarding the
nature of politics. Moral force, the paper noted, can mean nothing expect 'the
demonstration of the justice of a measure', since 'if a party can prove that its
view of a question is the correct one, it has moral force on its side'. However
as 'moral force, or demonstration, can never move an opponent to act against
his own interests', the paper noted that 'every political lever worthy of the
name is an example of physical force', irrespective of how this physical force,
or 'action', was employed. Most Irishmen's confusion over this point was seen
as proof that they had not developed 'the "brains" of a nation', not because of
'English despotism', but because of the existence of Irish Catholic elites that
feared change, were opposed to 'freedom of speech and a free press' and
desired to keep people 'in a state of complete political ignorance'. Since 'free
men supply no taxes and no soldiers for purposes over which they have no
control', the paper called upon all Irishmen to cease supporting Westminster
MPs of any kind. The paper proclaimed with certainty that 'the Irish will
always be serfs and Ireland will never be a nation' until the people received 'a
thorough political education' and accepted the reasoning of the republican
movement, for 'the principles of nationality cannot exist if the principles of
political liberty are unknown'.[34] It also quipped that the term 'advanced
nationalism' which Irish Party journalists had always used to describe the
politics of the supposed 'extreme Fenian party' made no literal sense ('nationalism cannot be any more or less advanced than nationalism') and was simply
a ploy designed to confuse the public mind and hide the fact that Westminster
MPs could not in any sense be Irish nationalists.[35]

The *United Irishman* was a forum for debate, rather than an adamantly
republican journal, and not all the enthusiasms of the paper's contributors
were inspired by republicanism. Many were also influenced greatly by the rise
of the Gaelic League and, in particular, by an 'Irish-Ireland' movement
launched by Catholic intellectuals associated with the league. This 'Irish-
Ireland' movement had several revolutionary connotations of which its
instigators were perhaps not fully aware.

The Gaelic League was a marginal, linguistic movement up until 1898,
when one of Ireland's leading Catholic intellectuals, Fr Tom Finlay SJ,
encouraged D.P. Moran, a member of the London Gaelic League, to write for
the Catholic University's *New Ireland Review* a series of articles on the
relevance of the Irish language to modern Ireland. These articles (later
published as a book entitled *The philosophy of Irish-Ireland*) would form the
inspirational basis for Moran's journalism in his paper entitled the *Leader*

29 Apr. 1899. **34** 'Political ignorance' by 'Z' (a Corkman), *United Irishman*, 3 Feb. 1900;
'What is constitutional agitation?' by 'Ollamh', *United Irishman*, 30 May 1903. **35** *United
Irishman*, 23 May 1903.

(Dublin), which was founded after the Irish Party reunited. The *Leader* was an instant great commercial success and soon influenced the journalism of other Irish newspapers in a manner comparable to the way *United Ireland* influenced its contemporaries during the early 1880s: through the sheer force of its populist rhetoric. Moran purposely distorted Douglas Hyde's rhetoric of the need to 'deanglicize' Irish culture by equating the supposed cancer of 'anglicization' not with culture but with English and even Irish Protestant monopolies over Irish business, an idea that naturally appealed greatly to the Catholic middle class and ambitious Catholic college students who supported the Irish Party. This was the reason why Moran's paper was a great commercial success and was essentially the main reason why, through the influence of his paper, the Catholic middle classes began enrolling in the Gaelic League, in both town and country. Parish priests also promoted the league, which, indeed, had been founded partly by Fr Eugene O'Growney, the professor of Irish at Maynooth College. Whilst teaching the Irish language in parish-based branches of the league, or in branches established in Catholic diocesan colleges (where most middle-class Irish Catholics had and would continue to receive their education from the 1840s until the mid twentieth century), priests championed Catholic social teaching on sexual mores, temperance, denominational education and secret societies. During the period 1899–1902, Catholic colleges also began setting up their own GAA clubs for the first time, thereby altering its previous, exclusively working-class social profile, making the clergy less suspicious of its influence and the middle classes less afraid of the risk of becoming social pariahs by joining it. The GAA had become 'respectable' for the first time, and the patronage of the Catholic middle classes allowed it to begin to prosper. By 1902, the Gaelic League's membership had risen to well over 20,000 members and its annual 'Irish Language Day' processions (held on St Patrick's Day and effectively launched by the *Leader*) became huge events. In Dublin, they frequently attracted over 25,000 people and often allowed the league to collect as much as £1,000 in a single day;[36] which was far more than the Irish Party or any political organization could possibly hope to collect at such short notice. The league also launched its own very successful newspaper, *An Claidheamh Solas* ('The Sword of Light'), which was edited by Patrick Pearse, a Catholic intellectual, lawyer and committed educationalist. Irish politicians could not ignore such a large organization for very long, and the fact that it campaigned after 1898 for local government bodies (as well as bodies such as the General Post Office and the national schools) to introduce the use of Irish meant that it was indisputably involved in politics.

Notwithstanding the fact that the 'Irish-Ireland' educational ethos of the Gaelic League was being shaped by Catholic intellectuals, some young Protestant nationalists became enthusiastic about the movement for much the

36 NAI, DMP Crime Department, Précis of Information, carton 6, 26591/s, 26819/s.

same reason as many of their Catholic counterparts. This mystery can be easily explained. The true reason why the Gaelic League became extremely popular during the post-1898 period (and would cease to be so popular once Ireland became independent) was not just its emphasis on Ireland's cultural or 'spiritual' separateness from England. Few people who joined the Gaelic League had linguistic skills. Rather many felt a deep compulsion to identify with the 'Irish-Ireland' movement because a central idea to D.P. Moran's journalism was that the entire society of nineteenth-century Ireland had been in a condition of 'slavery' due to the fact that it had been bowed down before the mysterious cultural-economic forces of 'anglicization'. In turn, this led Moran to argue that if there could ever be such a thing as 'a citizen' in Ireland, then he or she would need to develop the characteristic of a puritanical and Anglophobic figure who spoke, or professed a desire to speak, the Irish language. The appeal of the 'Irish-Ireland' movement was diverse. For priests, it could be a means of 'protecting' Irish society from secularist cultural influences, while to some intellectuals (both Catholic and Protestant) it could be a means of protesting subconsciously against the largely subsidiary nature of Irish intellectual life. For anyone with a real taste for power and politics, however, identifying with the Gaelic League was effectively a means of doing one thing only, and this was to express, consciously or unconsciously, their desire for some form of citizenship.

The origins of the 'Irish-Ireland' movement, which would be championed at all levels of the Catholic education system, undoubtedly lay in the Catholic Church's concern about the threat of anticlericalism and the presence of the new rival communal influence of local government. It is also probably not coincidental that the campaign was launched in the midst of the 1798 centenary, or that a new, intellectualist brand of Catholic fiction was created at this time by writers such as Canon P.A. Sheehan, whose most influential book *The Triumph of Failure* (1898) told the story of a young intellectual man in 1890s Dublin, the heartland of republican radicalism, who was 'led astray' from the faith by the 'false philosophies' of the time, only to finally realize 'the truth' and return to the church through reason. Fr Tom Finlay SJ was a leading light of the Catholic University during the 1890s and 1900s and continued to be so for a few decades after it was renamed as University College Dublin in 1908, when Whitehall formed the 'National University of Ireland'. As early as 1892, Finlay had joined the YIL, via Yeats' NLS, and purposely attempted to befriend or influence the IRB president John O'Leary,[37] the man whom many lesser-educated and perhaps more simply religious Catholic clergy seem to have considered as the root of all evil. Finlay would eventually succeed (albeit not until he was almost on his death-bed) in doing what no-one

---

37 NLI, Minute book of the NLS, MS 645.

thought could be done, and convert O'Leary, the stoic agnostic, to Catholicism,[38] no doubt in a suitably intellectual manner. Jesuits priests would also begin targeting James Connolly during the 1900s, challenging him to answer their interpretation of socialism in public debate. Connolly essentially did not succeed in meeting the challenge and so wrote a pamphlet to attempt to vindicate his arguments after the event.[39]

The Catholic bishops essentially developed the same idea at the time of the IRB's success in stage-managing the 1798 centenary as John O'Leary had fifteen years earlier, namely that Ireland's *political* future would be determined not by events at Westminster but by how this mostly pre-political and peasant society could be educated. The old tactic of asking lesser clergy to denounce the GAA, the YIS and other such bodies from the altar when they came under republicans' influence, or denouncing republicans as 'physical force men', was deemed as too risky or no longer sufficient, due to rising levels of education in the country and the potential role of local government in depriving priests of communal authority. Something intellectually coherent was needed. Consequently, it was decided to bring the full weight of the Catholic education system to bear and attempt to subsume republicans' longstanding work in spreading their principles by promoting a scheme of self-education through the medium of the church's own 'Irish-Ireland' movement, which would target the same social channels as had been used by republicans. Not until 1898 did the church feel this was opportune and the church could essentially not lose this struggle, due to its huge social and educational influence. In a few years, the Irish-Ireland movement would revolutionize, or rather grossly simplify, popular understanding in Ireland of what citizenship could, or did, mean, and in the process effectively ensure that a republican politics could not very well be revived in Ireland. Not surprisingly, these trends first began to influence nationalists' propaganda in London, which was generally the centre of Irish literary life under the Union because virtually all publishers, writers and civil servants had to move there to find work.

In January 1899, Mark Ryan formed the 'Irish National Club' in London, which, over the next ten years, would become the progenitor of all political, social and 'educational' clubs patronised by London-Irish separatists.[40] Many members of the London Gaelic League (from which D.P. Moran emerged) were closely associated with this club, which was also attended by Jesuit priests, who soon tried to befriend and indeed exercised a strong influence upon Mark Ryan.[41] The influence of the 'Irish-Ireland' movement within the London Gaelic League spread to Dublin during 1900, due to William Rooney's role in bringing the CLS and Gaelic League in Dublin into closer harmony. Rooney encouraged many London Gaelic Leaguers to write

---

38 *Gaelic American*, 26 Mar. 1907 (obituary).   39 James Connolly, *Labour, nationality and religion* (Dublin, 1910).   40 *United Irishman*, 1 July 1899; Ryan, *Fenian memories*, 190–200. 41 Ryan, *Fenian memories* (introduction by T.F. O'Sullivan).

columns for the *United Irishman*. Simultaneously, he gave CLS lectures claiming that the Irish people had clearly 'reached that height of intelligence when the greater section of our people believes that the created legislature of a foreign parliament cannot, by any chance, give us an Irish nation, in spite of all the ecstatics of the newspapers', but noted that 'these beliefs *I have chosen to denominate* [my italics] as Gaelicism.'[42] As the 'Irish-Ireland' movement spread, the republicanism of the *United Irishman* generally become less pronounced. Several articles written for the paper by London Gaelic Leaguers such as 'Sean Ghall' with *apparently* republican titles, such as 'Civic Debauchery' and 'The Duties of Patriotism', were actually nothing more than an reiteration of D.P. Moran's arguments. The growth of the 'Irish-Ireland' movement would soon have a very negative effect on the IRB's efforts to recruit members in several parts of the country, particularly in Cork and Belfast, despite the fact that republican activism generally increased in the country in the wake of the outbreak of the Boer War.

The Irish 'pro-Boer' movement began as early as June of 1899, once it became clear that Britain was going to invade the Boer Republic. The first bodies to support the launch of a pro-Boer movement were Mark Ryan's recently established 'Irish National Club' in London, James Connolly's ISRP and the 'Irish-Transvaal Committee', which was supported by the CLS and the Dublin '98 clubs and had some friends within the Transvaal itself, due to Arthur Griffith's former residency in South Africa.[43] John O'Leary was chosen as the president of the Irish-Transvaal Committee. When the war actually broke out in October 1899, some Irish Party MPs spoke against Britain's invasion of the Boer Republic in the House of Commons, three Irish Party members (William Redmond, T.D. Sullivan and Patrick O'Brien) made a subscription to the Irish-Transvaal Committee, but none except Michael Davitt (a somewhat reluctant Dillonite MP since 1892) was willing to take this protest as far as resigning their seat in the House of Commons. Immediately upon the outbreak of the war, resolutions of sympathy with the Boers were passed by six of the thirty-two county councils in Ireland (Limerick, Kilkenny, Mayo, Kings County, Sligo and Cork) and about two dozen urban and district councils, town commissions and board of guardians (mostly in the counties Monaghan, Tipperary, Clare and Galway), but the Irish Party leaders and 'the majority of the parliamentary party' were opposed to this campaign, fearing it would give a hand to the republicans.[44]

The Boer War made it more difficult for the Irish Party to maintain its former public image as a nationalist party, and this problem was created not

42 Seamus McManus (ed.), *Prose writings of William Rooney* (Dublin, 1909), 106–8. McManus was an academic at Notre Dame University at the time. 43 NAI, DMP files, carton 14, reports 5313 and 5339, Ass. Comm. Mallon, 21 Aug, 28 Sept. 1899. Griffith had acquired his first experience of being a newspaper editor while in South Africa. P.A. McCracken, 'Arthur Griffith's South African sabbatical' (1996). 44 PRO (London) 30/60/28, Gerald Balfour Papers, Inspector General of RIC to Under Secretary, 6 Jan. 1900.

least because of the fall–out from the defeat of the 'home rule bill' of 1893 by the House of Lords. Unlike any government, the authority of the House of Lords could never be questioned or challenged in the name of mere party politics. For this reason, the entire Irish Party had to emphasize repeatedly their complete loyalty to the British crown from October 1893 onwards whenever they were requested to do so by the two other British political parties. The republicans' pro–Boer campaign helped to highlight this fact, for the Irish Party had to respond to the pro–Boer campaign by disowning most of the nationalist enthusiasm in the country and trying (unsuccessfully) to persuade the UIL to side with it in expressing support for the British government, as it celebrated the bravery of Irish soldiers within the British army or organized regular royal visits to Ireland. Dublin Castle believed that the Irish Party and its supporters were 'not, at heart, anxious for the defeat of the British army' in the Transvaal and that it was 'solely in the revolutionary or secret organizations that any real effect of pro–Boer feeling is to be found'.[45] However, even figures who felt opposed to the republicans' pro–Boer campaign, such as T.W. Rolleston, believed that the Irish Party was being led to adopt a stance regarding Ireland's relationship with the empire that most young and educated figures in 'Catholic and nationalistic Ireland' found impossible to identify with:

> They don't understand a party which talks sedition in Ireland and America and takes the oath of allegiance in Westminster – which abuses the British Army and at the same time makes violent scenes in the House because Irish soldiers in it are not allowed to wear the shamrock – which denounces England's piratical wars and then tells her that Ireland will supply soldiers for them if only home rule is granted to her. This sort of thing disgusts them.[46]

The *United Irishman* certainly professed to believe that the Irish Party's now very evident monarchist and imperialist leanings were causing them to play 'a losing game': 'they have sat on two stools for twenty years. We are compelling them to choose one.'[47] The reality of the situation, however, was that the political credibility of the Irish Party in Ireland no longer rested on any of its claims to be an Irish nationalist party, but rather on its promise to pressurize the government into introducing reform legislation for the benefit of Catholic elites or the rural middle class.

The Boer War was the first prolonged war in which Britain was involved since the Sudanese war of the early 1880s and, consequently, Irish revolution-aries began to consider how they might take advantage of this situation. In America, O'Neill Ryan entered into communications with the Dutch and

45 Ibid.   46 C.H. Rolleston, *Portrait of an Irishman: a biographical sketch of T.W. Rolleston* (1939), 117–21.   47 *United Irishman*, 20 May, 20 June, 18 July and 25 July 1903.

Russian embassies, while Devoy and the UB were determined to give direct assistance to the Boers, but faced two problems: the restrictions of the American neutrality laws and the fact 'we knew that there were many British spies in the organization who would reveal what we were doing and enable the British government to take prompt measures to stop us'.[48] Indeed, in November 1899 John Merna, together with John Nolan, left Dublin for the United States and persuaded the former UB leader, Luke Dillon, to take part in a desperate enterprise. In the spring of 1900, Nolan and Dillon left for Canada and made a failed attempt to blow up Welland Canal Dock in Ontario, ostensibly to prevent Canadian ships bringing supplies to the British troops in southern Africa. Very shortly afterwards, Nolan and Dillon were arrested, put on trial for the outrage, convicted and sentenced to life imprisonment in Canada.[49] Both Nolan and Dillon were no doubt fully intent on committing this outrage (both of them had planted bombs in the past), but a surviving report by the Chief Commissioner of the DMP proves that the British secret service was behind the plot.[50] John Merna was subsequently assassinated by the Clan, which also discovered (albeit not until the agent's death in 1912) that one of Dillon's deputies in Philadelphia was in the pay of the British secret service;[51] a further indication of how easily British intelligence could manipulate the American organization.

Dublin Castle heard regular rumours that the IRB sought to import arms after the outbreak of the Boer War. The principal suspects believed to be involved were Joseph MacBride, who was in charge of Westport Harbour Board (and the founder of the Gaelic League in Castlebar), members of the 'Edward Duffy National Club'[52] in Castlerea, a team of Tipperary railway workers and Robert Johnston in Belfast.[53] In January 1900, after unveiling a memorial to P.W. Nally in Balla, Co. Mayo (the erection of which was previously forbidden by the Grand Jury, but was now allowed by the new Mayo county council), Mark Ryan of London and most Connacht IRB leaders (some of whom had formerly supported the INB experiment) held a secret meeting in Thomas Ryan's hotel in Claremorris and, according to an informer present, talked quite seriously about insurrectionary plans. This prompted Dublin Castle to ask the Royal Navy to place a gunboat in Clew Bay as a precaution to prevent the importation of arms.[54] In subsequent months, however, except for a few firearms 'surreptitiously brought in one-by-one from England by migratory pedlars' into north Leinster and south Ulster, little or no weapons

48 John Devoy, 'The story of Clan na Gael', *Gaelic American*, 6 June 1925. 49 Brannigan, 'The Luke Dillon case and the Welland Canal explosion of 1900', 36–44. 50 PRO 30/60/28, Gerald Balfour papers, Report of Chief Comm. J.J. Jones to Under Secretary, 9 Jan. 1900; NAI, DMP files, carton 7 (packet for 1900), report 5527, J.J. Jones, 28 March 1900; NAI, CBS files, Home Office précis, carton 3, 25520/s. 51 Sean Cronin, *The McGarrity papers* (1972), 34–5. 52 Edward Duffy was the founder of the IRB in Connacht during the mid 1860s, but died in prison in 1868 aged just twenty-five. 53 NAI, CBS files, Home Office précis, carton 2, 20989/s, 21270/s, 21614/s, carton 3, 23860/s, 24032/s. 54 PRO 30/60/28, Gerald Balfour papers, Report of Sir David Harrel to Lord Lieutenant, 11 Jan. 1900.

appear to have been imported, partly because nationalists were aware that agents of Dublin Castle were watching all the ports.[55] As it was in no situation to prepare for a rebellion and had very limited funds, the IRB reacted to the Boer War merely by distributing small batches of arms (to provide new recruits with instructions in loading and firing) and in the meantime engaged in a good deal of 'treasonable talk' as well as the 'wholesale dissemination of seditious literature', principally in an effort to dissuade Irishmen from enlisting in the British army.[56] With financial help from Maud Gonne, as many as 40,000 circulars were printed in Dublin during 1900 which proclaimed that enlisting in the British army was 'an act of treason to Ireland'. Many of these circulars were distributed in the country by IRB activists, but Dublin Castle was equally active in seizing this seditious literature. In many parts of the country, this anti-enlistment campaign was not successful, but it was undoubtedly helped by the fact that it won support from some of the clergy (most notably from Fr Kavanagh, who proclaimed the Boer War to be an 'unjust war' according to the teachings of the Catholic Church) and because fears of conscription existed in Ireland during the spring of 1900.[57]

The most pivotal factor in determining the course of Irish revolutionary politics at this time, and the reason why some began looking to the wealthy, eccentric and politically suspect figure of Maud Gonne for support, was the fact that most revolutionaries literally had 'not two-and-sixpence in the world to spare'. For example, in Dublin, Arthur Griffith (who, at this time, wore threadbare clothes and lived in a small tenement flat off Capel Street) was unable to save his destitute father from the shame of having to enter the workhouse, where he probably died, while in Cork, the ISRP could only advertise for protest meetings by writing with chalk on the city pavements.[58] Meanwhile the IRB was facing great difficulty in collecting subscriptions from its generally poor 'rank and file'. To help solve this problem, Devoy and the UB tried to get in contact with the Transvaal government to secure funds. This venture was thwarted, however, owing to the fact that F.H. O'Donnell, an eccentric but gifted former MP and a member of the London INA, had already contacted the Boers and acquired a good deal of funding to launch a pro-Boer campaign.[59] Most of this money was handed over to Mark Ryan, the leader of the London INA who also had some political friends in South Africa. Meanwhile in Paris, Maud Gonne used the political contacts of her lover, Lucien Millevoye, the leader of the 'League of Patriots' (a small right-wing French nationalist organization made up of 'the dregs of the Boulangist movement' of the late 1880s), to acquire extra funding for the Irish pro-Boer

55 NAI, CBS files, Home Office précis, carton 3, 24032/s, 24149/s, 24517/s (Jan-Apr. 1901). **56** NAI, DMP files, carton 7, Report 5504, Chief Comm. Jones, 2 Mar. 1900. **57** NAI, CBS files, Home Office précis, carton 2, 19132/s, 19650/s, 19740/s, 21614/s, 23671/s; carton 3, 24517/s. **58** NAI, DMP files, carton 14, report 5391, J.J. Jones, 15 Nov. 1899; NAI, CBS files, Home Office précis, carton 3, 22520/s (Sept 1901). **59** John Devoy, 'The story of Clan na Gael', *Gaelic American*, 13 June 1925.

movement.[60] As a result of these developments, by the summer of 1900, Ryan and Gonne virtually became the paymasters of all Irish separatist activities. One major consequence of this was that the *United Irishman* editors, Griffith and Rooney, believing that the UB and IRB had been 'too stingy' in their past financial support,[61] approached Ryan and Gonne to fund their paper, which they did. As Ryan officially held no rank in the IRB, and Gonne was not a member at all (not surprisingly, women were never allowed to become one of the 'brothers'), neither John Devoy in New York nor Fred Allan in Dublin were in a position to direct Irish revolutionary activities at this time, and this would generally continue to be the situation up until Ryan's Boer funding ran out during the summer of 1902.

In February 1900, while the Irish Party was nominally being reunited under John Redmond's leadership, Mark Ryan proposed that John MacBride be put forward for a South Mayo parliamentary by-election. The fact that MacBride was fighting as a rebel commando with the Boers was a major propaganda boost to the Irish pro-Boer movement, and the idea to nominate him (which was supported by O'Leary, the *United Irishman* and the Mayo IRB) was intended simply to make a protest against British rule.[62] However, due to lack of funds and the fact that MacBride was almost a complete political unknown who could do nothing for Mayo's interests he polled very badly, his only support coming from the Castlebar area, where his brother was a town commissioner. The *United Irishman* claimed to have expected this result,[63] but it was probably a big disappointment to all concerned. In the same month, the new lord mayor of Dublin, Thomas Pile, dismissed John Clancy as the city's sub-sheriff; an action that disappointed Dublin republicans who desired to have some men to represent their interests in City Hall.[64] The loss of Clancy was ameliorated to some degree by the simultaneous appointment of Fred Allan as the mayor's personal secretary, a development that was welcomed greatly by John Daly and Patrick Hoctor.[65] In early March 1900, however, it was announced in London that Queen Victoria was going to visit Dublin the following month and Pile immediately declared his intention to organise large welcoming celebrations. This placed Fred Allan in a very awkward position and so he consulted O'Leary and the IRB leadership as to whether or not he should immediately resign from his post, in protest.[66] The attitude of John O'Leary, as the IRB's president, towards the forthcoming visit of the queen was simply that he hoped 'the Irish people will look upon any future visit of her Britannic Majesty to this country with the same profound indifference with which they have regarded all her previous ones'.[67] He did not believe, however, that there was any need for protests or that the queen's visit was of

60 Ibid., 8 Sept. 1924. 61 Ibid. 62 *United Irishman*, 17 and 24 Feb. 1900; Mark Ryan to *United Irishman*, 5 May 1900. 63 *United Irishman*, 3 Mar. 1900. 64 NAI, DMP files, carton 7, Report 5521, Chief Comm. Jones, 20 Mar. 1900. 65 NAI, CBS files, Home Office précis, carton 2, 21270/s. 66 Lyons, *Recollections of Griffith*, 28. 67 *United Irishman*, 17 Mar. 1900.

any political significance. James Connolly and Arthur Griffith felt differently, however, and both men were also currently receiving funding from Maud Gonne. G.A. Lyons recalled that, four months earlier, Griffith had called on O'Leary, 'whose lightest word silenced opposition in those days', seeking his approval for an aggressive street protest demonstration that James Connolly was planning against a visit of Joseph Chamberlain to Dublin. O'Leary was opposed to the idea (just as was Robert Johnston) on the grounds that it would probably erupt into needless violence, which it did, but Griffith went ahead and supported Connolly's plans anyway.[68] This time around, Griffith did not call upon O'Leary but instead upon James Egan, the corporation's official 'sword-bearer' (a well-paid, but purely ceremonial role) since September 1898, and asked him to protest publicly against the mayor's decision to welcome the queen. As Egan, like Griffith, held no senior rank in the IRB, he wanted to know what Fred Allan was going to do first but Griffith told him to 'never mind anyone but yourself.'[69]

O'Leary and a slight majority of the IRB leadership decided that there was no need for Allan to resign, and it is very probable that Allan himself desired to remain in City Hall, partly because if he (the president of the WTMC) left the corporation, the future of the Wolfe Tone monument project would be hopeless. Following his municipal duties, Allan did whatever Pile asked him to do in preparing celebrations for the queen's visit and stood silently by the mayor on the platform when the queen was received. Egan, however, was persuaded to issue a protest statement (which was actually written by Griffith) to the national press announcing his unwillingness to take part in any event in honour of 'that aged lady'. Meanwhile, during the queen's visit, Griffith publicly horsewhipped a newspaper editor for supposedly slandering Maud Gonne, published bitter *United Irishman* editorials against the 'Famine Queen' (as the histrionic figure of Gonne was calling Victoria) and took part in ISRP-organized street brawls with the police, in the process putting two policemen in hospital. As a result, Griffith was arrested twice during the queen's visit and his newspaper was prosecuted.[70] Many republicans wrote to the *United Irishman* praising Egan for his actions, without mentioning or perhaps even noticing Allan's involvement in the event. Griffith himself, however, effectively blacklisted Allan by listing his name in an article ('which we request our readers to carefully preserve') alongside a host of political figures who attended the royalist demonstration and whom the paper demanded should be boycotted in the future.[71] According to G.A. Lyons, thereafter Egan in particular was so 'covered with glory' (he was granted the freedom of Limerick by John Daly) and Allan was 'covered with such odium' in Dublin republican circles that the latter 'never quite forgave Griffith's interference' once he 'learned the secret story of the case.'[72]

68 Lyons, *Recollections of Griffith*, 16–26. 69 Ibid., 29. 70 NAI, DMP files, carton 7 (packet for 1900), reports 5535–6 and 5548–9, 1–3 and 12 Apr. 1900; *United Irishman*, 7, 14 and 21 Apr. 1900. 71 *United Irishman*, 14 Apr. 1900. 72 Lyons, *Recollections of Griffith*, 30.

It is tempting to conclude that Griffith was seeking to oust Allan from his position as the leader of the republican movement in Dublin and assume this position for himself, but it is more likely that his actions were dictated by the fact that he was being funded by Mark Ryan and particularly by Maud Gonne. The fact that James Connolly was also entirely dependent financially upon their London circle may well have influenced his actions as well. While forming the ISRP in the autumn of 1896, Connolly argued in the *Shan Van Vocht* that 'it is not republicanism, but the counsel of insurrectionary effort to realise republicanism' that the Irish public was not prepared to accept.[73] Holding this belief, in the midst of the 'Wolfe Tone Day' celebrations in August 1898, with Gonne's financial support, Connolly formed his *Workers' Republic* newspaper, which republished some French republican literature that was socialist and anti-clerical in tone, and called for the creation of a socialist-republican party in Westminster. Although Fred Allan had helped found the 'May Day' tradition in Dublin and contributed to various British socialist publications during the mid 1890s,[74] Connolly did not approve of how Allan ran the 1798 Centenary Committee, and Gonne, who knew little and understood less of Irish revolutionary affairs, was aware that she was not supposed to like Allan either, due to her exposure to the gossip of the London INA. During the mid 1890s, Allan resolved to 'give up replying to newspaper criticisms' after his attempts to reply to the criticisms of the *Irish Republic* only helped to undermine his secret efforts to reorganize the IRB, particularly by alienating Mark Ryan's London party. Allan did not attempt to vindicate himself during the queen's visit affair partly for this reason, but also for personal reasons that he had made clear previously, when he responded to criticisms from James Connolly.

During the late 1890s, Allan was the treasurer of the Irish Journalists' Association, the national trade union for Irish journalists, and for this reason, Connolly's *Workers' Republic* denounced Allan in both 1898 and 1899 for allowing a toast to be made to the queen at the association's annual dinner. During 1898, in response to this criticism, Allan merely spoke with members of the Cork ISRP about the matter,[75] but after Connolly interrupted the June 1899 Bodenstown demonstration to heckle Allan personally on the same account, Allan felt it necessary to write to the *Workers' Republic* to defend both himself and the Journalists Association. With regards to the latter body, Allan noted that it was 'composed of all creeds and political sections, I am glad to say; otherwise it would be of very little practical use to journalism.' The association recognized that 'as long as the majority think it right to honour the toast of "the Queen", they are perfectly entitled to do so, just as the minority are entitled to refuse to honour it', and the existence of this ruling 'is no excuse for an Irish journalist [Connolly] for refusing to join an association which is the

---

73 James Connolly to *Shan Van Vocht*, November 1896. 74 NAI, British in Ireland microfilm, C.O.904/17/1. 75 *Workers Republic*, 13 Aug. 1898, 6 June 1899.

trade union of journalism', for in so doing, he was effectively acting as a 'blackleg', or an enemy of trade unionism among journalists. Connolly, unlike P.T. Daly (one of Allan's deputies, who had been a compositor with both the *Workers Republic'* and the *Daily Independent*), was not a member either of the Dublin printers' union. Allan argued that if the ISRP 'had taken the trouble to make the smallest enquiry', they would have known that at these events, just as at all press events he had attended over the past twenty years, he had never taken part in toasts to the queen when they were proposed. This was a form of 'silent protest' that he had always adopted in Ireland, as well as at Journalist Association events in England. He had enlisted support for the Irish repub- lican movement from 'a well-known English republican' in the Journalist Association by doing so, and 'why should an Irish republican attack me under precisely the same circumstances?'[76] Since 1885, the IRB had engaged in many such 'silent protests', essentially fearing a political backlash, but the crux of the matter, so far as Connolly and Griffith were concerned, was that the day of silent protests should be long over, particularly when the pro-Boer movement was such a major concern. Connolly, who also denounced Michael Davitt as a sham socialist at this time owing to his closeness to the Irish Party,[77] argued that Allan had a 'duty to *publicly* [my italics] reprove his trade union and disso- ciate himself from its acts when it strayed from the path of trade unionism to become the mouthpiece of flunkeyism', and he concluded his attack by arguing that:

> The nationalist principles (?) of Mr. Allan may be of secondary impor- tance to the harmony of a dinner party, but the revolutionary principles of the working-class democracy are to them a matter of life and death. We will in the future, as in the past, do our utmost to banish from public life every so called nationalist who takes part, or allows himself to be represented as taking part, in any function where colour is given to the idea that Ireland has relinquished the struggle for a real republican freedom.[78]

That many young republicans felt the same way is indicated by the fact that Allan was not re-elected as the leader of the Wolfe Tone Clubs in June 1900 and, as a result, he lost most of his influence in the Dublin republican movement. Following Griffith's and Connolly's lead instead, the new young Dublin 'rank and file' were preoccupied for most of that summer with working with the Irish-Transvaal Committee and the *United Irishman* in trying to prevent the UIL from being established in Dublin city. This activity was given some passive support by former members of the Irish National Amnesty Association, which formally disbanded in November 1899 because it had

---

76 Allan to *Workers Republic*, 1 July 1899.   77 *Workers Republic*, 2 Sept., 7 Oct. 1899.
78 Connolly's reply to Allan's letter, *Workers Republic*, 1 July 1899.

practically no reason to exist since September 1898, when the last significant political prisoner, Tom Clarke (by now a promoter of the WTMC), was released.[79]

In June 1900, the UIL set-up a central executive in Dublin for the first time and officially declared itself as the supporting body of the Irish Party. As did the National League of the 1880s, it granted the Catholic hierarchy the right to be *ex-officio* members of the executive, in the process giving the church the ability to veto any choice of Irish Party candidate of which they did not approve. This guaranteed that the Irish Party would continue to act as the Catholic party in British politics. In August 1900, the Transvaal Committee, several Dublin '98 clubs and the ISRP successfully broke up a meeting in the Rotunda that was supposed to inaugurate the UIL in Dublin. They also gathered a crowd of about 2,000 people to break up (what was intended to be) a monster meeting of the UIL in the Phoenix Park. This 'monster meeting' attracted only 6,000 people and thus the DMP felt that the pro-Boer party came off far better for the event.[80] Not until that winter did the UIL succeed in establishing itself in Dublin, and this was actually done by winning over John Clancy, by now a city councillor for Clontarf. Earlier that year, Clancy had mounted a propaganda campaign against Mayor Pile (for dismissing him) and was understood to be opposed to the queen's visit. In September, together with Maud Gonne and Griffith, he supported efforts by the Transvaal Committee and the Dublin '98 clubs to have Tom Clarke appointed to a junior clerical position in the corporation. A large meeting in the Phoenix Park was even held to muster support for Clarke's candidacy, but he failed to secure the post, prompting young republicans of the CLS to take over City Hall for thirty minutes once the election results were announced, shouting abuse at the councillors and cheering for the establishment of an Irish republic, before the mayor finally called the police to disperse the protesters.[81] In early November, again with the support of the Transvaal Committee, Clancy attempted, in vain, to get City Hall to confer the freedom of Dublin upon the president of the Boer Republic.[82] Once this failed, however, Clancy, probably acting on the advice of J.P. Nannetti (who shocked his old republican associates by joining the Irish Party and standing, successfully, for Dublin's College Green Division in October 1900), began to identify openly with the UIL. Thereafter Nannetti and Clancy helped ensure that the UIL became established in Dublin by making it supportive of a policy of removing the loyalists from the corporation, so scenes like the last royal visit would not occur again.[83] The fact that this was deemed necessary demonstrates that, although they created a

79 NAI, DMP files, carton 14, Report 5413, Chief Commissioner Jones, 1 Dec. 1899. 80 NAI, DMP Crime Dept, Précis of Information, carton 6, report 23203/s, Ass Comm Mallon, 7 Nov. 1900 (summary Aug-Oct). 81 NAI, DMP files, carton 7, Report 5686, Chief Comm. Jones, 2 Oct. 1900. 82 NAI, DMP précis of information, carton 6, Chief Comm. Jones, 5 Dec. 1900. 83 NAI, CBS files, Home Office précis, carton 3, 23504/s, C.C. Jones, 5 Dec. 1900.

spectacle, the royal visits did not have much popular approval in Dublin. Griffith, however, was not satisfied with the Dublin UIL's professed opposition to the visits. At the time, the IRB was still committed to building up a new republican movement around the basis of the centenary clubs. Griffith, however, now called for a new movement that would commit itself primarily to removing all 'flunkeys' from Irish municipal politics and started to ignore the centenary clubs.[84]

On 30 September 1900, a 'new organization' was tentatively established at a meeting in the CLS rooms that was chaired by James Egan, the hero of the hour. This was attended by only about two dozen members of the Dublin '98 clubs and some members of the CLS and Transvaal Committee. On this occasion, the CLS officially launched a body called 'Cumann na Gaedhael' (Confederation of the Gaels) and a non-elective 'provisional executive' was appointed, led by Griffith.[85] Neither Fred Allan nor any other IRB leader was invited to or present at this meeting, and Connolly (who now accused Griffith of attempting to claim the credit for all the protest demonstrations that the ISRP had organized) was not informed of the gathering either. A few days afterwards, a women's nationalist organization, the Daughters of Erin, was established at the CLS rooms under the leadership of Maud Gonne, Mrs James Egan and Mrs J.W. Power. Both organizations (which were no doubt funded by Ryan and Gonne in London, where the Gaelic League had become very popular) expressed total support for promoting the Irish language and all other aspects of the 'Irish-Ireland' movement. At the first convention of Cumann na Gaedhael (which ended in a 'ceidhli' with members of the two organizations), an official executive for the association was elected. Griffith failed to be elected, but William Rooney and Peter White of the CLS (his closest friends since the late 1880s) were elected as treasurer and secretary respectively, while James Egan was made vice-president. The remainder of the executive, John O'Leary (president), John MacBride, Robert Johnston and Fr Kavanagh (vice-presidents), were elected *in absentia*, and all owed their positions solely to their prominence in the pro–Boer agitation.[86] Fr Kavanagh subsequently wrote to the *United Irishman* in support of Cumann na Gaedhael, but stressed that the new movement must not be allowed to fall under the influence of men with 'unCatholic doctrines.'[87] Apart from giving perpetual support to the pro–Boer campaign, Cumann na Gaedhael expressed a desire to achieve political influence over all the local government boards in Ireland, particularly Dublin City Hall. Cumann na Gaedhael, however, was nothing more than another confederation of literary societies along the lines of the YIL and INA, both of which it effectively replaced, and thus it could not actively pursue this policy. Its plan to establish an executive council of the association (with 20 elected and 21 nominated members) also could not be

84 *United Irishman*, 4 and 21 Aug. 1900. 85 *United Irishman*, 6 Oct. 1900. 86 *United Irishman*, 1 Dec. 1900. 87 *United Irishman*, 23 Feb. 1901.

accomplished, for the various societies which expressed a desire to affiliate themselves with the association were totally isolated from each other. Their only real link was that they read the *United Irishman* or the *Leader* and identified with the ideals of the 'Irish-Ireland' movement.

Cumann na Gaedhael was not the 'national republican association' that was originally envisioned by the IRB during 1899. That was supposed to be based around the 1798 centenary clubs, of which there were many in Ireland and none in London, as Yeats' and Gonne's '1798 Centennial Association of Great Britain and France' (which was really just the London and Paris Irish Literary Societies) had disbanded. Instead Cumann na Gaedhael was the product of the London INA. Probably for this reason, or else just because of the rise of Irish-Irelandism, the *United Irishman* began criticizing various IRB activists in Ireland. In May 1900, T.B. Kelly, the aging Connacht IRB leader and the leader of several Mayo centenary clubs (which he had kept alive through the Ballina GAA), was accused of being a 'sham patriot' in the *United Irishman* for not having read in Irish at a 1798 commemorative event; a fact that naturally annoyed Kelly, who replied that 'Gaelic is not taught in this district' and that he and his followers had been promoting republican political beliefs 'since long before the editor of the *United Irishman* was born' and 'we will not now stand criticism, unjustly at least.'[88] However, two much younger activists in west Mayo, Joseph MacBride and Frank Dorr (a commercial traveller), were promoting the Gaelic League and, with financial support from Mark Ryan, soon began forming branches of Cumann na Gaedhael. The GAA president, Francis Dineen, had also expressed his support for Cumann na Gaedhael and the Gaelic League. Both MacBride and Dorr would soon be elected members of the executive of the GAA and Cumann na Gaedhael, while MacBride was also on the 'Oireachtas' of the Gaelic League. Consequently, T.B. Kelly completely lost his influence with the younger men and he soon gave up political activity altogether. Several IRB-led branches of YIS in Munster, such as Maurice Moynihan's branch in Tralee, John O'Keeffe's branch in Cork and John Daly's branch in Limerick, chose to affiliate with Cumann na Gaedhael, but they soon found themselves unable to adapt to its ethos. In October 1900, Moynihan took part in a parliamentary election campaign (as IRB men were allowed to do) in support of Thomas O'Donnell, a young Gaelic Leaguer and teacher who identified with the Irish-Ireland movement, but he was denounced by the *United Irishman* for doing so, as this was supposedly against the constitution of Cumann na Gaedhael (no such constitution existed). Moynihan, who was the leader of several small 1798 clubs in the Tralee and Listowel district, responded to criticism by noting that, while neither he nor his (IRB) followers supported the Irish Party or the UIL, they believed that 'if we have to have people inclined that way', it was as well using their influence to prevent Irish political representation being confined to men who had

---

88 Kelly to *United Irishman*, 12 May 1900.

entered politics only at the request of 'all the priests of the constituency and nearly all the people who have substantial balances in their banks.'[89] Moynihan's influence was waning, however, and when he lost his position as a Kerry GAA leader to a puritanical Irish Irelander journalist, some *United Irishman* contributors actually described this as having 'routed the forces of West-Britonism and miniòns of alien rule from the Gaelic ranks.'[90] John O'Leary, the nominal president of Cumann na Gaedhael, was also denounced by the *United Irishman*. This was because of his close association with the Protestant patriot T.W. Rolleston, who supported Horace Plunkett's co-operative movement, was a critic of the narrow-mindedness of aspects of the Irish-Ireland movement (he had left the London INA) and also opposed the excesses of the pro-Boer campaign on the grounds that it would alienate Ulster Protestants. At the time, O'Leary was working with a research team (which included Arthur Conan Doyle, the author of the Sherlock Holmes stories) in the British Library, London for Rolleston's anthology of Anglo-Irish literature – the first such work of its kind – and he was irritated by these criticisms, stating that he 'did not at all like' the intolerant attitudes now being championed by the paper, and defended Rolleston, 'who had served Irish literature well'.[91] What O'Leary did not realize, however, was that Rolleston was now championing the wrong literature, and belonged to the wrong political community in Ireland, as far as most young 'Irish-Irelanders' were concerned, who were writing columns for the *United Irishman* with titles such as 'Is an Anglo-Irish literature possible?'

During 1899–1900 IRB veterans in Munster such as P.N. Fitzgerald, John Daly and John O'Keeffe tried to persuade the Trade and Labour Association to oppose the UIL by calling upon the nationalist youth in Clare, Tipperary and Cork to join the 'Gaelic associations', rather than the UIL; a policy that generally succeeded because the local UIL's only concern was with the ongoing rivalries between the old Redmondite and Healyite factions in City Hall.[92] Fitzgerald did not know the Irish language and evidently did not desire to learn it, but his right-hand man in Cork city, O'Keeffe (who now began calling himself 'Séan') formed a new *partly* Irish-speaking branch of the YIS and managed to get himself elected as a leader of the Cork GAA. O'Keeffe's bodies expressed support for Cumann na Gaedhael and both he and Fitzgerald attempted to form new IRB circles of young men around this basis. However once Fitzgerald and O'Keeffe told their prospective new following they must not allow themselves to be influenced by 'the old enemies, the priests and the police' and that they should learn to use firearms, the young 'Irish-Irelander' members of the Cork YIS, who had nothing against priests nor any desire to use firearms, all resigned. Some, following the wishes of Fr Kavanagh, even informed the police of what Fitzgerald and O'Keeffe were

89 Moynihan to *United Irishman*, 28 Oct. 1900.   90 *United Irishman*, 11 Apr. 1903.
91 O'Leary to *United Irishman*, 9 Feb. 1901.   92 NAI, CBS files, Home Office précis, carton 2, 23367/s, carton 3, 23768/s.

doing.[93] Two members of the Cork Gaelic League, Liam de Róiste (William Roche) and T. MacSuibhne (Terence McSwiney), thereafter formed a breakaway society from the Cork YIS, the Cork Celtic Literary Society (CLS), elected Fr Kavanagh as their president, declared themselves as 'believers in the principles of Tone and Davis' and denounced the republicans as 'effete'.[94] Roche and McSwiney, however, took no part in politics, revolutionary or otherwise. They were both puritanical Catholic middle-class figures whose revolutionary enthusiasm was shaped purely by their identification with the narrow 'Irish-Ireland' ideal of citizenship; hence their contempt for men who had not been educated in 'Gaelicism' and belonged to that far from puritan class of publicans and commercial travellers who they believed were the very bedrock of Ireland's moral or spiritual 'slavery'.[95]

A comparable development occurred in Belfast. During 1900, the seventeen-year-old Denis McCullough was sworn into the IRB by his own father, Daniel, a west-Belfast publican and former Belfast IRB leader, who had been involved in numerous rough-and-tumble political quarrels over the past fifteen years shaped by failed arms importation efforts, Special Branch intrigues and conflicts with the priests arising from the Parnell Split and the struggle for control of the 1798 centenary movement. Once he became a 'brother', however, Denis, a young idealistic member of the Gaelic League, was bitterly disappointed at the sort of men he found in the organization, as they were invariably middle-aged figures debating Irish politics in public houses. This was not the 'Irish-Ireland' he so desperately wanted to find, and so, disillusioned, he ran home to his mother and cried.[96] Within Robert Johnston's 'Pioneer Branch' of Cumann na Gaedhael (a teetotaller branch financed by Mark Ryan), however, he would soon meet the talented figure of Bulmer Hobson, a young Quaker and friend of Alice Milligan who was involved in the Gaelic League, the GAA and the 'Protestant National Association'. Like McSwiney, Hobson was a literary contributor to the *United Irishman* and had ambitions to form a new theatre group. Eventually, McCullough would swear Hobson into the IRB and together they tried to reorganize the movement on a completely different basis, keeping only the company of their own young friends. Neither man realized that they technically belonged to an organization that had formerly been involved in arms importation efforts, or that the IRB had any firearms at all. This was not a concern, however, for their mutual object was to become effective propagandists for Cumann na Gaedhael.

The IRB's plan to capitalize upon the existence of the nationalist literary societies affiliated with the YIL or the INA had always faced problems. As W.P. Ryan, an influential Tipperary-born London journalist, noted, most Irish

93 Ibid., 22189/s (June 1900). 94 *United Irishman*, 19 Jan. 1901. 95 *United Irishman*, 20 Sept. 1902; NAI, CBS files, Home Office précis, carton 3, 27158/s (May 1902). 96 Donncha MacConnuladh (Denis McCullough), 'Chéad Uachtarán Phoblacht na hÉireann' (article supplied courtesy of Joseph McCullough).

literary societies of the 1890s lacked 'that missionary spirit, which did more than literary power, to make a force of the *Nation*'s "brave young men"', as well as 'that cohesion and fraternity without which a movement is, to a large extent, ineffectual ... Literary Ireland, in fact, does not know itself'.[97] Few young literary figures identified with the political morality of either the Young Irelanders or that of the IRB, which evidently seemed to them as dated or uninteresting. For example, Ryan read John O'Leary's recollections of the IRB but he interpreted it only as a literary text: 'virile, stern, startling sometimes in its candour, "each word direct as a blow", it has a nobility of its own, typical of that fine old Roman rectitude'. However, he found its political reasoning either difficult to understand or simply irrelevant:

> Work which moved an earlier generation – and which is not yet a spent force with the men of the 'Old Guard' – is inaccessible to the younger ones, quietly buried as it is in the open file of the newspaper tomb.[98]

Yeats had never taken political nationalisms seriously as he conceived of nations as imaginary cultural entities, rather than actual political units. He believed that 'what a nation imagines that is its history, there is its heart',[99] and consequently creating mythologies was the key to capturing the popular imagination. However, his efforts to celebrate mythical folk-cultures in poetry and especially drama failed to capture the popular imagination; a fact that he came to realise around 1904. That year, while speaking before a Clan na Gael Robert Emmet commemoration in New York, Yeats lamented the failure of his own movement and predicted that the 'Irish-Ireland' movement would soon sweep all before its path, because the myth that a Gaelic civilization was being reborn was extraordinarily powerful: 'Ireland is being transformed from end to end by that impracticable dream.'[100] The 'Irish-Ireland' movement effectively gave literary societies that 'cohesion and fraternity' and 'missionary spirit' which people like W.P. Ryan craved, although this occurred not only because of the cultural myths it involved or indeed its educational ethos. The 'Irish-Ireland' movement also had a strong economic nationalist dimension, owing to its emphasis on the 'buy Irish' campaign. In other words, it encompassed a political policy. The IRB veterans, by contrast, were seemingly prepared to appeal only to people's sense of political morality. Perhaps if they began championing socialism, they might well have appealed to many young intellectuals, but they refused to do so. P.N. Fitzgerald, for example, noted that the Irish Party's agitation 'serves only a class' and this could well 'separate and bring classes into conflict', but he refused to champion radical socialist views, which he believed were motivated by as much 'low opportunism' as the 'art of

97 W.P. Ryan, *The Irish literary revival* (London, 1894), preface, 130–1. The *Nation* referred to is the original publication of the 1840s. **98** Ryan, *The Irish literary revival*, 144–5. **99** Kelly, 'Aesthete among the athletes', 135 (Yeats to *The Gael*, 1887). **100** *Gaelic American*, 5 Mar. 1904.

political legerdemain' practised by the Irish Party. In principle he believed 'what we need in this country is a commingling of classes for the common benefit of all', but in practice he had no policy to bring this about. He just called on people 'to examine your political consciences and see if the so-called patriotism of the present day is at all comparable to that preached and practised by the United Irishmen.'[101]

In October 1900, the reunited Irish Party won 76 of the 103 Irish seats, but this was a deceptive victory. Those elected in the previous election simply reclaimed their seats because no-one could afford to stand against them, while most UIL branches ignored the demands of the central executive of the UIL to subscribe to the Irish Party's 'Parliamentary Fund' to pay the MPs' expenses. In the major towns and cities, the UIL was weak because the Catholic mercantile community had no interest in reviving a land agitation in the country and continued to be divided along Dillonite, Healyite or Redmondite lines, depending on which faction they believed could best assist their businesses. Meanwhile in rural areas, the UIL's membership was far more interested in working with county councillors to favour agrarian interests rather than with the future of the Irish Party at Westminster; a reality that William O'Brien, in particular, soon became well aware of and knew could not be ignored. Tim Healy and his followers were expelled from the Irish Party in December 1900 for calling for the UIL to be governed differently, while his chief supporter, William Martin Murphy, soon succeeded in buying the *Irish Daily Independent* and amalgamating it with the *Daily Nation* to create the *Irish Independent*, which often differed from the Irish Party line. As a result of these developments, the Irish Party was forced to send Joseph Devlin and P.A. McHugh to the United States looking for funding.[102] Republicans responded by calling upon the Clan to do all in its power to prevent the Irish Party from collecting money in Irish-America, distributed pamphlets declaring that the Irish Party was not worthy of financial support, while the *United Irishman* began reporting on the activities of the Irish Party in Westminster exclusively within its columns on foreign, international news.[103]

Republicans tried to publicize the idea that the Boer War might lead to a war between Britain and France. P.N. Fitzgerald, Maurice Moynihan and T.B. Kelly spoke to this effect at some 1798 commemorative events; the *United Irishman* published carefully selected extracts from Parisian journals every week to substantiate the theory; and the Old Guard Union, to express enthusiasm for the idea, carried 'the flags of the French and Irish Republics' and marched to La Marseillaise at the Manchester martyr and Bodenstown demonstrations that took place in Dublin and Kildare during 1899–1901.[104]

101 *Daily Independent*, 25 Nov. 1895 (speech at Tralee); *Leinster Leader*, 29 June 1901 (speech at Bodenstown). 102 NAI, CBS files, Home Office précis, carton 3, 24399/s (Mar. 1901), 25049/s (June 1901). 103 Ibid., carton 2, 21795/s. 104 *Daily Nation*, 11 Nov. 1899, *Freeman's Journal*, 20 Nov. 1899, 27 Nov. 1900, 25 Nov. 1901; *Leinster Leader*, 29 June 1901.

Some of these pro–Boer demonstrations were quite large, particularly one held in Limerick during November 1900 by John Daly (the mayor), who stated that he believed that those who believe 'in the policy of redeeming their country by paying £500 to win a parliamentary seat for a member of their family' would soon 'be trampled on by the people.'[105] During the same month, however, John MacBride had fled for his life from south Africa and this helped to take the steam out of the pro-Boer and pro-French campaigns. In fact, there had never been any real chance of an Anglo-French war in the first place. Although very serious tensions had arisen during 1898 between the British and French as a result of their mutual colonial exploits in the Sudan, by March 1899 the French (being the weaker of the two military forces) were forced to abandon their claims over Egypt once more, being far less equipped or eager for war. Ultimately, shortly after the end of the Boer War, an 'Entente Cordiale' was agreed between Britain and France to settle their quarrels over northern Africa, not least due to the efforts of Lord Lansdowne of Dublin, and there-after the chances of a war between the two countries virtually evaporated. Anticipating this, in Irish-America, the Clan had already been attempting to develop an understanding with the German-American community, now that Germany was clearly Britain's greatest political enemy. This work was aided by the fact that in 1899 a 'German National Alliance' was formed by the German-American community in an effort to emulate the INA's example of acting as an anti-British pressure group in American politics. Fearing the possibility of an Anglo-American alliance, they each adopted the motto of John Finerty's *Chicago Citizen* as their own: 'Europe, not England, is the mother-country of America.'[106]

In December 1900, Mark Ryan sent Maud Gonne and John MacBride to America to assist the Clan in undermining Irish Party fund collection efforts, while Fred Allan sent John Daly to America for the same purpose. Both these missions were undermined, however, by the fact that the Clan was in disarray. Six months earlier, the Clan had been nominally reunited for the first time in sixteen years during a Philadelphia convention that was attended by Patrick Hoctor and Anthony MacBride (brother of John) as representatives of the IRB.[107] At this convention, William Lyman was expelled for 'borrowing' Clan funds to save his business ventures from collapse and a new executive was appointed, led by O'Neill Ryan (chairman) and John Devoy (secretary), but the Clan found it very difficult to agree on any policy, owing to the existence of three distinct factions in the movement. One faction led by Patrick Egan and John Finerty, who were influential Irish-American politicians (Egan was a friend of Teddy Roosevelt) and not just Clansmen, had grown in popularity because they had managed a little spectacle by sending fifty Irish-Americans to the Transvaal as an ambulance corps, which was legal according to the

---

105 *Daily Independent*, 24 Nov. 1901.   106 Carl Wittke, *The Irish in America* (New York, 1956), 274–6.   107 John Devoy, 'The story of Clan na Gael', *Gaelic American*, 30 May 1925.

American neutrality laws, but on arrival they took firearms out of their medical supply kits and joined the Boer armed forces. Like Lyman (with whom they were still associated), Finerty and Egan were former leaders of the American INA and members of the US Republican Party, and were in favour of the Clan continuing to act in much the same way as the INB had done since the mid 1880s, as a sort of secret freemasonry in American politics. As a former leader of the INLA and INFA, Egan's attitude towards Irish politics was that the Irish Party was the only movement that was in a position to accomplish anything and therefore deserved to be supported, but were it ever possible for the Irish people to choose their own form of government democratically (a thing not possible under the Union), he believed that the vast majority of the population would elect to establish an Irish republic.[108] Another much more militant Clan faction, derived from the spy-ridden Brooklyn section of the former INB organization, was in favour of making the republican movement in Ireland completely subservient to the Clan Executive for obvious reasons. The third faction, of which Devoy was the most prominent figure, was in favour of the existing arrangement, allowing the 'home organization' complete independence of action, and continuing to finance and place their trust in the existing IRB leadership of John O'Leary, Fred Allan and P.N. Fitzgerald, although none of these figures were in a position to adopt any significant political initiatives in Ireland at this time.[109] With such widely different views prevalent among the Clan leadership it is not surprising that it split once more shortly after the Irish Party tried to form an auxiliary organisation to the UIL in the United States to solve the MPs' financial problems.

As they were considered to be political nobodies, MacBride and Gonne's tour was not taken seriously by the 'home rule' press, but Daly's American lectures did attract much attention in Ireland, as he was the mayor of Limerick. Daly was particularly aggressive in his denunciations of the Irish Party during his American tour and, as a result, after he returned to Limerick in March 1901 the *Limerick Leader*, William O'Brien's *Irish People* and the Catholic clergy mounted a strong propaganda campaign against him;[110] a fact that helped ensure he was not returned as mayor for another term. The *United Irishman* and the 'home rule' press issued wildly contradictory reports regarding the respective success of the Devlin-McHugh and the Daly-Gonne-MacBride tours, but it seems clear that the decision of the *Irish World* (New York) not to promote the Devlin-McHugh tour and the Clan's support for the MacBride-Gonne-Daly tour meant that the Irish Party's mission was initially far from successful.[111] The decisive factor in the struggle, however, had yet to arrive and a key player in bringing about its resolution was actually the semi-retired figure of Michael Davitt.

108 *United Irishman*, 31 Mar. 1900 (reprint of Egan interview in *New York World*). 109 John Devoy, 'The story of Clan na Gael', *Gaelic American*, 30 May 1925. 110 NAI, CBS files, Home Office précis, carton 3, 24517/s (Mar.-Apr. 1901). 111 Ibid., 24399/s (Mar. 1901).

While in south Africa as a reporter, Davitt befriended the Irish–Australian republican Arthur Lynch, who had held a higher-rank than MacBride in the Irish–Boer commando forces and had been an associate of Mark Ryan and Maud Gonne's circles of cultural nationalists in London ever since he was defeated in running as a Parnellite for Galway in 1892. Davitt succeeded in persuading Lynch to accept an Irish Party nomination (he was subsequently elected for Clare) and to go to America to boost Devlin and McHugh's efforts. Upon Lynch's arrival in America in early 1901, his lecture tour was organized by John Finerty of the *Chicago Citizen*, who spoke alongside him at all rallies. After twenty years of being the most famous and popular 'Lion's Tail Twister' in Irish–America, Finerty surprised many people by completely reversing his former political stance, denouncing the idea of rebellion in Ireland and championing the Irish Party's strategy in Westminster. As Finerty was not only a very influential Irish–American orator and journalist but was also a leading figure in the Clan, his actions caused the various factions in the movement to become violently hostile to each other. Most of the ex-INB party, which was the larger of the two wings based mostly in the mid-west, broke away to form a movement called the United Irish Brotherhood (UIB) which supported the idea of forming an American wing of the UIL, both as a means of creating an effective Irish–American pressure group in American politics and to give them some means of influencing the Irish Party's policy in Ireland, although this latter goal was an unrealistic expectation. The man who succeeded in persuading Finerty to change his tune was Patrick Egan, who at Davitt's request sought to win over Patrick Ford of the *Irish World* (who was prepared to send money for land agitation in Ireland, but not for the Irish Party), while Egan also generally kept Davitt informed of affairs in the Clan.[112] In his capacity as a life-long honorary member of the Old Guard Union, Davitt also organized and acted as the chief pallbearer in the funeral of James Stephens in March 1901. After the funeral, he was seen by DMP detectives inviting various IRB leaders, past and present, back to his room at the Gresham Hotel. Among those who accepted Davitt's invitation were John O'Leary, P.N. Fitzgerald, Mark Ryan, John Daly, Patrick Hoctor, James Egan, Charles Doran and Anthony Mackey, while Fred Allan, William McGuinness and James Mullet (now chairman of the Dublin board of guardians) had a separate meeting in the same hotel. The DMP did not know what took place at these meetings, which were virtually a reconvening of the IRB Supreme Council of 1879, but many were seen quarrelling with Mark Ryan afterwards who was believed to have attempted to 'boss the proceedings' due to the fact that only he had any revolutionary funds, due to his success in getting money from the Boer government.[113]

112 TCD, Davitt papers, MS 9483/4735–48 (Ford to Davitt, 1899–1900); MS 6569/13–16 (Egan to Davitt).   113 NAI, DMP Crime Dept, Précis of Information, carton 6, 24761/s (summary Apr-May 1901).

Mark Ryan supported the UIB in America, believing this could maximize Irish-American financial support for his various London-based endeavours. To this end, he experimented with forming an Irish wing of the UIB under the cover of Cumann na Gaedhael, which was supposed to have John MacBride as its president, William Rooney and Arthur Griffith as the leaders of the Irish wing of the organization, and finally with himself as the leader of the English wing.[114] During his visit to Dublin for Stephens's funeral in March 1901, Ryan asked Griffith and Rooney to support his plan but, according to the recollections of G.A. Lyons, they were indifferent to the suggestion.[115] Ryan, however, clearly did not abandon the idea, for it was presented to the centres of the Dublin IRB one year later at a meeting in James Egan's home in Chapelizod. Although the police were informed that the idea was rejected, it appears that an UIB organization of some kind was already in existence in England and Ireland at this time, acting under the cover of Cumann na Gaedhael.[116]

The UIB faction of the Clan was generally successful in winning support for the idea of forming an American wing of the UIL. In May 1902, John T. Keating (the new Clan chairman – O'Neill Ryan had retired to focus on his legal career), John Devoy and their new friend Senator Daniel Cohalan were contemplating resigning completely from the Clan, due to their inability to direct the organization.[117] When Devoy heard from the IRB leadership that Mark Ryan had launched a rival organization under John McBride's presidency, he wrote to MacBride complaining, but the 'major' dismissed the complaint. He replied that 'whoever informed you of the work of the newer or younger organization in Ireland [the UIB] informed you wrongly', for it was not really attempting to undermine the IRB, but rather seeking to gather the men 'who had dropped out through disgust at the way things were going' and were sending its agents 'to the younger men' in Cumann na Gaedhael, who he claimed were being 'entirely neglected' by the IRB.[118] As MacBride had not been in Ireland since 1896 and was closely associated with Maud Gonne and Mark Ryan (the leaders of the pro-Boer movement), he was naturally inclined to sympathize with all their endeavours. He had written to the *United Irishman* during January 1902 (and would do so again in May 1903) to emphasize his belief that public organizations identified with the 'Irish-Ireland' movement, such as Cumann na Gaedhael, as well as many branches of the Gaelic League and the GAA, were bringing 'a new soul into Erin'. He suggested that they should adopt a new motto of 'Sinn Féin' ('Ourselves Alone' or 'Self-Reliance') to describe their objectives.[119] This slogan became the title of a small journal of Cumann na Gaedhael in Meath and would soon become quite popular, at

114 NAI, CBS files, Home Office précis, carton 2, 19172/s, 19425/s, 19650/s (reports Major Gosselin); carton 3, 24896/s, 24928/s (June 1901); *DPB*, 2, 347–50. 115 G.A. Lyons, 'Arthur Griffith and the IRB' (1950), 6–7. 116 NAI, DMP Crime Dept, Précis of Information, carton 6, 26819/s, 27417/s (summary Apr.–July 1902) 117 *DPB*, vol. 2, 348. 118 Ibid., 347. 119 MacBride to *United Irishman*, 18 Jan. 1902, 20 May 1903.

least among the many young 'Irish-Irelander' separatists.[120] MacBride was not
totally dismissive of Devoy's complaints, but he believed that the formation of
the new movement was opportune, noting that 'from one point of view, the
starting of the younger branch was a good thing, as the older men were doing
then what they are doing now, sitting on their backsides and criticising and
abusing one another.'[121] MacBride felt that 'the *United Irishman* at present
supplies the place of [IRB] organisers in Ireland' and was 'at least equal to a
dozen'. As Ryan's pro-Boer funds had run out, MacBride also appealed to
Devoy to start funding the paper, which could not be sustained by its sales
alone, due to its failure to get businesses to advertise in the paper, a problem
that faced all seditious newspapers in Ireland under the Union for obvious
reasons. Devoy agreed and forwarded this funding to Griffith through
MacBride in Paris.[122]

In October 1902, John Finerty and Patrick Egan were finally able to launch
the 'United Irish League of America' (UILA) as a support body for the Irish
Party in the United States, with Finerty as president and Egan as vice-
president. Thereafter Finerty or Egan effectively disbanded the UIB
organization, for it had served its purpose as far as they were concerned. Many
former supporters of the UIB rejoined the Clan, which was now technically
reunited once more. This put an end to Mark Ryan's plans to affiliate his new
organization with the American UIB, while John MacBride, after marrying
Maud Gonne in February 1903, effectively withdrew from Irish revolutionary
affairs. By that time, owing to the defection of its former mid-western support
base to the UILA, the Clan had been reduced for the first time since 1879 to a
small organization confined to a few eastern cities.

From information received in Irish-America, British intelligence knew that
the IRB managed to increase its active, subscribing membership during
1898–9 to approximately nine thousand men.[123] No such information was
received by British intelligence after the Clan reunited, but it is likely that the
IRB lost a good deal of followers again between 1899 and 1902 as it had little
or no funds and also clearly lacked initiative. In the past, the IRB generally
tried to make an impact as a political movement through its sheer strength in
numbers. By the 1900s, this was no longer practicable and on a propagandist
level, as well as on a policy level, it had nothing left to offer people either. A
policy was needed, rather than a revolutionary strategy. As late as August 1902,
the plan of trying to create a new public republican movement around the basis
of the centenary clubs still existed, but it essentially came to nothing, outside
of Dublin, where the Wolfe Tone Clubs remained. A Robert Emmet centenary
demonstration the following year was supposed to have been an opportunity
to bring all the clubs together and be a republican 'show of strength', but by

---

120 The paper *Sinn Féin* (Navan) was edited by Patrick Bartley. *United Irishman*, 7 Feb. 1903.
121 *DPB*, vol. 2, 347. 122 Ibid., 347–50 (McBride-Devoy correspondence, 1902).
123 PRO (London), C.O. 903/7, Chief Secretary's Office miscellaneous intelligence notes (W
Series), 1–10, p. 44.

the time this event was held (20 September 1903), the only centenary clubs left in the country were evidently the Wolfe Tone Clubs in Dublin, which attended the demonstration along with about 6,000 people who were chiefly members of Cumann na Gaedhael, the GAA and Gaelic League.[124]

The IRB's relationship with Cumann na Gaedhael began to alter after the tragic death of William Rooney from tuberculosis in May 1901, aged just twenty-nine. Rooney had been the principal editor of the *United Irishman* up until his death and he was essentially responsible for giving the paper its Irish-Ireland bias. Griffith, by contrast, was not an Irish language enthusiast ('West Britonism is West Britonism, even if it wags in the Irish tongue'),[125] but he recognized that the backbone of the pro-Boer movement had been the young Irish-Irelanders, rather than the old republicans. Consequently he did not change the paper's editorial policy. After Rooney's death, P.T. Daly, the secretary of the Wolfe Tone Clubs, became a travelling organizer of the IRB and tried to link up the republican movement with Cumann na Gaedhael. This was difficult. In Cork city, for example, P.N. Fitzgerald, Sean O'Keeffe and the IRB were opposed to having anything to do with local branch of Cumann na Gaedhael because it was run by Fr Kavanagh.[126] Daly, however, was prepared to work with Cumann na Gaedhael and the priests regardless of the complaints of the old republicans, whom he generally ignored. When speaking before Cumann na Gaedhael meetings, Daly generally spoke in Irish as well as English, denounced the Irish Party for its 'lack of practical economics' and called upon the youth of the country to begin studying economics. Speaking before the Irish Trades Union Congress of 1902, Daly also called for the establishment of a new labour party in Irish politics,[127] which was his true desire.

In October 1902, Daly was appointed as a full-time travelling organizer for Cumann na Gaedhael,[128] and it is quite likely he became the IRB secretary around this time as well, replacing Fred Allan, who was weighed down with numerous other responsibilities. By 1901, Allan was the secretary of Dublin Corporation's new 'Electric Light Company' and secretary to about half of the corporation's 'improvement committees' (a fellow republican Patrick Tobin was made the permanent secretary of all other corporation improvement committees),[129] and thus he was tied down with this work. Allan also experimented with other activities, such as forming an agency for freelance journalists and publishing a short-lived entertainment magazine, the *Sporting Record*, to which his friend Joseph Holloway was the leading contributor.[130] By the end of 1902, branches of Cumann na Gaedhael existed in Dublin, Cork, Belfast, Dunleary (Kingstown), Tullamore,[131] Castlebar, Tralee, Liverpool,

---

124 *United Irishman*, 26 Sept. 1903. **125** *United Irishman*, 18 Jan. 1902. **126** NAI, Home Office précis, carton 3, 27804/s, 27881/s, 28005/s. **127** *United Irishman*, 4 Jan., 20 Sept. 1902. **128** *United Irishman*, 24 Oct. 1902. **129** *Thom's Directory* (1901–21). **130** NLI, Joseph Holloway papers, MS 22412, 23218; *Irish Times*, 17 and 22 Mar. 1937 (obituaries for Allan). **131** This was led by Patrick O'Loughlin, an IRB veteran and former Leinster arms

Glasgow, Manchester and London, but each was involved in promoting the 'Irish-Ireland' movement rather than the IRB. Only two IRB figures, Frank Dorr, a young commercial traveller from Mayo, and Michael Crowe, a Dublin clerk and the son of the long-time Limerick IRB leader John Crowe, sat on the executive of Cumann na Gaedhael. They assumed this position, however, because they were leaders of the GAA, not because of their IRB membership. In January 1903, with the support of P.N. Fitzgerald and Francis Dineen, Dorr and Crowe revived the GAA's ban against members of the RIC joining the association and extended it to include (for the first time) the army, militia and navy as well. In Crowe's estimation, this made the entire British state forces more obnoxious to the Irish people than mere anti-recruitment literature ever possibly could.[132] This move was made to counter the decline of the anti-enlistment campaign, which continued for many more years, but had ceased to be effective by 1901.[133] It is very unlikely, however, that these young men would have been able to introduce this ruling were it not for the fact that most 'Irish-Irelanders', including many priests, supported the anti-enlistment movement.

By 1903, Arthur Griffith was convinced that the only way any sort of nationalist agitation could be sustained in the country was if the republican movement committed itself entirely to the 'Irish-Ireland' movement and adapted itself to its ethos, even though this would mean compromizing its republican principles. He suggested that this could be a means of bringing about a political revolution in the country:

> The taking of the Bastille was an upheaval. A revolution is not an upheaval. A revolution is the silent, impalpable working of forces for the most part undiscerned in their action … That nationalists feel the working of a new order of things in Ireland at the present day, no-one will be prepared to doubt.[134]

The fact that Griffith had little conception of life in Ireland outside of Dublin led him to magnify the significance of the fact that, in Dublin, the leaders of Cumann na Gaedhael included local government officials, barristers (such as ex-Parnellites William O'Leary Curtis and L.E. O'Carroll), newspaper editors (J.W. Power, editor of the *Evening Telegraph*, and himself) and one of Ireland's leading economists, C.H. Oldham; all of whom identified with and admired Griffith's little oracle of patriotism. This led him to believe that a new political party could be launched in Irish politics, through Cumann na Gaedhael, so long as it identified with the 'Irish-Ireland' movement. As a result, he began formulating what would become known as 'the Sinn Féin policy'.

agent during the 1880s, who operated a branch of the CLS and Cumann na Gaedhael in his hometown and edited a little journal called *Saoirseacht. United Irishman*, 14 Mar. 1903. **132** Mandle, *GAA*, 123, 159. **133** Terence Denman, 'The red livery of shame: the campaign against army recruitment in Ireland, 1899–1914' (1994). **134** *United Irishman*, 27 June 1903.

10

The IRB, Sinn Féin and the birth
of an 'Irish-Ireland', 1903–10

land freed

In April 1903, the Tory government introduced a new land act that helped divide opinion in the Irish Party and the UIL. Under its terms, the government committed itself to offering loans to help tenant farmers buy their land, thereby potentially freeing all farmers from any direct responsibility to the landed aristocracy. This measure had been introduced partly because the great landowners had become prepared to hold conferences with UIL leaders, such as William O'Brien, to decide how a 'final arrangement' of the land question could be reached. O'Brien, as well as John Redmond, believed that if the great landowners were now willing to settle issues in this manner many other issues, perhaps even Ulster resistance to 'home rule', could be solved if the Irish Party began to work more with the aristocracy. John Dillon, however, felt differently. He feared that the passing of this act would cause the Irish Party's support base to evaporate throughout rural Ireland, since his party would have nothing left to offer them. He was also opposed to working with the aristocracy, mostly because they were invariably Tory, while the Irish Party was pro-Liberal. As William O'Brien was effectively the leader of the UIL Directory, this led to a quarrel within the Irish Party regarding the management of the UIL. Ultimately, in November 1903, O'Brien decided to resign from parliament and from the UIL Directory, thereby preventing himself from directing that political organization which he had largely built, although he still had great influence over very many branches of its organization, particularly in Munster. Thereafter, together with Tim Healy, O'Brien favoured decentralizing control of the UIL in order to make it more representative of political opinion in the provinces. John Dillon's solution to this challenge to his authority was to make his loyal supporter Joseph Devlin, the recently elected president of the AOH, the new leader of the UIL Directory. Devlin, who was also elected MP for West Belfast at this time, was a popular figure among many urban supporters of the Irish Party in Belfast and Dublin, but lacked commensurate popularity elsewhere. Consequently the urban-rural divide within both the Irish Party and UIL became more pronounced than ever. From 1904 onwards, the Irish Party and the UIL Directory essentially began to represent Catholic business and educational interests exclusively, and this caused many UIL branches in provincial Ireland (as well as provincial newspaper editors and local councillors) to become alienated from the party and follow either their own political intuition or side with Healy and O'Brien.

Following the introduction of the 'Wyndham Land Act' of 1903, the Tory government sent the new British monarch, Edward VII, to Ireland as a supposed patron of the act. Arthur Griffith responded by launching a campaign demanding that no local government bodies would welcome the king to Ireland. In May, a manifesto appeared in the press purportedly on behalf of the 'advanced nationalists of Ireland' proclaiming their support for the royal visit. Who wrote this manifesto is unclear, but it is quite probable that it was written by Griffith himself to incite people into opposing the royal visit. On 18 May, a couple of days after this manifesto appeared, Griffith, Henry Dixon and Tom Kelly (a Cumann na Gaedhael city councillor) disrupted a UIL meeting in Dublin by trying to force the lord mayor to express opposition to the visit. When he refused to answer, Griffith led a mob armed with sticks that attacked the UIL men present and, in the process put John O'Donnell (the AOH MP for South Mayo, who had defeated John MacBride for the seat in 1900) in hospital.[1] After this meeting Dixon and Kelly, together with Maud Gonne and the Irish-American writer Seamus McManus, formed a body called 'The People's Protection Association', supposedly to protect Irish nationalists from being politically misrepresented, but within days this body was renamed as the 'National Council for Defence' or, more simply, as the 'National Council', apparently at the instigation of Griffith. The National Council then issued a manifesto proclaiming its intention

> to gather in one loose organization, representative men in all parts of the country, whether they be home rulers only, or nationalists who believe in the absolute independence of their country, for one purpose on which both can agree – the stamping out of flunkeyism and toadyism in this land. Outside this object, the Council will, of course, interfere in no way with any members' actions.[2]

While the Irish Party press argued that Edward VII was full of good intentions towards Ireland and was a sincere 'home ruler', the *United Irishman* proclaimed that the very idea of kings was contrary 'to the principle of human equality' and declared that 'the King of England comes as a symbol of an alien rule, imposed by force'. The *United Irishman* noted that the Catholic hierarchy's invitation to the king to Maynooth College was a typical representation of the Catholic upper classes' politics.[3] Meanwhile at public rallies in Dublin, Henry Dixon argued that the Irish Party's press had lied when it proclaimed that the Dublin working classes welcomed Queen Victoria to Ireland in 1900, stressing the fact that she arrived 'under the protection of 20,000 soldiers and 5,000 armed police', whose job was 'to suppress every expression of dissent'. A free, public opinion did not exist in Ireland. The same argument was thereafter repeated in the *United Irishman*.[4]

Within a month of its establishment, the National Council had won the

---

1 NAI, DMP précis, carton 6, 28498/s (May 1903).   2 *United Irishman*, 23 and 30 May 1903.
3 *United Irishman*, 6 and 13 June, 4 July 1903.   4 *United Irishman*, 11 July, 25 July, 8 Aug.
1903.

support of W.B. Yeats and Edward Martyn of the Abbey Theatre, the editors of *Sinn Féin* (Navan), the *Derry People* and the *Monaghan Advocate*, Sigerson's students at the Catholic University Medical School, Fr Kavanagh and some former leaders of the Ladies Land League, such as Anna Parnell and Jennie Wyse Power.[5] Not surprisingly, much support for the National Council also came from IRB figures, including John O'Leary (president of Cumann na Gaedheal), Jack O'Hanlon (the leader of the Wolfe Tone Clubs), Mark Ryan (the leader of the Irish National Club in London), and three vice-presidents of Cumann na Gaedheal, Robert Johnston, John Daly and James Egan, the latter now being a member of the trade union for Dublin municipal officials. The campaign was soon augmented when John T. Keating, the Clan chairman, came to Ireland in mid June along with Patrick Hoctor (who was now a businessman in America) to give a short lecture tour.

Upon the arrival of the Clan leader, P.T. Daly, Jack O'Hanlon and P.N. Fitzgerald organized an open-air lecture for him outside Dublin City Hall and made him the principal speaker along with Patrick Hoctor at Bodenstown, two events that attracted a few thousand people, including many members of the Wolfe Tone Clubs, the GAA and the Gaelic League.[6] Like Seamus McManus, Keating was a leading figure in the Ancient Order of Hibernians of America, the single largest Irish-American organization, and was using this influence to turn Irish-Americans away from the UILA. The AOH in Ireland had become a large organization for the first time after 1898 when it started winning over the following of the *theoretically* non-sectarian Foresters. Keating desired that the AOH would affiliate itself with the American AOH and turn against the Irish Party. Patrick Hoctor brought circulars with him proclaiming that the Clan was succeeding in turning Irish-Americans away from the UILA and was willing to promote an independence movement in Ireland. These circulars were then distributed in Ireland mostly by P.N. Fitzgerald and Hoctor himself. In his speeches in Dublin and Bodenstown, Keating championed the 'People's Protection Association', proclaimed that the Irish Party's press was misleading the Irish public by claiming that the UILA was popular, and argued that the AOH in America was really only in favour of supporting Cumann na Gaedheal. Thereafter P.N. Fitzgerald held public meetings in Tipperary and Clare denouncing all 'title hunters and flunkeys' who were ready to welcome the King to Ireland, while T.J. O'Reilly (formerly president of the Dublin Trades Council) and his close friend William McGuinness, the old northern England IRB leader, left for Keating's hometown of Cork city and promoted the 'National Council'. James Mullet, the Dublin IRB leader in the Land League days, now a prominent figure in the Old Guard Union and chairman of the Dublin Board of Guardians, was asked to do the same, but he refused, in deference to the wishes of Michael Davitt, who was the co-leader alongside

---

5 *United Irishman*, 23 May, 30 May, 6 June, 13 June, 4 July 1903. 6 *United Irishman*, 27 June 1903; NAI, CBS précis reports to Home Office, carton 3, 28765/s (July 1903).

Mullet of the 'Newgate Prison Memorial Committee'.[7] Meanwhile Keating, along with Hoctor and P.T. Daly, travelled to Belfast, where they met Robert Johnston and Bulmer Hobson, both of whom had recently held (under Cumann na Gaedhael auspices) their own small protest meeting about the king's visit at Cave Hill near Belfast. After speaking before various branches of Cumann na Gaedhael, the AOH and the Gaelic League in Ulster, Keating travelled to Glasgow, where he met the Scottish IRB leader John Geraghty and the ex-Cavan IRB leader Terence Fitzpatrick, and spoke before a branch of Cumann na Gaedhael, before returning to America in mid July.[8]

A couple of days after Keating left for America, Dublin City Council voted against making a welcoming address to the king by a narrow margin (40 votes to 37). As had been the case in 1892, when the corporation refused to welcome a lord lieutenant, it was the votes of the representatives of the working-class districts on the council that tipped the balance in the nationalists' favour.[9] The *United Irishman* claimed this as a victory for the National Council, but it was J.P. Nannetti MP (still a member of the Old Guard Union) who actually played the decisive role in defeating the motion by persuading many figures in the Dublin UIL to take a nationalist stand. Thereafter Nannetti, who was elected mayor the following year, encouraged the Dublin UIL to adopt a more radical political stance to ensure that he could maintain his political support, and prevent the Dublin UIL from continuing to lose ground to the young radicals.[10] As a result, a few independent branches of the UIL soon began to emerge in Dublin, most notably the 'Young Ireland Branch' led by Tom Kettle (son of Andrew, a former Land League leader). This consisted of several young Catholic University men who shared similar sensibilities to Cumann na Gaedhael, although their real desire was to become the new leaders of the Irish Party and commit it to an 'Irish-Ireland' policy. Outside of Dublin, however, the king's visit did not evoke a similar response; a fact which seems to have surprised P.N. Fitzgerald, who denounced all the more violently the 'flunkeys' and 'so-called nationalists in Cork and Limerick' municipal authorities who seconded addresses of welcome to the king.[11]

The campaign against the royal visit did not do much to revitalize the IRB, but a pattern was established of UIL dissenters in the provinces expressing some support for Griffith's Dublin party. In Connacht, mostly through the medium of the Gaelic League and the GAA, Frank Dorr, as well as two old IRB activists of the Parnell era, Maurice Shine and Thomas Egan, a baker and John Lavin's former right-hand man in the Roscommon IRB (who had started

7 NAI, CBS précis reports to Home Office, carton 3, 29218/s. The foundation stone for this was laid by Charles Doran in 1899. Doran, Davitt and Mullet were honorary leaders of the Old Guard Union.   8 *United Irishman*, 27 June 1903; NAI, CBS précis reports to Home Office, carton 3, 28765/s (July 1903).   9 *United Irishman*, 18 July 1903.   10 NAI, DMP précis, carton 6, 28772/s (July 1903).   11 NAI, Home Office precis, carton 3, 28899/s (summary of events, Aug. 1903).

calling himself 'Tomas O'Aodhgain'), persuaded some influential local newspaper editors, most notably the fiercely independent Jasper Tully MP of the *Roscommon Herald*, to adopt a sympathetic attitude towards Cumann na Gaedhael and the National Council.[12] In turn, P.A. McHugh MP, the editor of the *Sligo Champion* (the great rival of the *Roscommon Herald*), demanded that the personnel of the leadership of the GAA and Gaelic League must be altered and brought entirely under the control of the MPs;[13] McHugh was again waging war against the 'factionists'. Frank Dorr made great efforts to establish branches of Cumann na Gaedhael in rural Ireland at this time, but this rarely worked. In fact, only one active branch appears to have been established. This was in the village of Carron, Co. Clare, and was led by new young Clare IRB leader, Tom O'Loughlin.[14] O'Loughlin's Cumann na Gaedhael following was very different to that in the rest of the country. In response to a demand within the Clare UIL, he engaged in arms distribution and arms importations during 1903. Frank Dorr assisted in this activity by distributing firearms through the medium of the Galway GAA.[15] In the west of Ireland, irrespective of the introduction of the Wyndham Land Act, a demand was made to clear cattle off land, which impoverished tillage farmers desired and perhaps needed, and many evidently desired arms to bolster this agitation. Many local branches of the UIL (but not the Irish Party or the UIL Directory) supported this demand and eventually Laurence Ginnell, another fiercely independent MP, would create an 'independent UIL' organization in the mid-west in an attempt to direct the agitation in the west of Ireland as a whole. Tom O'Loughlin later imported 200 rifles into Clare for the purposes of what became known as the 'ranch war',[16] but such arms importation work also had some negative consequences for the IRB. For example, Frank Dorr was not generally active in this work, but as it was known by the community that he had distributed arms, he was accused by the parish priest of his hometown of Foxford, Co. Mayo, of being a government spy. This naturally made it very difficult for Dorr to acquire customers in his capacity as a commercial traveller and thus, by 1906, he was forced to emigrate to the United States. There, he joined his brother, who was in the Clan in Brooklyn, and helped to set up the GAA in America.[17]

By the autumn of 1903, Griffith's propaganda in the *United Irishman* had altered considerably in tone. He noted with great curiosity that, among the many contemporary dissenters from the Irish Party's politics, there were 'many law bachelors who are Gaelic Leaguers ... These are the stuff of which politicians are made ... Their influence could permeate every phase of Irish

---

12 NAI, CBS files, Home Office précis, carton 3, 26763/s, 27019/s, 27804/s, 29702/s. 13 *United Irishman*, 12 Sept. 1903 (public speech of McHugh). 14 *United Irishman*, 20 May 1903. 15 NAI, CBS files, Home Office précis, carton 3, 27881/s, 28005/s, 29427/s. 16 NAI, British in Ireland microfilm collection, DMP and RIC précis, report for May 1910 on history of the 'ranch war'. 17 Ibid., reports for Aug. 1905, Oct. 1907 and May 1909.

life.'[18] Reports of Gaelic League *feiseanna* now dominated the front page of his paper every week, while elements of D.P. Moran's anti-Protestant rhetoric began to surface as well in its editorial columns. Although Griffith did not abandon his essential political thinking, he clearly played down his republican political beliefs at this time to make his paper more appealing to the new Irish-Irelander, Catholic middle class. In Ireland at this time, as in most of Europe, France was seen as both the cultural and political symbol of republican liberty, but owing to republicans' attempts to break the church's monopoly over the education system, the Pope had ordered all French Catholics to withdraw their allegiance to the state. Irish Catholics, whether 'Irish-Irelanders' or not, generally detested the Third Republic for this very reason. Indeed, after attending a Bastille Day demonstration in 1900, Griffith and some IRB veterans were denounced by the Irish press for simply attending a national celebration of the supposedly 'priest-eating' republic.[19] Griffith's growing Irish-Irelander bias also reflected the fact that, following John T. Keating's visit to Dublin in June 1903, IRB circles began to be set up around the basis of the local Gaelic League for the first time. This work was possibly initiated by G.A. Lyons, a former IRB recruiting agent in the CLS (a society which had grown moribund after Rooney's death). Among the men recruited through this means were young Irish-Irelanders such as Sean T. O'Kelly and Ernest Blythe, as well as a few young Protestant working-class radicals like Lyons himself, including Sean O'Casey.[20]

In America, Irish revolutionaries began to alter the tone of their propaganda at this time as well. To defend the Clan from the ever-growing criticisms in the Irish-American press, Devoy decided to relaunch his *Irish Nation* newspaper, but John MacBride warned him that, if he did so, he should make sure that its propaganda was in concert with the 'Irish-Ireland' propaganda of the *United Irishman* and Cumann na Gaedhael so it would be understood by the young men.[21] Devoy was not enthused by this idea, but Keating and Cohalan believed that it was necessary. Against Devoy's wishes, the proposed paper was renamed at the insistence of Cohalan, its principal shareholder, as the *Gaelic American*, instead of the *Irish Nation*, to reflect the growing popularity of the Irish-Ireland movement in Ireland and Irish-America.[22] Most of the papers' contributors were young American 'Irish-Irelanders'.

Although Devoy was the editor of the *Gaelic American*, unlike the *Irish Nation* twenty years previously, he did not dominate its editorial policy and he effectively did whatever his paymaster, Cohalan, told him to do. The principal

18 *United Irishman*, 6 June, 12 Sept. 1903. 19 NAI, CBS files, Home Office précis, carton 3, 22489/s (quote from *Daily Nation*). In actual fact, the men they associated with in Paris were Gonne's ex-Boulangist political friends, who were not at all popular in Paris among republicans, communists or any other radical democrats, as they were simply old French nationalists who had supported their country's colonial exploits of the 1880s. 20 Sean O'Tuama (ed.), *The Gaelic League idea* (1972), 34 (recollections of Ernest Blythe, IRB). 21 *DPB*, vol. 2, 350. 22 John Devoy, 'The story of Clan na Gael', *Gaelic American*, 6 June 1925.

purpose of the *Gaelic American* was to win over the readership of the Ancient Order of Hibernians of America, the single largest Irish-American organization (it reputedly had over a million members) and a body over which the UILA exercised little influence east of Pittsburgh. By focusing on this goal, the paper quickly became a great commercial success and a serious rival to the New York *Irish World* as the principal mouthpiece of Irish-American nationalism. In America, the AOH was the principal promoter of 'the philosophy of Irish-Ireland' because some of its leaders, like Seamus McManus (the former founder of the 'People's Protection Association'), were closely associated with Notre Dame University in Ohio. One of the chief contributors to the *Gaelic American* was Patrick MacCartan, a native of Tyrone and graduate of a Catholic private college in Belfast, who moved to Philadelphia in 1901 and by 1903 had become a leader of the Clan in Philadelphia alongside Joseph McGarrity, an unscrupulous businessman and Irish-Irelander whom MacCartan had befriended. Two years later, upon moving to Dublin to study at the medical school of the Catholic University, MacCartan became the Dublin correspondent of the *Gaelic American* and a member of the IRB. He began working with fellow northerners Bulmer Hobson and Denis McCullough in boosting Cumann na Gaedhael specifically in Ulster by promoting 'Dungannon Clubs'. In this work, they found much assistance from an AOH and Gaelic League activist, Sean MacDermott, a native of Leitrim and former assistant-teacher in Belfast who had reputedly lost his job owing to a quarrel with the clergy. MacCartan corresponded very regularly with McGarrity and, to a much lesser extent, with Devoy. It was largely through him alone that the *Gaelic American* and the Clan kept in touch with what was happening in nationalist circles in Ireland from 1905 onwards, owing to the fact that P.T. Daly did not correspond regularly with the Irish-Americans.[23]

P.T. Daly was the chief travelling organizer of the IRB from 1902 onwards, but he faced many problems. In Dublin, he was unpopular in several circles because it was rumoured that he had stolen WTMC funds. The IRB was still split while British intelligence also knew that Mark Ryan was the chief instrument of distributing Clan funds to the IRB. Ryan's letters of instruction and funds sent to Daly from London were 'traced' by British intelligence and detailed reports were also received of several IRB meetings chaired by Daly, possibly indicating that one of Mark Ryan's intermediaries with Daly was working for British intelligence.[24] As had been the case since the 1880s, Major Gosselin remained extraordinarily well informed of IRB activity in northern England at this time. Information was received regularly about conventions of IRB centres in a Liverpool public house run by James Murphy, who ran a local branch of the CLS and Cumann na Gaedhael. Murphy also replaced William McGuinness (who died in April 1905) as the northern England IRB leader

23 Cronin, *McGarrity papers*; *DPB*, vol. 2., passim.   24 NAI, Home Office précis, carton 3, monthly reports dated 17 Oct. 1902, 9 Dec. 1902. *DPB*, vol. 2, 570.

around this time.[25] From the spring of 1903 onwards, British intelligence received regular reports of conventions of IRB centres in south Ulster, apparently owing to the fact that the IRB had begun recruiting ex-AOH men. These men had been active in the 1798 centenary movement but had no loyalty to 'the organization'.[26] During 1903 an informer in Belfast and another in Derry gave the Special Branch the names of the local IRB leadership and stated what P.T. Daly had told them, indicating that discipline within the organization was declining rapidly.[27]

In September 1903, Griffith's idea of forming a new political party received a significant boost when he succeeded in persuading P.T. Daly to stand (successfully) as the first ever 'National Council' candidate for Dublin City Hall, thereby signifying that the National Council was going to be a permanent political organization and not merely a temporary alliance of diverse people who were opposed to royal visits. Immediately after Daly's election, Griffith called upon all Cumann na Gaedhael followers to run as National Council candidates. He argued that if they 'realised at its proper value the weapon which the assimilation [equalization] of the municipal and parliamentary franchises placed in their hands', they could 'capture the municipal administration of all Ireland' and govern Ireland from *this* basis and prompt the Irish public to ignore Westminster MPs altogether, thereby forcing them to withdraw or retire.[28] Griffith's idea was a novel modification of what John O'Leary had described during 1879–81 as 'the Hungarian policy', owing to the fact that Griffith was suggesting making local governmental office the platform upon which to base the abstentionist policy, rather than just trying to persuade the MPs to withdraw. The hope of the republican supporters of the 'new departure' that the Irish Party itself might adopt the 'abstentionist policy' and thereafter ally itself with the republicans had died during 1885–6. Parnell's intimations during 1890–1 that he would 'adopt other means' were not believed by the IRB, and republicans' political calculations during the 'split' were not shaped by this consideration.[29] John MacBride expressed great doubts as to the practicality of Griffith's strategy, noting that even if the abstentionist policy worked, Irishmen would need to be able to back up the provisional government by force and they did not have this capacity.[30] Although John O'Leary, the nominal IRB and Cumann na Gaedhael president, took part in discussions held after P.T. Daly's election as to whether or not the 'National Council' and Cumann na Gaedhael should amalgamate and support Griffith's plan,[31] he probably did not play any significant role in inspiring Griffith to champion the new policy. The controversy surrounding his role as president of the 1798 Centenary Committee had essentially broken

25 NAI, Home Office precis, carton 3, 23860/s, 25049/s, 28150/s, 28377/s. 26 Ibid., 28377/s. 27 Ibid., 28429/s, 28634/s. 28 *United Irishman*, 12 Sept 1903. 29 Fred Allan to *Irish Weekly Independent*, 6 Oct. 1894. 30 MacBride to *United Irishman*, 9 Oct. 1904. 31 NAI, DMP reports, précis of information, carton 6, 1899–1905, report 5 Oct. 1903, 28965/s, summary for September.

O'Leary's political resolve and his health, like that of P.N. Fitzgerald, was very poor. After twenty years of being a frequent letter-writer, from 1899 until his death, O'Leary wrote no more political letters to the press. If he attended meetings at all, he generally attended only those of George Sigerson's NLS, rather than Cumann na Gaedhael. It was up to Griffith to put some flesh onto 'the Hungarian policy' idea.

Over the first six-months of 1904, Griffith wrote a series of *United Irishman* articles that were soon republished as a top-selling book, *The Resurrection of Hungary* (1904). Although it took the form of a history of Hungary, this book was written with two very specific political purposes. First, to spell out to the Irish public 'the obvious truth' that a nation cannot exist if 'the political centre of the nation' is not 'within the nation', and thus the Irish Party's policy was inherently anti-nationalist. Second, to 'point out to his compatriots [in the IRB] that the alternative to armed resistance to the foreign government of this country' was not necessarily 'acquiescence in usurpation, tyranny and fraud', since the National Council could become a practical forum for launching the abstentionist policy.[32] To illustrate why the Irish Party's policy was worthy only of 'condemnation', Griffith stated that, over a generation, the Irish public had expended over £600,000 to keep the Irish Party in Westminster, only to see a constant fall in the population through emigration and a commensurate growth in imperial taxation, while the Irish Party had led itself into a political 'cul-de-sac' and the 'vanity and selfishness' of its leaders was 'preventing them from admitting the truth and retracing their steps.'[33] This was an argument that could appeal to many young Irish-Irelanders, who may not have actually felt opposed to the Irish Party, but favoured D.P. Moran's idea of protecting Irish industries and building up a completely new forum of public opinion in the country. By contrast, much of the traditional support base of the Irish Party since the 1880s and the existing Irish mercantile community (Catholic and Protestant) had no inherent problems with the existing colonial system of taxation, or the fact that the Irish economy was being managed purely for the benefit of the empire, for they had already prospered solely because they had adapted to this system. The new young rising Catholic middle class of the 1900s, however, were generally hostile to the previous generation of business leaders and felt that if 'home rule' was to be worth anything, a different brand of economics needed to be championed. This trend played a large part in inspiring Griffith to create his 'Sinn Féin policy' for the National Council the following year, which was designed to persuade the new middle class that their desire for greater economic self-determination could best be fulfilled by following a political programme designed to bring about Irish independence.

On 28 November 1905, Griffith spelt out 'the Sinn Féin policy' at the first annual convention of the National Council in a long lecture that was later

---

32 Arthur Griffith, *The resurrection of Hungary* (1904), preface.   33 Ibid., 90–1.

republished as a top-selling pamphlet. The most notable aspect of Griffith's programme was his emphasis on the intrinsic link between a people's capacity for citizenship and their levels of education, and what this indicated the 'Irish-Ireland' movement could achieve. Griffith denounced the British government as completely tyrannical and claimed that its chief instrument of tyranny was its educational system in Ireland, which he believed was purposely 'designed to make them oblivious of their rights as men and their duties as citizens.' Griffith believed that this anti-republican bias existed even at the highest level: 'the young men who go to Trinity College are told by Aristotle that the sole end of education is to make men patriots; and by the professors of Trinity not to take Aristotle seriously ... [I]f he lived in our times and in our country, Aristotle would be a seditious person in the eyes of the British government in Ireland.' Griffith called on the Irish people to 'take over the primary education system themselves' by forming their own voluntary schools and he praised the new Christian Brothers' schools as an example of this. This may well indicate that he had abandoned his former hostility to denominational education, or else that he simply felt obliged to recognize that the Christian Brothers' schools were those where most young 'Irish-Irelanders' were being educated. After education, Griffith considered the most important issue in the country to be the state of the economy, and he championed the ideas of 'national political economy' held by an old German economist named Frederich List. In Griffith's opinion, List had ingeniously managed to 'brush aside the fallacies of Adam Smith and his tribe' by emphasizing that if any political society or government allows civic life to become a secondary consideration to the blind forces of a free-trade economy, the inevitable result will sooner or later be the destruction of the civil basis of that society. Griffith believed that Irish business leaders needed to adopt a protectionist policy to undo the effect which the British imperial economy was having on Irish life and argued that this policy could be advanced if the county, urban and district councillors, as well as the poor law guardians, used their collective influence to protect the interests of Irish manufacturers. As far as Griffith was concerned, this was an imperative duty of all local government officials. Furthermore, he proposed the formation of a 'Council of Three Hundred' (a 'National Council'), to be composed of the members of the county, urban and rural district councillors of Ireland who would 'sit in Dublin and form a *de facto* Irish parliament' in defiance of the British government and force the Irish MPs in Westminster to obey the ruling of this *de facto* government:

> The basis of the policy is national self-reliance ... If we realise the duties and responsibilities of the citizen and discharge them, we shall win ... Let each man do so much, and I have no fear for the ultimate triumph of our policy. I say ultimate, because no man can offer Ireland a speedy and comfortable road to freedom, and before that goal is attained [the creation of an Irish civil society], many may have fallen and all will have suffered

... We go to build up the nation from within, and we deny the right of any but our own countrymen to shape its course ... We shall not justify our course to England. The craven policy that has rotted our nation has been this policy of justifying ourselves in our enemies eyes ... If we realise this conception of citizenship in Ireland – if we place our duty to our country before our personal interests, and live not each for himself but each for all, the might of England cannot prevent our ultimate victory.[34]

The Sinn Féin policy did not essentially introduce an economic dimension to Irish republican political thought. Rather it introduced a republican dimension to Irish-Irelanders' political thought, by linking the demand for economic self-determination with a coherent philosophy of citizenship, not some romantic ideal of the rebirth of a Gaelic civilization that had been imagined by some Catholic priests. This was Griffith's objective and to do this he knew he had to present the policy in such a way so as to appeal to Irishmen 'whether they be republicans or whether they be not'.[35] One way he attempted to do this was by giving the Sinn Féin policy a supposed 'constitutional basis' by claiming, nonsensically, that the Renunciation act of 1783, whereby Westminster declared that it would not override the legislation of the Irish House of Commons and House of Lords, was still legally binding and so the Act of Union was illegal. This led many members of Cumann na Gaedheal to criticize Griffith for seemingly demanding only the restoration of the Protestant parliament of 1782, but what Griffith was trying to do was to convince many Irish Party supporters to abandon the politics of 'home rule', as it operated since 1885, by developing the will to make a demand for Irish independence, rather than just allowing Westminster to decide how Ireland should be governed. He believed this policy could eventually allow Sinn Féin to replace the Irish Party as the principal political party in the country, launch the abstentionist policy and create a *de facto* independent Irish state. Griffith may have placed *some* hope in the possibility that if Sinn Féin officially committed itself to recognizing the crown, Britain would not declare war on Ireland should his policy succeed, but he certainly was not prepared to shirk the possibility of the more likely outcome of a full-scale Anglo-Irish conflict. This is why he noted that 'many may have fallen and all will have suffered' before Sinn Féin's policy could possibly succeed. To Griffith's mind, Sinn Féin's policy was republican because its policy was rooted strictly in a civic philosophy. He believed that demanding an Irish republican state was politically impractical, as well as unnecessary: 'what the form of an Irish national government should be is an interesting, but not a material question. It is the thing itself, regardless of its form, that Ireland wants.'[36] No IRB man essentially disagreed with him on

34 Speech of Griffith before first annual convention of the National Council, 28 Nov. 1905, reproduced in Griffith (ed.), *The resurrection of Hungary* (3rd ed., 1918), 139–40, 160–3.
35 *Sinn Féin*, 18 May 1907. 36 Ibid.

this point, but some young Cumann na Gaedhael members believed that Griffith (like Connolly before him) was making a mistake in trying to commit all republicans' energies into launching a new political party and chose instead to launch a propagandist campaign which they felt would be more effective in boosting Irishmen's desire for republican liberty. The foremost of these was Bulmer Hobson, who had been influenced deeply by the _Shan Van Vocht_ and the writings of Fintan Lalor. He had been sworn into the IRB in Belfast during 1904 and was a strong supporter of the anti-enlistment movement.

In March 1905, Hobson formed the first 'Dungannon Club' in Belfast with the support of some local writers and over the next eighteen months, other branches were formed in Dublin, Derry, Armagh, Wexford, Kerry, Tyrone, Newcastle-upon-Tyne and London, mostly on the basis of Cumann na Gaedhael.[37] Unlike the stoic and unsociable Griffith, who was really only a journalist, Hobson was capable of appealing to men of all classes and creeds in person. By December 1906, the Belfast Dungannon Club had launched a short-lived journal called the _Republic_, to which Hobson, the Belfast Presbyterian writers Robert Lynd and J.W. Good, as well as P.S. O'Hegarty, a rising London IRB leader and civil servant, were the principal contributors. The _Republic_ emphasised that it stood 'not for a republican party', as Griffith was trying to create, but to rally the intelligent manhood of Ireland behind the broader ideal of 'building up an Irish republic', or building up the basis of an Irish civil society, without engaging in party politics. Like many an IRB propagandist over the past forty years, Hobson declared confidently that 'the governmental system of England – the armed garrison she keeps in the land – will go down as grass before the reaper before the first generation in Ireland that trusts in itself and starts to work out its own salvation, relying on itself alone' and turning their attention completely away from Westminster. This was a 'battle not with England, but with the people of Ireland – it is the battle of self-respect, self-reliance and courage against the moral cowardice, the slavishness, the veneration for any authority however and by whoever assumed – that have marked the people of this country for generations.' He emphasized that 'the social and political institutions of Ireland, as in any country, are simply the outward visible expression of the people', and that 'when the mind of a people has outgrown the conditions existing in any country, the old conditions are cast off.' For this reason, he believed that 'a revolution has already begun, not merely a revolution that will achieve political independence, but a revolution in the mind of the nation': 'the future is ours to make and to mould as we would have it … this is the creed of The Republic'.[38]

The new propaganda campaign of Hobson, O'Hegarty and like-minded men was notable for its great enthusiasm and was based on the old IRB idea that a 'young republic' actually lived in the country. In the _Shan Van_

37 Bulmer Hobson, _Ireland: yesterday and tomorrow_ (1968), 21. 38 Bulmer Hobson, _The creed of the Republic_ (1907), reprint of article in _The Republic_, entitled 'The mind of the nation'.

Vocht, Patrick McManus even went so far as to argue that, by the 1890s, 'all Irishmen are at heart, with very few exceptions, republicans'.[39] In making this argument, however, McManus did not mean that all Irishmen, or even a majority, were adamant that there was a need for a republican state. What he meant was that Irishmen felt a deep desire to create the basis of a civil society in the country for the first time, and to do this in Ireland, as in any country, necessitated propagating republicanism. He was also expressing a belief that Irishmen were intrinsically opposed to the existing aristocratic social order in the country. On paper, Hobson and O'Hegarty essentially made similar arguments as IRB organizers used to make in their public speeches at Manchester-martyr and Land League rallies during the nineteenth century, but the context of Irish politics had changed. A wide scale democratic-republican agitation no longer existed in the country and the nineteenth-century ideal of creating movements of citizen-soldier democrats no longer had political relevance to people. Like past IRB organizers, Hobson and O'Hegarty frequently denounced the general public for their lack of 'self-reliance' in the same breath as they were calling upon them to take control of their own political destinies, but in championing this republican political morality they were not addressing workers and peasants, but rather fellow middle-class literary individuals like themselves. For this reason, their propaganda had no real political context. They were simply attempting to create a broader literary-political movement based upon the same ideals as their own. In effect, they were following O'Leary's ideal for the YIS.

Neal O'Boyle, a middle-aged Antrim farmer and the Ulster IRB leader, supported Hobson's Dungannon Clubs as well as Cumann na Gaedhael in Belfast and Antrim, along with Louis Smyth and John Clarke. O'Boyle, however, also attempted to direct the IRB's new working-class following in south Ulster, centred in east Tyrone, with which Hobson and the Dungannon Clubs refused to associate, since they were former AOH men. At one such Tyrone meeting in March 1905, the new local IRB leader, James Devlin (a former member of the AOH, who was probably recruited by John T. Keating) demanded that O'Boyle provide his following with firearms in return for their subscriptions; a demand that O'Boyle had probably not heard of for some time. He replied that the IRB had used funds in the past in an effort to repair arms it had acquired many years ago, but that these firearms were now virtually useless owing to recent developments in rifle technology. Consequently this practice was given up and it was decided instead to use the money only for 'organizing purposes'.[40] The Tyrone IRB were not satisfied with this, however, and so O'Boyle did distribute some firearms to the south Ulster IRB over the coming months, but a Special Branch informer who inspected the arms noted that they clearly all dated from the early 1880s.[41]

39 *Shan Van Vocht*, Aug. 1898. 40 NAI, British in Ireland microfilm, DMP and RIC précis, report of Crime Department Special Branch, 10 Apr. 1905. 41 Ibid., report of D.I. Wilkins, 4 July 1905.

This may well explain why few demands for firearms were made thereafter. A few thousand of such rifles were no doubt still hidden in various parts of the United Kingdom by those middle-aged republicans in Ireland who had acted under John O'Connor and P.N. Fitzgerald's direction during the early to mid 1880s, but from their recollections, it is clear that the young middle-class Irish-Irelanders who joined the IRB in Dublin or Belfast during the 1900s through the Gaelic League/Cumann na Gaedhael had no idea that they belonged to an organization that possessed firearms, or for that matter that the IRB used to collect subscriptions to fund arms importation efforts and be subject to Special Branch intrigues. They belonged to a different social world and effectively belonged to a different nationalist movement.

Hobson and O'Hegarty's revolutionary enthusiasms were rooted in their belief that the 'Irish-Ireland' movement could easily be directed towards nationalist ends and, in this respect, they did not differ radically from Griffith. The difference was that they had no faith in the practicality of his party-political policy. As Hobson recalled, they believed that Griffith's policy 'was all very well if there had been the remotest chance of our getting the town or county councils to accept and work the new policy; but to anyone with knowledge of local politics in the provinces at that period, this seemed quite out of the question',[42] not least because local politicians were resisting party politics of any kind. P.S. O'Hegarty believed that Griffith's reliance on the economic nationalist policy of the 'Irish-Irelanders' could end up making Sinn Féin nothing more than a party of 'the priests or the mythical commercial "'82 men"',[43] meaning a non-existing community of patriotic businessmen. These criticisms of the practicality of the Sinn Féin policy were undoubtedly justified – there were just nine National Council local government officials in the country during 1905, all based in Dublin – but the reality of the situation was that there was no other workable policy open to separatists.

By 1906, when the Liberals had been returned to power for the first time in over a decade, Griffith had become fully committed to making his Sinn Féin policy a forum for all dissenters from the Irish Party's politics, no matter how conservative they may have been. Among his new supporters were some men the *United Irishman* had denounced in 1900 for opposing the pro-Boer movement, but had been trying ever since the mid 1890s to make the rural, southern Irish community economically self-sufficient and more appealing to northern businessmen by promoting the co-operative movement. The most notable of these was T.W. Rolleston, who believed that the Sinn Féin movement was 'a relic' of the old IRB movement he knew during the 1880s. Writing during 1906 to Lady Aberdeen, a patron of the co-operative movement, Rolleston noted that 'I long ago saw that the ideal feeling, the sense

---

42 Hobson, *Ireland yesterday and tomorrow*, 20.   43 Michael Laffan, *The resurrection of Ireland* (1999), quoted 25.

of principle and of logic' of 'these people' made their minds immune to 'mere utilitarian arguments' or 'the brute force either of the State or of ecclesiasticism'. He viewed the rise of the new intellectual movement as proof that 'their great and growing influence over all the active young minds is now coming to maturity in Ireland' owing to the fact that, for the first time, 'they are getting the education now, in Catholic and nationalistic Ireland' and, consequently, the general public naturally 'don't understand a party which talks sedition in Ireland and America and takes the oath of allegiance in Westminster.'[44] Rolleston believed that 'unless the parliamentary movement can offer on its side a programme equally clear, honest and self-consistent' to Sinn Féin, 'it must inevitably go down before its antagonist' because 'young Ireland is now educated' while the Irish Party was supporting 'a self-reliant nationalism nowhere'. Indeed, Rolleston believed that *all* forms of Irish parliamentary representation at Westminster, including Ulster Unionists (who also formed a council of local government officials during 1905) would soon 'be forced back on its first principles' and have to face constituents who demanded rather more than they were capable of giving.[45]

While the Irish Party still spoke of politics in terms of 'leaders and followers', an independent public opinion was developing in Ireland at this time that helped negate this old style of politics. During the nineteenth century, republicans always used to celebrate their large public commemorations by arguing that 'there were no "leaders" - the people came themselves to do what every man or woman considered their duty, and they did it successfully.'[46] This, however, was generally reading into a populace a form of republican political reasoning that, more often than not, was not shared by those who attended these events. Such efforts by republicans to implement Davis's ideal of 'fostering a public opinion' in the country were fundamentally flawed for this very reason. The IRB's efforts to mobilize men within its own organization, distribute arms, issue circulars and find a foothold in the press had been more constructive. Meanwhile, the complaint of John Dillon during 1906 that 'Irish politics' had become 'a much more complex problem than it used to be'[47] reflected the fact that the Irish Party could no longer receive the public's total compliance with its politics by simply referring to Redmond as 'the Leader', as Parnell used to be known as 'the Uncrowned King'. The percentage of the population that were politically ignorant had declined significantly since the 1880s, due to rising levels of education in the country, and the growth of a full range of political papers in the country of diverse leanings was an illustration of this reality. The fact that 'Irish politics' had come to be seen as a 'problem' by some Irish Party leaders was rooted in the fact that its politics, based as it was solely upon the practicalities of British party politics, could not easily accommodate the existence of a public opinion within Ireland

44 Rolleston, *Portrait of an Irishman*, 117–20. 45 Rolleston, *Portrait of an Irishman*, 121.
46 Davis (ed.), *J.K. Casey*, 238. 47 F.S.L. Lyons, *John Dillon* (1968), 313.

that had both the will and the education to make up its own mind what politics in Ireland itself should be about without reference to Westminster.

In April 1906, Neal O'Boyle told the Ulster IRB that the IRB Supreme Council (and presumably the Clan as well) had now officially adopted the programme of Sinn Féin, although it did not accept Griffith's emphasis on the Renunciation Act.[48] When exactly Griffith left the IRB is unknown, but it is quite likely that he left at this time, as he did not want to change the programme he felt *he* invented at the dictates of the IRB. Another reason to believe this is that Griffith closed the *United Irishman* down in April 1906 and the following month launched a similar literary-political journal called *Sinn Féin* that was financially supported not by the IRB but instead by John Sweetman, a Healyite former MP, member of the Catholic landed gentry, propagandist of the Catholic Truth Society and enthusiastic supporter of the anti-enlistment campaign and the Gaelic League. Sweetman had recently become a vice-president of the National Council,[49] but he supported Griffith's initiative not to bring about Irish independence or a political revolution, but rather to express opposition to the Irish Party and the UIL Directory for failing to support the Liberals' idea of establishing an 'Irish Council', which would allow the public to elect men to govern a few select departments of the Dublin Castle administration. The Irish Party split once more as a result of this quarrel, several MPs resigning and a few others actively identifying themselves with the National Council for essentially the same reasons as Sweetman.[50] Griffith played up the significance of this in *Sinn Féin*, but the development failed to arouse the interest of republicans. Seventeen Dublin city councillors now supported the National Council, but only a few other small branches existed in Waterford, Kilkenny, Cavan and Belfast, and these generally involved literary rather than political people. This is hardly surprising, considering that the president of the National Council was Edward Martyn, the director of the Abbey Theatre and a member of the executive of the Gaelic League. The first branch of the National Council in Cork was established in September 1906, and its president was the 70-year-old republican C.G. Doran,[51] by now a leader of the Cork Historical and Archaeological Society, although he retired shortly thereafter and ultimately died in 1909.

As the IRB secretary, P.T. Daly was primarily responsible for pushing the new policy of supporting Griffith's movement. He did this by trying to reorganize the IRB solely among those directly linked with Sinn Féin, even if this meant alienating the older men. In the summer of 1906, he called for a Belfast IRB convention and asked Denis McCullough to chair the meeting. McCullough announced that all IRB 'circles under the auspices of Robert Johnston and Henry Dobbyn' were going to be expelled from the organization

48 NAI, British in Ireland microfilm, DMP and RIC précis, report of 7 May 1906.   49 Ibid., report 1 Nov. 1905.   50 Patrick Maume, *The long gestation* (1999), 89.   51 *Sinn Féin*, 3 Nov. 1906.

because they had been trying to build up new circles based around the AOH, which McCullough and Hobson detested. A bitter argument ensued. As a ruse, Johnston and Dobbyn were led out of the hall to discuss the matter further and, in their absence, P.T. Daly announced that he had appointed McCullough onto the Supreme Council as an honorary member to replace Johnston, who had been appointed to this position in October 1902 in order to restore unity in the Ulster IRB, but he had failed to do so. This gave McCullough the leverage necessary to expel all Johnston and Dobbyn's followers from the organization and to form a new Belfast IRB Directory based solely around Cumann na Gaedhael;[52] the price of this ritualistic purging of the ranks being to reduce the once-numerous Belfast IRB organization down to a very small size, consisting of three small circles of young men. Neal O'Boyle was not very happy with this development, but he stepped down voluntarily as Ulster IRB leader in favour of McCullough in 1908.[53]

By the time John O'Leary died in March 1907, a new IRB leadership had effectively been put in place, centred on P.T. Daly, the secretary. Following O'Leary's death, Cumann na Gaedhael and the Dungannon Clubs decided to unite and call themselves the 'Sinn Féin League' under the presidency of Daly. Three months later, one of the Irish Party defectors to the National Council, C.J. Dolan of north Leitrim, announced that he was going to seek re-election to parliament as a 'National Council' or abstentionist candidate. Most prominent Sinn Féin figures in the country took part in Dolan's campaign, not because they cared whether or not he was elected (they knew he had no chance of doing so), but rather to capitalize upon the fact that numerous UIL branches in the north-west had turned against the Irish Party and therefore campaigning in this area could help win them over to the Sinn Féin League. Indeed, several new rifts in the UIL emerged that year. Laurence Ginnell (an independent MP for Longford and a passive supporter of Sinn Féin)[54] and his 'Independent UIL' organization, which had launched the 'ranch war', was rapidly becoming the most popular political movement in the mid-west. Several provincial newspapers had expressed support for the Sinn Féin policy, most notably William O'Brien's *Irish People*, which called for a new national movement to be established that would incorporate Sinn Féin and truly reflect popular opinion in the country by turning away from the Dillon and Devlin's centralized oligarchy. The AOH (American Alliance), a breakaway body from Devlin's AOH, was also growing quickly, expressing opposition to the Irish Party and supporting Sinn Féin and William O'Brien.[55] The AOH (Board of Scotland), in which Henry Dobbyn was involved, supported Sinn Féin as early as 1905,[56] while a vocal minority of Joseph Devlin's AOH (Board of Erin) was also against supporting the Irish Party.[57] This may well help to explain why

52 UCD, Denis McCullough papers, P120/29 (1), statement to Bureau of Military History 14 Oct. 1957. 53 Ibid. 54 Bulmer Hobson claimed some credit for himself for making Ginnell sympathetic towards the Dungannon Clubs. Hobson, *Ireland yesterday and tomorrow*, 28. 55 Maume, *Long gestation*, 94–5. 56 *United Irishman*, 20 July 1905. 57 NAI, British

Devlin felt it necessary to argue at some public events during 1907 that he believed 'the majority of Irishmen' were correct in judging that, if it was possible, the idea of armed rebellion and the 'complete destruction' of British rule in Ireland was 'by the law of God, of nature and of nations ... fully justified', since Ireland had never been 'governed by the consent of the governed'.[58]

In September 1907, the Sinn Fein League and the National Council amalgamated and officially became known as the 'Sinn Féin Party'. Griffith, however, succeeded in keeping the Renunciation Act clause in its constitution; a clear illustration of how the influence of the moderates in the Dublin National Council outweighed that of the IRB. In October 1907, Terence McSwiney's Cork CLS championed William O'Brien's ideas on the land question and affiliated itself with Sinn Féin. Ex-IRB men of the Parnell era who were now aldermen in Cork City Hall, as well as Sean O'Keeffe and his following, who now left the IRB, began promoting Sinn Féin as well.[59]

On 6 October 1907, the sixteenth anniversary of Parnell's death, P.N. Fitzgerald died at the age of fifty-six in St Vincent's Hospital, Dublin, where he had been for several months. He had expressed passive support for the National Council, but failed in his efforts to maintain the IRB as a secret revolutionary underground. The last public initiative he had been involved in was trying to establish a GAA newspaper, the first since the demise of the *Gael*. This paper, the *Champion*, first went to print in December 1903, was edited by Michael Crowe and promoted Cumann na Gaedhael and the Gaelic League. P.S. O'Hegarty was one of its leading contributors. The *Champion* called for the establishment of 'Irish Brigade Clubs' of the GAA, which would affiliate themselves with the 'Major MacBride Athletics Club of Dublin', which was controlled by young republicans. This initiative was supported by a few figures in Dublin City Hall, but due to lack of funding, the *Champion* ceased publication as early as February 1904, while the attempt to form 'Irish Brigade Clubs' failed to win public interest.[60] The 60-year-old Mark Ryan funded this activity, but he was replaced as IRB treasurer shortly afterwards and was effectively retired. Although Ryan was made the honorary president of the first Sinn Féin branch in London when it was established in 1908,[61] its actual leader was P.S. O'Hegarty, who became a Supreme Councillor, as did Michael Crowe, who replaced 'P.N.', possibly not until after the Corkman died. Fitzgerald's funeral was a large affair. A large gathering of Dublin republican and trade union activists of his generation brought his remains to Kingstown station, and his funeral in rural east Cork was attended by many old IRB activists, some ex-Parnellites now on the executive of Cumann na Gaedhael, the mayor of Cork and many city councillors, as well as many town

in Ireland microfilm, DMP and RIC précis, 2 Aug. 1905, 3 Sept. 1905.   **58** *Freeman's Journal*, 23 Nov. 1907 (speech in Tipperary).   **59** *Sinn Féin*, 5 Oct. 1907.   **60** Mandle, *GAA*, 153–4. **61** Ryan, *Fenian memories*, 206.

councillors, journalists and GAA figures from Cork, Tipperary and Clare and even a few O'Brienite MPs. Cork City Hall voted to inscribe Fitzgerald's name on the 'National Monument' erected in the city centre the previous year, and collections were made for his family by the National Monuments Committee, supported by Mark Ryan, Sean O'Keeffe, Maurice Moynihan, Patrick Meade and J.C. Flynn MP.[62] Obituaries described Fitzgerald as a lifelong 'fearless propagandist of advanced views in Irish politics' who 'was identified with every movement which had for its object the physical and intellectual regeneration of the Irish people', and, 'although he held very strong views in Irish politics, he was always tolerant of other people's opinions.'[63] Thus ended the career of the chief travelling organizer of the IRB during the Parnell era. Except for Crowe and P.T. Daly (who claimed that Fitzgerald had a negative influence on the IRB during the 1900s)[64] no young IRB activist was present at his funeral, indicating that he was either an unpopular or an unknown figure to them. He certainly belonged to an earlier generation of Irish republican activists who, like James Stephens and the Land League organizers, possessed a missionary belief that by simply organizing 'the people' on a democratic basis and appealing to the general public to take control of their own destinies 'anything can be accomplished' and a new political order could be created.[65] This old IRB style of politics was still an inspirational and practicable brand of popular politics in Ireland during the 1880s, but by the 1900s there was essentially no longer any place in Irish popular politics for 'republican brothers' of this kind, who had virtually become just as politically irrelevant as the corpse of James Stephens rotting in Glasnevin cemetery. Instead of trying his hand at writing republican propaganda (something at which he might perhaps have excelled), Fitzgerald continued to rely on the spoken word, both as an IRB organizer and as a public figure, and evidently dreamed of the IRB becoming a mass political movement once more, as in former days. As late as 1898, he was still making Stephens-style platform statements like 'political "leaders" do not trouble me. I have set out since my early life with fixed purposes and my interests, while I live, will be the interests of humanity; the raising up and the bettering of the masses to higher conceptions of national duty and honour.'[66] By 1901, however, while speaking at Bodenstown, Fitzgerald admitted that he felt he was probably a bit of 'a dreamer', as 'some agrarian socialists' (probably meaning Davitt) were telling him, but, still, 'I would prefer to dream honestly than preach self-interested political claptrap'.[67]

Neal O'Boyle appears to have replaced John O'Leary as the nominal IRB president following the latter's death, and he subsequently took the lead in establishing a monument for O'Leary at Glasnevin in memory of 'the Fenian

62 TCD, Dillon papers, MS 1121. **63** *Evening Telegraph*, 7 Oct. 1907 (obituary); *Cork Examiner*, 8 and 9 Oct. 1907 (report of funeral). **64** *DPB*, vol. 2, 354. **65** *Irish Daily Independent*, 25 Nov. 1895. **66** *Freeman's Journal*, 18 April 1898. **67** *Leinster Leader*, 29 June 1901.

leader'.[68] Some Irish-American revolutionaries could not believe that O'Leary had held such a position, although Devoy stated categorically that O'Leary had been the IRB president 'for many years before he died and up to the day of his death'.[69] Devoy noted of O'Leary that 'he was essentially a critic' who 'seldom found himself in full agreement with the majority of the advanced nationalists [IRB], but in his own way, he conducted a most effective propagandistic campaign . . . He died literally in harness.'[70] Reputedly, O'Leary once said during the mid 1880s that he believed Ireland could be better served by 'fifty Thomas Davises' than 'fifty-thousand Joseph Bradies'. How far he truly believed this is unclear, for much though O'Leary prioritized the YIS policy, he clearly found the gradual dismemberment of the IRB during the later nineteenth century just as demoralizing as the rest of the organization. Certainly by the time P.N. Fitzgerald and John O'Leary died during 1907, the IRB organization they had known during the nineteenth century was dead, and 'fifty Thomas Davises' or journalists had effectively taken the place in Irish life that was formerly occupied by the IRB.

When John O'Connor, the IRB secretary of the 1880s, died in Paris in November 1908, both the Clan and the IRB were evidently concerned about what would happen to certain documents he held,[71] indicating that (as British intelligence suspected) he may have been called out of retirement once more to perform some IRB clerical duties shortly before his death.[72] Whatever the case, Devoy was certainly correct to say when O'Connor died that 'no man in recent Irish history showed a greater ability in doing under the very noses of the police things which it was their special business to prevent.'[73]

The IRB's decision to support Sinn Féin was undoubtedly shaped by the fact that Clan na Gael (principally due to Daniel F. Coholan's influence) had become wholly supportive of the Irish-Ireland movement and the Gaelic League. Coholan played a major role in organizing an American fund-collection tour of Douglas Hyde during early 1906 and he also visited Dublin in June 1906, encouraging IRB leaders to concentrate on the Gaelic League.[74] This had effectively already happened, as members of the Wolfe Tone Clubs and all republican societies were clearly involved in the Gaelic League at this time, as was virtually every other nationalist organization in the country for exactly the same reason: to attempt to capture the middle ground of Irish public opinion.

After his divorce from Maud Gonne in early 1905, John MacBride returned to Ireland, was granted work with Dublin Corporation by Fred Allan (MacBride also moved in with the Allan family) and became a fairly regular public speaker at republican commemorative events. Allan also became involved in republican activities for the first time in a few years, after Coholan

---

68 *Gaelic American*, 5 Dec. 1908. **69** *Gaelic American*, 12 Dec. 1908. **70** *Gaelic American*, 26 Mar. 1907. **71** *DPB*, vol. 2, 372–3. **72** NAI, Home Office précis, carton 3, 29621/s. **73** *Gaelic American*, 5 Dec. 1908. **74** NAI, British in Ireland microfilm, DMP and RIC precis, 2 July 1906.

encouraged him to do so. At the 1905 Bodenstown demonstration, which was attended by Jack O'Hanlon's Wolfe Tone Clubs, P.T. Daly, Arthur Griffith and Denis McCullough, MacBride re-emphasized a point that he had made earlier in 1902 while writing to the *United Irishman*, that while the IRB had always 'been accused of foolishly arguing in the country the necessity of appealing to arms' or 'of trying to sow discord amongst Irish nationalists', these accusations 'had never been true'. Rather the IRB 'lamented, and still lament, the waste of money upon the parliamentary movement' and was just pointing out to people that 'if that wealth was spent on arms' over the past few decades, 'we would be in a position to add another republic to the republics of the world'.[75] During 1905–7, however, he added another qualification to this argument, noting that 'we have no deep-rooted quarrel with men who earnestly think otherwise and seek no quarrel with them' even though 'we cannot see eye to eye with them'. As republicans had generally done since the mid 1880s, MacBride argued that in the IRB only 'was any real effort made to carry into effect the high principles of liberty embodied in the teachings of the Young Ireland party' of the 1840s, and the ideology of both movements was 'inseparably linked': 'give us an educated Ireland and no power on earth can stop her from gaining her liberty'.[76]

During 1907, while P.T. Daly committed himself to labour politics, helping James Larkin and others to set up the Irish Transport and General Workers Union (ITGWU), Bulmer Hobson tried to convince the public of the necessity of supporting Sinn Féin by arguing that 'to express confidence in the policy of the Irish Party is absurd, because it is expressing confidence in something which does not exist ... the Irish Party has no policy'.[77] While forming dozens of small new branches of the Sinn Féin party, similar arguments were made during 1908–9 by young party activists, such as Sean McDermott, Sean T. O'Kelly TC, Richard O'Carroll TC, Sean Milroy and G.A. Lyons. However most new branches of Sinn Féin established at this time consisted only of UIL deserters who just as quickly disbanded these branches and joined William O'Brien's All-for-Ireland League instead, as soon as that body was established in March 1910. Some old republicans of the Parnell era, such as Maurice Moynihan (who became the electoral registrar of Tralee in 1908) formed the first branches of Sinn Féin in Kerry and promoted both it *and* the All-for-Ireland League until he was struck down by tuberculosis in 1912.[78] While Arthur Griffith was favourable to the idea of Sinn Féin and O'Brien's party working together, however, most young Sinn Féin activists were against it. As a result, the Sinn Féin party essentially came to a complete standstill by 1910.

If Sinn Féin had not succeeded in benefitting from the political divisions in

75 *Leinster Leader*, 15 July 1905; *United Irishman*, 18 Jan. 1902.   **76** *Gaelic American*, 14 Dec. 1907.   **77** *Sinn Féin*, 5 Oct. 1907.   **78** J.A. Gaughan, *Thomas O'Donnell* (Dublin, 1983), 22–3 (biographical note on Moynihan); NAI, British in Ireland microfilm, DMP and Home Office précis, summary July 1910.

Ireland during 1908–10, a number of other factors helped to foment dissent. In April 1909, Matthew Cummings, the president of the AOH in America, came to Ireland with Seamus McManus to unite the AOH (Board of Erin), the AOH (Board of Scotland) and the AOH (American Alliance) in favour of the latter, which, like the AOH in America, was pro-Sinn Féin. In this work, he was supported by Henry Dobbyn, Robert Johnston (McManus's uncle) and his son James, all of whom had joined the AOH (Board of Scotland). As Cummings was a prominent member of the Clan, he also called upon all Dublin IRB/Sinn Féin leaders when he arrived in Ireland, including the Clan's most recent envoy to the IRB,[79] Tom Clarke, who was sent back to Ireland after P.N. Fitzgerald's death, arriving in Dublin on 10 December 1907. Dobbyn and Johnston's decision to get involved in the AOH was purely opportunistic, for they knew that it was the single most numerous Irish organization on both sides of the Atlantic and it would be a devastating blow to the Irish Party if it became pro-Sinn Féin, owing to John Dillon's heavy reliance upon Joseph Devlin and the AOH (Board of Erin) in attempting to impose discipline upon the urban followers of the Irish Party. Both Bulmer Hobson and Denis McCullough were very opposed to this strategy, but Patrick MacCartan from Dublin (a Sinn Féin T.C. who corresponded with Joseph McGarrity in Philadelphia) supported it, probably because he was more familiar with the cosmopolitan, middle-class and well-educated leaders of the AOH in America than he was with the parochial and intensely sectarian body that was the AOH in Ulster. With the help of the old Tyrone IRB activist Michael McGinn, Robert Johnston managed to contact John Devoy, the Clan secretary, appealing for the Clan to support his strategy of the IRB getting involved in the AOH 'with the object of leading them in the right direction.'[80] Cummings' arrival would indicate that the Clan agreed with the idea. John Nugent, the secretary of the AOH (Board of Erin) and a keen 'Irish-Irelander', also sympathised with the plan of allying the AOH with Cummings and McManus' American organization,[81] centred around Notre Dame University.

On 21 April 1909, a secret convention of all wings of the AOH was held in the Gresham Hotel and Cummings chaired the meeting. He argued that as 'only nationalists are fit to be called Hibernians', all AOH men should withdraw from the UIL and join with the American AOH and Johnston and Dobbyn's body in supporting Sinn Féin. Nugent was uncertain how to respond, but Joseph Devlin, the president of the AOH (Board of Erin), reacted by hurling vicious abuse at Cummings, Johnston and Dobbyn for attempting to 'cause disunion' and subsequently invited them to leave the hotel and settle the matter with their fists. This led to an uproar, during which the Irish and Irish-

---

79 NAI, British in Ireland microfilm, DMP and RIC precis, 3 May 1909.　80 *DPB*, vol. 2, 357–8.　81 NAI, British in Ireland microfilm, DMP and RIC precis, 1 April 1909.

American clergy present criticized Devlin, who withdrew his following from the meeting and the convention ended inconclusively.[82] The matter was far from settled, however, as the AOH in America was not unanimous in supporting Sinn Féin. For example, its leader in Boston, John O'Callaghan, was actually the treasurer of the UILA. After the convention, Devlin tried to strengthen his control over the UIL Directory, while Eoin MacNeill organized Gaelic League fund-raising events for Cummings, McManus and the American AOH in gratitude for their role in promoting the Irish-Ireland movement. Before leaving for America, Cummings called upon the IRB and Sinn Féin leadership in Dublin. However, he was also invited to Maynooth College, which gave him a sympathetic interview, a great illustration of the shifting trends in Irish politics.[83]

In September 1909, to counter the impact of Cummings' visit, Joseph Devlin arranged for John O'Callaghan to come to Ireland and to bring with him the 64-year-old Edward O'Meagher Condon, a former Irish-American revolutionary best known for the fact that it was he who first uttered the cry 'God save Ireland' from the dock with the Manchester martyrs in 1867. Condon was now an honorary official of the New York UILA. A number of large public rallies were held, where O'Callaghan and Condon spoke alongside Redmond in calling for all Irishmen to continue supporting the Irish Party. Meanwhile, the *Freeman's Journal* argued that Condon's support for the Irish Party proved that it, rather than Sinn Féin, was the true political successor to 'the Fenians'.[84] In early October, Condon was granted the freedom of Dublin, Cork, Sligo, Waterford and Wexford, while Redmond persuaded the Liberal Home Secretary, Winston Churchill, to allow Condon visit the spot where the Manchester martyrs were buried in Salford Jail in an attempt to convince the public of the reality of the 'union of hearts'.[85] Not surprisingly, both the Tories and Sinn Féin opposed the Condon tour. Most members of the Old Guard Union (who were not fully aware of the political context of the visit) actually welcomed the honour paid to Condon, although this sentiment was not shared by one of its leaders, James Mullet, the chairman of the Dublin board of guardians and associate of the socialist trade unionist William O'Brien. Mullet denounced the AOH (Board of Erin) as a 'bad lot' and wrote that 'no one from Antrim to Cork has a greater admiration than I have for O'Meagher Condon but if he lends himself out as a showman for a political organization, I object.'[86] These sentiments were also shared by Eamonn Ceannt, Mullet's successor as leader of the South Dock Union, a Gaelic Leaguer and Sinn Féiner who was a leader of the Dublin Municipal Officers Association and sought to ally it with the County Council Officers Association; something that was not achieved until 1920, with the formation of the Local Government and Public Services Union.[87]

82 Ibid., 3 May 1909. 83 Ibid., 4 May, 2 June, 4 June, 6 July, 2 Sept. 1909. 84 *Freeman's Journal*, 6 Sept. 1909. 85 *Freeman's Journal*, 5 and 6 Oct. 1909, 17 Dec. 1915 (obituary for Condon). 86 *Freeman's Journal*, 2 Sept. 1909. 87 Martin Maguire, *Servants to the public:*

After the January 1910 general elections, when the Irish Party (combined with eleven independent O'Brienite MPs) were able to keep the Liberals in power in return for a promise to introduce another 'home rule bill', the quarrel regarding the AOH effectively ceased. While the minority continued to denounce the Irish Party, the AOH (Board of Erin) generally remained supportive, although its interest in the future of the Irish Party, as was the case with virtually all movements at this time, was very conditional. In May 1910, for example, John D. Nugent, the national secretary of the AOH (Board of Erin), argued that the AOH (which had 70,000 members) was prepared to support the Irish Party at the present, but if it 'did not seem to be winning', the AOH would be willing to support different parties instead.[88] Remarks like these help to explain the confidence of men like Patrick Hughes, a leader of Sinn Féin, the AOH and Gaelic League in Dundalk, who proclaimed confidently that the Irish Party would receive 'a rude awakening' in the very near future regarding the *actual* level of popular support it had in the country.[89] These hopes of Sinn Féin were not based on its actual strength as a party – it was still just a loose alliance of town councillors, nationalists and members of literary and GAA clubs rather than a political party – but rather on its belief that it was far more in line with the political views of the Irish-Ireland movement and the young, rising Catholic middle class than Redmond, Dillon or Devlin. What was perhaps closer to the truth was that the Gaelic League and Irish-Ireland movement possessed a political power that was virtually beyond the control of either party. This was perhaps best demonstrated by Eoin MacNeill's success in getting the introduction of Irish as a compulsory subject for matriculation to the new National University of Ireland (NUI), despite the fact that the Irish Party and some of the Catholic hierarchy criticised or were unhappy with this policy.

By creating the NUI in 1908, the Liberals fulfilled the promise made by their Tory predecessors to give state recognition to the Catholic University, which now became known as University College Dublin (UCD) and maintained its Jesuitical ethos. Although the Catholic hierarchy was uncomfortable with the Irish language clause (which they feared might prompt non Irish-speaking, upper-class Catholics to attend Trinity), the establishment of UCD, the *Ne Temere* decree of 1908, combined with the huge growth of Christian Brothers' schools at a primary and secondary level in recent years (all of which maintained an 'Irish-Ireland' ethos), guaranteed the future wellbeing of Catholic Ireland, as far as the church was concerned. Furthermore, after the creation of UCD, the Catholic hierarchy no longer had any real reason to be concerned with the politics of 'home rule' or the future of the Irish Party, for it was known that no 'home rule bill' introduced by the British state would ever allow an Irish parliament interfere with the strictly non-

a history of the Local Government and Public Service Union 1901–1990 (Dublin, 1998), 17–8.
88 NAI, British in Ireland microfilm, DMP and RIC precis, report for May 1910 (speech of Nugent at Roscommon).   89 Ibid., report for April 1910 (speech of Hughes at Dundalk).

denominational status of the national schools. Indeed, like the mostly working or lower-middle class AOH in urban Ireland, or the land agitators in the mid-west and west of Ireland, the church now had every reason to support a different party than Redmond's if it was in a better position, or seemed more inclined, to comply with its desires.

During 1910, the Irish Party undoubtedly still had good support in Ireland among the Catholic business community and rural middle class. After the Liberals' return to power in 1906, it managed to collect some funds in Ireland again and it had very good success in doing so after the Liberals promised to introduce a 'home rule' bill in 1910.[90] The budget crisis of 1909–10 and the subsequent moves by the Liberals (with the Irish Party's cautious support) to limit the powers of veto of the House of Lords also made the passing of a 'home rule bill' a possibility for the first time. The Tories' response to this situation, however, did not help the Irish Party's public image. Once the Irish Party sided with the Liberals on the House of Lords issue, the Tories sought to gain political capital against the Liberals by protesting against the supposed 'republicanism of John Redmond', the Liberals' ally. This forced the 'home rule' press in Ireland and England to try and convince the British voting public that, 'when the last word has been said', the Irish Party were 'the strongest pillars of the Throne – certainly far stronger than even the authority of the Lords could make it.' The Irish Party also argued that the Irish people believed an independent Ireland could only mean disaster, as the country would 'be industrially ruined in a month'.[91] This economic argument was perhaps of some significance, although it was also missing a very important point. In 1886 and 1893, the fact that the proposed 'home rule bill' gave Ireland no autonomy and control over taxation may have been discussed and debated by the Irish Party and the government (on the government's terms), but it created no active debate in Ireland itself upon the issue of how Irish taxes were spent. The Parnellite press was purposely silent about the matter, just as it was about all other limitations of the bill. Little or no journals for debating the issue even existed in the country. By 1911, however, numerous journal articles and newspaper articles were being written, arguing that any such 'home rule' measure would be useless, since it gave the parliament no fiscal or legislative autonomy. Although John Dillon appealed to the public to 'make peace with England without any reserves' and welcome home rule, many newspapers (even the provincial *Sligo Champion*, which altered its tone when the factionist-baiter McHugh died in 1909) pointed out that the proposed 'home rule bill' was a sham.[92] Only those papers controlled by 'The Party' generally attempted to put a positive face on the matter, by adopting the same old Parnell era style rhetoric that the public should place their trust in the 'leaders

90 Ibid., report for June 1910. 91 L.G. Redmond Howard, *John Redmond* (London, 1910), 339–40, 330 (quoting the *Daily Nation*). 92 Boyce and O'Day (eds.), *Ireland in transition*, 64–7.

of the Irish nation' in the British imperial parliament. The reality, however, was that by 1910 much more than a few supposed 'extremists' or 'physical force men' refused to ignore the basic fact that 'free people supply no taxes or soldiers for purposes over which they have no control.' An educated Catholic polity now existed in Ireland that, unlike Redmond's 'Irish Party' or Carson's 'Ulster Party', was independent in both its thought and its action from the Liberal and Tory parties of the British political establishment, and believed it had the right to become Ireland's governing elite. Whatever occurred after 1910, this was not going to change. In effect, the politics of 'home rule' was dead and a nationalist politics had been born.

CONCLUSION

What was the role of the IRB in the 'Irish revolution' and Irish history?

The IRB's history could well be broken into three distinct phases, the first, covering the period from its inception up until the time of the 1798 centenary; the second, dating from the birth of the Irish-Ireland movement up until the formation of the Irish Volunteers in 1913; and the third, covering the era of the 'Irish revolution'. For reasons which will be explained in this chapter, of these three phases in the IRB's history, the first was essentially the most pivotal in determining the role that republicanism would, or would not, play in twentieth-century Irish life.

The greatest element of continuity in the IRB's history was that it always thought and acted like an underground republican party, which attempted to sustain the legacy of the Confederate Clubs of 1848. During the nineteenth century, the IRB tried to change the structure of Irish political society 'from below' through the medium of its organization and by propagating republican principles, thereby (it was hoped) creating a virtual 'young republic', or democracy, within Irish society that could change the political order in the country and become the basis of an independence movement. In so doing, the IRB was attempting to compensate for the fact that, literally speaking, there was no democracy in Ireland under the Union: the government, or administration, at Dublin Castle was completely unaccountable to the Irish public and it was also largely unaccountable to the imperial parliament, excepting the members of the cabinet at Whitehall. The IRB believed that its ideal of becoming, and remaining, a revolutionary 'nucleus' of Irish political life was always practicable because, under the circumstances, a republican 'brotherhood' or party operating outside of the arena of electoral politics was thought to be no less a practical method of political organization than anything else in the country. In fact, it was considered a much *more* practical and constructive action, as it responded exclusively to the situation within Ireland itself, was permanently in touch with popular political and social organizations and thus its political support base could remain strong. The moment a democratic political order could be established in Ireland, or that Irish politics began, as Griffith put it, to 'revolve on its own axis', the IRB felt it had every reason to believe that it would triumph politically over the Irish members of the unaccountable, imperial parliament. It was this eventuality that the IRB leaders were essentially betting, or counting, upon.

The IRB's perpetual great distrust of, or refusal to cooperate with, any political movement governed by the MPs, or by the bishops, was based upon its awareness that any such leadership would inherently endeavour to keep the focal point of Irish politics at Westminster and, thereby, ensure that the nature of political society in the country would not change. The IRB's shifting relationship with all popular political movements in the country, from the NBSP to the Amnesty Association, from the Land League to the United Irish League, hinged on this fixed point. This commitment was in fact what the IRB's definition of a 'nationalist' was in practice, and its use of that term was always based upon the presumption that the truth of this reasoning would be self-evident to contemporaries. To a very significant extent, it was. It was not in the interest of the Irish Catholic establishment, however, to acknowledge or champion such a viewpoint because it had already largely accommodated its interests with the Union. Contrary to the claims of sections of the Irish press, Catholicism and nationalism were not at all synonymous in Ireland under the Union, and Catholic Ireland itself embodied numerous divisions on class, cultural and ideological lines. It is significant that many leaders of the GAA and the Dublin Trades Council opted to become members of the underground republican party, often simply because they identified with democratic and egalitarian principles, and it is surely not coincidental that those few Irish Party politicians who defied the British parliament by championing a democratic brand of politics within Ireland itself during the 1880s were almost invariably former members of the IRB.

The reality of the political situation in nationalist circles in nineteenth-century Ireland was often completely different to that picture presented by the Tory, Catholic or 'home rule' press, each of which inherently represented the interests of those sections of the business community, or the propertied class, which had prospered under the Union and that consequently had reason to fear the rise of an Irish nationalism or 'separatism'. Newspapers are inherently commercial enterprises that cannot survive without advertising, and the small circulation or short-lived nature of virtually all Irish seditious newspapers under the Union was due to the fact that it was never possible to persuade businesses to advertise in them, since this would have been far too commercially risky for any business in a Whitehall-controlled economy. Ever since the 'Fenian fever' of the late 1860s, all mainstream papers had used the unexplainable word of 'Fenianism' to make contrapositive arguments to justify their own political positions or interests. What this 'Fenianism', which they defined their politics against, actually meant was something that was left conveniently unexplained. Irish Tory papers generally always represented 'Fenianism' as any threat to the existing social order posed by the proverbial rabble. Meanwhile, from 1870 onwards, newspapers representing the Catholic establishment in Ireland always referred to the 'Fenian movement' in the past tense, primarily because the Catholic 'National' Association wanted the Catholic population to view 'the men of '67' as having represented a politics that may have been idealistic, but was entirely impractical and which had consequently failed and was now past. The reality, of course, was that for at least another twenty-five years after the supposed demise of 'the Fenians' in 1867, party struggles between the IRB and the Irish establishment, including both the Tory-Anglican and Catholic-Whig/liberal ones, continued to take place, while the eventual outcome of these struggles was by no means certain to contemporaries.

By championing a different politics to that of the establishment, the IRB was neither engaged in 'crime' nor was it making people irresponsible or forcing them to adopt dangerous vices. This was something that Irish MPs privately knew to be the case, even if they were totally opposed to the IRB's revolutionary nationalist politics. Although they were dependent on (and thus responded exclusively to) the propertied classes, leading politicians from G.H. Moore to Isaac Butt, C.S. Parnell to John Redmond often engaged with the IRB because they knew this seditious party had very strong influence within Ireland, even if it had to stay mostly underground to stop it from being crushed by the imperial administration. Social interaction between republicans and MPs was not unusual, so long as the established politicians did not fear dealing with popular political activists. Each party generally knew where the other stood politically and the wording of their respective arguments, made for public consumption, was geared accordingly in an attempt to outmanoeuvre the other by winning away their respective followings. The IRB, for example, always denounced the MPs for being willing to waste people's money on paying the personal expenses for members of the 'talking-shop' at Westminster, instead of launching an independence movement in the country and truly serving the interests of 'the people'. This was effectively the party political statement of the IRB. By contrast, the MPs always argued that the nationalists and republicans were foolishly attempting to 'force' people into a rebellion that could not possibly succeed and so were living in a dreamland, whereas the MPs knew that the IRB was not 'forcing' people to do anything. The IRB leadership was generally aware of all possible methods of political action that might serve nationalist ends and judged the political situation in the country accordingly, to the best of its abilities.

For republicans, the self-evident fact that Irish MPs in Westminster could not exercise any control over their country's destiny was their greatest trump card. If they believed that 'history was on their side', this was because of their faith in the eventual evolution of a new democratic political order in the western world. For Catholic MPs, in particular, their greatest trump card was the fact that the Catholic Church was determined to ensure that all Irish resources would be channelled into pressurizing Whitehall to introduce reforms to guarantee the future well-being of a relatively insecure church and, in particular, enhance its control over the education system in the country. Lay as much as clerical elites of Catholic Ireland shared this latter ambition, since access to education was the key to social mobility. Furthermore, wherever the church and its schools led, the Irish Catholic community was generally sure to follow, not least because, particularly after the 1890s, Catholicism was perhaps the only truly powerful collective identity in the country.

During the early to mid 1860s, the IRB had no definite political strategy (though the British-infiltrated Fenian Brotherhood attempted to force one upon it in 1865) other than seeing how far it could successfully establish a democratic-republican and nationalist agitation in the country. After the IRB began to make real progress by the late 1860s, it became officially committed to the revolutionary strategy of the so-called 'abstentionist policy', which was the only means whereby Irish independence could be brought about short of an outright military defeat of Britain, which the IRB knew to be impossible. The abstentionist policy was the favoured revolutionary strategy of the IRB Supreme Council from the very beginnings of the 'home rule' movement in 1873 and an underlying idea of the republicans' 'new departure' of 1879, upon which the nationalist reputation of Charles Stewart Parnell and the Irish Parliamentary Party was largely based. The 'other means' that most Irish Party MPs felt it necessary to intimate that they would be prepared to adopt during the early 1880s was the independence strategy of the IRB, and they needed to make such statements for party-political reasons, that is, so long as they wished to win nationalist support. In this respect, the reason why public debate on the 'new departure' idea essentially gave an edge to Parnell (and why John O'Leary and some other IRB leaders felt distaste for the introduction of this debate into Irish politics) was simply that it allowed Westminster MPs greater flexibility in wording their political statements to the general public, thereby potentially allowing them to mislead nationalist opinion and outmanouevre the IRB. The Catholic hierarchy understood this very quickly, and so threw its weight behind the new 'Irish Party' as soon as the republicans began to achieve greater public influence. The politics of the 'new departure' had nothing to do with the verbal nonsense invented by O'Connell of 'constitutional' and 'physical force' methods, even though some parties might still use that language now and then whenever it suited them to adopt a more polemical stance to distinguish their politics from that of their opponents. Likewise, the politics of the 'new departure' had nothing to do with Parnell's own nonsensical verbal invention, drawing an imaginary distinction between 'ordinary nationalism' and 'advanced nationalism'. The 'new departure' had everything to do with conflicting ideas as to how a democratic politics in Ireland might be allowed to develop and, in this respect, the Land League agitation played the central role in giving the 'new departure' idea some substance and, indeed, in changing the whole shape of Irish politics.

Prior to the formation of the Land League, the IRB was by far the single largest political organization in Ireland, possessing over 30,000 members while the Home Rule League had only a few hundred. It was because the political leadership of the Land League was based largely on the underground party of the IRB and republicans played the lead in forming its branches that it became the first purely tenant-biased, as well as the most popular, land agitation ever established in Ireland. Upon this basis, a powerful independence movement came into being in Irish public life that was organized by men who proclaimed that they stood for an independent Ireland that would be democratic and republican, a development that would have been inconceivable five or ten years earlier. Gladstone, however, suppressed the Land League by force, formed the Special Branch almost thirty years before any other permanent British secret service body was ever formed and spent as much money on intelligence work in counteracting republicans during 1882–86 as Britain would spend between 1919 and 1921. Such was the political reality of 'the union of hearts'. Irish democratic, as much as Irish nationalist, aspirations were evidently incompatible with the Union and the aristocratic political institutions of Victorian Britain, not least because the Union was never designed to accommodate such interests, but rather to suppress or contain them.

The Land League was a very different organization to its self-professed successor organizations, the Irish National League and its offspring, Justin McCarthy's Irish National Federation (a title presumably modelled on Gladstone's National Liberal Federation in England) and the United Irish League. The Land League was not only independent of Westminster MPs authority but unlike all the later movements, it was a democratically-governed organization whose leadership subscribed to a republican social ideal: it was designed to allow the peasantry themselves take complete control over their own political future and aimed to launch an independence struggle on *this* basis. The IRB supported the Land League, but in a rather selfish way. While the Irish Party called on the Irish public to place its hopes in 'the English democracy' (or that working-class community in northern England that supported the Liberals rather than the Tories), the IRB attempted to build up 'an Irish democracy', but it could not do so effectively because there was no real basis in society upon which this objective could be built, or properly achieved. This is why 'the organization' had always sought to encompass all democratic radicals in the country within its own ranks and jealously attempted to keep a central, directing influence over their activities through maintaining an underground party. When the IRB saw that the Land League was beginning to be pulled in a different direction, or be directed by different parties, it withdrew its active support, although it by no means became opposed to the league, much though Kickham and O'Leary questioned the morality of some of its members' methods and sought to counter the propaganda campaign that the MPs and bishops had launched, blaming the IRB party (mistakenly) for the agrarian outrages in an attempt to discourage the public from listening to the nationalists and republicans.

The democratic, or 'revolutionary', uprising of the Land League was defeated by government coercion as well as Parnell's subsequent reaching of an agreement with the same Liberal Premier who suppressed it. To a very significant extent, with the establishment of the National League and then its alliance with the Catholic hierarchy and (through the 'Kilmainham Treaty') with Gladstone, Parnell managed to outmanoeuvre the IRB. The reasoning behind Michael Davitt's claim that the formation of the National League marked 'the counter-revolution' was that its eclipse of the Land League effectively reinforced the existing aristocratic social order in the country against all those who were in favour of championing a new democratic or republican one, even if this was for nationalist purposes only. Many historians have interpreted the Liberals and Tories' subsequent efforts to address the land question, from the Ashbourne Act of 1885 to the Wyndham Act of 1903, as a summation, or an achievement, of the demands of the original Land League, since these acts of the government helped bring about the eventual establishment of a peasant-proprietary in Ireland. However, apart from the fact that the Land League certainly did not die a natural death, this is ignoring the fact that, politically, these measures did not change the situation in the country at all, whereas the Land League was designed to empower people politically, not just to relieve distress. The undemocratic structure of the National League and all subsequent support bodies of the Irish Party was designed to act as a safeguard against potential democratic uprisings taking place against an unaccountable government; a measure deemed necessary to guarantee political stability. This also ensured that even if the existing complete monopoly of land rights held by the aristocracy or gentry was challenged (through piecemeal Westminster agitation, for Ireland as was the case for the rest of the United Kingdom*), the structure of political society in Ireland would undergo no fundamental changes, because Westminster would remain in total control of the country and of how the land question would be addressed. The greatest single proof that the various land acts did not even fulfil the material interests of those social classes that had formerly supported the Land League is that dissent from the UIL became strong in rural Ireland after 1903, once its national leadership began to ignore their desires. In turn, it is not coincidental that as soon as the Irish Party collapsed in the 1910s, the backbone of popular support that the new nationalist radicals won came from that same rural community (as well as from the long-ignored, urban working class) which had always a great reason to identify with a democratic, or egalitarian, social ideal.

The relationship between the Irish Party and its support organizations, such as the National and United Irish Leagues, was rather complex. If the national executive of the leagues (which attempted to enforce discipline) was always controlled by the MPs and designed purely to serve their ends (particularly in terms of collecting funds to salary the MPs), local branches of the leagues often followed their own political intuition. While bishops and parish priests unequivocally called upon the public to support the MPs financially up until 1898, or 1908, the relationship between non-clerical branch leaders and the MPs fluctuated in proportion to which they identified with, or were looked with favour upon by, the national executive. Particularly in the original Land League heartland of Connacht, the careers of well-known newspaper-proprietor politicians such as James Daly, Jasper Tully and P.A. McHugh always reflected this reality, and their editorial policies (particularly Tully's)

---

* See Roy Douglas, *Land, people and politics: a history of the land question in the United Kingdom 1878–1952* (London, 1976).

were subject to frequent change, depending upon whether they put local concerns, or the MP's concerns, first. McHugh, for instance, was exceptionally popular for his role in championing the 'Plan of Campaign' and local concerns in Sligo during the late 1880s, but the executive of the National League marginalized him, because he was considered too radical. Only later, when McHugh decided to champion a more emphatically clericalist brand of politics did the executive ask him to stand for parliament, and henceforth he and his *Sligo Champion* newspaper became the chief proponent of 'anti-factionist' propaganda in the west of Ireland. As soon as McHugh lost footing as an MP and died, however, the *Sligo Champion* began to focus on local concerns again and became critical of the Irish Party and executive of the United Irish League. The complex history of the National and United Irish Leagues, the provincial Irish press and the role of local government officials in late nineteenth and early twentieth-century Ireland cannot be properly understood without much greater analysis being done upon the fact that democratic politics in Ireland was generally localized and community based, and reflected shifting relationships between local and national elites within Ireland itself, rather than the course of political debate on the 'Irish question' that took place in London. This dynamic to Irish politics was the true legacy of the Land League, not the land law reform legislation that was introduced at Westminster.

Contrary to the popular perception, the fall of Parnell was not the real turning point in the history of the Irish Party. Rather this occurred following the 'home rule' negotiations of 1885–1886. From 1880 to 1885, the Irish Party often proclaimed that it was willing to follow the revolutionary nationalist ideals of the republicans' 'new departure' programme, and perhaps at no time did Irish nationalists spend more of their limited financial resources for political purposes than during the early 1880s. The Irish Party attained its hegemony on the Irish benches in Westminster during 1885 while proclaiming that it stood for an independent Ireland, possibly even a republic, and intimated that it would be willing to adopt the abstentionist policy if this demand was not met. It did this, however, only for electoral gain and to outmanoeuvre the IRB. Instead, following Gladstone's secret negotiations with the Catholic hierarchy and Parnell, the Irish Party cooperated fully with the government and its political course was effectively set in stone thereafter. Parnell's attempt to restore a pre-1885 political situation once his authority was threatened during 1890–91 was but a brief interlude, and no-one was prepared to support his efforts except the IRB, some urban Irish Party supporters (who disliked the agrarian radical MPs that were involved in the Plan of Campaign) and a handful of Irish Party MPs (most notably John Redmond) who had not yet made any mark in politics, but knew they could use the party split to enhance their political profile and acquire greater powers of leverage in making future bids to enter the higher echelons of the Irish Party. After 1885, the Irish Party was able to retain its seats perpetually simply because no party could possibly afford to stand candidates against it, except the landed gentry, and so no contests needed to be held and, indeed, generally were not held until the party's total collapse in 1918. By the early 1890s, the funds to sustain the Irish Party were coming mostly from English Liberals and Catholic bishops, not from the general Irish public, and thereafter this pattern was interrupted only intermittently.

The year 1884 was the greatest turning point in the IRB's history and in Irish nationalist politics under the Union generally, prior to the 1916 rising. In the spring and summer of 1884, the IRB was paralysed by Gladstone's administration with the assistance of Clan envoys in British pay, a leverage which enabled the Special Branch to hunt down and pounce on P.N. Fitzgerald, John Daly and the IRB just before Gladstone decided to introduce a bill that tripled the Irish franchise and gave Parnell and his party their great political opportunity. It was not until after the whole future of the IRB was placed in jeopardy during the spring and summer of 1884 that Parnell openly committed his party to the educational policy of the Catholic hierarchy (and gave it power over the National League executive) for the first time; a fact that enabled the Irish Party to draw fully on the church's huge political influence and enhanced greatly its capacity to triumph at the polls during November 1885. Parnell had engaged in political discussions with the IRB secretary John O'Connor in London sometime during 1884 and he would confer closely with P.N. Fitzgerald in Cork thereafter,[1] but by the time these discussions had taken place, he had already committed himself fully to working with the Catholic hierarchy rather than the nationalists, and was not about to go back on his 'Kilmainham Treaty' promises to Gladstone either, which had saved his political career in 1882. The real backdrop to Gladstone's introduction of the strange and unworkable 'home rule' measure of 1886 was not the triumph of the Irish Party at the polls in December 1885. The government legally could not, and never did, give more weight to that seventh of the membership of the House of Commons which constituted the Irish Party than to any other seventh of the total membership of the house. The Liberals and the Tories' motive in engaging in private negotiations with Parnell and the Catholic hierarchy for several months prior to the 1885 general election was that they naturally feared that the Irish Party might do in 1885 what Sinn Féin did in 1918 since it claimed to be a nationalist party, while the IRB still had a very strong influence in Irish popular politics. Parnell could, at best, use this fear to help persuade the government to do something in the interests of the Irish Party and the church, and this is why the 'home rule' negotiations took place.

The purpose of the 'home rule' negotiations of 1885–86 was to limit the chances of the lower-class Irish Catholic community ever supporting nationalists' abstentionist policy by politically empowering the Catholic

---

1 *Special Commission Report*, vol. 7, p. 6, 93, 97, 276–7 (evidence of Parnell).

establishment and the church, which feared the democratic-republican nationalists perhaps even more so than the government. This was because while the IRB posed only a distant security threat to the British state (which could probably be defeated easily in an open conflict), the church and the propertied Catholic classes considered them as a direct threat to their ideal of community life in their own parishes. As the government well knew, the church's only concerns related to denominational education, peace and property, and it also (perhaps inherently) subscribed to an aristocratic social ideal and this could guarantee political stability.

In the absence of representative political institutions, the only factor that kept political society together, or that prevented elites from feeling they were operating in a complete political no-man's land in Ireland under the Union was the preservation of an aristocratic, or pyramidical, social order in the country. This reality affected all aspects of Irish political, cultural and social life under the Union, and the government as well as the Catholic and Protestant establishments in the country naturally desired to keep this aristocratic social order intact. Hence once it was threatened by a democratic-republican political agitation during the 1880s, people felt themselves to be in a revolutionary political situation and all the root political divisions of twentieth-century Ireland essentially came into being. Both the British government and the Catholic Church desired to increase the capacity of various lay Catholic elites to create political uniformity within the Irish Catholic community as a whole. This is precisely why, after 1886, the government (both Liberal and Tory) began committing itself to fufilling the Catholic hierarchy's interests by providing Catholics with greater access to denominational education, assisted the development and rise in the number of prestiguous Catholic private colleges in Ireland and ultimately provided state recognition for the Catholic University/UCD in 1908; institutions which would play a pivotal role in shaping twentieth-century Irish life. Many of Ireland's modern Catholic cathedrals were also built at this time. The ideal of the old Catholic Association (which still operated as an organization at an elite level and worked closely with the hierarchy and the undemocratic central committees of Irish Party's supporting machines), of achieving equality of status for Catholics within the empire, was now seemingly coming true and the government and the Irish Party hoped that Ireland's future would be determined accordingly.

Fundamentally, the 'independence' of the Irish Party, like that of G.H. Moore's small party during the 1850s, was only ever an instrument to prioritize the interests of the minority Catholic community in the state, and, in particular, to maximize its power to pressurize the minority party in Westminster (invariably the Whigs or Liberals) to do the otherwise unthinkable in British politics, and champion sectional Catholic interests. Neither before nor after the Irish Party's formation was the championing of Irish nationalism in Westminster a practicable option.

By the late Victorian period, the greatest appeal of the British constitution in the minds of the lay leaders of Irish Catholic society was essentially its perceived success in guaranteeing, or accommodating, more balanced church-state relations in matters of education and property rights than any other state in Europe. Apart from questions of prosperity, this is mostly why the lay leaders of Catholic Ireland not only began to embrace the standards and ethics of British political life more enthusiastically, but attempted (and would continue to attempt) to envision the future evolution of Irish political life according to these same standards, and did not want to be disturbed by the 'Fenian troublemakers'. The advent of the 'Irish-Ireland' movement did little or nothing to alter this anti-republican bias of Catholic elites in Ireland, due to Catholics' opposition to the republican principle of separating church and state, while the IRB had only ever exercised an influence in Ireland in the popular political sphere. Unlike some democratic and republican political societies on the continent (which admired British prosperity, but little else of the British state), the would-be 'governing classes' of Ireland viewed political 'stability' as inherently a virtue, and generally identified with the British political system for much the same social, cultural and intellectual reasons as their English counterparts; namely, because of its unrivalled stability throughout history. Put simply, an 'unwritten constitution' was inherently more conducive to harmonious church-state relations than any republican form of government could possibly be.

The *realpolitik* of the politics of 'home rule' after 1885–86 was fundamentally no different from the politics practised by Irish MPs at Westminster at *any* time during the nineteenth century, since the formation of deals between the imperial cabinet and very select Irish political elites was still the only medium whereby Irish MPs could have any real say in determining their country's future, short of adopting the abstentionist policy. By the mid 1880s, this reality did not reflect the political demands of many people living within Ireland itself, whether or not they considered themselves as 'nationalists' or 'unionists'. Ulster Protestants were alienated politically in 1886 because the leaders of the Irish Catholic community had temporarily assumed much greater bargaining powers with the government, but their position was essentially no less secure. Later, in 1912, it would be the Catholic community's turn to protest when Ulster Protestants managed to assume greater bargaining powers, but the *realpolitik* of 'home rule' had not changed at all. Once more, British state interests simply decided who would acquire greater bargaining powers. The IRB nationalists, by contrast, naturally had no bargaining powers with the British government whatsoever. Consequently, after 1886, they were left high and dry for the first time, while the Parnellite movement now felt that it could safely throw its weight against them, since the Liberals and the church had promised to safeguard the Irish Party's future. The IRB faced a bitter struggle for survival as a result of concerted campaigns by the Catholic Church, which insinuated that its leaders were government agents, while the

Liberals and Tories, with some of the Irish Party's support, were equally
determined and successful in crushing that democratic nationalist movement
in Ireland which came into being in 1879 and was built mostly upon that IRB
organization which had been developing over the previous twenty years. The
theatrical farce of the Special Commission (1888–1890), when the Irish Party
collectively repented for their past 'criminality' in associating with IRB men
through the Land League, was essentially an expression of what had been
happening in private for a few years previously, although the general Irish
public had no understanding of this, not least because they were completely
unaware of what was happening at a high political level.* As P.N. Fitzgerald
discovered in 1887, professedly to his surprise, the days of 'felon-setting' were
certainly not over, and, as John O'Leary lamented greatly in 1896, there was a
very strong possibility that they would never come to an end at all.2

The IRB went from a position of great political confidence in 1884 to a
position of great political demoralization in 1894 and the organization all but
disbanded, facing the final insult of not even being allowed by the Catholic
Cemeteries Committee to erect a monument in memory of its 'Fenian dead' in
Glasnevin. The IRB's goal of directing a national revolution in Ireland
through the medium of an underground party naturally faced great obstacles,
but its failure was by no means inevitable, and it was not until the late 1880s
that its effectiveness as a revolutionary method of political organization
passed. What exactly was this revolution in question?

All supposed 'revolutions' are inherently shaped by the idea that a revolutionary consensus has, or would soon, come about within society as a whole. In
reality, however, this consensus invariably does not really exist, but this does
not generally become evident to revolutionaries until after the 'revolution' has
failed. During the mid-to-late Victorian era, IRB revolutionaries and the many
young radical Irish democrats associated with the Land League (who were
generally IRB men as well) often spoke about the onward march of 'the people'
who would effectively destroy feudal political institutions, make citizens out of
slaves and 'write on the tablets of the age: *republican!*'. This radical democratic
and egalitarian ideal was essentially the consensual idea behind that
'revolution' which was the hope of Irish nationalist revolutionaries during the
mid to late Victorian era, but ultimately an independence movement did not
come into being on this basis, due to governmental oppression, inept political
leadership and, perhaps most of all, class and social divisions within Ireland
itself; divisions which the IRB had hoped it could eliminate by forcing elites
(through its sheer numerical strength as a party) into becoming advocates of a
new egalitarian socio-political order, in the name of 'the nation' or 'the people'.
This is why, by 1894, when the 'young republic' was virtually dead rather than
virtually established, the IRB felt that the revolution envisioned by its

* See Emmet Larkin, *The Roman Catholic Church and the making of the Irish State 1878–1886*
(Dublin, 1975). 2 O'Leary, *Recollections*, vol. 2, 209.

founders had failed, and men like Fred Allan and P.N. Fitzgerald claimed that a counter-revolution had effectively taken place the previous decade; a view later taken up and elaborated upon by Michael Davitt in his book *The fall of feudalism* (1904) and would also inform some of the musings of William O'Brien in his later books, once he knew he could safely throw in his lot with Sinn Féin and leave all his 'constitutional' and 'physical force' rhetoric (which he always knew to be a complete nonsense) behind. Davitt and O'Brien, the two most popular ex-'republican brothers' in Irish politics, could interact and be friends with P.N. Fitzgerald, John Clancy and other republican figures in Irish popular politics, but if they wanted to establish and maintain successful political careers for themselves, they knew (particularly after 1886) that they needed to modify their politics to suit the Catholic hierarchy and representatives of the Catholic establishment at Westminster and, in particular, adopt its rhetoric about the impracticality of 'Fenianism'. This is why their political careers ultimately diverged greatly from the IRB and they were able to acquire much greater fame than their former 'brothers'. Not surprisingly, however, they both wrote political memoirs in their later years in an attempt to validate, and differentiate from the Irish Party movement generally, their respective contributions as democratically-biased nationalists in the eyes of future Irish historians.

During the mid to late 1880s, it was not the growth of the National League that weakened the republican movement so much as the evident impracticality after 1884 (and particularly after the Special Commission) of maintaining the the old IRB model of popular political organization in its own right. Many of those who deserted the IRB at this time were not so much throwing in their lot with the Irish Party as recognizing, or resigning themselves to, this very fact. The IRB may have been very influential as a revolutionary party in Ireland during the mid-to-late Victorian era, but it simply could not withstand a full onslaught by the British secret service, on top of the hostility to which the political establishment in Ireland itself already felt for 'the organization', and could now more freely express. Within about a decade, the thought of any return to the IRB method of political organization seemed unrealistic to many, since the republican party had evidently achieved all it could achieve. Only the young YIS stalwarts tended to hold a different view. Not surprisingly, they also took the line that Irish nationalist politics had fundamentally been perverted in 1885–86.

Particularly during the nineteenth century, the conflict between those who championed a republican social ideal and an aristocratic social ideal was the key issue around which the IRB's nationalist politics revolved. As a result of the events of the mid 1880s, this struggle was effectively lost by the republicans and the Irish Party reigned triumphant, while the clergy, taking advantage of the situation, attempted to monopolize control of whatever land agitation existed in the country in an attempt to ensure that no leverage remained available to enable republicans to reverse the situation. It is very important to note, however, that the stimulus for all significant political cleavages born during the mid 1880s was this same conflict that emerged in Ireland between republican and aristocratic social ideals. The most important of these new developments was the creation of the 'Ulster unionist' political tradition, which came into being as a direct result of the Liberals and Tories' eagerness during the mid 1880s to reach an agreement with the Irish Catholic establishment in an attempt to negate the threat of the underground Irish nationalist party. The Tories shared this objective every bit as much as the Liberals, since they both knew that the empowerment of Catholic elites in what was a predominantly Catholic country was a sure means of keeping the nationalist threat down, perhaps for good. However, the Tories professed not to agree with how the Liberals sought to achieve this (and pretended to be far more opposed to the political ambitions of Catholic elites than they actually were) simply because they knew that, this way, they could win that sizeable Irish Protestant vote which Gladstone had just alienated permanently.

During the 1880s and beyond, Ulster or southern Irish Protestants did not oppose the Irish Party because it was 'Irish'. They opposed it because, rather than portraying its politics truthfully (namely as that of the Catholic party in British politics), the Irish Party claimed to represent the politics of 'Ireland a Nation' whereas, in reality, it just wanted to modify the power structures of the Union more in Catholics' interests. This prompted the previously liberal Presbyterian community in Ulster (some of the Land League's most active promoters were actually Belfast Presybterians) to follow the lead of the local, aristocratic Tories in 1886 and to join (for the first time) the small Orange Order organization, which they had previously detested. In turn, most Ulster Presbyterians began to adopt a militantly confessional brand of politics and, slowly but surely, the Tories were able to make the Orange Order the bedrock for a new Ulster-centred politics.

Like the Irish Party, the politics and ethos of the emerging Ulster unionist movement was necessarily designed to reinforce the pyramidical socio-political order, which alone could maintain political stability in the country in the absence of parliamentary government. For this reason, the politics of the 'Ulster party' that began to rise to prominence after 1886 inherently rested on a consensus that the Tories would always be relied upon to provide the necessary leadership, and negotiate with the government, on behalf of the Ulster Protestant community as a whole. In this respect, the basis upon which 'Ulster unionist' politics was built after 1886 was virtually the same as that upon which the Irish Party's politics was based, with the exception that, within the Irish Party movement, the power held by the Tories in Ulster tended to be wielded instead by the Catholic hierarchy and a few members of the Catholic gentry class (such as Redmond and Dillon) for exactly the same reason: by virtue of their social standing. The 'Ulster Party' would never have existed were it not for the peculiar politics of the 'Irish Party' and, in many respects, their politics were mirror images of each other.

The fundamental reason why the 'two nations' Tory propaganda, born in 1886, could be slowly but surely moulded into a politico-religious reality was that political leadership in Ireland was being provided by two diametrically-opposed yet equally socially conservative interest groups, each of which claimed to be guardians of 'national traditions' and who, collectively, took it upon themselves to represent (or were expected by Whitehall to represent) the interests of the entire country in their bargaining with the government. Parliamentary election results for constituencies in Ireland were, ultimately, irrelevant to this true *realpolitik* of 'home rule', owing to the very fact of the government's unaccountability. Although great political diversity existed within both the Irish Party and Ulster Party camps, in practice, these always became negated, because they each had to rely upon particular elites to achieve *any* influence with the government. In turn, this allowed the Catholic hierarchy and the Tories to shape the political culture of the Irish Party's and Ulster Party's respective supporters as they saw fit, thereby reinforcing the respective 'nations' they claimed to represent, in terms of people's politics, culture and even their sense of their own history. It is not at all coincidental that the Tories and Catholic hierarchy respectively were the two parties which were most determined to misrepresent (and most consistently did misrepresent) the IRB's nationalist politics, and the supposed 'threat' it posed, from the early 1860s onwards.

It could be said that the story of the 'two nations' in the partitioned Ireland of the early twentieth century and the internal problems, or progress, of each was shaped significantly by this legacy of the 'home rule' negotiations of 1885–6. Once the Irish Party's long faltering political power was finally broken during the 1910s, the politics of 'home rule' inevitably disappeared in most of the island and political change slowly but surely was brought about through the gradual emergence of nationalist politicians who championed a more egalitarian social ideal, similar to that championed during 1879–82. By contrast, in what became Northern Ireland, the politics of 'home rule' lived on, as exemplified by the Ulster Unionist Party's attempts from 1920 onwards to reinforce and strengthen that political consensus that was established in 1886, as well as the existing socio-political order, by any and every means. On a socio-political level, the dynamics of political change, or resistance to political change, on both parts of the island had the same historical roots, and the principal cause of their ultimate divergence was simply that the 'Ulster Party' survived while the 'Irish Party' did not.

Directly or indirectly, the Catholic Church often played the most central role in determining the political divisions that emerged within the country during the nineteenth century, not least because Whitehall was determined to win its favour and vice versa. It is not coincidental that the Irish Party, right from its establishment in the autumn of 1880, always relied upon the clergy to keep republicans' influence in Irish popular politics to a minimum. The fact that the clergy, as well as the education system, were naturally inclined to favour the existing social order always played a large part in weighing the balance of interests in the country in favour of the conservatives, for as one tenant-farmer observed in 1887, 'the clergy are horribly afraid of republicanism and anything unknown' and this, more than anything, ensured that 'the Catholic Church is really the greatest friend to England in this country.'[3] When Parnell gave the Catholic hierarchy effective powers over both the National League and the selection of Irish Party candidates (something over which Irish voters and ordinary members of the National League had no influence whatsoever), those few republicans within his own party (most notably J.J. O'Kelly) were effectively marginalized.

The fact that the 'Parnell Split' evoked intense passions in urban Ireland (which some historians have seen as directly mirroring those which came about during the 'Treaty Split' of 1921) stemmed not from the actual merits or failings of Parnell as a politician or as a man. Rather it emanated from the role the split played in shattering the illusion that a nationalist consensus had come into being during 1879–85, after the Irish Party claimed to identify with the democratic, egalitarian and nationalist ideals of the republicans. During 1891 the public realized for the first time that the bishops and Gladstone controlled the Irish Party, and could make or break it at will (a situation Parnell himself was responsible for creating, particularly between 1882 and 1886), but most of the propertied Catholic community naturally had no problem with this situation. It was thus essentially inevitable that the 'uncrowned king' invented by the Catholic press would be thrown back into the arms of the 'republican brothers' that had originally launched his career and who, in reality, were far more responsible for that 'uprising of the Irish democracy' which occurred during the early 1880s, but for which the contemporary press in Britain and Ireland had made Parnell alone the symbol, since he was the only Land League figure of sufficiently high social standing to be taken seriously by the 'recognized leaders' of society in the United Kingdom.

The IRB had always been critical of the Irish Party and attempted to forward its own politics independently, but it was not until 1887–9 that it began to see how fully the Irish Party desired to crowd republicans' influence out of Irish politics altogether, with assistance from the church. Among republicans, the Parnell Split was seen as a welcome opportunity to reverse this trend and to revive their propaganda traditions in the country once more, but this was possible only to a relatively slight degree and the outcome of the struggle only demoralized the organization all the more. Parnell's adoption of a position of political self-isolation after 1886 may have been partly motivated by an awareness of the fact that he had misled the Irish public, particularly during 1885, and had effectively burnt several of his own political boats, for the enigmatic reputation he acquired between 1879 and 1885 rested entirely on the fact that he *seemingly* represented, or was willing to represent, a democratic

3 George Pellew, *In castle and cabin* (London, 1888), 50 (interview with a tenant-farmer).

The Irish Republican Brotherhood

or republican brand of Irish political nationalism (if only because of William O'Brien's 'Parnellite' journalism), whereas, in reality, he conformed entirely to the aristocratic political system of Victorian Britain and sought with much success (by engaging in private negotiations with Gladstone during 1882 and 1885–6) to redirect Irish popular political activity accordingly, in order to safeguard the Union. In so doing, Parnell was simply acting in line specifically with the interests of the upper and upper middle-classes (the propertied classes), since it guaranteed political stability, which was something that he himself also desired. He was not necessarily acting in line with the interests of those newly-enfranchised men who had voted for the Irish Party in 1885.

For the IRB, after several years of being subject to constant Special Branch intrigues, 'Fenian fever' propaganda in the Tory press and informer accusations thrown against its chief travelling organizer by the Catholic clergy and by highly-paid Special Branch agents like 'Nero', the 'most moving' of Parnell's remarks during his final days was his speech before 'P.N. Fitzgerald and his men' at the IRB's National Club in December 1890, that he knew that 'you have been sought to be intimidated by every device which the ingenuity of man could invent',[4] and his remarks in London five months later that Gladstone had 'tried by imprisonments, by prosecutions, by penal servitude, aye, and by executions, to destroy the unity of our race and the independence of our people. That is the history of Irish reform.'[5] Parnell knew the secret history of Irish politics during the mid 1880s much better than any of his Irish contemporaries, but by the time he made these emotive appeals to the IRB to save his own career during 1890–1, the Irish nationalist movement of the 1880s had effectively already been defeated as a result of his own past actions, while neither Fitzgerald nor any IRB leaders had the means, or ability, to reverse this situation.

In practical terms, like many other revolutionary or democratic political movements in nineteenth-century Europe, the IRB generally succeeded in making its lasting presence felt in the popular political sphere without actually being able to topple the ascendancy of established political interest groups, who feared that democracy would overturn civilization as they knew it and unleash forces of anarchy. Indeed, the dynamics of the IRB's impact on Irish life at this time could well be contrasted with the role republicans generally played in nineteenth-century France, notwithstanding the fact that France was a long-established and powerful nation state, while Ireland had never been, and was only half-heartedly 'struggling for nationality' against an unaccountable and distant imperial government, as well as an 'unwritten constitution' that remained completely incomprehensible to most Irish contemporaries in its actual application.

The IRB's rationale of creating, sustaining and building up a 'young

4 Allan to *Weekly Independent*, 6 Oct. 1894 (quoting Parnell) 5 Ryan, *Fenian memories*, 155.

republic' (this was the 'Irish Republic' originally referred to in its constitution) was an idea borrowed directly from France, where the phrase 'the republic' always signified an ideal of liberty, rather than an actual state. Hence, French people spoke about 'the doctors' republic', 'the lawyers' republic', 'the workers' republic' (the idea Connolly borrowed) and various other 'republics', all of which were supposedly collectively helping to keep 'democracy' and 'liberty' alive even during the years when monarchical, or imperial, governments dominated the country. French Catholic elites, subscribing to an aristocratic social ideal, were intensely contemptuous of 'the republic' and all it signified, regardless of what form of government might ever exist in the country. The IRB's politics was never openly characterized by a stereotypical, continental style of anticlericicialism, but nevertheless, like various nineteenth-century French republican movements, its politics and propaganda was always defined against the political culture of the existing aristocratic-minded Catholic establishment in the country, which in turn invariably defined its propaganda against that of the IRB. This political tradition was effectively sparked off in 1843, during the Davis-O'Connell quarrel, and reached maturity by the 1860s, a decade after Rome and Whitehall had re-established the Catholic hierarchy in the United Kingdom in the wake of the Europe-wide rebellions against aristocratic elites during 1848. French, as well as Irish, Catholic elites saw Catholicism as inherently the right formula, or model, for creating political and social uniformity, and generally viewed the philistine, republicans' baneful political influence as akin to that of other 'outsiders', like Jews and Protestants. Indeed, were it not that Allen, Larkin and O'Brien were denied Catholic burial rites in 1867, the IRB's relative 'outsider' status in relation to nineteenth-century Irish Catholic political life, first made evident during the early 1860s, quite probably would have received much more constant publicity and virulent criticism in the 'home rule' press thereafter. As it was, the execution of the 'Manchester martyrs' often helped to make the IRB immune to outright denunciations in the popular Catholic press because the folk-religious appeal of the concept of martyrology was too powerful among the general public to be criticized in any way by Catholic elites.

During the nineteenth century, Irish Catholic clergymen generally looked to experienced French and Belgian clergymen for advice as to how they might combat secularist or radical democratic trends in politics and, in particular, organizations like the IRB, which the clergy felt presented a grave moral danger to their flocks and their ideals for the existing social order, often simply because it was feared to be a fermenter of dissent. It is not coincidental that, after 1886, when the Irish Party, the Catholic hierarchy and Gladstone reached an agreement and called their own politics that of 'Ireland a Nation', denouncing that of all others as 'factionists', many Irish Protestants found themselves attracted to the IRB's propagandist endeavours, at least up until the republican movement was superceded in Irish nationalist debate by the Catholic-inspired 'Irish-Ireland' movement around 1902; a fact that prompted many Protestants to latch instead onto a romanticized memory of the aristo-cratic figure of Parnell, who could be turned from the enemy they generally considered him to be during the 1880s into an icon simply as a result of his fall amidst a divorce scandal. Cultural, communal and political conflicts between competing Catholic and republican (or nationalist) social ideals were rampant in most European political societies during the nineteenth century. The fact that this found no reflection in the cultural and political life of nineteenth-century Britain should not obscure the fact that, directly or indirectly, a very similar dynamic was often the pivotal feature in shaping the communal, cultural and political life of nineteenth-century Ireland, just as it was throughout Catholic Europe. This, in turn, naturally affected most aspects of the lives of Irish Protestants almost as much as those of Irish Catholics since they each were fortunate, or unfortunate, enough to live in the same political society, even if their social interaction was sometimes limited.

John O'Leary's claim in 1886 that religious polarization in Irish political and social life could easily be avoided by keeping priests and the question of denominational education out of politics undoubtedly had much truth in it. The raising of such questions always had a see-saw effect on political life in nineteenth-century Ireland. It is perhaps not entirely coincidental, for example, that Ulster Protestants did not speak out against the Land League until early November 1880, the same week as the IRB leadership withdrew its active support, owing to the league's falling under what the IRB felt to be too much clerical control. Albeit from purely sectarian motives, the Orange Order often praised those who had begun to resist the priests' role in politics during the 1890s, and it no doubt would have been surprised to learn that the men they were praising were actually the dreaded 'Fenians', for the endless 'Fenian fever' propaganda of Irish and English Tory newspapers since 1867 (as well as the Irish Party's nonsensical talk of its being the heirs of the 'men of '67' in the same breath as it praised its 'patriot priests') naturally led them to believe something very different. John O'Leary's claim during the mid 1890s, as part of his recollections of the IRB, that 'we meant to kill clerical dictation and we did kill it ... if it has come to life again ... the fault is not ours'[6] did reflect a reality of the IRB's politics, even if O'Leary presented it in rather dramatic terms. Several sections of the Connacht IRB, while reportedly being ready to call it a day during the mid 1890s, surmised before disbanding that the one hope for the republican cause in the future was that the current generation were much more willing to defy the clergy in politics than any previous ones, and thus the next generation would probably possess a completely firm resolve to do the same.[7] However, their prediction could essentially not have been more wrong and, within a few years, numerous IRB leaders would be denounced as effete, sham patriots by would-be separatists for not living up to the puritan ideals of Fr Kavanagh and the 'Irish-Ireland' movement.

6 O'Leary, *Recollections*, vol. 2, 53.   7 NAI, Home Office precis, carton 1, 10466/s.

Paradoxically, it was thus that the seeds of the 'Irish revolution' of the early twentieth century were first sown.

It was fitting that when the old IRB threatened, for the last time, to dominate Irish popular politics through the existence of the 1798 centenary movement that the Tory government finally decided to fulfil the hierarchy's dream by giving state recognition to the Catholic University, set up by the former Anglican John Henry Newman in 1854. This was something which a Liberal administration formally did with the formation of the National University of Ireland ten years later. The granting of official recognition to the Catholic University also meant that its students could now acquire greater access to prestigious English colleges, like Cambridge and Oxford, to do their postgraduate work and potentially acquire higher positions in the civil service. After the death of James Stephens in March 1901, the 'home rule' press, the ideological successors of the Catholic-Whig press of the 1860s, printed newspaper editorials that were virtually identical to those printed in the early 1870s on the legacy of 'the Fenians' or 'the men of '67', all of which were written in the past tense. This time, however, the reality was that the 'Fenian movement' *had* essentially passed from the Irish political scene. Be that as it may, the IRB's actual political purpose or legacy was something that the 'home rule' press still did not want to be truthfully portrayed. This was because the Irish Party (after all its former denunciations of the supposed 'physical force party') now wanted to claim the 'Fenians' legacy as its own as a means of calling for the public to continue supporting its politics, despite the fact that it was entirely dependent on the whims of the two larger British parties and had no workable policies of its own. Old Catholic MPs at Westminster pointed to the few ex-IRB men in their party ever since the early 1880s (such as the ailing J.J. O'Kelly, now permanently bound in a wheelchair in London) and claimed to be 'standing in the same place today as were the men of '67', while new Liberal Party leaders like Lloyd George and Winston Churchill were supposedly becoming 'Irish nationalists' just as much as Gladstone supposedly did before them. As evidence of the onwards march of 'Ireland a Nation', the 'nationalist' *Freeman's Journal* (which, not surprisingly, died with the Irish Party) cited with joy John Mallon's appointment as the first-ever Catholic assistant-commissioner of the DMP in 1894 and paid great honours to him when he retired in 1901, while few events were celebrated more ecstatically by the 'home rule' press in 1910 than the election of the first-ever Catholic mayor of Manchester, for a Mayo man had 'made it' and become the most 'respectable figure' in England's second city (and the Liberal party's heartland) for one whole year. Catholic Ireland was truly coming into its own. Henceforth, while the lower middle and working classes in Irish Catholic society were fed the story by the 'home rule' press that the Irish Party followed 'the men of '67' (whether they ever believed this is far from clear), the Catholic upper classes, the 'natural leaders' of society, who attended prestiguous Catholic private schools and were schooled to identify with an aristocratic social ideal, were taught to believe that 'the Fenians' of the nineteenth century were simply uneducated ruffians whose lives revolved around public houses. The reality, however, was that the IRB had simply been Irish nationalists who also subscribed to a democratic or republican social ideal, who were completely independent politically from the church and so were feared by the Catholic hierarchy and, in turn, the clergy.

In its last days, the old IRB organization could call the Irish Party's politics and its rhetoric as 'politically deranged', 'a satire on Irish nationalism' and as being based upon a 'will-o-the-wisp' as much as it liked, but it could no longer hope to change the existing political order in the country, or achieve John O'Leary's hope of setting up a kind of rival education system, which, indeed, was its greatest failure. The clergy's desire to defeat this ambition of the IRB, however, inadvertently caused the Irish-Ireland movement to become the kernel of early twentieth-century Irish radicalism. Students of Catholic private schools who understood (or were successfully schooled into accepting) Catholic ideals of education and principles of social order naturally had no time for the secular nationalist ideology of republicanism, but middle and lower sections of Catholic Ireland who attended cheaper Catholic schools could easily be made to identify with a new, cultural and religiously-inspired separatism.

In its initial conception, the post-1898 'Irish-Ireland' movement could perhaps be best described as the Catholic Church's response to worrying, attitudinal trends evident in Irish politics ever since 1891. While Catholic schools propagated a particular idea of respectability that was perfectly in line with the aristocratic social order of the United Kingdom, the church feared that if the ethos of Irish Catholic schools was not distinguished from those of other schools in the state, then, in the long term, the political trend of Irishmen denouncing clericalist politics might grow. After all, most schools in the state were nominally Protestant, just like the adulterer Parnell, and some had now reputedly become secularist in their ethos as well. Something was needed to prevent this trend from affecting 'this Catholic nation', and so the choice made was to emphasize Ireland's cultural and 'spiritual' separateness from Britain. The birth of the 'Irish-Ireland' movement was also influenced by the church's fears of the consequences of the IRB's monopoly of the 1798 centenary celebrations, which were planned as early as 1894, and what influence this might have in shaping people's idea of the origins and the meaning of 'Irish nationalism' and, more specifically, the role of Catholicism therein. By the time of the 1798 centenary, various Irish writers, radicals and intellectuals were evidently looking for a new Irish civic ideal and the demoralized IRB, while it engaged in wholesale political commemorations, was clearly struggling or else simply unable to provide one. This search was very important to many people because, as ever, notwithstanding the Irish Party's hegemony on the Irish benches at Westminster, there was no central focus to Irish politics, and the radical democratic and egalitarian ideal which was the basis of the popular political consensus of the early to mid 1880s was evidently dead. While William O'Brien (who was eager to re-enter politics) toyed with the idea of reviving that 'Plan of Campaign' agitation which had made his name during the late 1880s, the church resolved to use the influence of its education system to fill this void in Irish politics to make sure that nothing potentially disturbing could possibly emerge in its place.

The popularity of the 'Irish-Ireland' ideal never reflected the influence of republicans, but rather the great educational influence of the Catholic Church. While the members of the nineteenth-century IRB were generally self-educated men, or educated at national schools or at evening classes, the Edwardian generation of radical nationalists were invariably educated at newly-established private Catholic schools, or by the Christian Brothers schools which had grown rapidly since the mid 1880s. This is essentially why, during the Edwardian era, most young Irish radicals, though vaguely conscious of the ideals, or rather the failures, of the past generation, did not speak about democratic uprisings, 'the people' or republican liberty. Rather they spoke of the rebirth of a 'Gaelic civilization', which was supposedly filling the Irish people with great self-respect, as not only did they the Irish people possess a superior moral, spiritual and cultural sense to all 'English ways' but Ireland was about to become a beacon for the world by reviving its ancient resources of civilization. The Irish-Irelanders were also armed with a new sense of history, provided to them by the Christian Brothers schools and that was imbued with the same moral viewpoint. The Irish-Ireland movement effectively completely supplanted the influence of the old IRB during 1899–1902 and assumed the role the IRB formally played in shaping popular nationalist discourse in Ireland. If this had not been the case, the anti-clerical or 'doctrinaire' republican Arthur Griffith would never have felt it necessary to ape D.P. Moran's rhetoric; a change on his part that, had he been able to see into the future ten years earlier, he no doubt would never have believed he would need to take. Fred Allan may have been more of a republican than William Rooney, but there was certainly no place in Irish politics by the early to mid 1900s for men who were calling for an end to 'kid gloves' approaches in combatting the political influence of the Catholic bishops.[8] There was certainly plenty of room, however, for men who spoke (in English) in the language of 'Gaelicism'. The emergence of would-be separatists like Terence McSwiney, a representative figure of the new 'Irish-Ireland' nationalists, was a case in point. He denounced the IRB as 'effete' and saw Fr Kavanagh (who warned that Cumann na Gaedhael must not be exposed to any 'unCatholic doctrines') as a 'disciple' of Wolfe Tone and Thomas Davis. Virtually all future leaders of the 'Irish revolution', including figures such as Patrick Pearse, Eamon de Valera, Liam Lynch and Rory O'Connor, were Irish-Irelanders educated at Catholic private schools, all of which championed an aristocratic

8 Allan to *Weekly Independent*, 6 Oct. 1894.

social ideal, and saw Catholicism and the Irish language as the basis of Irish 'nationality'.

The importance of the Gaelic League in early twentieth-century Irish political life and in shaping the 'Irish revolution' should not be underestimated. Indeed, it is arguably of fundamental importance in understanding the dynamics of the 'Irish revolution of the early twentieth century to focus on the fact that all Irish contemporaries who expressed belief in the idea that a revolutionary consensus had come into being in Ireland did so by referring specifically to the popularity of the *new* brand of 'self-reliant' ideals championed by the Irish-Ireland movement. These long predated both the first world war and the formation of the volunteer movements, both in their origins and in terms of the great impact they were having on popular social or political life. For this reason, one cannot reasonably view the 'Irish revolution' as something that was shaped simply by the militarisation of Irish society during the 1910s or the first world war. Like any perceived 'revolution' in history, it was the product of longstanding political trends, and its power rested on the void at the heart of Irish politics, stemming not least from the frustration of democracy in the country since the mid 1880s.

During the 1900s, many Irish writers spoke of a coming 'revolution' and those who did not generally commented simply on the rising levels of education in the country and noted the great political consequences this was having, breaking down all the old nonsensical jargons of 'home rule' politics, creating much more political diversity in the country and raising the prospect of a very uncertain future. This very sense of uncertainty was important in creating the mentality of the 'revolutionary generation', and the Gaelic League seemingly offered an appealing vision for the future to answer this felt anxiety. The Gaelic League became the greatest single unifier of social classes among the young generation in Edwardian Ireland, attracting colleges students, clerks and workers alike. In this respect, on a purely socio-political level, it made a similar impact upon Irish social life to the old IRB and filled much the same void, but it never became an IRB recruiting ground, outside of a few select circles in Dublin based around the Wolfe Tone Clubs. In fact, most young Irish-Irelanders had only total contempt for the IRB, whose members fitted into D.P. Moran's conceptual model of anglicized slaves and the baseness of the whole nineteenth-century past. P.N. Fitzgerald and the old IRB had expected that a democratic-republican ideal would eventually 'sweep all before its path' and create a nationalist Ireland, and ultimately were to be disappointed. One major reason for this was that no education system existed in the country that would support or abet the IRB's politics. By contrast, the Irish-Ireland movement, centred on the Gaelic League, did, as Yeats predicted, 'sweep all before its path', for the simple reason that it did have an educational system to support it, namely virtually all the Catholic schools in the country.

The Clan and the *Gaelic American* had a very good relationship with the

Gaelic League, since they were collecting funds for it in America, and this had a significant impact on the course of Irish 'revolutionary', or nationalist, politics during the 1900s. One significant illustration of how things had changed in Irish nationalist circles at this time is that Fr Eugene Sheehy (the man Eamon de Valera credited for having made him a nationalist) was a fierce critic of the IRB and verbal abuser of P.N. Fitzgerald and John O'Leary during the GAA controversies of 1887, but he could befriend the Irish-Irelander Joseph McGarrity and the staff of the *Gaelic American* during the 1900s and, eventually, willingly acted as a courier of letters between the Clan and the small IRB organization of 1910.[9] Arthur Griffith's motive in fomulating 'the Sinn Féin policy' in 1905 was essentially to reach a balance between the old republican and new Irish-Irelander ideals, but in this he was never very successful. Meanwhile the IRB itself had become a very small organization of a little over a thousand men and had altered greatly in some respects from what it had formerly been. In this respect, if the role of the IRB in the 'Land League revolution' of the 1880s was very considerable, its role in shaping the 'Irish revolution' of the 1910s was certainly not as great as is often supposed. It provided neither the manpower nor the ideals of the 'revolution', although, as an organization, it did provide an important political nucleus, or medium, to push an independence movement through, and its general ideology played a significant part in shaping its outcome as well.

Retrospectively, Clan na Gael propagated the view that their sending Tom Clarke to Ireland in 1907 effectively launched the 'revolution'. The fact that the young republican journalists of the 1900s later told the Irish State's 'Bureau of Military History' that they found Clarke an inspirational ally has prompted some historians to give credence to this view. Indeed, it has been argued that Clarke's arrival in Dublin on 10 December 1907 had a dramatic effect in revitalizing the IRB, making it more militant and eventually leading it into rebellion in 1916, and that this rebellion was *ipso facto* an IRB affair and the defining feature of its republicanism. The reality of the situation, however, was much more complex. By the time Tom Clarke arrived in Dublin not only did the IRB barely exist, except on paper, but its old style of republicanism was virtually dead as a factor in Irish popular politics. By 1906, when he decided to commit 'the organization' entirely to the public Sinn Féin movement P.T. Daly had abandoned what was left of the old IRB and reduced the organization to little more than 1,000 members, three quarters of which were confined to the Wolfe Tone Clubs of Dublin, which Fred Allan had founded and were led by Jack O'Hanlon, another veteran of the organization of the 1880s. Except for P.S. O'Hegarty (a critic of Sinn Féin), who knew Allan and

---

9 Cronin, *McGarrity papers*, 36. Fr Sheehy of Bruree, Co. Limerick, it might be noted, had been one of the few priests to champion the 'no rent manifesto' whilst a delegate to a Land League of America conference, but he modified his views thereafter after getting into trouble with his bishop, and was sent 'permanently' to America. Shortly after he returned in 1904, he no longer served as a priest.

Robert Johnston quite well and credited Allan for having kept the IRB alive,[10] the young propagandists of the time were all 'rank and file' figures. Like P.T. Daly, they were concerned first and foremost with pursuing their own personal political activities in public life and the IRB only existed nominally as a revolutionary underground thereby ensuring that 'the organization' exercised little or no influence upon the young members' actions or thought. Tom Clarke, who joined the Tyrone IRB in 1878 at the request of John Daly and Michael McGinn, was a member of the Clan since 1880 and had been given a job by John Devoy as an assistant manager with the *Gaelic American* in 1903 (the same year as he was made, briefly, an honorary vice-president of Cumann na Gaedhael) because the Clan felt responsible for his welfare after he spent fifteen years in prison as a result of its mishaps.[11] Simultaneously Clarke's sister was made the only distributor of the *Gaelic American* in Dublin. Therefore, two 'rank and file' IRB contributors to that paper, Hobson and Patrick MacCartan (a Sinn Féin T.C.), looked to him for news of American affairs once he came to Dublin, even though Clarke associated mostly with fellow ex-prisoners of the 1880s who were virtually at death's door, John Daly (1845–1916) and James Egan (1845–1909).

In April 1910, the IRB secretary P.T. Daly was removed from authority when it was discovered that he was misappropriating and using the IRB's funds (most of which had come from the Clan, since very few people were paying subscriptions anymore) only to fund Sinn Féin city councillors' electoral campaigns;[12] a policy that began in 1906, but had ceased to be popular in the IRB by 1909. This forced John Geraghty, the IRB treasurer, to retire, and also prompted Neal O'Boyle, the IRB president, to resign, though Daly was the real instigator of the policy. Only then did the Clan discover to its horror that a numerous IRB following or disciplined organization simply did not exist anymore. After the IRB Executive resigned in April 1910, Clarke was promoted be the new IRB treasurer, partly because of his popularity and partly because the Clan knew and trusted him best. Meanwhile a very reluctant Fred Allan (who had not joined Sinn Féin) was persuaded to come back to perform his former duties as IRB secretary and try to put the IRB on a 'business footing' for the first time since the late 1890s, as he was effectively the only man who had the experience and know-how to run such an organization.[13] From this date onwards, the IRB was supposed to exercise total independence from the faltering Sinn Féin party, which had all but died. The 'Supreme Council', however, still only existed on paper, and had little or no

---

10 P.S. O'Hegarty, 'Obituary: Robert Johnston and Fred Allan', *Dublin Magazine*, 12 (July-Sept. 1937), p. 94.   11 Clarke's motive in taking part in the 'dynamite war' is unknown, but it is very probable he was persuaded to do so by an *agent provocateur* because the Land League had been suppressed and all its leaders imprisoned without trial, as this was the principal grievance of the New York extremists.   12 UCD, Denis McCullough papers, P120/24 (4), statement of Patrick McCartan; *DPB*, vol. 2, 570.   13 *DPB*, vol. 2, 401–2.

power over Irish separatists' activities which, indeed, were very disparate. John MacBride was appointed the nominal representative of Connacht, but he seems to have never visited the province. He worked everyday in his Dublin corporation office and lived permanently in Allan's home. M.F. Crowe was the nominal representative of Munster (mostly because he was the son of John Crowe), but he lived and worked in Dublin, the only IRB work he did being to occasionally swear in a few members of the Dublin GAA, for which he was a referee at weekends. The Munster IRB had died with P.N. Fitzgerald. Denis McCullough (Ulster), P.S. O'Hegarty (South of England), James Murphy (North of England) and John Mulholland (Scotland, and nominal IRB president) were each just leaders of very small branches of Cumann na Gaedhael or Sinn Féin. Only Jack O'Hanlon (Leinster) had an actual IRB organization behind him, while the young journalists, except for O'Hegarty, did not care about the existence of the IRB Supreme Council.[14]

Owing to the demise of *Sinn Féin* and the *Irish Nation and Peasant* during early 1910, papers to which they formerly contributed, Patrick MacCartan and Bulmer Hobson wanted to launch a new newspaper. Fred Allan and Tom Clarke agreed to support this initiative, so long as it would be an official journal of O'Hanlon's Wolfe Tone Clubs, which would fund the paper and thereby exercise control over its editorial policy, effectively on behalf of the IRB. As they were both 'rank and file' figures, neither MacCartan nor Hobson had any authority in the Wolfe Tone Clubs. Allan at first wanted to be the editor, but probably due to his extensive duties at Dublin City Hall, he and O'Hanlon instead asked MacCartan to be the editor. As a result, *Irish Freedom*, or *Saoirse na Éireann*, a monthly paper of the Wolfe Tone Clubs, went to print in November 1910, with MacCartan as editor and O'Hegarty and Hobson as the chief writers. Allan and Crowe also wrote several articles, but most of its contributors were not IRB men, but rather friends of its editor or chief writers. These included Terence McSwiney, Patrick Pearse, Piaras Beaslai, J.W. Good and Roger Casement,[15] individuals who were not products of the IRB's organizational or political traditions.

Fred Allan wanted *Irish Freedom* to be kept under strict control of 'the organization', which he was trying to revive and rediscipline. Its chief contributors, however, viewed it as simply another vehicle to allow them to write separatist propaganda, and had little other concerns. During 1911, MacCartan came into conflict with Allan after he disobeyed orders (at the instigation of the Countess Markievicz) by introducing resolutions, without the IRB's permission, at a Robert Emmet commemoration organized by the Wolfe Tone Clubs. This prompted Allan to threaten to dismiss MacCartan as editor for his disobedience of IRB orders and assume greater control of the paper on behalf of the Wolfe Tone Clubs. MacCartan had never had to 'follow orders' in this

---

14 UCD, Denis McCullough papers, P120/24 (4), statement of Patrick McCartan. 15 Ibid.

manner before and he resented this disciplinary action, partly because Allan was a less socially mobile fellow, and not in touch with the 'Irish-Ireland' school as much as himself (MacCartan was a Catholic University student with an evidently very bright future). Subsequently, Allan was incapacitated in his role as IRB secretary since Joseph McGarrity, the treasurer and effective leader of the Clan, refused to answer his correspondence, presumably at the request of his close friend MacCartan, his former deputy as Clan leader in Philadelphia.[16] The 70-year-old John Devoy, the nominal Clan secretary, may well not have known what was going on, since he was going deaf and blind and preoccupied with fulfilling his responsibilities as editor of the *Gaelic American*, a job done since 1905 mostly by James Reidy, a protégé and the real principal editor of the *Gaelic American* up until the 1930s. Allan did not take any action against MacCartan until November 1911, when he deposed him as editor of *Irish Freedom* and assumed this responsibility himself. MacCartan responded by appealing to Clarke (as IRB treasurer) to support him, but Clarke, a believer in 'the organization', naturally refused to disobey the Supreme Council's orders.[17] Consequently, MacCartan cabled McGarrity looking for funds, which he immediately received. As a result, the following month, two editions of the paper appeared, one edited by Allan and the other edited by MacCartan. Amazed at how this had happened, in January 1912 the Supreme Council called upon MacCartan to explain himself. He informed the Supreme Council that McGarrity, the Clan treasurer, had financially supported him in bringing out the rival edition of the paper. Realizing that the Supreme Council's authority now seemingly counted for nothing as McGarrity was completely ignoring the IRB's independence from the Clan (a fundamental principle upon which the entire IRB organization had always been based), Allan, O'Hanlon, MacBride, Crowe and many members of the Wolfe Tone Clubs resigned from the IRB in March 1912 as a protest. The sole travelling organizer of the IRB at this time, Cathal Brugha (who had been sent by Crowe to inspect what was left of the IRB's following in Munster during 1911), also resigned.[18] This meant that there was almost no Supreme Council or IRB left.

Tom Clarke, the nominal IRB treasurer, had never been more than a 'rank and file' man in the Irish revolutionary movement. He had only ever followed orders and never gave them, though he possessed a very charismatic and persuasive personality. He decided to follow the recommendation of the ambitious *Irish Freedom* journalists to make the paper's assistant-manager and the former principal organizer of the Sinn Féin party, Sean MacDermott, the new IRB secretary. 'Rank and file' IRB men who were contributors to *Irish Freedom*, like Bulmer Hobson and Seamus Deakin, a Protestant chemist and Gaelic Leaguer, were suddenly made Supreme Councillors, although this

16 Ibid. *DPB*, vol. 2, 401–2. 17 Ibid. 18 Ibid. Diarmuid Lynch, *The IRB and the 1916 insurrection* (1957), 22.

meant very little by 1912. Hobson (another man with an apparently very bright future) replaced O'Hanlon (a mere compositor by day) and so had an actual IRB following of sorts, while Deakin was made the nominal IRB president, although he never attended any Supreme Council meetings and soon dropped out. His replacement, Denis McCullough, could play little or no part in IRB affairs, since he was based in Belfast, while the IRB itself was now confined almost entirely to Dublin.

By April 1912, when a home rule bill was introduced by the Liberal government, the IRB in Ireland was essentially nothing more than the *Irish Freedom* newspaper, three small circles led by Denis McCullough in Belfast and Hobson's following. Tom Clarke did not revitalize the IRB. The journalists, to their delight, had merely been freed from any responsibilities, given total control over *Irish Freedom* and greater room for their talents, and Clarke accepted this situation in his usual sanguine manner mostly because he had no choice. What Clarke did help to do was to encourage several young IRB men (most notably MacDermott) that the moribund Sinn Féin party was no longer worth bothering about, but this trend was already in place due to the perpetual weakness of the Sinn Féin party between 1906 and 1910. As was the case during the 1870s, most IRB members could not tolerate the idea that their subscriptions might be used only to fund individual politicians' political careers, and this was essentially the real issue at stake. Both the Clan and *Irish Freedom* issued statements regarding the 'home rule' bill that were not unlike those being issued by many 'Irish-Irelander' newspapers at the time, noting that 'while we do not object to the Irish people making whatever use they can of the very limited powers given to them by this measure', they believed that regardless of whether or not it passed, 'Ireland will stand, not for an Empire, but for her own national development' and, consequently, Irishmen would ultimately make a nationalist stand and reject the idea of a devolved British government or 'home rule'.[19]

Since December 1906, several of the arms acts were no longer in operation but the new young IRB and Sinn Féin activists made no attempt to acquire any, nor did P.T. Daly, the labour party activist, attempt to collect subscriptions for this purpose. The deposed IRB veteran John MacBride had written to *Irish Freedom* in November 1912 calling for men to avail of the situation, as he had in 1907, but this evoked no immediate response.[20] In January 1913, however, the Ulster Volunteer Force was established and this prompted Bulmer Hobson (co-founder of the nationalist boy-scouts, Fianna Eireann) to tell his Dublin IRB following that they should use this as an excuse to try to persuade the public to form an Irish volunteer force. James Stritch, an old IRB activist of the Parnell era who grew up with Jim Boland in Manchester, immediately had

---

19 *Irish Freedom*, Feb. 1913 (editorial); NLI, John Devoy papers, MS18000 (6), Clan na Gael circular, Mar. 1913. **20** John MacBride, 'Home rule and an appeal to arms', *Irish Freedom*, Nov. 1912.

a drilling hall built behind the Wolfe Tone Clubs headquarters (41 Parnell Square, the former site of the National Club, now the Foresters' Hall) and he, together with some much younger members of Fianna Eireann, began drilling a small number of IRB followers associated with the Dublin GAA, which was led by Jim Boland's son, Harry.[21] Not long afterwards, Dublin labour leaders called for the establishment of a citizens' defence force in the wake of the lock out of strikers in August 1913. Three months later, on 1 November, Eoin MacNeill of UCD and the Gaelic League wrote an article for *An Claidheamh Solus* suggesting the formation of an Irish volunteer force with the encouragement of Deakin, Hobson and others. The thought of the 'Irish-Ireland' generation seemed to be travelling along the same tracks. Within a few weeks, the Irish Citizens' Army was formed and the Irish Volunteers were established, under MacNeill, with the support of fellow staff of *An Claidheamh Solus*, Patrick Pearse and Michael O'Rahilly, as well as D.P. Moran of the *Leader*: the spokesmen for the new 'Irish-Ireland' generation. Not surprisingly, ten days later all the arms acts (which were dropped completely to faciliate the formation of the Ulster Volunteers in 1912) were renewed, while *Irish Freedom* was suppressed by the government a few months later, along with various other nationalist newspapers.

The soon to be famous figure of Michael Collins, who joined the IRB in 1909, was a great admirer of the writings of William Rooney and Thomas Davis and, as O'Hegarty noted, his political thinking was essentially a 'welding of IRB and Gaelic League principles'.[22] In other words, Collins was influenced very significantly by the IRB political tradition (evidenced partly by his completely non-sectarian attitudes and curiosity regarding the history of the Land League), but first and foremost he was essentially an Irish-Irelander and a man of his generation. Collins claimed, as did several other young IRB figures, that the formation of the Irish Volunteer movement was not merely a knee-jerk reaction to the government's allowing the Ulster Volunteers to be established, as is often supposed, but was actually 'the old Irish Republican Brotherhood in fuller force'.[23] Although several IRB men, such as MacDermott, Hobson and Deakin, assisted in the formation of the Irish Volunteers, this claim of Collins was essentially true in one sense only. By resolving to take up arms to assert or defend their liberties like 'free citizens', the men who constituted the Irish Volunteer and Irish Citizen Army movements demonstrated a political resolve that had not been exhibited in the Irish political community at large since the days of the 'old IRB' organization during the Land League era. As Peter Hart has noted, the formation of the volunteer forces was the single greatest factor in the creation of a spirit of direct, active citizenship in Ireland during the early twentieth century,[24] and it

---

21 David Fitzpatrick, *Harry Boland's Irish revolution* (2004), 34; Hobson, *Ireland yesterday and tomorrow*, 42. 22 *Sunday Independent*, 28 Nov. 1948 (O'Hegarty review of *Kevin O'Higgins*, by T. de Vere White). 23 Michael Collins, *The path to freedom* (1922), 54. 24 Peter Hart, 'The language of revolutionary republicanism 1913–22', paper delivered at

is not coincidental that as soon as the general public demonstrated this resolve, their desire for political freedom became actualized, rather than just an aspiration, as the IRB organization of the nineteenth century had always claimed it would. This, rather than just a concern over what was happening in Ulster, was essentially the reality behind the Irish-Irelanders' decision to form the Irish Volunteer movement, which created a vibrant nationalist culture in the country more powerful than anything that had existed since the early 1880s. However, the Irish Volunteer movement was organized among and led by that new Catholic middle-class community (including AOH men) which believed in the ideals of the 'Irish-Ireland' movement, not the republicanism of the old IRB, which was a political tradition that had died out.

During the nineteenth century, the IRB sought to acquire arms to create democratic 'citizen-soldiers' in the country and, potentially, a prospective revolutionary force. Their purpose, however, was never simply a rebellion, nor was the IRB leadership ever a revolutionary, military junta. They simply wanted to bring about political change and create a nationalist movement. A fundamental rule of the IRB was always that what it termed as its 'military organization', in so far as it had one, was to be entirely subordinate to its 'civil organization' (including the IRB executive), 'less anarchy supplant liberty'.[25] The movement was always organized on that basis. Like the IRB leaders of the nineteenth century, early twentieth-century IRB propagandists such as P.S. O'Hegarty and Bulmer Hobson spoke about 'building up an Irish republic' and they had a similar purpose as had James Stephens. They wished to 'build up' a republican political society in Ireland, and viewed the civil/military principle of the organization as being that upon which the entire IRB was based, both in terms of its ideology and how the movement could work and progress. By 1913, however, the IRB had little or no organization left, 'civil' or 'military', its experienced leadership had resigned and it had no initiatives except for keeping *Irish Freedom* in print, and this was achieving very little. Consequently, once the Irish Volunteers were formed, an excited Clarke and MacDermott decided to bank all their hopes for the future upon the volunteer movement. Their goal was to build up new IRB circles within the volunteers and to make these new circles alone the future of 'the organization'; a task in which they were remarkably successful. From 1913 onwards, however, the IRB's personnel tended to fluctuate very regularly, with people often being recruited or dismissed as leaders, nationally or locally, solely on the basis of what influence they had within the volunteers, rather than how much they were suited to be members of the IRB. As a result, the organization had much less of a centre of gravity than before.

Notwithstanding the role that the Clan played in encouraging a rebellion after the outbreak of the First World War, in essence, the 1916 rising was not

NUI Maynooth, 11 May 2002. **25** NAI, British in Ireland microfilm, reel 4, box 10, Secret Societies 1882–4, p.200 (copy of IRB circular, 1883).

a national insurrection, but a citizens' revolt or the last 1848-style rebellion in European history, when would-be 'free citizens' simply 'manned the barricades' in a capital city in defence of a cause of 'national' liberty against an unaccountable, monarchical government and virtually waited to be shot to pieces. This was reflected by the fact that when Tom Clarke, the old Irish republican rebel of the 1870s and 1880s, was asked why he was determined to proclaim a republic, he answered that 'you must have something striking to appeal to the imagination of the world.'[26] The fact that the rising took place in Dublin is not surprising, as it was the only town or city in the country where republicans' level of influence remained consistent in preceding decades. After the outbreak of the First World War, the idea of launching a protest rising could not have taken off the ground were it not that a diverse number of officers of the Irish Volunteers, as well as members of the Irish Citizens' Army (which generally idolized the 1848 propagandists Mitchel and Lalor) favoured the idea, unlike the doubting figures of Hobson, MacCartan and the Irish-Irelander journalists. Most historians have described the 1916 revolt as a purely IRB affair, but this could be said to be a misnomer. Clarke and MacDermott may have presented the idea of the rising to various volunteers, swore some of them into the IRB and formed a 'military council' which was *in theory* something to do with an IRB organization, but Patrick Pearse, Thomas McDonagh, Joseph Mary Plunkett, Eamon de Valera, Countess Markievicz and many other figures who were leaders of the rising never had anything to do with the IRB and were certainly not a product of 'the organization' or its political traditions. In this respect, it should be emphasized that the motives of the participants in the 1916 rising were diverse. While Clarke evidently wanted a citizens' revolt to draw international attention to Irishmen's desire for independence (just as republicans had attempted to do with the 'new departure' of 1879), others like Pearse were essentially Irish-Irelander fanatics, who could hardly be described as republicans, even if Pearse (a supporter of 'home rule') had begun to emulate republican rhetoric in some of his writings a few months prior to the rising. Curiously, very few IRB veterans had any association with the rising. The only real exception was John MacBride, who joined the rising (despite Allan's pleas with him not to) a day after it began, while the Daly-Clarke and Boland families could well have been described as 'Fenian' families. Michael McGinn had been the manager of Clontarf Town Hall (a job given him by Allan and John Clancy)[27] when the rising was planned there, but he does not appear to have taken part. Others like the Dublin corporation official Eamonn Ceannt had 'come in' only very recently through the Volunteers. By 1910, however, a broad and very different independence movement to the IRB now existed, and the three Catholic poets, McDonagh,

---

26 Annie Ryan, *Witnesses: inside the Easter rising* (Dublin, 2005), quoted 157.   27 Clancy was elected mayor of Dublin on 23 January 1915, but died six days later, aged 74, before he could take office. *Weekly Freeman*, 2 Feb. 1915.

Plunkett and Pearse (whose writings were appropriately first published posthumously by a priest at Maynooth College), were undoubtedly its most symbolic representatives. Their deaths, in particular, played a large part in determining the Irish public's reaction to the rising.

For the most part, the Irish public did not believe that the 1916 rebels had fought and died for the old IRB ideal of calling on the Irish people to create a great democratic republic amongst themselves. This was an ideal of liberty that few people really understood or, indeed, identified with. Instead, it was felt that they died for all the ideals of the Irish-Ireland generation, its envisioned rebirth of a Gaelic civilization or, in other words, for the ideals of Pearse, who was immediately made the symbolic icon of the rising by the Catholic press, despite the fact that he had essentially been employed by Clarke in 1916 (as at Rossa's funeral) to act simply as an orator. This is the main reason why the 1916 rising ended up receiving strong retrospective approval from the Irish-Ireland generation at large, and in particular from many young men who joined the Irish Volunteers *after* 1916, who literally felt it was 'their' rebellion, since the public's reaction to the execution of Irish Volunteer officers like Pearse and MacDonagh gave that organization a very dramatic appeal. From a long-term perspective, the significance of the citizens' revolt of 1916 in Irish history was essentially that it caused the democratic idea, that Irishmen had a right to determine their own political future, to be reborn in the country, effectively for the first time in thirty years and, in this respect, it attained Clarke and MacDermott's original objective, just as the 'new departure' of 1879 had made a similarly dramatic impact. Many of the 1916 rebels, however, may well not have comprehended the significance attributed to the rising after the event by the Irish-Ireland generation as a whole.

While the Catholic Church was the great bastion against the rise of the IRB and democratic-republican radicalism in Ireland during the nineteenth century, the clergy had little fear of the rapidly-growing post-1917 Sinn Féin party.[28] The clergy recognized that its ideology, in so far as it had one, was based first and foremost upon the 'philosophy of Irish-Ireland', which was the creation of its own Catholic schools. Furthermore, the new Sinn Féin leader, Eamon de Valera (nicknamed 'the Chief'), a product of Blackrock College and UCD, made clear that he had no desire to lessen the church's control of the education system in the country or separate church and state within an independent Ireland. It was felt, therefore, that Sinn Féin could be trusted as much as the old Irish Party, even if the new Irish Volunteer movement, with which Sinn Féin was associated, attracted many embittered urban workers and members of the rural poor, the potential 'troublemakers'.

The new IRB organization, established in 1917 by Michael Collins, Harry Boland and others, had relatively few IRB veterans within its ranks and was governed differently, giving the president in particular more power than he

---

28 Laffan, *Resurrection of Ireland*, 198–201.

had had in the past and lessening the authority of the secretary. Like the organization of 1914–16, Collins' IRB maintained a great focus upon the Irish Volunteers, but first and foremost it was essentially concerned with the rise of the Sinn Féin party, as it knew, as did Griffith (and as had the old IRB), that no independence movement could be launched, let alone succeed, unless it was based around the abstentionist strategy. As the British government was bound to suppress Sinn Féin once this policy was implemented, the IRB understood (better than others) the necessity of keeping its underground party alive, to keep Sinn Féin alive. The IRB also considered that it was probably best equipped in terms of political experience to act as a co-ordinating nucleus for the new independence movement as a whole and to help push the abstentionist policy through. Indeed, apart from the IRB, there was no established political organization in Ireland available to co-ordinate Sinn Féin party management, now that the Irish Party was dead, and this played a large part in allowing the IRB to play an important role in the independence struggle, despite the small size of its membership. During 1917–8, Collins, Boland and other IRB men managed to play a significant role in selecting candidates for the new Sinn Féin party (which included a couple of old figures like Henry Dixon and Arthur Griffith), while Fred Allan returned to work with Collins and others in collecting funds through the Irish National Aid and Volunteer Dependants Fund and became a leader of Sinn Féin in south County Dublin. A handful of other surviving IRB men of the Parnell era (most of whom were well over 60 years old) merely watched the course of events from a distance.[29]

Following the triumph of Sinn Féin at the polls on the abstentionist ticket in 1918 (which was the first general election with universal suffrage, including women, thereby more than doubling the old electorate), it established an Irish parliament and provisional government in an attempt to force the British government to come to its terms. Not surprisingly, and as the IRB expected, Dublin Castle immediately imprisoned the abstentionist MPs, or TDs (or as many of them as they could find) and established auxiliary forces to aid the police suppress the Sinn Féin organization. The struggle for independence had now effectively begun, as far as the revived IRB organization was concerned, which soon reached a peak membership of about 3,000 men and effectively saw itself as entering a final chess match with the British government. Collins took a leading role in attempting to sustain the Dáil

29 Patrick Hoctor (1861–1933), who ran as an independent pro-Sinn Féin MP in 1915, and Robert Johnston (1840–1937) seem to have held pro-Fianna Fáil views when they died in the 1930s (*Nenagh Guardian*, 11 Nov. 1933; *Irish Press*, 15 May 1935), while Henry Dobbyn (1842–1939) was reputedly more pro-IRA, as were Patrick Tynan (1851–1936) and Luke Dillon (1848–1930) in the Clan. William Carroll (1835–1926) and John Devoy (1841–1928) were pro-Cumann na Gaedhael while Fred Allan (1861–1937) was arrested and imprisoned several times for trying to organize Sinn Féin in south county Dublin during 1919–21 and became a (pro-republican) founder of Cumann na Gaedhael in 1923. McGee, 'Frederick James Allan', *History Ireland* (spring 2002), 29–33.

underground, though his espionage work in counteracting British intelligence did not extend beyond attempts to infiltrate, and make attacks upon, the 'G-Men' of the DMP, that same force which Jim Boland and others (including the twelve-man 'squad' of John Nolan)[30] had attempted to infiltrate, or undermine, during the late 1880s and early 1890s. Several intelligence agents were killed, including Alan Bell, the Special Branch leader in counteracting the IRB in the midlands during the 1880s, who had been called out of retirement by Dublin Castle now that men of his experience were needed to co-ordinate British intelligence work once more.

In January 1919, mostly as a propagandist exercise, Dáil Eireann decided (nonsensically) to declare itself as the successor to the purely theoretical 'provisional government' of 1916 (which never came into existence, as the rebels were defeated and executed), rather than simply proclaiming itself a *de facto*, operative parliament in its own right. This action was taken to draw the sympathy of all who identified with the idealism of the 1916 rebels and thereby give the actual provisional republican government of 1919 a strong moral authority. However, the fact that the TDs had taken an oath to the provisional government, which in turn was seen to be a successor of the 1916 rebels, gave 'The Republic' a significance to many young Irish Volunteers that was very different from that maintained by the IRB. While the IRB viewed 'the republic' simply as their ideal of political liberty for an independent Ireland, to young Irish-Irelanders who idolized the executed 1916 'martyrs' as passionately (and for effectively the same reasons) as Catholic youths had celebrated the Manchester 'martyrs' in the past, 'the republic' which had been proclaimed in 1916 acquired an almost religious significance, symbolizing the entire 'Irish-Irelander' separatist ideal, with all its connotations. Even some low-ranking, Irish-Ireland clergymen began talking enthusiastically about 'the republic' after 1916, without evidently being aware of what a republic meant in practice (their bishops were not so ignorant). This extraordinary birth of an association between a popular Catholic sense of Irish identity and the phrase 'the republic' played a very significant role in influencing the manner in which many people reacted to the Anglo-Irish Treaty of 1921.

It was only because Sinn Féin adopted the abstentionist policy in 1918 and the Irish public subsequently defended the authority of an Irish provisional government and forced Britain to come to (most of) its terms that Ireland was ever able to win independence, with a government where the executive was wholly responsible to the parliament and the elective house; the form of government John O'Leary desired.[31] The 'home rule' bills of 1886, 1893 and

30 John, or 'Jackie' Nolan (1857–1920), was released from a Canadian prison in 1915 after the Luke Dillon case was reopened, and returned to Dublin, where he was given a job with the corporation by Fred Allan and renewed his friendship with W.T. Cosgrave TD, who knew him well whilst both men were growing up on James Street and was one of the few men, along with Joseph McGrath TD and Allan, to attend his funeral. *Irish Independent*, 7 Dec. 1920. 31 *Gaelic American*, 12 Dec. 1908 (biographical article on O'Leary by Devoy). This article

1912 did not grant Ireland the slightest form of autonomy, nor could *any* pieces of Westminster legislation have granted Ireland autonomy as they were inherently the prerogative of Westminster alone: it was not within the British parliament's power to pass legislation denying itself the right to subsequently repeal this legislation. The only way Sinn Féin (or the Irish Party before it, had it meant what it said in 1885) could attempt to claim a right to national self-determination or actual Irish independence (as opposed to a devolved British government) was by adopting the abstentionist policy, which inherently meant forcing the British government into recognizing the authority of the Irish parliament and, thereafter, attempting to force as many of the Irish government's terms upon the British cabinet as were possible in subsequent treaty negotations between the two governments. This is what occurred during 1920–1. Contrary to what some historians have argued in recent years, the 'dominion status' of Canada and Australia (neither of which were part of the United Kingdom) was no more a legal possibility for Ireland under the Union than it was for Yorkshire, Scotland, Kent, or any other part of the United Kingdom of Great Britain and Ireland. The Anglo-Irish Treaty of 1921, which broke the connection of 'southern Ireland' with the United Kingdom (if not the 'Commonwealth') and provided for the separation of church and state, was drafted by and legally required ratification from *both* governments. Its significance was that it ensured that the Irish state had a written constitution (which it could modify) to define its laws and citizens' liberties in the republican fashion, unlike the United Kingdom and completely unlike northern Ireland, which after thirty-five years protesting against the idea of 'home rule' was granted a 'home rule' settlement by Westminster in 1920, which possessed all the inherent shortcomings, or imbalances, of any such measure.

Sinn Féin, like the Irish Party, did not want the country to be partitioned, the former for nationalistic reasons and the latter more for economic reasons. The reality, however, was that partition was a question beyond Sinn Féin's control not primarily because of the military power of the British state, but because the political polarization brought about within Ireland itself over the last thirty-five years was very real. Just as Ulster Protestants always resisted the Catholic politics of the Irish Party, so too did they react against its 'Ireland a Nation' rhetoric by essentially developing, albeit with the Tories' patronage, their own sense of nationalism, which was based upon parallel socio-economic and religious standards to the Irish Party's sense of nationalism, and identified equally with the empire. Sinn Féin, being an outgrowth of an Irish-Irelander Catholic middle class (educated mostly at those schools which the Irish Party had appealed, on behalf of the bishops, to the government to set up), was not only no more appealing to Ulster Protestants than the Irish Party had been, but its very character meant that it was certainly not equipped to deal with the

explains O'Leary's attitude towards republicanism and other constitutional matters particularly well.

previous thirty-five years of politico-religious polarization on the island, which, being a party of young 'Irish-Irelanders' with a very shortsighted and confessional view of the past, Sinn Féin did not even understand. So long as this was the case, nothing was likely to change in the relationship between 'north' and 'south'.

As far as the IRB was generally concerned, it was the fight for an Irish constitution, or the right for the Irish people to make their own laws without British interference, that made the struggle for independence between 1919 and 1921 a republican one and which ensured that, thereafter, republican liberty could thrive in Ireland so long as Irish citizens and, in turn, their politicians, were determined that it would. This is why the IRB generally supported the treaty, notwithstanding its perceived shortcomings, although, as Michael Collins soon discovered, Britain was determined to do everything in its power to prevent the Free State from adopting an explicitly republican constitution, while other problems soon emerged.

Collins' Supreme Council issued a statement following the signing of the treaty noting that all members of the IRB were completely free to make up their own minds about it, but the Supreme Council believed it should be accepted, as 'it has always been the policy of this organization to make use of all instruments, political or otherwise, which are likely to aid the attainment of its final end – a free, independent republican government in Ireland'. However this circular was immediately denounced by the IRB's very recent Irish Volunteer recruits (most notably Liam Lynch, the nominal representative of Munster on the Supreme Council) 'as being utterly at variance with the principles of the IRB' because it was 'treason to the republic established in 1916'.[32] Collins pointed out the simple fact that the purpose of the leaders of the 1916 rising in proclaiming a republic was to make 'a wonderful gesture – throwing down the gauntlet of defiance to the enemy, expressing to ourselves the complete freedom we aimed at',[33] but the vast majority of the young Irish Volunteers could not understand this reasoning and definition of the purpose of the rising, which reflected the nineteenth-century republican tradition. Many felt that the separatist ideal (or even the 'bones of the martyrs' of 1916, particularly Pearse's), was somehow being desecrated. Some bewildered young Irish Volunteers (virtually all of whom, like de Valera, had no connection with Irish politics prior to 1917) began propagating conspiracy theories regarding the meaning of that other 'Irish Republic' referred to in the IRB's constitution and accused the IRB of being traitors and seeing itself as the only authority in the country. To the chagrin of the IRB, these men now denied that the Dáil had a right to vote on the Treaty which its plenipotentiaries had co-drafted (it voted narrowly to accept it) or to maintain civil control over what was described as 'the army'. In effect, to use IRB parlance,

32 Florence O'Donoghue, *No other law* (Dublin, 1954), 192–4. 33 Collins, *Path to freedom*, 55.

the 'military organization' of the Irish revolution (the Irish Volunteers, which was becoming known as the 'Irish Republican Army') was not willing to be kept under the control of the 'civil organization' (Dáil Eireann). The first loyalty of the IRB, however, as per its ideology and constitutional rules, was inherently to the Dáil.

De Valera's decision, because he lost a vote for the presidency of the Dáil, to withdraw from the Dáil, set up his own rival (un-elected) government and to proclaim that his government was the 'legitimate', true successor of the first Dáil (and by inference of the 1916 rebels as well) prompted much of the IRA to swear allegiance to it, and thus a new Irish revolutionary tradition was born based upon the principle of legitimism; a political philosophy which is rooted entirely in monarchical and anti-republican conceptions of liberty and government. This is why the IRB veteran P.S. O'Hegarty denounced the anti-treaty party as 'pseudo-republicans', who were defiling principles of liberty which they did not even understand and, in all probability, would end up destroying republicanism as an ideal of Irish political liberty for good.[34] Certainly, from an IRB perspective, the legacy of 1916 was now turned completely on its head. The withdrawal of de Valera and other TDs from the Dáil due to their refusal to take an oath of allegiance to the Free State constitution and an oath of fidelty to the King as head of the commonwealth may have been a means of championing the ideal that Irishmen must have a complete right to define their own conception of citizenship, and O'Hegarty and others (notwithstanding their anger at the TDs' withdrawal) believed that, in so doing, they could nevertheless work with the Dáil in bringing such a situation about. However De Valera's setting up of a rival form of government in the country and basing its existence on a theory of legitimism could serve no purpose whatsoever but to obscure republicanism as an ideal of liberty in Ireland, and to appeal to the public and the IRA to turn directly against the supposedly 'illegitimate' Dáil, which a sizeable percentage of the IRA did, while de Valera shocked his former associates by assuming the mantle as the IRA's spokesman in a subsequent attempted *coup d'état*. The IRA could not possibly have defeated the British army in an actual war, but it could very easily defeat itself, the IRB and the whole republican movement by adopting a self-destructive ideology.

Apart from polluting the Irish body politic in its very infancy, the civil war of 1922–3 essentially turned the very notion of a 'republican' in Ireland into a sectional and comparatively meaningless political badge, for people were now defined as republicans based solely on their attitudes towards 'the treaty' and on 'which side' they took in the civil war. The attempted summary of Ernie O'Malley (a leader of the anti-Treaty IRA who denounced the IRB as British imperialists and traitors) of what the IRA were fighting for, that 'freedom comes religious, political and economic; we were at the political

---

34 O'Hegarty, *Victory of Sinn Fein*, 84, 85, 118–20.

stage',[35] reflected the fact that in the minds of many of the anti-Treaty IRA (and evidently deValera as well), 'the republic' had much more to do with the Irish-Ireland, separatist ideal in which they had been schooled by priests than a republican ideal of liberty.

The fact that the British government attempted to pressurize the Irish government into accepting the treaty settlement by issuing strange 'ultimatum warnings' was undoubtedly a cause of the civil war. Not only are ultimatums inherently a denial of political liberties, but the very fact that the treaty could thereby be presented to the Irish public as an enforcement of Britain's will made it seem an intolerable measure to many, regardless of its contents. In so doing, Whitehall was effectively motivated by a desire to humiliate Irish separatists by attempting to deny them any claim to victory, and to incite the IRA by highlighting that if the British government had reached an impasse in trying to deny Irishmen political independence, it most certainly had not lost any 'war', in a military sense.

The IRB was naturally divided in its opinion regarding the Anglo-Irish Treaty, as was most of the country, but it was nevertheless very conscious of the need for republican unity, no matter what happened, to prevent the old Irish Party establishment from reasserting its political authority in the country. De Valera ('the chief'), by contrast, seems to have been determined that he personally, rather than the IRB (whose influence he resented), would be able to determine the outcome of the 'revolution' and so he attempted to win the IRA away from the IRB.

It is very unlikely that the IRB, being as small as it was at the time, could have become a medium for uniting various political factions and pulling off its old trick of 'leading them in the right direction' once more, as Collins attempted to do in the months prior to the civil war, mostly through the instrument of (the ambivalent mind of) Harry Boland. Some IRB men placed blame for the civil war upon de Valera and particularly Liam Lynch, whose role in breaking the chain of command in the IRB (and subsequently instituting the IRA as a distinct organization, sworn to uphold de Valera's un-elected Dáil) undoubtedly helping bring about the whole catastrophe. Indeed, Lynch reputedly realized before his death that he made a great mistake in deliberately sending the country into civil war, without any awareness (or, indeed, apparent consideration) of the consequences this would have.

It is conceivable that no political organization may have been better equipped, at least in terms of its ideology and experience, to bring harmony to republican factions in the country during the 1920s than the IRB, had its leaders not been shot in the civil war and the organization subsequently outlawed and suppressed by Kevin O'Higgins, who killed off the IRB not because it was a 'threat' to the state or to democracy (it was neither), but

35 Ernie O'Malley, *The singing flame* (Tralee, 1978), 286.

because, in the wake of the civil war, O'Higgins believed the only way to guarantee political stability in the insecure young state was to rely on the old Catholic establishment that had supported the Irish Party and whose influence still pervaded the civil service and higher education system that had been originally set up in the country by the British government to accommodate the possibility of a new Dublin Castle administration being set up consisting predominantly of Irish Catholics. O'Higgins, the nephew of Tim Healy (who in turn was a nephew of A.M. Sullivan), effectively stayed true to his political roots by attempting to build up an Irish state in this rather reactionary manner. This in turn helped negate the possibility that Cumann na Gaedheal (which Fred Allan and G.A. Lyons helped establish) might become the sort of republican party that the few IRB survivors desired it would be, since the party soon tried (successfully) to incorporate remnants of old Irish Party political networks into its ranks. Whether or not this development should be seen as a 'counter-revolution', as one historian has recently termed it,[36] is questionable. It might better be described simply as a belated victory of the Catholic establishment over the republican political traditions of the IRB, the supposed 'physical force party', which the Catholic establishment had always asked the public to view as a threat to decent society, or as 'wildmen screaming through the keyhole' of the civilised Catholic world and the social ideal it represented. The days of 'republican brothers' in Irish politics were thus brought to an end.

The outbreak of civil war not only shattered the unity of Sinn Féin and the republican movement, but it inherently discredited (and indeed distorted) republicanism in the eyes of many, prompting many anxious political figures to react against what Sinn Féin had been attempting to do in recent times. If the civil war had been prevented, this might not have happened. Whatever the case, it is clear that once the civil war broke out most of those who had no time for the idea of establishing a new republican socio-political order in the country (including many old Irish Party supporters, who literally 'sat on the fence' during the recent conflict, and of course the bishops, who excommunicated the anti-Treaty IRA) invariably rallied to the Free State's standard, very often simply by default, thereby bringing about a political situation the IRB party feared and had essentially being doing its best to prevent from coming about since 1919. The post-1917 Irish Volunteer movement, which gave birth to the IRA, had drawn heavily upon those same sections of the community who had once supported the Land League and had never been allowed political empowerment. After the civil war, what became known as the 'anti-Treaty' party was generally able to draw its popular support from these same classes who had most reason to desire the establishment of a republican social order in the country, again often simply by a process of default, since the Free State had been tarnished during the civil war by its willingness to execute IRA

36 John Regan, *The Irish counter revolution, 1921–1936* (Dublin, 1999).

prisoners. Such a division of party interests in the country in the wake of the 'revolution' was perhaps inevitable (de Valera was certainly counting on this eventuality), although the manner by which these divisions were expressed, and what 'The Republic' came to symbolize in the minds of many Irish people after 1922, was something that had no historical precedents.

From the 1920s onwards, the IRA liked to think of itself as the successor of a 'Fenian tradition' in Irish politics, but it was the first to admit that it had little or no understanding of what the IRB political tradition actually was, as it could only perceive the history of Irish republicanism through the prism of the civil war or what significance de Valera chose to attribute retrospectively to the 1916 rising. Its sense of history was rooted in the same Irish-Ireland outlook of the past that was championed by the Free State which it detested. One significant consequence of this myopia was that the IRA claimed, presumably from its reading of popular Catholic histories like *Speeches from the Dock* (which the IRA reprinted in new additions),[37] the existence of a continuous 'physical force tradition' in Irish history and used this idea to legitimize its political stance. It was completely unaware that this very rhetorical tradition of 'physical force' actually stemmed from some meaningless verbal gymnastics concocted by Catholic MPs in the imperial parliament during the nineteenth century in an attempt to 'legitimize' their politics, to rationalize that moral authority which the 'unwritten constitution' of the British state had in their own eyes and to crowd nationalists out of Irish life by portraying them as criminals. The reality of the history of the IRB, just as was the case for the 'Young Ireland' fraternity and the 'Society of the United Irishmen', was that it was an Irish republican brotherhood committed to bringing about an Irish nationalist society through propagating republican principles of political liberty by whatever means were possible, whether this took the form of promoting democratic (or 'revolutionary') movements, propagating political literature, combating sectarianism, speaking out against parliamentary corruption or encouraging a volunteering tradition among Irishmen. However, popular Catholic journalisms and histories, which referred to these movements (just as the Irish Party did) only at those moments of '1798', '1848', '1867' or '1916', deliberately presented a very obscure and much more simplistic picture. If a 'physical force tradition' exists as a feature of Irish history (as that term is now generally understood), then the post-1923 IRA was essentially responsible for creating it, by attempting to sustain the legitimist stance of de Valera during the civil war, claiming that an army alone has a right to represent a public's will. The IRA's false sense of republican history, culminating in its strange marrying of a popular Catholic view of history with an essentially Marxist idea of what a 'revolutionary' must be (indoctrinating men into holding certain rigid attitudes towards history and politics), could

---

37 Incidentally, this book was written by A.M. Sullivan, the original 'felon-setter'.

well be described as a negation of the entire Irish republican tradition prior to 1922.

Notwithstanding the deep contradictions and anti-republican (legitimist) elements in the post-1922 IRA's ideology, it had some obvious parallels with the IRB: its obsession with the question of Ireland achieving complete political self-determination without British interference and, more significantly, its felt need to maintain a radicalism through its own organization, acting as a sort of revolutionary 'nucleus', since the structure of Irish political society as a whole was perceived to be inimicable to 'the republic'. The manner by which it attempted to put such ideals into practice, however, were again a negation of the IRB political tradition and were rooted entirely in the politics of the civil war. After 1923, being embittered by the civil war and seeking to 'restore' a republic which was only ever provisionally established, the IRA denounced and sometimes shot many people as 'traitors' and 'imperialists' (the growing popularity of the latter rhetoric being something that soon attracted IRA men to communism) and evidently desired to suppress any aspect of Irish political life (most notably Remembrance Day commemorations) that did not correlate with the revolutionary consensus which it believed to have existed during the preceding years. The fact (which Griffith and IRB veterans had generally been well aware of) that a republican ideal of liberty was actually largely missing from the ideals of the 'revolutionary generation' as a whole was something the IRA did not understand, as all its young recruits from 1923 onwards (who were not allowed to be older than nineteen) were literally indoctrinated into thinking otherwise, almost as an article of faith.

The reality was that no matter what the outcome of the 'Irish revolution' might have been, the very educational system in the country that had produced the 'revolutionary generation' (including the IRA) in the first place had a Catholic and 'Irish-Ireland' ethos. It most certainly did not have a republican ethos, and this perhaps naturally determined what type of political establishment would eventually come into being in Ireland, as well as the manner by which opposition to that establishment would very often be expressed. Popular political activists, whether they had been in the IRB or IRA, could not overcome this reality, which not all of them understood. Certainly, those IRA activists who believed that 'Irish-Irelander' nationalism and republicanism were somehow synonymous were bound to be blind to this reality of Irish society as a whole.

The weakness of republicanism as a factor in the 'Irish revolution' was reflected in the fact that except in the case of the primary 'national schools' (which were handed over to the Catholic Church), the formation of the Irish state would bring about virtually no changes in the education system in the country, which was simply inherited from the days of British rule. Irish intellectual life had always been characterized by a largely subsidiary nature, drawing from Catholic or English sources, and it was symptomatic of the origins and nature of the 'Irish revolution' that most writers associated with it assumed the antidote to this latter trend was to champion 'Gaelicism', or the Irish language, and viewed the language as somehow the basis of a lost Irish civic ideal or 'civilization'. Patrick Pearse may have been adopted temporarily as a sort of spokesman for the IRB during the 1916 rising, but he represented a very different ideal, which was essentially akin to that of de Valera. It might be noted that a significant percentage of the intellectual leaders of the 'revolutionary generation' in early twentieth-century Ireland expressed admiration for English Catholic intellectuals like G.K. Chesterton for similar reasons as they did for men like Pearse or de Valera. For this reason, it is perhaps not at all coincidental that as soon as figures like Chesterton disappeared from the Irish intellectual landscape, so too did Pearse and the whole 'philosophical' (as opposed to the purely linguistic) dimension to the Gaelic League/Irish-Ireland ideal, which essentially originated with D.P. Moran's perceptibly anti-Protestant branch of the Gaelic League in London. If the ideals of 'Irish revolution' eventually began to seem neither relevant nor very comprehensible to many people in Ireland by the mid-to-late twentieth century, this was essentially the historical reason why. The demise of Irish-Irelandism was also a contributory reason why historical perceptions of the 'Irish revolution' began to alter greatly.

The history of the 'Irish revolution' was generally not examined by academics until the state's commemoration of the fiftieth anniversary of the 1916 rising and the outbreak of sectarian violence in Northern Ireland not long afterwards. Irish historiography itself had no real antecedents as a professional discipline prior to the creation of *Irish Historical Studies*, a north-south publication founded by academics of TCD and UCD in 1938, the year after de Valera produced his controversial constitution with a legitimist claim over Northern Ireland and guaranteeing Ireland's status as a Catholic-biased state. The conceptual framework these academics adopted (and subsequently popularized in Ireland) for interpreting the political history of life under the Union was the same as that employed in Britain; namely, placing primary, or sometimes total, focus upon parliamentary representation at Westminster. Analysis of Ireland was not generally extended beyond 1910. If the imbalances of the Union were sometimes noted by historians, they were not analysed, while the importance of extra-parliamentary agitations in Ireland (where there was no parliament) was not recognized; 'democratic' politics was identified exclusively with parliamentary procedures and the formation of governments, despite the very fact that the country was governed by an unaccountable administration in a pre-democratic age. Irish Catholic MPs' rhetoric during the nineteenth century about 'constitutional' and 'physical force' methods were also repeated by historians at face value, without any explanation or analysis. More recent historiography of the political history of Ireland under the Union has focused to a much greater degree upon the era of the First World War, although the great emphasis placed upon the militarism of the 1910s has arguably obscured the fact that the Irish independence movement both before and after the war was not only democratically-based, but possessed an extra-parliamentary focus simply by virtue of the government's unaccountability. The struggle for Irish independence itself during 1919–21 was, first and foremost, an episode in defensive warfare and a democratic attempt to set up an accountable, Irish government.

If the history of Ireland under the Union cannot be understood without reference to Whitehall's treatment of the 'Irish question', there is much to be said for the evolution of a historiography of Ireland under the Union which recognizes that the origins of the Irish polity of the early twentieth century (whether it was nominally labelled as 'nationalist' or 'unionist' – Ulster Protestants solemnly adopted their own brand of 'abstentionist' policy in 1912) cannot be understood without far greater emphasis being placed upon all those dimensions to politics outside the range of the imperial parliament; a politics which, in Ireland, was more often than not an expression of democratic aspirations and was what made the creation of an Irish state possible. If historians are well aware of the theories of 'responsible government' which formed an intellectual preoccupation for many officials at Dublin Castle and Whitehall, whatever notions, or perceptions, of political liberty that may have been held, or championed, in any locality in Ireland under the Union have not generally been deemed worthy of analysis from historians. Indeed, it could well be argued that many aspects of the history of Ireland under the Union have been completely obscured through this very neglect. Meanwhile, the history of the Irish Party, and, indeed, of parliamentary representation under the Union generally, undoubtedly should begin to be examined far more so in terms of the shifting relationship between Westminster MPs and community life in Ireland, the distance between government and the governed, the contrasts between contemporary British and Irish perceptions of the proper role of various 'classes' in political life and the inherent limitations of electoral politics in Ireland under the Union.

The idea that the 'Irish revolution', or the rise of an independence movement in Ireland, was an unnatural 'aberration' in the history of Ireland under the Union, caused simply by the outbreak of the First World War or the 1916 rising, is essentially misleading. The 'Irish revolution' was, if nothing else, the triumph of the Irish-Ireland party and its ideals in Irish politics, and it acquired the label of being a 'revolution' by virtue of this very fact. The Irish-Ireland ideal owed its prevalence partly to a rise in levels of education in Ireland but mostly because of its ability as early as the 1900s to assume the mantle of expressing Irish nationalist aspirations through capturing the middle ground of Irish public opinion, just as the Land League agitation had done during the early 1880s, that is before the politics of 'home rule' was taken up by Gladstone in an attempt to undo the 'uprising of the Irish democracy' that took place in 1879. The First World War marked the end of 'the age of empire' and the birth of new democratic political orders in Europe, while it also essentially ended the *belle époque* in the history of Britain, which reached the apogee of its cultural and political influence and power in the pre-war period.[38] Before the impact of the First World War on *Irish* life can be fully understood, however, much greater analysis will need to be done on the full range and complexities of Irish political experiences before, just as much as after, 1914.

The Irish state's own sense of its historical origins and its desire to have something to celebrate about Ireland's past has arguably played a significant role in obscuring the complexities of Irish history under the Union as well as the history of Irish republicanism. The very fact that a 'Bureau of Military History' was eventually set up by de Valera to examine the history of the 'Irish revolution' reflected the state's growing acceptance of the post-1922 IRA's rationale that the 'Irish revolution' was first and foremost a war, or 'military' conflict, led by an actual army, rather than a democratic struggle for independence involving various voluntary citizens' defence forces, for which a republican brotherhood, among others, tried to act as a co-ordinating medium. Somewhat similar attitudes surrounded the state receptions that were given to the two most well-known survivors of the IRB of the 1860s, John Devoy and Mark Ryan, during the 1920s and 1930s.[39] Both men were subsequently asked to write (or in Ryan's case, dictate) books of recollections specifically about '1867' and '1916' (the supposed high points of 'Fenianism') and the individual 'military' valour of the men involved. Devoy, in particular, seemingly complied, exaggerating the extent to which the Irish language was a concern of the IRB (or himself) during the 1860s, and playing up an idea that a successful rising might have been possible at that time owing to the number of IRB recruits in the British army, despite the fact he had always completely dismissed this idea previously.[40] It was not pointed out in his posthumously edited and arranged *Recollections* (New York, 1929) what he effectively admitted in previous newspaper recollections during 1924, that the height of his own political career and the height of IRB activism did not occur at the time of the 1867 or 1916 risings, but rather during that long period of radical, democratic activity in the intervening years when the IRB strained its capabilities and resources to the absolute limit, accomplished many small political goals but failed to accomplish its great revolutionary goal. However this was a tale that could not possibly be celebrated and that could not be easily explained, partly because Devoy was a very old, dying and blind man (who was never entirely informed of what was happening in Ireland) and most of all because the political audiences of the 1920s would simply not have understood such terms of reference.

It is curious, but not entirely surprising, that after the IRB disbanded in 1924, Devoy surmised, in retrospect, that 'the most efficient secretary it ever had', or the most efficient 'chief organizer of the Irish Republic', was not

---

38 Eric Hobsbawm, *The age of empire, 1875–1914*, (London, 1987), 6–7. 39 Devoy was given a state reception in 1924 and state funeral in 1929, while all political parties in the Dáil came together to make an official tribute to Ryan in 1936. Ryan, *Fenian memories*, appendix IV.
40 John Devoy, 'Stephens and his secretary', *Irish Nation* (New York), 7 June 1884.

James Stephens, Sean MacDermott, Harry Boland, Michael Collins or other such celebrated and famous figures, but rather John O'Connor,[41] the secretary from 1878 to 1895. It was at this time, particularly from 1880–1884, when the 'young republic' of the IRB was at its greatest strength, numerically, financially and even 'militarily', although it had no pretensions of being an army and viewed 'the will of the people' as its master. It was also at this time when republicans succeeded in launching the Land League political tradition of a self-sustaining, radical agrarian politics, which completely transformed the Irish political landscape and created a vibrant democratic political culture, which the British government found it very difficult to, and ultimately failed to, contain or suppress. The Young Ireland Societies founded at this time became the basis for the republican movement of the early twentieth century and were effectively the precursors of the Anglo-Irish literary movement, as well as the Irish-Ireland movement. The IRB also played a major role at this time in launching and shaping the nationalist ethos of the GAA, a central force in Irish social, communal and popular political life and an organization that was increasingly viewed by many of its supporters as a democratic alternative to the National League bureaucracy (or that of the National Federation or United Irish League) in representing Irish nationalist aspirations. It was also during this time when the IRB came closest to bringing about what happened during 1918 purely as a result of its own numerical strength as an organization, or party. Were it not for several major setbacks that prevented it from progressing towards this end, it may perhaps have been able to accomplish this goal ultimately without recourse to the dramatic gesture of the 1916 rising in an attempt to vindicate its 'Fenian dead'. In his journalism, Devoy continued up until 1914 to follow the reasoning of the 'new departure' that he had helped initiate in 1879, and curiously it was not until he came to Ireland for the first time in forty-five years for an official state reception during 1924 that he seems to have come to the conclusion that his having placed his trust in Parnell as custodian of the 'new departure' ideal was the one great mistake of his political career.[42] Certainly, the *actual* underlying, root cause of the divisions in Irish politics during the twentieth century was that the 'Irish revolution' did not alter the socio-political order in the country, which, indeed, had not essentially changed since those who championed a democratic and nationalist political ideal lost the conflict with those who championed an aristocratic and religious social ideal during the later nineteenth century. It could well be said that this particular outcome during the later nineteenth century determined, directly or indirectly, the ethos of the power structures in Irish political life, both north and south, well into the twentieth century.

The nineteenth-century IRB organization had a significant debt to the example of mid-nineteenth century French republicanism, and the eventual outcome of the IRB's role in sustaining a republican ideal of any kind in Irish political life over three generations can perhaps best be understood with

41 Devoy, 'Story of the Clan', *Gaelic American*, 6 Dec. 1924.   42 Ryan, *Fenian memories*, 65.

reference to this very fact. Like the Irish state that was created partly by IRB activists amidst great turmoil during 1922, the 'Third Republic' that was established in France amidst civil war during 1871 (and which was dismissed as a sham republic by more hardline revolutionaries) embodied a mass of political contradictions, inspired by great class, intellectual, religious and cultural differences that were deep-rooted in society for generations. For very many years after France technically became a republican state in 1871, many people still spat when 'La Marseillaise' (which became the national anthem only several years later) was played as much as others cheered, because they either detested or identified with the social ideal that a simple musical symbol (as well as various other symbols) could represent in the public mind. In France, this represented the persistence of the conflict between a Catholic and aristocratic social ideal with a democratic-republican one within the country. Although democratic republics virtually became an accepted norm in European society in the post-1918 world, on a cultural level (and in terms of the nature of the education system in the country), the political divisions in Ireland after 1922 could well be said to have been shaped by a similar dynamic, not least owing to the uncertain outcome of the old conflict between the Irish Party and IRB. To some extent, the rise of the Irish-Ireland movement actually reversed the terms of reference by which this conflict of interests was expressed.

As did many of the French during the nineteenth century, many twentieth-century Irish citizens would attempt to rationalize the mass of political contradictions they saw around them in terms of a supposedly all-embracing ideal of 'The Republic' and view this ideal as either the root of all their society's problems, or the basis for all their hopes in the future, more often than not on grounds of the manner in which they were educated (or educated themselves), or perhaps their general class prejudices, rather than in the name of any doctrinaire ideology. Beneath the surface of the 'Irish revolution' and the subsequent 'doctrinaire' rhetoric of its self-professed chief protagonists after the event, a similar political and social dynamic could be said to have been at work. As was the case in France, however, the *true* historical origins of the Irish ideal of 'The Republic' that was given forcible expression in 1916 was simply the desire of a sizeable percentage of the ordinary community to see the creation of a new form of society that might be transfigured by a democratic and egalitarian (or 'republican') ideal of liberty and thereby allow 'the people', or 'the nation', to achieve political self-determination. The continued appeal and popularity of such an ideal in Irish life might well be said to be the single greatest reason why an Irish revolutionary brotherhood that began with just six bohemian figures in the Liberties area of Dublin in 1858 eventually managed to encompass tens of thousands of people during the would-be 'revolution' of the early to mid 1880s and survived for another forty years to carry through the establishment of an Irish state, before being immediately thwarted by the treaty split and then suppressed by the political representatives of an Irish Catholic establishment, first moulded by Cardinal Cullen during the 1850s. The fact that the Irish polity eventually managed to outgrow the United Kingdom, as the IRB always claimed it would, and thereby achieve political independence, was determined by the persistence of this democratic and nationalist tradition in Ireland, which the Union was never designed to accommodate and stood in direct conflict with the British state.

The age when revolutionary, republican brotherhoods could be popular mediums for championing democratic liberty in Europe may not have outlasted the demise of the proverbial 'long nineteenth century' of 1789–1914 (or in Ireland's case, perhaps one should say 1789–1916), but if one can rightly speak of republicanism, or even a 'young republic', as having been an active factor in Irish life after 1916, then its basis no doubt rested upon a very similar dynamic. By contrast, if debate upon republicanism for much of twentieth-century Ireland came to rest upon very different premises, one might postulate that a very false or distorted view of republicanism somehow entered Irish political and, subsequently, Irish historical discourse.

Select bibliography

MANUSCRIPTS AND NEWSPAPERS

NATIONAL ARCHIVES OF IRELAND
Crime Special Branch (CSB) reports, B files 1880–3, South East and Northern Divisions 1882–4
Land and National League reports, 1879–87
District Inspector Crime Special (DICS) reports, all RIC divisions 1887–95
Crime Branch Special (CBS) reports, S files 1890–1910, Précis to Home Office 1894–1905
Fenian Papers (A files, F files, Police Reports), 1871–83
Dublin Metropolitan Police (DMP) files, 1882–1900
Chief Secretary Office Registered Papers (CSORP), 1877–1890
British in Ireland microfilm catalogue (CO 904):
DMP and RIC précis 1901–11
Registers of secret society suspects in Ireland and America
Register of informers
Register of Foreign Associations
Register of Home Associations

NATIONAL LIBRARY OF IRELAND
Fred Allan papers (includes John MacBride papers)
John Devoy papers
Leon O'Broin papers
Jeremiah O'Donovan Rossa papers
John O'Leary papers
John Redmond papers
James Stephens papers
Minute-books of Young Ireland Society, Leinster Literary Society, Celtic Literary Society and National Literary Society

UNIVERSITY COLLEGE DUBLIN
Desmond Ryan papers
Denis McCullough papers
Tim Healy papers
Richard Mulcahy papers (Sean O'Muirthile memoir)

TRINITY COLLEGE DUBLIN
Michael Davitt papers (includes James Stephens papers)
John Dillon papers

PUBLIC RECORD OFFICE (LONDON)
Sir Robert Anderson papers
Arthur Balfour papers
G.W. Balfour papers
Colonial Office, confidential print series (CO 903)
Foreign Office, Fenian Brotherhood files, vols. 46–8
London Metropolitan Police Records (MEPO files)

MANUSCRIPTS IN PRIVATE POSSESSION
James Boland papers (courtesy of Annraoi O'Beolain)

NEWSPAPERS

Citizen (Chicago)	*Irish World (New York)*
Dublin University Review	*Nation*
Evening Herald	*Northern Patriot*
Freeman's Journal	*Sinn Fein*
Gaelic American (New York)	*Shan Van Vocht*
Irish Daily Independent	*Times*
Irish Freedom	*Pilot (Boston)*
Irishman	*United Ireland*
Irish Nation (New York)	*United Irishman*
Irish People	*Weekly Freeman*
Irish Weekly Independent	

BOOKS, PAMPHLETS AND ARTICLES

Agulhon, Maurice, *Marianne into battle: republican imagery and symbolism in France 1789–1880* (Cambridge, 1981)

Appleby, Joyce, *Liberalism and republicanism in the historical imagination* (Cambridge, Mass., 1992)

Billington, James, *Fire in the minds of men: the revolutionary faith* (New York, 1981)

Boyce, D.G., and Alan O'Day (eds.), *Ireland in transition, 1867–1921* (London, 2004)

Boyce, D.G., *Nationalism in Ireland* (3rd ed., London, 1995)

Boyle, J.W., *The Irish labour movement in the nineteenth century* (Washington D.C., 1988)

Brannigan, C.J., 'The Luke Dillon case and the Welland Canal explosion of 1900', *Niagara Frontier*, 24 (summer 1977), 36–44

Callanan, Frank, *The Parnell split, 1890–91* (Cork, 1992)

Campbell, Christy, *Fenian fire* (London, 2002)

—— *The Maharajah's box* (London, 2000)

Clark, Samuel, *Social origins of the Irish land war* (Dublin, 1979)

Comerford, R.V., *Fenianism in context: Irish politics and society, 1848–82* (2nd ed., Dublin, 1998)

Cronin, Sean, *The McGarrity papers* (Tralee, 1972)

Clarke, Thomas, *Glimpses of an Irish felon's prison life* (Dublin, 1922)

Collins, Michael, *The path to freedom* (Dublin, 1922)

Cullen, Patrick, 'James Stephens and the *Irish People* in the evolution of Irish nationalist politics in the 19th century' (unpublished MPhil thesis, UCC, 1997)

D'Arcy, William, *The Fenian movement in the United States 1858–86* (Washington D.C., 1947)

Daly, Dominic, *The young Douglas Hyde: the dawn of the Irish revolution and renaissance, 1874–93* (Dublin, 1974)

Davis, Eugene ['Owen Roe'] (ed.), *Reliques of John K. Casey* (Dublin, 1878)

Davis, R.P., *Arthur Griffith and non-violent Sinn Fein* (Tralee, 1974)

—— *The Young Ireland movement* (Dublin, 1987)

Davitt, Michael, *The fall of feudalism* (London, 1904)

Denieffe, Joseph, *A personal narrative of the Irish Revolutionary Brotherhood* (New York, 1906)

Denman, Terence, 'The red livery of shame: the campaign against army recruitment in Ireland, 1899–1914', *IHS*, 29 (1994), 208–33

Denvir, John, *Life story of an old rebel* (Dublin, 1910)

Devoy, John, *Recollections of an Irish rebel* (New York, 1929)

Doyle, D.N., *Irish Americans, native rights and national empires* (New York, 1976)

Fanning, M.F. (ed.), *The new movement convention which gave birth to the Irish National Alliance* (Chicago, 1896)

Feingold, W.L., *The revolt of the tenantry* (New York, 1984)

Fitzpatrick, David, *Harry Boland's Irish revolution* (Cork, 2003)

Fogarty, L. (ed.), *James Fintan Lalor: patriot and essayist* (Dublin, 1918)

Funchion, M.F., *Chicago's Irish nationalists, 1881–1890* (New York, 1976)

—— (ed.), *Irish American voluntary organisations* (Westport, Conn., 1983)

Geary, L.M., *The Plan of Campaign* (Cork, 1986)

—— (ed.), *Rebellion and remembrance in Ireland* (Dublin, 2001)

Golway, Terry, *Irish rebel: John Devoy and America's fight for Ireland's freedom* (New York, 1998)

Griffith, Arthur, *The resurrection of Hungary* (1904, 3rd ed., Dublin, 1918)

—— (ed.), *Thomas Davis: the thinker and teacher* (Dublin, 1914)

Haller, S.W., *William O'Brien and the Irish land war* (Dublin, 1990)

Harrison, Rodyen, *Before the socialists* (London, 1965)

Healy, T.M., *Leaders and letters of my day*, 2 vols. (London, 1928)

Hobson, Bulmer, *Ireland yesterday and tomorrow* (Tralee, 1968)

—— *The creed of the republic* (Belfast, 1907)

Johnson, Maurice, 'The Fenian amnesty movement, 1868–79' (unpublished MA thesis, Maynooth, 1980)

Jordan, Donald, *Land and politics in Ireland: County Mayo from the plantation to the land war* (Cork, 1994)

—— 'The Irish National League and the unwritten law: rural protest and nation building in Ireland, 1882–1890', *Past and Present*, 158 (1998), 146–171

—— 'John O'Connor Power, Charles Stewart Parnell and the centralisation of popular politics in Ireland', *IHS*, 25 (1986), 46–66

Julienne, Janick, 'La question Irlandaise en France de 1860 a 1890' (unpublished PhD thesis, University of Paris VII, 1997)

—— 'John Patrick Leonard (1814–89): chargé d'affaires d'un government Irlandais en France', *Etudes Irlandaise*, 25 (2000), 48–65

King, Carla, *Michael Davitt* (Dundalk, 1999)

Lane, Fintan, *The origins of modern Irish socialism, 1881–1896* (Cork, 1997)

Leech, H.B., *The continuity of the Irish revolutionary movement* (2nd ed., London, 1912)

Legg, M.L., *Newspapers and nationalism: the Irish provincial press, 1850–1892* (Dublin, 1999)

—— (ed.), *Alfred Webb: the autobiography of a Quaker nationalist* (Cork, 1999)

Loughlin, James, 'The Irish Protestant Home Rule Association and nationalist politics 1886–93', *IHS*, 24 (1985), 341–60

Lyons, F.S.L., *Charles Stewart Parnell* (London, 1977)

—— *The Irish parliamentary party, 1890–1910* (London, 1951)

—— *John Dillon* (London, 1968)

Lyons, G.A., *Some recollections of Griffith and his times* (Dublin, 1923)

—— 'Arthur Griffith and the IRB', *Forum* (Jan. 1950), 7–8

Lynch, Arthur, *My life story* (London, 1924)

Lynch, Diarmuid, *The IRB and the 1916 insurrection* (Cork, 1957)

MacBride, Maud Gonne, *A servant of the queen* (London, 1938)

MacManus, Seamus (ed.), *William Rooney: prose writings* (Dublin, 1909)

Mandle, W.F., *The GAA and Irish nationalist politics, 1884–1924* (Dublin, 1987)

Maume, Patrick, *The long gestation: Irish nationalist life, 1891–1918* (Dublin, 1999)

—— 'Young Ireland, Arthur Griffith and republican ideology: the question of continuity', *Éire-Ireland* (summer 1999), 155–74

Maye, Brian, *Arthur Griffith* (Dublin, 1997)

McBride, L.W. (ed.), *Images, icons and the Irish nationalist imagination* (Dublin, 1999)

McCarthy, Pat, 'James Francis Xavier O'Brien (1828–1905): Dungarvan-born Fenian', *Decies*, 54 (1998), 107–38

McCracken, P.A., 'Arthur Griffith's South African sabbatical', *South African Irish Studies*, 3 (1996), 227–62
McGee, Owen, 'God save Ireland: Manchester-martyr demonstrations in Dublin, 1867–1916', *Eire-Ireland* (fall/winter 2001), 39–66
—— 'Fred Allan (1861–1937): Republican, Methodist, Dubliner', *Dublin Historical Record*, 66 (autumn 2003), 205–16
Meehan, Helen, 'Shan Van Vocht', *Ulster Local Studies*, 19 (summer, 1997), 80–90
Mitchel, John, *Jail Journal* (Glasgow, n.d., *c*.1870)
Moody, T.W., and Leon O'Broin (eds.), 'The IRB Supreme Council, 1868–78', Select Documents XXXII, *IHS*, 19, (1974), 286–332
Moody, T.W., *Davitt and Irish revolution* (2nd ed., Oxford, 1984)
—— (ed.), *The Fenian movement* (Cork, 1967)
—— 'The Times versus Parnell and Co., 1887–90', *Historical Studies*, 6 (1968), 147–82
—— 'The new departure in Irish politics, 1878–9' in Cronne, Moody, Quinn eds., *Essays in British and Irish history* (1949), 303–33
Murray, Nancy, 'Joseph K. Bracken: GAA founder, Fenian and politician', *Tipperary: history and society* (1985), 379–93
Newsinger, John, *Fenianism in mid-Victorian Britain* (London, 1994)
Nord, Phillip, *The republican moment: struggles for democracy in nineteenth century France* (Cambridge, Mass., 1994)
O'Baoighill, Padraig, *Nally as Maigh Eo* (Dublin, 1998)
O'Brien, C.C., *Parnell and his party, 1880–90* (2nd ed., Oxford, 1964)
O'Brien, R.B., *The life of Parnell* (2nd ed., London, 1910)
O'Brien, W., and Desmond Ryan (eds.), *Devoy's post bag*, 2 vols. (Dublin, 1979)
O'Brien, William, *Evening memories* (Dublin, 1926)
O'Broin, Leon, *Revolutionary underground* (Dublin, 1976)
—— *The prime informer* (London, 1971)
—— *Fenian fever: an Anglo-American dilemma* (London, 1971)
O'Day, Alan, *Irish home rule, 1867–1921* (Manchester, 2003)
—— (ed.), *Reactions to Irish nationalism* (London, 1987)
O'Donovan Rossa, Jeremiah, *Recollections* (New York, 1898)
O'Grady, J.P., *Irish-Americans and Anglo-American relations, 1880–88* (New York, 1976)
O'Halpin, Eunan, 'The British secret service vote and Ireland, 1868–1922', *IHS*, 23 (1983), 348–53
O'Hegarty, P.S., *The victory of Sinn Fein* (Dublin, 1924)
O'Leary, John, *Young Ireland: old and new* (Dublin, 1885)
—— *What Irishmen should know and how Irishmen should feel* (Dublin, 1886)
—— 'Some guarantees for the Protestant and unionist minority', *Dublin University Review*, 2 (Dec. 1886), 959–65
—— *Recollections of Fenians and Fenianism*, 2 vols. (London, 1896)
O'Riordain, Tomas, 'GAA and Fenian pioneer: the story of P.N. Fitzgerald', *Cork Holly Bough* (Christmas, 1984), 20, 29
O'Tuama, Sean (ed.), *The Gaelic League idea* (Dublin, 1972)
Owens, Gary, 'Nationalist monuments in Ireland, 1870–1914: symbolism and ritual' in Gillespie and Kennedy (eds.), *Ireland: art into history* (Dublin, 1994), 103–17
Piggott, Richard, 'Ireland and the Franchise Bill' (published under pseudonym 'James Stephens'), *Contemporary Review* (1884), 687–97
Quinlivan, P., and Paul Rose, *The Fenians in England, 1865–72* (London, 1982)
Rafferty, O.P., *The church, the state and the Fenian threat, 1861–75* (Oxford, 1999)
Redmond, J.E., *Historical and political addresses, 1883–97* (Dublin, 1898)
Rodechko, J.P., *Patrick Ford and his search for America* (New York, 1976)
Rolleston, C.H., *Portrait of an Irishman: a biographical sketch of TW Rolleston* (London, 1939)
Roney, Frank, *Irish rebel and California labor leader* (San Francisco, 1931)
Ryan, Desmond, *The Fenian chief: a biography of James Stephens* (Dublin, 1967)

Ryan, Mark, *Fenian memories* (Dublin, 1945)

Sigerson, George, *Modern Ireland* (2nd ed., London, 1869)

—— *Political prisoners: at home and abroad* (London, 1890)

Shannon, Catherine, *Arthur J. Balfour and Ireland, 1874–1922* (Washington D.C., 1988)

Short, K.R.M., *The dynamite war: Irish-American bombers in Victorian Britain* (Dublin, 1979)

Souvenir journal of the Amnesty Association of America (New York, 1893)

Special Commission Act, 1888: reprint of the shorthand notes of the speeches, proceedings and evidence taken before the commissioners appointed under the above-named act, 12 vols. (London, 1890)

Sullivan, T.D., *Recollections of troubled times in Irish politics* (Dublin, 1905)

Swift, R., and S. Gilley (eds.), *The Irish in Britain, 1815–1939* (Oxford, 1989)

Takagami, Shin-ichi, 'The Dublin Fenians, 1858–79' (unpublished PhD thesis, TCD, 1990)

Tynan, P.J.P., *The Irish National Invincibles and their times* (London, 1894)

Walker, B.M. (ed.), *Parliamentary election results in Ireland, 1801–1922* (Oxford, 1978)

Williams, T.D. (ed.), *Secret societies in Ireland* (Dublin, 1973)

Yeats, W.B., *Autobiographies* (London, 1955)

Zimmermann, G.D., *Irish political street ballads and rebel songs, 1780–1900* (Geneva, 1966)

Index